# mugen SPIRAL

## Volume 1

### Created by Mizuho Kusanagi

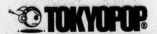

HAMBURG // LONDON // LOS ANGELES // TOKYO

## *Mugen Spiral Vol. 1*
## Created by Mizuho Kusanagi

Translation - Nan Rymer
English Adaptation - Christine Schilling
Retouch and Lettering - Bowen Park
Production Artist - Courtney Geter
Cover Design - Jose Macasocol, Jr.

Editor - Katherine Schilling
Digital Imaging Manager - Chris Buford
Pre-Production Supervisor - Erika Terriquez
Art Director - Anne Marie Horne
Production Manager - Elisabeth Brizzi
VP of Production - Ron Klamert
Editor-in-Chief - Rob Tokar
Publisher - Mike Kiley
President and C.O.O. - John Parker
C.E.O. and Chief Creative Officer - Stuart Levy

A 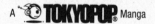 Manga

TOKYOPOP Inc.
5900 Wilshire Blvd. Suite 2000
Los Angeles, CA 90036

E-mail: info@TOKYOPOP.com
Come visit us online at www.TOKYOPOP.com

ISBN: 978-1-59816-829-7

First TOKYOPOP printing: January 2007
10 9 8 7 6 5 4 3 2 1
Printed in the USA

# mugen SPIRAL

## Volume 1

Mizuho Kusanagi

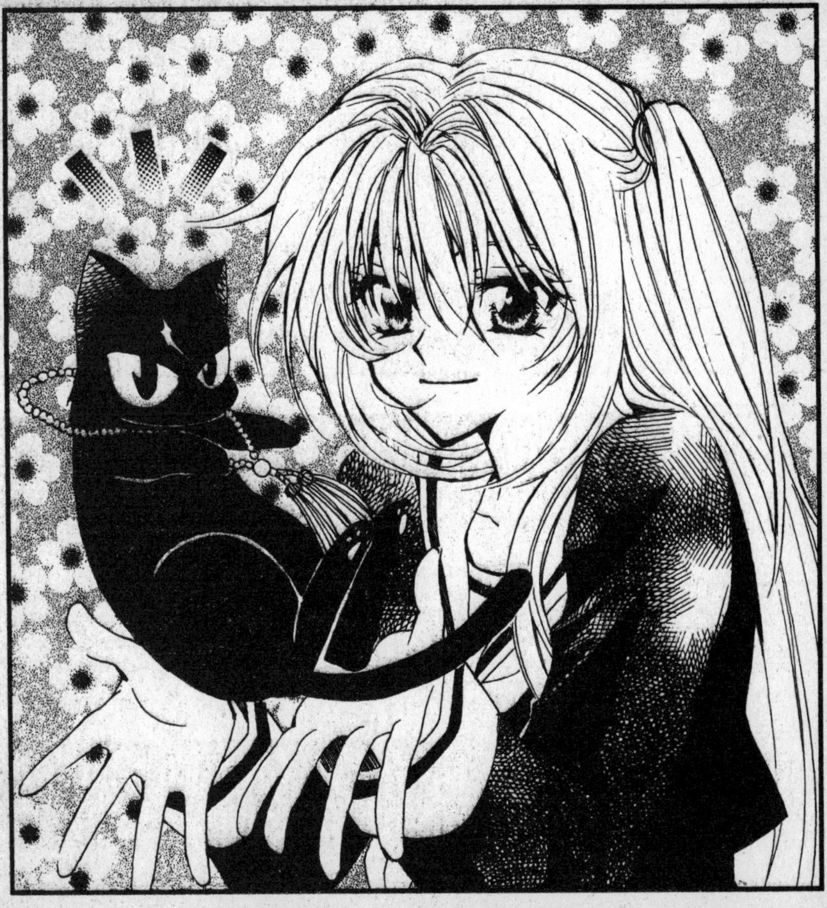

# mugen SPIRAL

## Table of Contents

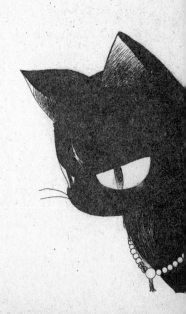

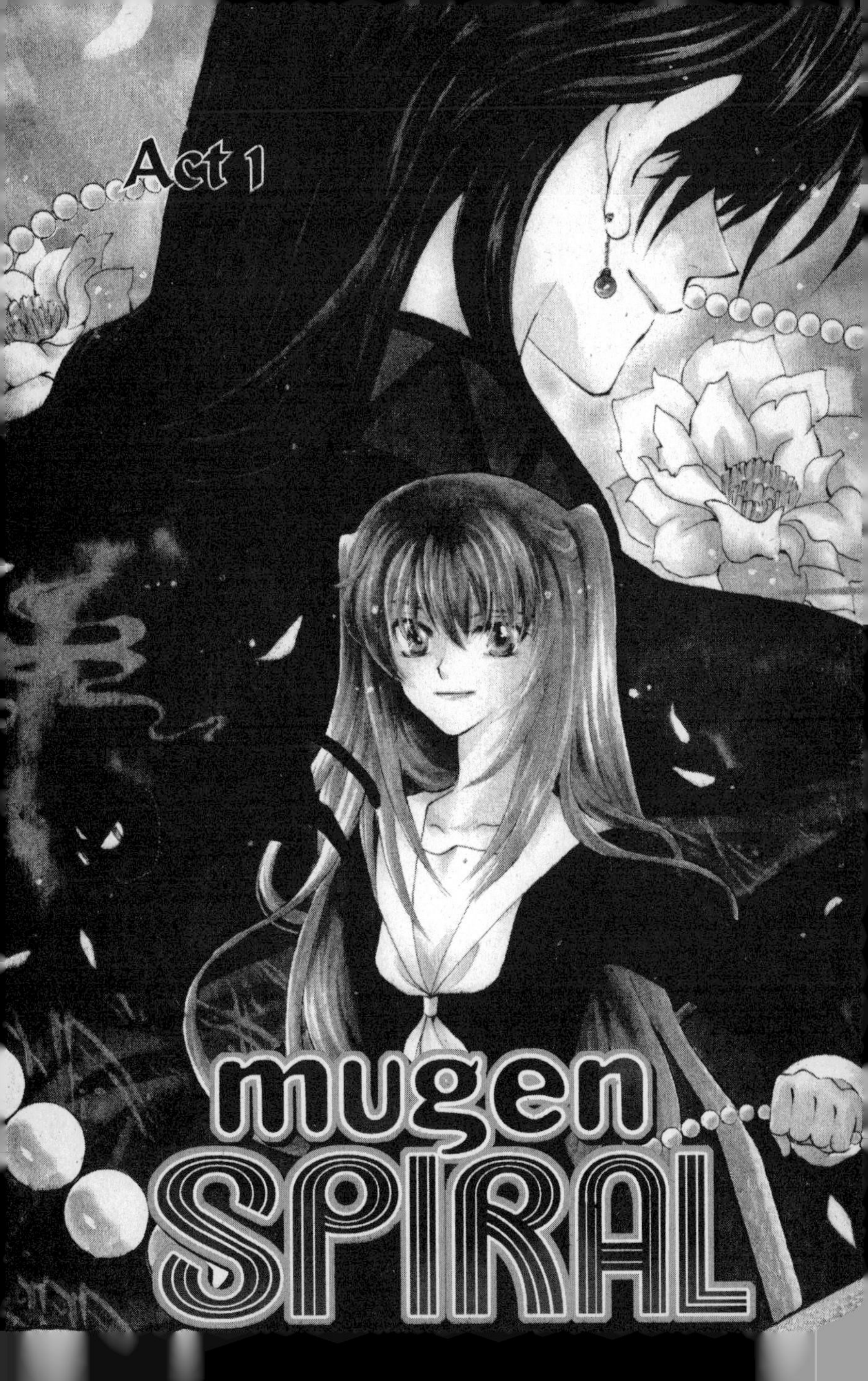
Act 1
mugen
SPIRAL

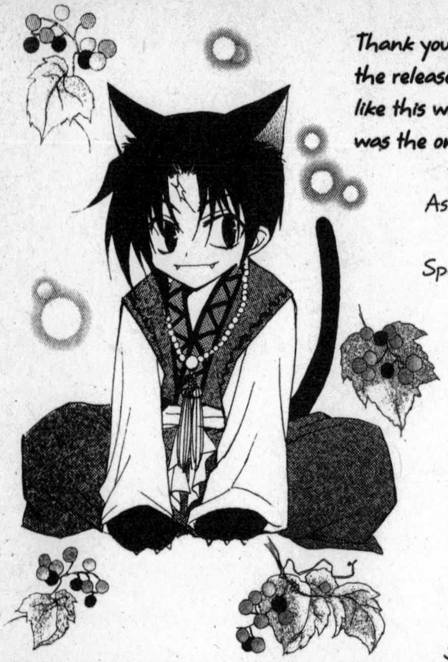

Thank you so much to everyone who helped make the release of this book possible! Normally, a notice like this would go at the end of the book, but this was the only space I had so...

| | |
|---|---|
| Assistants | Mikorun-sama |
| | Akira Sakura-sama |
| Special Thanks | Rurunga-sama |

To my manager, to the entire editorial staff at Hana to Yume, to the designers and everyone involved in the printing of this book, thank you and forgive me for all the trouble I've put you through.
To my family, friends, and all you readers, thank you, thank you so much! I hope you continue to support me here and there in the future.

True story. I know it's a really sad drawing, but that's just how I draw.

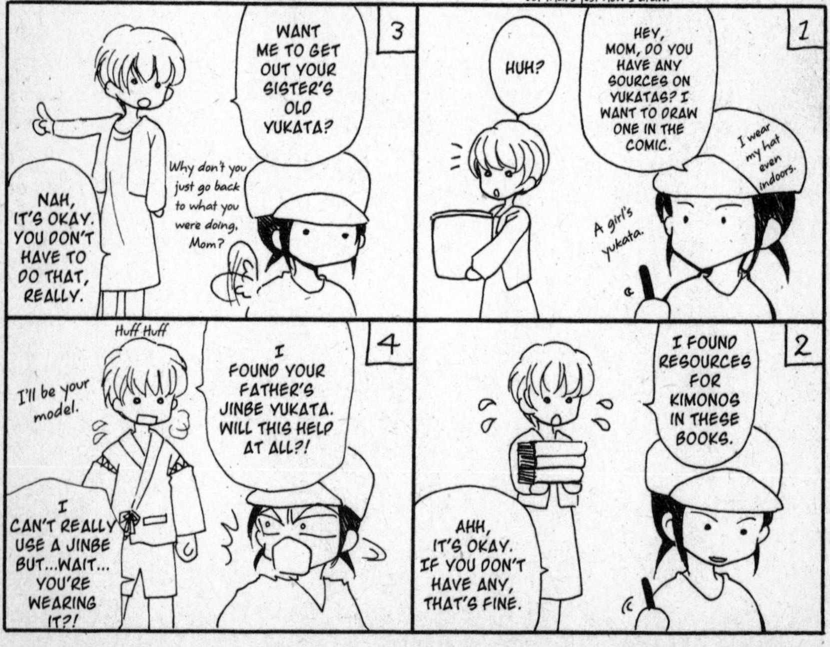
1
HEY, MOM, DO YOU HAVE ANY SOURCES ON YUKATAS? I WANT TO DRAW ONE IN THE COMIC.
HUH?
I wear my hat even indoors.
A girl's yukata.
2
I FOUND RESOURCES FOR KIMONOS IN THESE BOOKS.
AHH, IT'S OKAY. IF YOU DON'T HAVE ANY, THAT'S FINE.
3
WANT ME TO GET OUT YOUR SISTER'S OLD YUKATA?
Why don't you just go back to what you were doing, Mom?
NAH, IT'S OKAY. YOU DON'T HAVE TO DO THAT, REALLY.
4
I FOUND YOUR FATHER'S JINBE YUKATA. WILL THIS HELP AT ALL?!
Huff Huff
I'll be your model.
I CAN'T REALLY USE A JINBE BUT...WAIT... YOU'RE WEARING IT?!

MY MOTHER WAS ON STANDBY, WEARING THE JINBE. SO, THE YAYOI-CHAN I DREW WITH A YUKATA WAS BASED ON MY MOTHER'S MODELING OF A JINBE... (IT'S NOT IN THIS COMIC HOWEVER.)

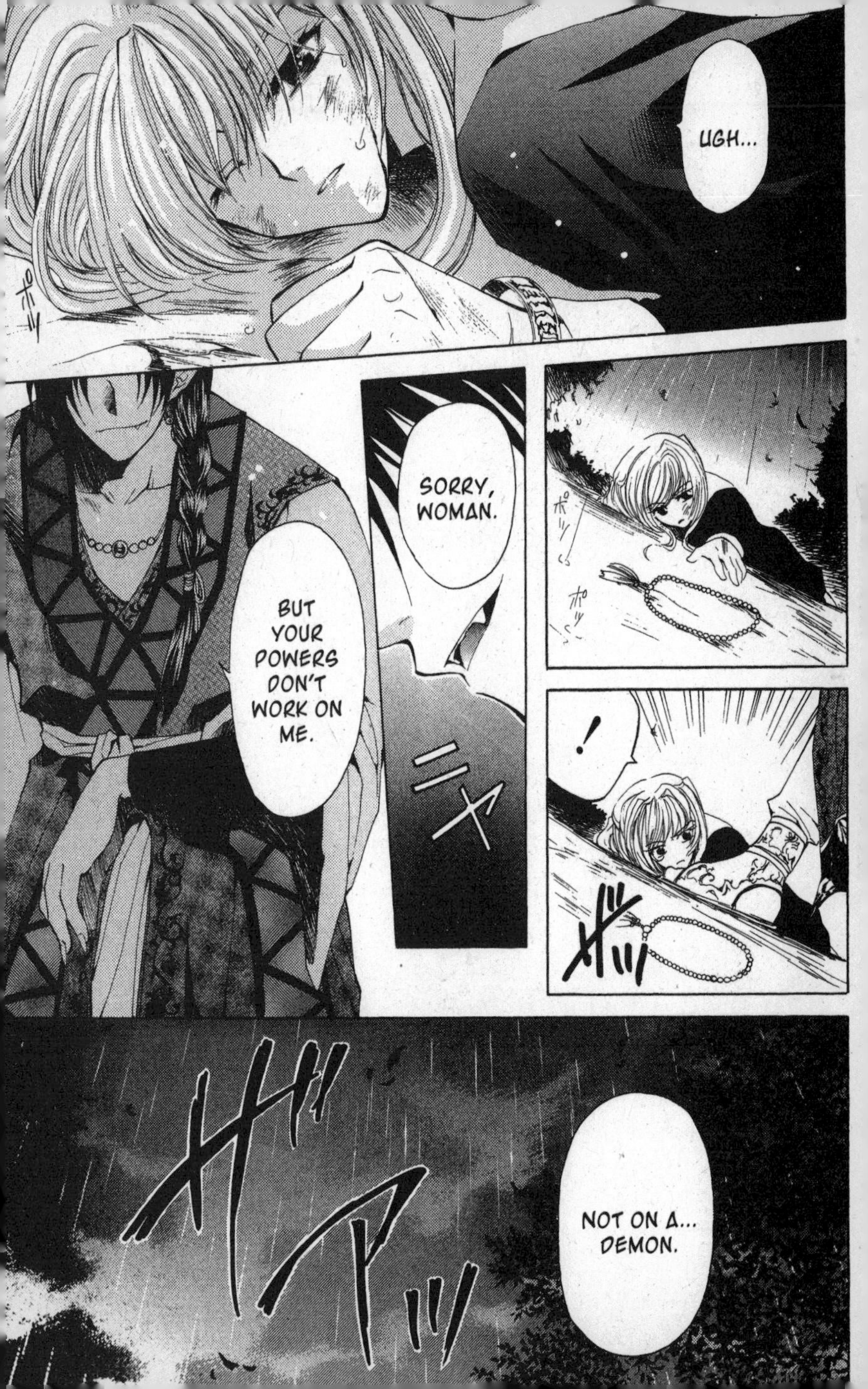
UGH...
SORRY, WOMAN.
BUT YOUR POWERS DON'T WORK ON ME.
!
NOT ON A... DEMON.

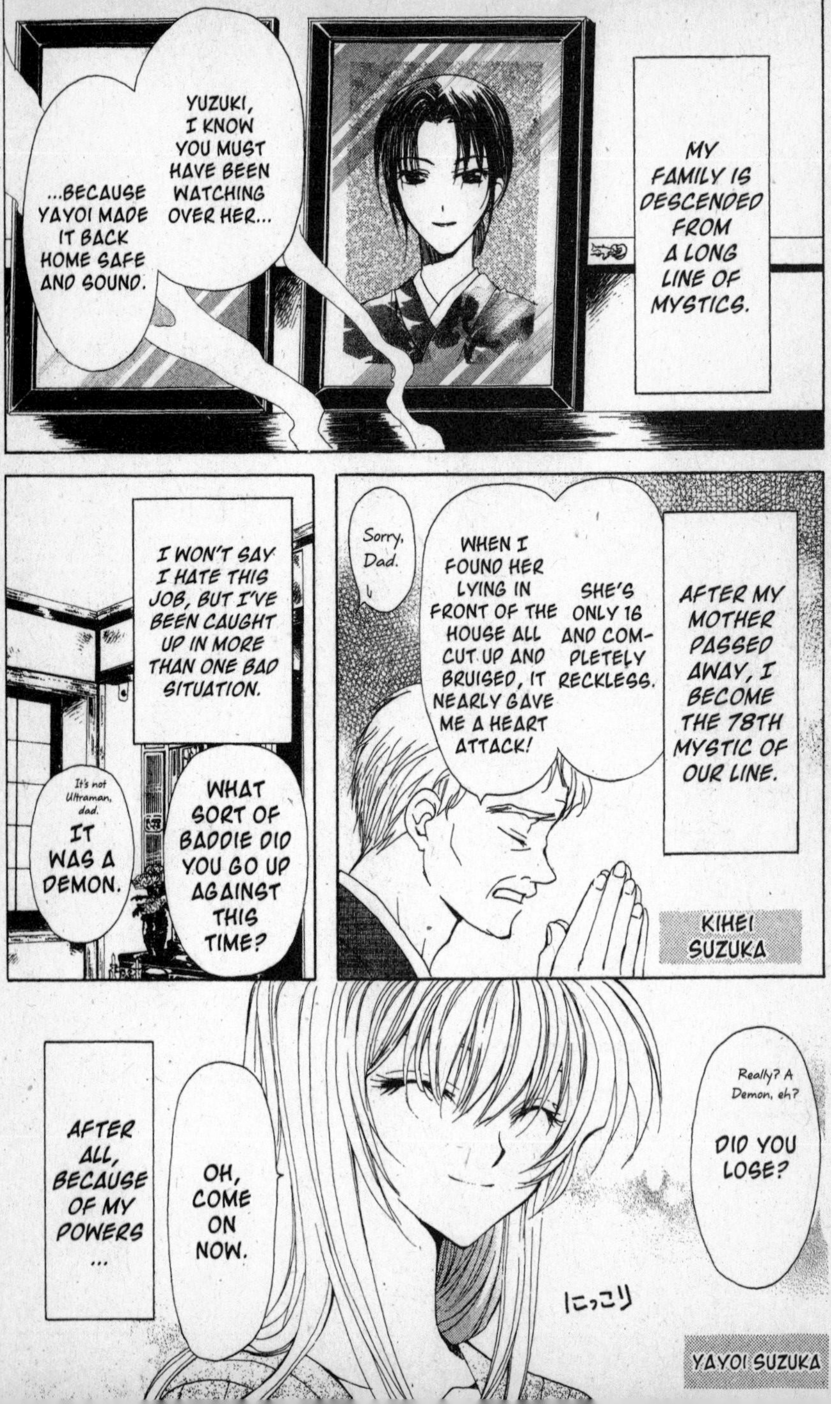
MY FAMILY IS DESCENDED FROM A LONG LINE OF MYSTICS.
YUZUKI, I KNOW YOU MUST HAVE BEEN WATCHING OVER HER...
...BECAUSE YAYOI MADE IT BACK HOME SAFE AND SOUND.
AFTER MY MOTHER PASSED AWAY, I BECOME THE 78TH MYSTIC OF OUR LINE.
SHE'S ONLY 16 AND COMPLETELY RECKLESS.
WHEN I FOUND HER LYING IN FRONT OF THE HOUSE ALL CUT UP AND BRUISED, IT NEARLY GAVE ME A HEART ATTACK!
Sorry, Dad.
KIHEI SUZUKA
I WON'T SAY I HATE THIS JOB, BUT I'VE BEEN CAUGHT UP IN MORE THAN ONE BAD SITUATION.
WHAT SORT OF BADDIE DID YOU GO UP AGAINST THIS TIME?
It's not Ultraman, dad.
IT WAS A DEMON.
Really? A Demon, eh?
DID YOU LOSE?
にっこり
OH, COME ON NOW.
AFTER ALL, BECAUSE OF MY POWERS ...
YAYOI SUZUKA

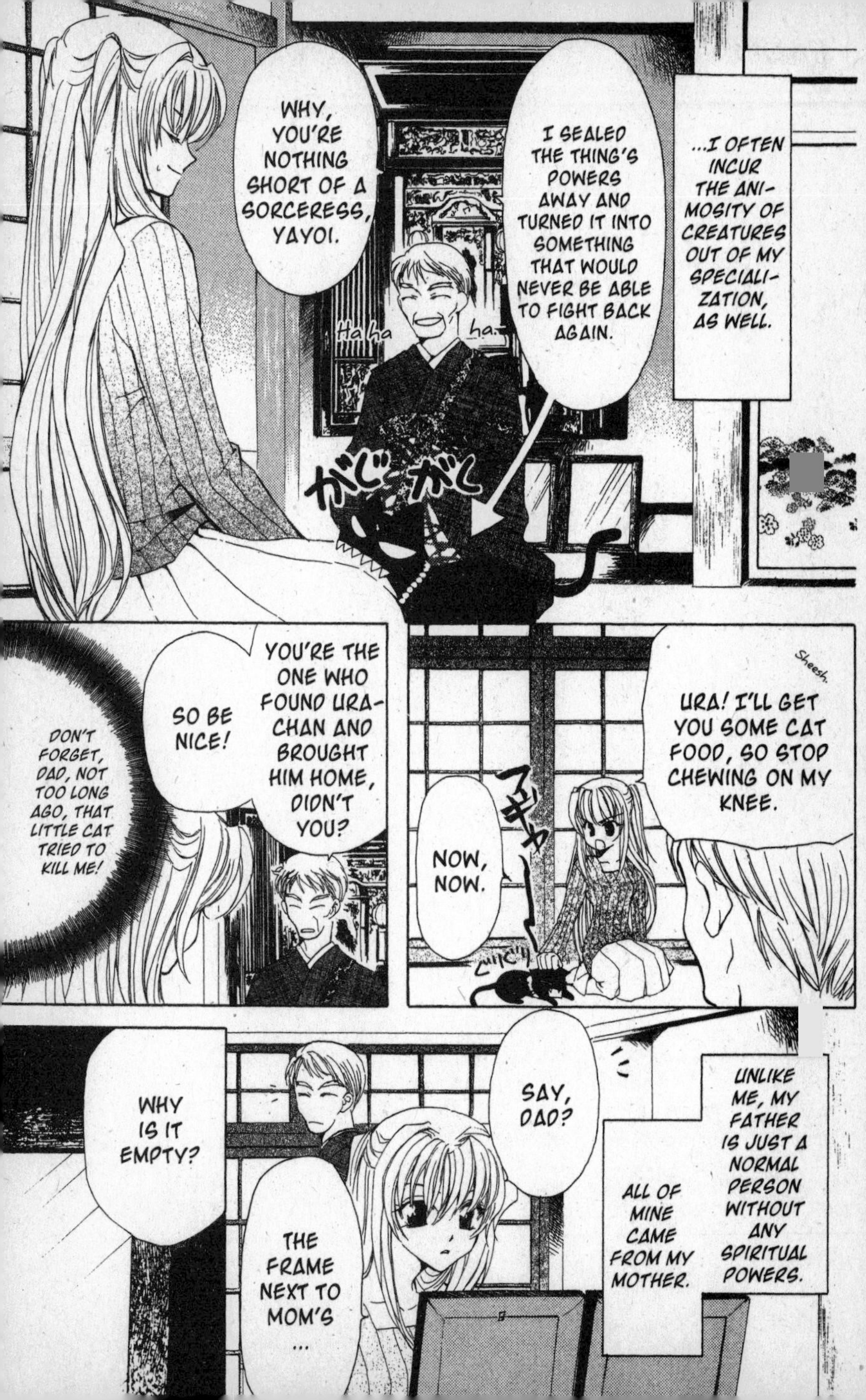
...I OFTEN INCUR THE ANI-MOSITY OF CREATURES OUT OF MY SPECIALI-ZATION, AS WELL.
I SEALED THE THING'S POWERS AWAY AND TURNED IT INTO SOMETHING THAT WOULD NEVER BE ABLE TO FIGHT BACK AGAIN.
WHY, YOU'RE NOTHING SHORT OF A SORCERESS, YAYOI.
Ha ha ha.
Sheesh.
URA! I'LL GET YOU SOME CAT FOOD, SO STOP CHEWING ON MY KNEE.
NOW, NOW.
YOU'RE THE ONE WHO FOUND URA-CHAN AND BROUGHT HIM HOME, DIDN'T YOU?
SO BE NICE!
DON'T FORGET, DAD, NOT TOO LONG AGO, THAT LITTLE CAT TRIED TO KILL ME!
UNLIKE ME, MY FATHER IS JUST A NORMAL PERSON WITHOUT ANY SPIRITUAL POWERS.
ALL OF MINE CAME FROM MY MOTHER.
SAY, DAD?
WHY IS IT EMPTY?
THE FRAME NEXT TO MOM'S
...

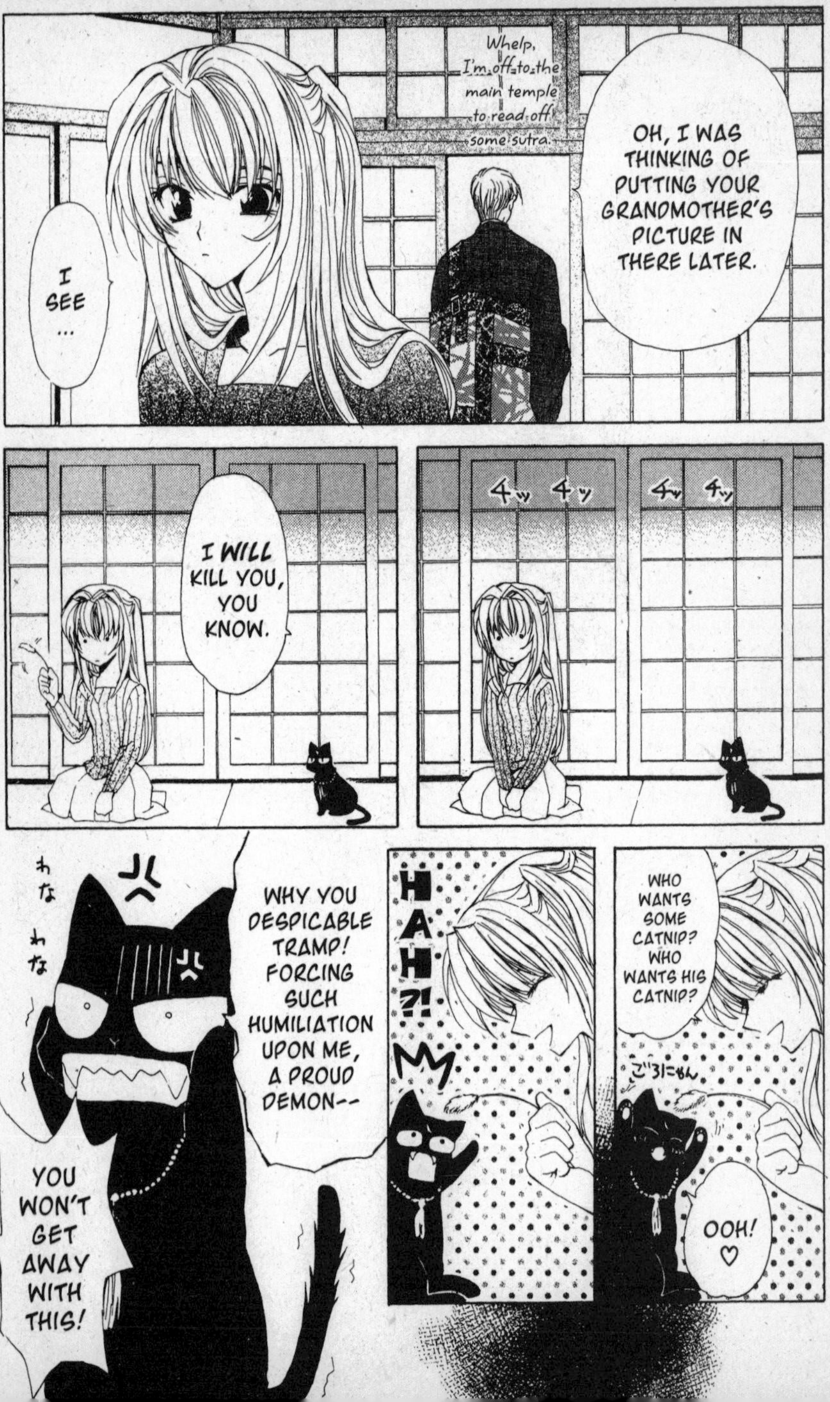
OH, I WAS THINKING OF PUTTING YOUR GRANDMOTHER'S PICTURE IN THERE LATER.
Whelp, I'm off to the main temple to read off some sutra.
I SEE ...
I WILL KILL YOU, YOU KNOW.
WHO WANTS SOME CATNIP? WHO WANTS HIS CATNIP?
ごろにゃん
OOH! ♡
HAH?!
わなわな
WHY YOU DESPICABLE TRAMP! FORCING SUCH HUMILIATION UPON ME, A PROUD DEMON--
YOU WON'T GET AWAY WITH THIS!

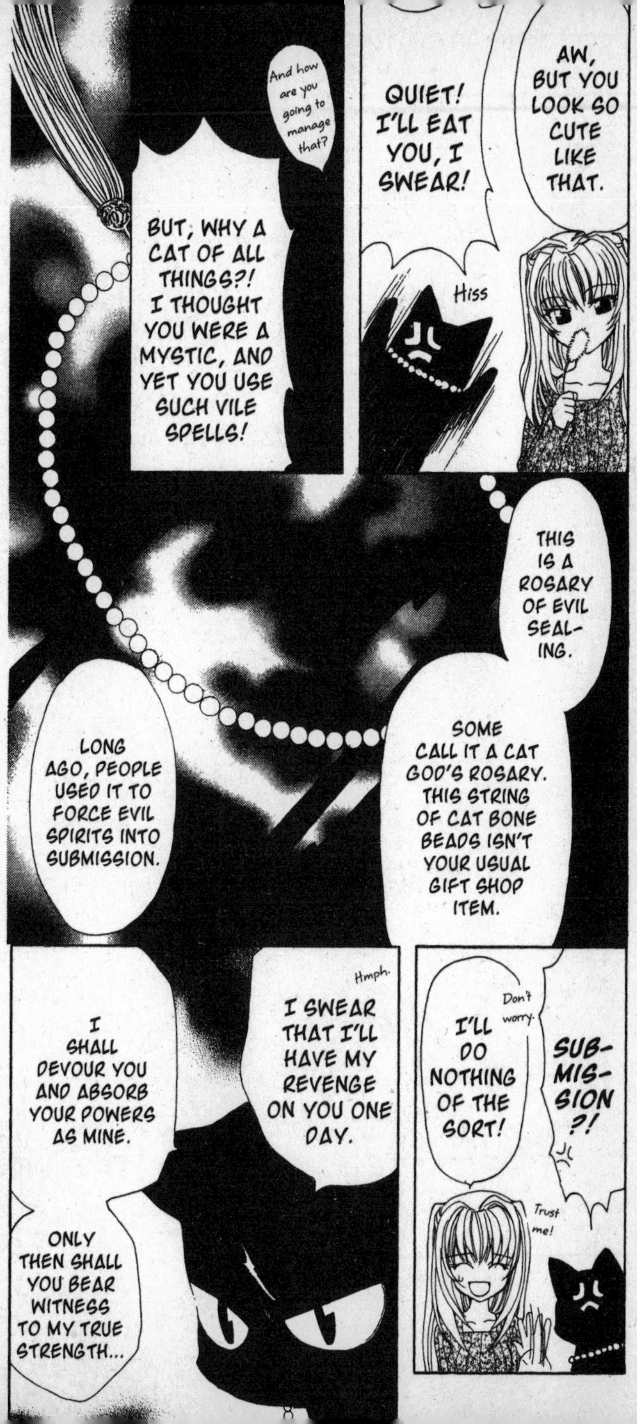
AW, BUT YOU LOOK SO CUTE LIKE THAT.
QUIET! I'LL EAT YOU, I SWEAR!
Hiss
And how are you going to manage that?
BUT, WHY A CAT OF ALL THINGS?! I THOUGHT YOU WERE A MYSTIC, AND YET YOU USE SUCH VILE SPELLS!
THIS IS A ROSARY OF EVIL SEAL-ING.
SOME CALL IT A CAT GOD'S ROSARY. THIS STRING OF CAT BONE BEADS ISN'T YOUR USUAL GIFT SHOP ITEM.
LONG AGO, PEOPLE USED IT TO FORCE EVIL SPIRITS INTO SUBMISSION.
SUB-MIS-SION?!
Don't worry.
I'LL DO NOTHING OF THE SORT!
Trust me!
Hmph.
I SWEAR THAT I'LL HAVE MY REVENGE ON YOU ONE DAY.
I SHALL DEVOUR YOU AND ABSORB YOUR POWERS AS MINE.
ONLY THEN SHALL YOU BEAR WITNESS TO MY TRUE STRENGTH...

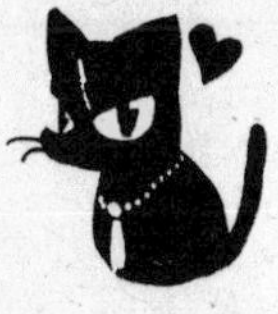

Thank you so much for purchasing Mugen Spiral Volume 1! And if you're only borrowing it from someone, thanks nonetheless! This is Mizuho Kusanagi. But wow, things sure are happening fast. I'm terribly sorry that due to the lack of extra pages, I'm not able to draw a lot of originals for the comic, but I still hope that you find at least one small part of the book you've enjoyed regardless. Nothing could make me happier!

Now then, some of you may know that this is indeed my second project. I had just as much trouble with it as I did my previous work ("Yoiko no Kokoroe - The Good Girl's Guide") for different reasons. For example, it took me quite a while to get the story to come together. It took over a month to think up the new story. Whenever you're in brainstorming mode for a new story line, not only is your body drained, but your soul, too! Sometimes it feels like there's no escape--it's neither this way nor that and at times, you just want to storm around the house screaming, "Somebody help me! I'm sorry I'm an idiot! I'm sorry I was ever born!" But if you were able to find at least a little piece of happiness out of what I have gone through, then that would make doing this job completely worthwhile for me.

To be continued...

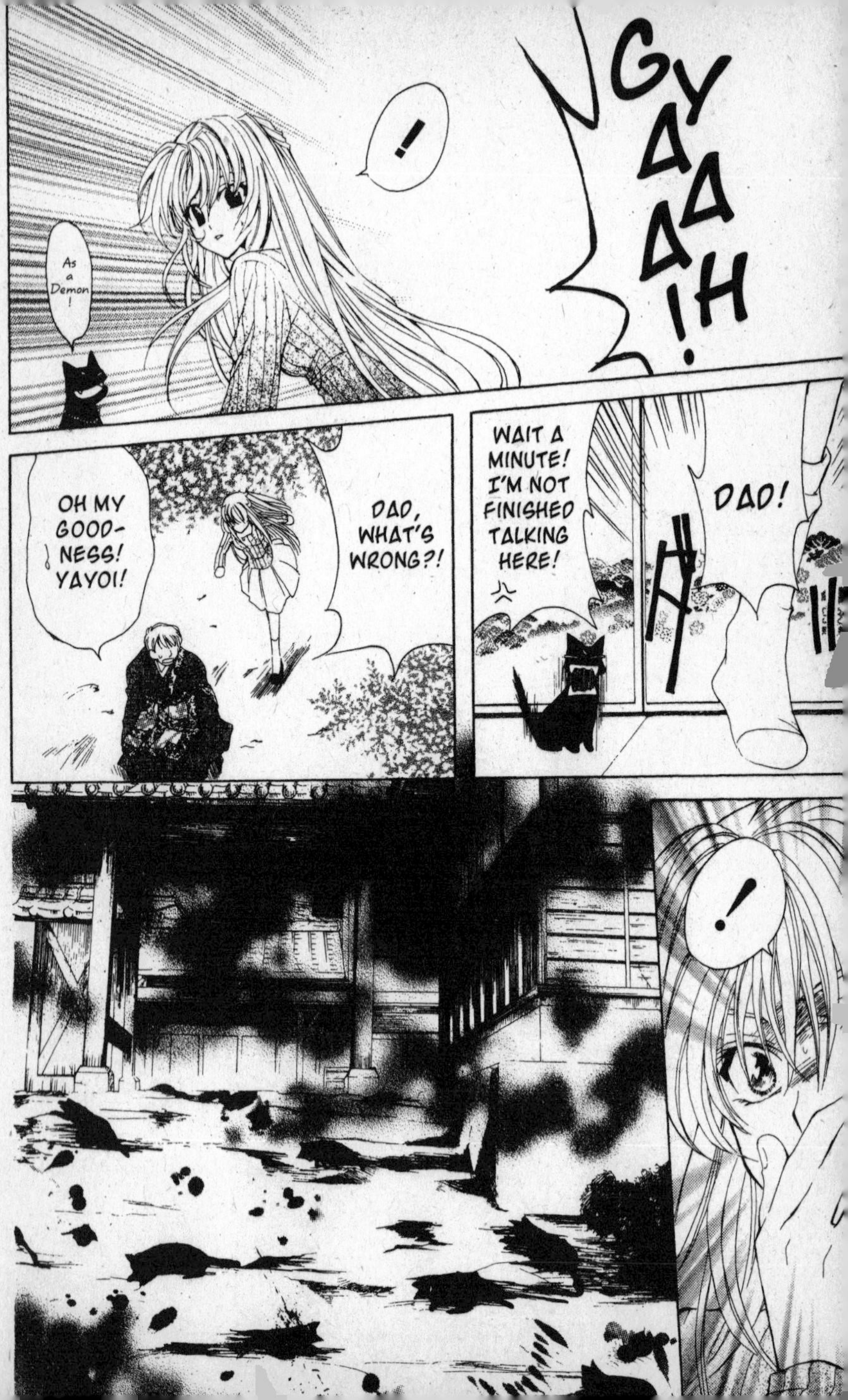
GYAAAH!
!
As a Demon!
DAD!
WAIT A MINUTE! I'M NOT FINISHED TALKING HERE!
DAD, WHAT'S WRONG?!
OH MY GOODNESS! YAYOI!
!

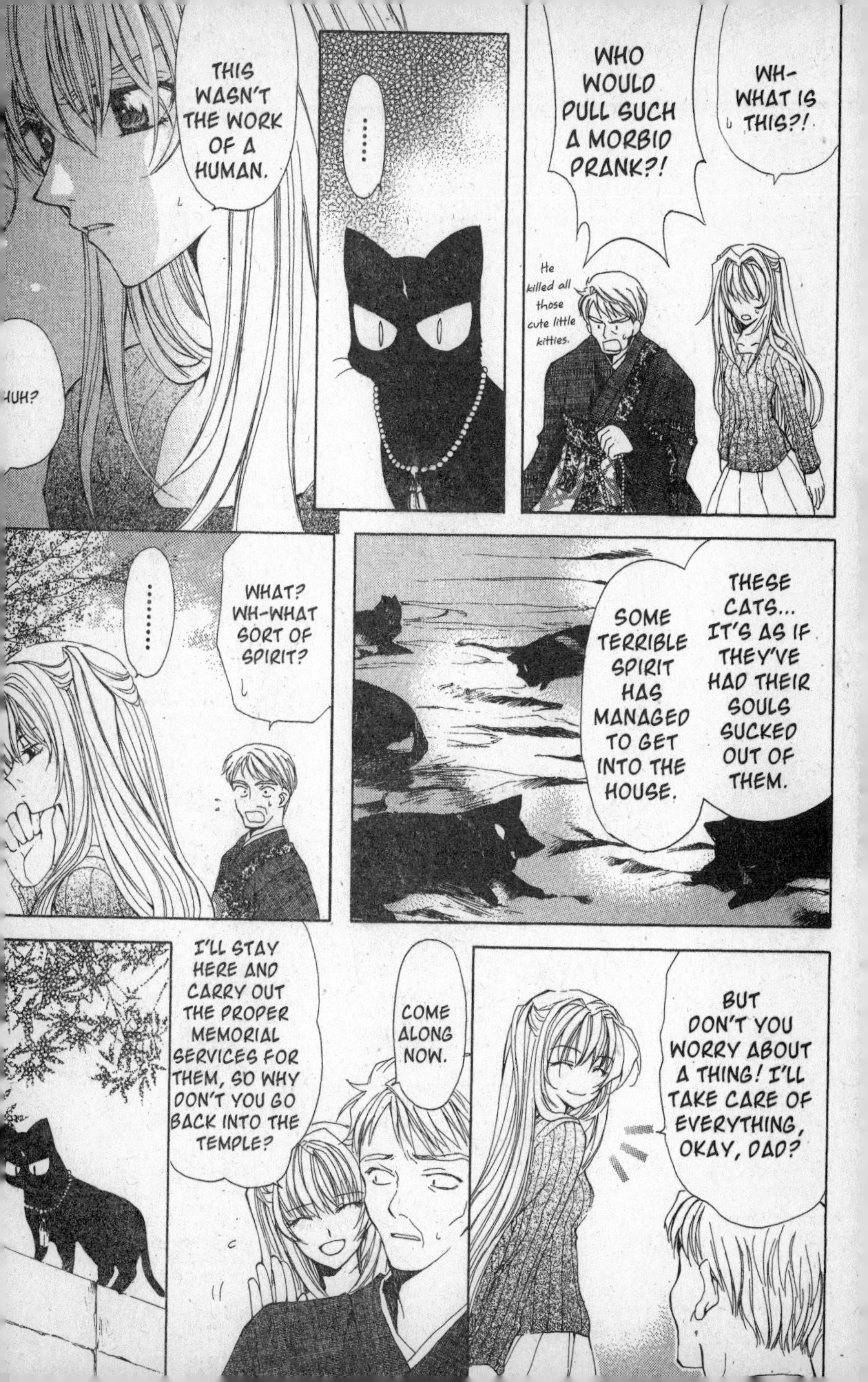
WH- WHAT IS THIS?!
WHO WOULD PULL SUCH A MORBID PRANK?!
He killed all those cute little kitties.
......
THIS WASN'T THE WORK OF A HUMAN.
HUH?
THESE CATS... IT'S AS IF THEY'VE HAD THEIR SOULS SUCKED OUT OF THEM.
SOME TERRIBLE SPIRIT HAS MANAGED TO GET INTO THE HOUSE.
WHAT? WH-WHAT SORT OF SPIRIT?
......
BUT DON'T YOU WORRY ABOUT A THING! I'LL TAKE CARE OF EVERYTHING, OKAY, DAD?
COME ALONG NOW.
I'LL STAY HERE AND CARRY OUT THE PROPER MEMORIAL SERVICES FOR THEM, SO WHY DON'T YOU GO BACK INTO THE TEMPLE?

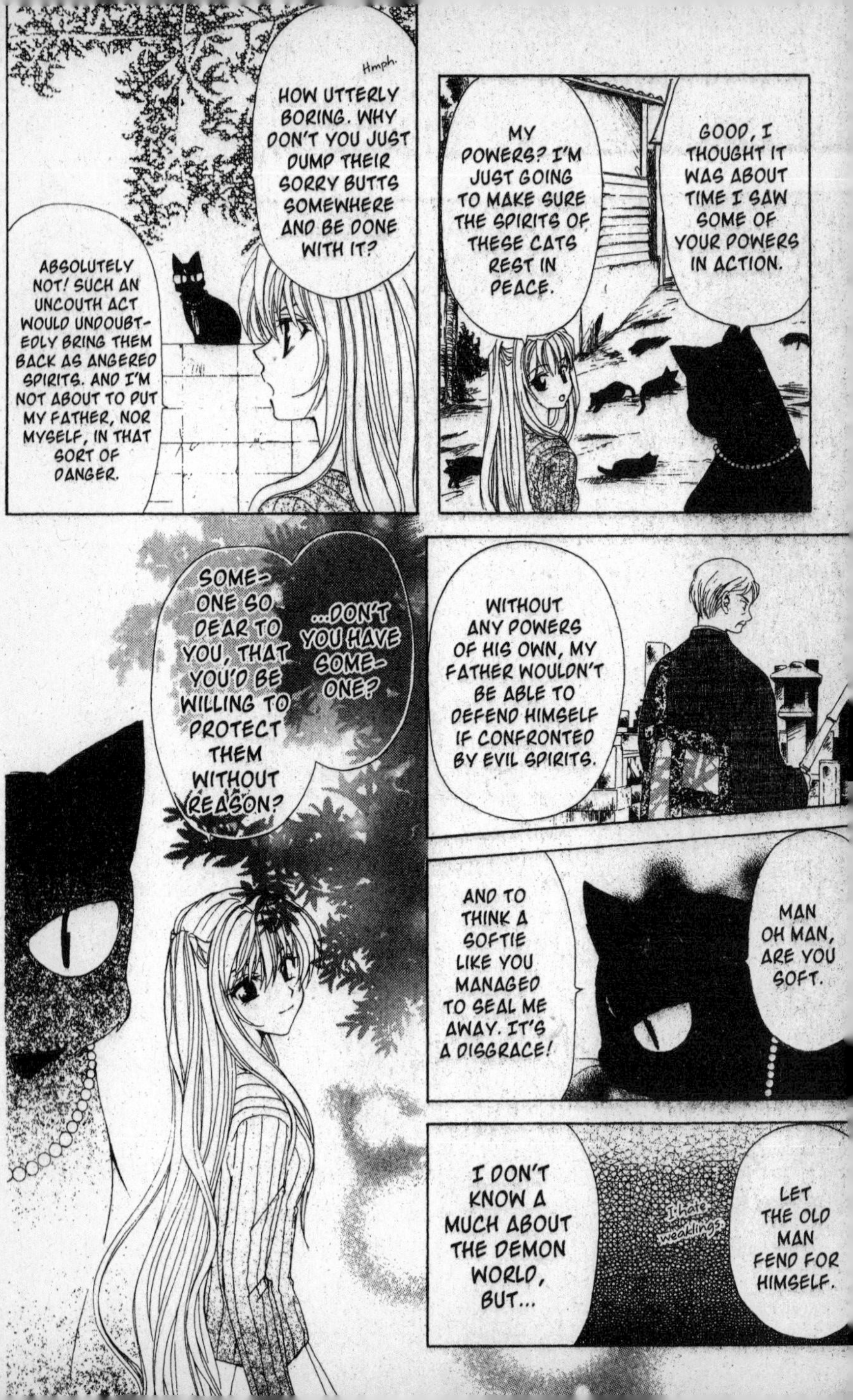
GOOD, I THOUGHT IT WAS ABOUT TIME I SAW SOME OF YOUR POWERS IN ACTION.
MY POWERS? I'M JUST GOING TO MAKE SURE THE SPIRITS OF THESE CATS REST IN PEACE.
Hmph.
HOW UTTERLY BORING. WHY DON'T YOU JUST DUMP THEIR SORRY BUTTS SOMEWHERE AND BE DONE WITH IT?
ABSOLUTELY NOT! SUCH AN UNCOUTH ACT WOULD UNDOUBTEDLY BRING THEM BACK AS ANGERED SPIRITS. AND I'M NOT ABOUT TO PUT MY FATHER, NOR MYSELF, IN THAT SORT OF DANGER.
WITHOUT ANY POWERS OF HIS OWN, MY FATHER WOULDN'T BE ABLE TO DEFEND HIMSELF IF CONFRONTED BY EVIL SPIRITS.
MAN OH MAN, ARE YOU SOFT.
AND TO THINK A SOFTIE LIKE YOU MANAGED TO SEAL ME AWAY. IT'S A DISGRACE!
LET THE OLD MAN FEND FOR HIMSELF.
I hate weaklings.
I DON'T KNOW A MUCH ABOUT THE DEMON WORLD, BUT...
...DON'T YOU HAVE SOMEONE?
SOMEONE SO DEAR TO YOU, THAT YOU'D BE WILLING TO PROTECT THEM WITHOUT REASON?

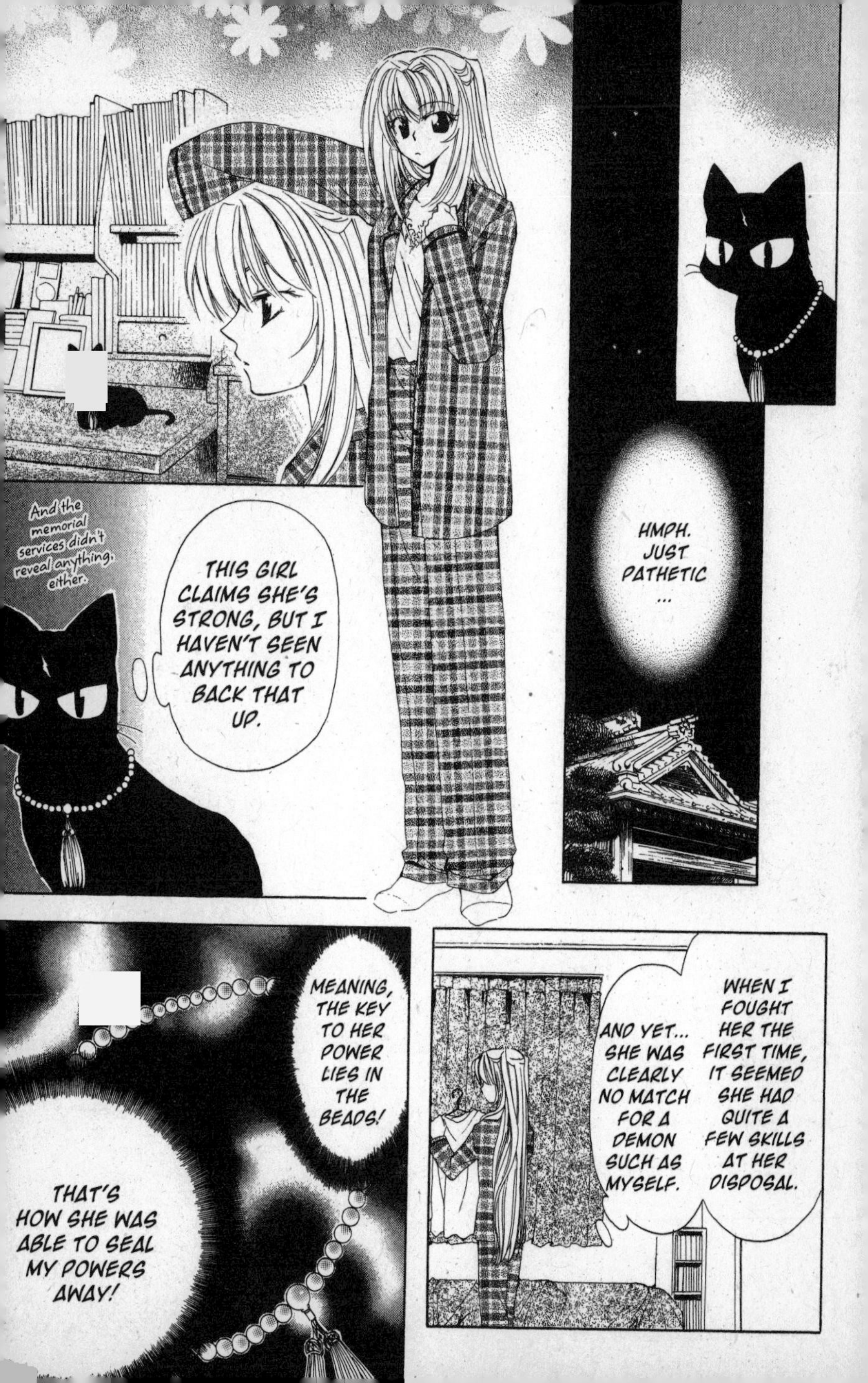
HMPH. JUST PATHETIC ...
And the memorial services didn't reveal anything, either.
THIS GIRL CLAIMS SHE'S STRONG, BUT I HAVEN'T SEEN ANYTHING TO BACK THAT UP.
WHEN I FOUGHT HER THE FIRST TIME, IT SEEMED SHE HAD QUITE A FEW SKILLS AT HER DISPOSAL.
AND YET... SHE WAS CLEARLY NO MATCH FOR A DEMON SUCH AS MYSELF.
MEANING, THE KEY TO HER POWER LIES IN THE BEADS!
THAT'S HOW SHE WAS ABLE TO SEAL MY POWERS AWAY!

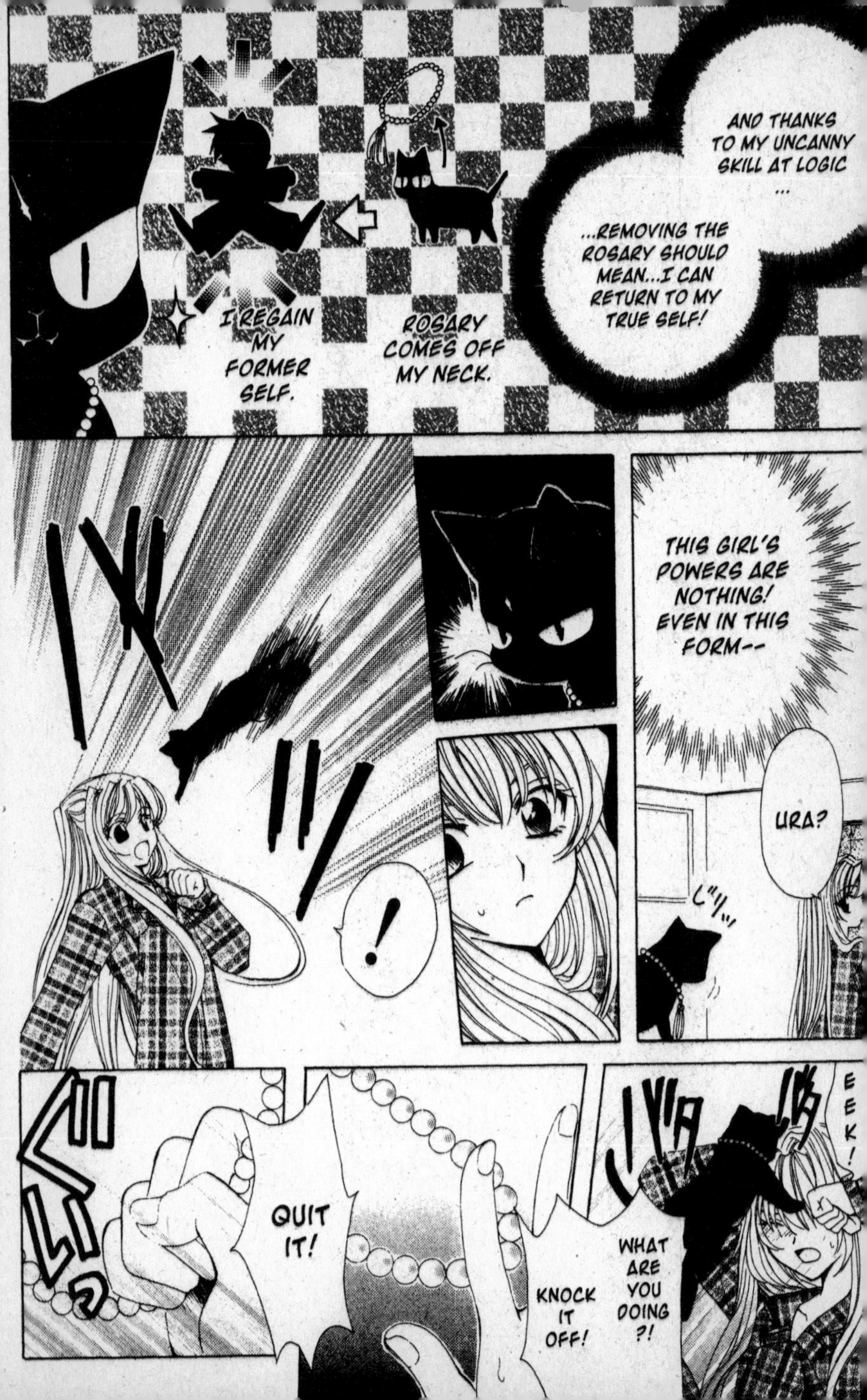
AND THANKS TO MY UNCANNY SKILL AT LOGIC ...
...REMOVING THE ROSARY SHOULD MEAN...I CAN RETURN TO MY TRUE SELF!
ROSARY COMES OFF MY NECK.
I REGAIN MY FORMER SELF.
THIS GIRL'S POWERS ARE NOTHING! EVEN IN THIS FORM--
URA?
!
EEK!
WHAT ARE YOU DOING ?!
KNOCK IT OFF!
QUIT IT!

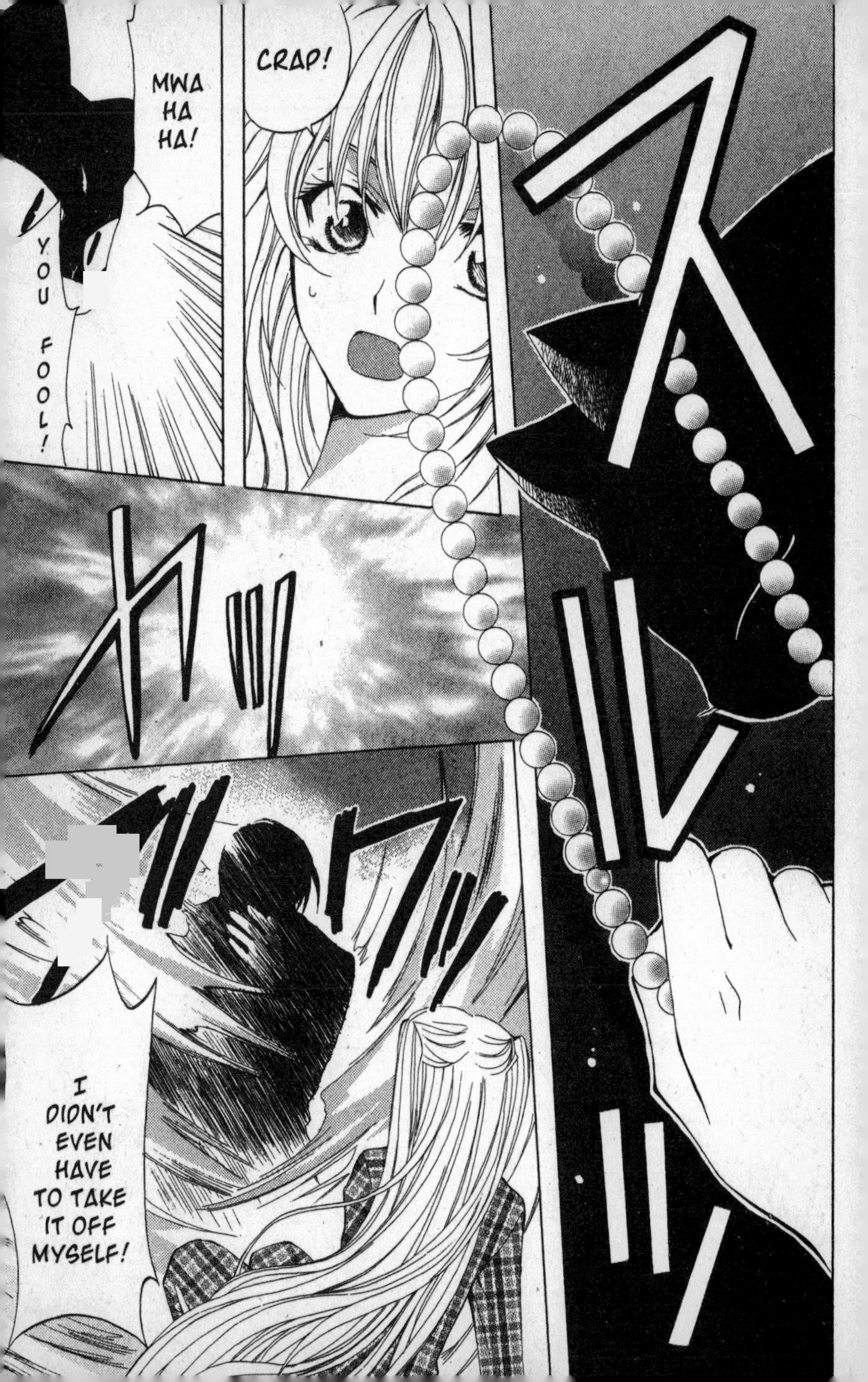
CRAP!
MWA HA HA!
YOU FOOL!
I DIDN'T EVEN HAVE TO TAKE IT OFF MYSELF!

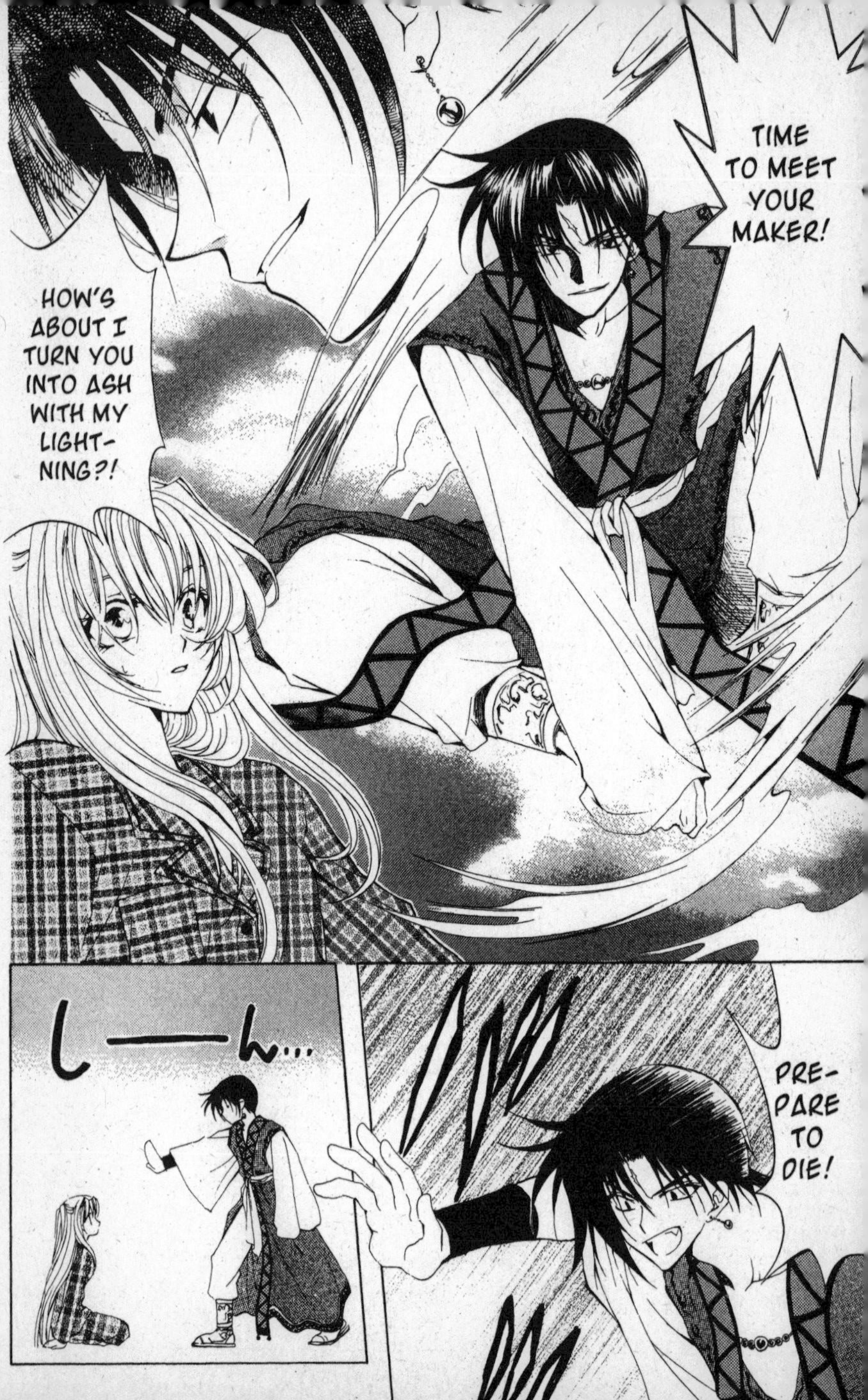
TIME TO MEET YOUR MAKER!
HOW'S ABOUT I TURN YOU INTO ASH WITH MY LIGHTNING?!
PREPARE TO DIE!
し——ん…

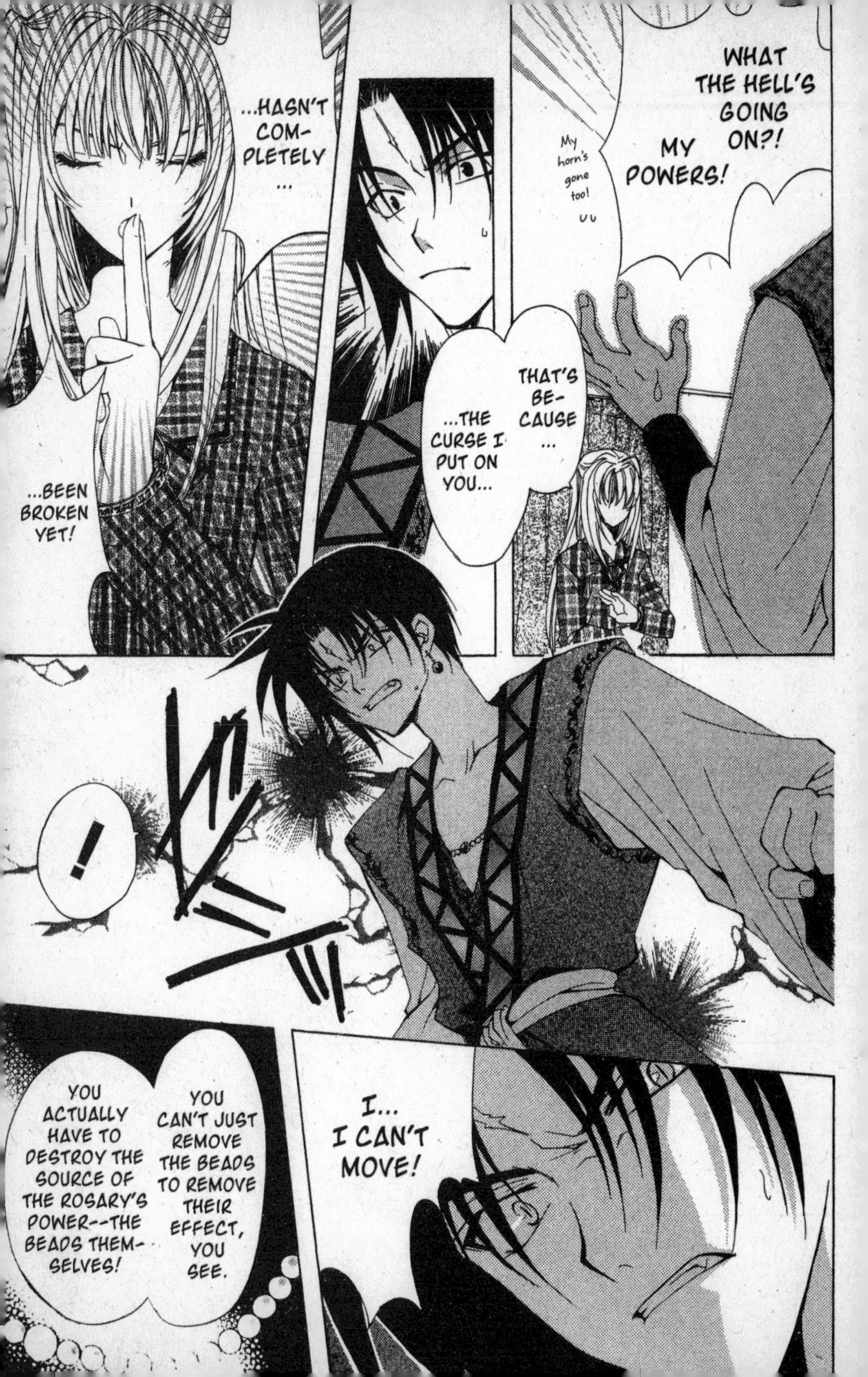
WHAT THE HELL'S GOING ON?!
MY POWERS!
My horn's gone too!
THAT'S BE-CAUSE ...
...THE CURSE I PUT ON YOU...
...HASN'T COM-PLETELY ...
...BEEN BROKEN YET!
!
I... I CAN'T MOVE!
YOU CAN'T JUST REMOVE THE BEADS TO REMOVE THEIR EFFECT, YOU SEE.
YOU ACTUALLY HAVE TO DESTROY THE SOURCE OF THE ROSARY'S POWER--THE BEADS THEM-SELVES!

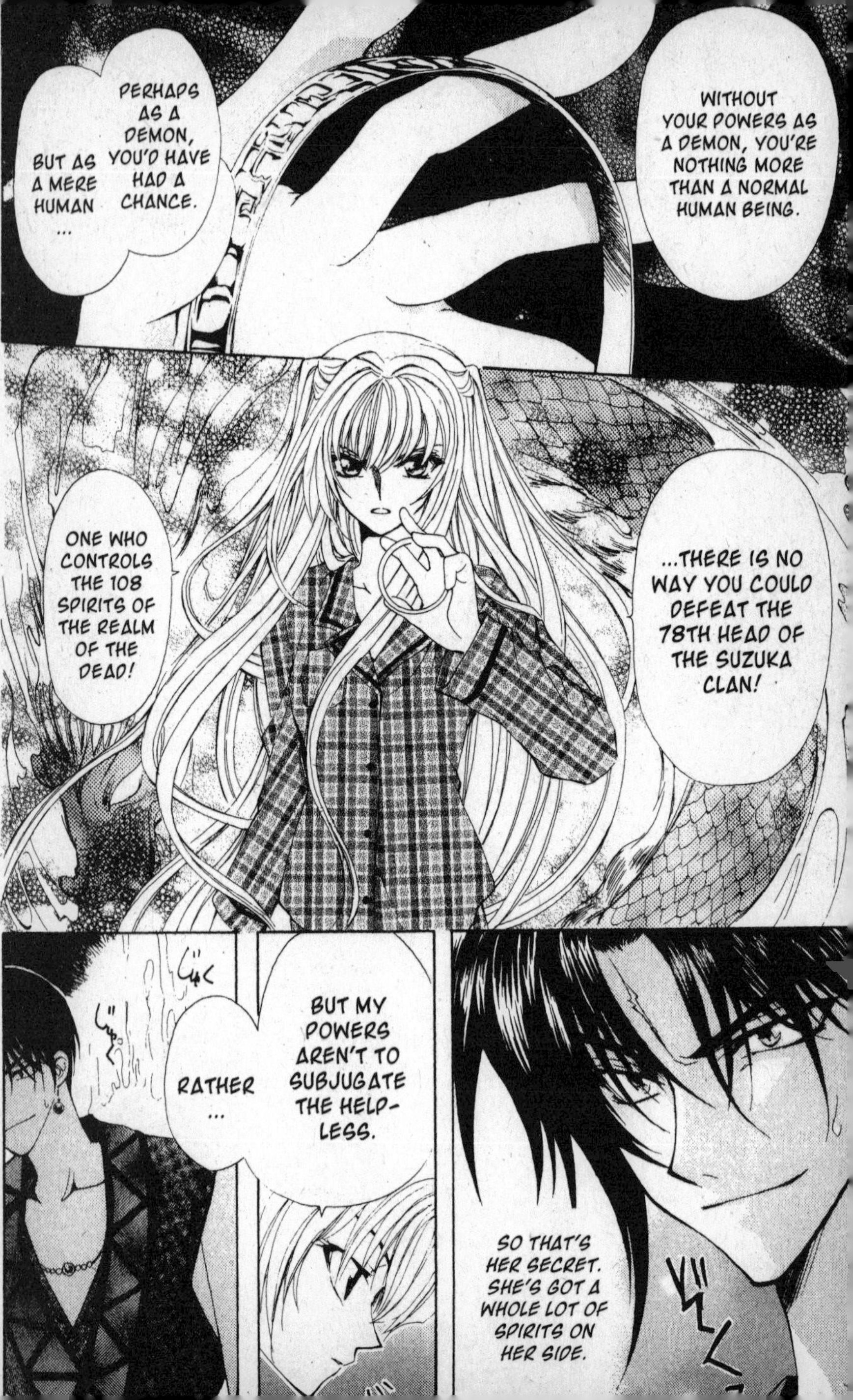
WITHOUT YOUR POWERS AS A DEMON, YOU'RE NOTHING MORE THAN A NORMAL HUMAN BEING.
PERHAPS AS A DEMON, YOU'D HAVE HAD A CHANCE.
BUT AS A MERE HUMAN ...
...THERE IS NO WAY YOU COULD DEFEAT THE 78TH HEAD OF THE SUZUKA CLAN!
ONE WHO CONTROLS THE 108 SPIRITS OF THE REALM OF THE DEAD!
SO THAT'S HER SECRET. SHE'S GOT A WHOLE LOT OF SPIRITS ON HER SIDE.
BUT MY POWERS AREN'T TO SUBJUGATE THE HELP-LESS.
RATHER ...

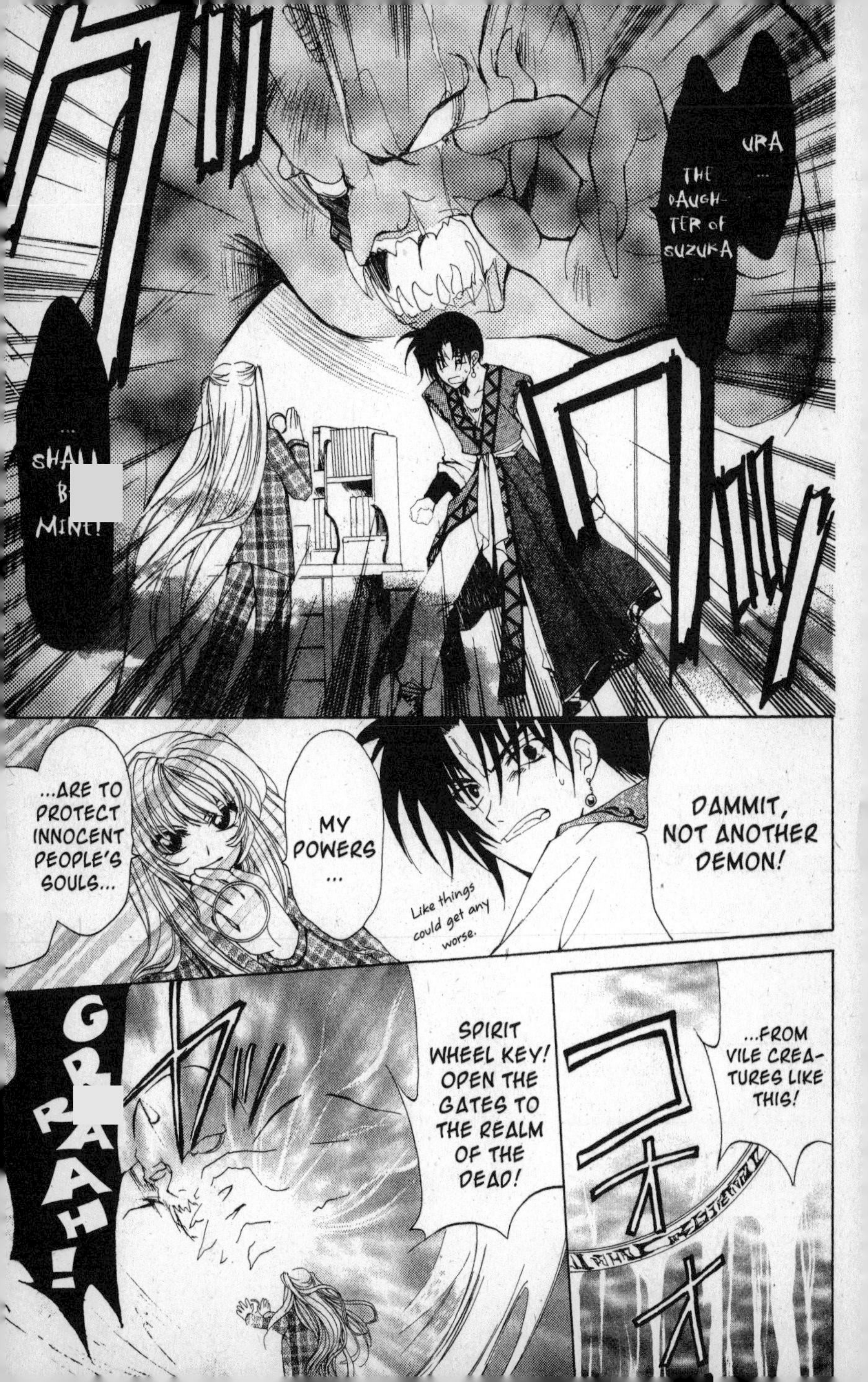
URA ... THE DAUGHTER of SUZUKA ...
... SHALL B MINE!
DAMMIT, NOT ANOTHER DEMON!
Like things could get any worse.
MY POWERS ...
...ARE TO PROTECT INNOCENT PEOPLE'S SOULS...
...FROM VILE CREATURES LIKE THIS!
SPIRIT WHEEL KEY! OPEN THE GATES TO THE REALM OF THE DEAD!
GRAAH!!

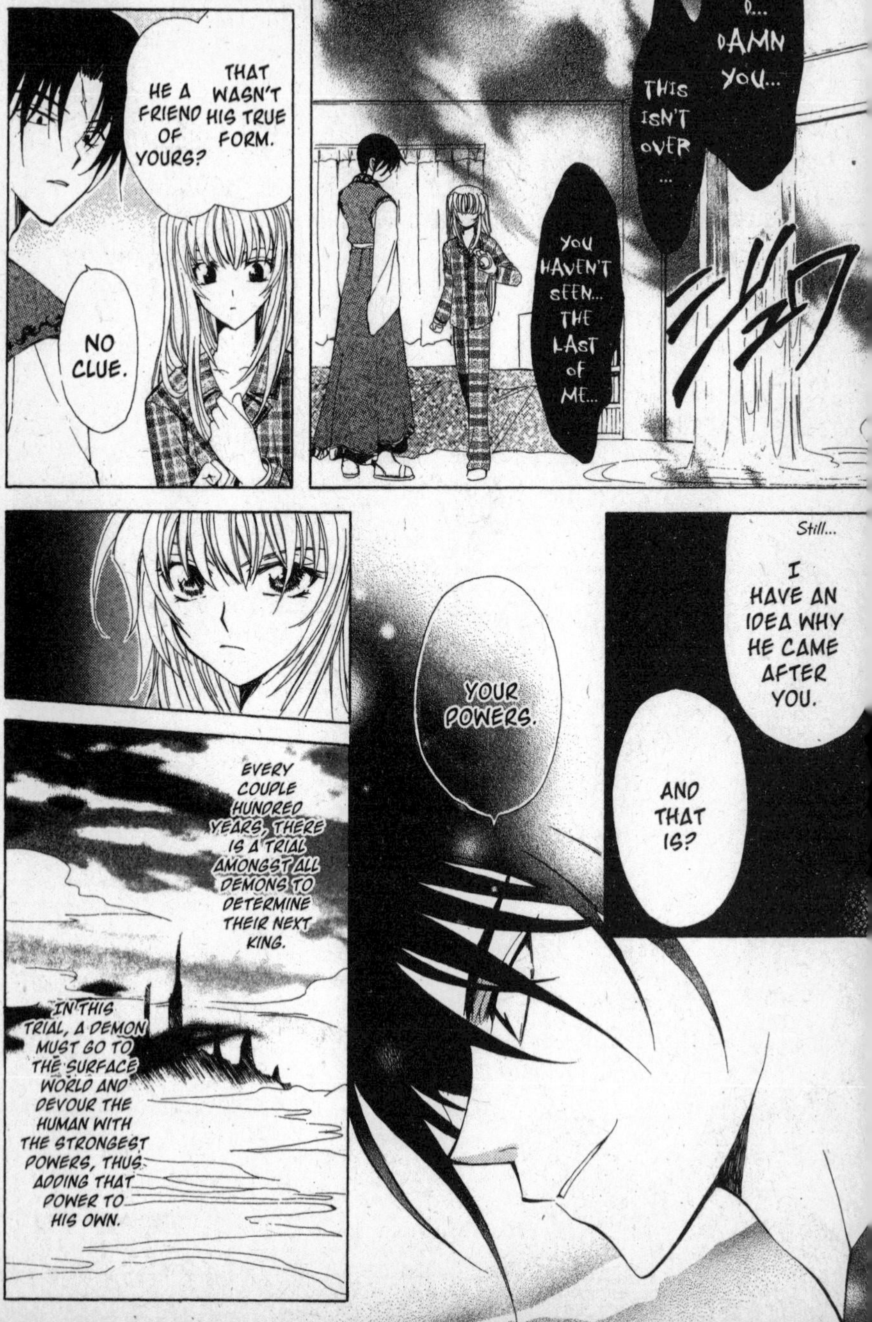
D... DAMN YOU...
THIS ISN'T OVER ...
YOU HAVEN'T SEEN... THE LAST OF ME...
THAT WASN'T HIS TRUE FORM.
HE A FRIEND OF YOURS?
NO CLUE.
Still... I HAVE AN IDEA WHY HE CAME AFTER YOU.
AND THAT IS?
YOUR POWERS.
EVERY COUPLE HUNDRED YEARS, THERE IS A TRIAL AMONGST ALL DEMONS TO DETERMINE THEIR NEXT KING.
IN THIS TRIAL, A DEMON MUST GO TO THE SURFACE WORLD AND DEVOUR THE HUMAN WITH THE STRONGEST POWERS, THUS ADDING THAT POWER TO HIS OWN.

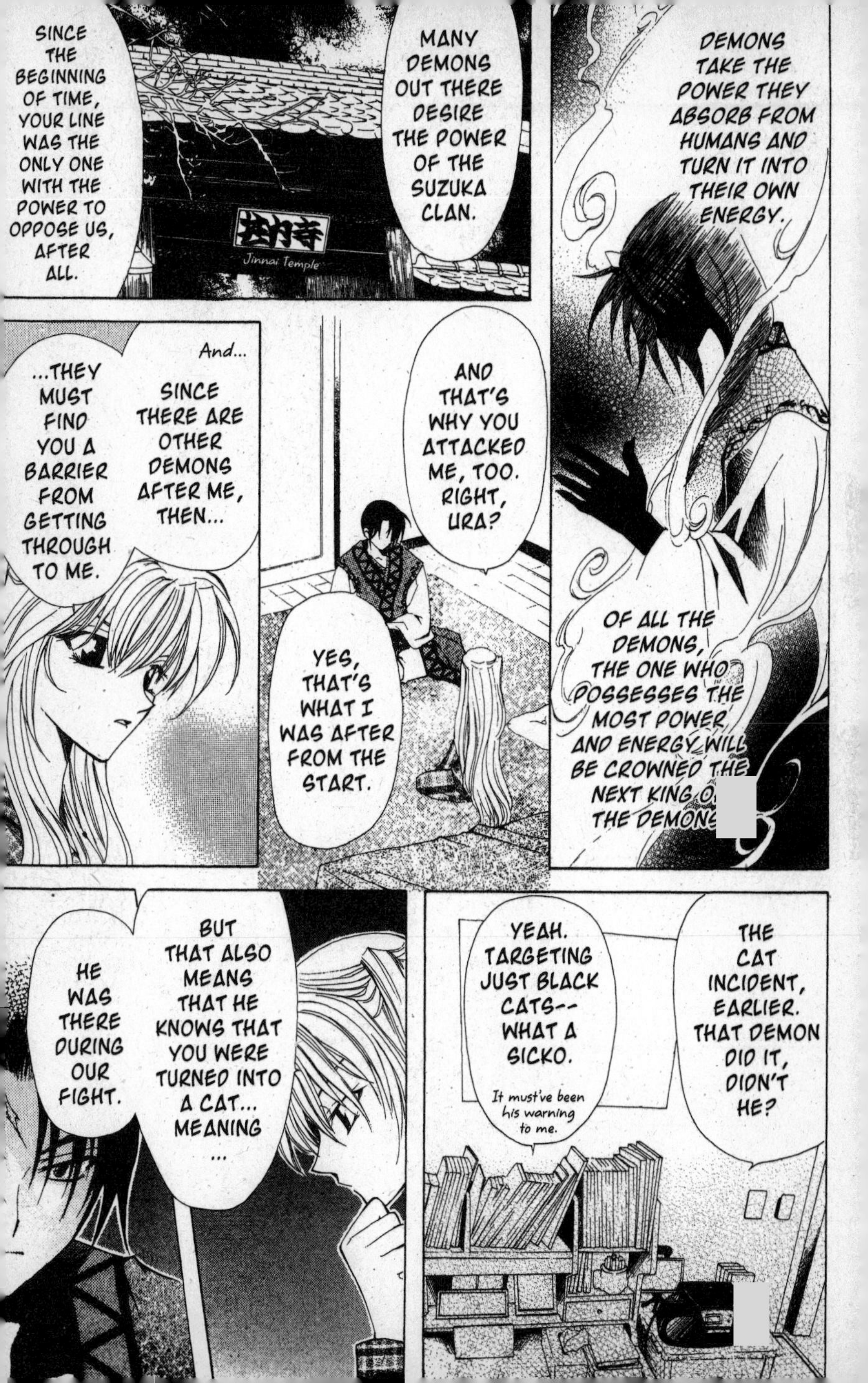
MANY DEMONS OUT THERE DESIRE THE POWER OF THE SUZUKA CLAN.
SINCE THE BEGINNING OF TIME, YOUR LINE WAS THE ONLY ONE WITH THE POWER TO OPPOSE US, AFTER ALL.
Jinnai Temple
DEMONS TAKE THE POWER THEY ABSORB FROM HUMANS AND TURN IT INTO THEIR OWN ENERGY.
OF ALL THE DEMONS, THE ONE WHO POSSESSES THE MOST POWER AND ENERGY WILL BE CROWNED THE NEXT KING OF THE DEMONS.
AND THAT'S WHY YOU ATTACKED ME, TOO. RIGHT, URA?
YES, THAT'S WHAT I WAS AFTER FROM THE START.
And...
SINCE THERE ARE OTHER DEMONS AFTER ME, THEN...
...THEY MUST FIND YOU A BARRIER FROM GETTING THROUGH TO ME.
THE CAT INCIDENT, EARLIER. THAT DEMON DID IT, DIDN'T HE?
YEAH. TARGETING JUST BLACK CATS-- WHAT A SICKO.
It must've been his warning to me.
BUT THAT ALSO MEANS THAT HE KNOWS THAT YOU WERE TURNED INTO A CAT... MEANING ...
HE WAS THERE DURING OUR FIGHT.

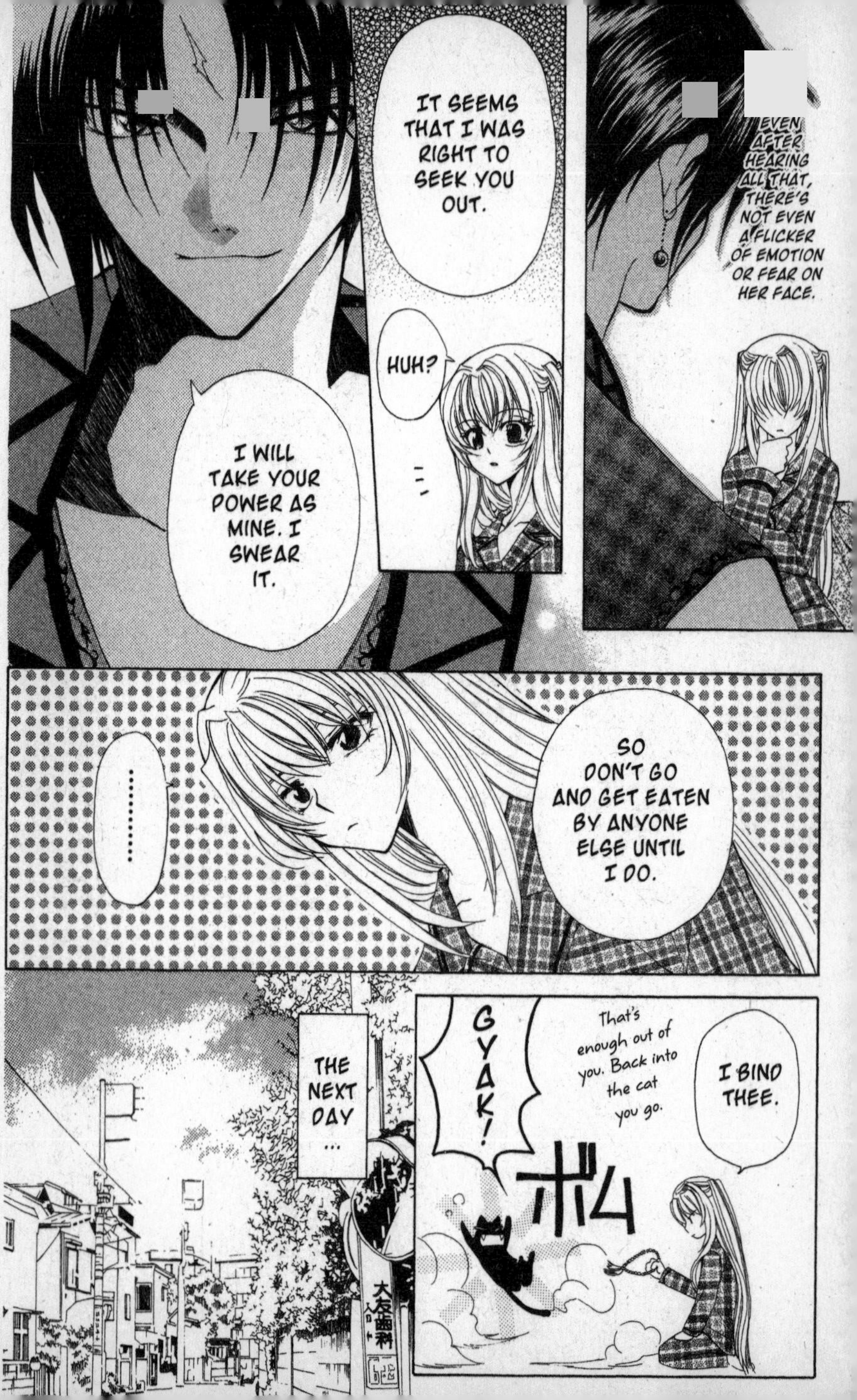
EVEN AFTER HEARING ALL THAT, THERE'S NOT EVEN A FLICKER OF EMOTION OR FEAR ON HER FACE.
IT SEEMS THAT I WAS RIGHT TO SEEK YOU OUT.
HUH?
I WILL TAKE YOUR POWER AS MINE. I SWEAR IT.
SO DON'T GO AND GET EATEN BY ANYONE ELSE UNTIL I DO.
……
I BIND THEE.
That's enough out of you. Back into the cat you go.
GYAK!
ボム
THE NEXT DAY ...

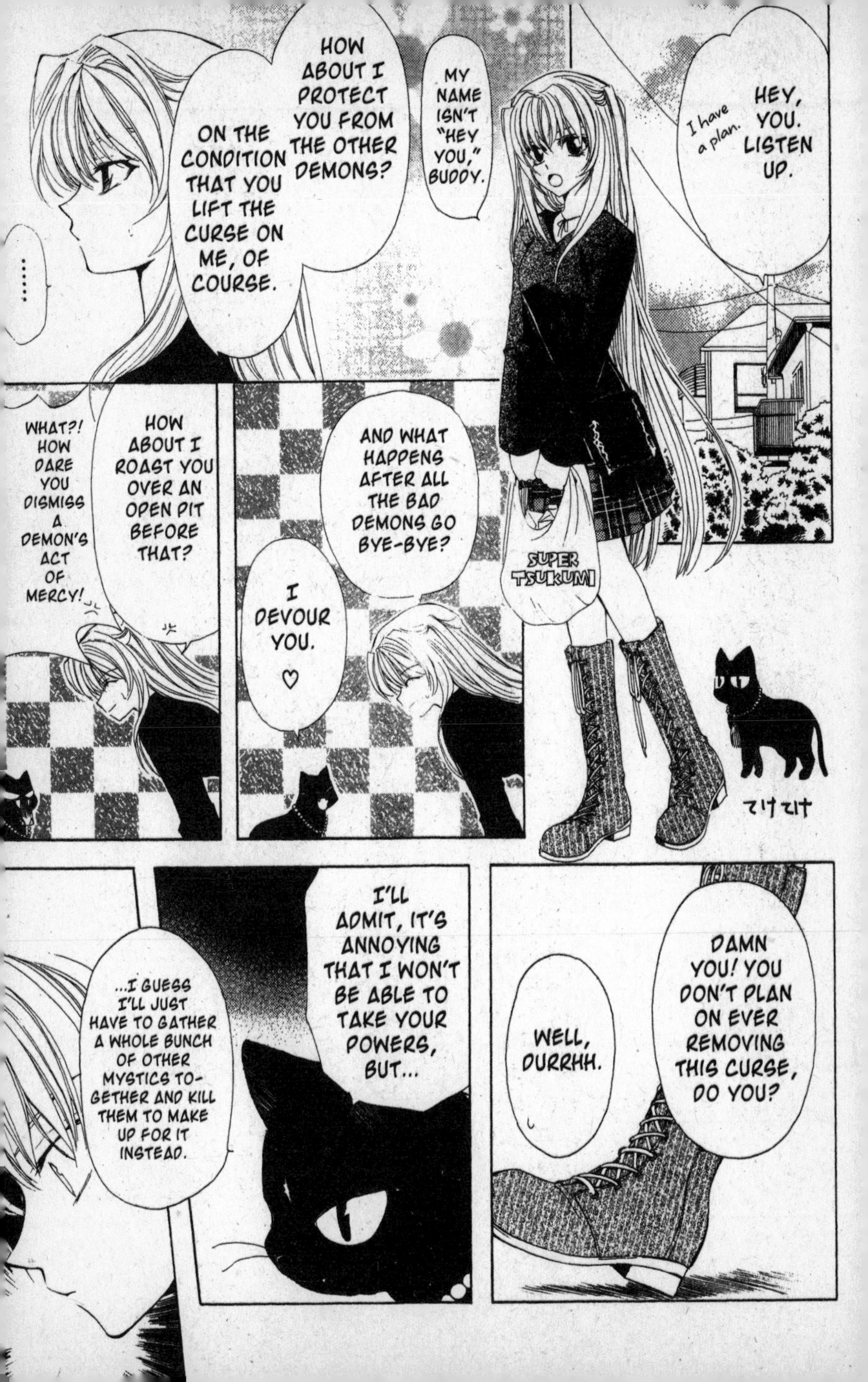
HEY, YOU. LISTEN UP.
I have a plan.
MY NAME ISN'T "HEY YOU," BUDDY.
HOW ABOUT I PROTECT YOU FROM THE OTHER DEMONS?
ON THE CONDITION THAT YOU LIFT THE CURSE ON ME, OF COURSE.
SUPER TSUKUMI
てけてけ
……
AND WHAT HAPPENS AFTER ALL THE BAD DEMONS GO BYE-BYE?
I DEVOUR YOU. ♡
WHAT?! HOW DARE YOU DISMISS A DEMON'S ACT OF MERCY!
HOW ABOUT I ROAST YOU OVER AN OPEN PIT BEFORE THAT?
DAMN YOU! YOU DON'T PLAN ON EVER REMOVING THIS CURSE, DO YOU?
WELL, DURRHH.
I'LL ADMIT, IT'S ANNOYING THAT I WON'T BE ABLE TO TAKE YOUR POWERS, BUT...
...I GUESS I'LL JUST HAVE TO GATHER A WHOLE BUNCH OF OTHER MYSTICS TO-GETHER AND KILL THEM TO MAKE UP FOR IT INSTEAD.

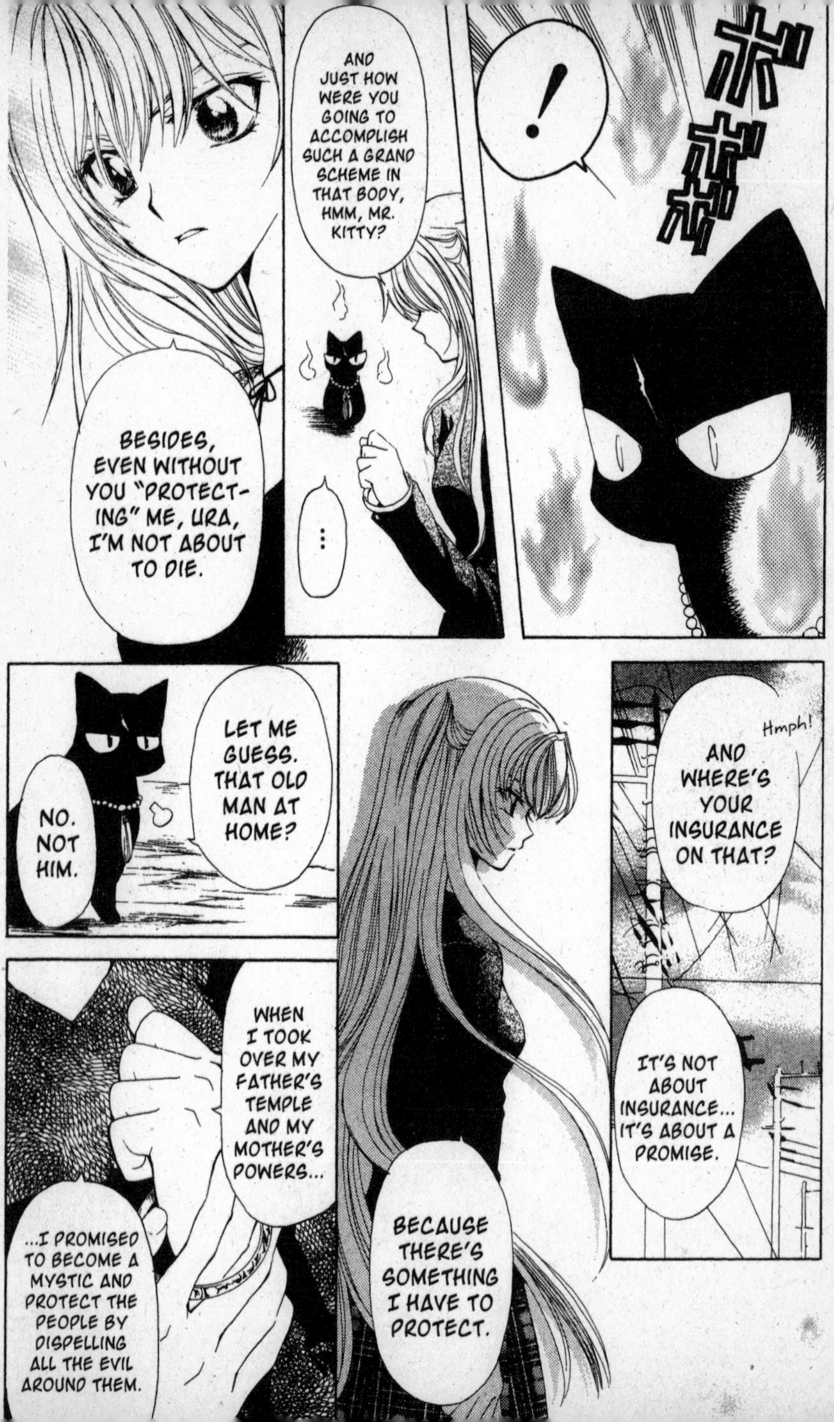
!
AND JUST HOW WERE YOU GOING TO ACCOMPLISH SUCH A GRAND SCHEME IN THAT BODY, HMM, MR. KITTY?
...
BESIDES, EVEN WITHOUT YOU "PROTECTING" ME, URA, I'M NOT ABOUT TO DIE.
Hmph!
AND WHERE'S YOUR INSURANCE ON THAT?
IT'S NOT ABOUT INSURANCE... IT'S ABOUT A PROMISE.
BECAUSE THERE'S SOMETHING I HAVE TO PROTECT.
LET ME GUESS. THAT OLD MAN AT HOME?
NO. NOT HIM.
WHEN I TOOK OVER MY FATHER'S TEMPLE AND MY MOTHER'S POWERS...
...I PROMISED TO BECOME A MYSTIC AND PROTECT THE PEOPLE BY DISPELLING ALL THE EVIL AROUND THEM.

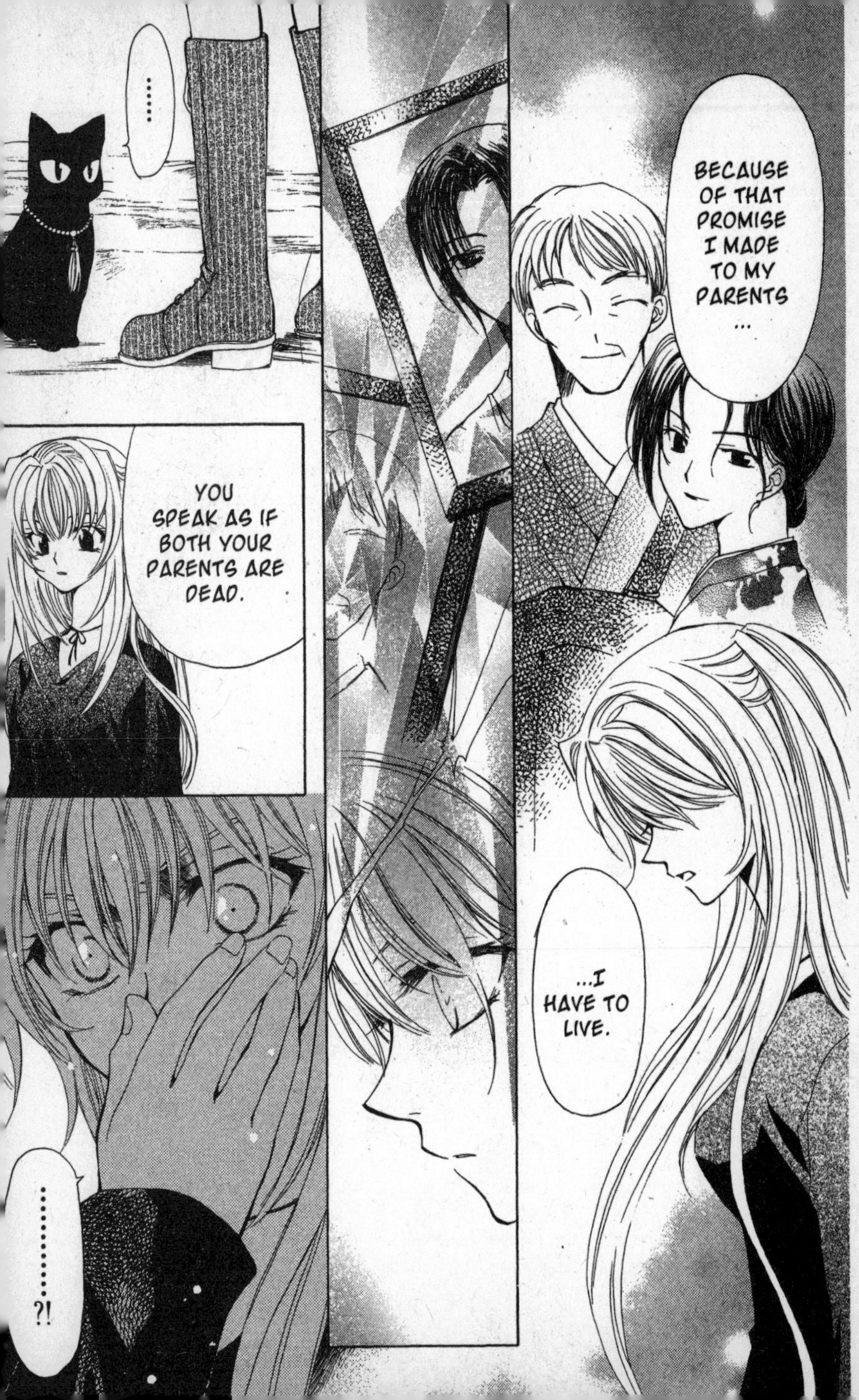
BECAUSE OF THAT PROMISE I MADE TO MY PARENTS ...
...I HAVE TO LIVE.
......
YOU SPEAK AS IF BOTH YOUR PARENTS ARE DEAD.
.........?!

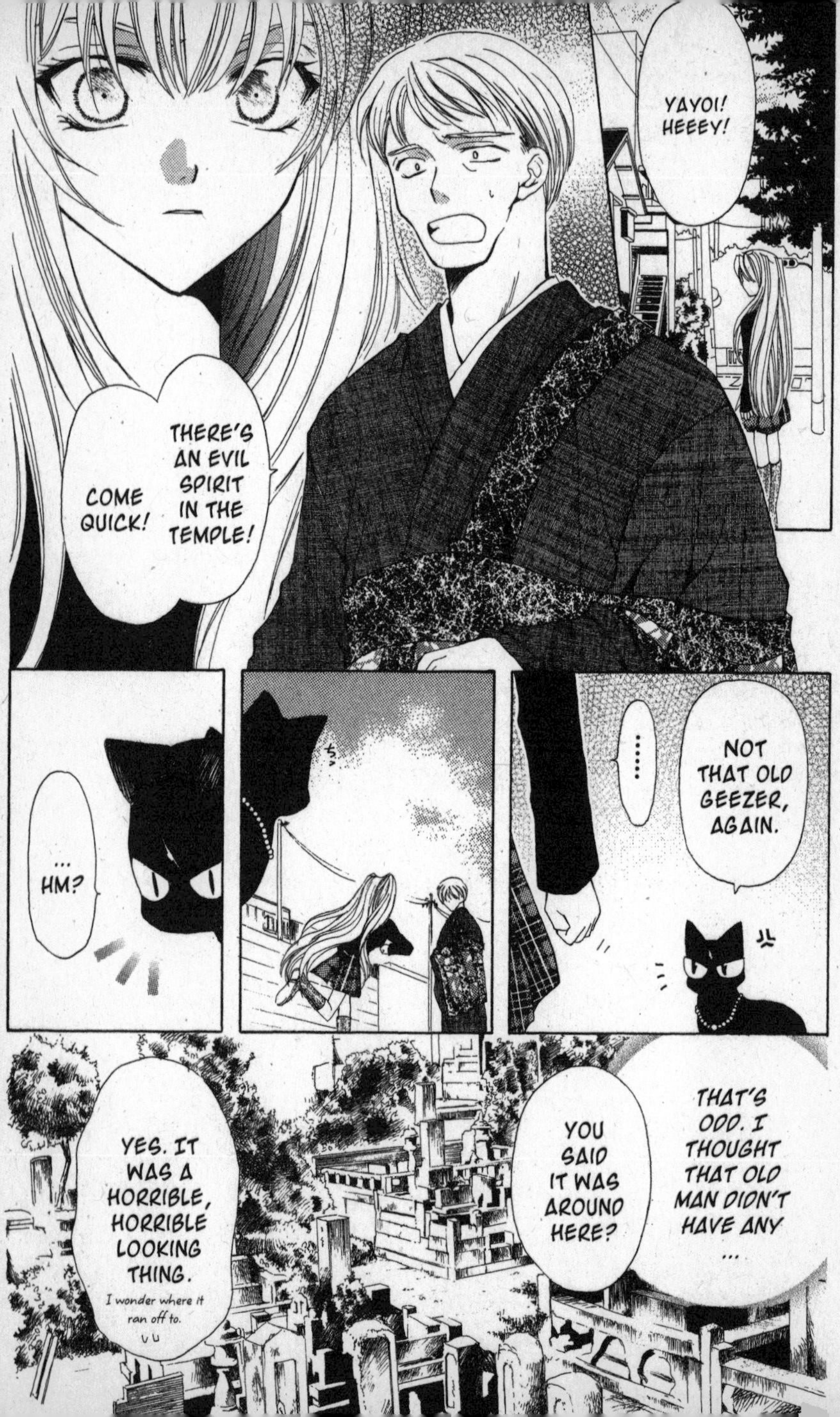
YAYOI! HEEEY!
THERE'S AN EVIL SPIRIT IN THE TEMPLE!
COME QUICK!
NOT THAT OLD GEEZER, AGAIN.
......
... HM?
THAT'S ODD. I THOUGHT THAT OLD MAN DIDN'T HAVE ANY ...
YOU SAID IT WAS AROUND HERE?
YES. IT WAS A HORRIBLE, HORRIBLE LOOKING THING.
I wonder where it ran off to.

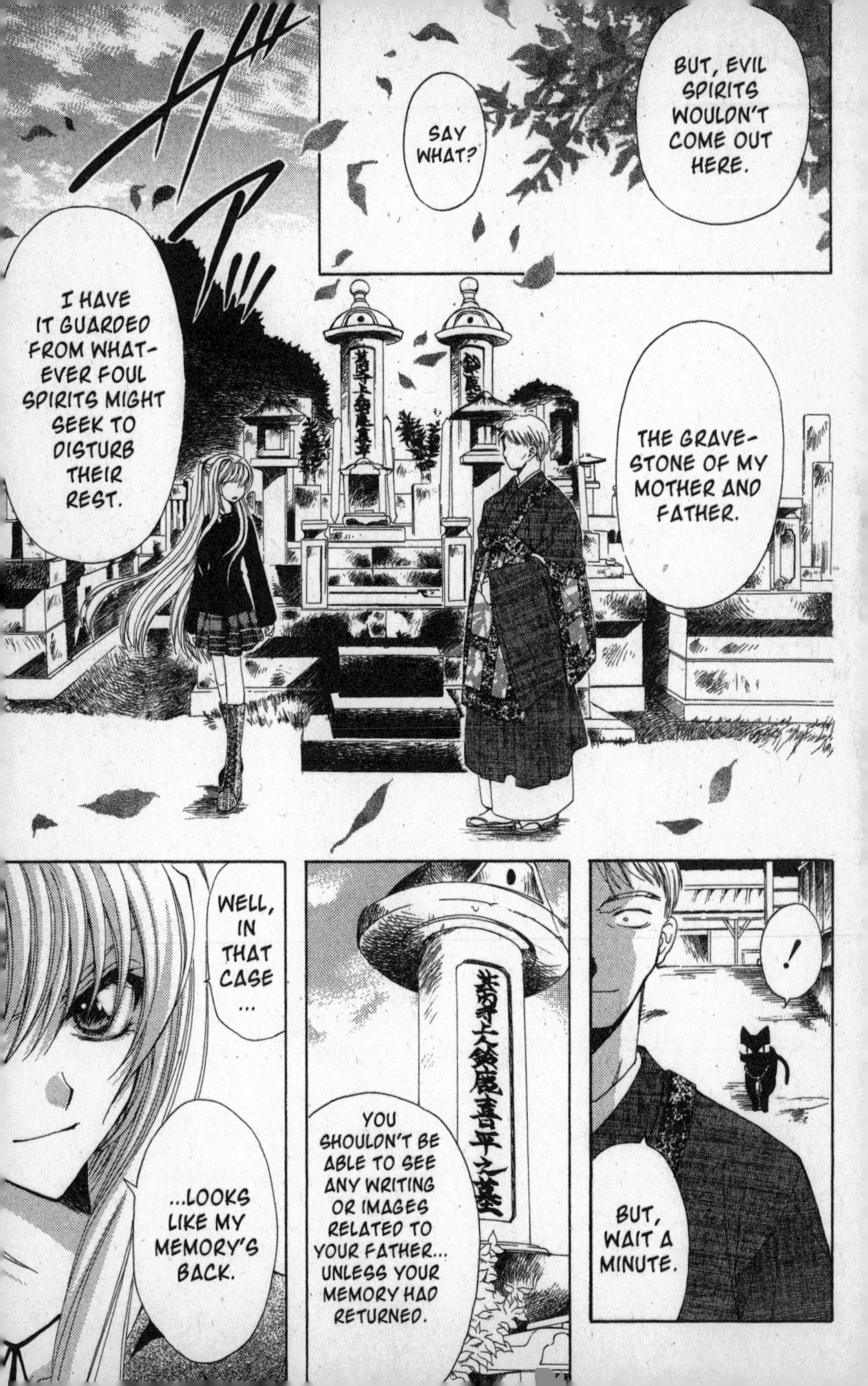
BUT, EVIL SPIRITS WOULDN'T COME OUT HERE.
SAY WHAT?
THE GRAVESTONE OF MY MOTHER AND FATHER.
I HAVE IT GUARDED FROM WHATEVER FOUL SPIRITS MIGHT SEEK TO DISTURB THEIR REST.
!
BUT, WAIT A MINUTE.
YOU SHOULDN'T BE ABLE TO SEE ANY WRITING OR IMAGES RELATED TO YOUR FATHER... UNLESS YOUR MEMORY HAD RETURNED.
WELL, IN THAT CASE ...
...LOOKS LIKE MY MEMORY'S BACK.

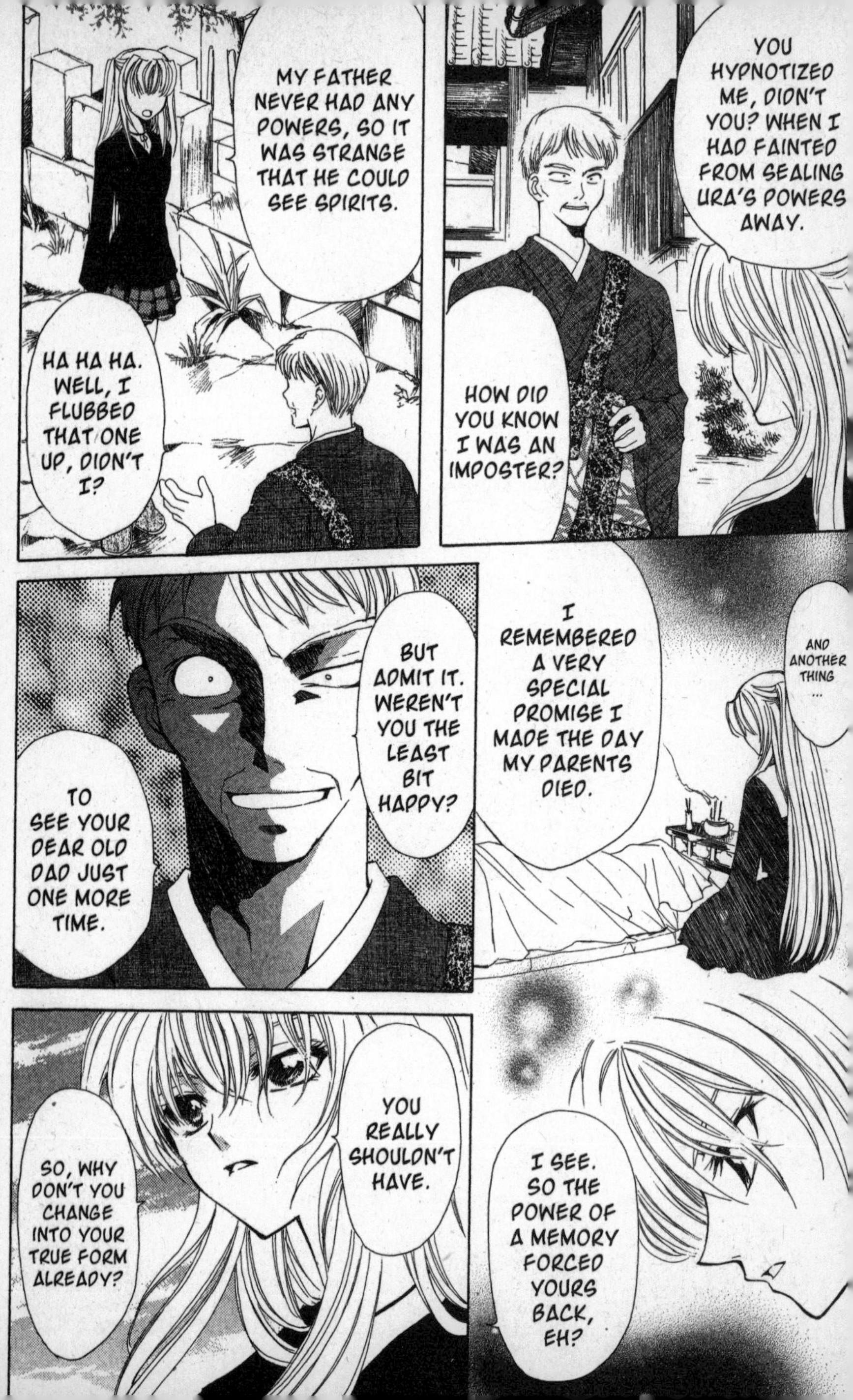
YOU HYPNOTIZED ME, DIDN'T YOU? WHEN I HAD FAINTED FROM SEALING URA'S POWERS AWAY.
HOW DID YOU KNOW I WAS AN IMPOSTER?
MY FATHER NEVER HAD ANY POWERS, SO IT WAS STRANGE THAT HE COULD SEE SPIRITS.
HA HA HA. WELL, I FLUBBED THAT ONE UP, DIDN'T I?
AND ANOTHER THING ...
I REMEMBERED A VERY SPECIAL PROMISE I MADE THE DAY MY PARENTS DIED.
BUT ADMIT IT. WEREN'T YOU THE LEAST BIT HAPPY?
TO SEE YOUR DEAR OLD DAD JUST ONE MORE TIME.
I SEE. SO THE POWER OF A MEMORY FORCED YOURS BACK, EH?
YOU REALLY SHOULDN'T HAVE.
SO, WHY DON'T YOU CHANGE INTO YOUR TRUE FORM ALREADY?

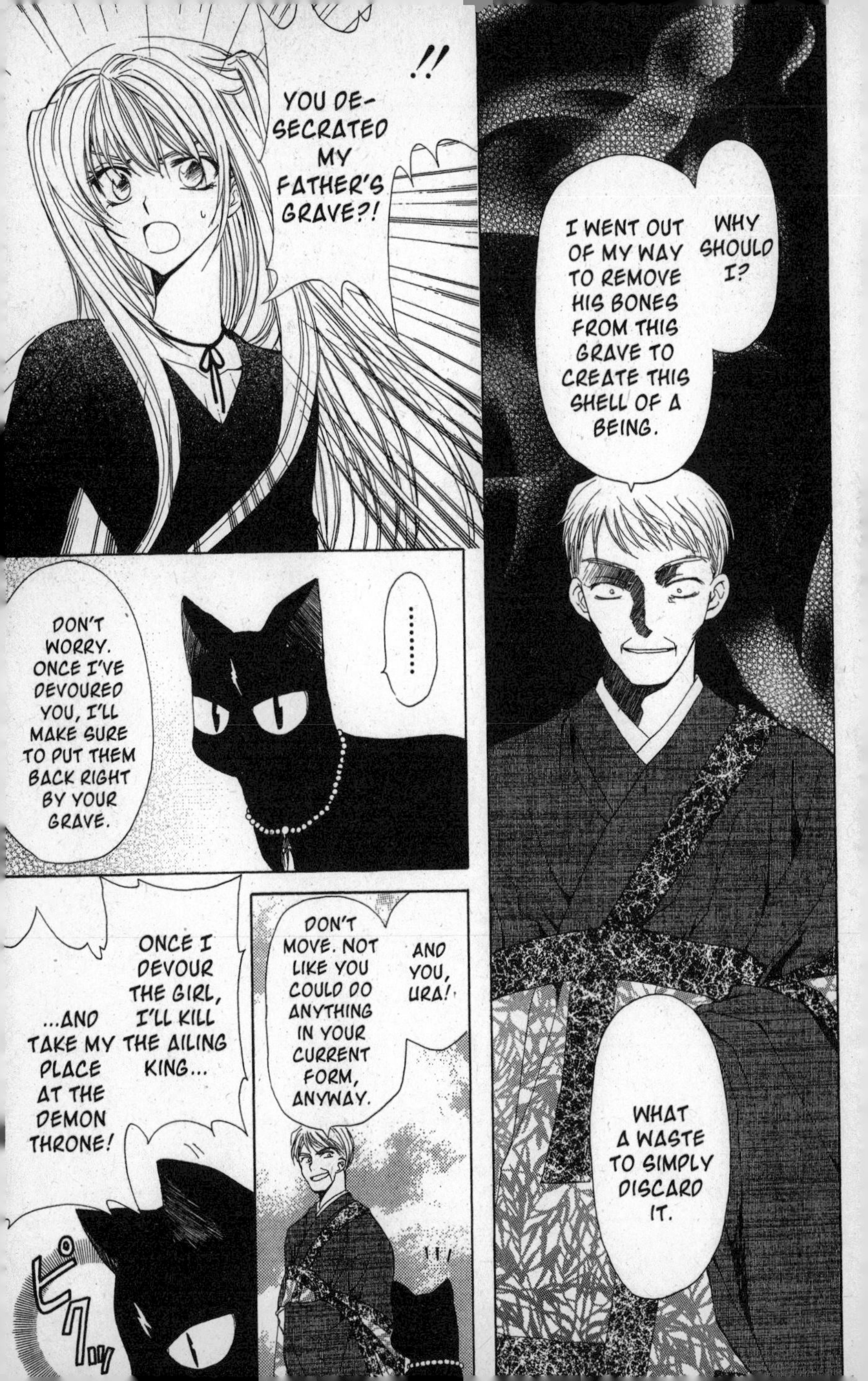
WHY SHOULD I?
I WENT OUT OF MY WAY TO REMOVE HIS BONES FROM THIS GRAVE TO CREATE THIS SHELL OF A BEING.
WHAT A WASTE TO SIMPLY DISCARD IT.
!!
YOU DE-SECRATED MY FATHER'S GRAVE?!
......
DON'T WORRY. ONCE I'VE DEVOURED YOU, I'LL MAKE SURE TO PUT THEM BACK RIGHT BY YOUR GRAVE.
AND YOU, URA!
DON'T MOVE. NOT LIKE YOU COULD DO ANYTHING IN YOUR CURRENT FORM, ANYWAY.
ONCE I DEVOUR THE GIRL, I'LL KILL THE AILING KING...
...AND TAKE MY PLACE AT THE DEMON THRONE!

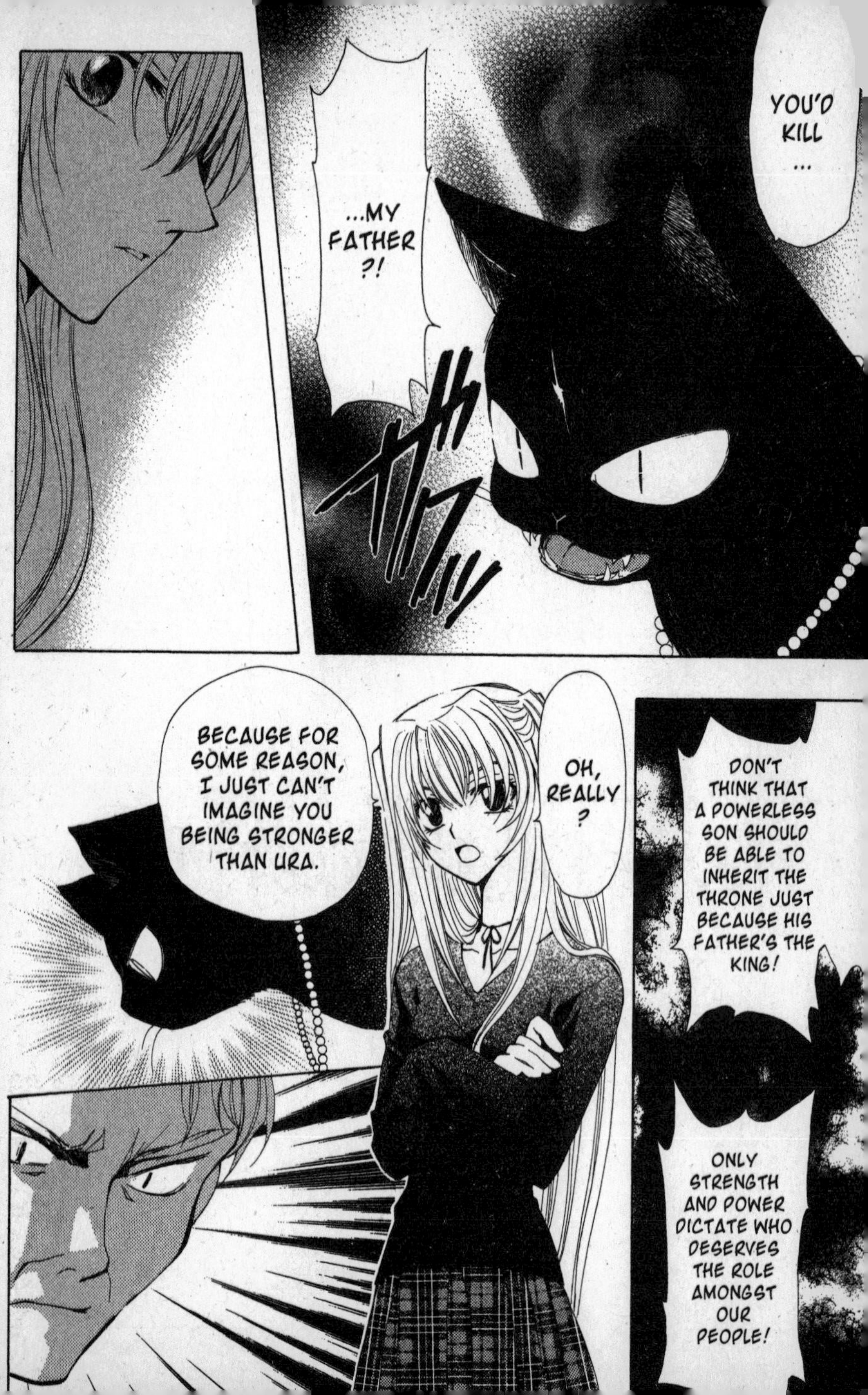
YOU'D KILL ...
...MY FATHER ?!
DON'T THINK THAT A POWERLESS SON SHOULD BE ABLE TO INHERIT THE THRONE JUST BECAUSE HIS FATHER'S THE KING!
ONLY STRENGTH AND POWER DICTATE WHO DESERVES THE ROLE AMONGST OUR PEOPLE!
OH, REALLY ?
BECAUSE FOR SOME REASON, I JUST CAN'T IMAGINE YOU BEING STRONGER THAN URA.

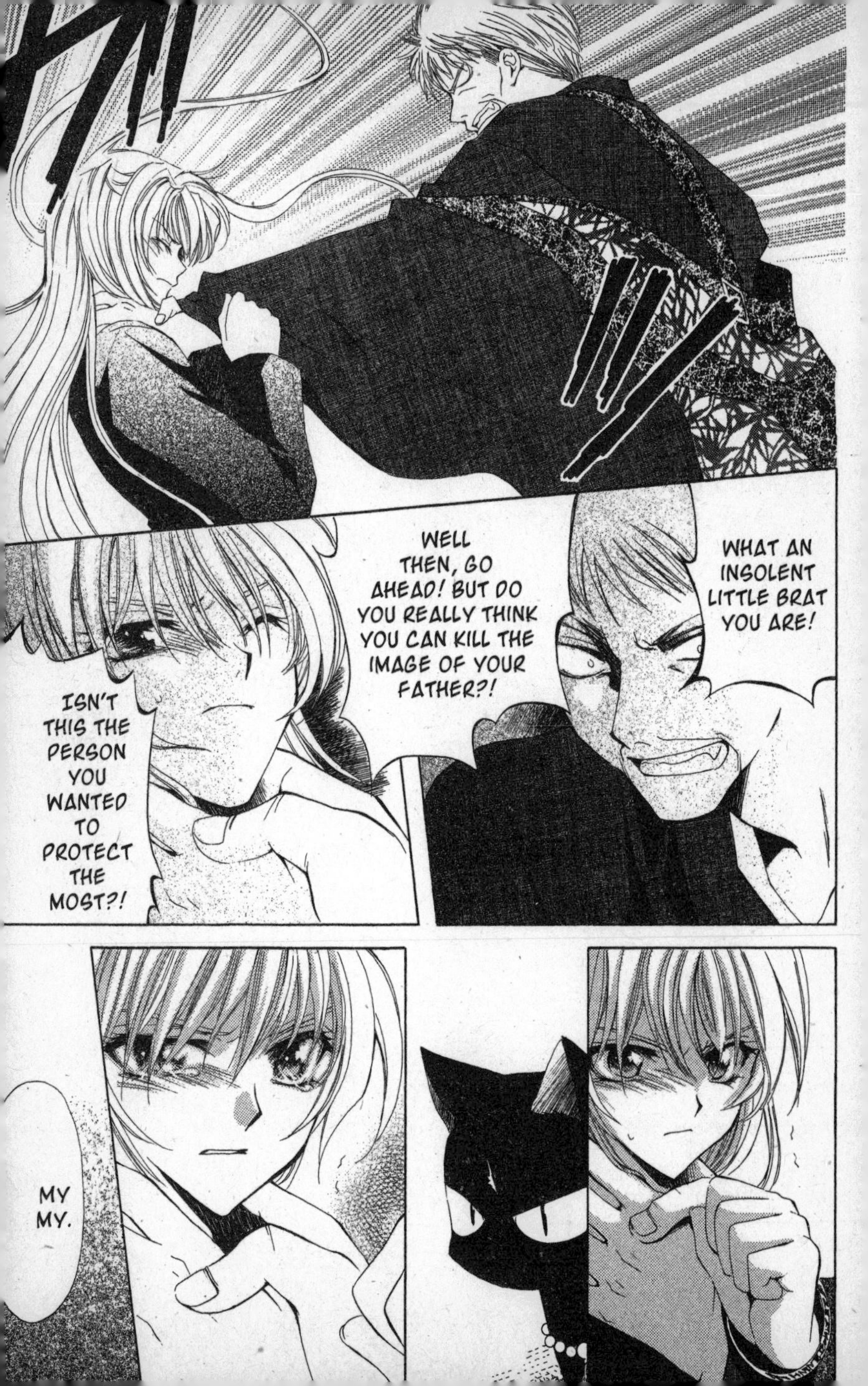
WHAT AN INSOLENT LITTLE BRAT YOU ARE!
WELL THEN, GO AHEAD! BUT DO YOU REALLY THINK YOU CAN KILL THE IMAGE OF YOUR FATHER?!
ISN'T THIS THE PERSON YOU WANTED TO PROTECT THE MOST?!
MY MY.

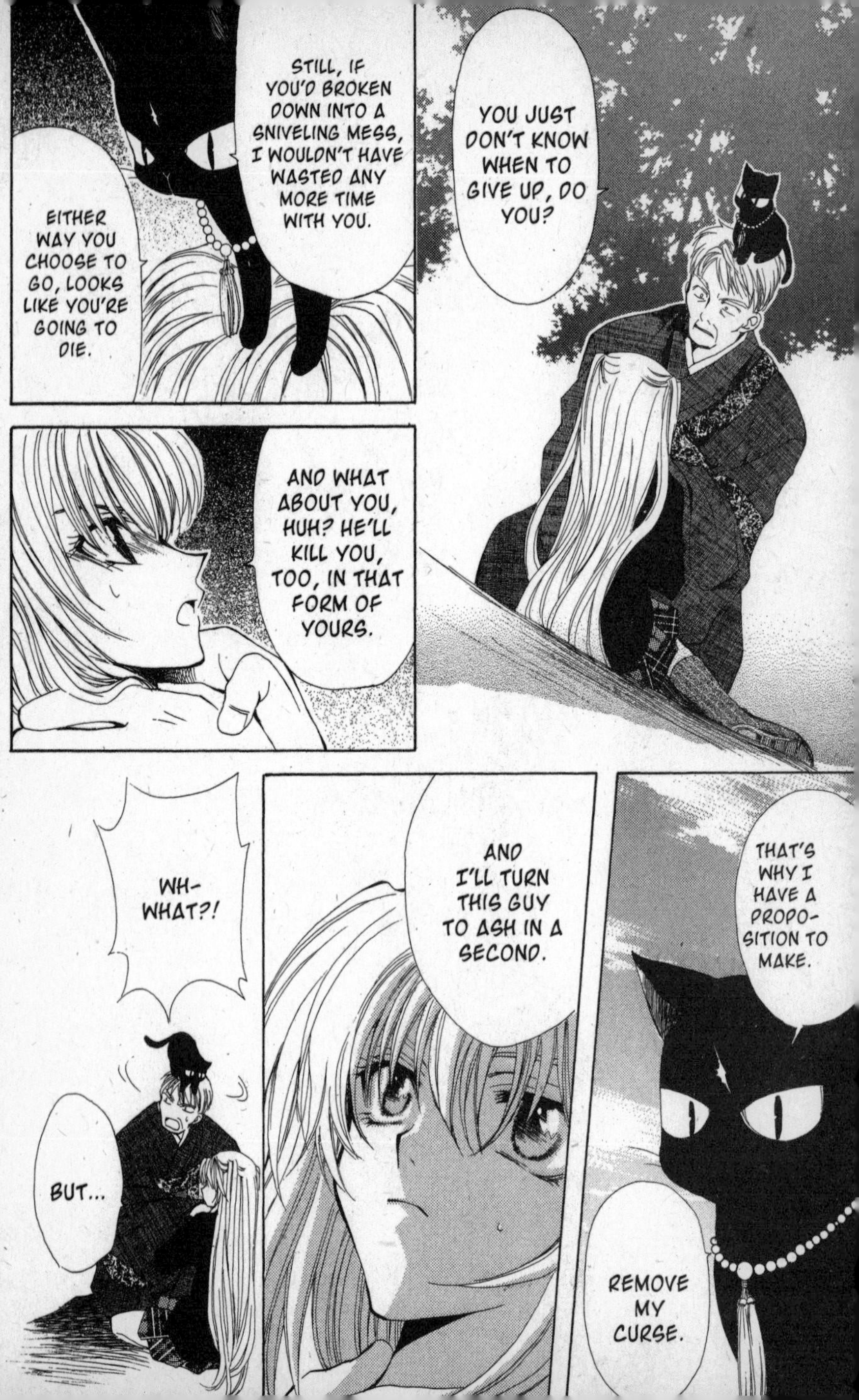
YOU JUST DON'T KNOW WHEN TO GIVE UP, DO YOU?
STILL, IF YOU'D BROKEN DOWN INTO A SNIVELING MESS, I WOULDN'T HAVE WASTED ANY MORE TIME WITH YOU.
EITHER WAY YOU CHOOSE TO GO, LOOKS LIKE YOU'RE GOING TO DIE.
AND WHAT ABOUT YOU, HUH? HE'LL KILL YOU, TOO, IN THAT FORM OF YOURS.
THAT'S WHY I HAVE A PROPO-SITION TO MAKE.
REMOVE MY CURSE.
AND I'LL TURN THIS GUY TO ASH IN A SECOND.
WH-WHAT?!
BUT...

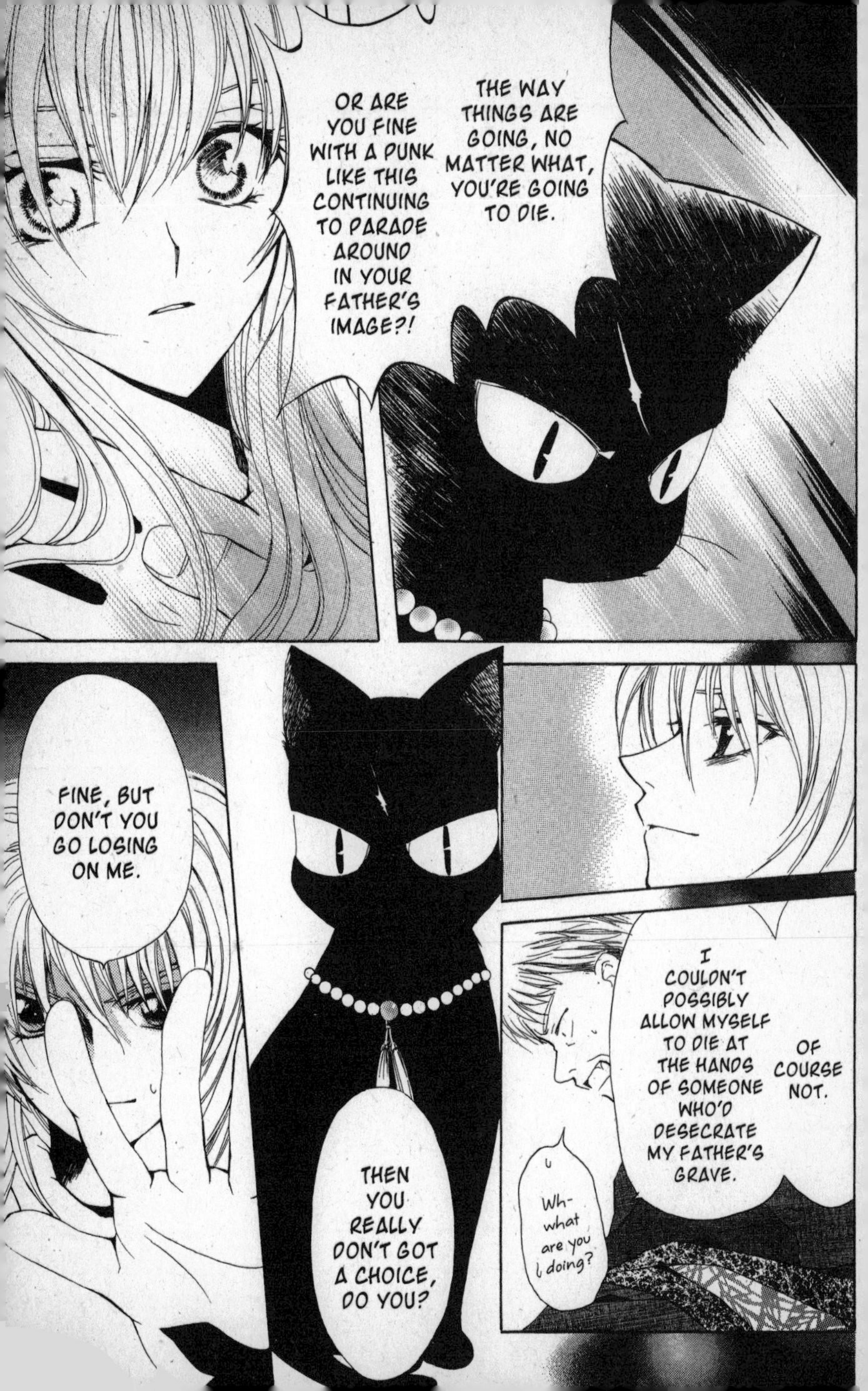
THE WAY THINGS ARE GOING, NO MATTER WHAT, YOU'RE GOING TO DIE.
OR ARE YOU FINE WITH A PUNK LIKE THIS CONTINUING TO PARADE AROUND IN YOUR FATHER'S IMAGE?!
OF COURSE NOT.
I COULDN'T POSSIBLY ALLOW MYSELF TO DIE AT THE HANDS OF SOMEONE WHO'D DESECRATE MY FATHER'S GRAVE.
Wh-what are you doing?
THEN YOU REALLY DON'T GOT A CHOICE, DO YOU?
FINE, BUT DON'T YOU GO LOSING ON ME.

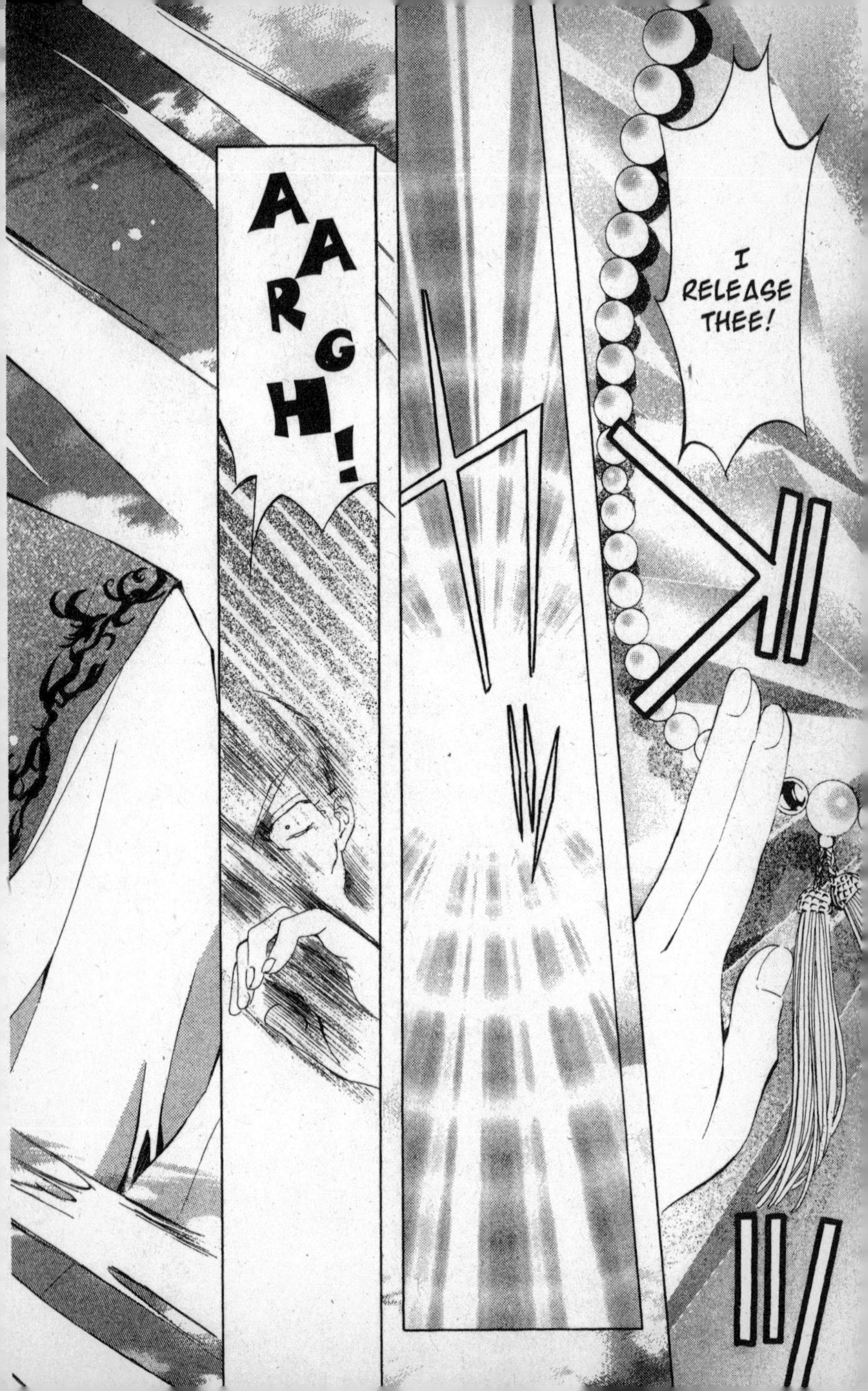
I RELEASE THEE!
AARGH!

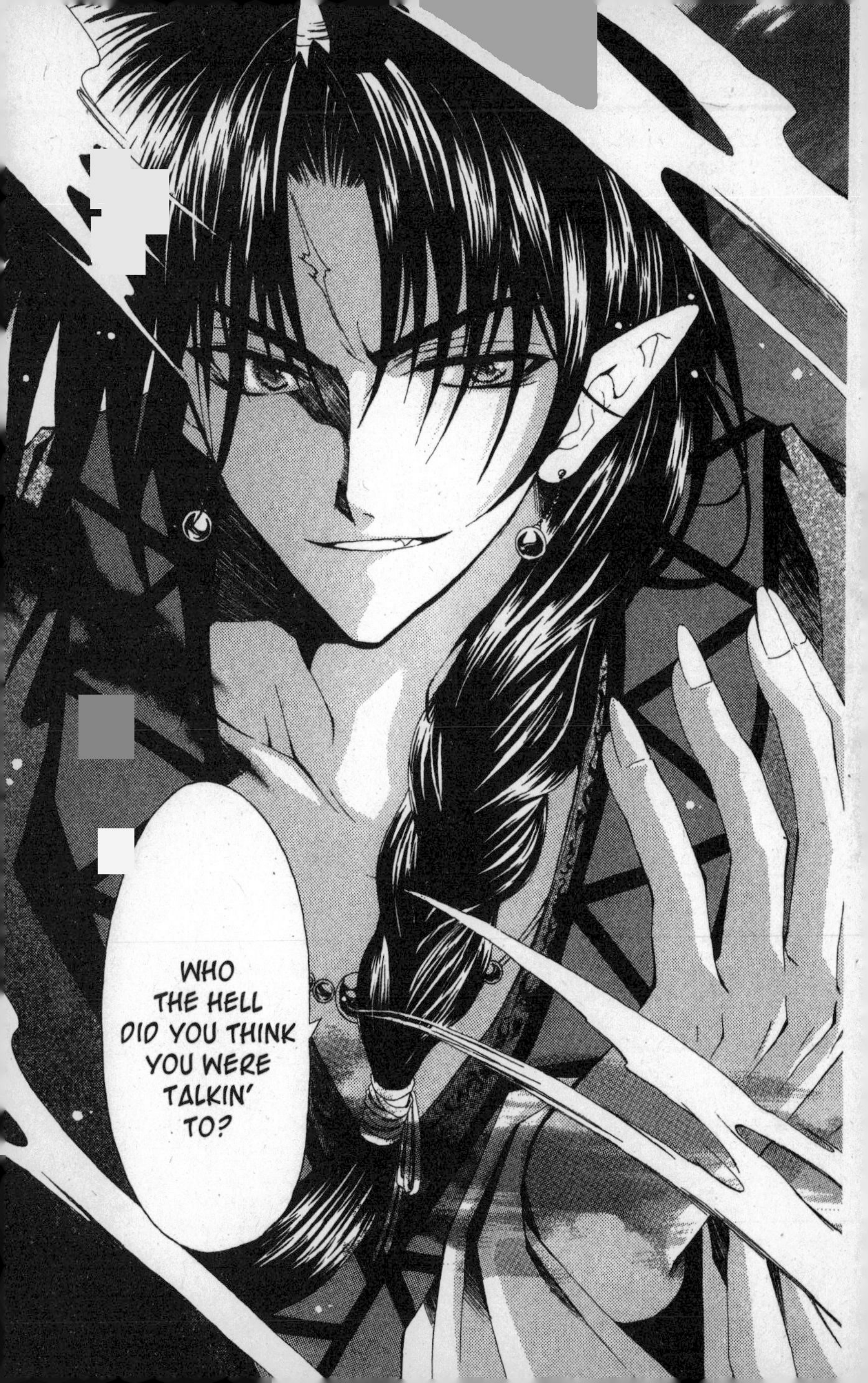
WHO THE HELL DID YOU THINK YOU WERE TALKIN' TO?

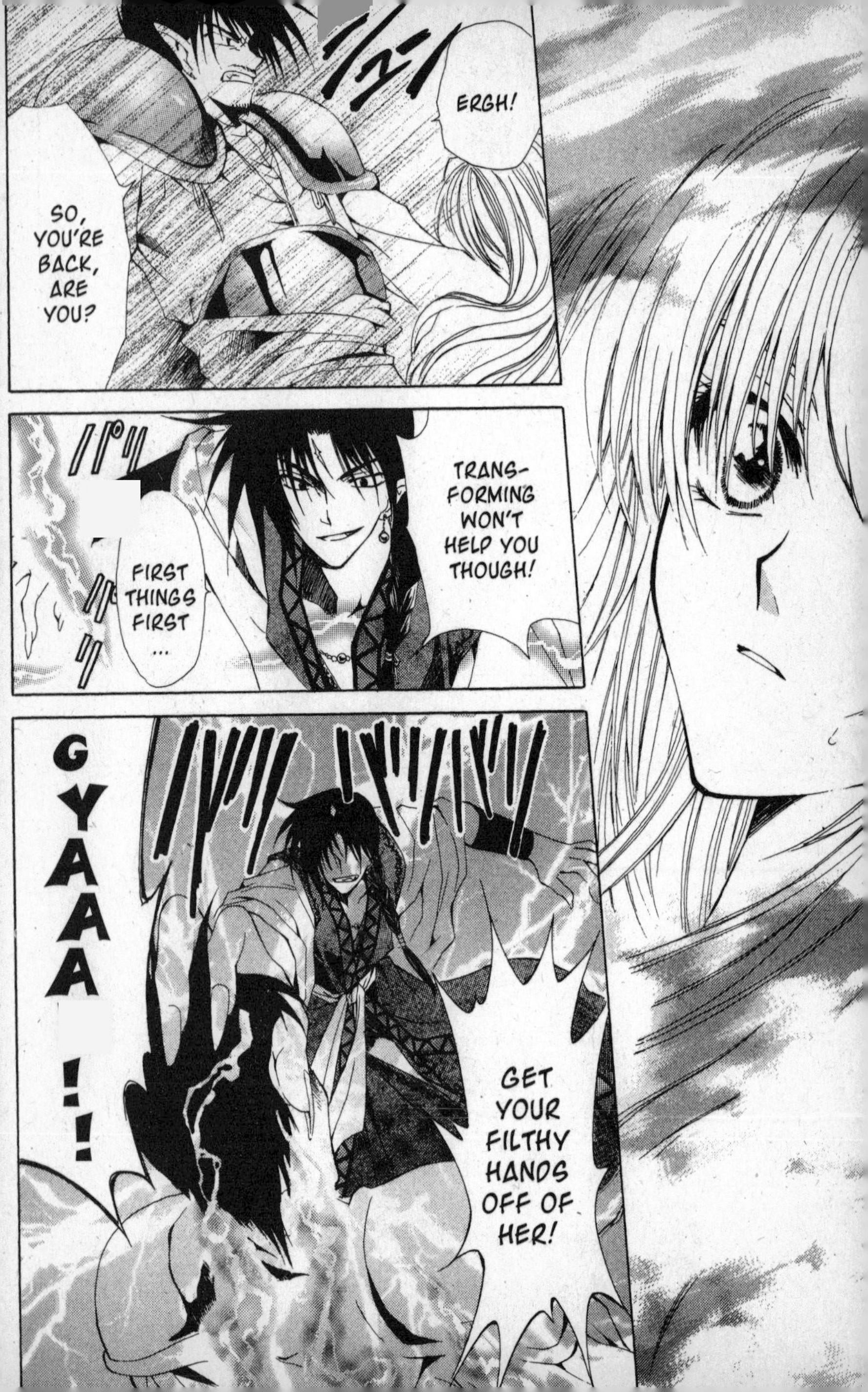
ERGH!
SO, YOU'RE BACK, ARE YOU?
TRANS-FORMING WON'T HELP YOU THOUGH!
FIRST THINGS FIRST ...
GET YOUR FILTHY HANDS OFF OF HER!
GYAAA!!!

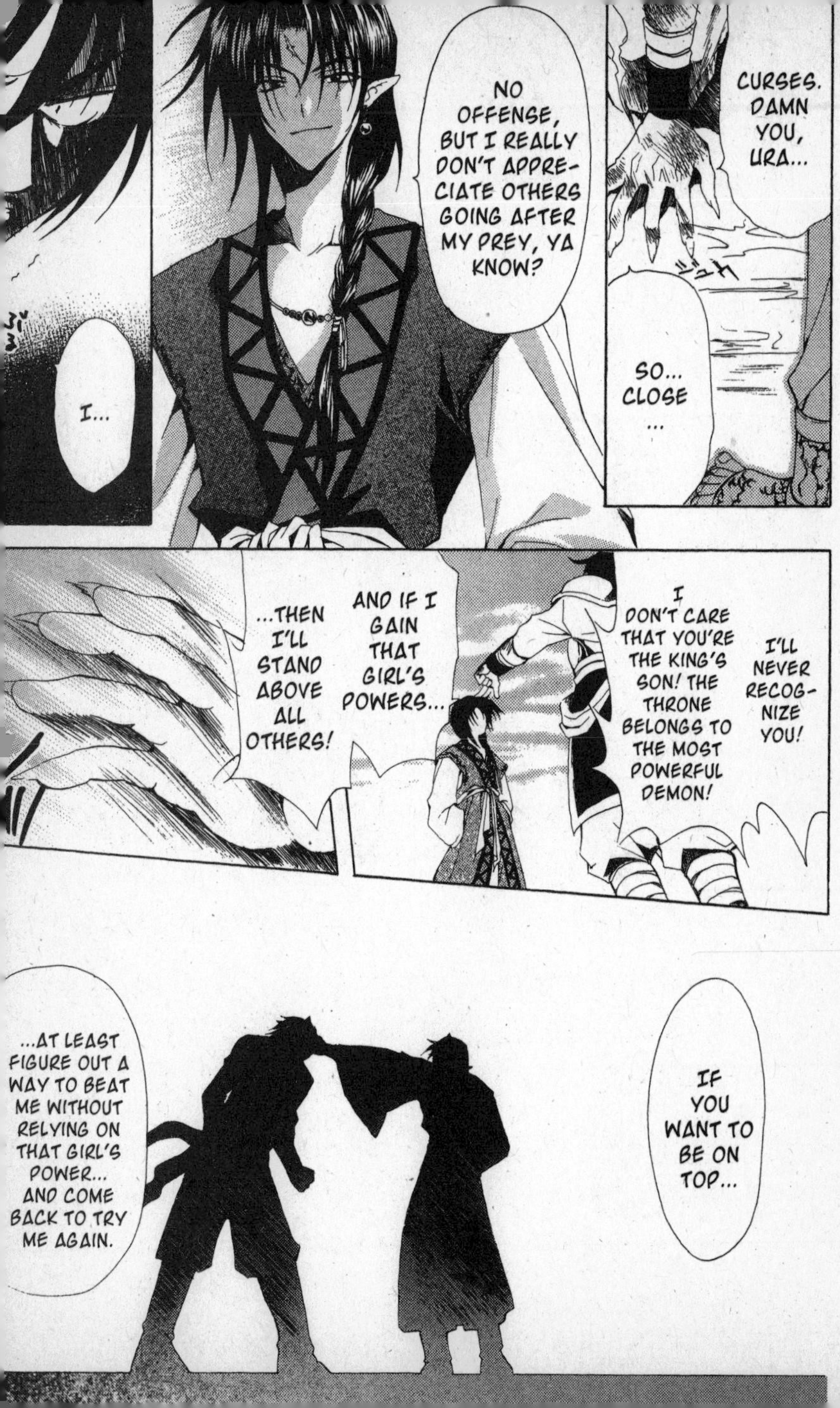
CURSES. DAMN YOU, URA...
SO... CLOSE ...
NO OFFENSE, BUT I REALLY DON'T APPRECIATE OTHERS GOING AFTER MY PREY, YA KNOW?
I...
I'LL NEVER RECOGNIZE YOU!
I DON'T CARE THAT YOU'RE THE KING'S SON! THE THRONE BELONGS TO THE MOST POWERFUL DEMON!
AND IF I GAIN THAT GIRL'S POWERS...
...THEN I'LL STAND ABOVE ALL OTHERS!
IF YOU WANT TO BE ON TOP...
...AT LEAST FIGURE OUT A WAY TO BEAT ME WITHOUT RELYING ON THAT GIRL'S POWER... AND COME BACK TO TRY ME AGAIN.

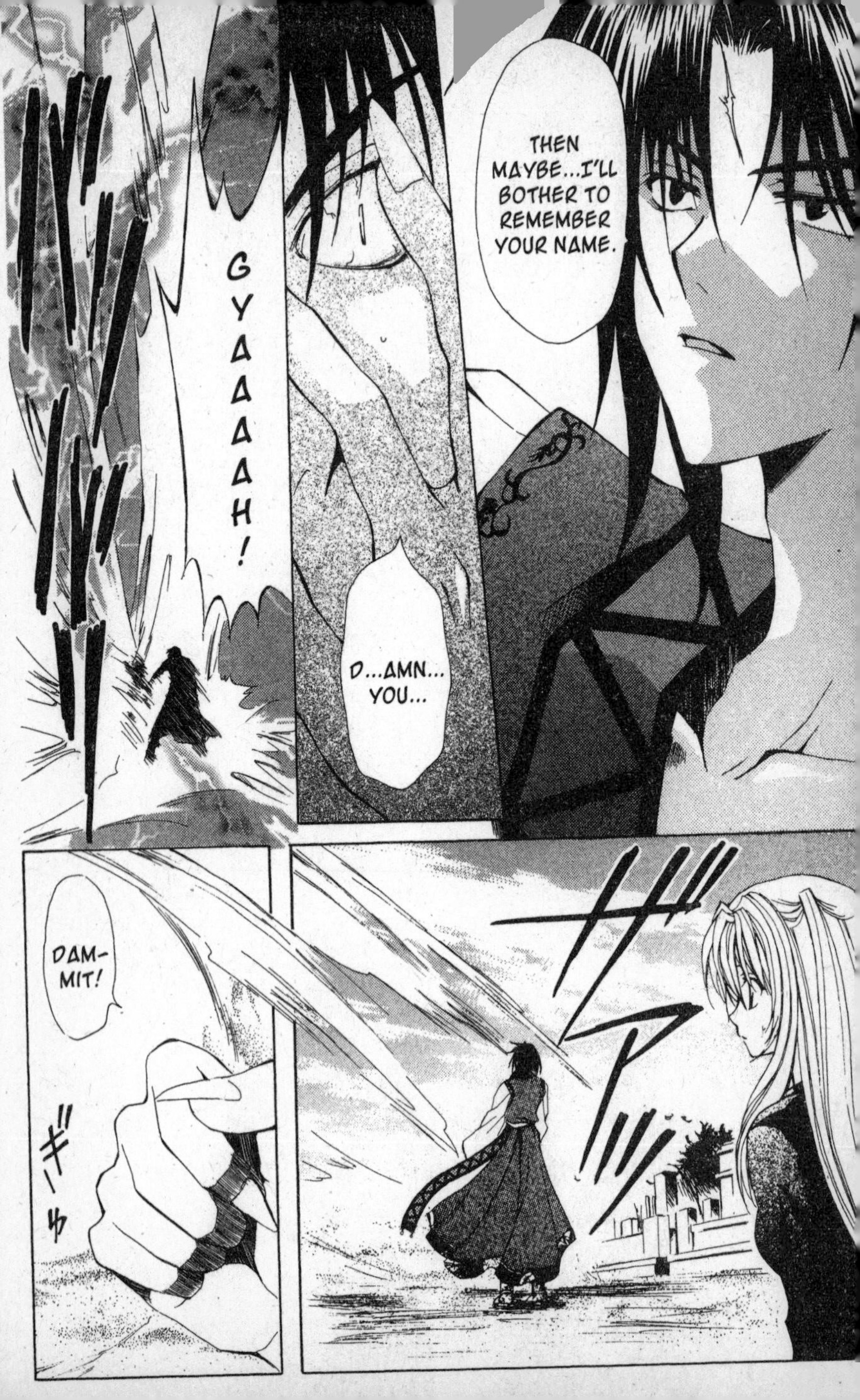
THEN MAYBE...I'LL BOTHER TO REMEMBER YOUR NAME.
D...AMN... YOU...
GYAAAAAH!
DAM-MIT!

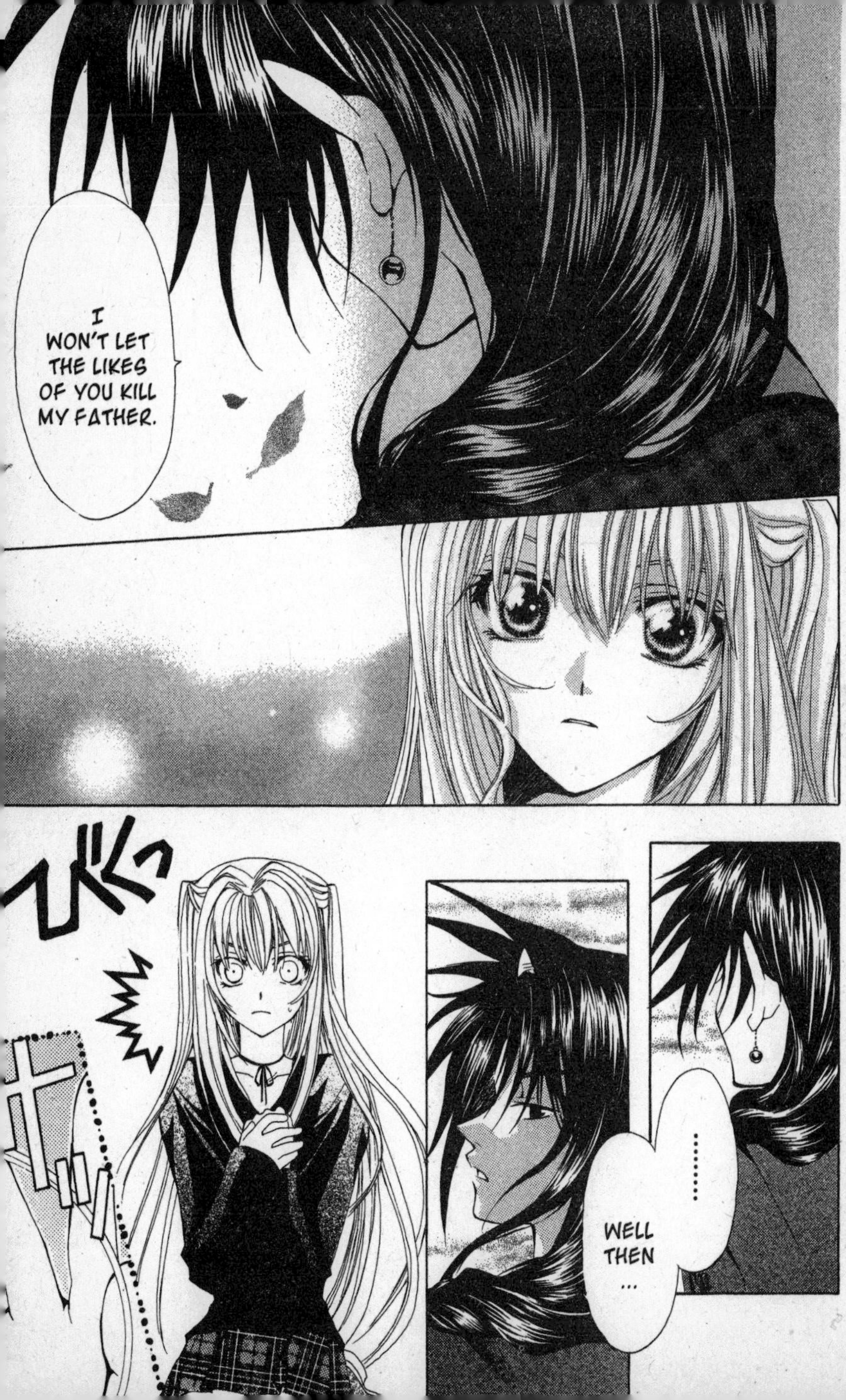
I WON'T LET THE LIKES OF YOU KILL MY FATHER.
......
WELL THEN ...
びくっ

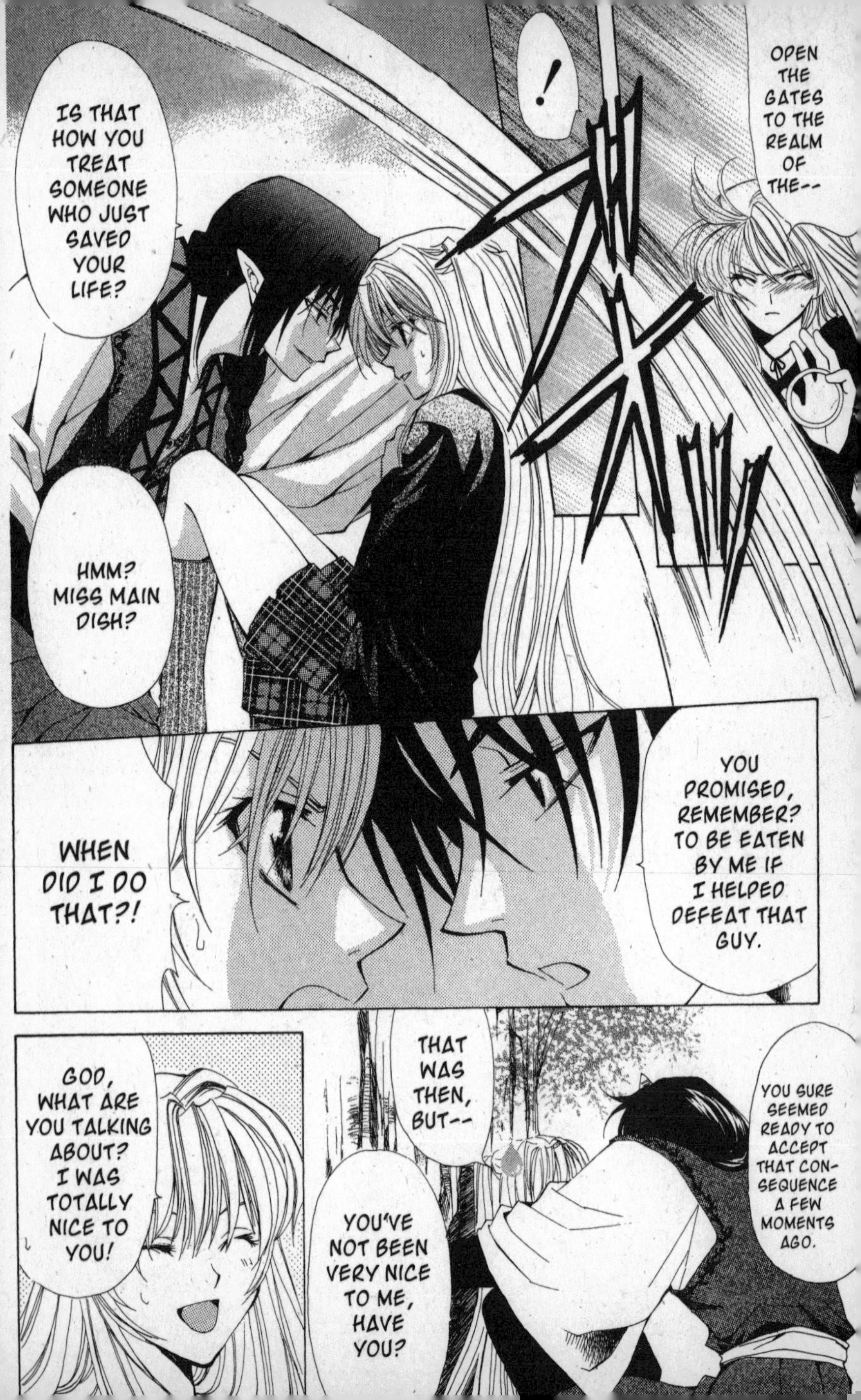
OPEN THE GATES TO THE REALM OF THE--
!
IS THAT HOW YOU TREAT SOMEONE WHO JUST SAVED YOUR LIFE?
HMM? MISS MAIN DISH?
YOU PROMISED, REMEMBER? TO BE EATEN BY ME IF I HELPED DEFEAT THAT GUY.
WHEN DID I DO THAT?!
YOU SURE SEEMED READY TO ACCEPT THAT CON-SEQUENCE A FEW MOMENTS AGO.
THAT WAS THEN, BUT--
YOU'VE NOT BEEN VERY NICE TO ME, HAVE YOU?
GOD, WHAT ARE YOU TALKING ABOUT? I WAS TOTALLY NICE TO YOU!

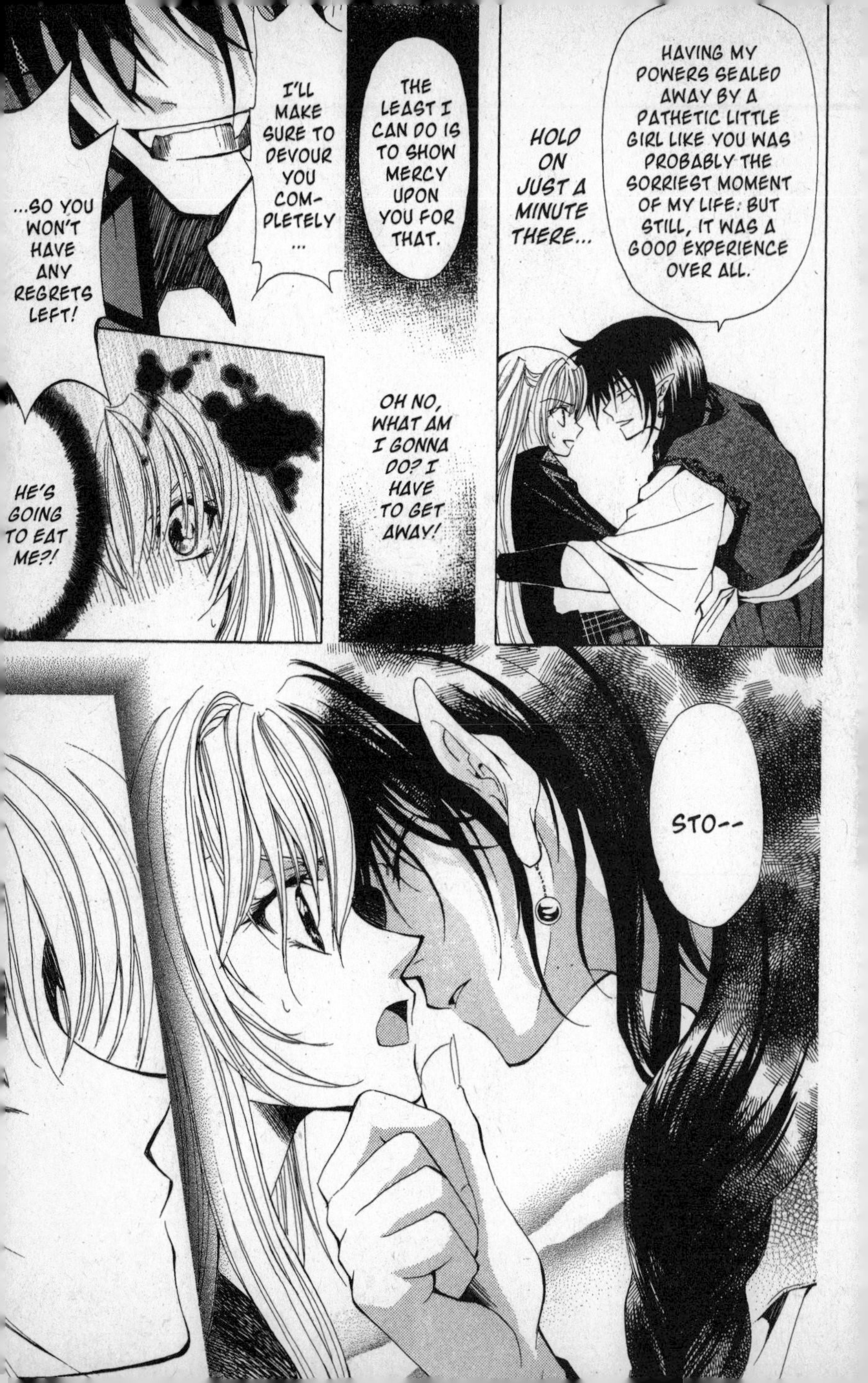
HAVING MY POWERS SEALED AWAY BY A PATHETIC LITTLE GIRL LIKE YOU WAS PROBABLY THE SORRIEST MOMENT OF MY LIFE. BUT STILL, IT WAS A GOOD EXPERIENCE OVER ALL.
HOLD ON JUST A MINUTE THERE...
THE LEAST I CAN DO IS TO SHOW MERCY UPON YOU FOR THAT.
I'LL MAKE SURE TO DEVOUR YOU COM-PLETELY ...
...SO YOU WON'T HAVE ANY REGRETS LEFT!
HE'S GOING TO EAT ME?!
OH NO, WHAT AM I GONNA DO? I HAVE TO GET AWAY!
STO--

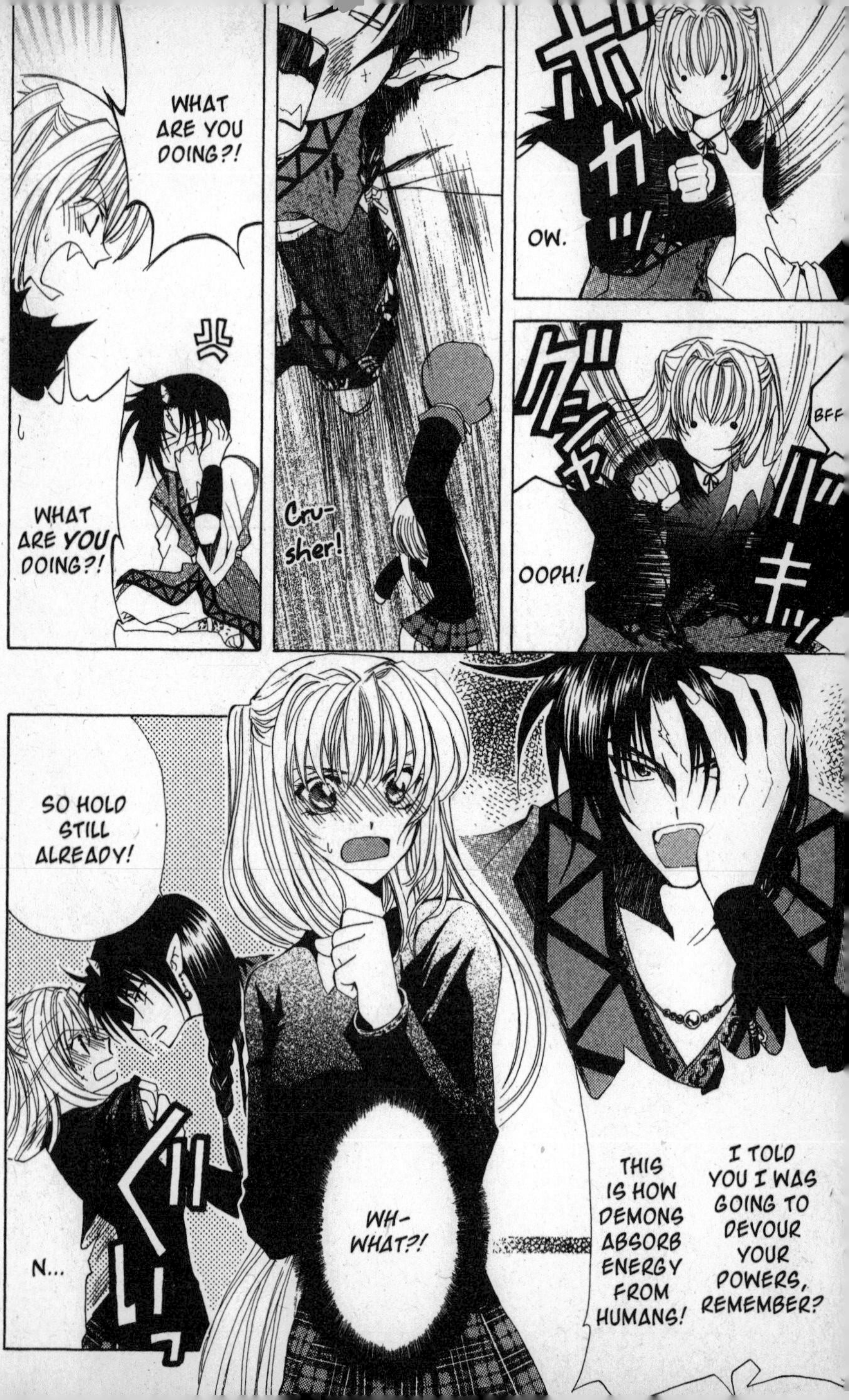
OW.
BFF
OOPH!
Cru-sher!
WHAT ARE YOU DOING?!
WHAT ARE YOU DOING?!
I TOLD YOU I WAS GOING TO DEVOUR YOUR POWERS, REMEMBER?
THIS IS HOW DEMONS ABSORB ENERGY FROM HUMANS!
WH-WHAT?!
SO HOLD STILL ALREADY!
N...

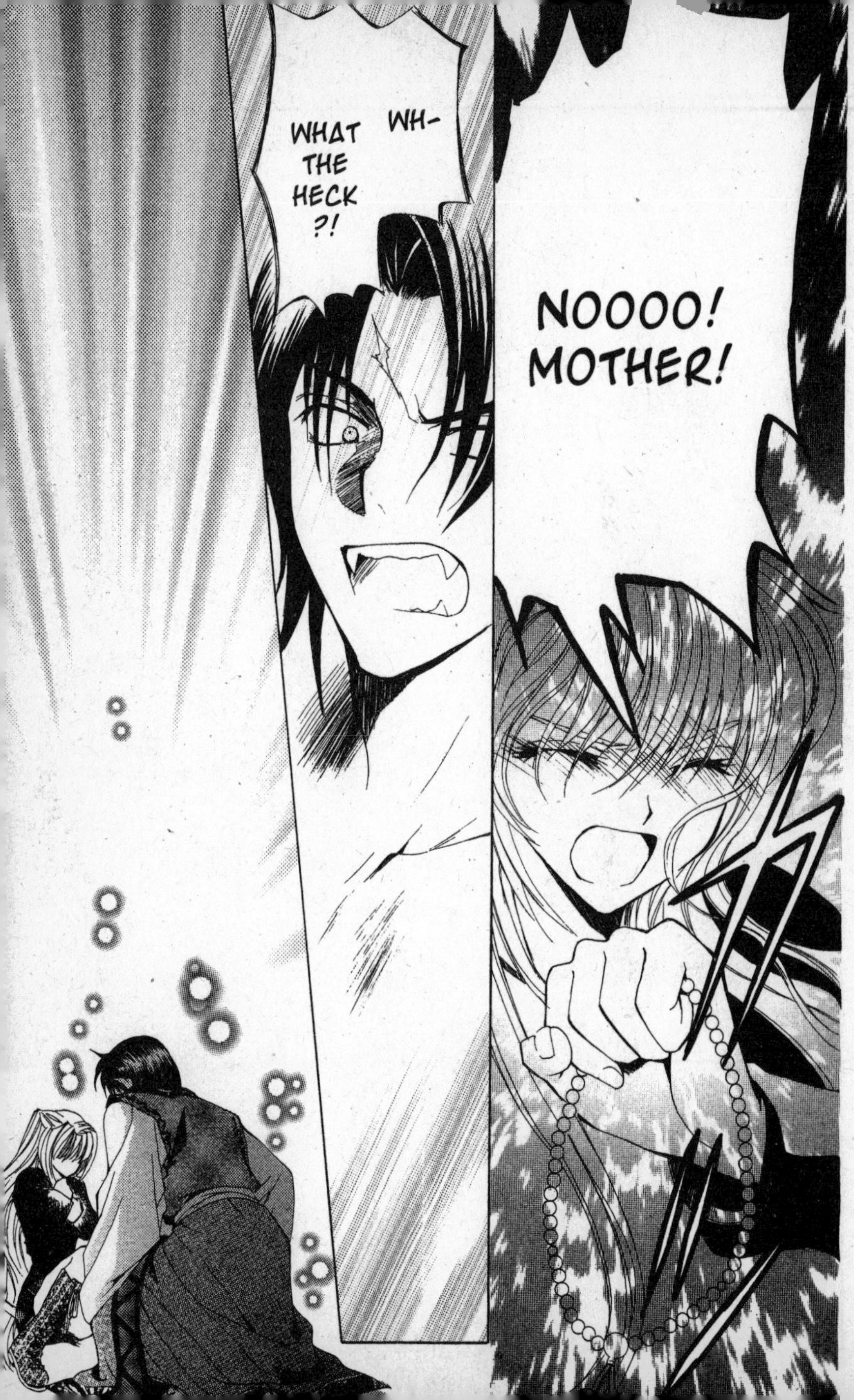
NOOOO! MOTHER!
WH-
WHAT THE HECK ?!

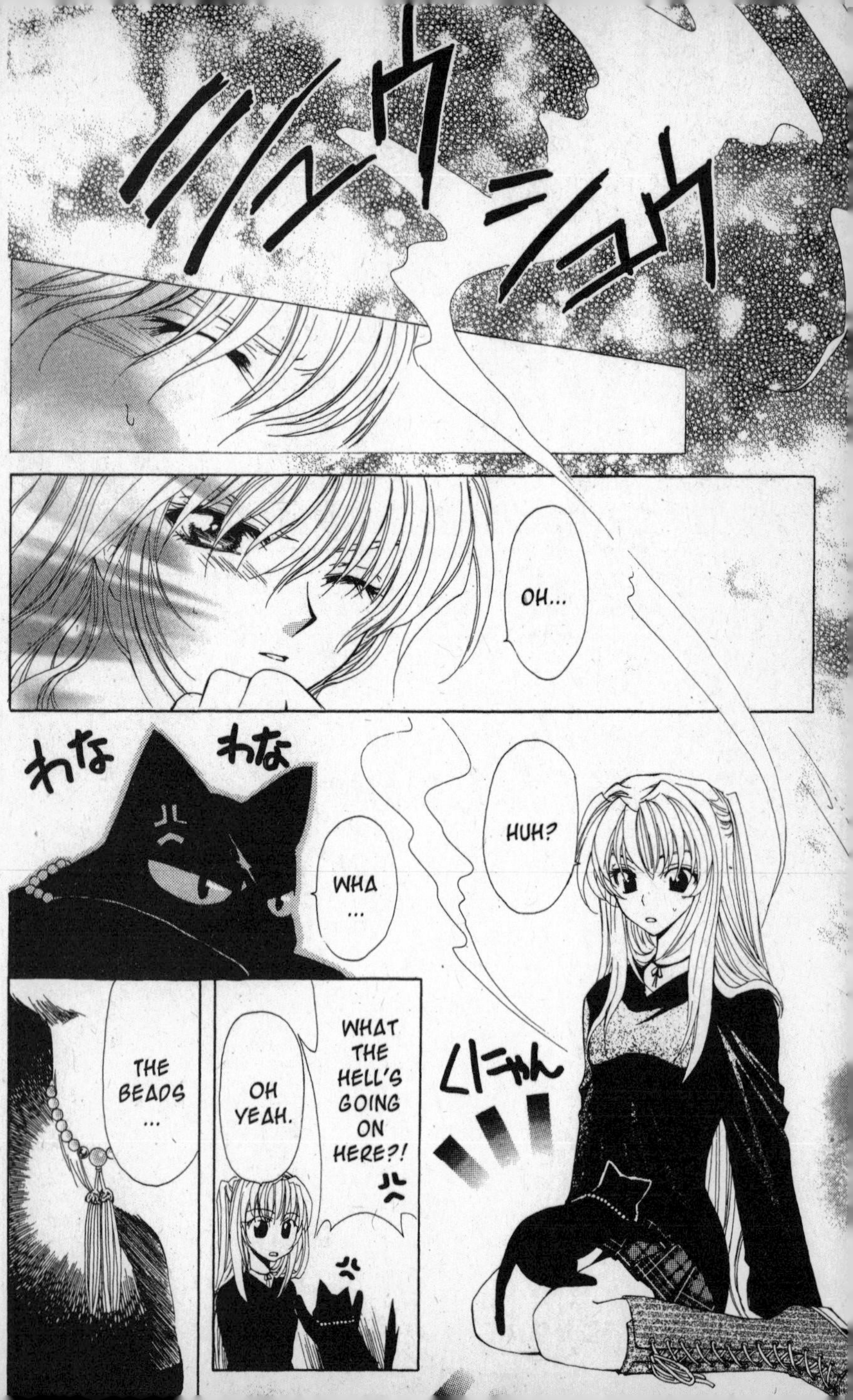

OH...
HUH?
わな わな
WHA ...
くにゃん
WHAT THE HELL'S GOING ON HERE?!
OH YEAH.
THE BEADS ...

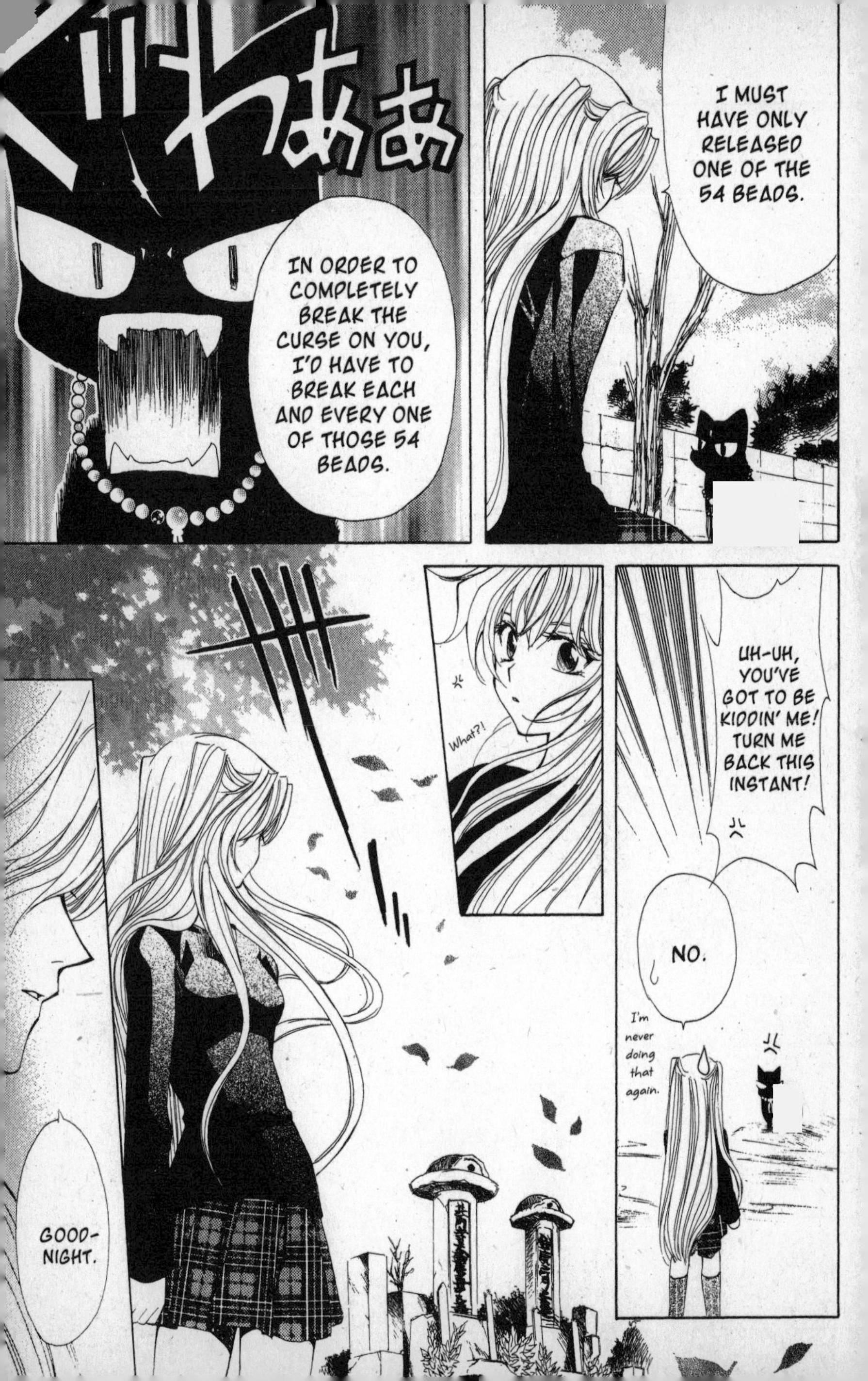
I MUST HAVE ONLY RELEASED ONE OF THE 54 BEADS.
わああ
IN ORDER TO COMPLETELY BREAK THE CURSE ON YOU, I'D HAVE TO BREAK EACH AND EVERY ONE OF THOSE 54 BEADS.
UH-UH, YOU'VE GOT TO BE KIDDIN' ME! TURN ME BACK THIS INSTANT!
NO.
I'm never doing that again.
What?!
GOOD-NIGHT.

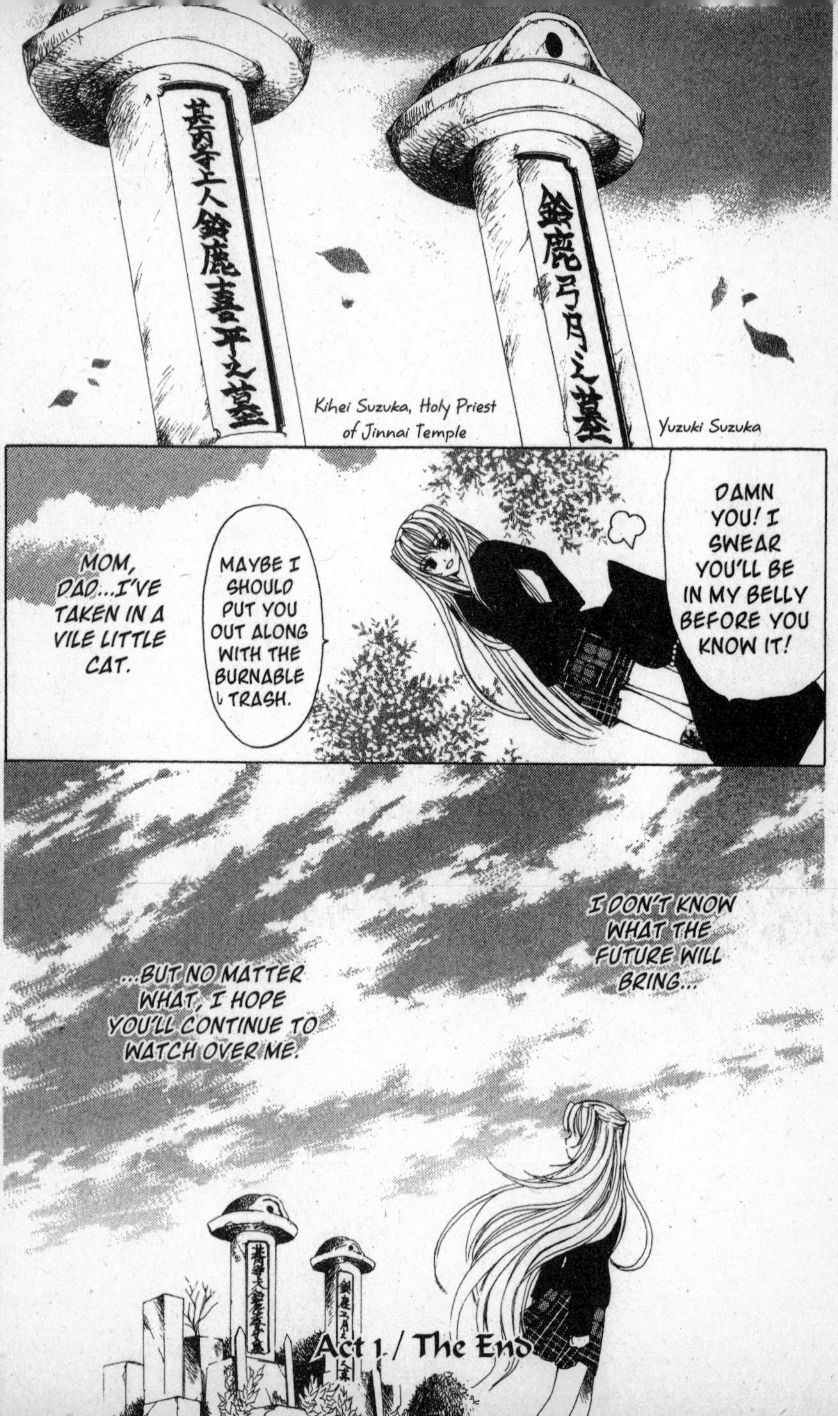
鈴鹿弓月之墓
Yuzuki Suzuka
甚内寺上人鈴鹿喜平之墓
Kihei Suzuka, Holy Priest of Jinnai Temple
DAMN YOU! I SWEAR YOU'LL BE IN MY BELLY BEFORE YOU KNOW IT!
MAYBE I SHOULD PUT YOU OUT ALONG WITH THE BURNABLE TRASH.
MOM, DAD...I'VE TAKEN IN A VILE LITTLE CAT.
I DON'T KNOW WHAT THE FUTURE WILL BRING...
...BUT NO MATTER WHAT, I HOPE YOU'LL CONTINUE TO WATCH OVER ME.
Act 1 / The End

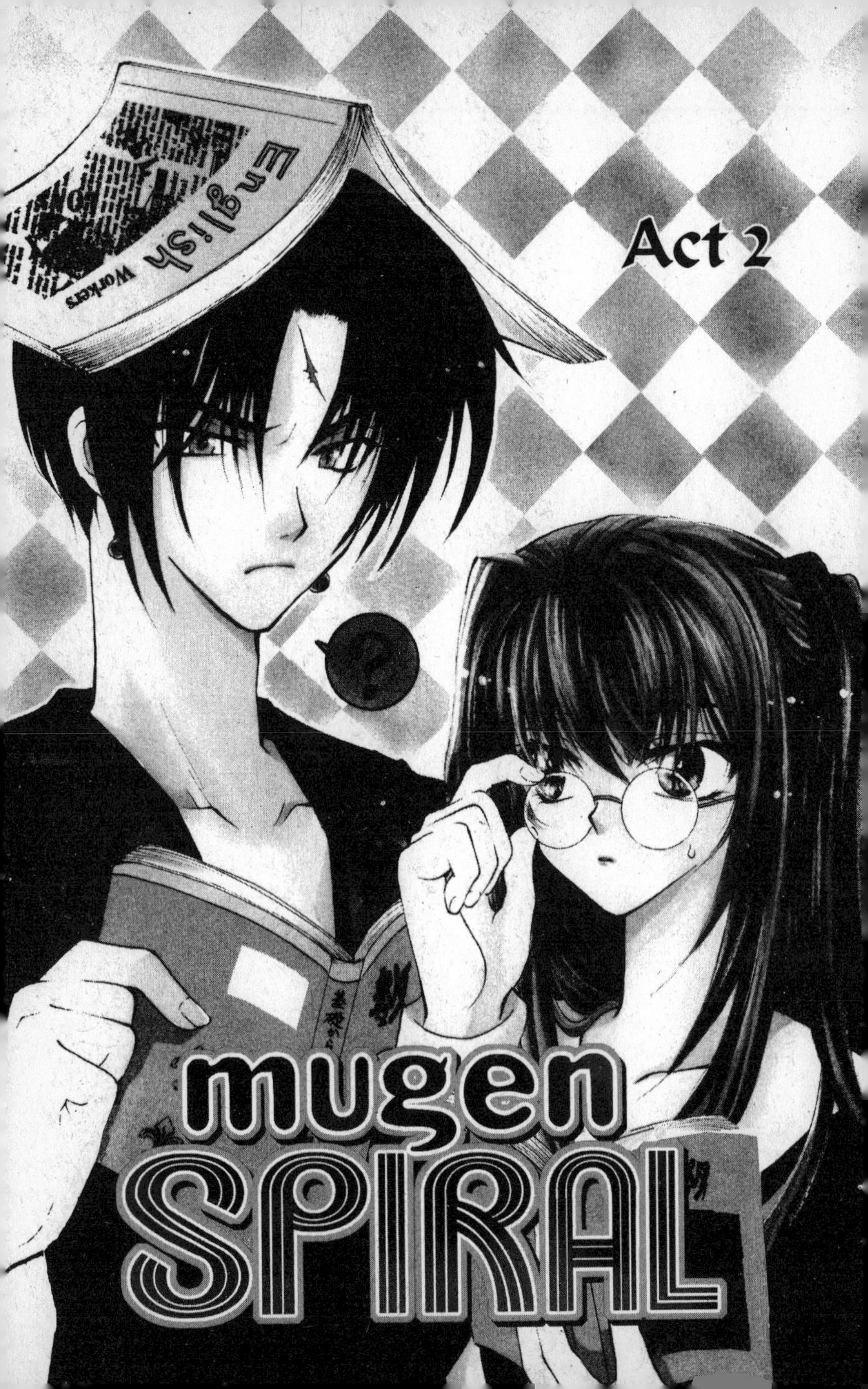
English Workers
Act 2
mugen
SPIRAL

# Character Memo.

## Yayoi Suzuka

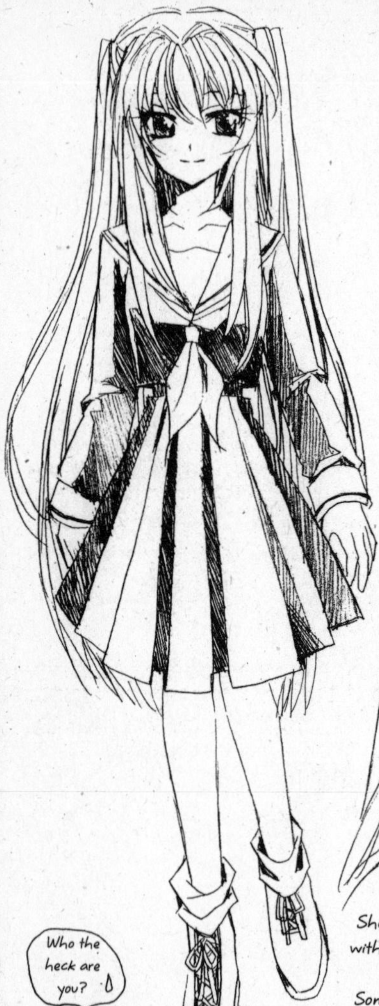

A lot of tweaking took place before this girl became the "Yayoi" that we know. In the original setting, she was a crybaby Mystic who was afraid of ghosts. But crying wasn't going to keep the story moving (ha ha,) so we decided on pulling a complete 180-degree spin to bring you "invincible Yayoi" instead. She's even on par with Demons now. But I'm sure that in order to gain the trust of 108 spirits, she had to go through quite an ordeal. Regardless of her past struggles, she is the type of girl who tries her best to mask any possible weakness from others.

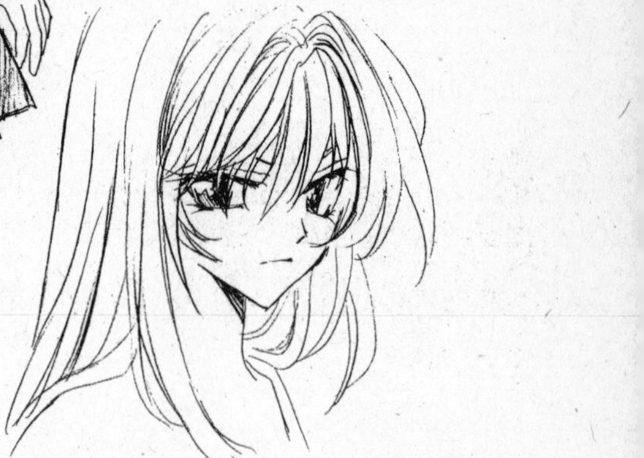

She grew up in a home with a kind father and a stern mother. Somehow she became a very aloof little girl. Although she has family, she prefers to do things on her own, and therefore lives alone.

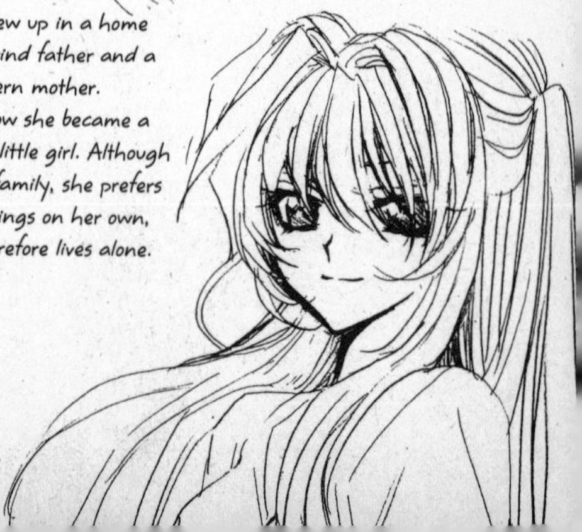

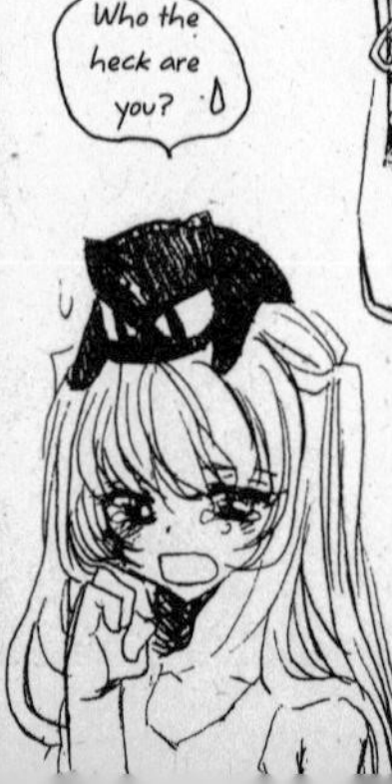
Who the heck are you?
I'm so scared!

← The original Yayoi.

I'm so glad she got stronger.

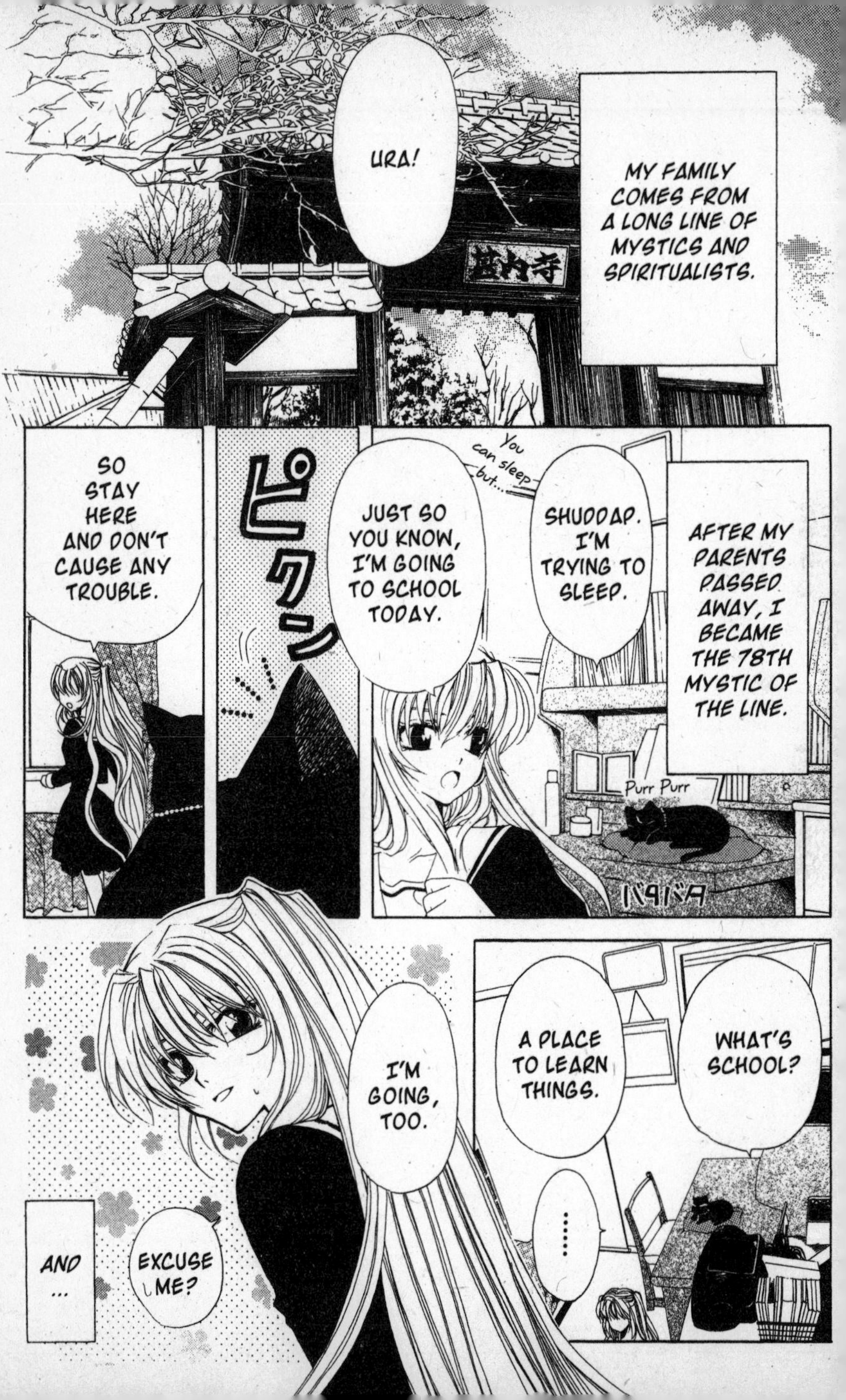
MY FAMILY COMES FROM A LONG LINE OF MYSTICS AND SPIRITUALISTS.
URA!
AFTER MY PARENTS PASSED AWAY, I BECAME THE 78TH MYSTIC OF THE LINE.
SHUDDAP. I'M TRYING TO SLEEP.
Purr Purr
バタバタ
You can sleep but...
JUST SO YOU KNOW, I'M GOING TO SCHOOL TODAY.
ピクーン
SO STAY HERE AND DON'T CAUSE ANY TROUBLE.
WHAT'S SCHOOL?
A PLACE TO LEARN THINGS.
......
I'M GOING, TOO.
EXCUSE ME?
AND ...

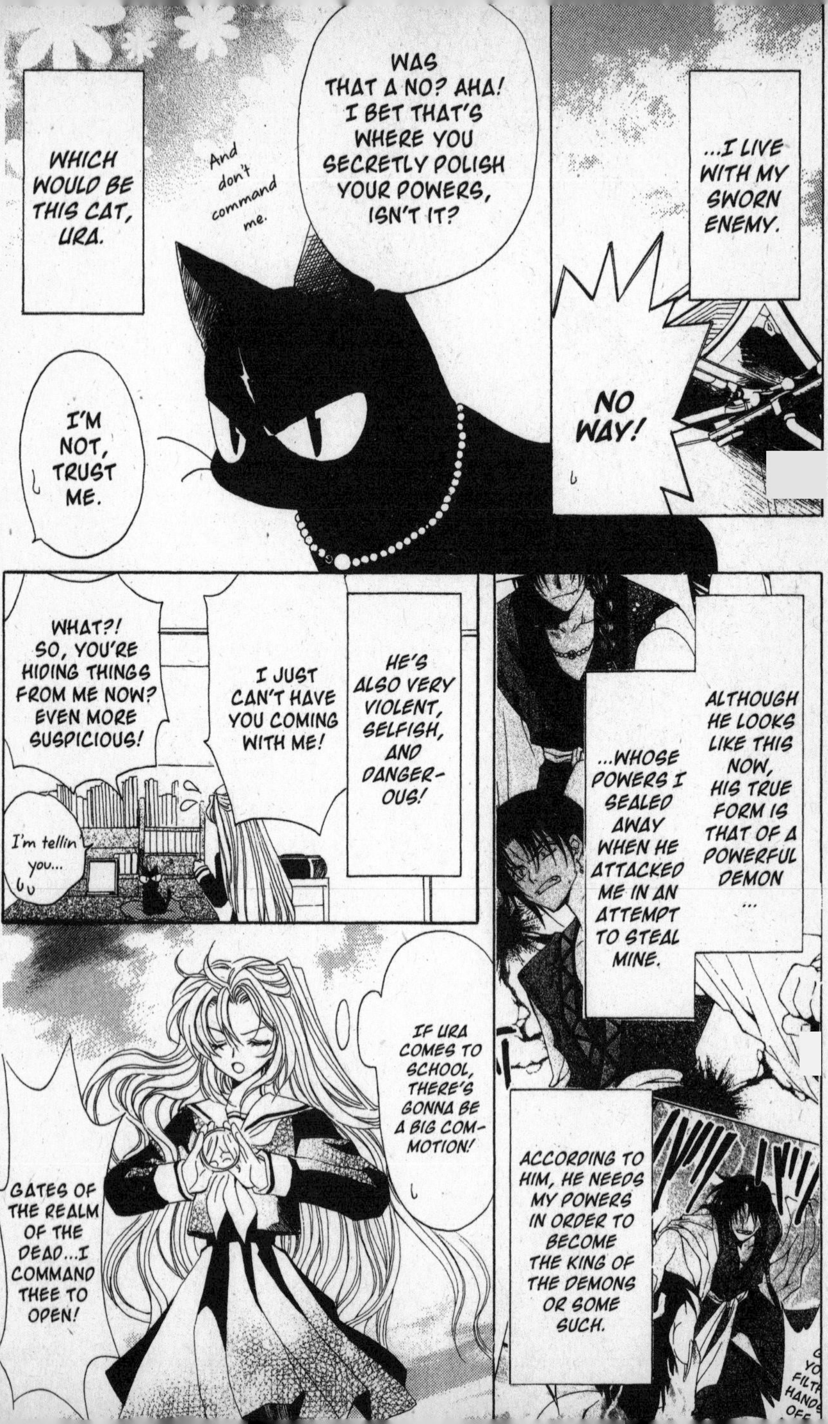
...I LIVE WITH MY SWORN ENEMY.
NO WAY!
WAS THAT A NO? AHA! I BET THAT'S WHERE YOU SECRETLY POLISH YOUR POWERS, ISN'T IT?
And don't command me.
WHICH WOULD BE THIS CAT, URA.
I'M NOT, TRUST ME.
ALTHOUGH HE LOOKS LIKE THIS NOW, HIS TRUE FORM IS THAT OF A POWERFUL DEMON ...
...WHOSE POWERS I SEALED AWAY WHEN HE ATTACKED ME IN AN ATTEMPT TO STEAL MINE.
ACCORDING TO HIM, HE NEEDS MY POWERS IN ORDER TO BECOME THE KING OF THE DEMONS OR SOME SUCH.
HE'S ALSO VERY VIOLENT, SELFISH, AND DANGER-OUS!
I JUST CAN'T HAVE YOU COMING WITH ME!
WHAT?! SO, YOU'RE HIDING THINGS FROM ME NOW? EVEN MORE SUSPICIOUS!
I'm tellin' you...
IF URA COMES TO SCHOOL, THERE'S GONNA BE A BIG COM-MOTION!
GATES OF THE REALM OF THE DEAD...I COMMAND THEE TO OPEN!

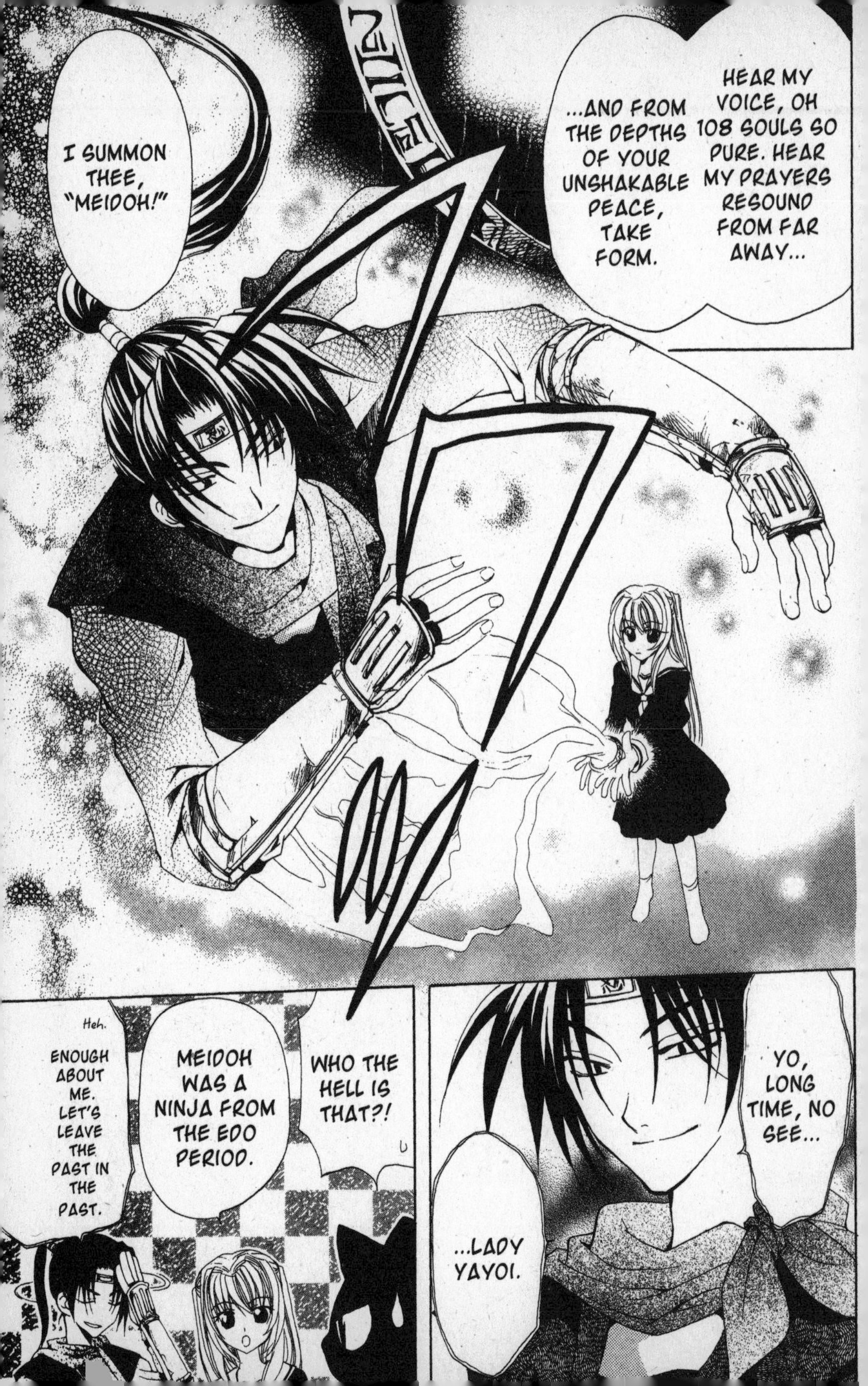
HEAR MY VOICE, OH 108 SOULS SO PURE. HEAR MY PRAYERS RESOUND FROM FAR AWAY...
...AND FROM THE DEPTHS OF YOUR UNSHAKABLE PEACE, TAKE FORM.
I SUMMON THEE, "MEIDOH!"
YO, LONG TIME, NO SEE...
...LADY YAYOI.
WHO THE HELL IS THAT?!
MEIDOH WAS A NINJA FROM THE EDO PERIOD.
Heh.
ENOUGH ABOUT ME. LET'S LEAVE THE PAST IN THE PAST.

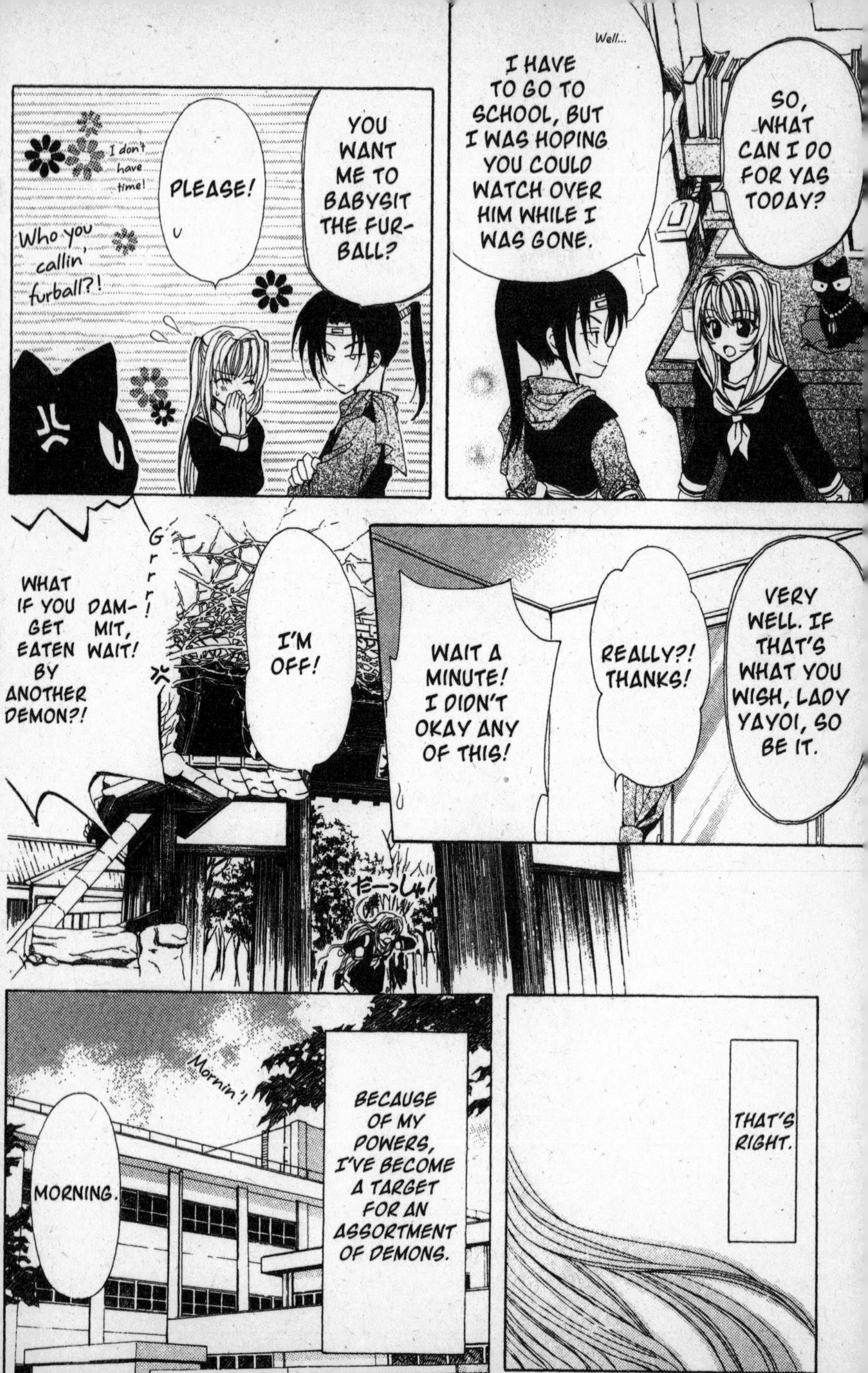
SO, WHAT CAN I DO FOR YAS TODAY?
Well...
I HAVE TO GO TO SCHOOL, BUT I WAS HOPING YOU COULD WATCH OVER HIM WHILE I WAS GONE.
YOU WANT ME TO BABYSIT THE FUR-BALL?
PLEASE!
I don't have time!
Who you callin' furball?!
VERY WELL. IF THAT'S WHAT YOU WISH, LADY YAYOI, SO BE IT.
REALLY?! THANKS!
WAIT A MINUTE! I DIDN'T OKAY ANY OF THIS!
I'M OFF!
Grrr!
DAM-MIT, WAIT!
WHAT IF YOU GET EATEN BY ANOTHER DEMON?!
THAT'S RIGHT.
BECAUSE OF MY POWERS, I'VE BECOME A TARGET FOR AN ASSORTMENT OF DEMONS.
Mornin'!
MORNING.

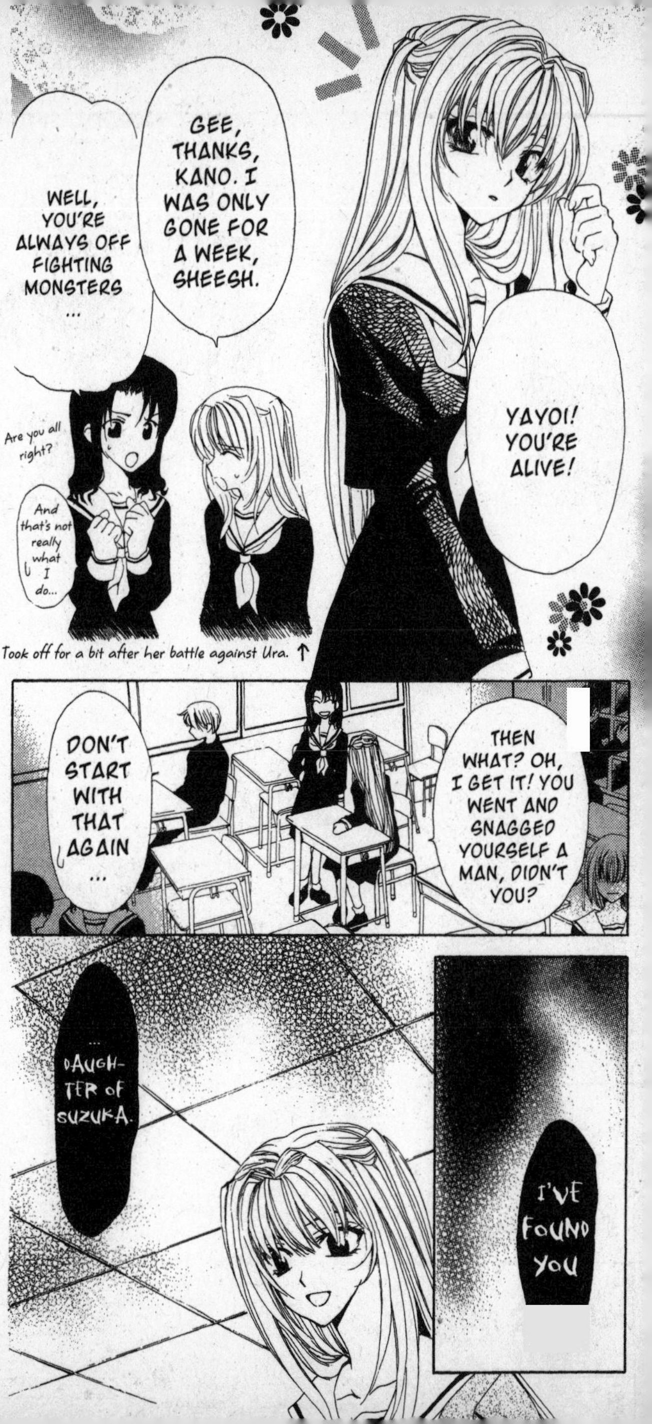
YAYOI! YOU'RE ALIVE!
GEE, THANKS, KANO. I WAS ONLY GONE FOR A WEEK, SHEESH.
WELL, YOU'RE ALWAYS OFF FIGHTING MONSTERS ...
Are you all right?
And that's not really what I do...
Took off for a bit after her battle against Ura. ↑
THEN WHAT? OH, I GET IT! YOU WENT AND SNAGGED YOURSELF A MAN, DIDN'T YOU?
DON'T START WITH THAT AGAIN ...
I'VE FOUND YOU
... DAUGH-TER OF SUZUKA.

Before I turned pro, I read a lot of good manga. But once I began drawing my own, I suddenly couldn't tell what was "good" and what wasn't anymore. Perhaps because I have read so many good mangas, I just have a higher, almost unattainable standard. One day, however, I'd like to create something I can just gloat over. (Ha ha!) I guess I better keep trying so I can reach that goal!

It was quite a long process of trial and error to bring "Mugen Spiral" to what it is today. For one, the characters just didn't fall into place so easily. And even though I had always thought of making it a story that involved some sort of creature-banishing, I really debated whether it should be more Western or Eastern influenced. But since I like kanji names, I decided on Demons instead. I even debated whether to make the protagonist a boy or a girl. Of course, I'm very happy that I was ultimately able to have a heroine!

The other thing I had a lot of trouble with was the page limit. That was probably my biggest obstacle. It's just so hard to represent a fantasy setting in such a limited space. I was forever running out of pages.

To be continued...

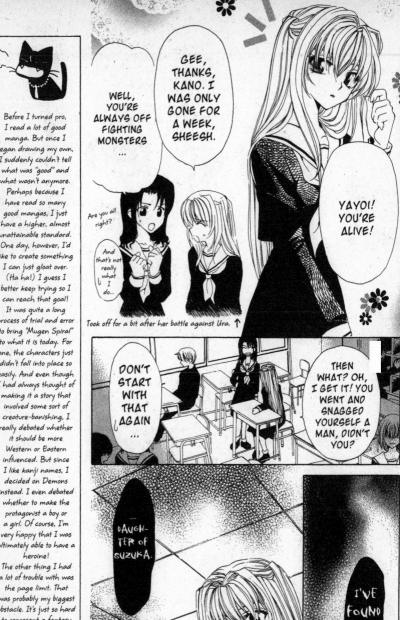

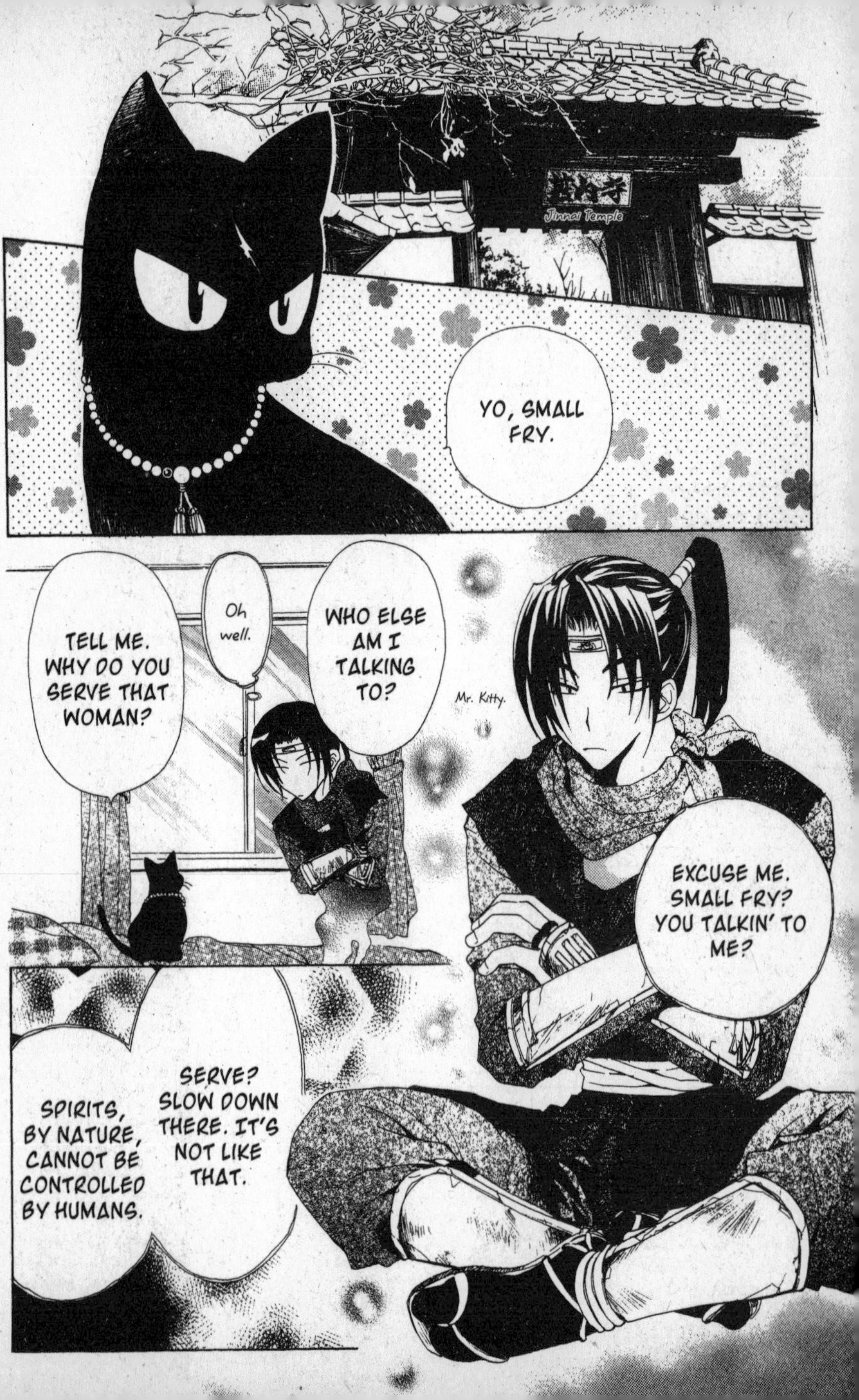
Jinnai Temple
YO, SMALL FRY.
EXCUSE ME. SMALL FRY? YOU TALKIN' TO ME?
WHO ELSE AM I TALKING TO?
Mr. Kitty.
Oh well.
TELL ME. WHY DO YOU SERVE THAT WOMAN?
SERVE? SLOW DOWN THERE. IT'S NOT LIKE THAT.
SPIRITS, BY NATURE, CANNOT BE CONTROLLED BY HUMANS.

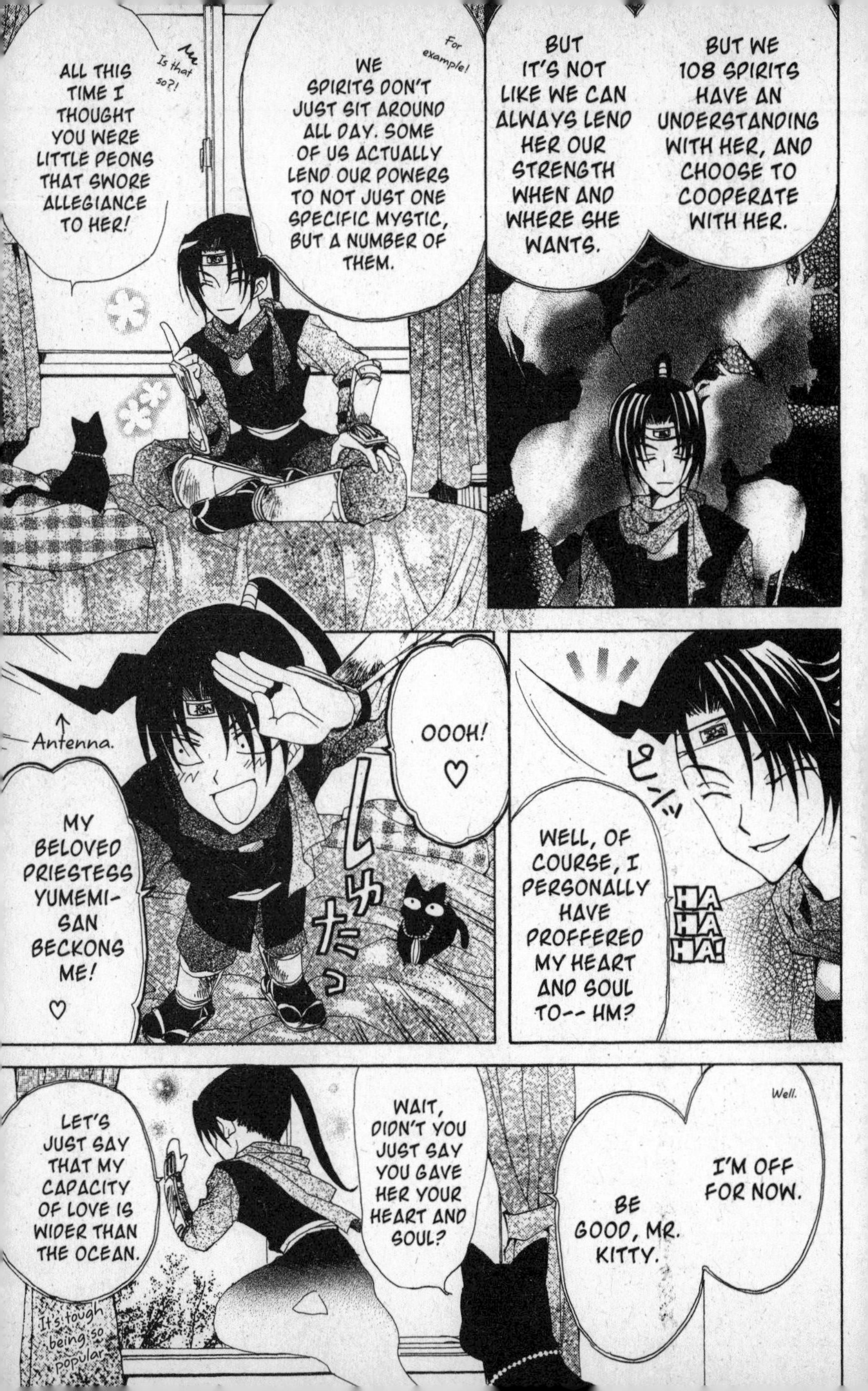
BUT WE 108 SPIRITS HAVE AN UNDERSTANDING WITH HER, AND CHOOSE TO COOPERATE WITH HER.
BUT IT'S NOT LIKE WE CAN ALWAYS LEND HER OUR STRENGTH WHEN AND WHERE SHE WANTS.
ALL THIS TIME I THOUGHT YOU WERE LITTLE PEONS THAT SWORE ALLEGIANCE TO HER!
Is that so?!
WE SPIRITS DON'T JUST SIT AROUND ALL DAY. SOME OF US ACTUALLY LEND OUR POWERS TO NOT JUST ONE SPECIFIC MYSTIC, BUT A NUMBER OF THEM.
For example!
WELL, OF COURSE, I PERSONALLY HAVE PROFFERED MY HEART AND SOUL TO-- HM?
HA HA HA HA!
ピンッ
OOOH! ♡
しゅたっ
MY BELOVED PRIESTESS YUMEMI-SAN BECKONS ME! ♡
Antenna.
Well.
I'M OFF FOR NOW.
BE GOOD, MR. KITTY.
WAIT, DIDN'T YOU JUST SAY YOU GAVE HER YOUR HEART AND SOUL?
LET'S JUST SAY THAT MY CAPACITY OF LOVE IS WIDER THAN THE OCEAN.
It's tough being so popular.

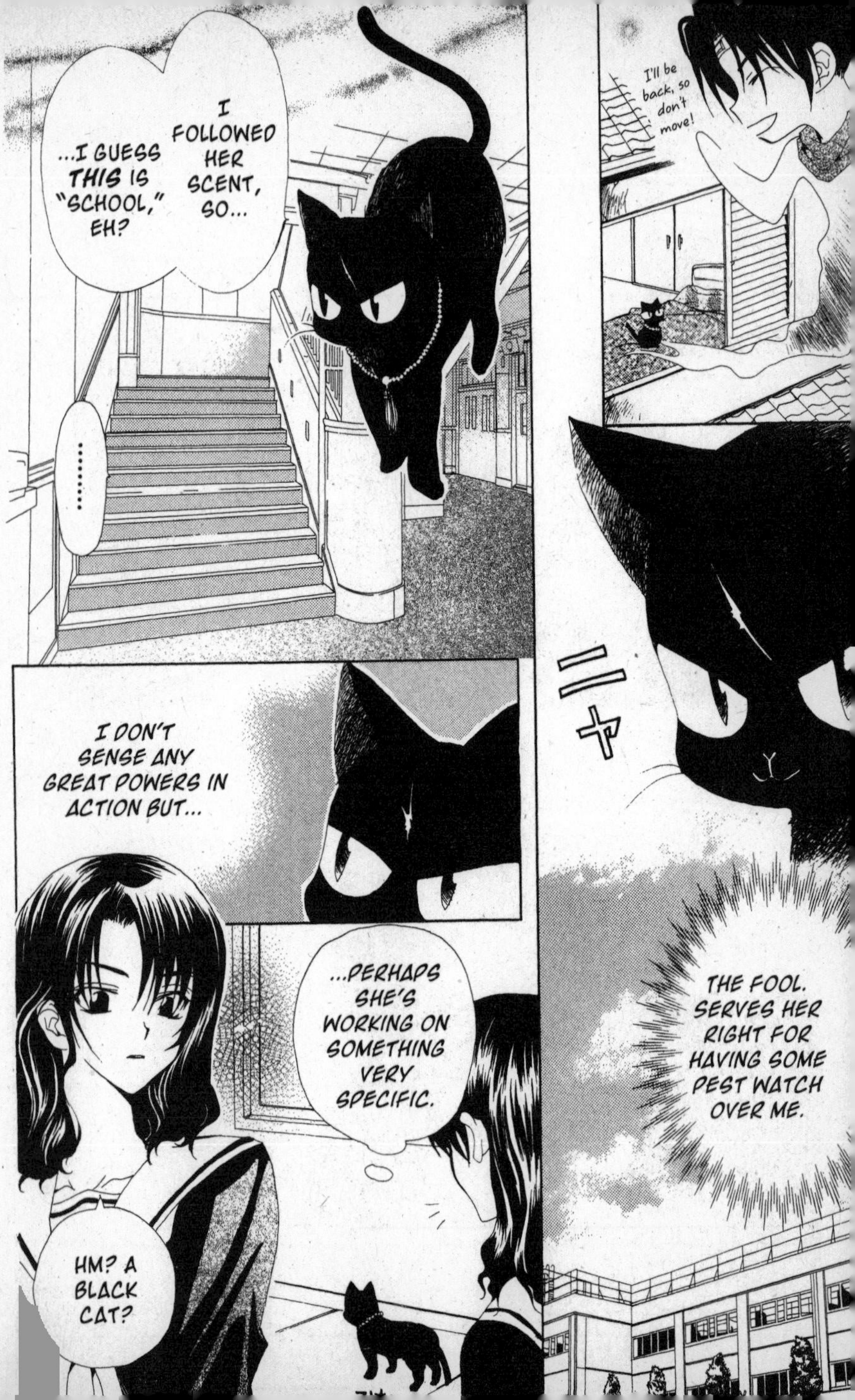
I'll be back, so don't move!
ニヤ
THE FOOL. SERVES HER RIGHT FOR HAVING SOME PEST WATCH OVER ME.
I FOLLOWED HER SCENT, SO...
...I GUESS THIS IS "SCHOOL," EH?
......
I DON'T SENSE ANY GREAT POWERS IN ACTION BUT...
...PERHAPS SHE'S WORKING ON SOMETHING VERY SPECIFIC.
HM? A BLACK CAT?

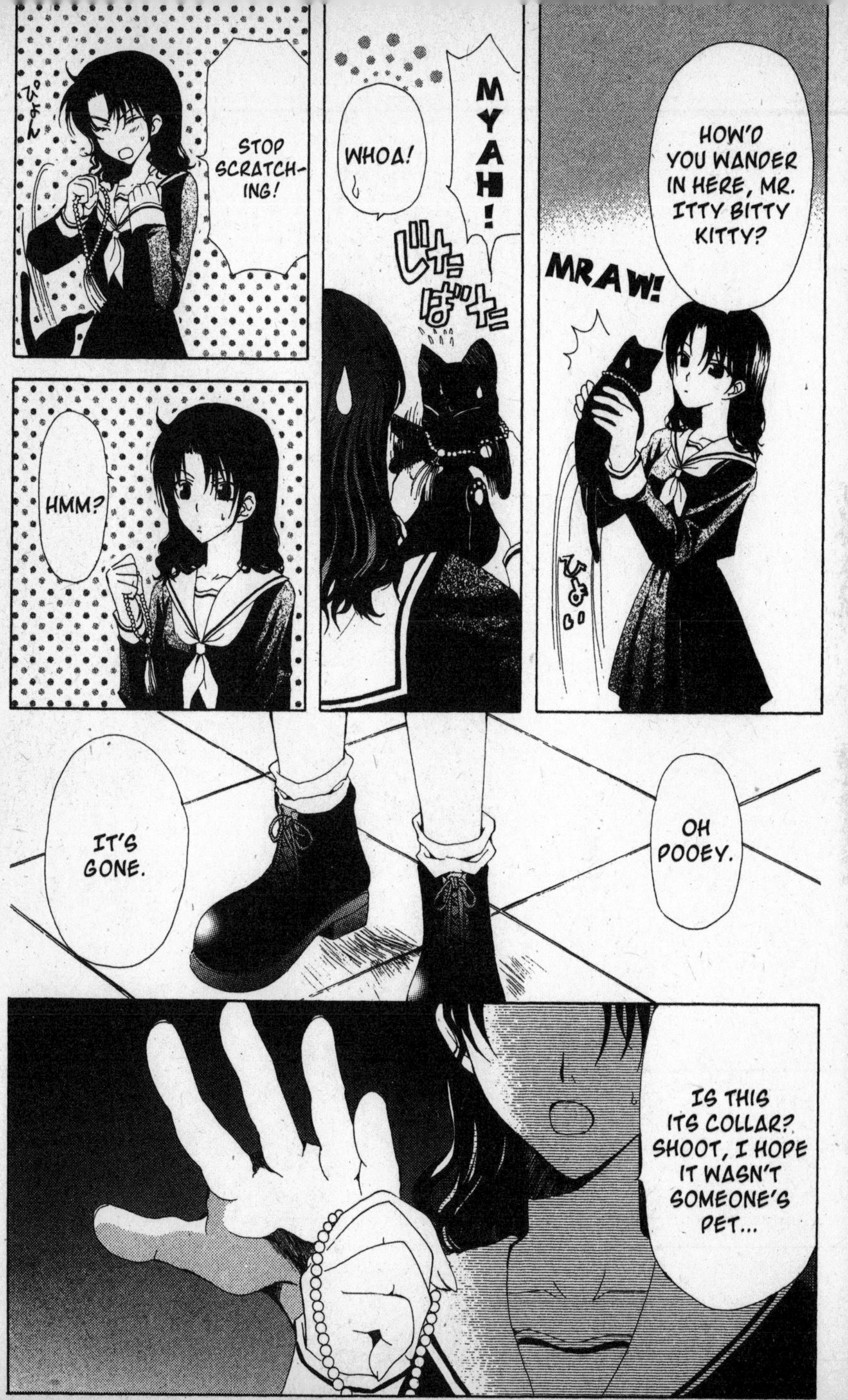
HOW'D YOU WANDER IN HERE, MR. ITTY BITTY KITTY?
MRAW!
MYAH!
WHOA!
じたばた
ぴょん
STOP SCRATCH-ING!
HMM?
OH POOEY.
IT'S GONE.
IS THIS ITS COLLAR? SHOOT, I HOPE IT WASN'T SOMEONE'S PET...

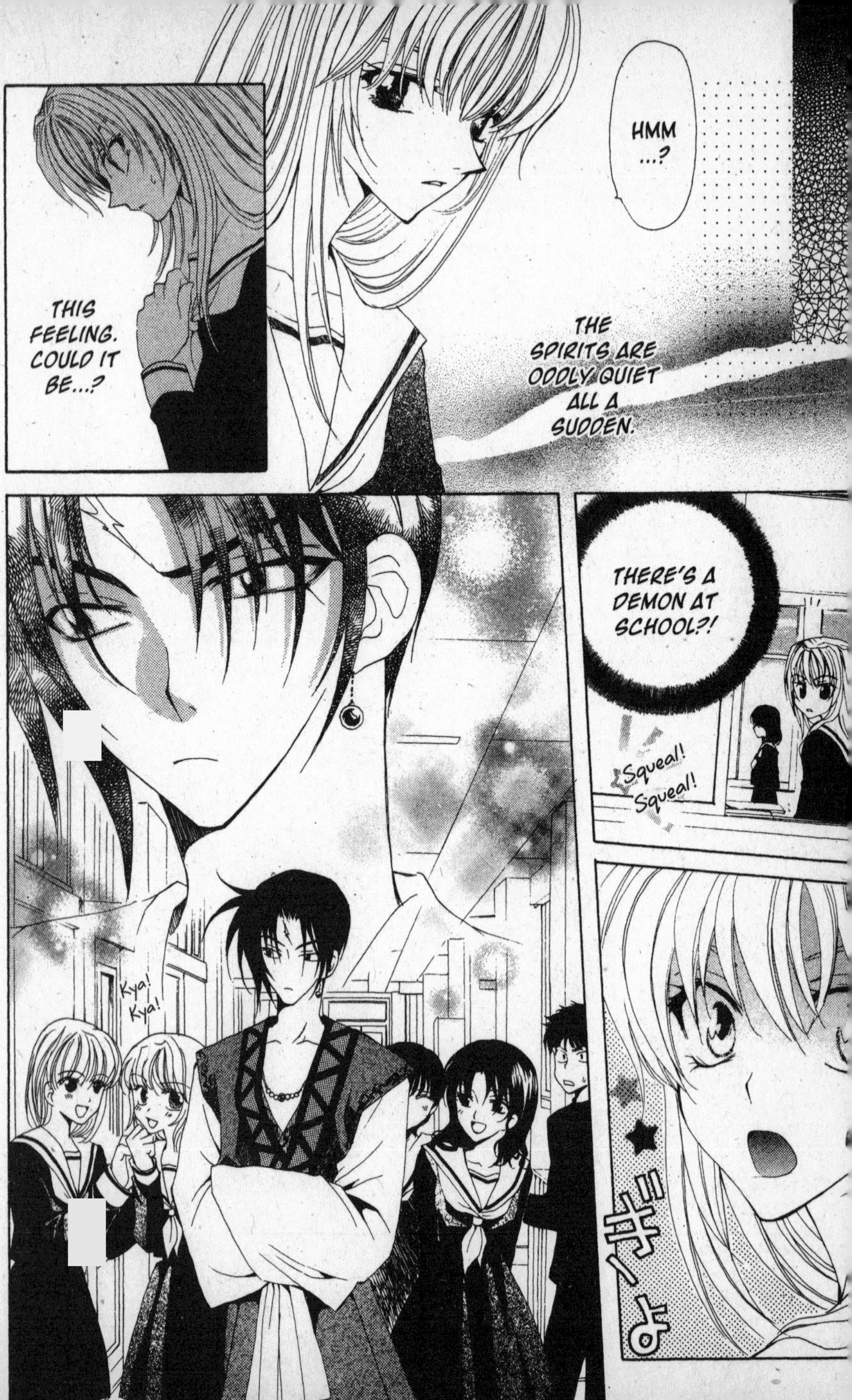
HMM ...?
THE SPIRITS ARE ODDLY QUIET ALL A SUDDEN.
THIS FEELING. COULD IT BE...?
THERE'S A DEMON AT SCHOOL?!
Squeal! Squeal!
Kya! Kya!

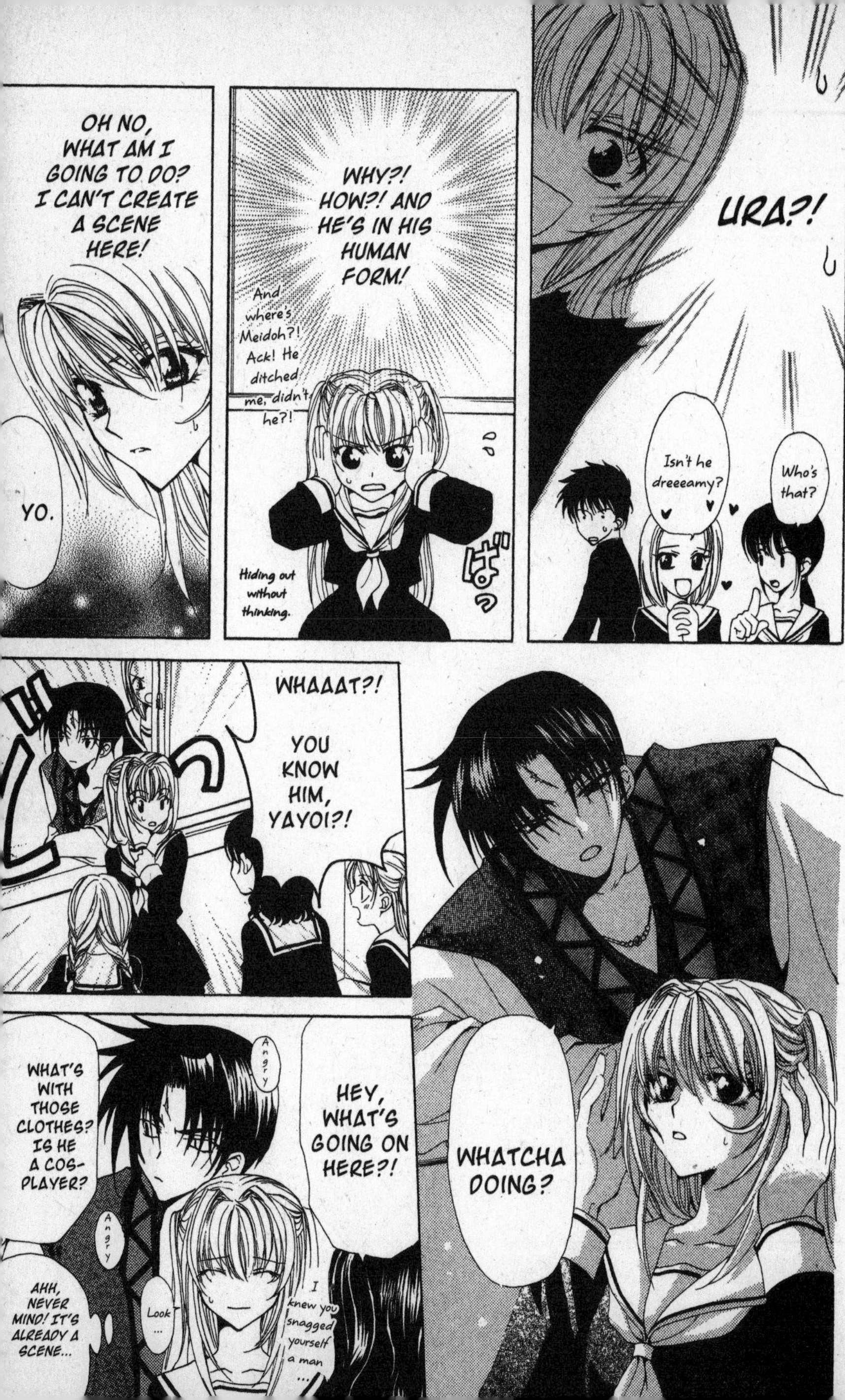
URA?!
Who's that?
Isn't he dreeeamy?
WHY?! HOW?! AND HE'S IN HIS HUMAN FORM!
And where's Meidoh?! Ack! He ditched me, didn't he?!
ぱっ
Hiding out without thinking.
OH NO, WHAT AM I GOING TO DO? I CAN'T CREATE A SCENE HERE!
YO.
WHATCHA DOING?
WHAAAT?!
YOU KNOW HIM, YAYOI?!
HEY, WHAT'S GOING ON HERE?!
Angry
WHAT'S WITH THOSE CLOTHES? IS HE A COS-PLAYER?
Angry
I knew you snagged yourself a man ...
Look ...
AHH, NEVER MIND! IT'S ALREADY A SCENE...

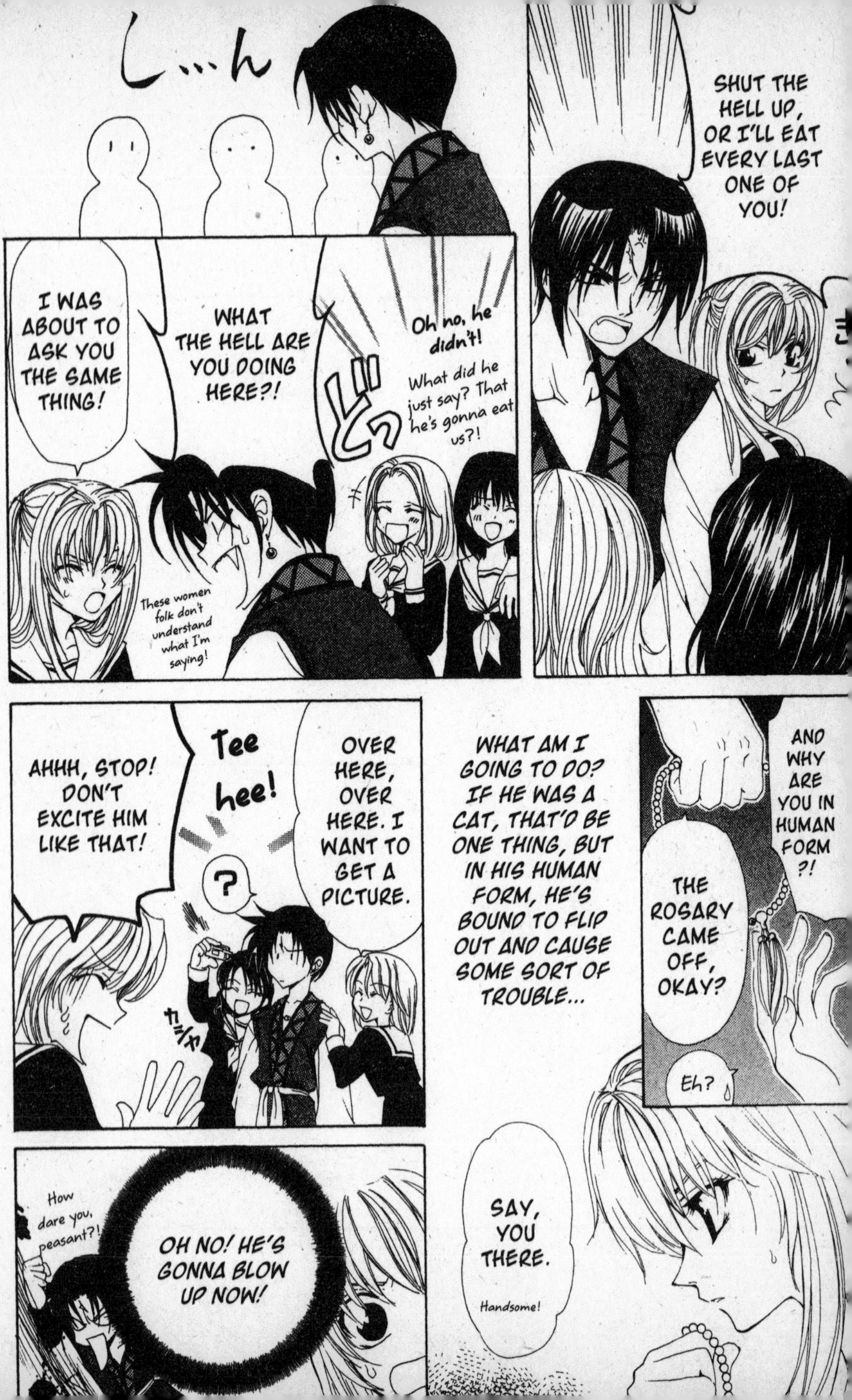
SHUT THE HELL UP, OR I'LL EAT EVERY LAST ONE OF YOU!
し…ん
WHAT THE HELL ARE YOU DOING HERE?!
Oh no, he didn't!
What did he just say? That he's gonna eat us?!
どっ
I WAS ABOUT TO ASK YOU THE SAME THING!
These women folk don't understand what I'm saying!
AND WHY ARE YOU IN HUMAN FORM?!
THE ROSARY CAME OFF, OKAY?
Eh?
WHAT AM I GOING TO DO? IF HE WAS A CAT, THAT'D BE ONE THING, BUT IN HIS HUMAN FORM, HE'S BOUND TO FLIP OUT AND CAUSE SOME SORT OF TROUBLE...
OVER HERE, OVER HERE. I WANT TO GET A PICTURE.
Tee hee!
?
カシャ
AHHH, STOP! DON'T EXCITE HIM LIKE THAT!
SAY, YOU THERE.
Handsome!
OH NO! HE'S GONNA BLOW UP NOW!
How dare you, peasant?!

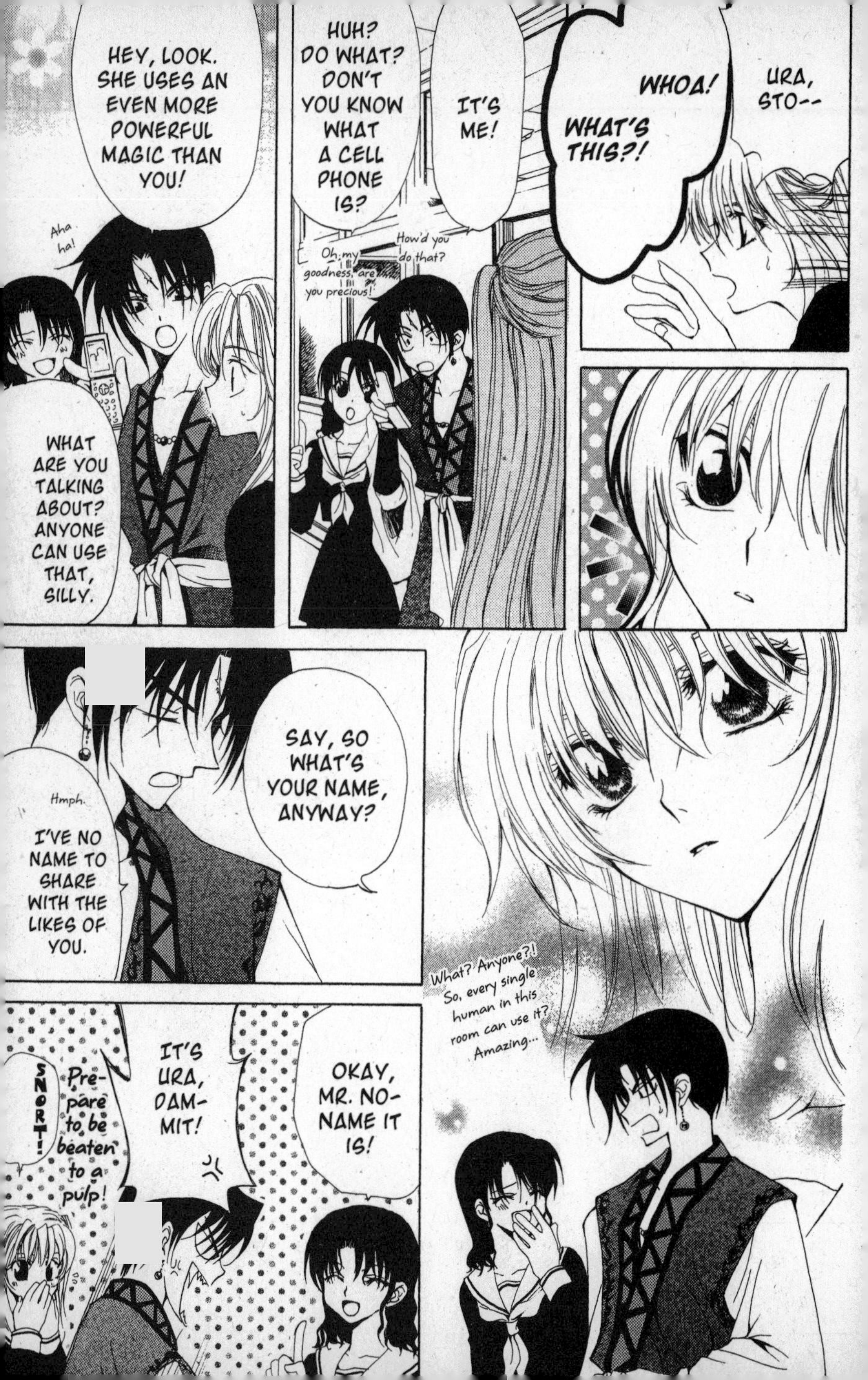
URA, STO--
WHOA!
WHAT'S THIS?!
IT'S ME!
HUH? DO WHAT? DON'T YOU KNOW WHAT A CELL PHONE IS?
How'd you do that?
Oh, my goodness, are you precious!
HEY, LOOK. SHE USES AN EVEN MORE POWERFUL MAGIC THAN YOU!
Aha ha!
WHAT ARE YOU TALKING ABOUT? ANYONE CAN USE THAT, SILLY.
What? Anyone?! So, every single human in this room can use it? Amazing...
SAY, SO WHAT'S YOUR NAME, ANYWAY?
Hmph.
I'VE NO NAME TO SHARE WITH THE LIKES OF YOU.
OKAY, MR. NO-NAME IT IS!
IT'S URA, DAM-MIT!
SNORT!
Pre-pare to be beaten to a pulp!

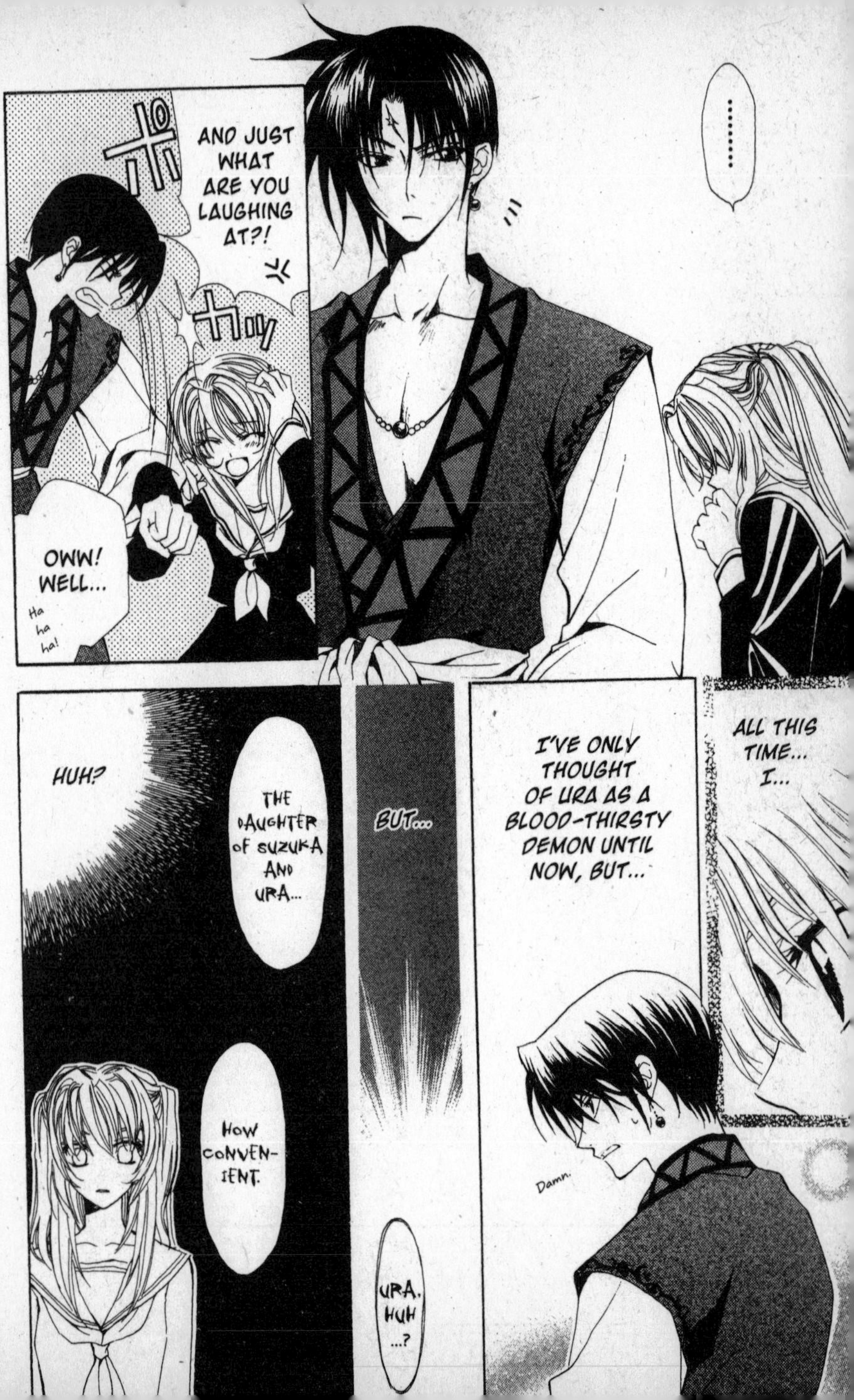
......
AND JUST WHAT ARE YOU LAUGHING AT?!
OWW! WELL...
Ha ha ha!
ALL THIS TIME... I...
I'VE ONLY THOUGHT OF URA AS A BLOOD-THIRSTY DEMON UNTIL NOW, BUT...
Damn.
BUT...
URA, HUH ...?
THE DAUGHTER OF SUZUKA AND URA...
HUH?
HOW CONVEN-IENT.

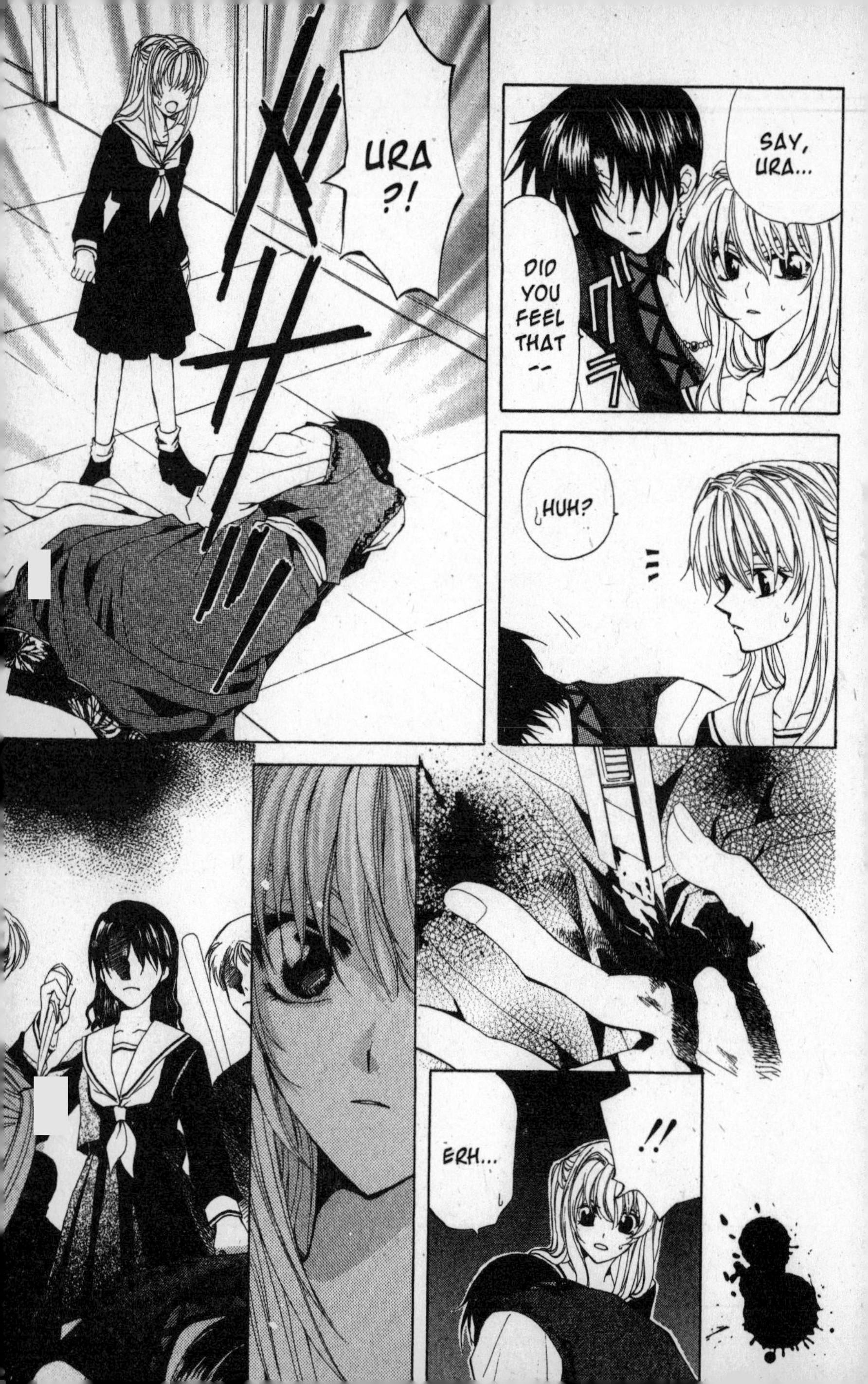
SAY, URA...
DID YOU FEEL THAT --
HUH?
URA ?!
!!
ERH...

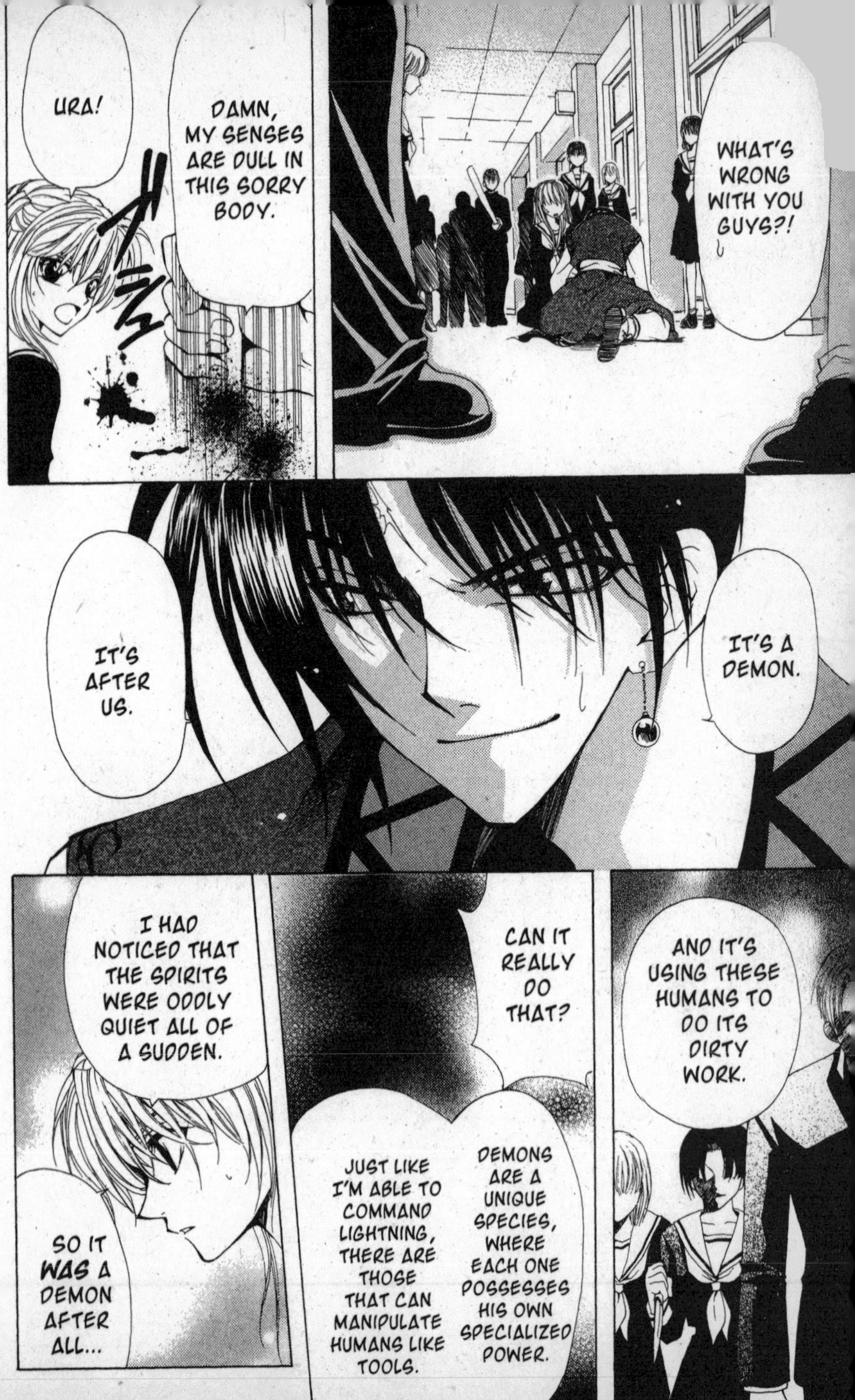
WHAT'S WRONG WITH YOU GUYS?!
DAMN, MY SENSES ARE DULL IN THIS SORRY BODY.
URA!
IT'S A DEMON.
IT'S AFTER US.
AND IT'S USING THESE HUMANS TO DO ITS DIRTY WORK.
CAN IT REALLY DO THAT?
DEMONS ARE A UNIQUE SPECIES, WHERE EACH ONE POSSESSES HIS OWN SPECIALIZED POWER.
JUST LIKE I'M ABLE TO COMMAND LIGHTNING, THERE ARE THOSE THAT CAN MANIPULATE HUMANS LIKE TOOLS.
I HAD NOTICED THAT THE SPIRITS WERE ODDLY QUIET ALL OF A SUDDEN.
SO IT WAS A DEMON AFTER ALL...

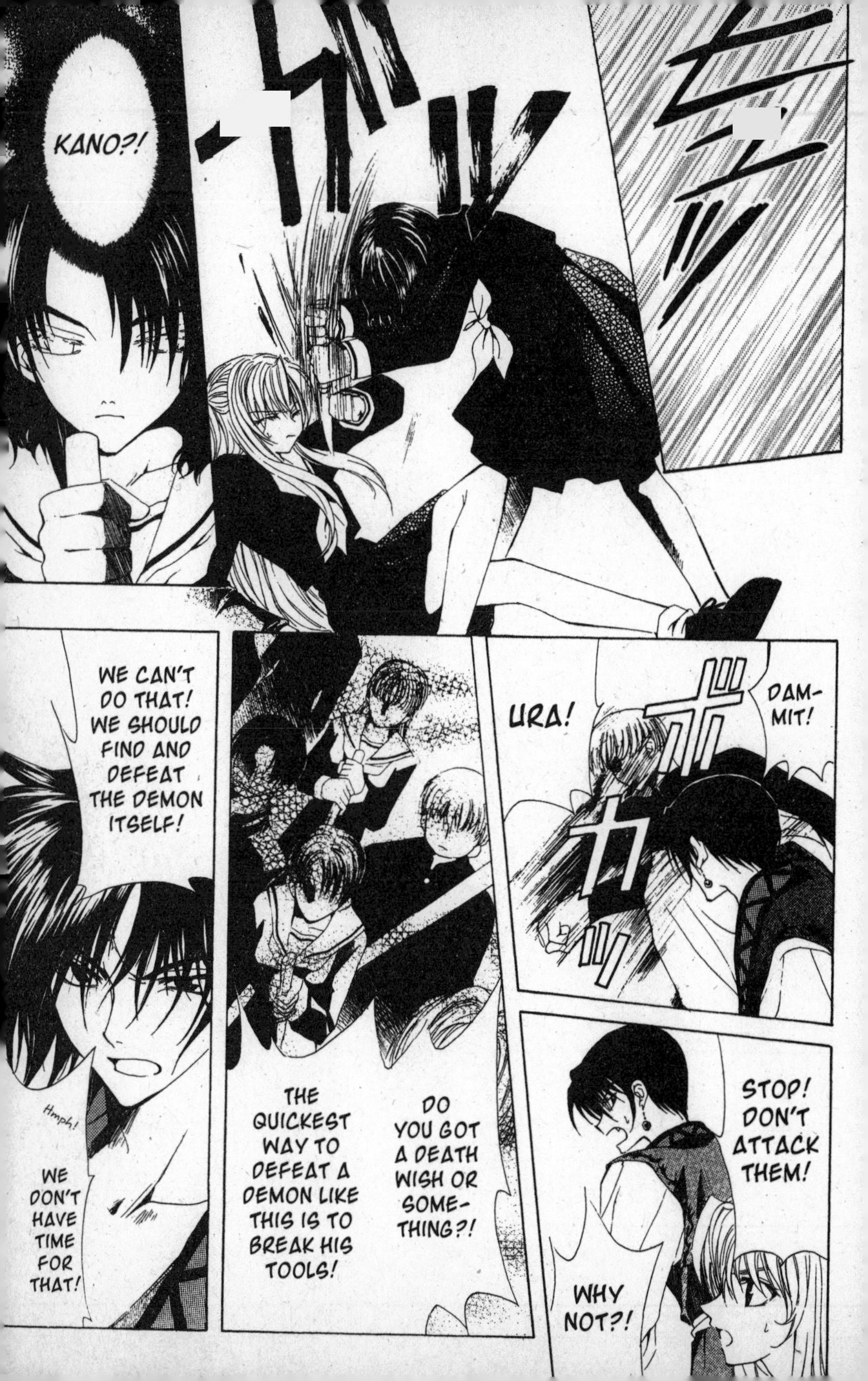

KANO?!
DAM-MIT!
URA!
ボカッ
STOP! DON'T ATTACK THEM!
WHY NOT?!
DO YOU GOT A DEATH WISH OR SOME-THING?!
THE QUICKEST WAY TO DEFEAT A DEMON LIKE THIS IS TO BREAK HIS TOOLS!
WE CAN'T DO THAT! WE SHOULD FIND AND DEFEAT THE DEMON ITSELF!
Hmph!
WE DON'T HAVE TIME FOR THAT!

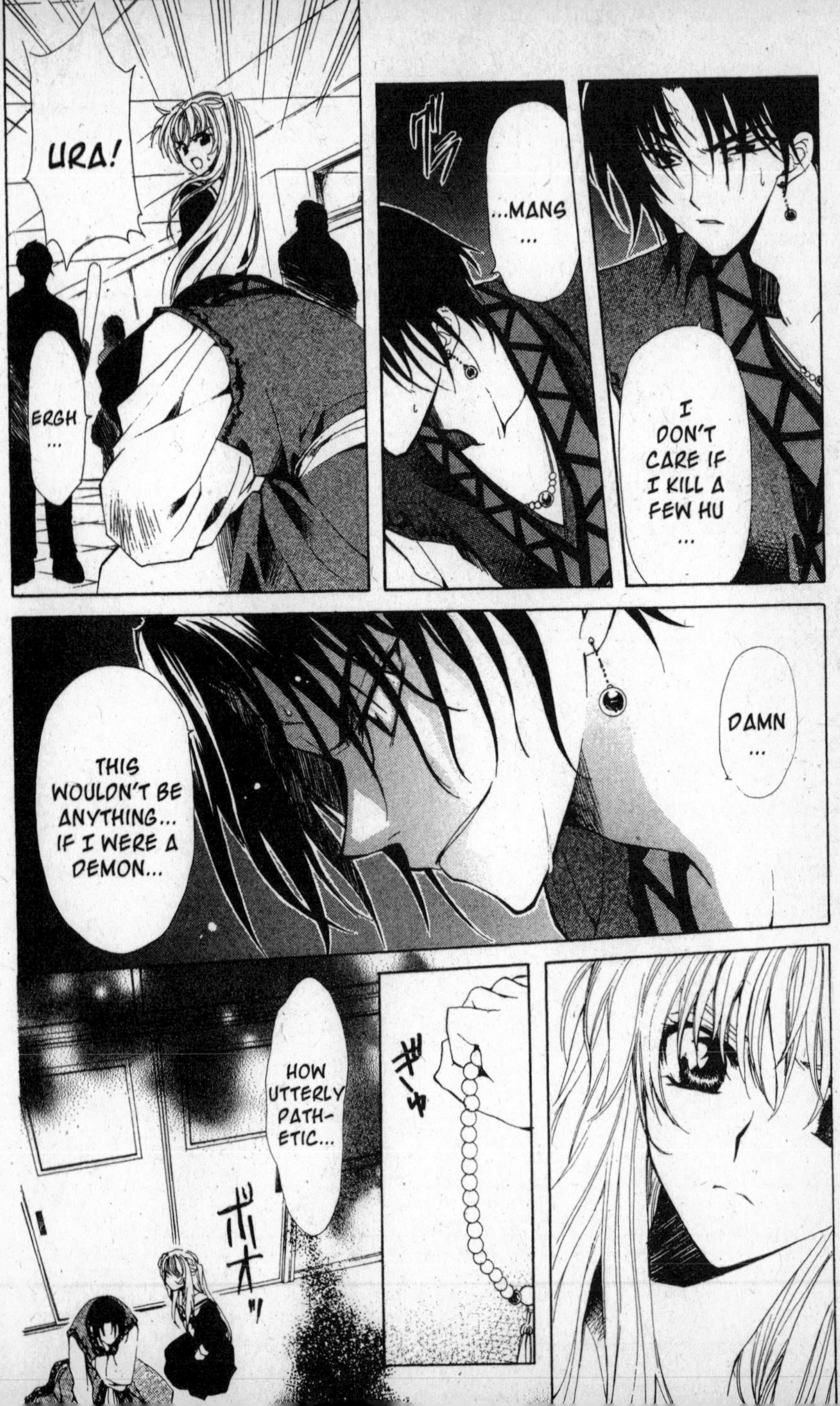
I DON'T CARE IF I KILL A FEW HU ...
...MANS ...
URA!
ERGH ...
DAMN ...
THIS WOULDN'T BE ANYTHING... IF I WERE A DEMON...
HOW UTTERLY PATH-ETIC...

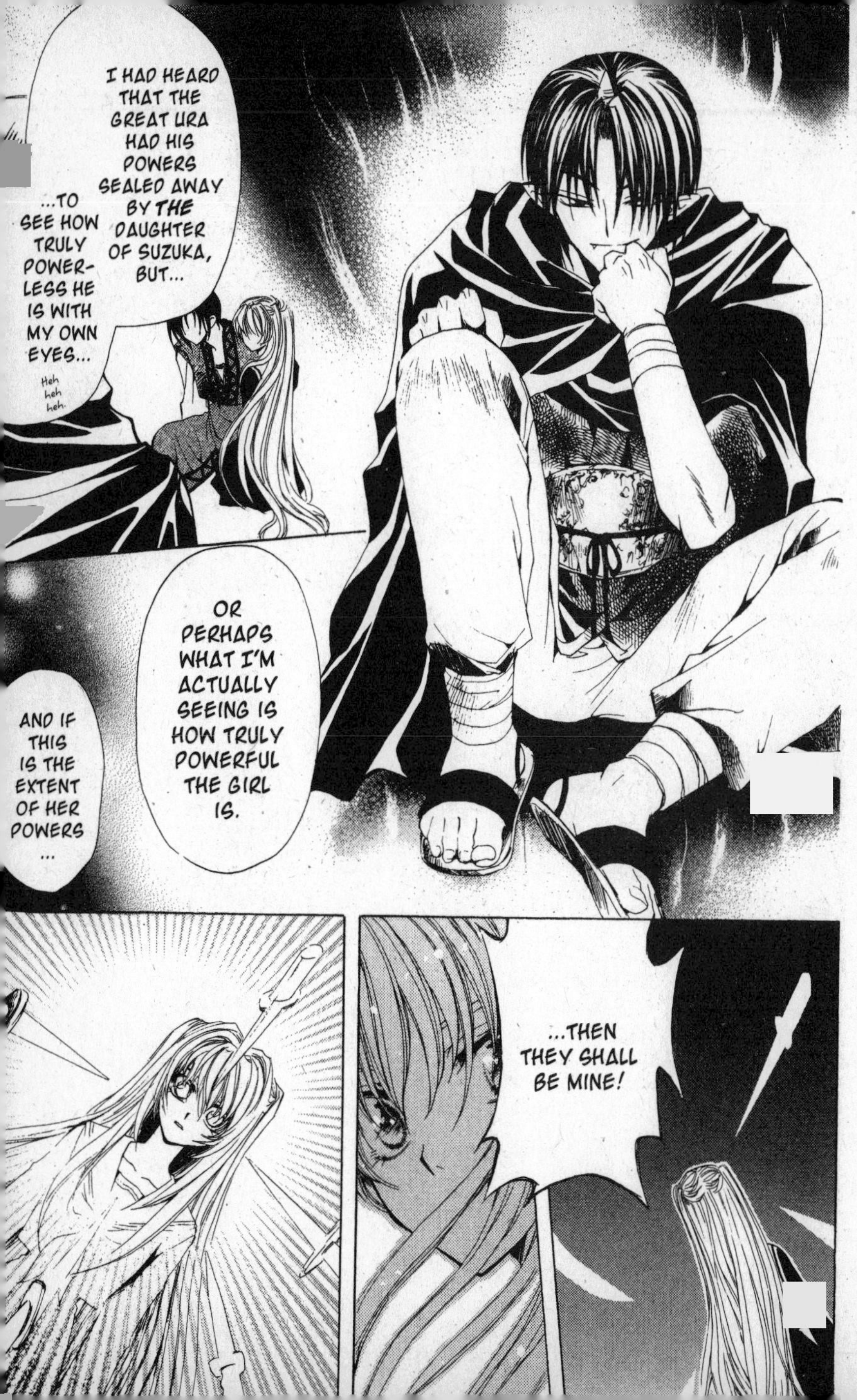
I HAD HEARD THAT THE GREAT URA HAD HIS POWERS SEALED AWAY BY THE DAUGHTER OF SUZUKA, BUT...
...TO SEE HOW TRULY POWER-LESS HE IS WITH MY OWN EYES...
Heh heh heh.
OR PERHAPS WHAT I'M ACTUALLY SEEING IS HOW TRULY POWERFUL THE GIRL IS.
AND IF THIS IS THE EXTENT OF HER POWERS ...
...THEN THEY SHALL BE MINE!

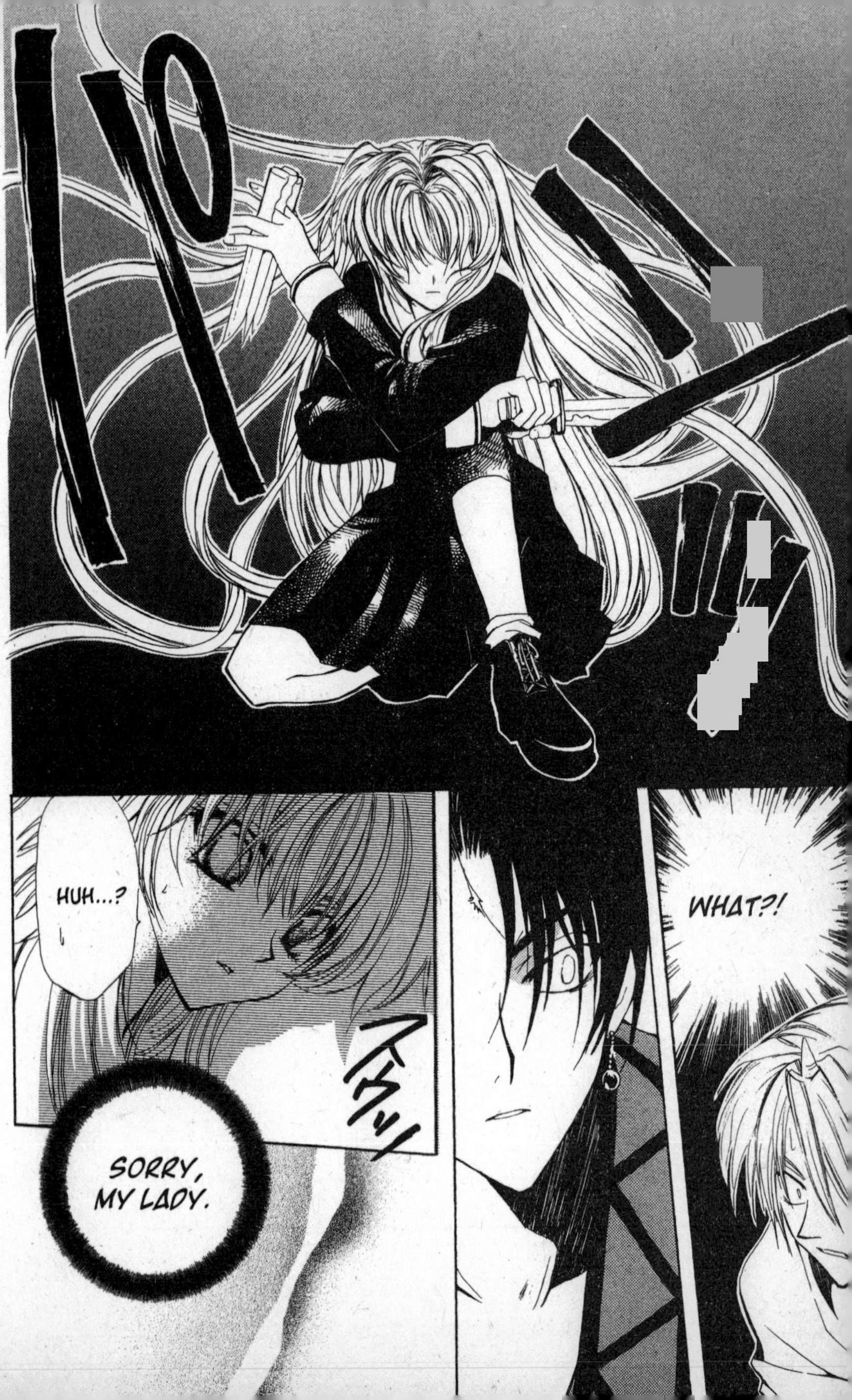
WHAT?!
HUH...?
SORRY, MY LADY.

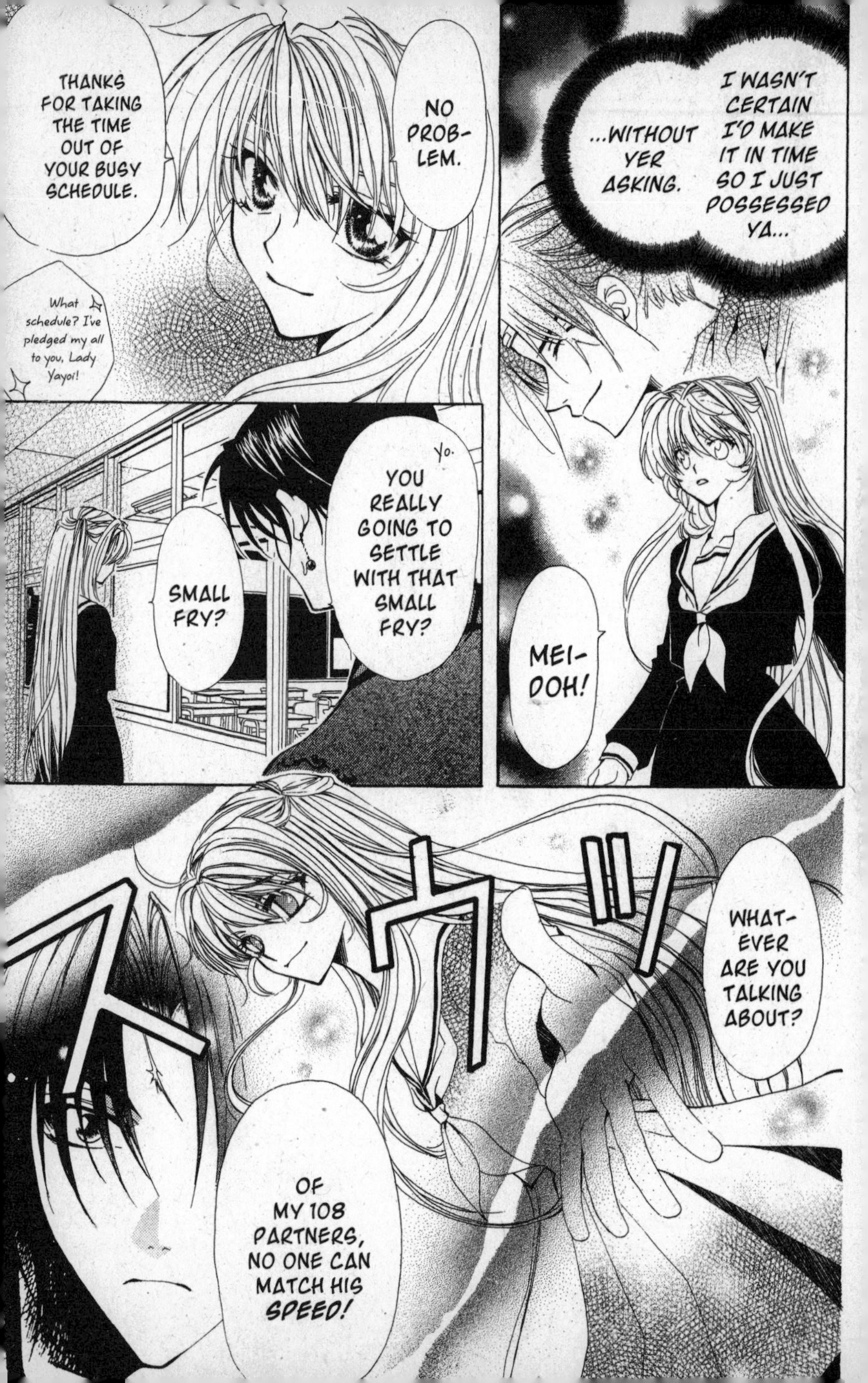
I WASN'T CERTAIN I'D MAKE IT IN TIME SO I JUST POSSESSED YA...
...WITHOUT YER ASKING.
MEI-DOH!
THANKS FOR TAKING THE TIME OUT OF YOUR BUSY SCHEDULE.
NO PROB-LEM.
What schedule? I've pledged my all to you, Lady Yayoi!
Yo.
YOU REALLY GOING TO SETTLE WITH THAT SMALL FRY?
SMALL FRY?
WHAT-EVER ARE YOU TALKING ABOUT?
OF MY 108 PARTNERS, NO ONE CAN MATCH HIS SPEED!

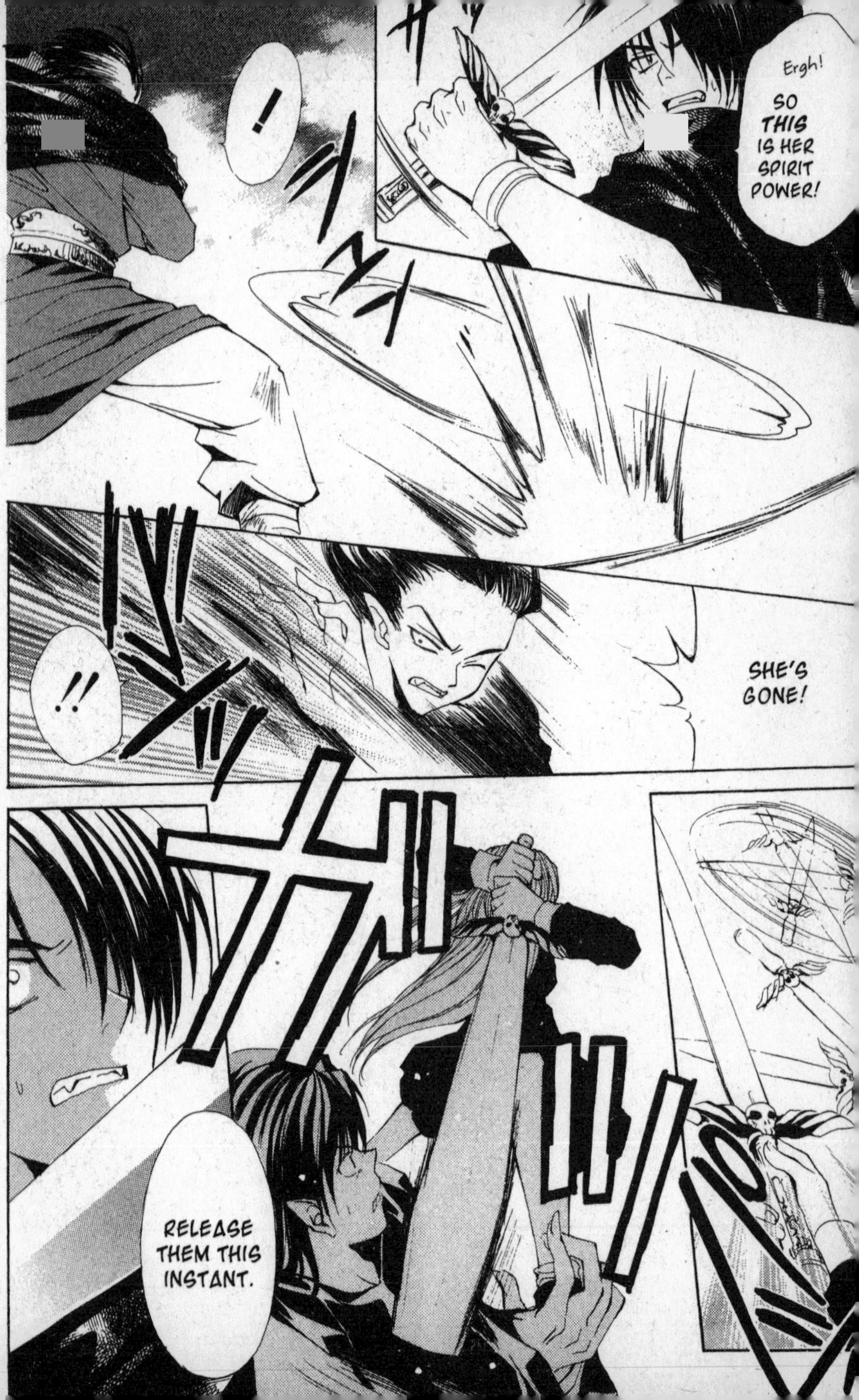
Ergh!
SO THIS IS HER SPIRIT POWER!
!
SHE'S GONE!
!!
RELEASE THEM THIS INSTANT.

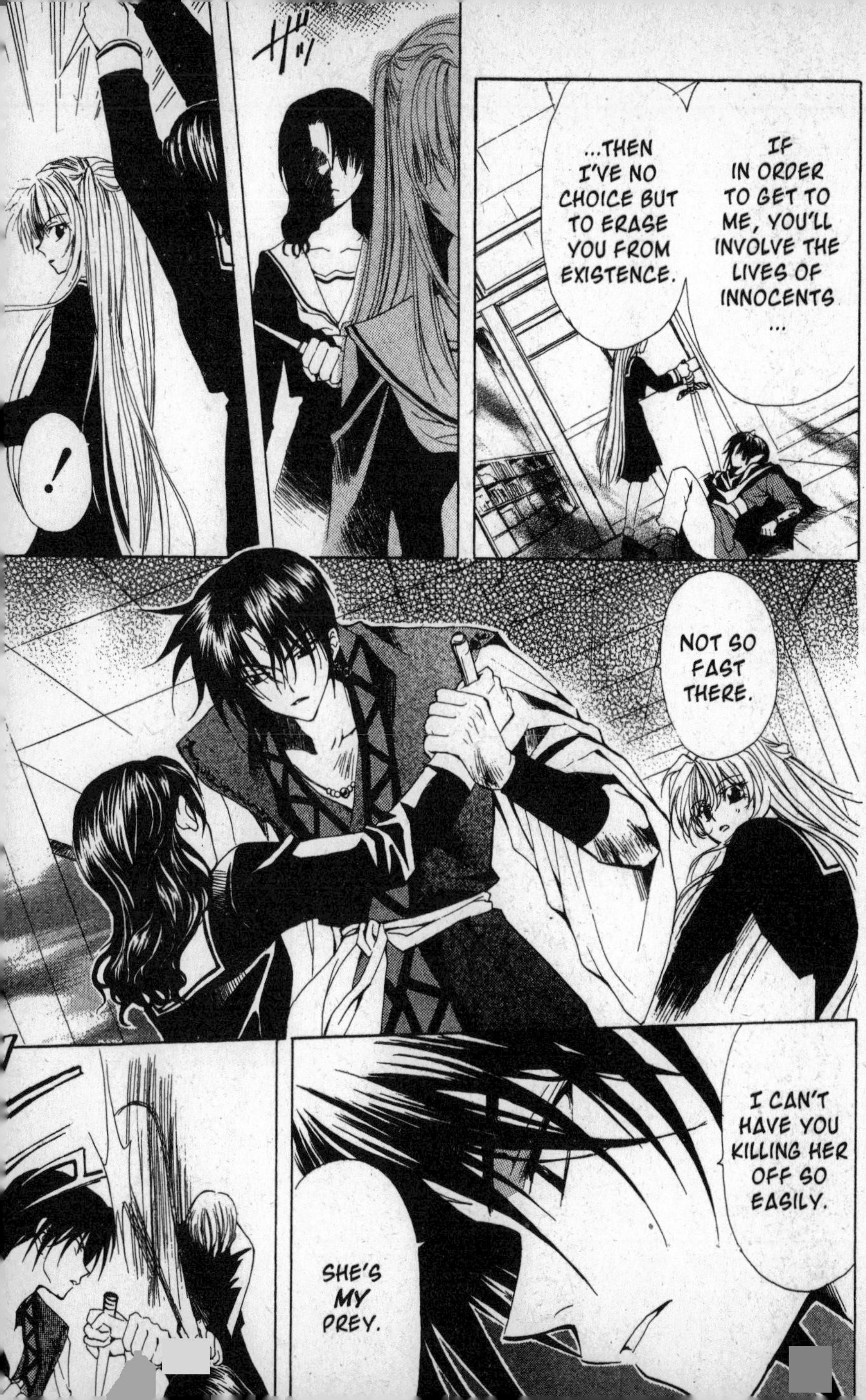
IF IN ORDER TO GET TO ME, YOU'LL INVOLVE THE LIVES OF INNOCENTS ...
...THEN I'VE NO CHOICE BUT TO ERASE YOU FROM EXISTENCE.
!
NOT SO FAST THERE.
I CAN'T HAVE YOU KILLING HER OFF SO EASILY.
SHE'S MY PREY.

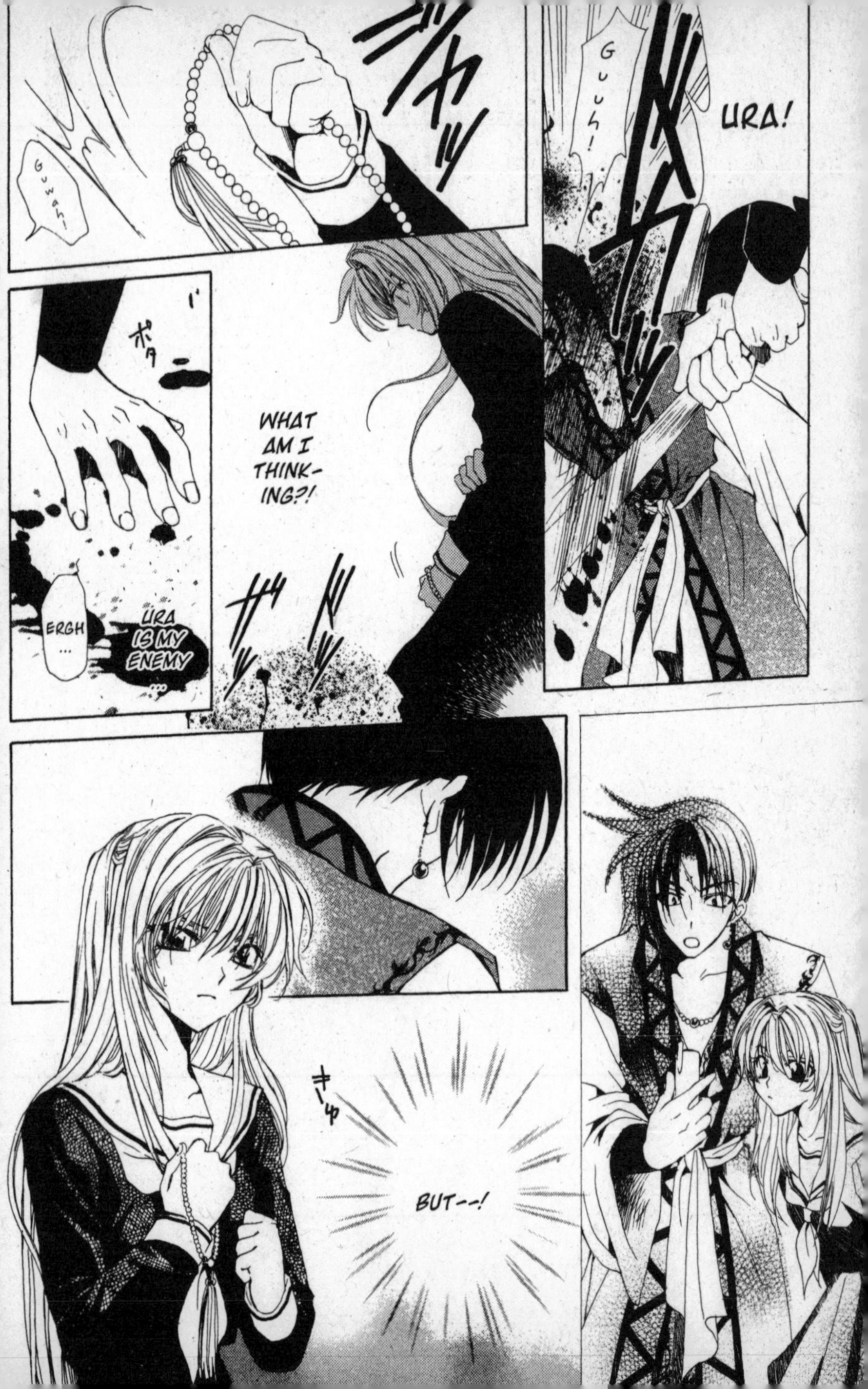
Guuh!
URA!
Guwah!
WHAT AM I THINKING?!
ERGH...
URA IS MY ENEMY...
BUT--!

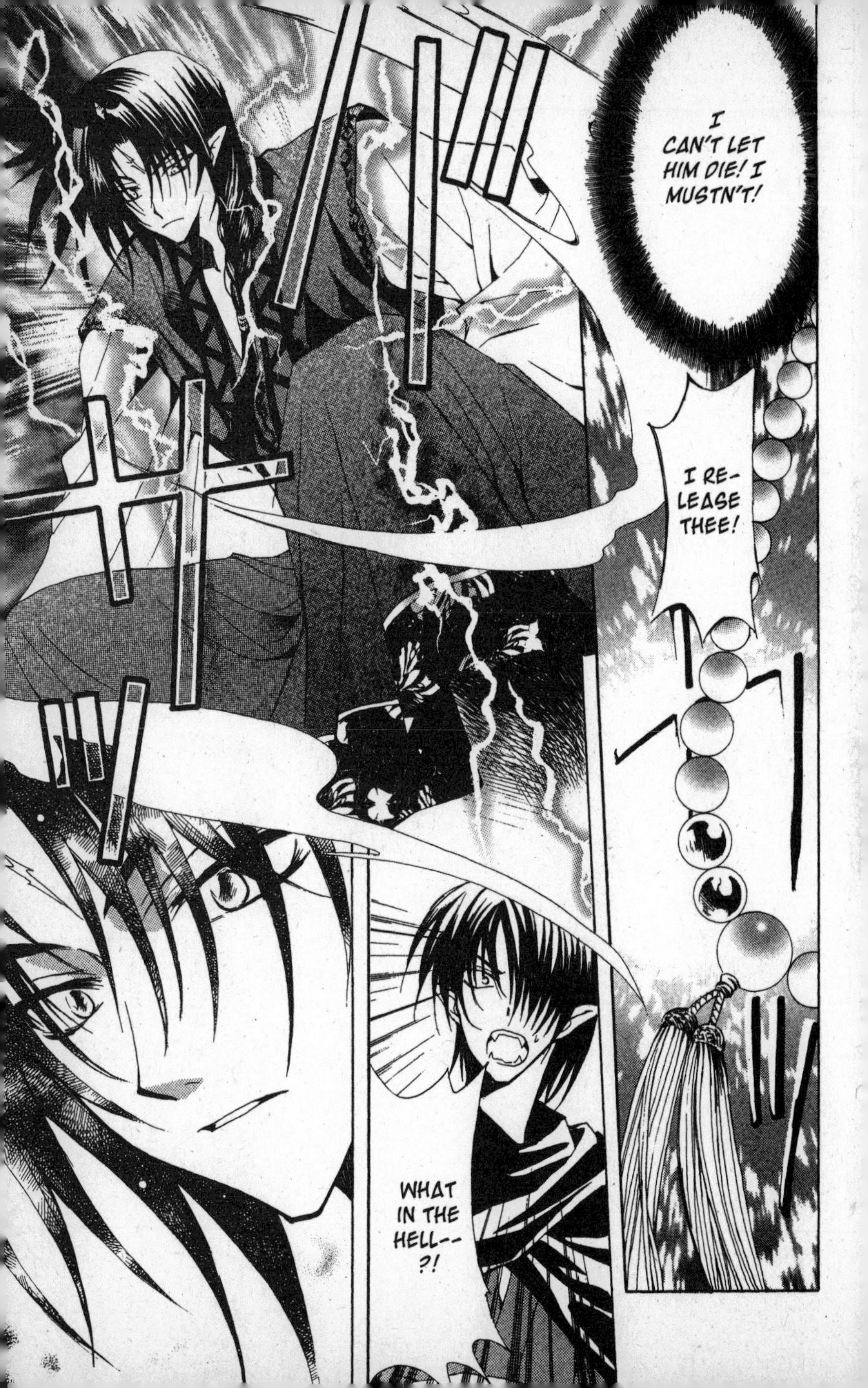
I CAN'T LET HIM DIE! I MUSTN'T!
I RE-LEASE THEE!
WHAT IN THE HELL-- ?!

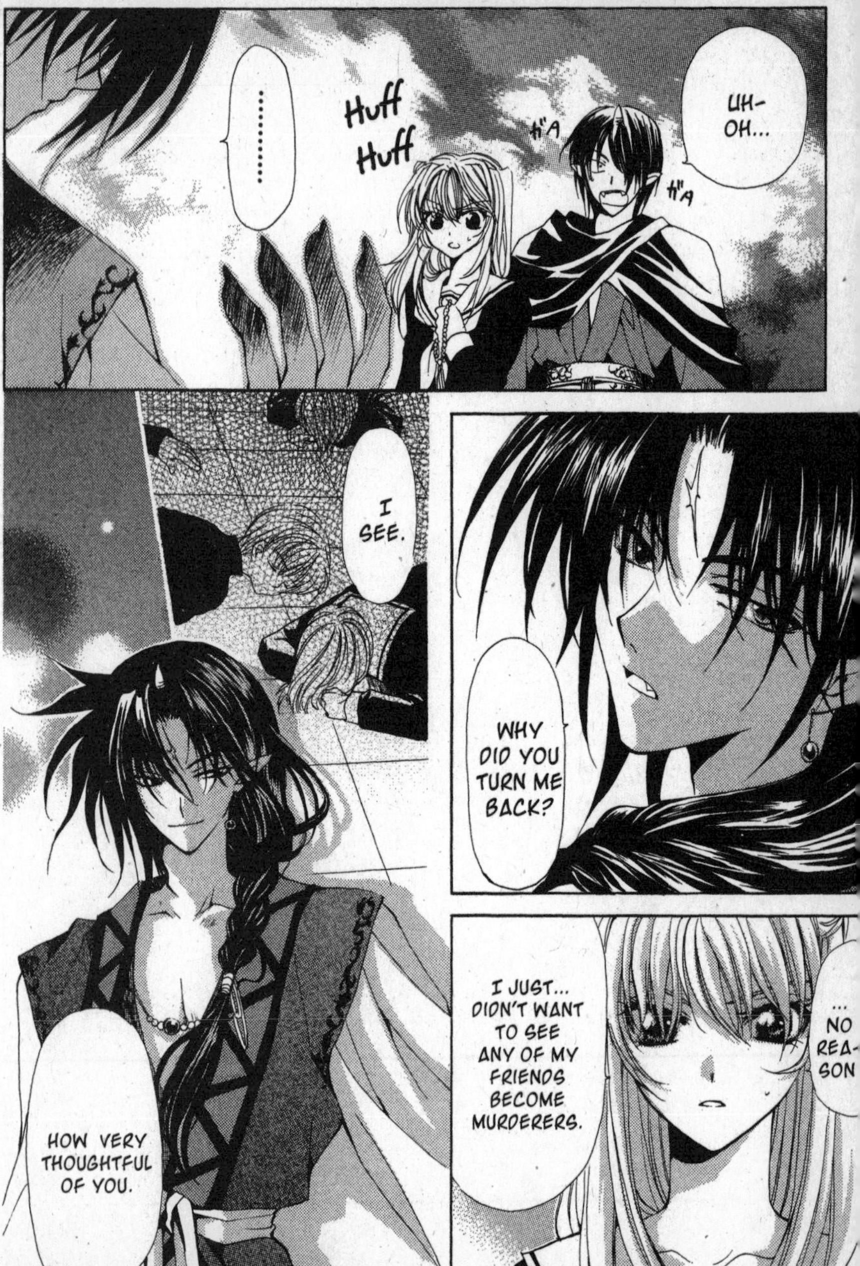
UH-OH...
Huff Huff
......
WHY DID YOU TURN ME BACK?
...NO REASON
I JUST... DIDN'T WANT TO SEE ANY OF MY FRIENDS BECOME MURDERERS.
I SEE.
HOW VERY THOUGHTFUL OF YOU.

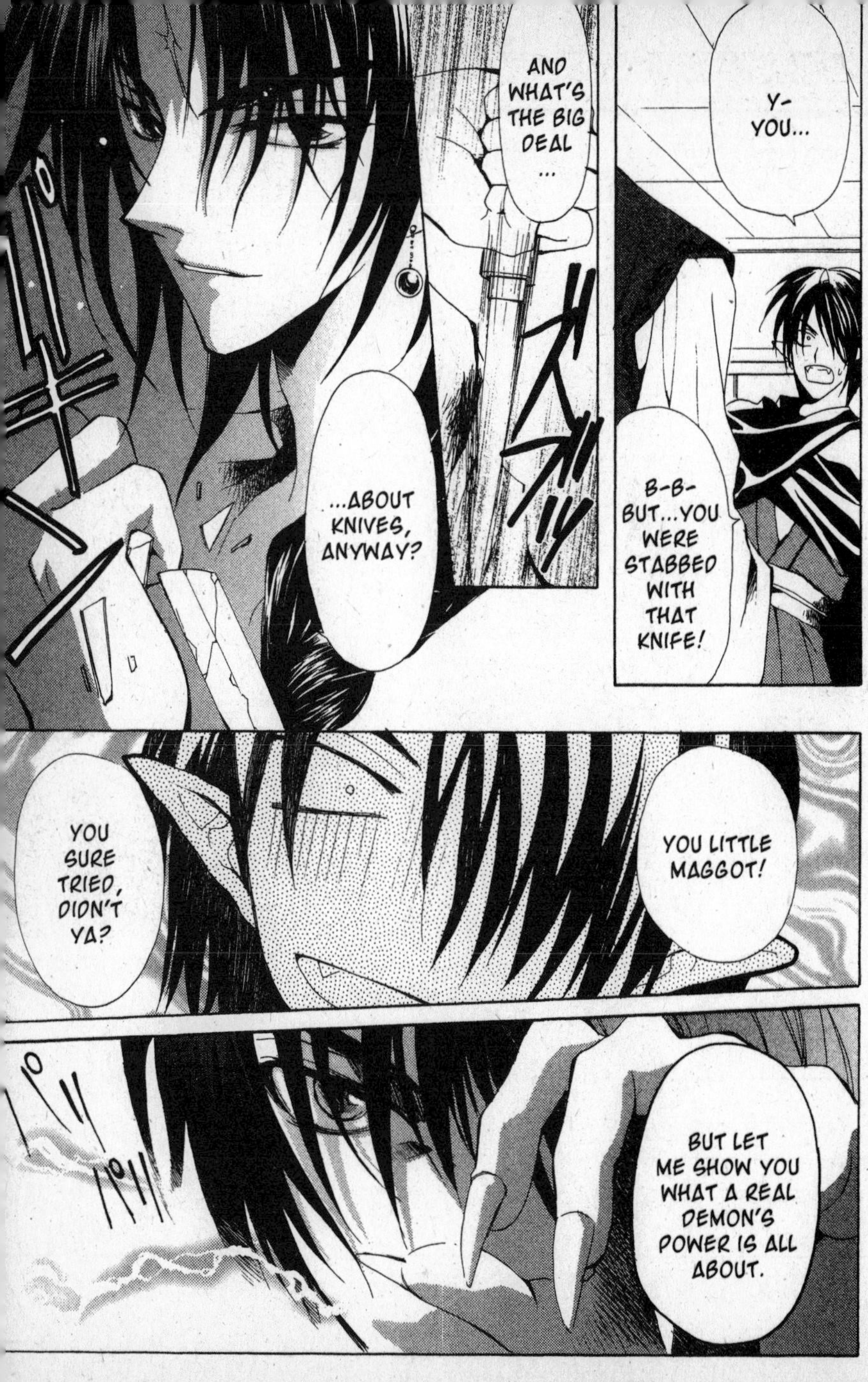
Y-YOU...
B-B-BUT...YOU WERE STABBED WITH THAT KNIFE!
AND WHAT'S THE BIG DEAL ...
...ABOUT KNIVES, ANYWAY?
YOU LITTLE MAGGOT!
YOU SURE TRIED, DIDN'T YA?
BUT LET ME SHOW YOU WHAT A REAL DEMON'S POWER IS ALL ABOUT.

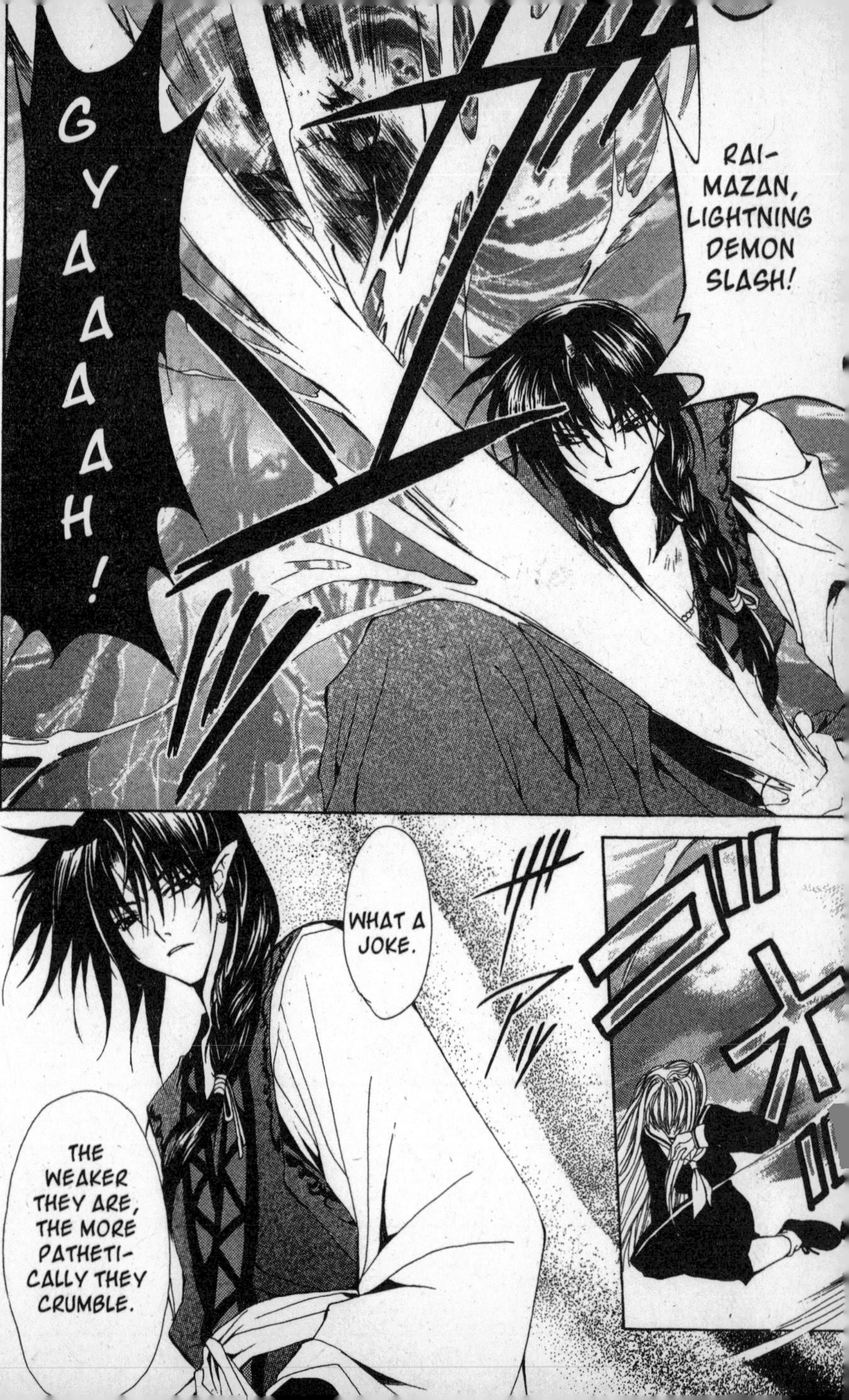
RAI-MAZAN, LIGHTNING DEMON SLASH!
GYAAAAH!
WHAT A JOKE.
THE WEAKER THEY ARE, THE MORE PATHETICALLY THEY CRUMBLE.

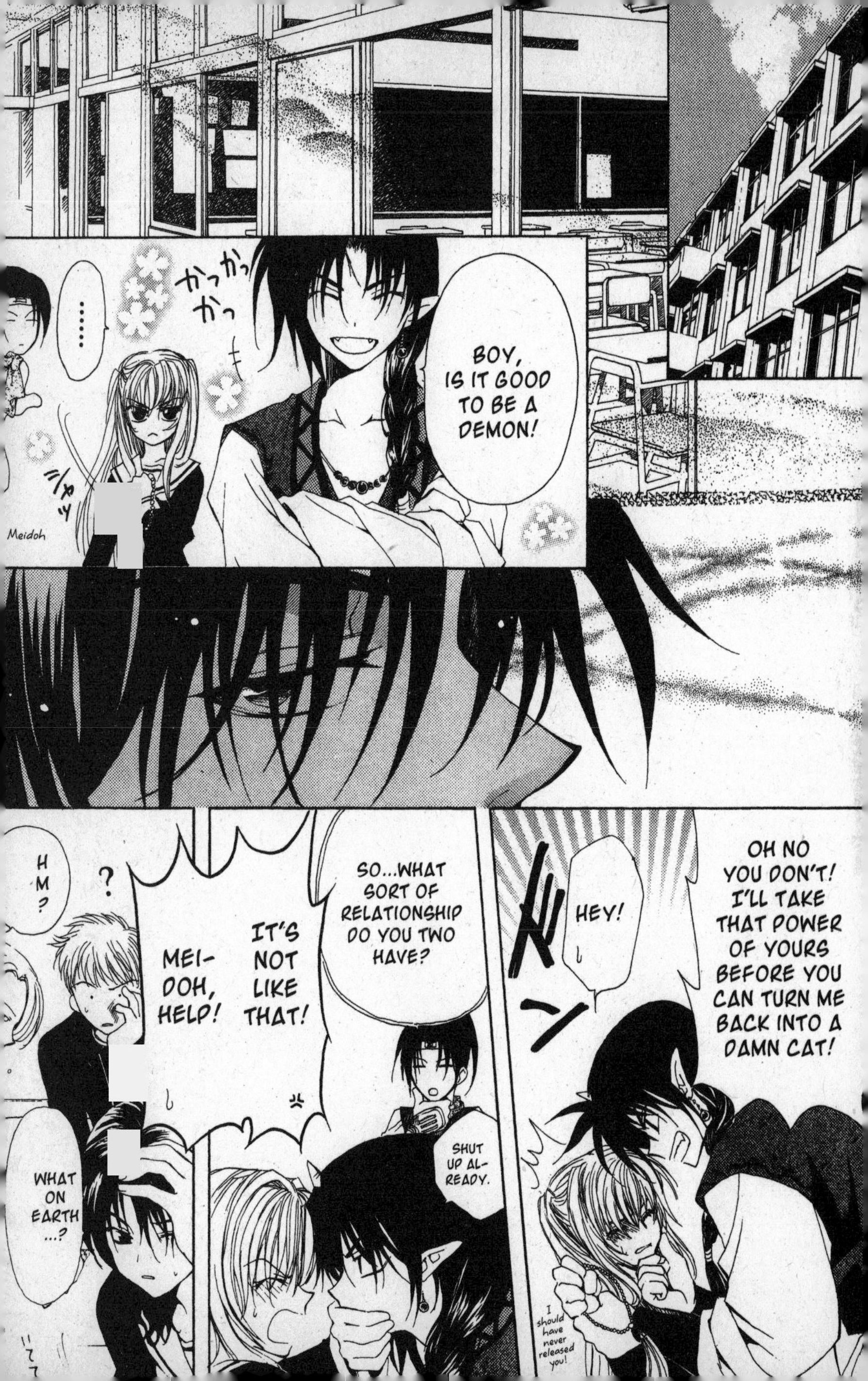
BOY, IS IT GOOD TO BE A DEMON!
かっかっかっ
……
シャッ
Meidoh
HEY!
OH NO YOU DON'T! I'LL TAKE THAT POWER OF YOURS BEFORE YOU CAN TURN ME BACK INTO A DAMN CAT!
I should have never released you!
SO...WHAT SORT OF RELATIONSHIP DO YOU TWO HAVE?
SHUT UP AL-READY.
IT'S NOT LIKE THAT!
MEI-DOH, HELP!
HM?
WHAT ON EARTH ...?
いてて

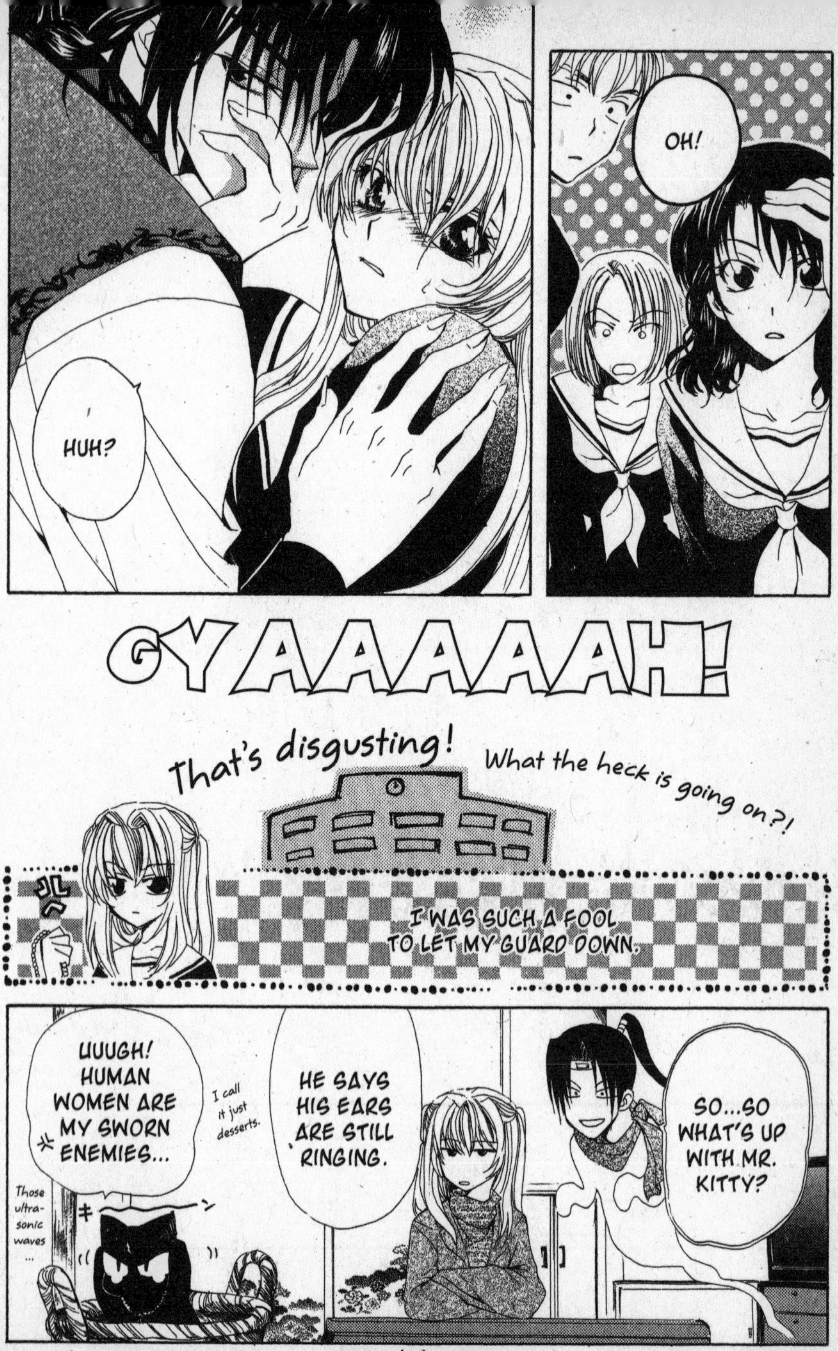
OH!
HUH?
GYAAAAAH!
What the heck is going on?!
That's disgusting!
I WAS SUCH A FOOL TO LET MY GUARD DOWN.
SO...SO WHAT'S UP WITH MR. KITTY?
HE SAYS HIS EARS ARE STILL RINGING.
I call it just desserts.
UUUGH! HUMAN WOMEN ARE MY SWORN ENEMIES...
Those ultra-sonic waves...

Act 2/The End

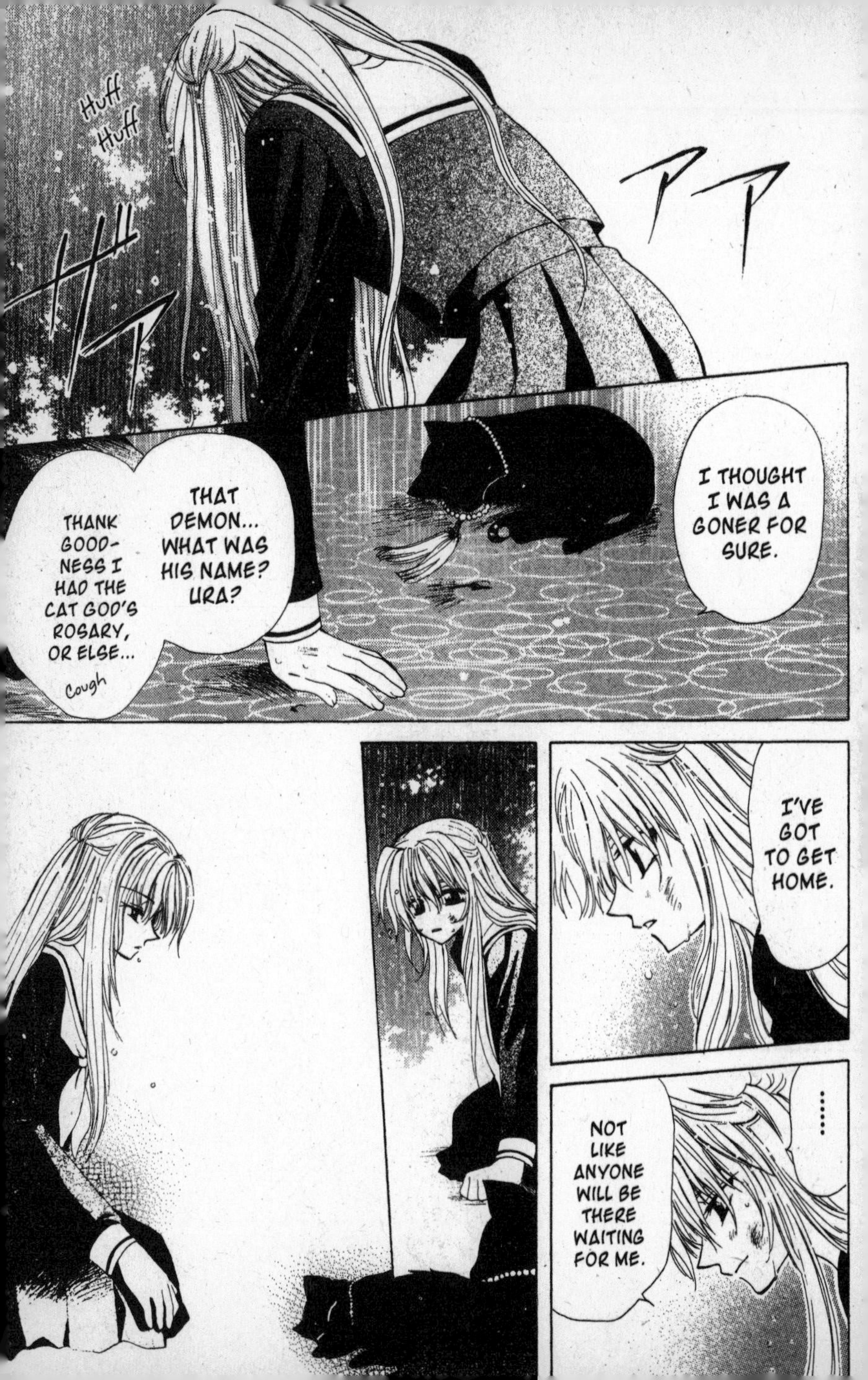
Huff Huff
I THOUGHT I WAS A GONER FOR SURE.
THAT DEMON... WHAT WAS HIS NAME? URA?
THANK GOODNESS I HAD THE CAT GOD'S ROSARY, OR ELSE...
Cough
I'VE GOT TO GET HOME.
......
NOT LIKE ANYONE WILL BE THERE WAITING FOR ME.

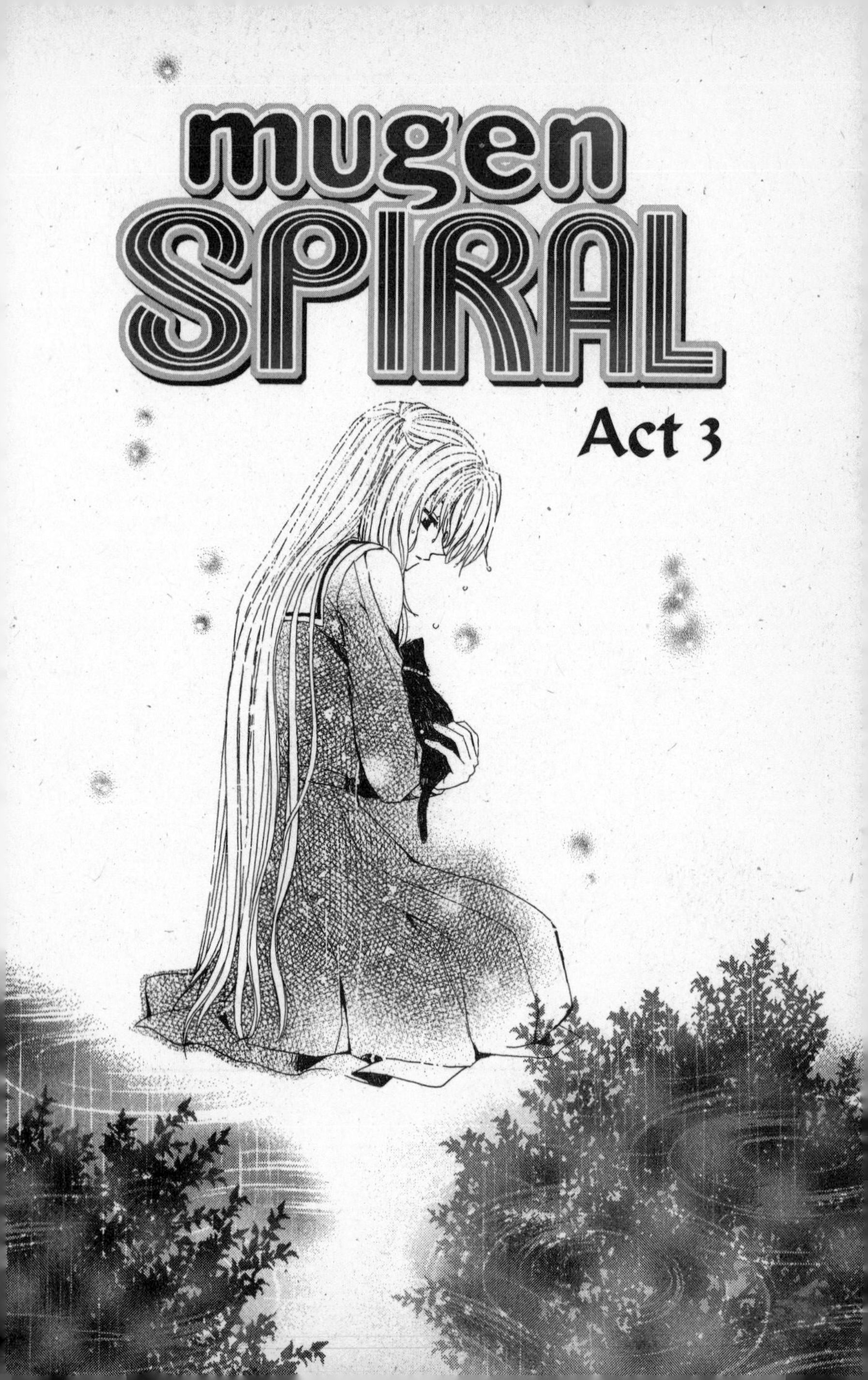
mugen SPIRAL
Act 3

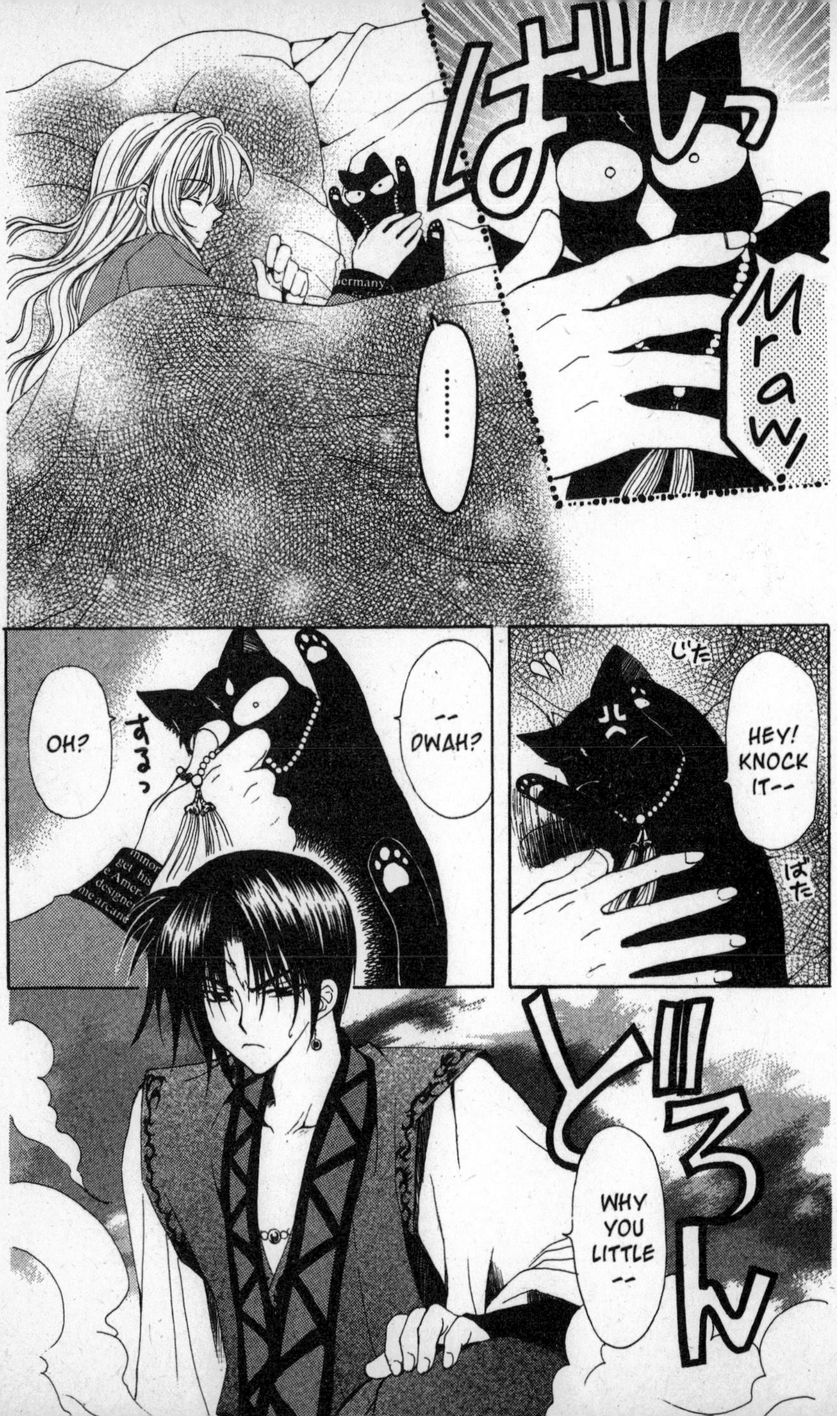
ばしっ
Mraw!
......
じた
HEY! KNOCK IT--
ばた
--OWAH?
するっ
OH?
どろん
WHY YOU LITTLE --

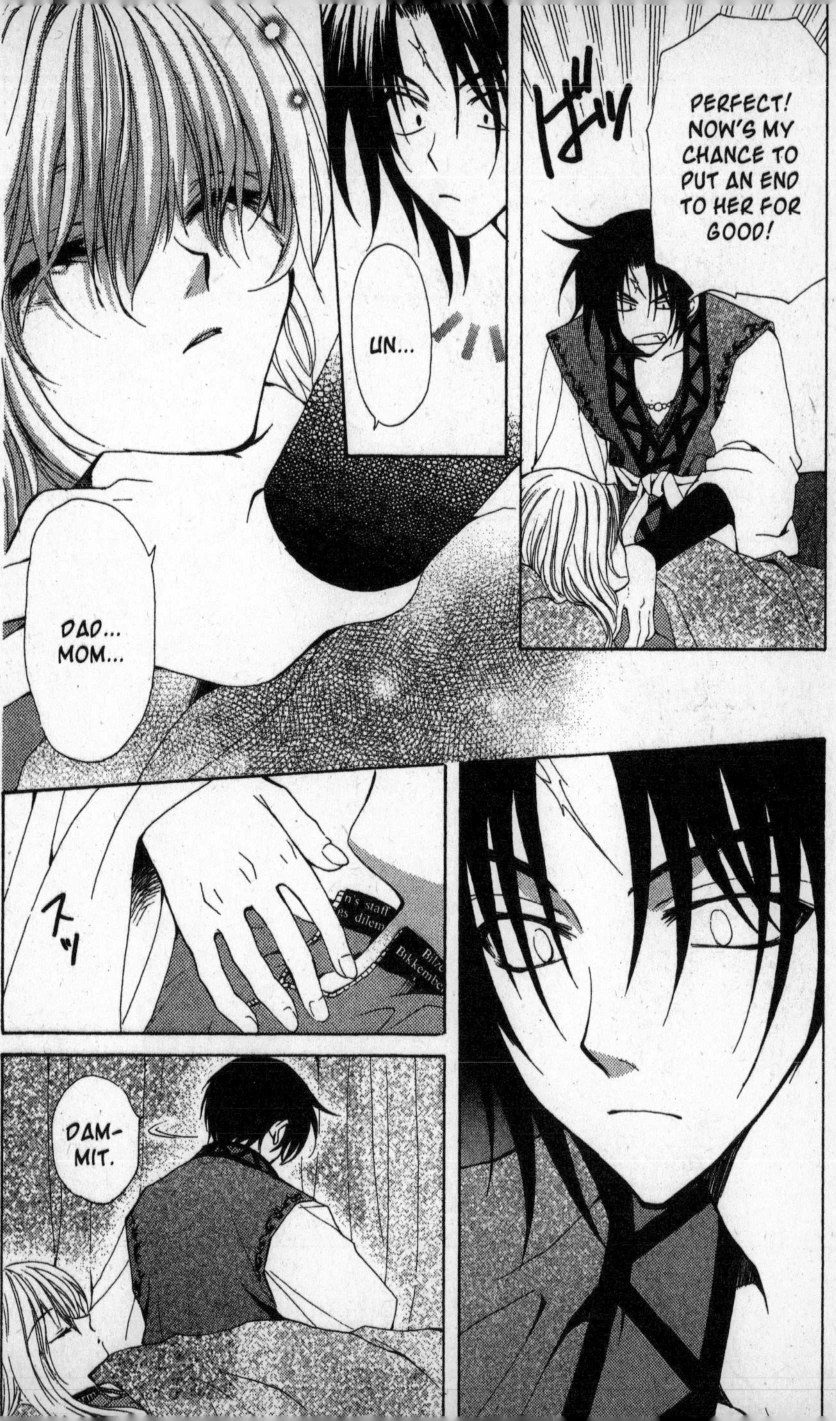
PERFECT! NOW'S MY CHANCE TO PUT AN END TO HER FOR GOOD!
UN...
DAD... MOM...
スッ
DAM-MIT.

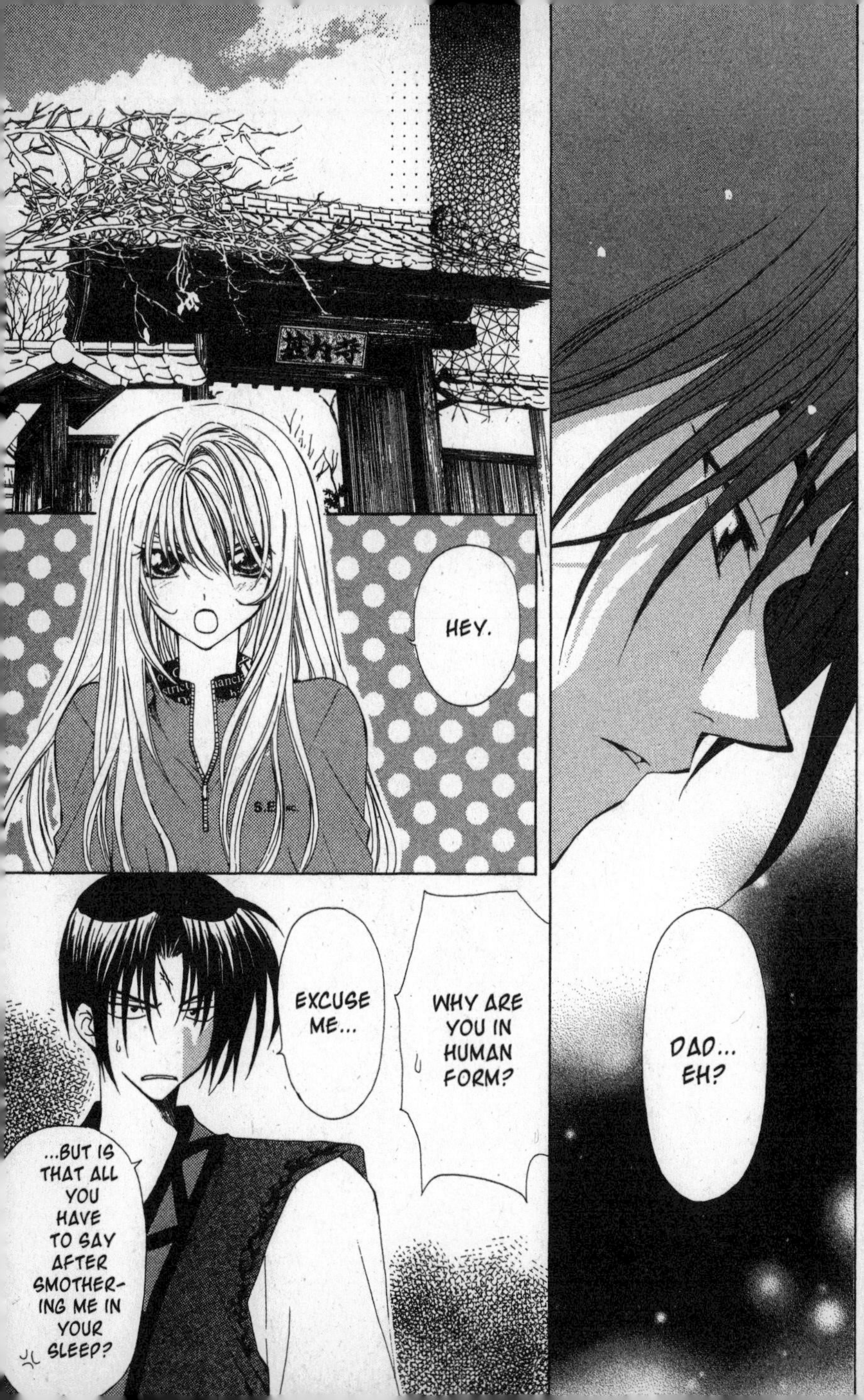
DAD... EH?
HEY.
WHY ARE YOU IN HUMAN FORM?
EXCUSE ME...
...BUT IS THAT ALL YOU HAVE TO SAY AFTER SMOTHERING ME IN YOUR SLEEP?

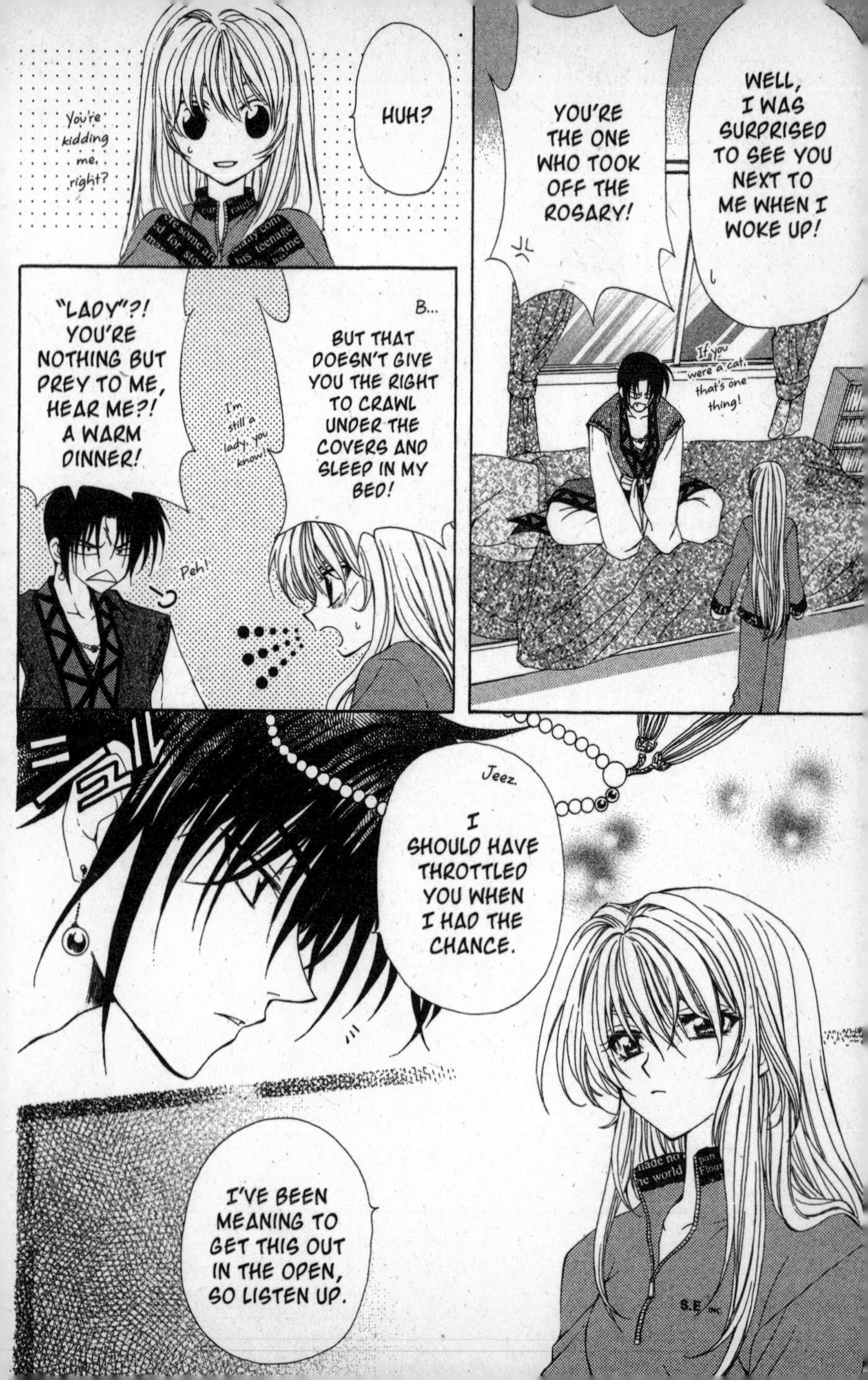

WELL, I WAS SURPRISED TO SEE YOU NEXT TO ME WHEN I WOKE UP!
YOU'RE THE ONE WHO TOOK OFF THE ROSARY!
If you were a cat, that's one thing!
HUH?
You're kidding me, right?
B...
BUT THAT DOESN'T GIVE YOU THE RIGHT TO CRAWL UNDER THE COVERS AND SLEEP IN MY BED!
I'm still a lady, you know!
"LADY"?! YOU'RE NOTHING BUT PREY TO ME, HEAR ME?! A WARM DINNER!
Peh!
Jeez.
I SHOULD HAVE THROTTLED YOU WHEN I HAD THE CHANCE.
I'VE BEEN MEANING TO GET THIS OUT IN THE OPEN, SO LISTEN UP.

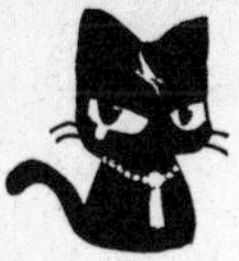

The first three acts of Mugen Spiral were run as three consecutive showcase episodes. Meaning that each had to be a standalone story. It was a little hard introducing a new enemy to fight each episode, but since I like action/battle manga to begin with, next thing you know, all my characters are fighting, anyway! In this act, a ghost makes an appearance, but the story is still centered around Demons. To be honest, I try to avoid drawing ghosts as much as possible, and if you ask me why...it's because I'm scared of them! It's not like I see dead people or anything, but I hear that if you draw or talk too much about ghosts, then they become drawn to you. (Kyaahhh!) Then maybe they'd start to look at what I'm drawing and criticize it (which would be awful in so many ways.)
I'm the type of person that's terrible with horror movies, novels, comics, and even horror games. And I'm totally bad when it comes to splatter movies or anything with a lot of murder scenes in it. When I even think about drawing a story about ghosts, I start to scare myself (not to say that I'll stop drawing them.) That's why the ghosts that do show up in my stories are oddly giddy. (Like Meidoh.)

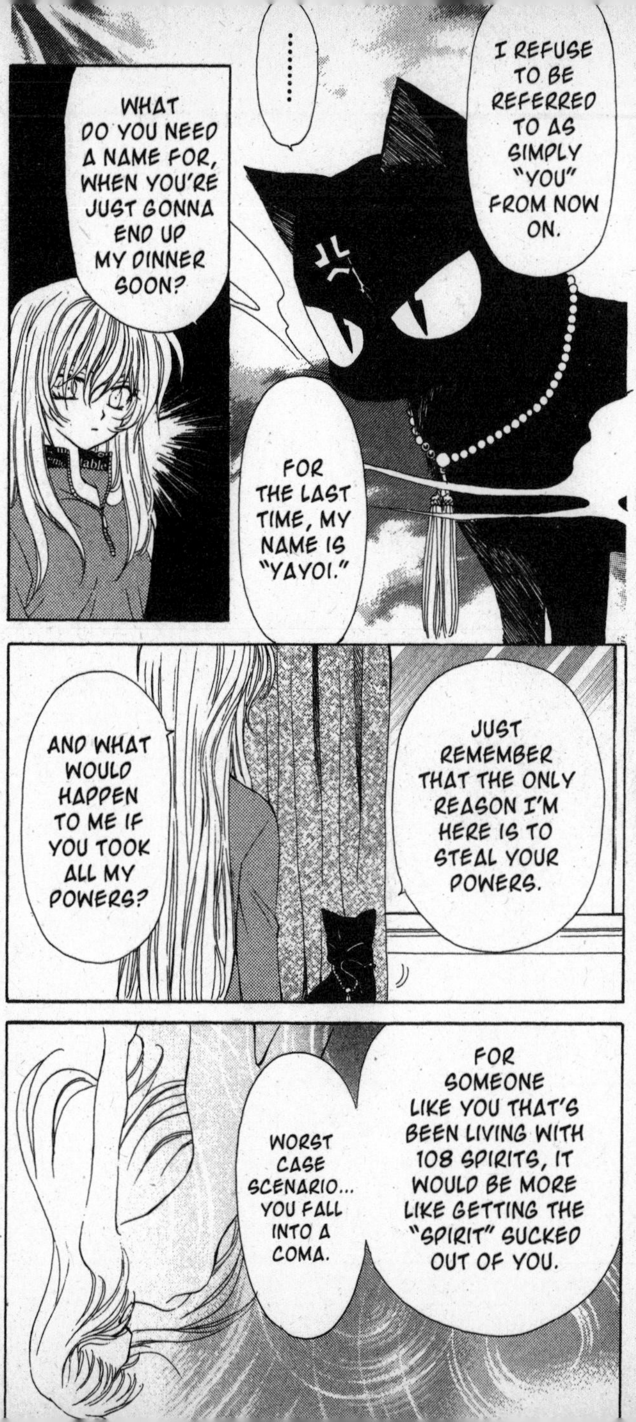
I REFUSE TO BE REFERRED TO AS SIMPLY "YOU" FROM NOW ON.
......
WHAT DO YOU NEED A NAME FOR, WHEN YOU'RE JUST GONNA END UP MY DINNER SOON?
FOR THE LAST TIME, MY NAME IS "YAYOI."
JUST REMEMBER THAT THE ONLY REASON I'M HERE IS TO STEAL YOUR POWERS.
AND WHAT WOULD HAPPEN TO ME IF YOU TOOK ALL MY POWERS?
FOR SOMEONE LIKE YOU THAT'S BEEN LIVING WITH 108 SPIRITS, IT WOULD BE MORE LIKE GETTING THE "SPIRIT" SUCKED OUT OF YOU.
WORST CASE SCENARIO... YOU FALL INTO A COMA.

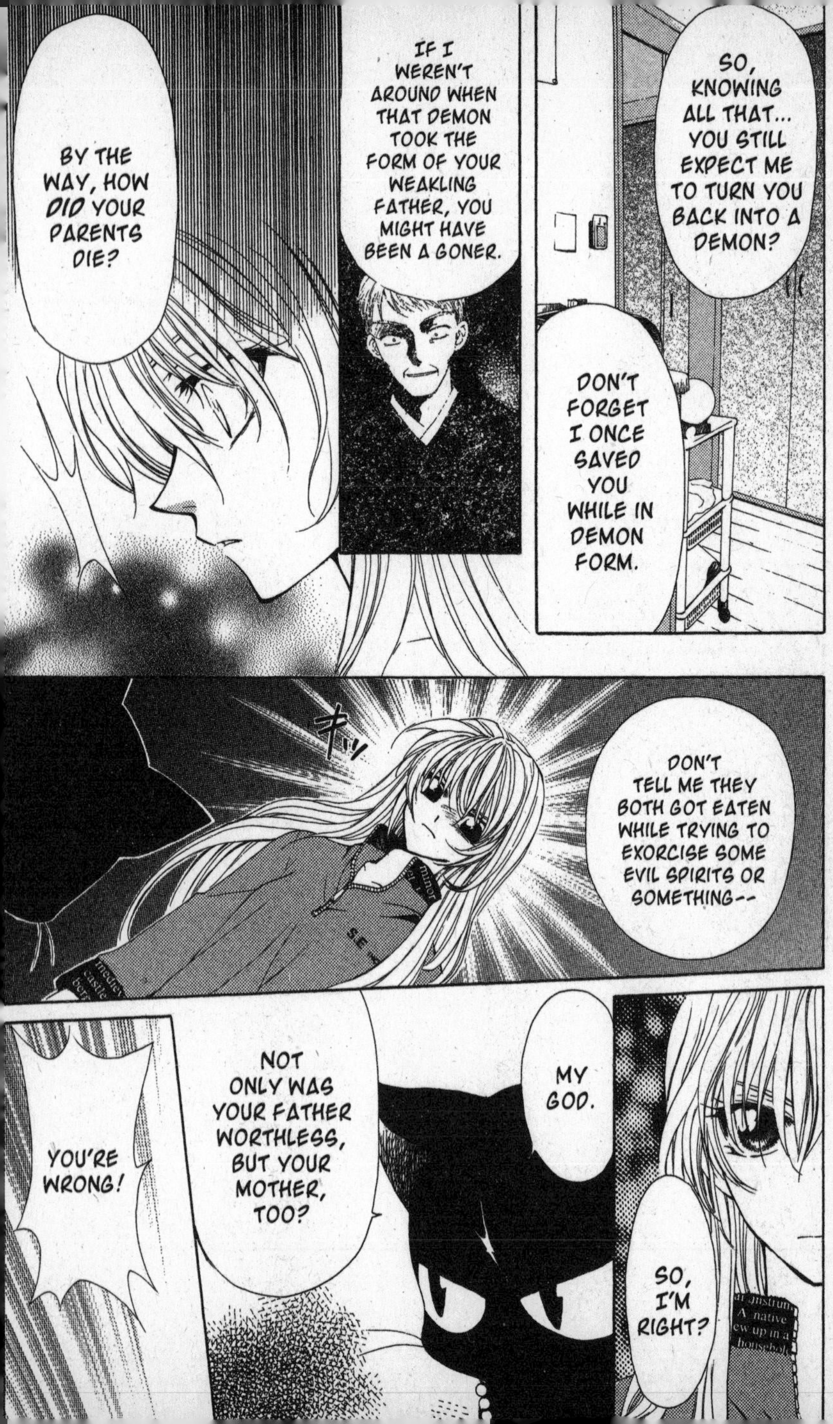
SO, KNOWING ALL THAT... YOU STILL EXPECT ME TO TURN YOU BACK INTO A DEMON?
DON'T FORGET I ONCE SAVED YOU WHILE IN DEMON FORM.
IF I WEREN'T AROUND WHEN THAT DEMON TOOK THE FORM OF YOUR WEAKLING FATHER, YOU MIGHT HAVE BEEN A GONER.
BY THE WAY, HOW *DID* YOUR PARENTS DIE?
DON'T TELL ME THEY BOTH GOT EATEN WHILE TRYING TO EXORCISE SOME EVIL SPIRITS OR SOMETHING--
MY GOD.
SO, I'M RIGHT?
NOT ONLY WAS YOUR FATHER WORTHLESS, BUT YOUR MOTHER, TOO?
YOU'RE WRONG!

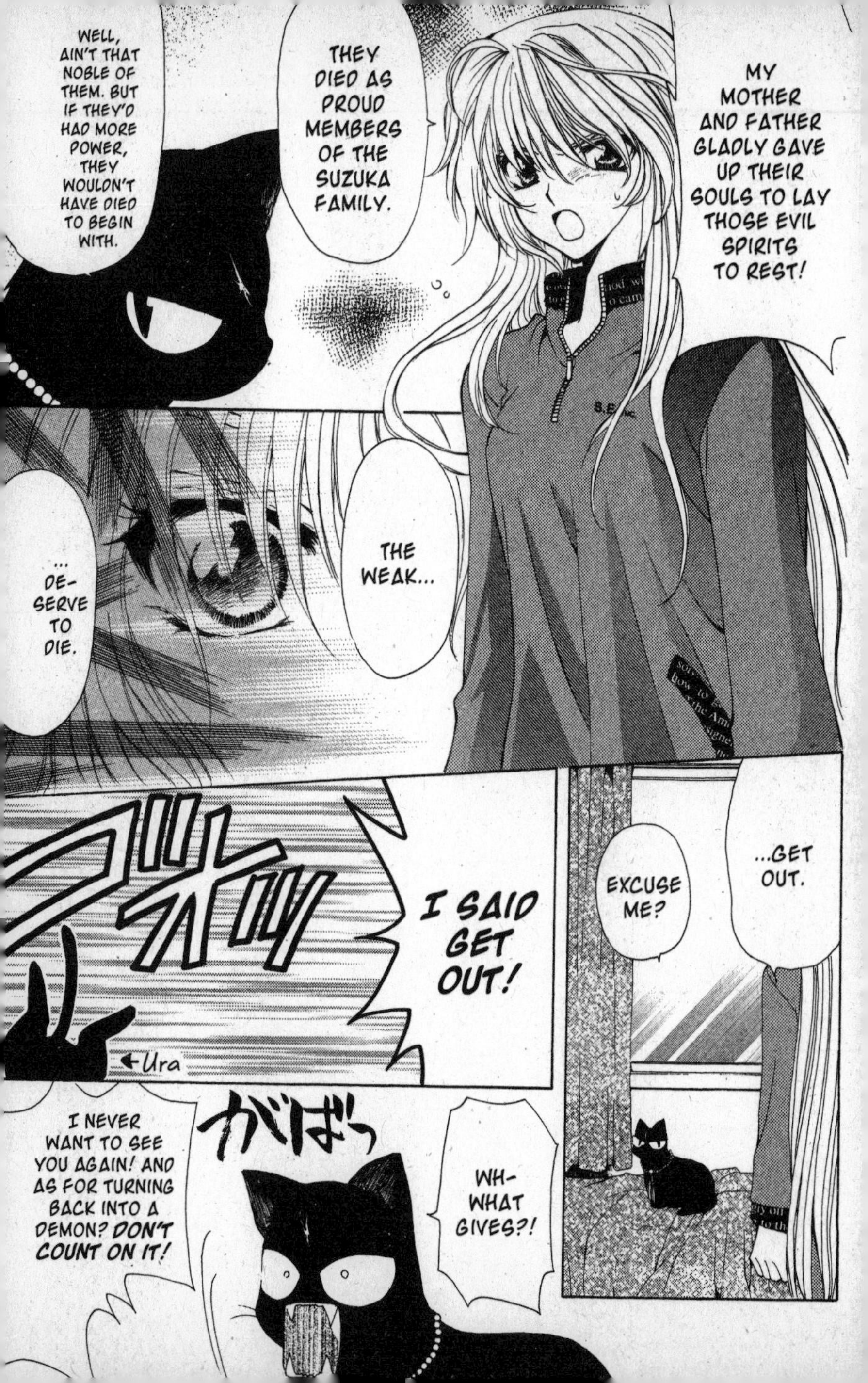
MY MOTHER AND FATHER GLADLY GAVE UP THEIR SOULS TO LAY THOSE EVIL SPIRITS TO REST!
THEY DIED AS PROUD MEMBERS OF THE SUZUKA FAMILY.
WELL, AIN'T THAT NOBLE OF THEM. BUT IF THEY'D HAD MORE POWER, THEY WOULDN'T HAVE DIED TO BEGIN WITH.
THE WEAK...
...DESERVE TO DIE.
...GET OUT.
EXCUSE ME?
I SAID GET OUT!
←Ura
WH-WHAT GIVES?!
がばっ
I NEVER WANT TO SEE YOU AGAIN! AND AS FOR TURNING BACK INTO A DEMON? DON'T COUNT ON IT!

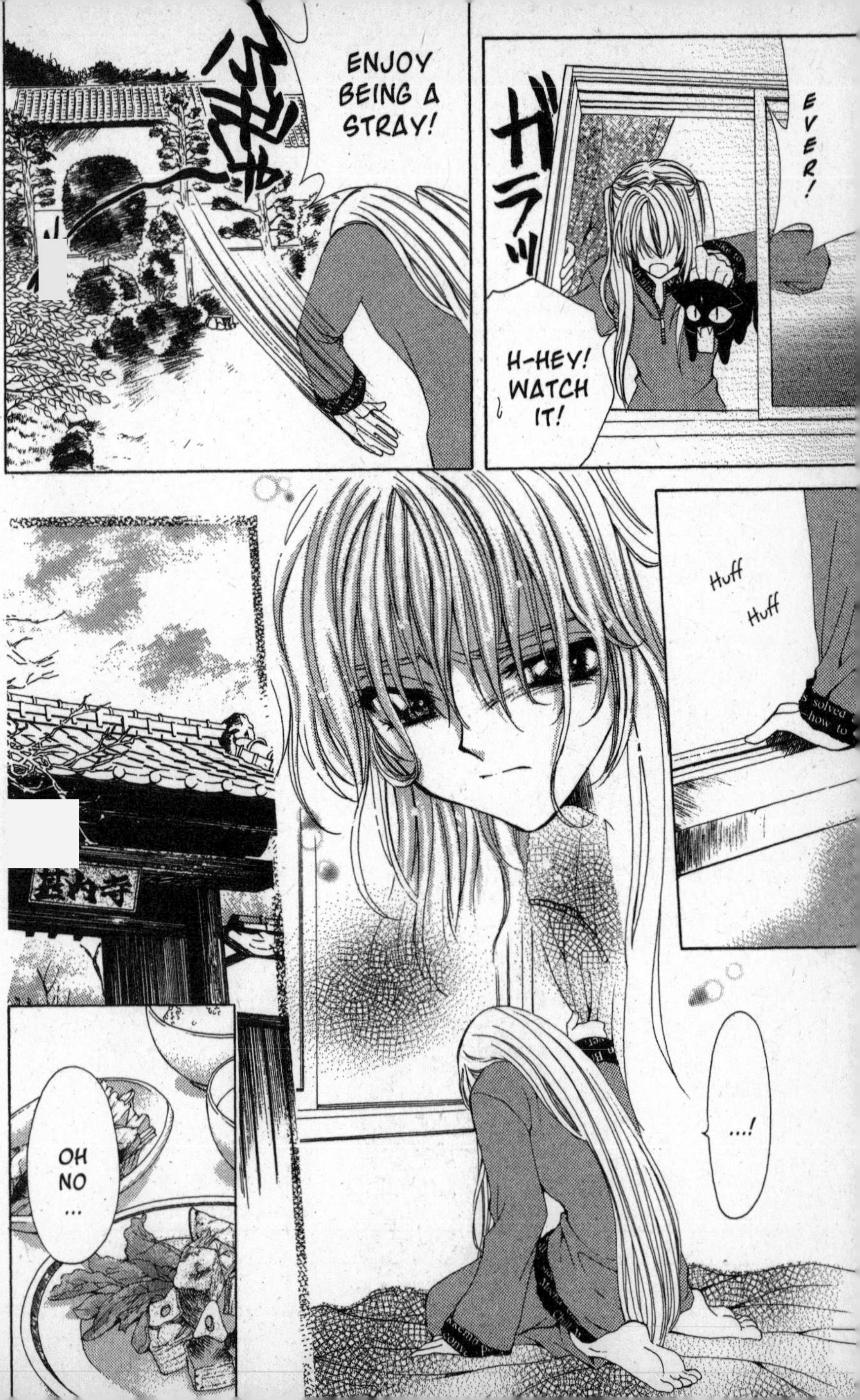
EVER!
H-HEY! WATCH IT!
ENJOY BEING A STRAY!
Huff
Huff
...!
OH NO ...

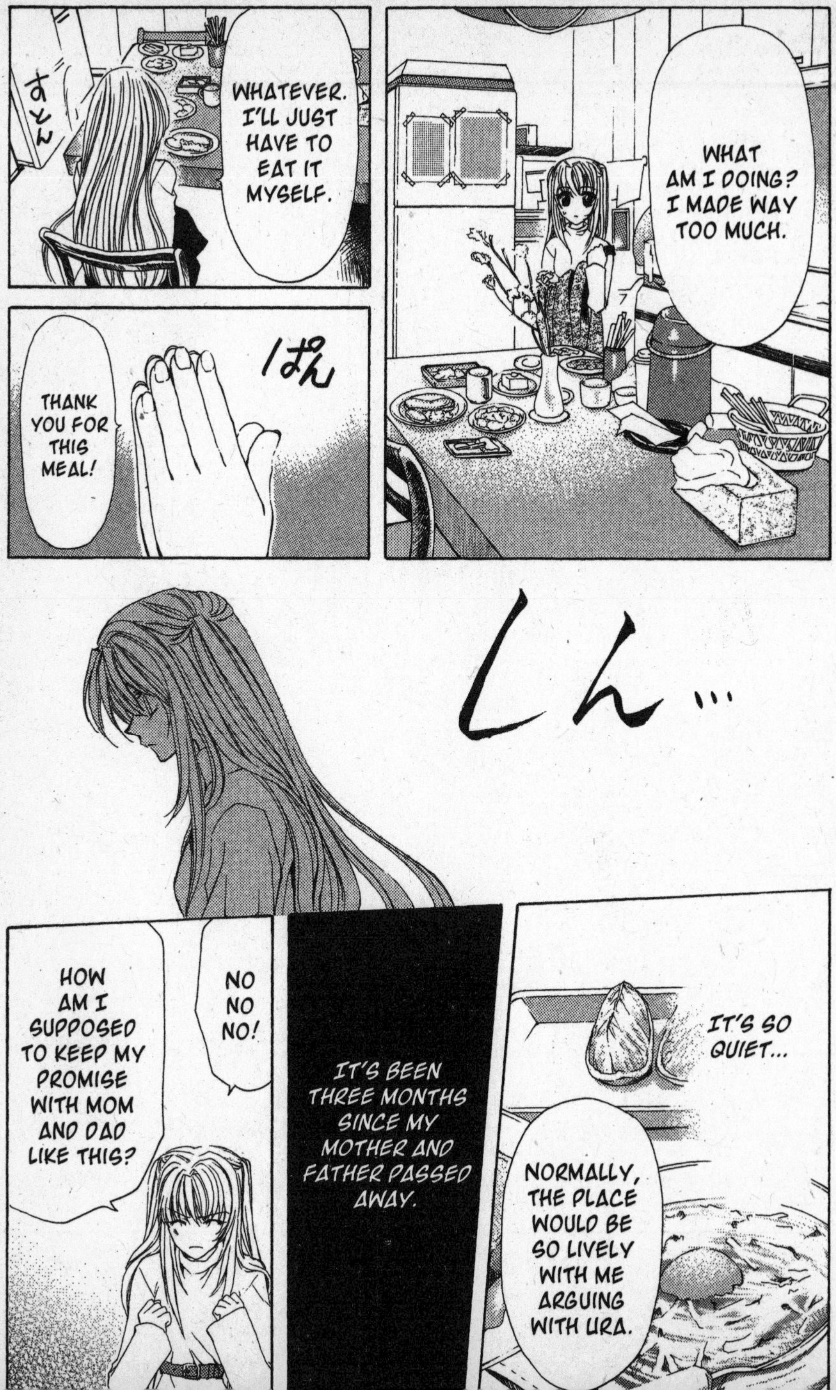
WHAT AM I DOING? I MADE WAY TOO MUCH.
すとん
WHATEVER. I'LL JUST HAVE TO EAT IT MYSELF.
ぱん
THANK YOU FOR THIS MEAL!
しん…
IT'S SO QUIET...
NORMALLY, THE PLACE WOULD BE SO LIVELY WITH ME ARGUING WITH URA.
IT'S BEEN THREE MONTHS SINCE MY MOTHER AND FATHER PASSED AWAY.
NO NO NO!
HOW AM I SUPPOSED TO KEEP MY PROMISE WITH MOM AND DAD LIKE THIS?

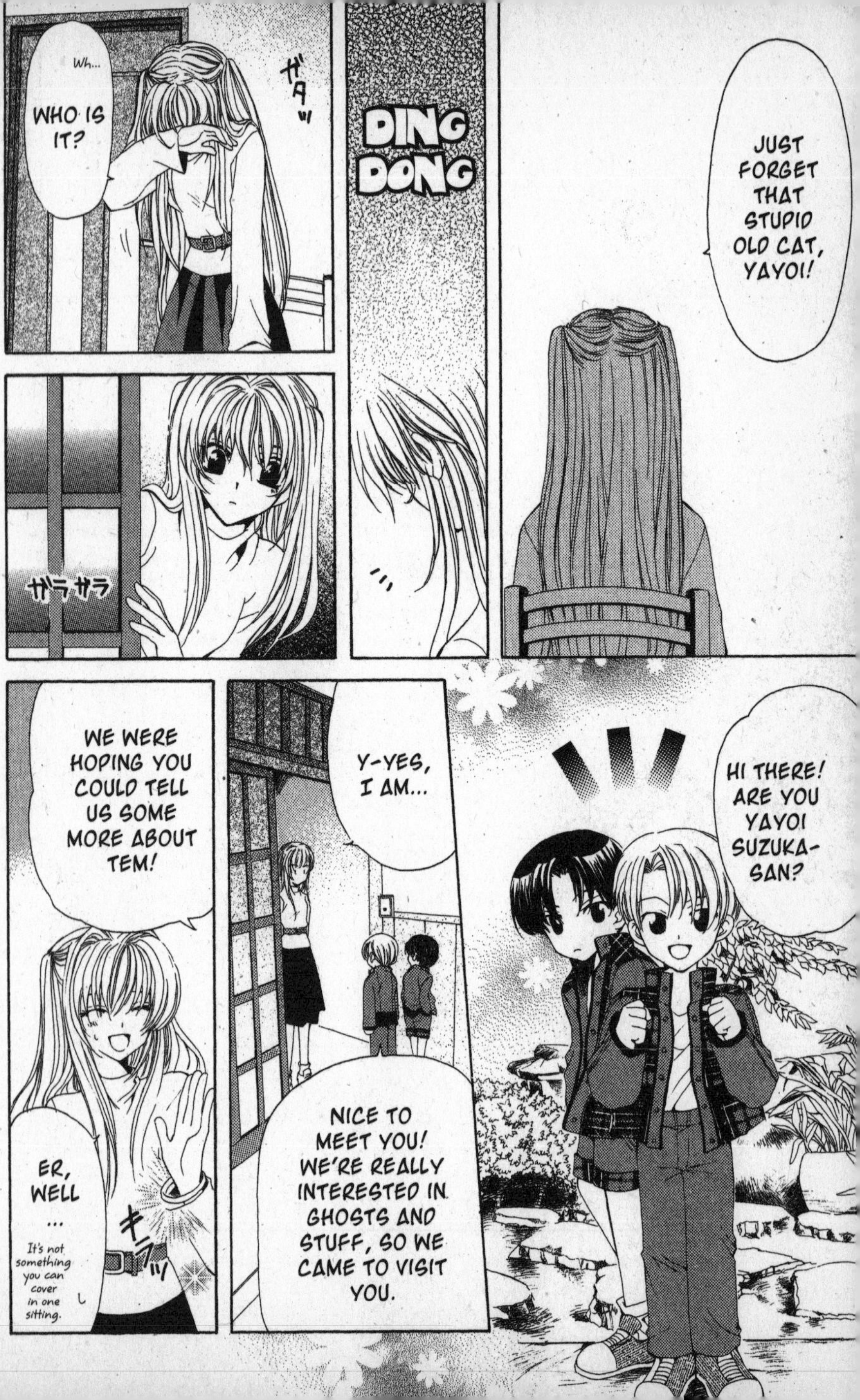

JUST FORGET THAT STUPID OLD CAT, YAYOI!
DING DONG
Wh...
WHO IS IT?
ガタッ
ガラガラ
HI THERE! ARE YOU YAYOI SUZUKA-SAN?
Y-YES, I AM...
NICE TO MEET YOU! WE'RE REALLY INTERESTED IN GHOSTS AND STUFF, SO WE CAME TO VISIT YOU.
WE WERE HOPING YOU COULD TELL US SOME MORE ABOUT TEM!
ER, WELL ...
It's not something you can cover in one sitting.

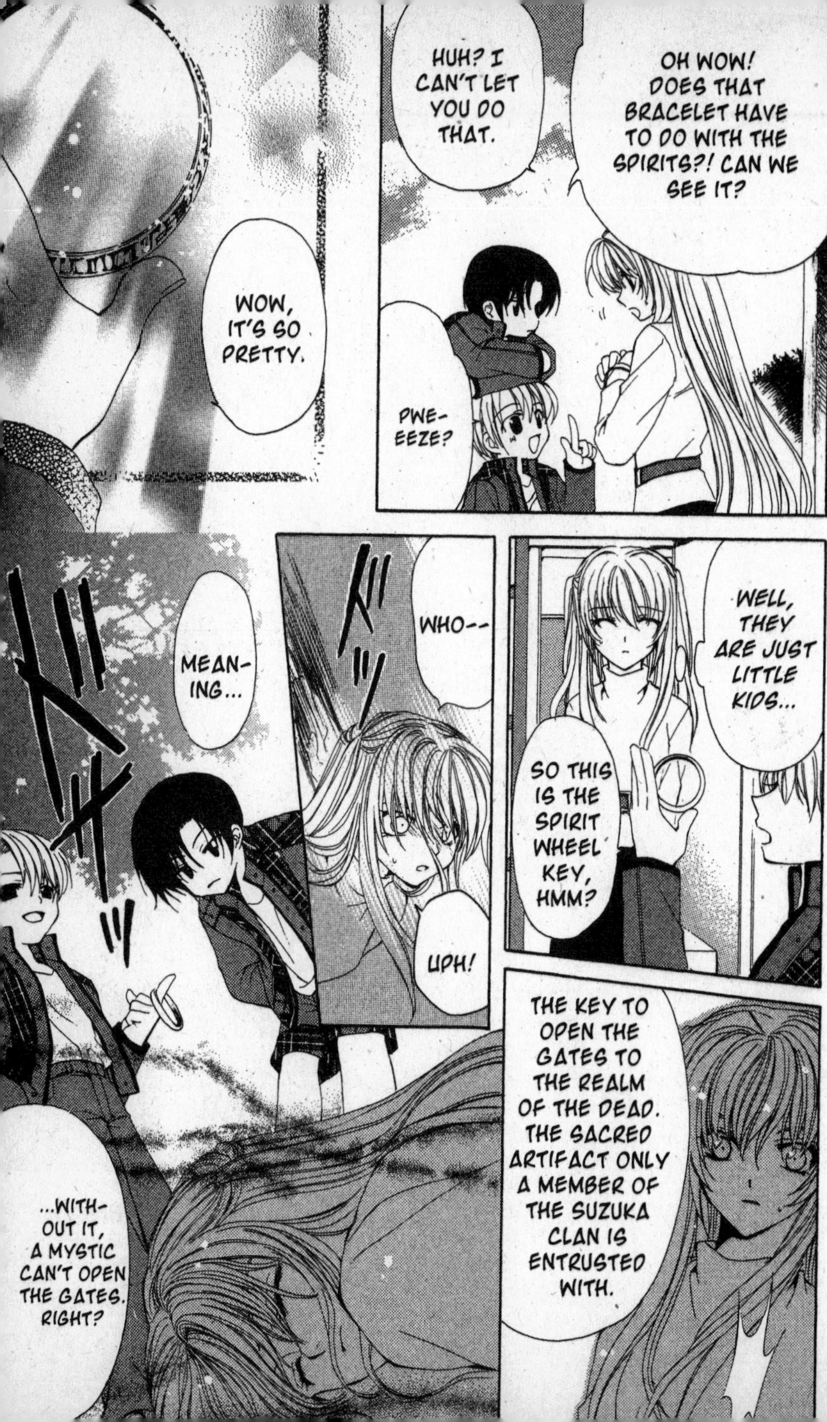
OH WOW! DOES THAT BRACELET HAVE TO DO WITH THE SPIRITS?! CAN WE SEE IT?
HUH? I CAN'T LET YOU DO THAT.
PWE-EEZE?
WOW, IT'S SO PRETTY.
WELL, THEY ARE JUST LITTLE KIDS...
SO THIS IS THE SPIRIT WHEEL KEY, HMM?
WHO--
UPH!
THE KEY TO OPEN THE GATES TO THE REALM OF THE DEAD. THE SACRED ARTIFACT ONLY A MEMBER OF THE SUZUKA CLAN IS ENTRUSTED WITH.
MEAN-ING...
...WITH-OUT IT, A MYSTIC CAN'T OPEN THE GATES. RIGHT?

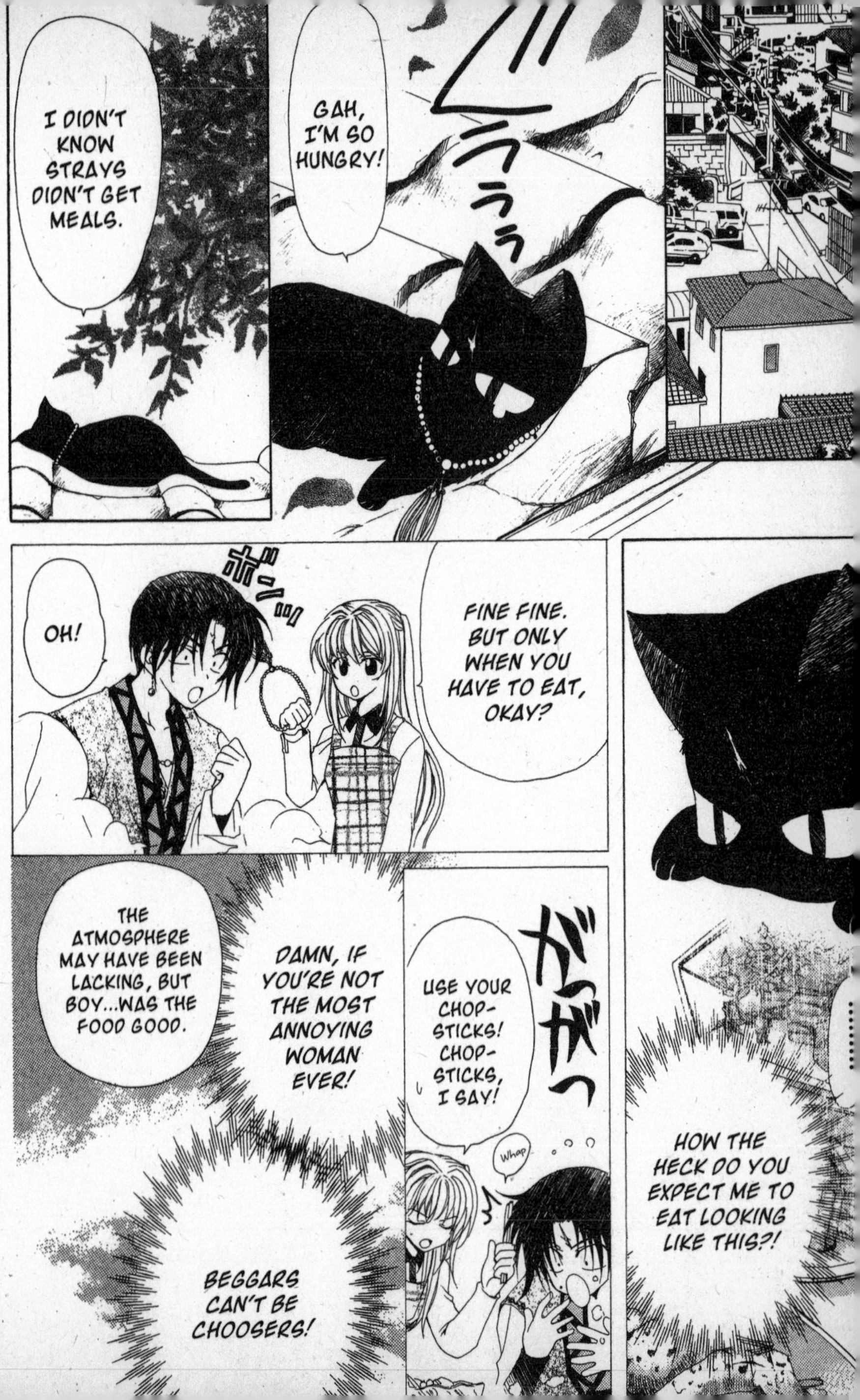
GAH, I'M SO HUNGRY!
I DIDN'T KNOW STRAYS DIDN'T GET MEALS.
HOW THE HECK DO YOU EXPECT ME TO EAT LOOKING LIKE THIS?!
FINE FINE. BUT ONLY WHEN YOU HAVE TO EAT, OKAY?
OH!
USE YOUR CHOP-STICKS! CHOP-STICKS, I SAY!
Whap
DAMN, IF YOU'RE NOT THE MOST ANNOYING WOMAN EVER!
THE ATMOSPHERE MAY HAVE BEEN LACKING, BUT BOY...WAS THE FOOD GOOD.
BEGGARS CAN'T BE CHOOSERS!

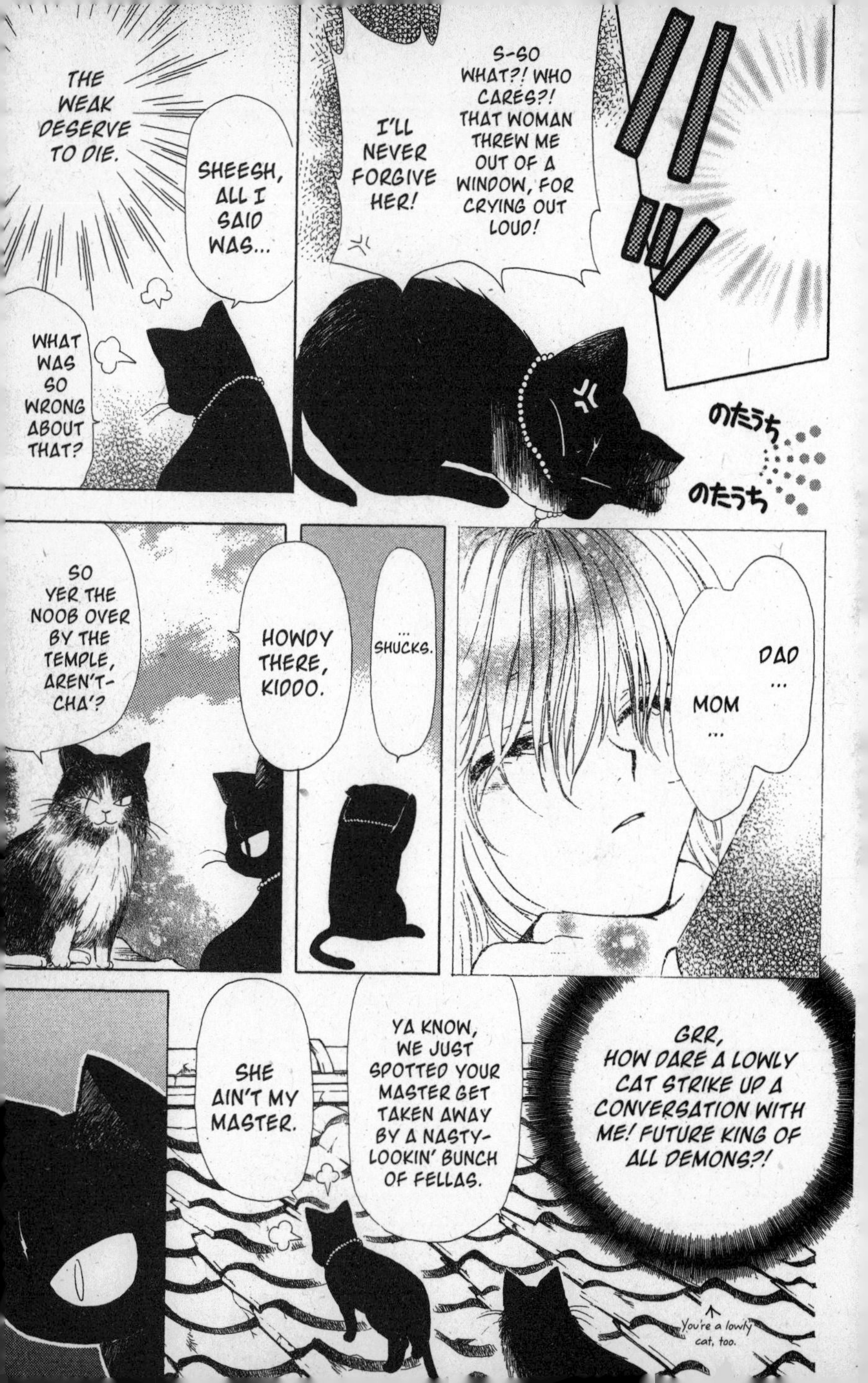
のたうち
のたうち
S-SO WHAT?! WHO CARES?! THAT WOMAN THREW ME OUT OF A WINDOW, FOR CRYING OUT LOUD!
I'LL NEVER FORGIVE HER!
THE WEAK DESERVE TO DIE.
SHEESH, ALL I SAID WAS...
WHAT WAS SO WRONG ABOUT THAT?
DAD ... MOM ...
... SHUCKS.
HOWDY THERE, KIDDO.
SO YER THE NOOB OVER BY THE TEMPLE, AREN'T-CHA'?
GRR, HOW DARE A LOWLY CAT STRIKE UP A CONVERSATION WITH ME! FUTURE KING OF ALL DEMONS?!
You're a lowly cat, too.
YA KNOW, WE JUST SPOTTED YOUR MASTER GET TAKEN AWAY BY A NASTY-LOOKIN' BUNCH OF FELLAS.
SHE AIN'T MY MASTER.

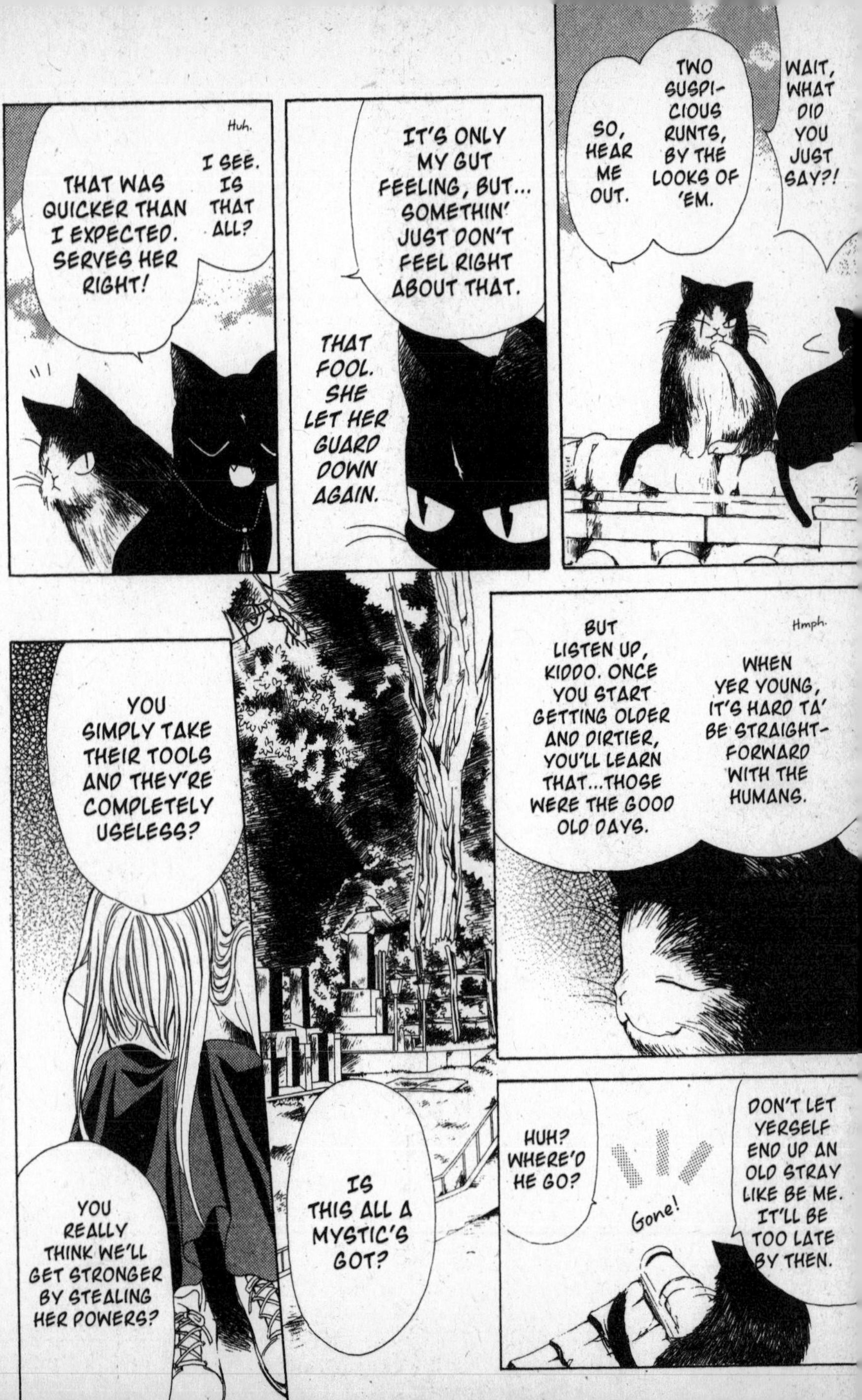
WAIT, WHAT DID YOU JUST SAY?!
TWO SUSPICIOUS RUNTS, BY THE LOOKS OF 'EM.
SO, HEAR ME OUT.
IT'S ONLY MY GUT FEELING, BUT... SOMETHIN' JUST DON'T FEEL RIGHT ABOUT THAT.
THAT FOOL. SHE LET HER GUARD DOWN AGAIN.
Huh.
I SEE. IS THAT ALL?
THAT WAS QUICKER THAN I EXPECTED. SERVES HER RIGHT!
Hmph.
WHEN YER YOUNG, IT'S HARD TA' BE STRAIGHTFORWARD WITH THE HUMANS.
BUT LISTEN UP, KIDDO. ONCE YOU START GETTING OLDER AND DIRTIER, YOU'LL LEARN THAT...THOSE WERE THE GOOD OLD DAYS.
DON'T LET YERSELF END UP AN OLD STRAY LIKE BE ME. IT'LL BE TOO LATE BY THEN.
HUH? WHERE'D HE GO?
Gone!
YOU SIMPLY TAKE THEIR TOOLS AND THEY'RE COMPLETELY USELESS?
IS THIS ALL A MYSTIC'S GOT?
YOU REALLY THINK WE'LL GET STRONGER BY STEALING HER POWERS?

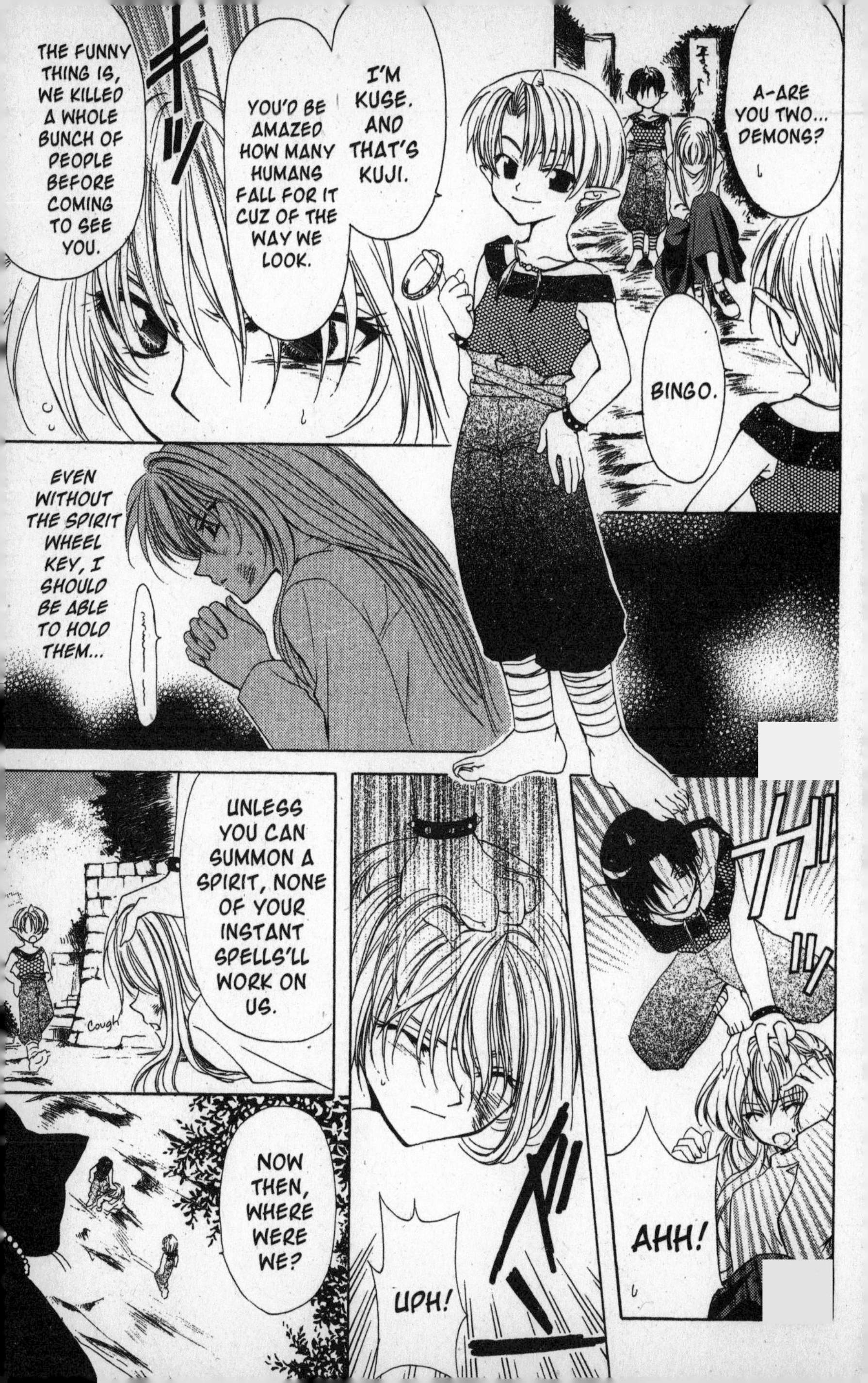
A-ARE YOU TWO... DEMONS?
BINGO.
I'M KUSE. AND THAT'S KUJI.
YOU'D BE AMAZED HOW MANY HUMANS FALL FOR IT CUZ OF THE WAY WE LOOK.
THE FUNNY THING IS, WE KILLED A WHOLE BUNCH OF PEOPLE BEFORE COMING TO SEE YOU.
EVEN WITHOUT THE SPIRIT WHEEL KEY, I SHOULD BE ABLE TO HOLD THEM...
AHH!
UPH!
UNLESS YOU CAN SUMMON A SPIRIT, NONE OF YOUR INSTANT SPELLS'LL WORK ON US.
Cough
NOW THEN, WHERE WERE WE?

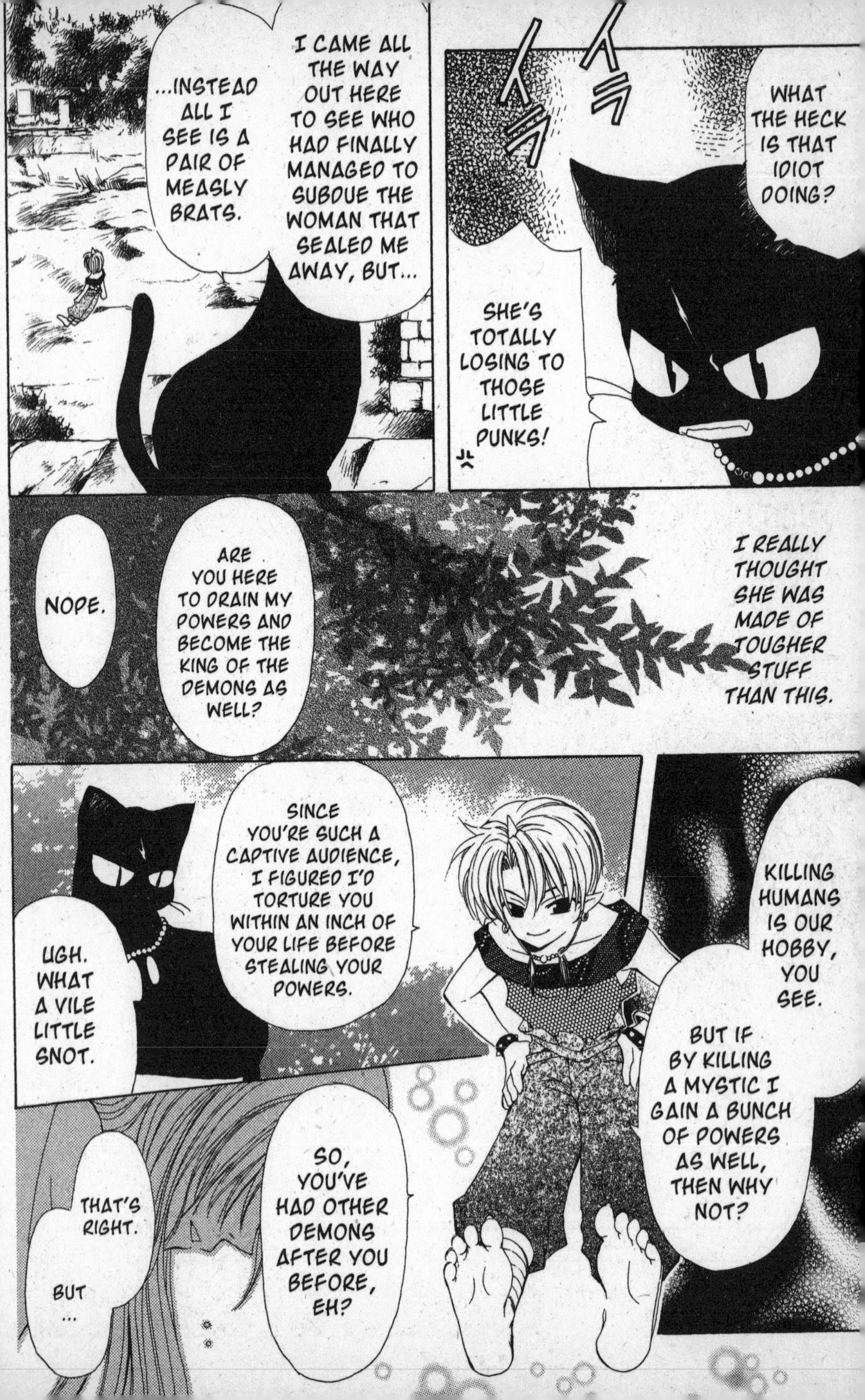
WHAT THE HECK IS THAT IDIOT DOING?
SHE'S TOTALLY LOSING TO THOSE LITTLE PUNKS!
I CAME ALL THE WAY OUT HERE TO SEE WHO HAD FINALLY MANAGED TO SUBDUE THE WOMAN THAT SEALED ME AWAY, BUT...
...INSTEAD ALL I SEE IS A PAIR OF MEASLY BRATS.
I REALLY THOUGHT SHE WAS MADE OF TOUGHER STUFF THAN THIS.
ARE YOU HERE TO DRAIN MY POWERS AND BECOME THE KING OF THE DEMONS AS WELL?
NOPE.
KILLING HUMANS IS OUR HOBBY, YOU SEE.
BUT IF BY KILLING A MYSTIC I GAIN A BUNCH OF POWERS AS WELL, THEN WHY NOT?
SINCE YOU'RE SUCH A CAPTIVE AUDIENCE, I FIGURED I'D TORTURE YOU WITHIN AN INCH OF YOUR LIFE BEFORE STEALING YOUR POWERS.
UGH. WHAT A VILE LITTLE SNOT.
SO, YOU'VE HAD OTHER DEMONS AFTER YOU BEFORE, EH?
THAT'S RIGHT.
BUT ...

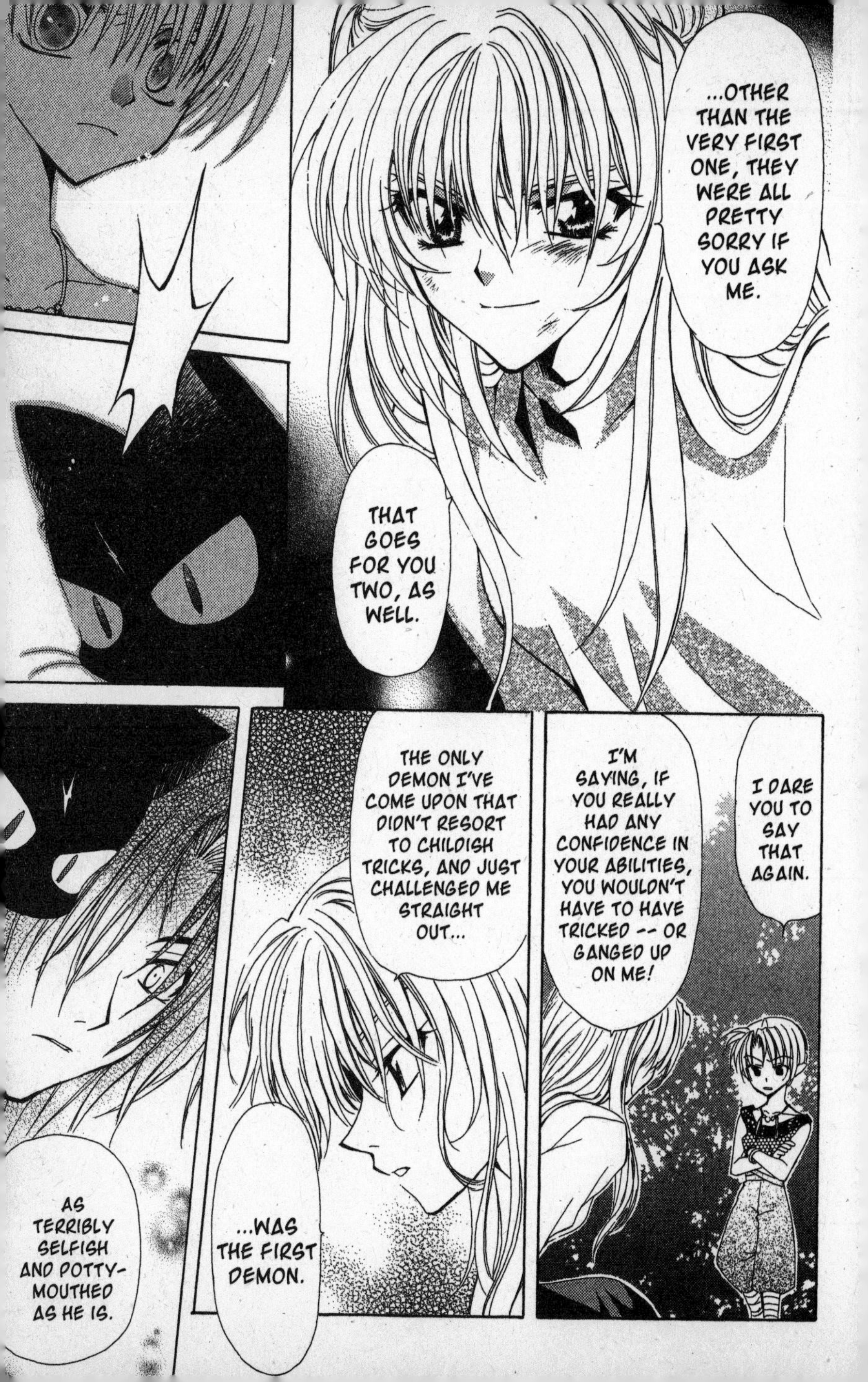
...OTHER THAN THE VERY FIRST ONE, THEY WERE ALL PRETTY SORRY IF YOU ASK ME.
THAT GOES FOR YOU TWO, AS WELL.
I DARE YOU TO SAY THAT AGAIN.
I'M SAYING, IF YOU REALLY HAD ANY CONFIDENCE IN YOUR ABILITIES, YOU WOULDN'T HAVE TO HAVE TRICKED -- OR GANGED UP ON ME!
THE ONLY DEMON I'VE COME UPON THAT DIDN'T RESORT TO CHILDISH TRICKS, AND JUST CHALLENGED ME STRAIGHT OUT...
...WAS THE FIRST DEMON.
AS TERRIBLY SELFISH AND POTTY-MOUTHED AS HE IS.

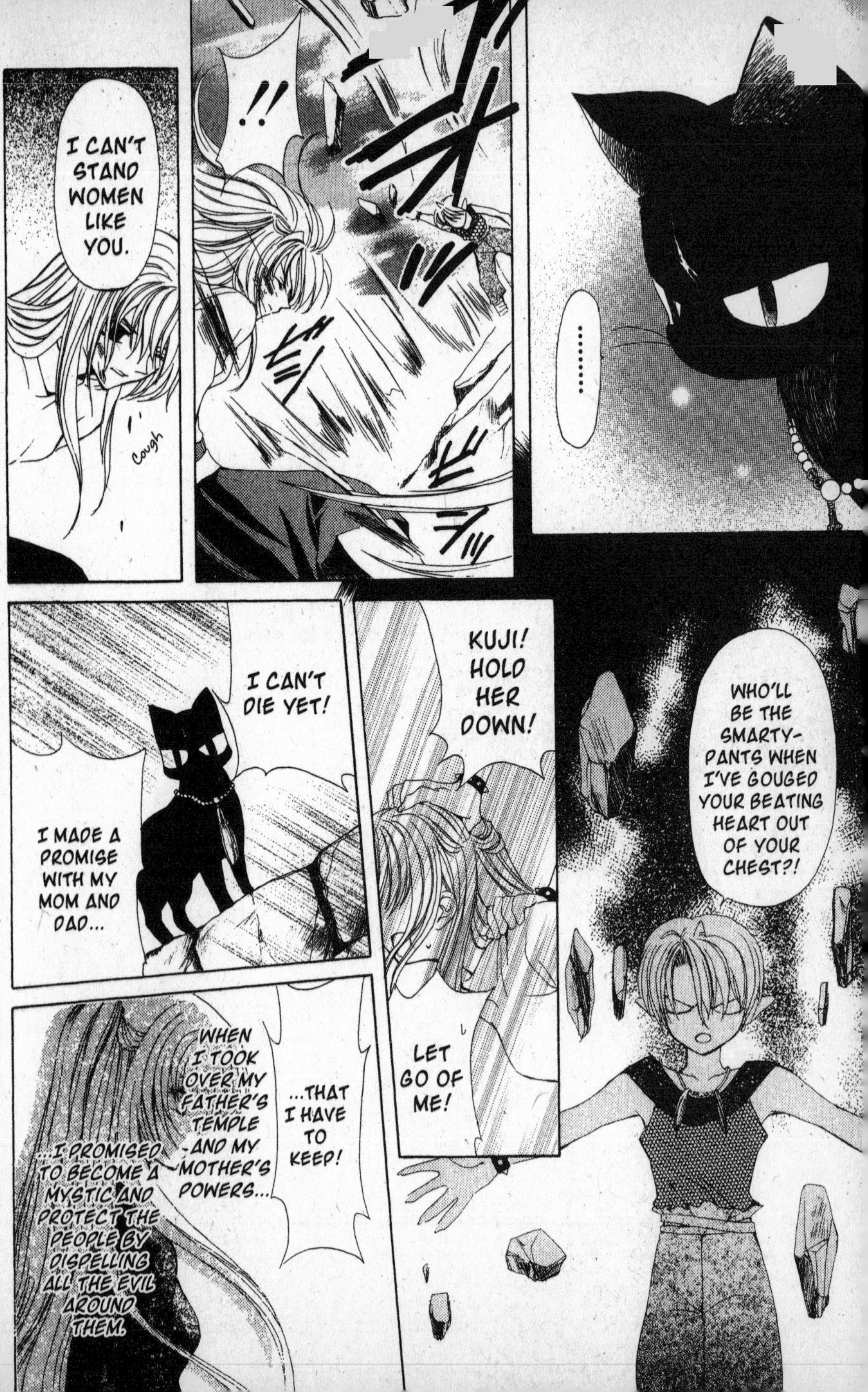
......
!!
I CAN'T STAND WOMEN LIKE YOU.
Cough
WHO'LL BE THE SMARTY-PANTS WHEN I'VE GOUGED YOUR BEATING HEART OUT OF YOUR CHEST?!
KUJI! HOLD HER DOWN!
LET GO OF ME!
I CAN'T DIE YET!
I MADE A PROMISE WITH MY MOM AND DAD...
...THAT I HAVE TO KEEP!
WHEN I TOOK OVER MY FATHER'S TEMPLE AND MY MOTHER'S POWERS...
...I PROMISED TO BECOME A MYSTIC AND PROTECT THE PEOPLE BY DISPELLING ALL THE EVIL AROUND THEM.

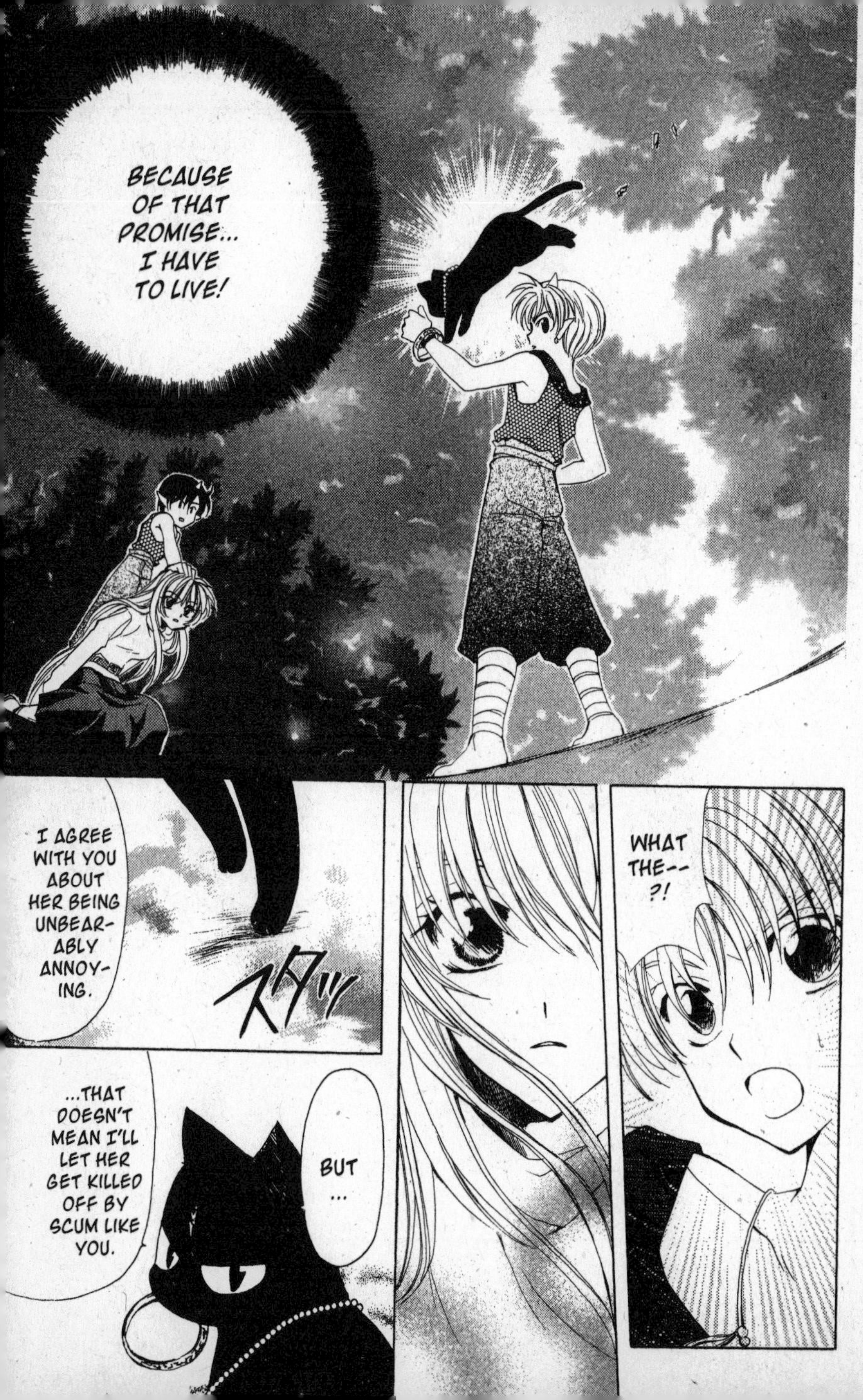
BECAUSE OF THAT PROMISE... I HAVE TO LIVE!
WHAT THE--?!
I AGREE WITH YOU ABOUT HER BEING UNBEARABLY ANNOYING.
スタッ
BUT...
...THAT DOESN'T MEAN I'LL LET HER GET KILLED OFF BY SCUM LIKE YOU.

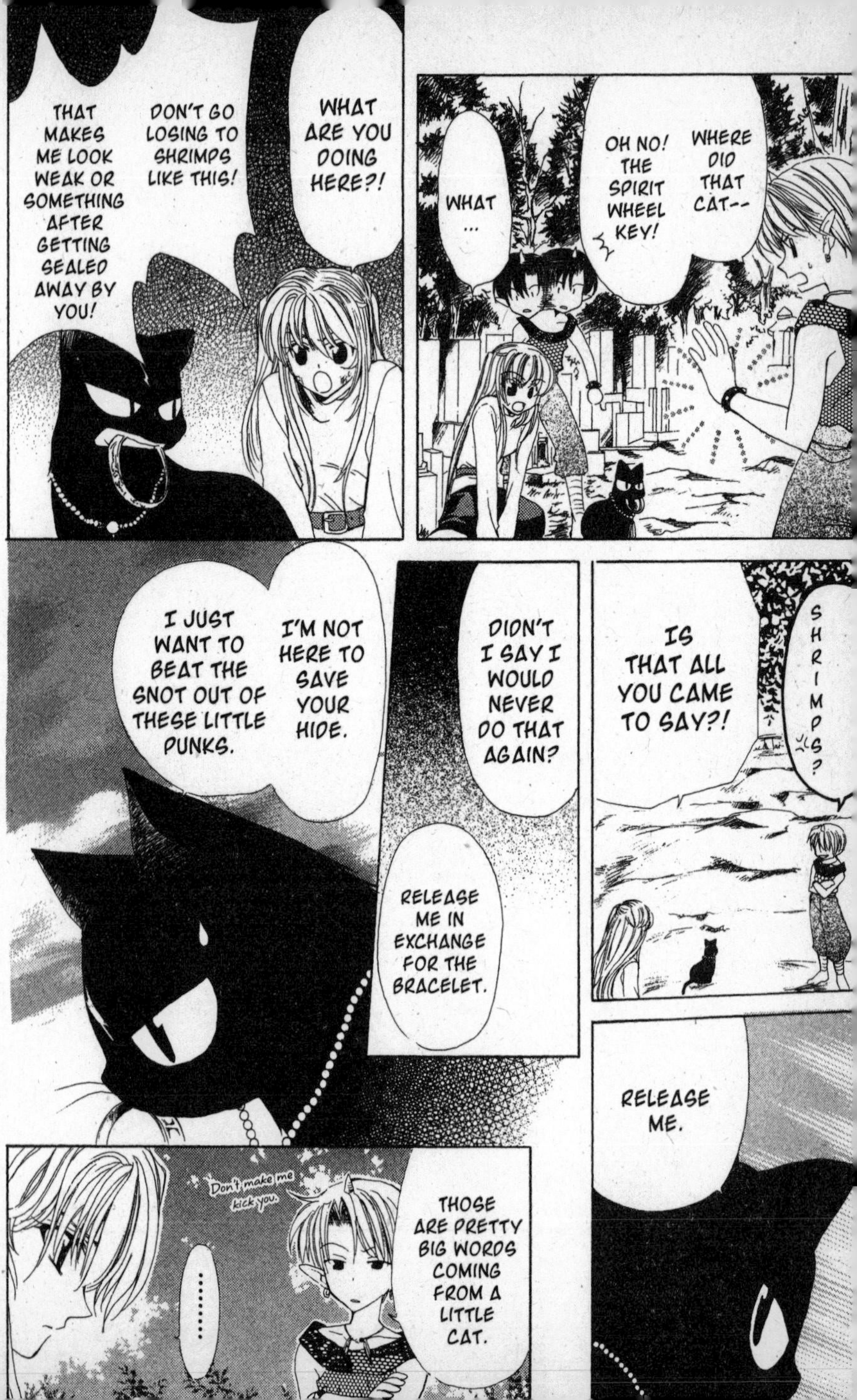
WHERE DID THAT CAT--
OH NO! THE SPIRIT WHEEL KEY!
WHAT ...
WHAT ARE YOU DOING HERE?!
DON'T GO LOSING TO SHRIMPS LIKE THIS!
THAT MAKES ME LOOK WEAK OR SOMETHING AFTER GETTING SEALED AWAY BY YOU!
SHRIMPS?
IS THAT ALL YOU CAME TO SAY?!
DIDN'T I SAY I WOULD NEVER DO THAT AGAIN?
I'M NOT HERE TO SAVE YOUR HIDE.
I JUST WANT TO BEAT THE SNOT OUT OF THESE LITTLE PUNKS.
RELEASE ME IN EXCHANGE FOR THE BRACELET.
RELEASE ME.
THOSE ARE PRETTY BIG WORDS COMING FROM A LITTLE CAT.
.......
Don't make me kick you.

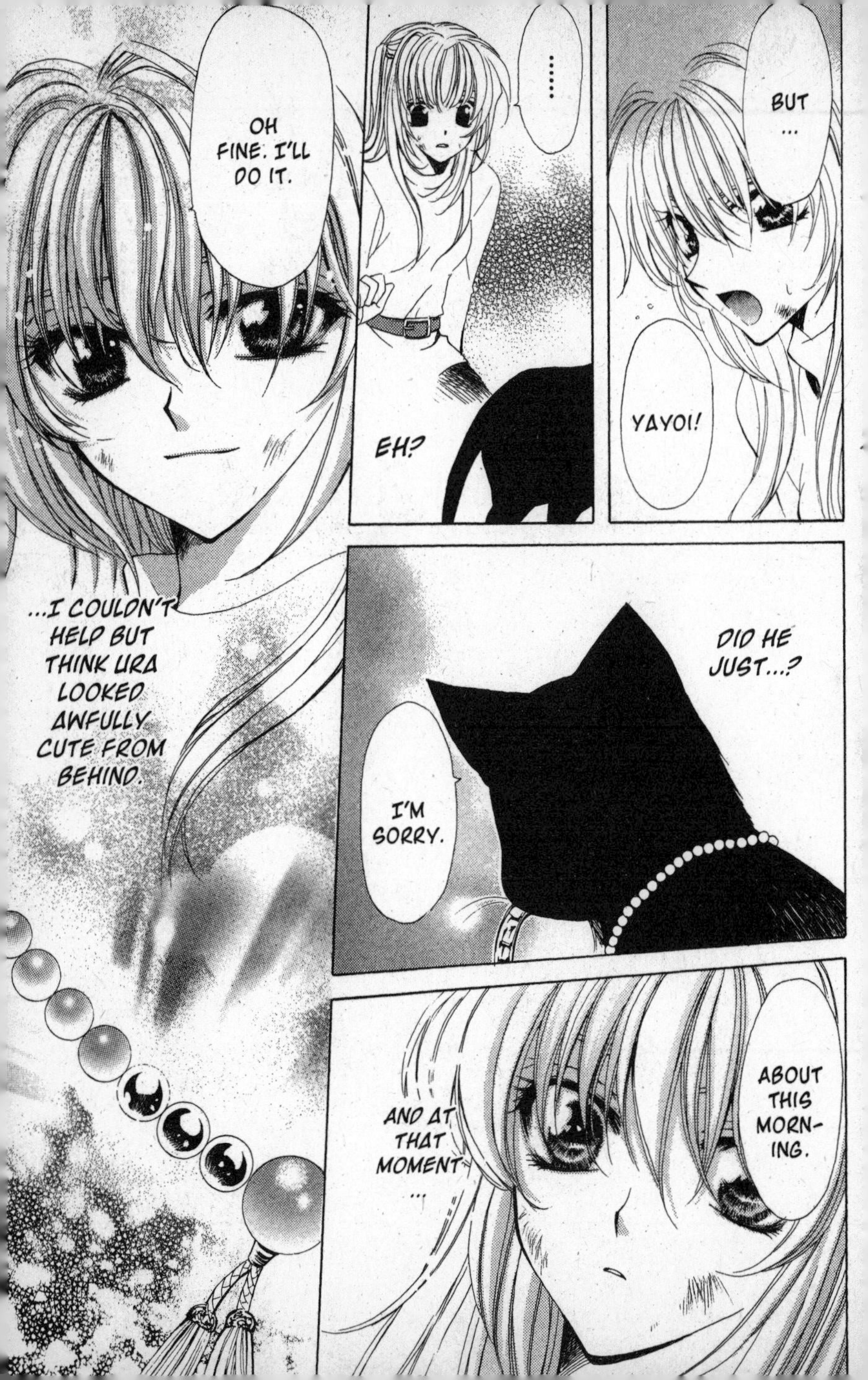
BUT ...
YAYOI!
......
EH?
DID HE JUST...?
I'M SORRY.
ABOUT THIS MORN-ING.
AND AT THAT MOMENT ...
OH FINE. I'LL DO IT.
...I COULDN'T HELP BUT THINK URA LOOKED AWFULLY CUTE FROM BEHIND.

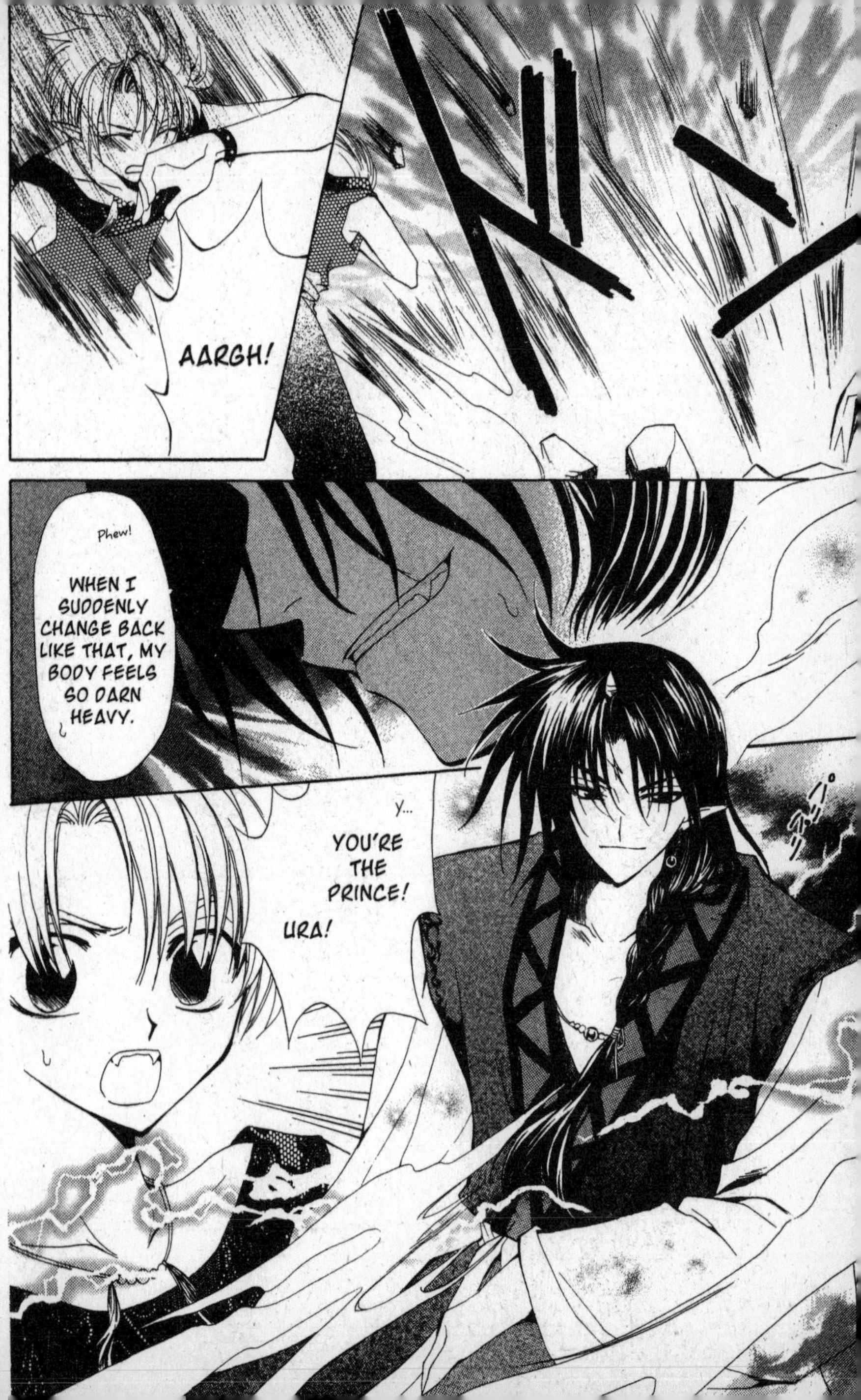
AARGH!
Phew!
WHEN I SUDDENLY CHANGE BACK LIKE THAT, MY BODY FEELS SO DARN HEAVY.
Y...
YOU'RE THE PRINCE!
URA!

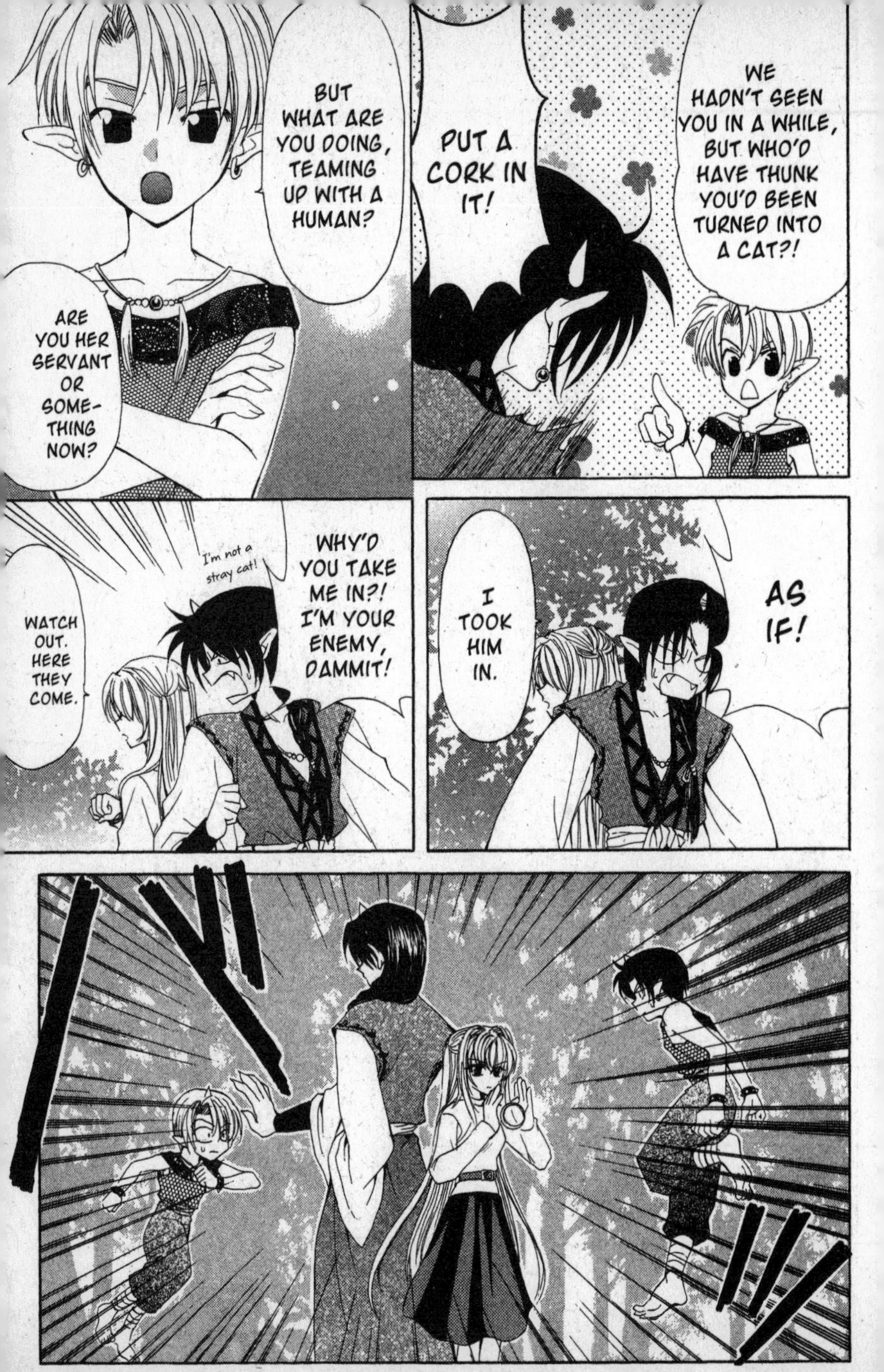

WE HADN'T SEEN YOU IN A WHILE, BUT WHO'D HAVE THUNK YOU'D BEEN TURNED INTO A CAT?!
PUT A CORK IN IT!
BUT WHAT ARE YOU DOING, TEAMING UP WITH A HUMAN?
ARE YOU HER SERVANT OR SOME-THING NOW?
AS IF!
I TOOK HIM IN.
WHY'D YOU TAKE ME IN?! I'M YOUR ENEMY, DAMMIT!
I'm not a stray cat!
WATCH OUT. HERE THEY COME.

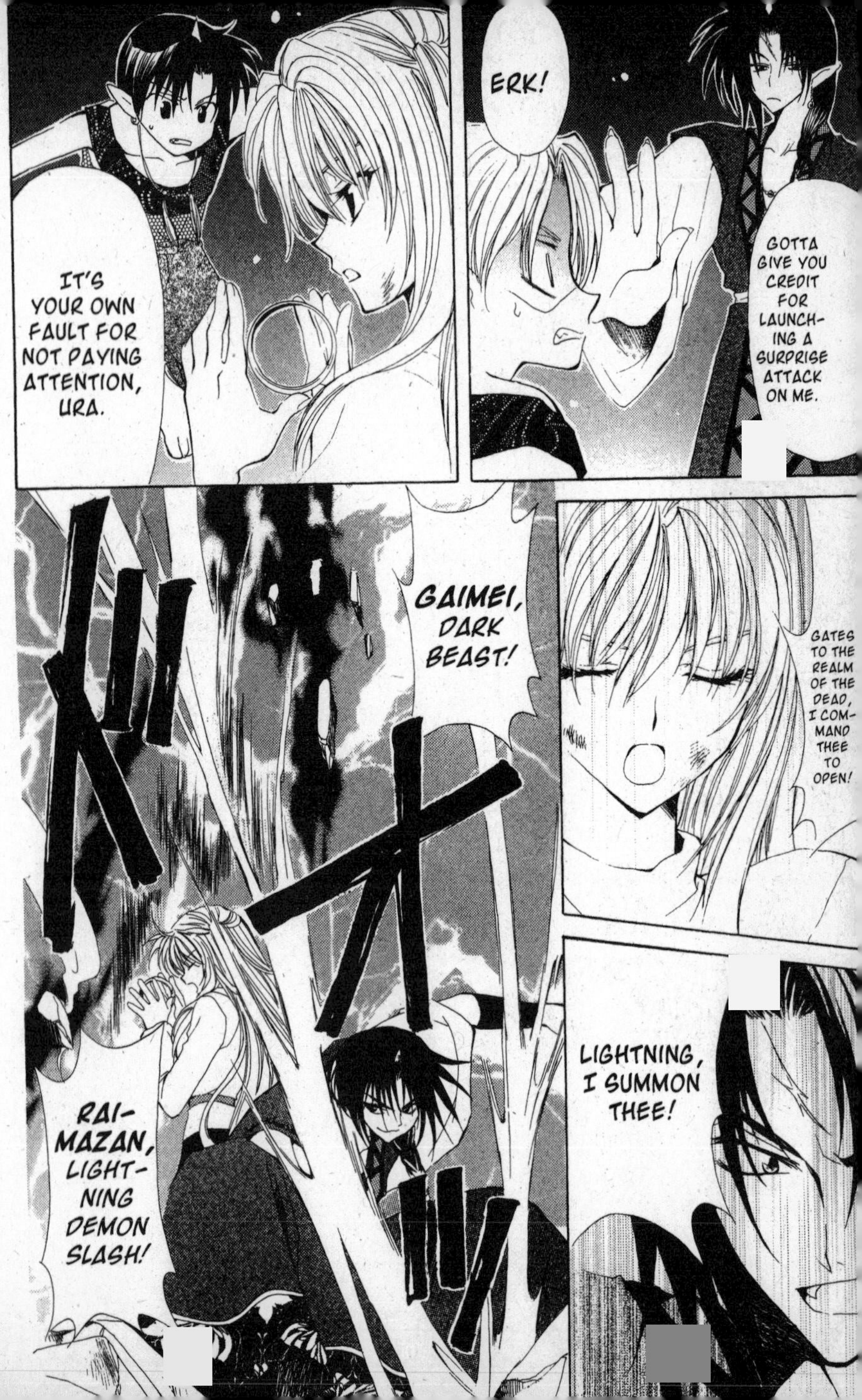
ERK!
GOTTA GIVE YOU CREDIT FOR LAUNCHING A SURPRISE ATTACK ON ME.
IT'S YOUR OWN FAULT FOR NOT PAYING ATTENTION, URA.
GATES TO THE REALM OF THE DEAD, I COMMAND THEE TO OPEN!
LIGHTNING, I SUMMON THEE!
GAIMEI, DARK BEAST!
RAI-MAZAN, LIGHTNING DEMON SLASH!

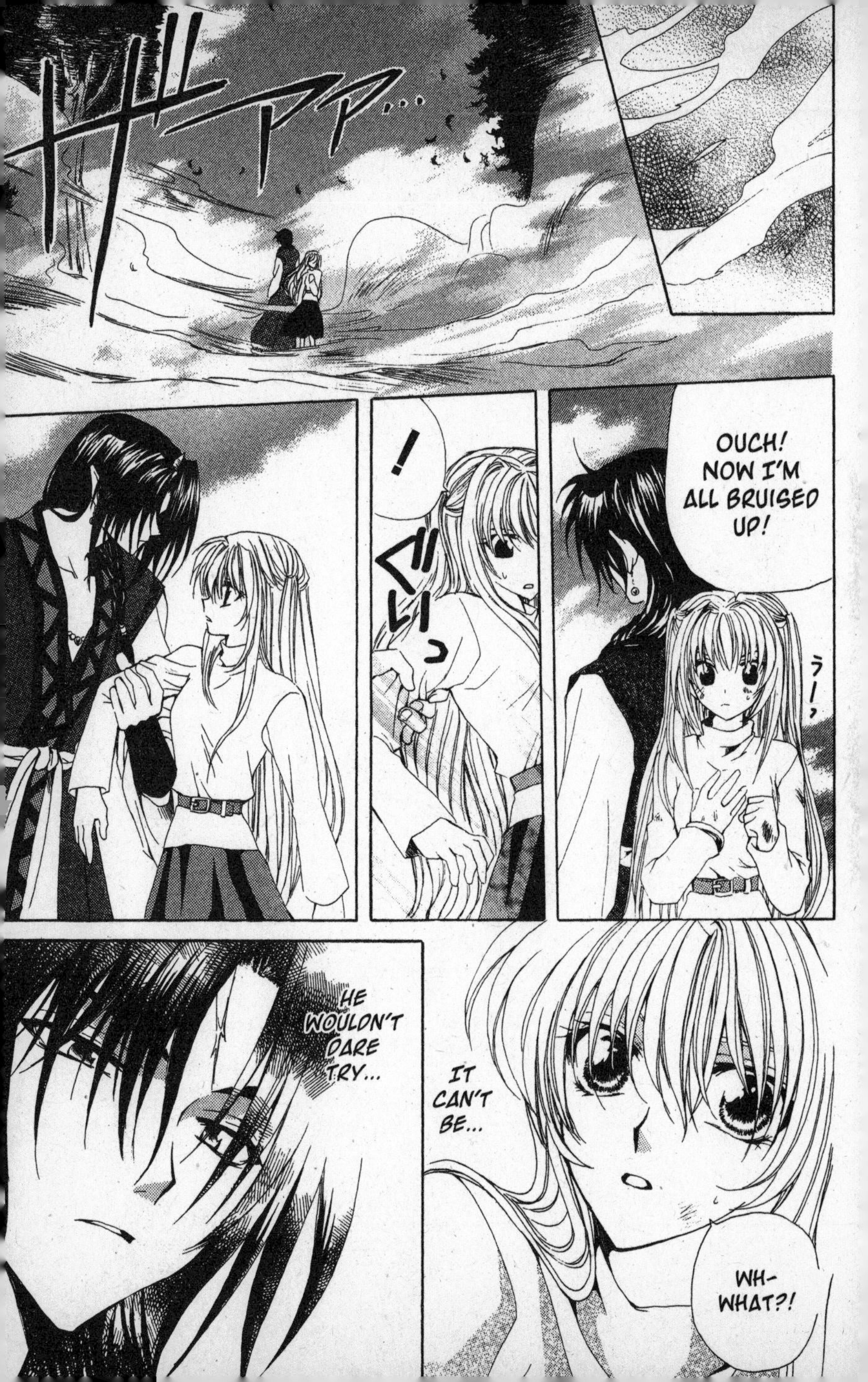
OUCH! NOW I'M ALL BRUISED UP!
!
WH-WHAT?!
IT CAN'T BE...
HE WOULDN'T DARE TRY...

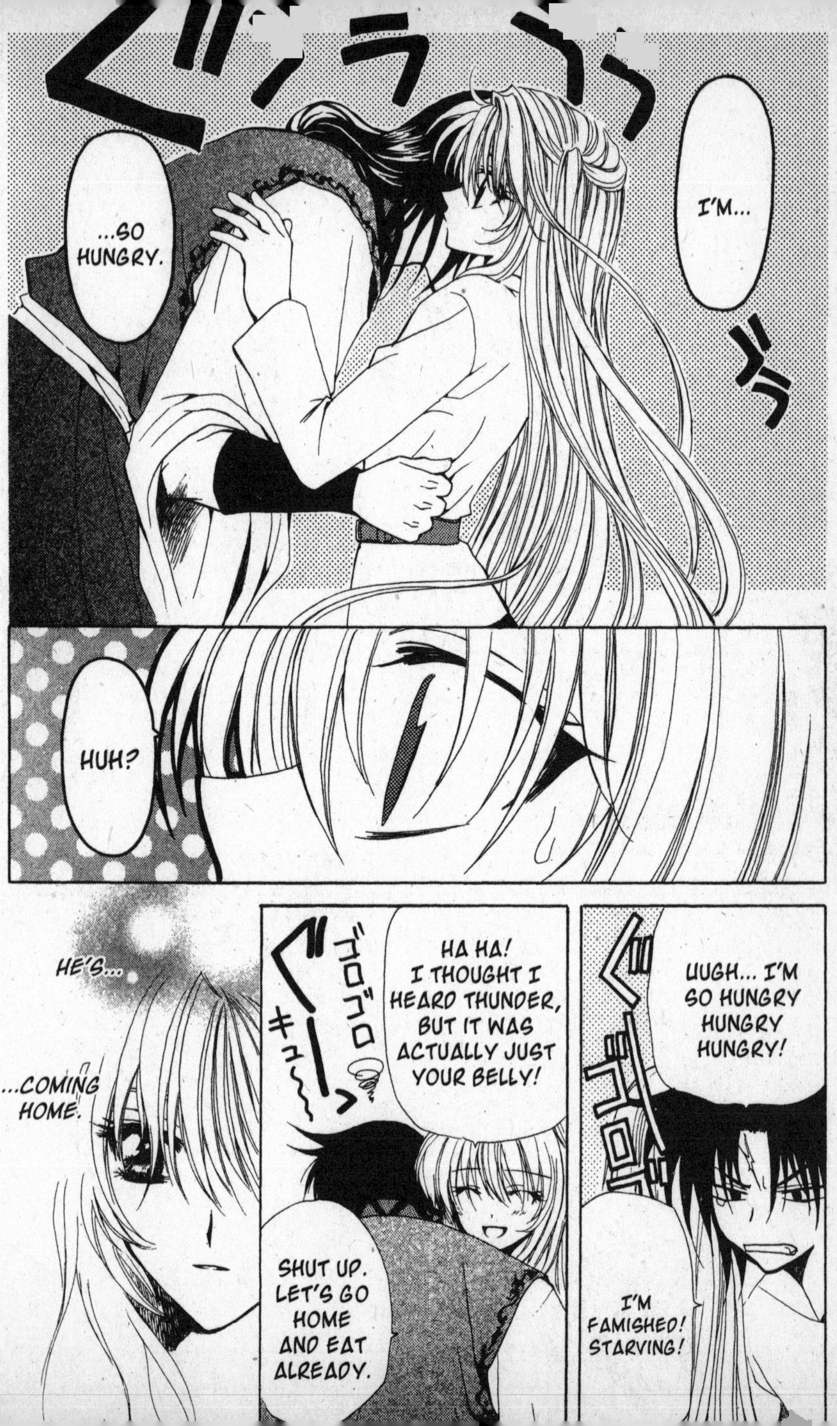
I'M...
...SO HUNGRY.
HUH?
UUGH... I'M SO HUNGRY HUNGRY HUNGRY!
I'M FAMISHED! STARVING!
ゴロゴロ
HA HA! I THOUGHT I HEARD THUNDER, BUT IT WAS ACTUALLY JUST YOUR BELLY!
SHUT UP. LET'S GO HOME AND EAT ALREADY.
HE'S...
...COMING HOME.

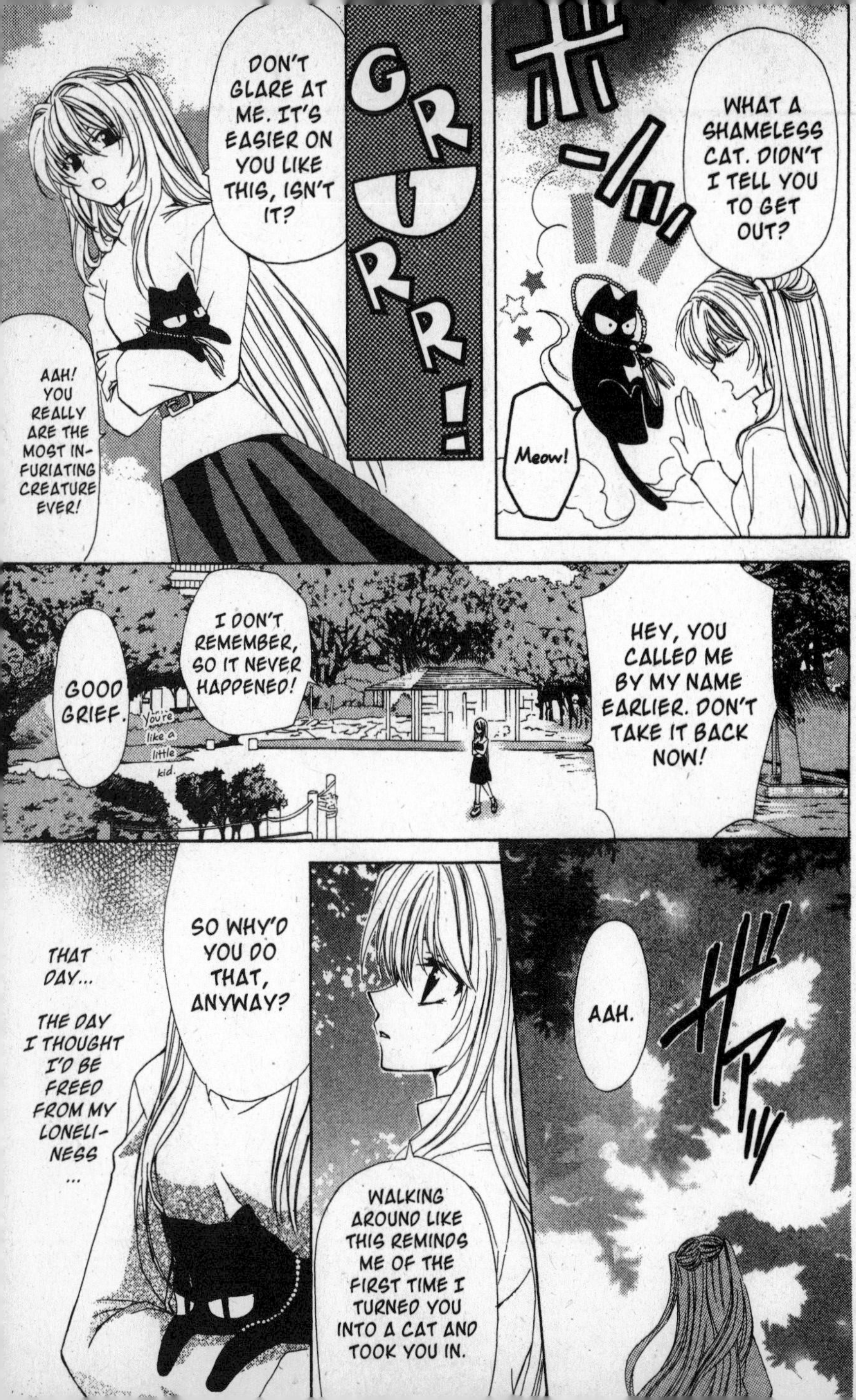
WHAT A SHAMELESS CAT. DIDN'T I TELL YOU TO GET OUT?
Meow!
GRURR!
DON'T GLARE AT ME. IT'S EASIER ON YOU LIKE THIS, ISN'T IT?
AAH! YOU REALLY ARE THE MOST IN-FURIATING CREATURE EVER!
HEY, YOU CALLED ME BY MY NAME EARLIER. DON'T TAKE IT BACK NOW!
I DON'T REMEMBER, SO IT NEVER HAPPENED!
GOOD GRIEF.
You're like a little kid.
AAH.
WALKING AROUND LIKE THIS REMINDS ME OF THE FIRST TIME I TURNED YOU INTO A CAT AND TOOK YOU IN.
SO WHY'D YOU DO THAT, ANYWAY?
THAT DAY...
THE DAY I THOUGHT I'D BE FREED FROM MY LONELI-NESS ...

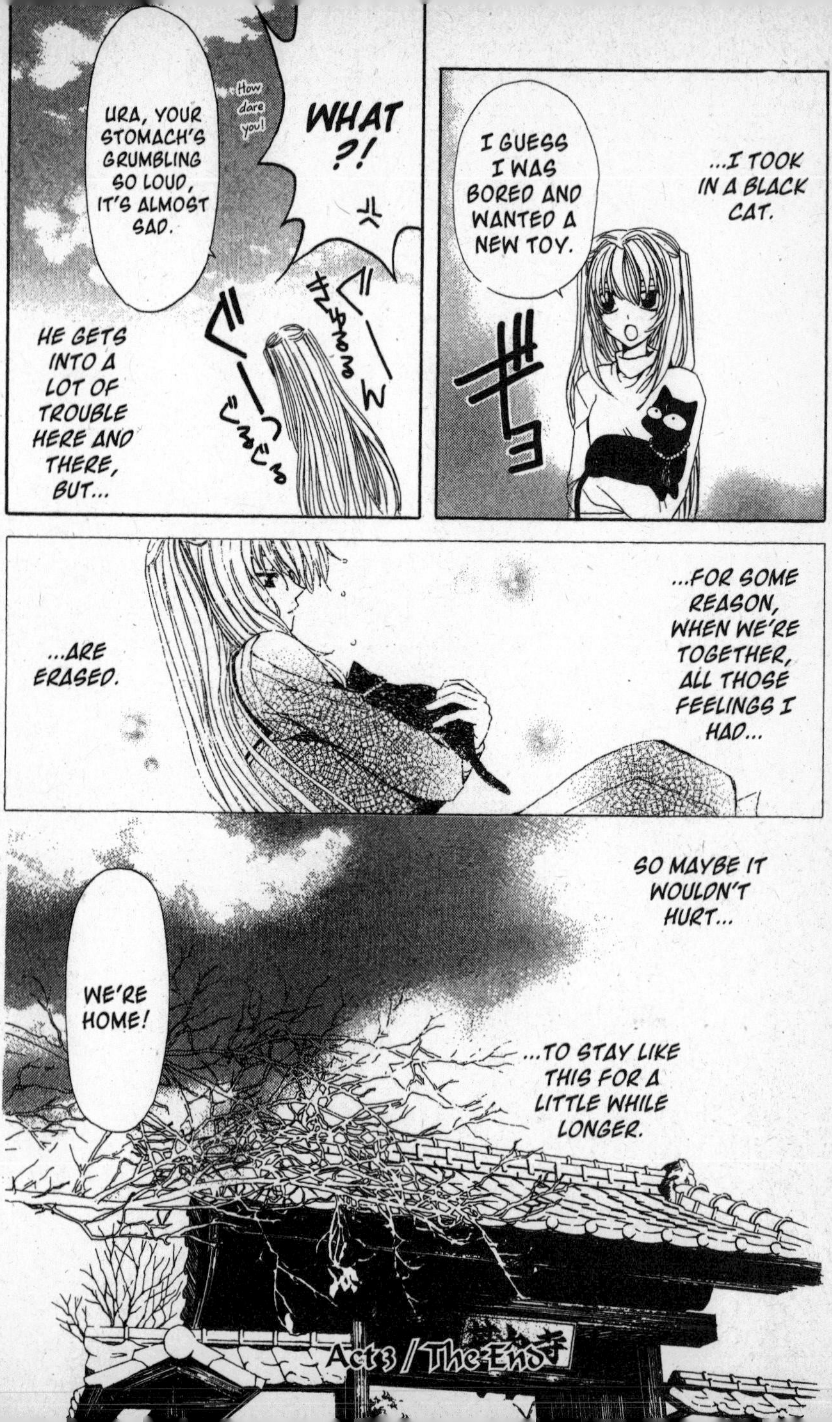
...I TOOK IN A BLACK CAT.
I GUESS I WAS BORED AND WANTED A NEW TOY.
ギュ
URA, YOUR STOMACH'S GRUMBLING SO LOUD, IT'S ALMOST SAD.
WHAT?!
How dare you!
ぐーーー
きゅるる
ぐーっ
ごろごろ
HE GETS INTO A LOT OF TROUBLE HERE AND THERE, BUT...
...FOR SOME REASON, WHEN WE'RE TOGETHER, ALL THOSE FEELINGS I HAD...
...ARE ERASED.
SO MAYBE IT WOULDN'T HURT...
WE'RE HOME!
...TO STAY LIKE THIS FOR A LITTLE WHILE LONGER.
Act 3 / The End

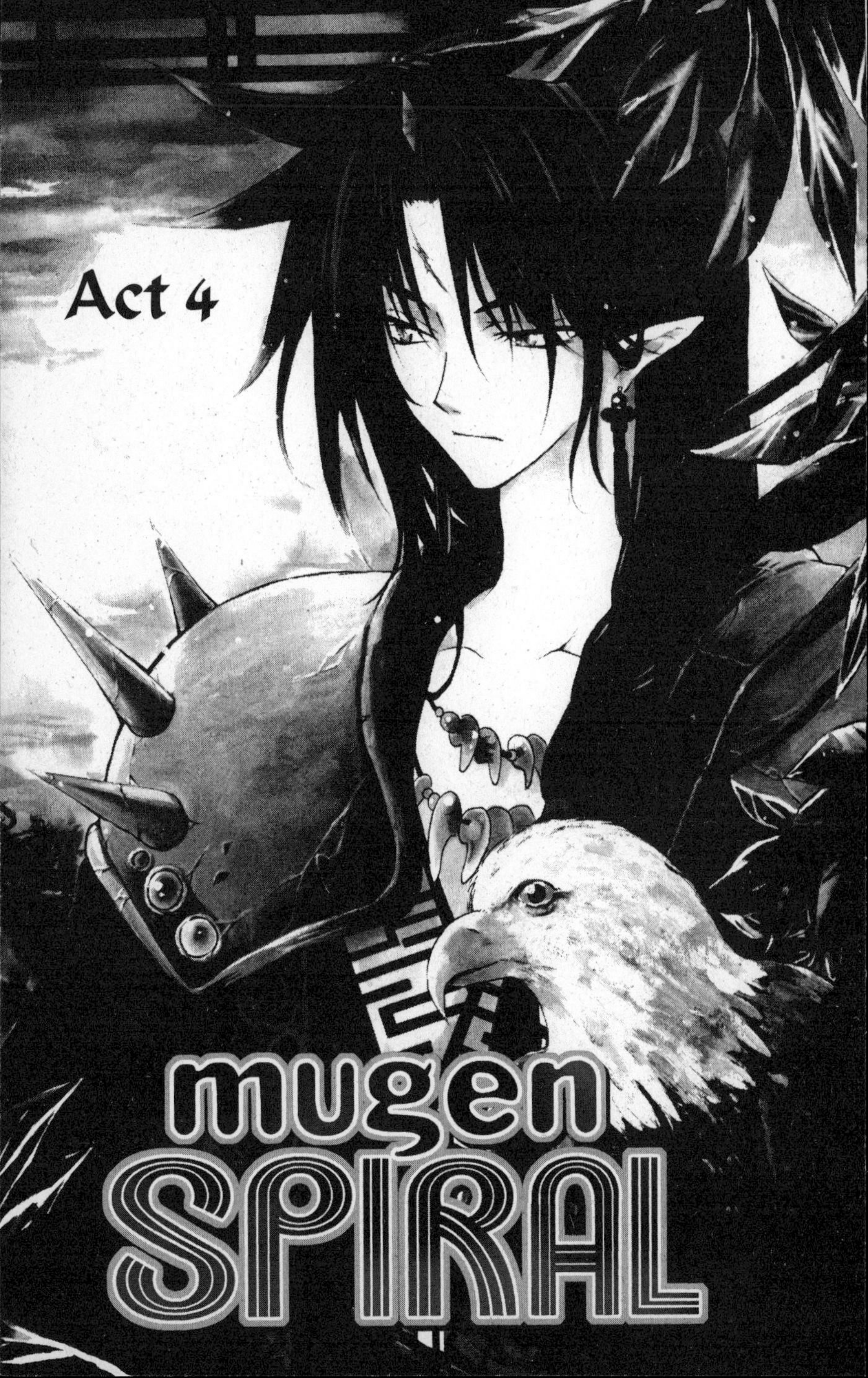
Act 4
mugen
SPIRAL

# Ura

The flow of time in the Demon World and the Human World are different so his age is unknown. But he was definitely born in an era far before Yayoi's time.
In the Demon World, he was quite renowned and pampered, so he was more like an idol than a prince. (Ha ha!) But since coming to the human world, he's either letting loose a bit or regressing (heh).

He's slightly ill mannered and rough, but when it comes to his family or those that he recognizes as friends, he tends to lower his guard and accept openly.
In the original setting, he was even more different than Yayoi. He always spoke very politely, but behaved like a brute.

He used to be a narrow-eyed cat who loved picking on cry baby Yayoi. He also was dressed a lot nicer. But it was hard to move the story along with a secondary protagonist like that, so he was changed. And the original character was instead passed down to Ouga.

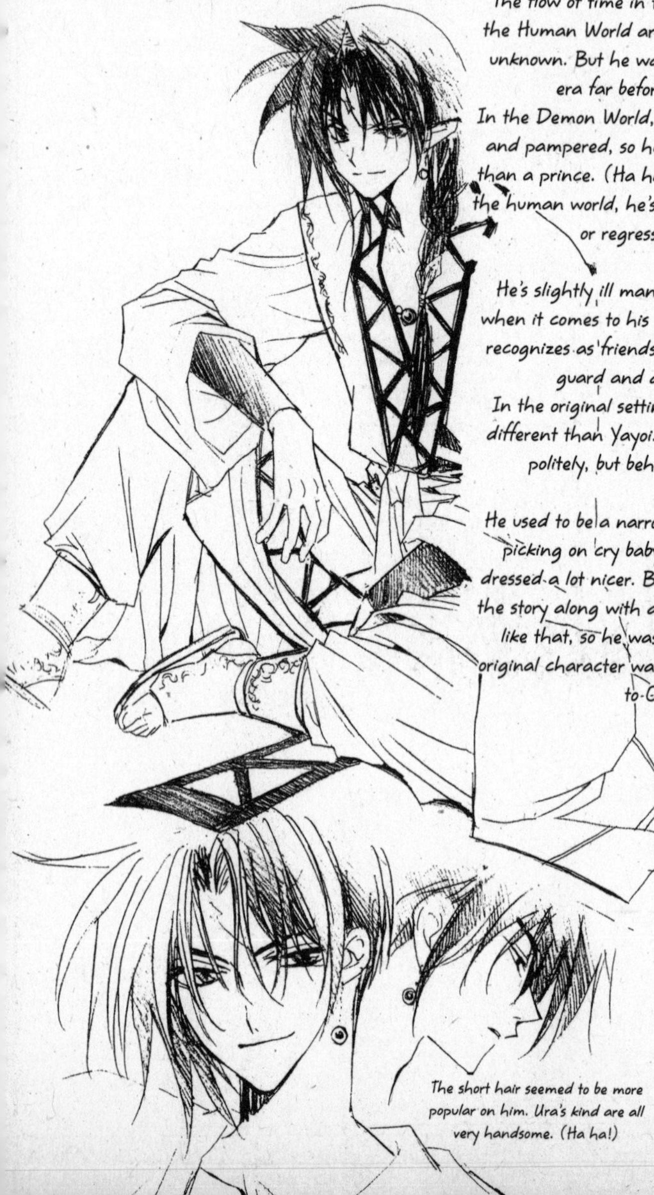

The short hair seemed to be more popular on him. Ura's kind are all very handsome. (Ha ha!)

Weak for cat toys and catnip.

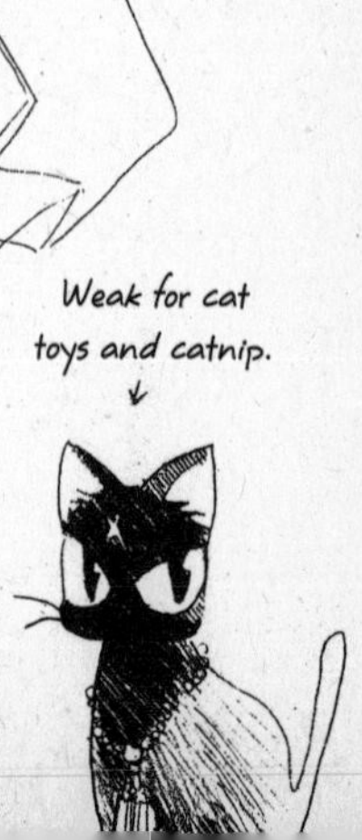

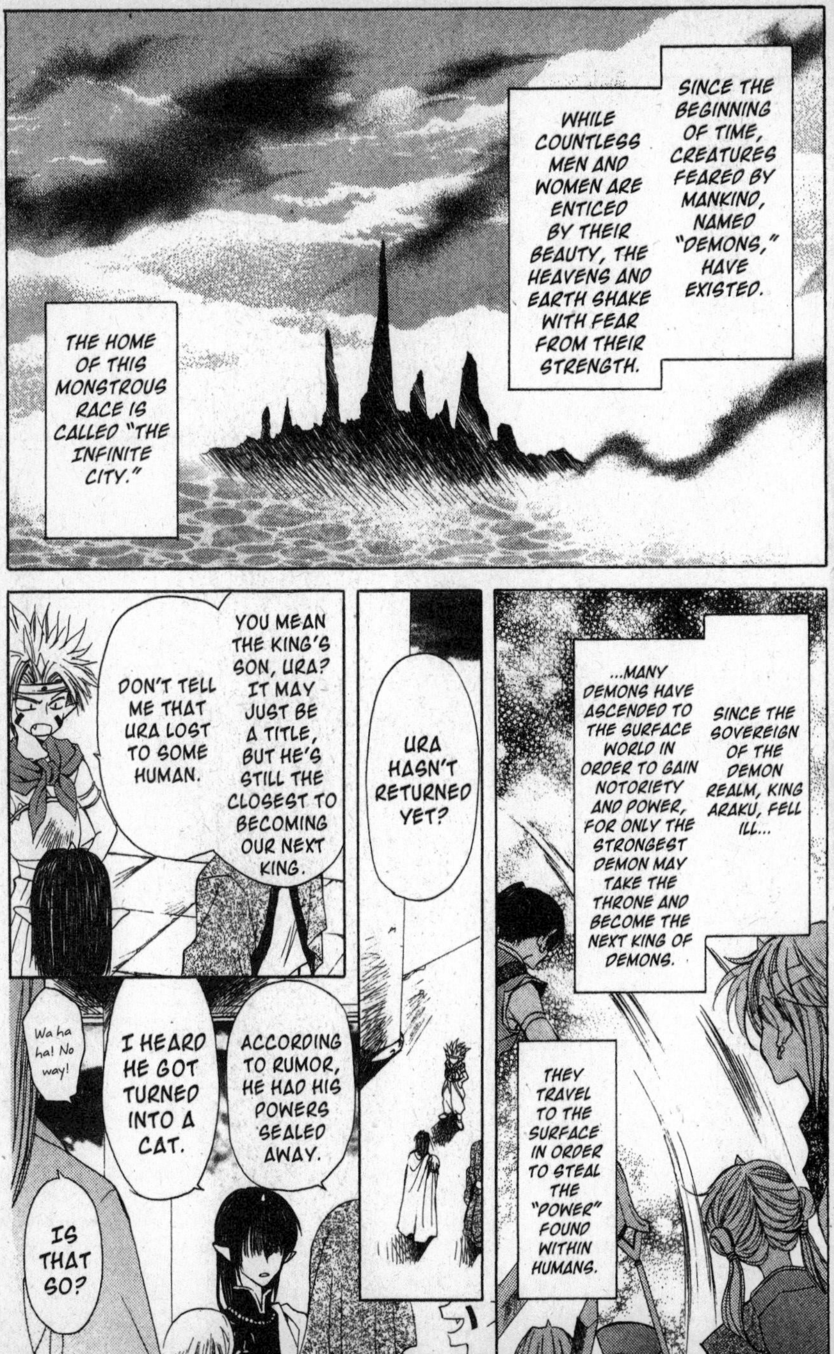
SINCE THE BEGINNING OF TIME, CREATURES FEARED BY MANKIND, NAMED "DEMONS," HAVE EXISTED.
WHILE COUNTLESS MEN AND WOMEN ARE ENTICED BY THEIR BEAUTY, THE HEAVENS AND EARTH SHAKE WITH FEAR FROM THEIR STRENGTH.
THE HOME OF THIS MONSTROUS RACE IS CALLED "THE INFINITE CITY."
SINCE THE SOVEREIGN OF THE DEMON REALM, KING ARAKU, FELL ILL...
...MANY DEMONS HAVE ASCENDED TO THE SURFACE WORLD IN ORDER TO GAIN NOTORIETY AND POWER, FOR ONLY THE STRONGEST DEMON MAY TAKE THE THRONE AND BECOME THE NEXT KING OF DEMONS.
THEY TRAVEL TO THE SURFACE IN ORDER TO STEAL THE "POWER" FOUND WITHIN HUMANS.
URA HASN'T RETURNED YET?
YOU MEAN THE KING'S SON, URA? IT MAY JUST BE A TITLE, BUT HE'S STILL THE CLOSEST TO BECOMING OUR NEXT KING.
DON'T TELL ME THAT URA LOST TO SOME HUMAN.
ACCORDING TO RUMOR, HE HAD HIS POWERS SEALED AWAY.
I HEARD HE GOT TURNED INTO A CAT.
Wa ha ha! No way!
IS THAT SO?

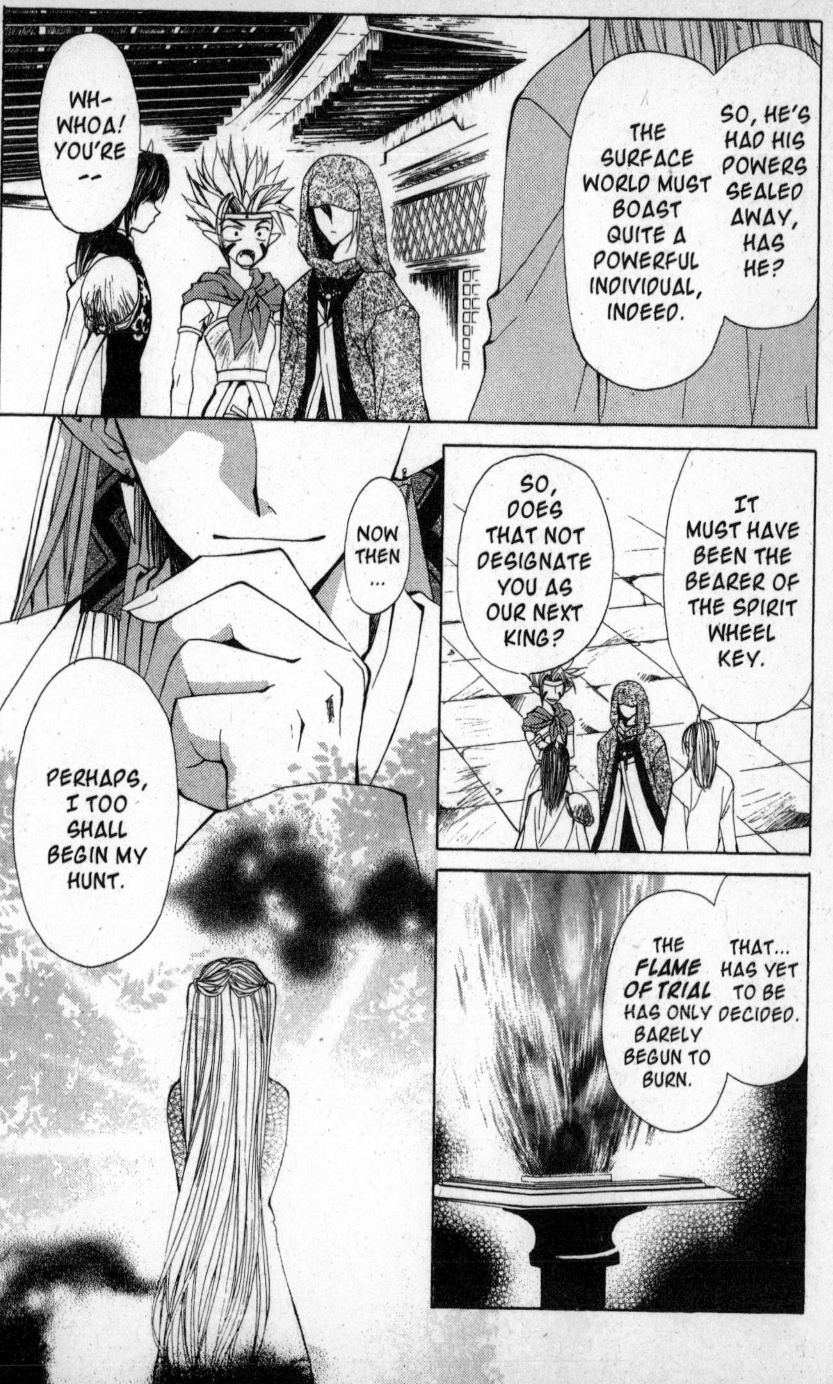
SO, HE'S HAD HIS POWERS SEALED AWAY, HAS HE?
THE SURFACE WORLD MUST BOAST QUITE A POWERFUL INDIVIDUAL, INDEED.
WH-WHOA! YOU'RE --
IT MUST HAVE BEEN THE BEARER OF THE SPIRIT WHEEL KEY.
SO, DOES THAT NOT DESIGNATE YOU AS OUR NEXT KING?
THAT... HAS YET TO BE DECIDED.
THE *FLAME OF TRIAL* HAS ONLY BARELY BEGUN TO BURN.
NOW THEN ...
PERHAPS, I TOO SHALL BEGIN MY HUNT.

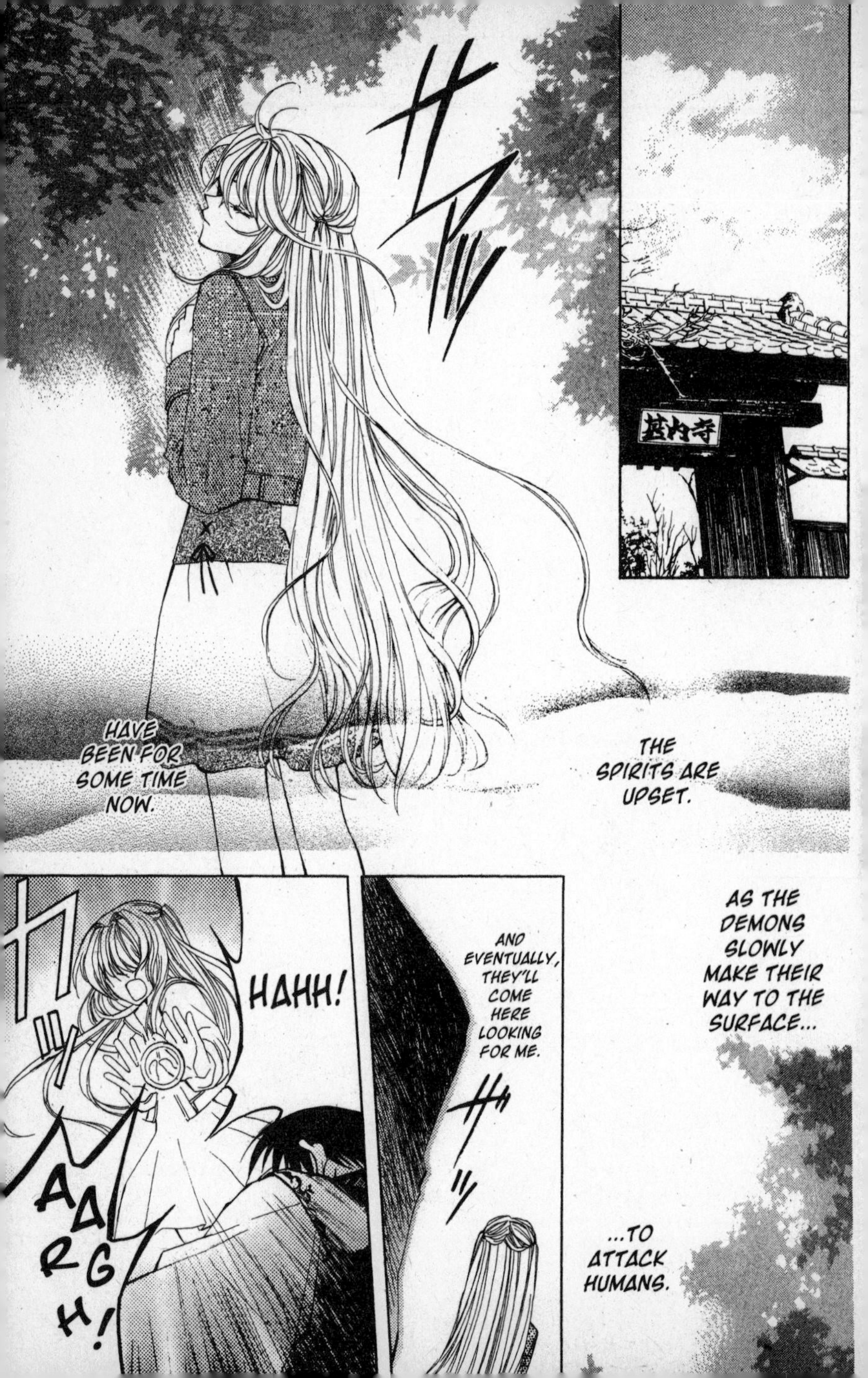
THE SPIRITS ARE UPSET.
HAVE BEEN FOR SOME TIME NOW.
AS THE DEMONS SLOWLY MAKE THEIR WAY TO THE SURFACE...
...TO ATTACK HUMANS.
AND EVENTUALLY, THEY'LL COME HERE LOOKING FOR ME.
HAHH!
AARGH!

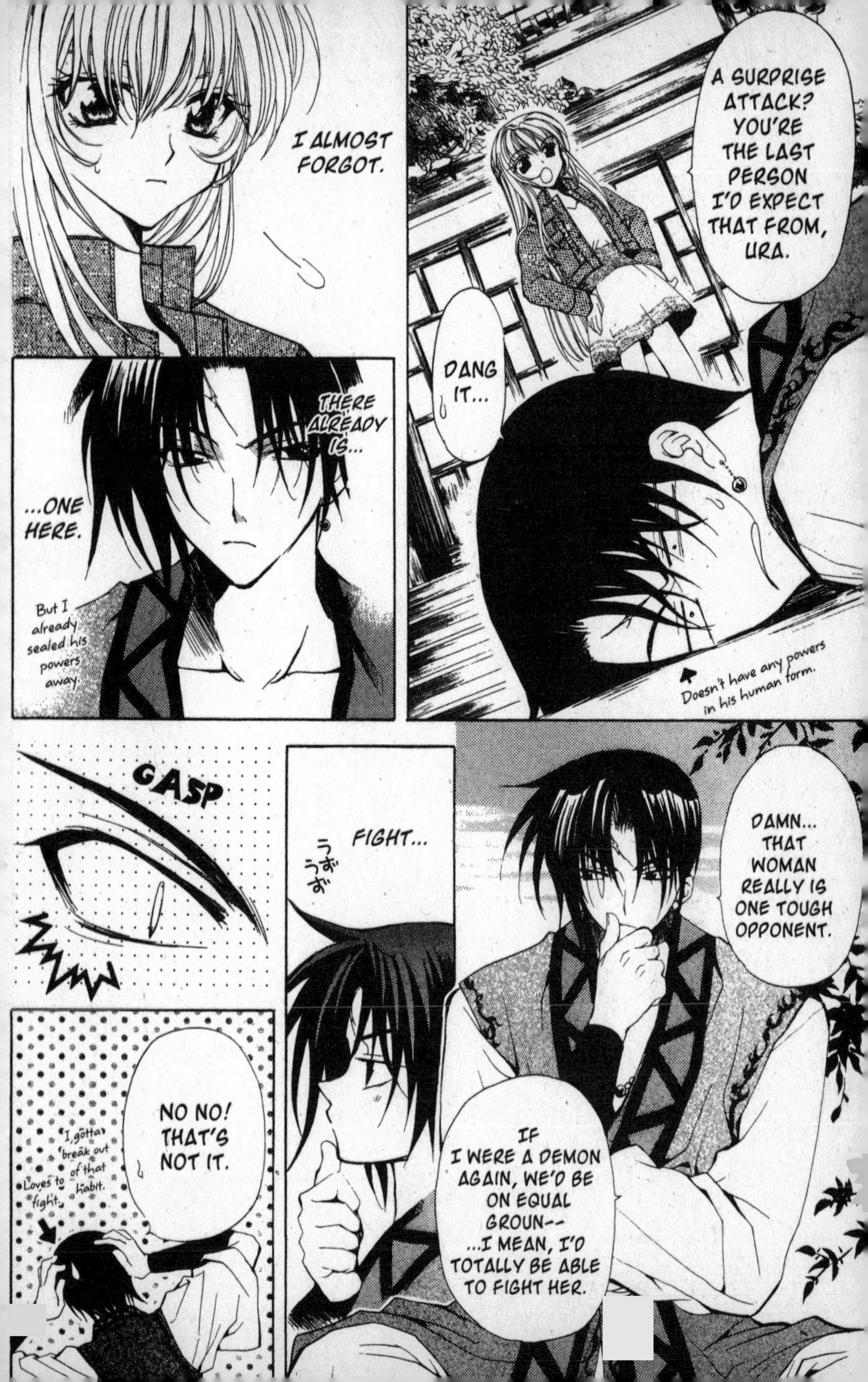
A SURPRISE ATTACK? YOU'RE THE LAST PERSON I'D EXPECT THAT FROM, URA.
DANG IT...
Doesn't have any powers in his human form.
I ALMOST FORGOT.
THERE ALREADY IS...
...ONE HERE.
But I already sealed his powers away.
DAMN... THAT WOMAN REALLY IS ONE TOUGH OPPONENT.
IF I WERE A DEMON AGAIN, WE'D BE ON EQUAL GROUN-- ...I MEAN, I'D TOTALLY BE ABLE TO FIGHT HER.
FIGHT...
うずうず
GASP
NO NO! THAT'S NOT IT.
I gotta break out of that habit.
Loves to fight.

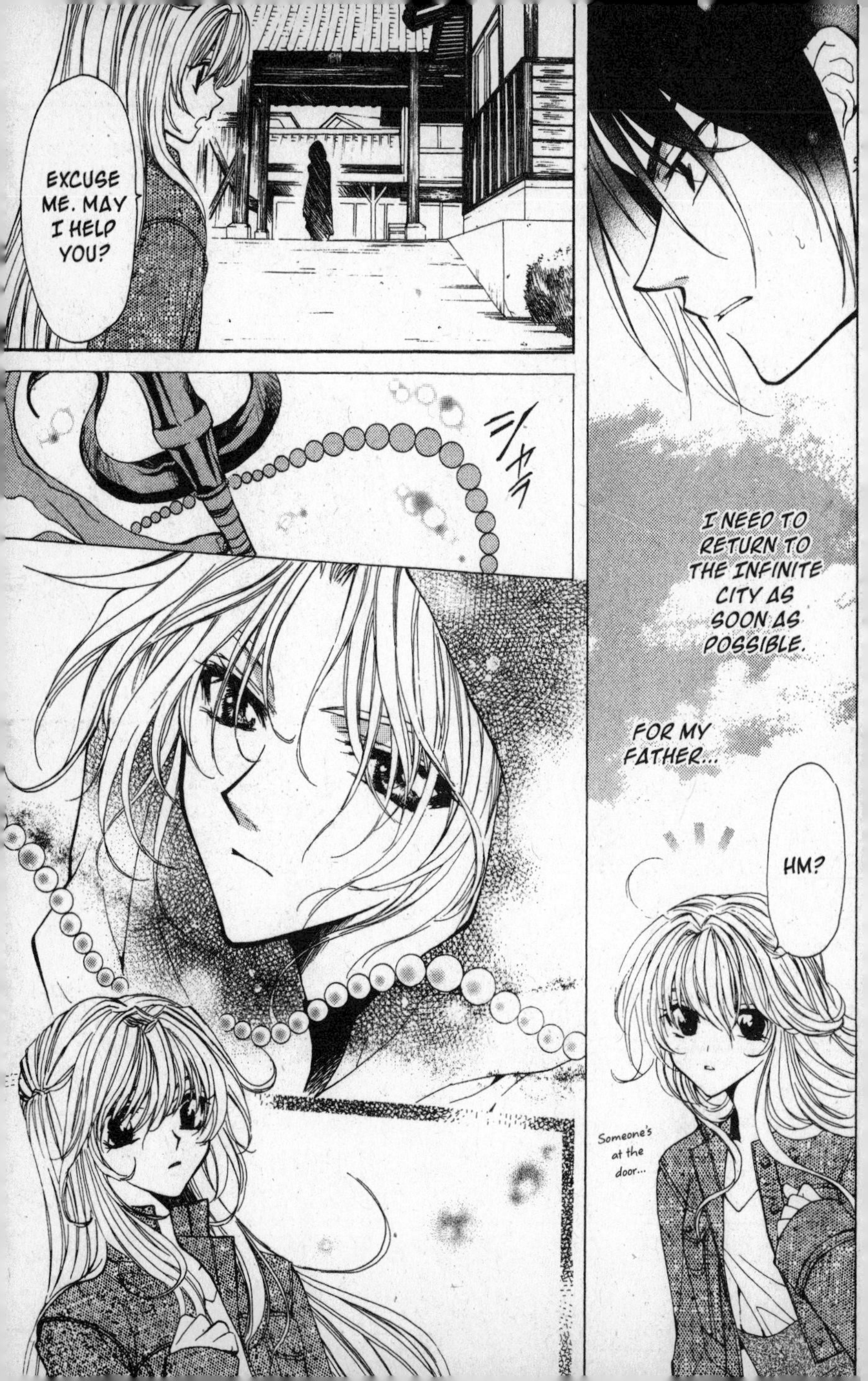
I NEED TO RETURN TO THE INFINITE CITY AS SOON AS POSSIBLE.
FOR MY FATHER...
HM?
Someone's at the door...
EXCUSE ME. MAY I HELP YOU?
シャラ

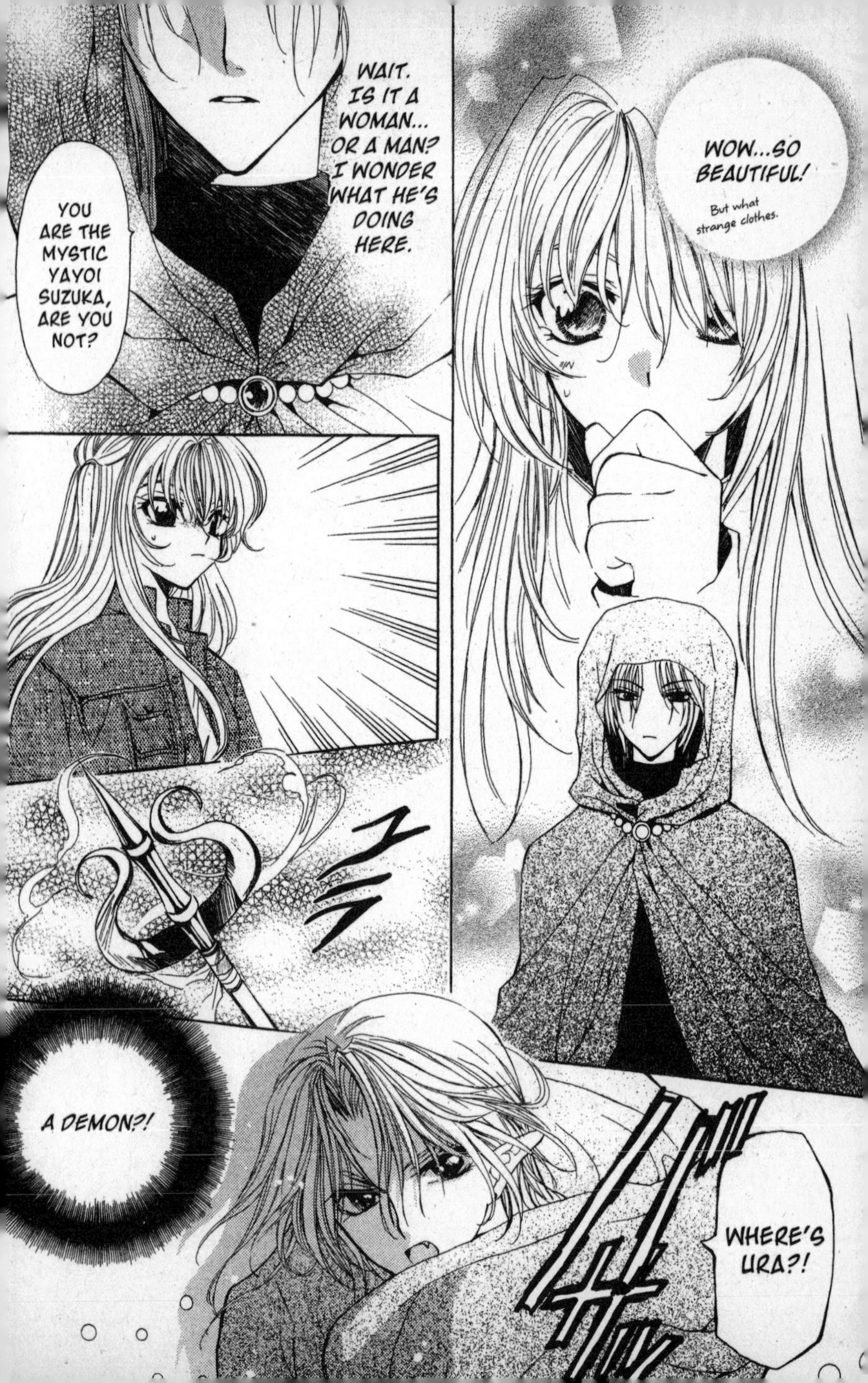
WOW...SO BEAUTIFUL!
But what strange clothes.
WAIT. IS IT A WOMAN... OR A MAN? I WONDER WHAT HE'S DOING HERE.
YOU ARE THE MYSTIC YAYOI SUZUKA, ARE YOU NOT?
A DEMON?!
WHERE'S URA?!

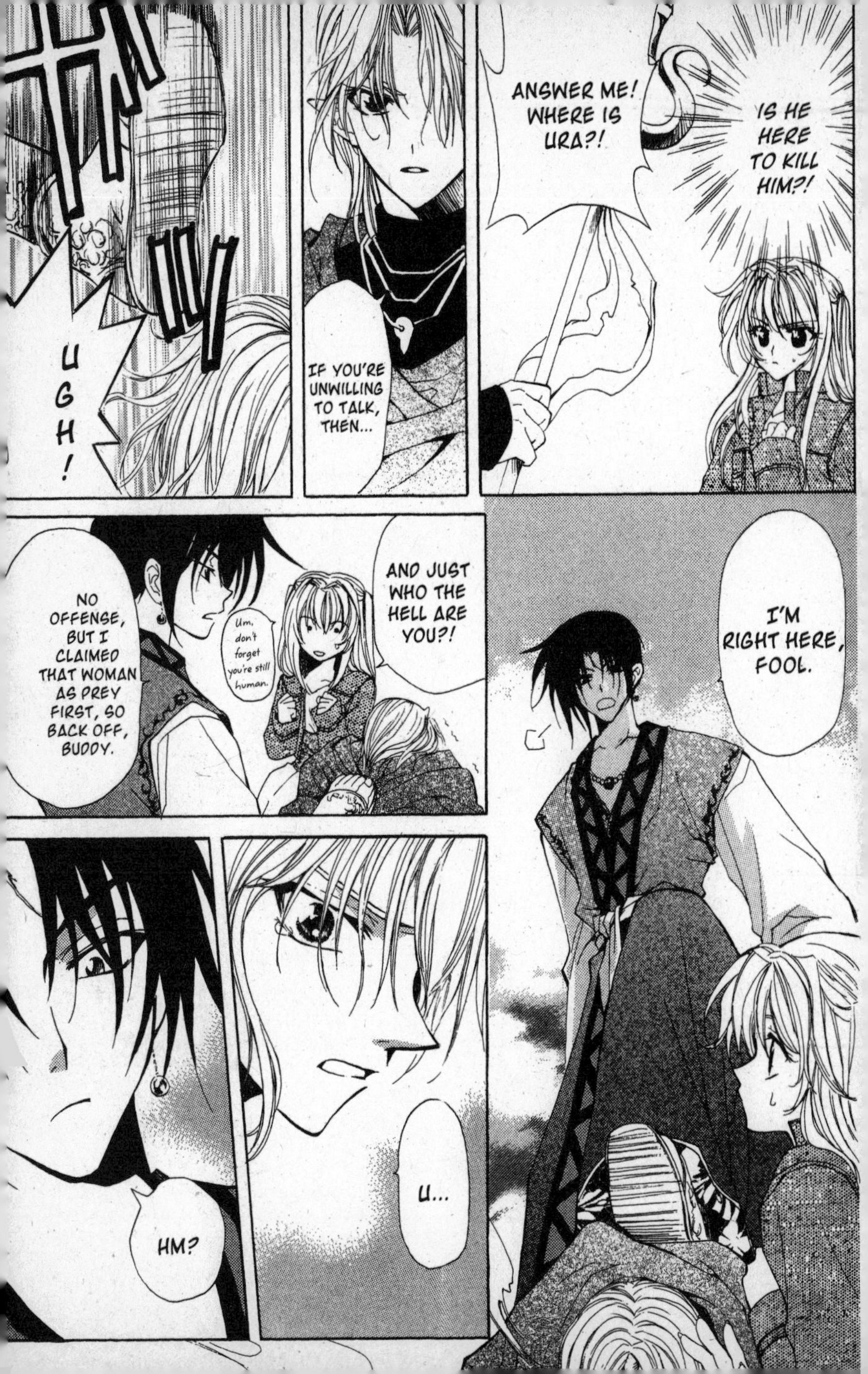
IS HE HERE TO KILL HIM?!
ANSWER ME! WHERE IS URA?!
IF YOU'RE UNWILLING TO TALK, THEN...
UGH!
I'M RIGHT HERE, FOOL.
AND JUST WHO THE HELL ARE YOU?!
Um, don't forget you're still human.
NO OFFENSE, BUT I CLAIMED THAT WOMAN AS PREY FIRST, SO BACK OFF, BUDDY.
U...
HM?

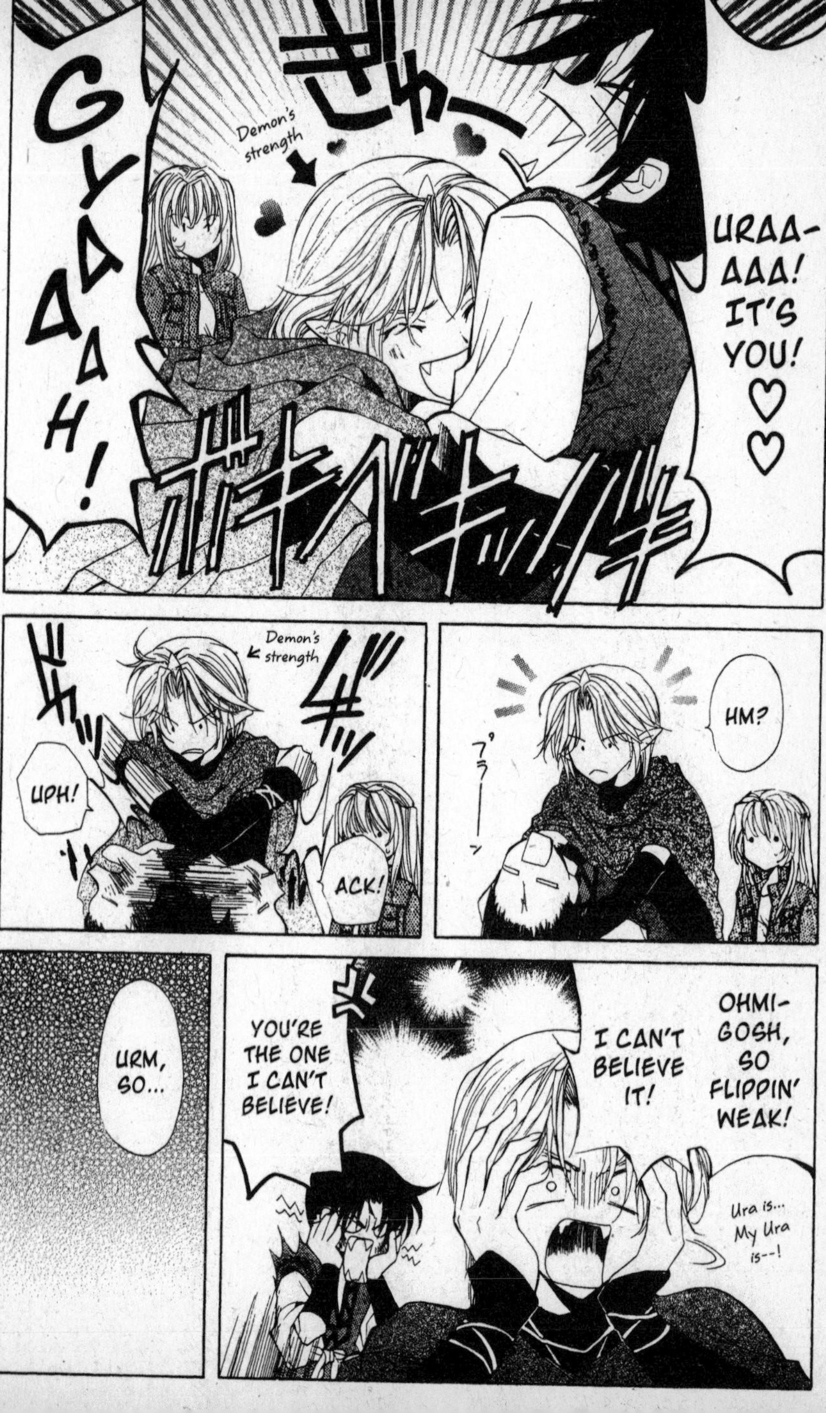
ぎゃー
URAAA-AAA! IT'S YOU! ♡ ♡
Demon's strength
GYAAAAH!
HM?
Demon's strength
UPH!
ACK!
OHMI-GOSH, SO FLIPPIN' WEAK!
I CAN'T BELIEVE IT!
YOU'RE THE ONE I CAN'T BELIEVE!
Ura is... My Ura is--!
URM, SO...

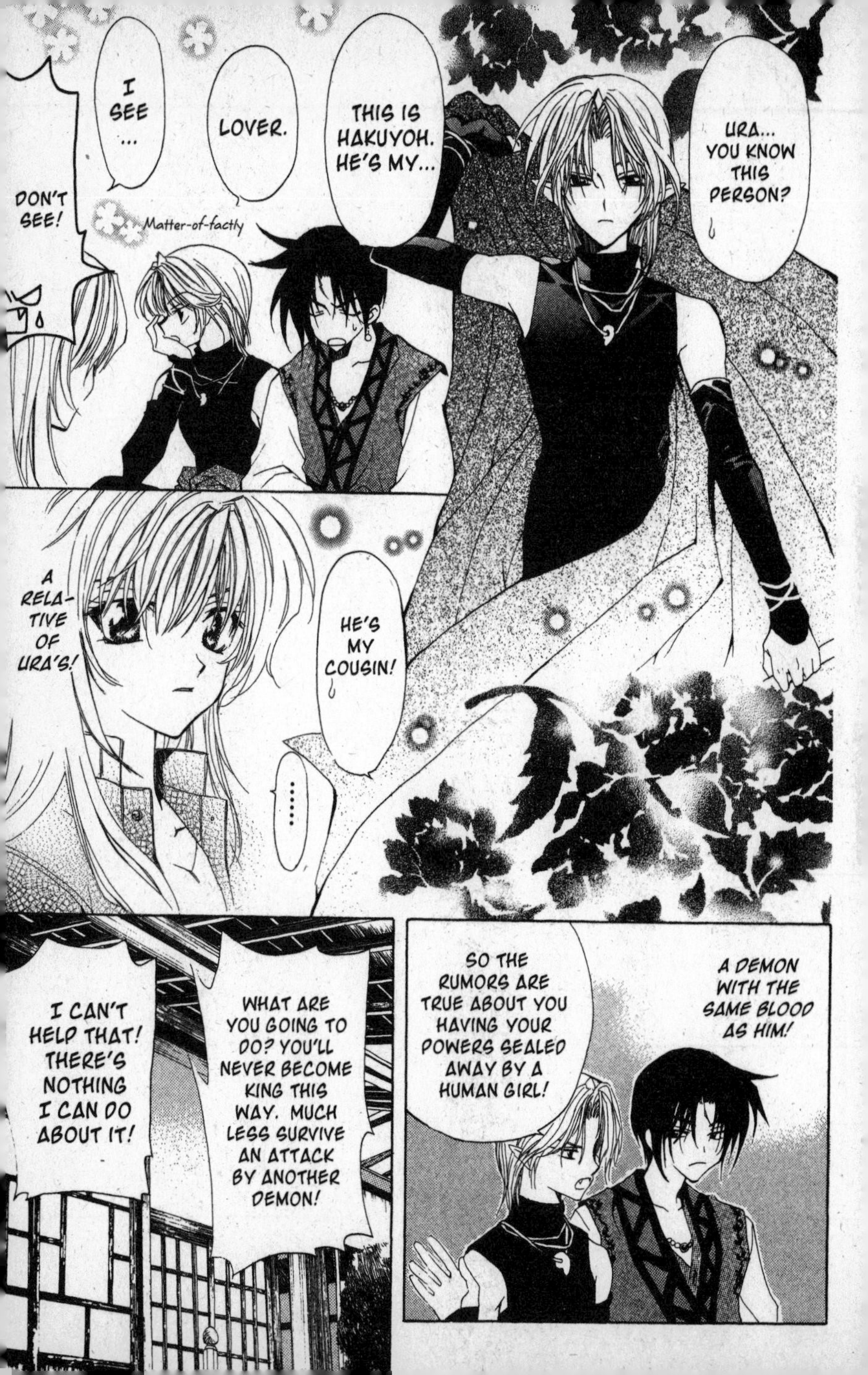
URA... YOU KNOW THIS PERSON?
THIS IS HAKUYOH. HE'S MY...
LOVER.
I SEE ...
DON'T SEE!
Matter-of-factly
HE'S MY COUSIN!
......
A RELA-TIVE OF URA'S!
A DEMON WITH THE SAME BLOOD AS HIM!
SO THE RUMORS ARE TRUE ABOUT YOU HAVING YOUR POWERS SEALED AWAY BY A HUMAN GIRL!
WHAT ARE YOU GOING TO DO? YOU'LL NEVER BECOME KING THIS WAY. MUCH LESS SURVIVE AN ATTACK BY ANOTHER DEMON!
I CAN'T HELP THAT! THERE'S NOTHING I CAN DO ABOUT IT!

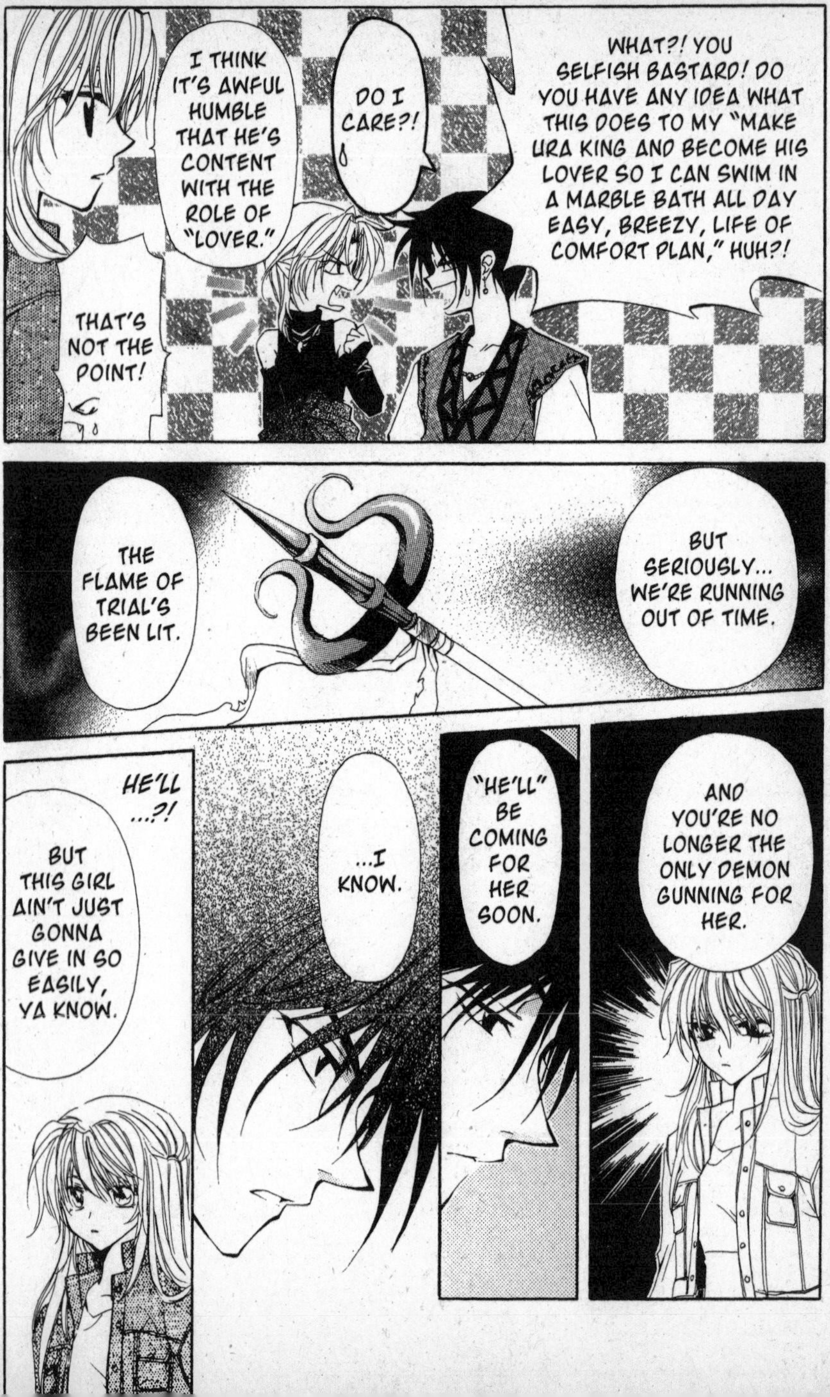
WHAT?! YOU SELFISH BASTARD! DO YOU HAVE ANY IDEA WHAT THIS DOES TO MY "MAKE URA KING AND BECOME HIS LOVER SO I CAN SWIM IN A MARBLE BATH ALL DAY EASY, BREEZY, LIFE OF COMFORT PLAN," HUH?!
DO I CARE?!
I THINK IT'S AWFUL HUMBLE THAT HE'S CONTENT WITH THE ROLE OF "LOVER."
THAT'S NOT THE POINT!
BUT SERIOUSLY... WE'RE RUNNING OUT OF TIME.
THE FLAME OF TRIAL'S BEEN LIT.
AND YOU'RE NO LONGER THE ONLY DEMON GUNNING FOR HER.
"HE'LL" BE COMING FOR HER SOON.
...I KNOW.
HE'LL ...?!
BUT THIS GIRL AIN'T JUST GONNA GIVE IN SO EASILY, YA KNOW.

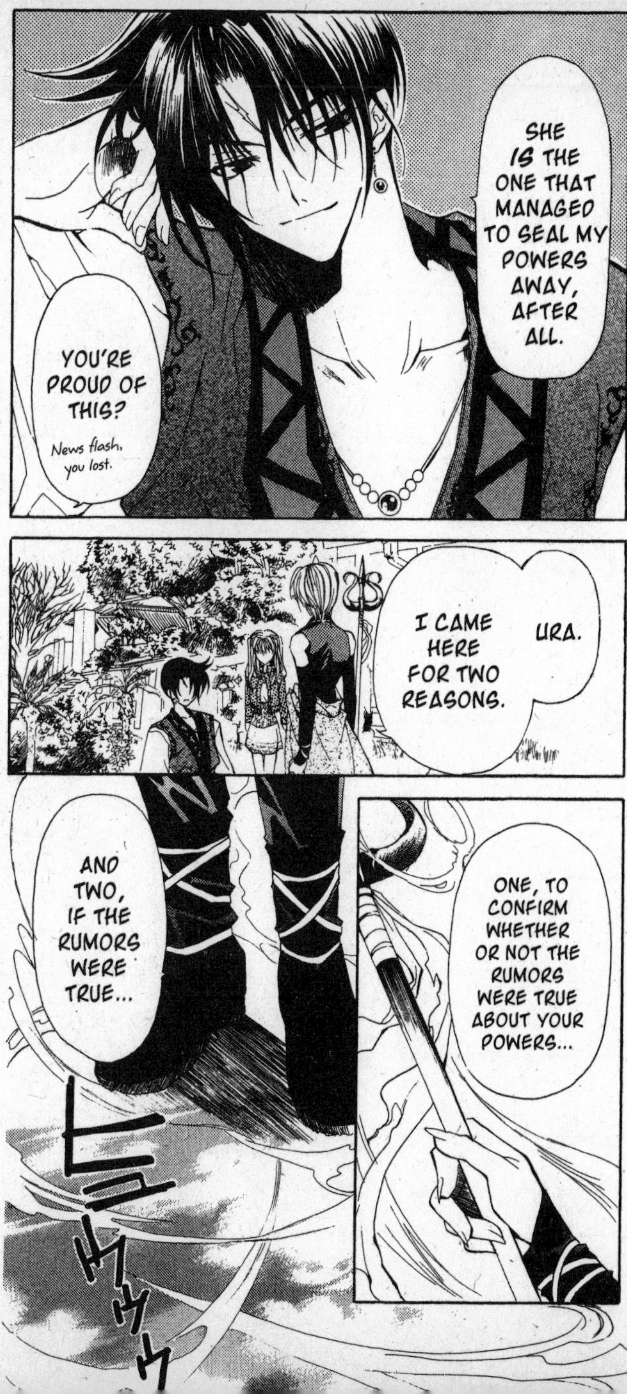
SHE IS THE ONE THAT MANAGED TO SEAL MY POWERS AWAY, AFTER ALL.
YOU'RE PROUD OF THIS?
News flash, you lost.
URA.
I CAME HERE FOR TWO REASONS.
ONE, TO CONFIRM WHETHER OR NOT THE RUMORS WERE TRUE ABOUT YOUR POWERS...
AND TWO, IF THE RUMORS WERE TRUE...

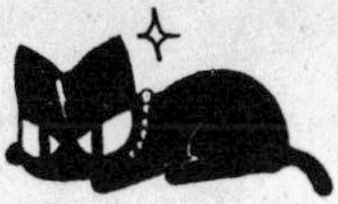

About my drawings.

I often receive letters from my readers asking how to get better at drawing. Hmm. The only thing I can tell you is to keep drawing. Nowadays, I think there are a lot of young girls and non-professionals who just suddenly are really good at drawing. But when I was in elementary and middle school, things were pretty bad for me. So even if you can't draw the way you want to draw now, don't worry. Just take your time and draw lots of things you like to draw. I, too, want to get better at drawing. I'm really bad with design, so try to study things like that everyday. When it comes to drawings, it's not so much how well you draw, but the power of your pictures. Even if you're not good with design, if the image has power, then you want to stare at it all day. That's the type of drawing I aspire towards. And by the way, this is the sort of picture I used to draw in Elementary school.

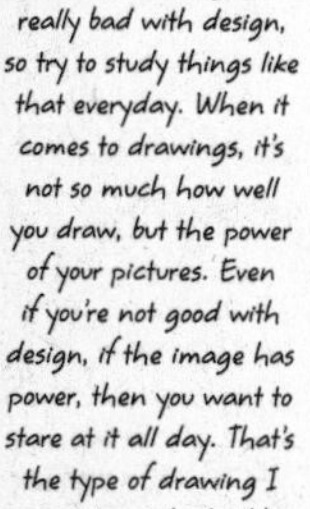

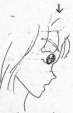

This girl's name is Nanako-chan. I even created a bit of background for her, where she's an orphan.

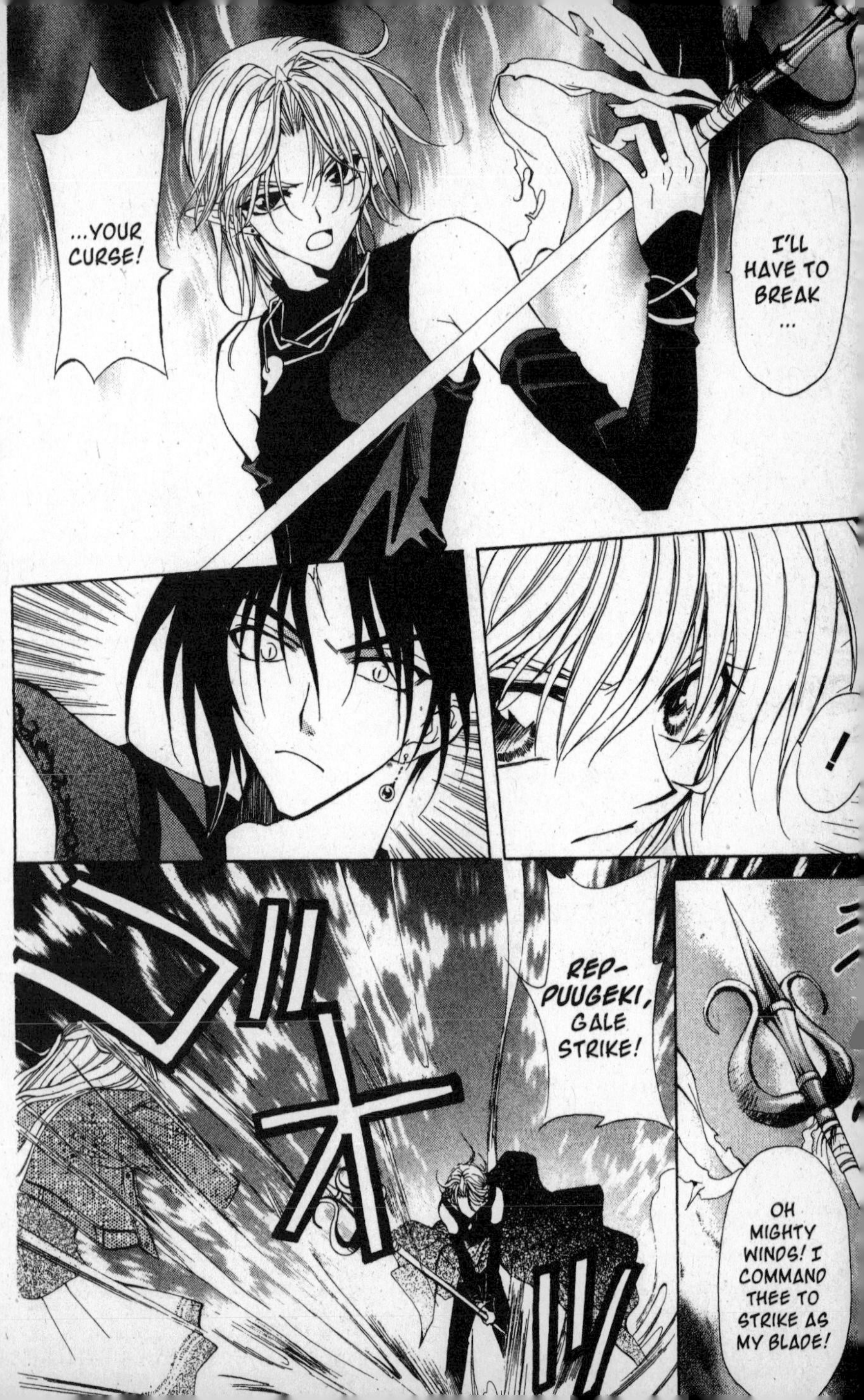
I'LL HAVE TO BREAK ...
...YOUR CURSE!
!
OH MIGHTY WINDS! I COMMAND THEE TO STRIKE AS MY BLADE!
REP-PUUGEKI, GALE STRIKE!

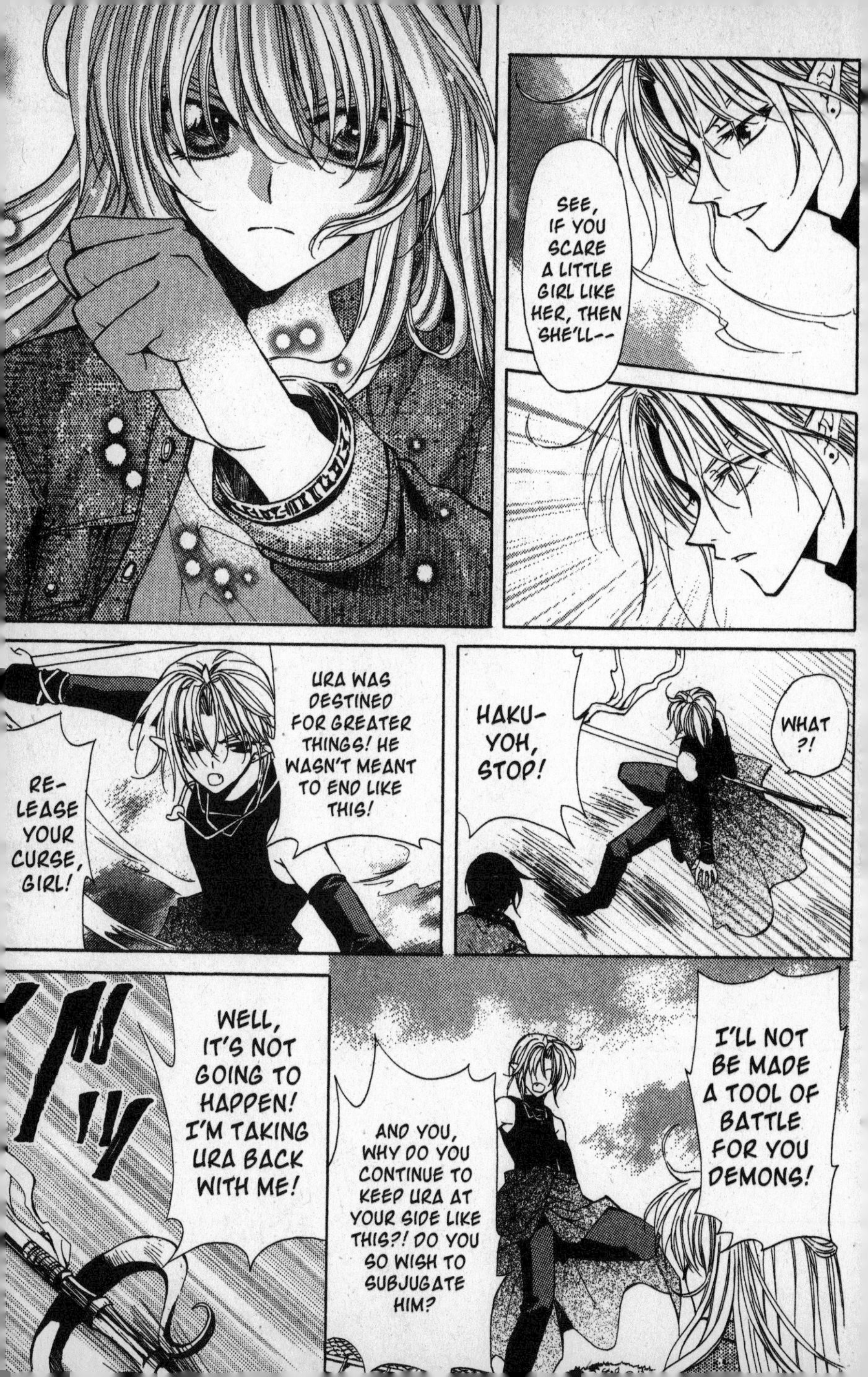
SEE, IF YOU SCARE A LITTLE GIRL LIKE HER, THEN SHE'LL--
HAKU-YOH, STOP!
WHAT?!
URA WAS DESTINED FOR GREATER THINGS! HE WASN'T MEANT TO END LIKE THIS!
RE-LEASE YOUR CURSE, GIRL!
I'LL NOT BE MADE A TOOL OF BATTLE FOR YOU DEMONS!
AND YOU, WHY DO YOU CONTINUE TO KEEP URA AT YOUR SIDE LIKE THIS?! DO YOU SO WISH TO SUBJUGATE HIM?
WELL, IT'S NOT GOING TO HAPPEN! I'M TAKING URA BACK WITH ME!

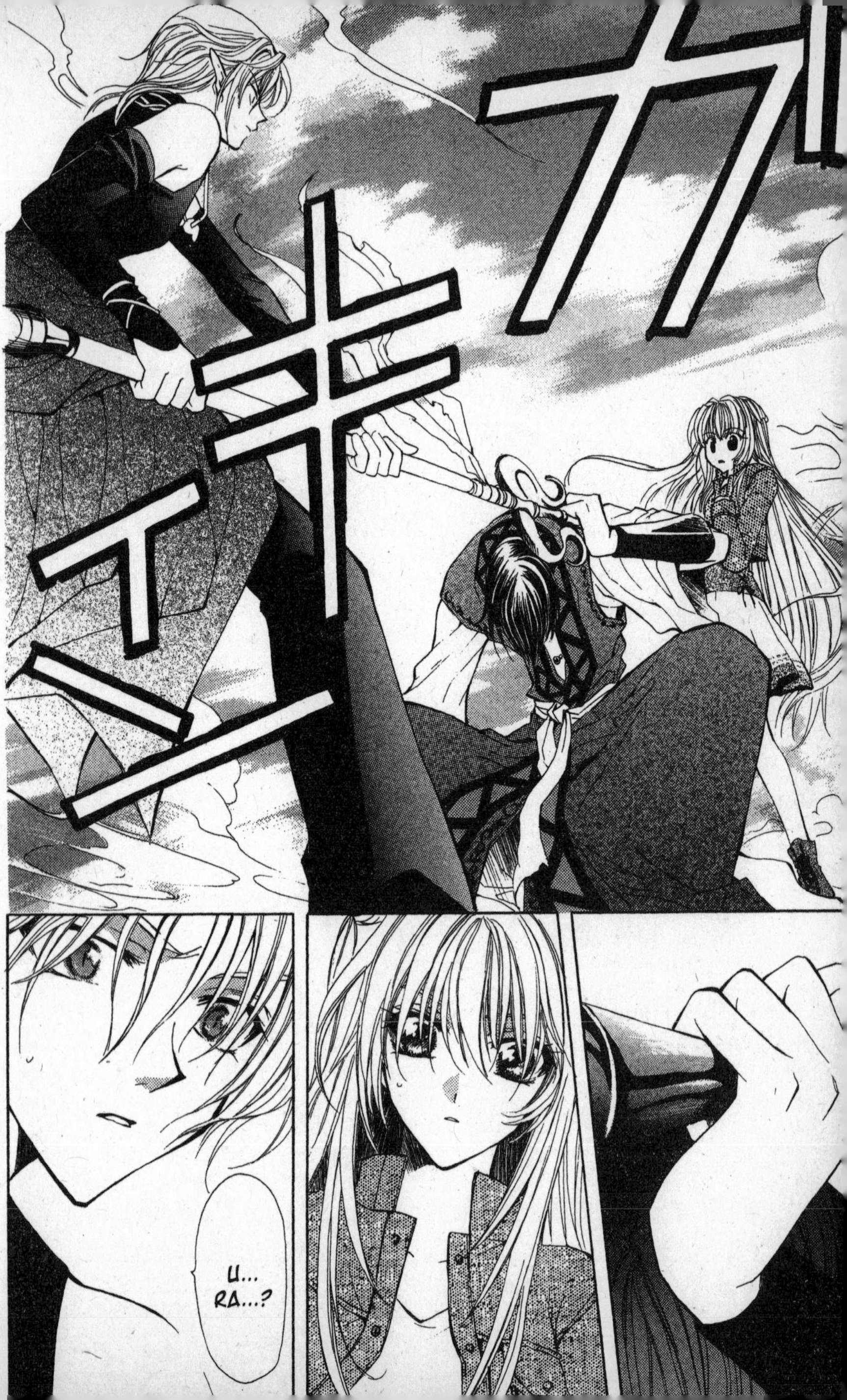
ガキイン
U... RA...?

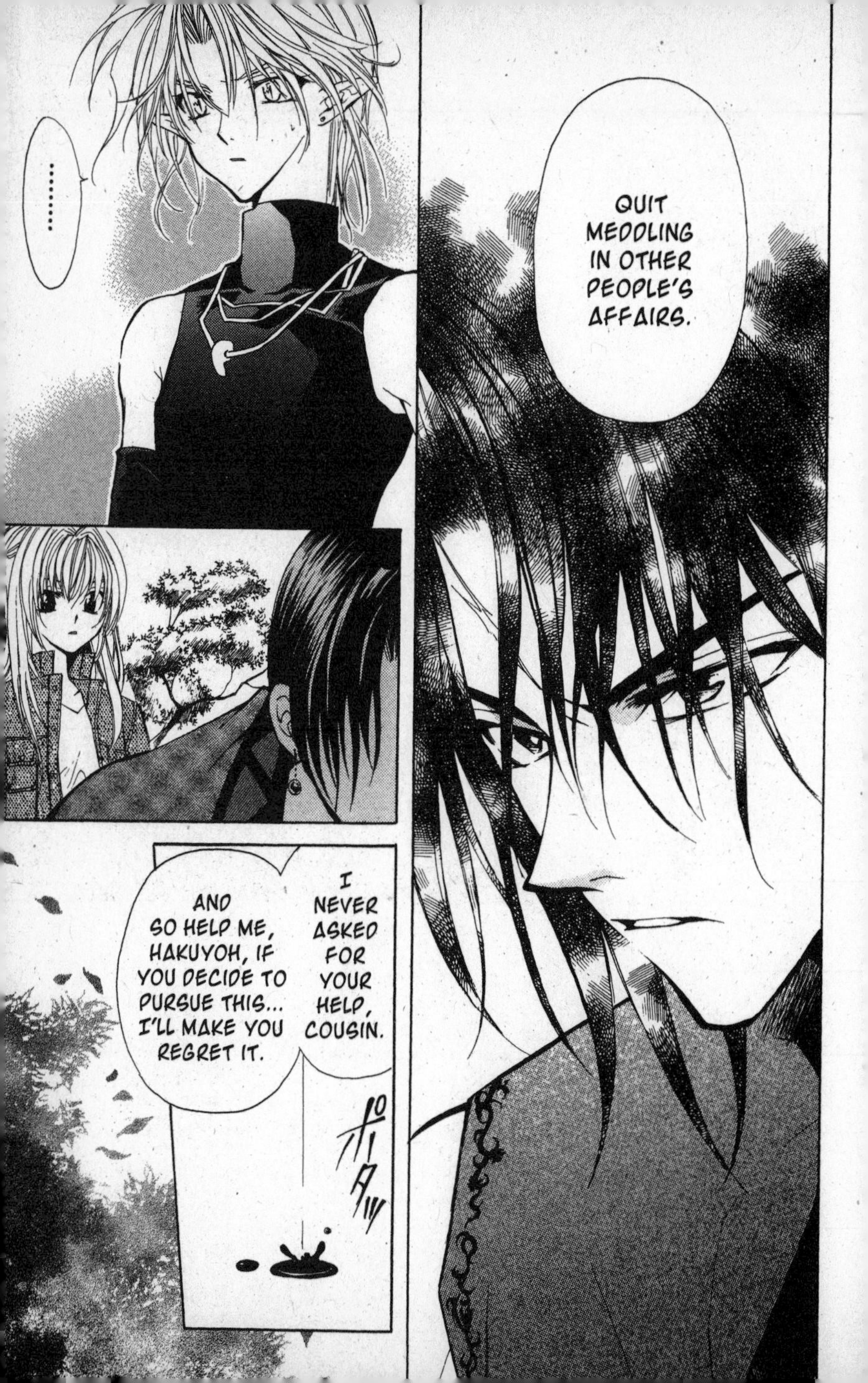
QUIT MEDDLING IN OTHER PEOPLE'S AFFAIRS.
........
I NEVER ASKED FOR YOUR HELP, COUSIN.
AND SO HELP ME, HAKUYOH, IF YOU DECIDE TO PURSUE THIS... I'LL MAKE YOU REGRET IT.

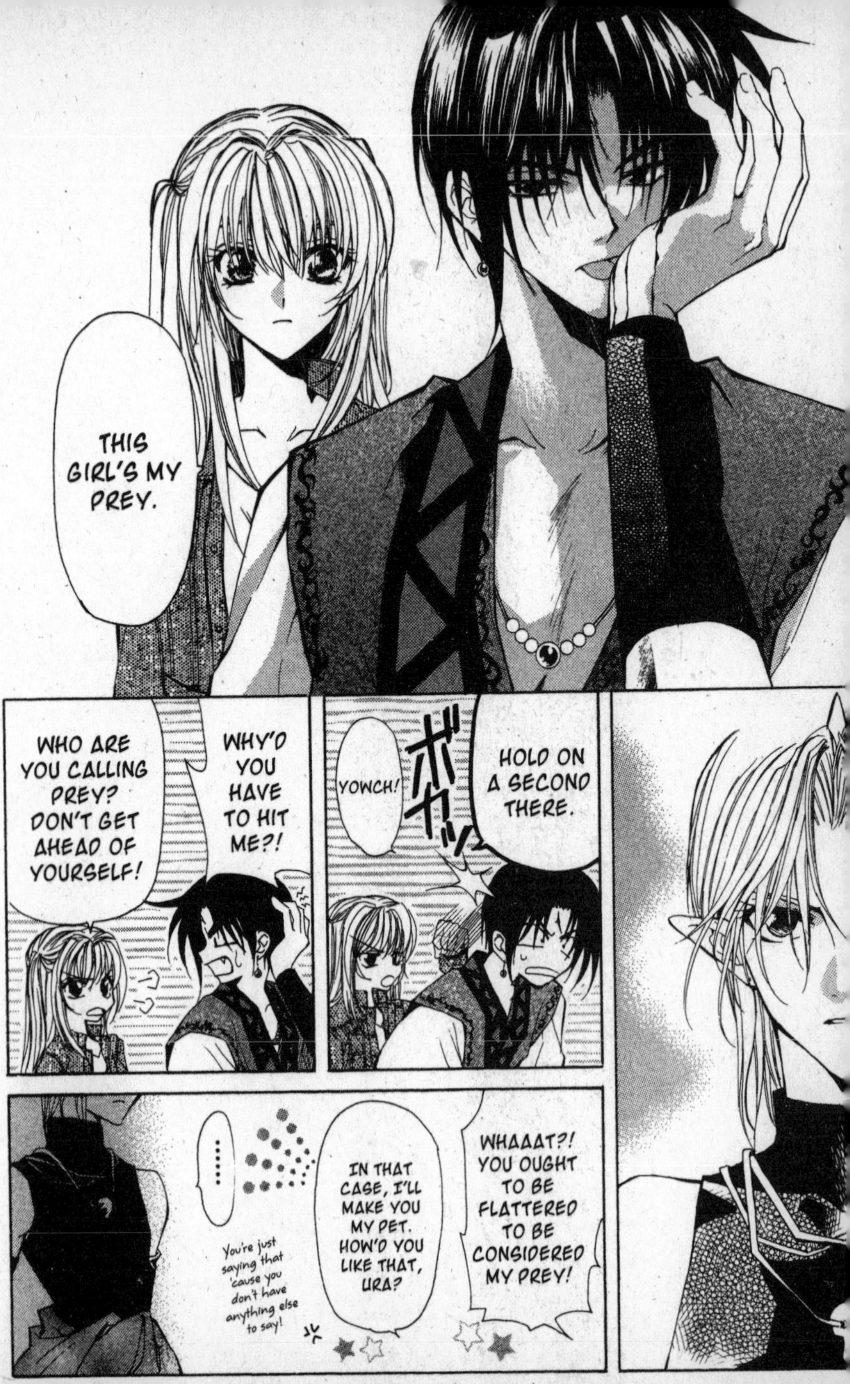
THIS GIRL'S MY PREY.
HOLD ON A SECOND THERE.
ボカッ
YOWCH!
WHY'D YOU HAVE TO HIT ME?!
WHO ARE YOU CALLING PREY? DON'T GET AHEAD OF YOURSELF!
WHAAAT?! YOU OUGHT TO BE FLATTERED TO BE CONSIDERED MY PREY!
IN THAT CASE, I'LL MAKE YOU MY PET. HOW'D YOU LIKE THAT, URA?
You're just saying that 'cause you don't have anything else to say!
......

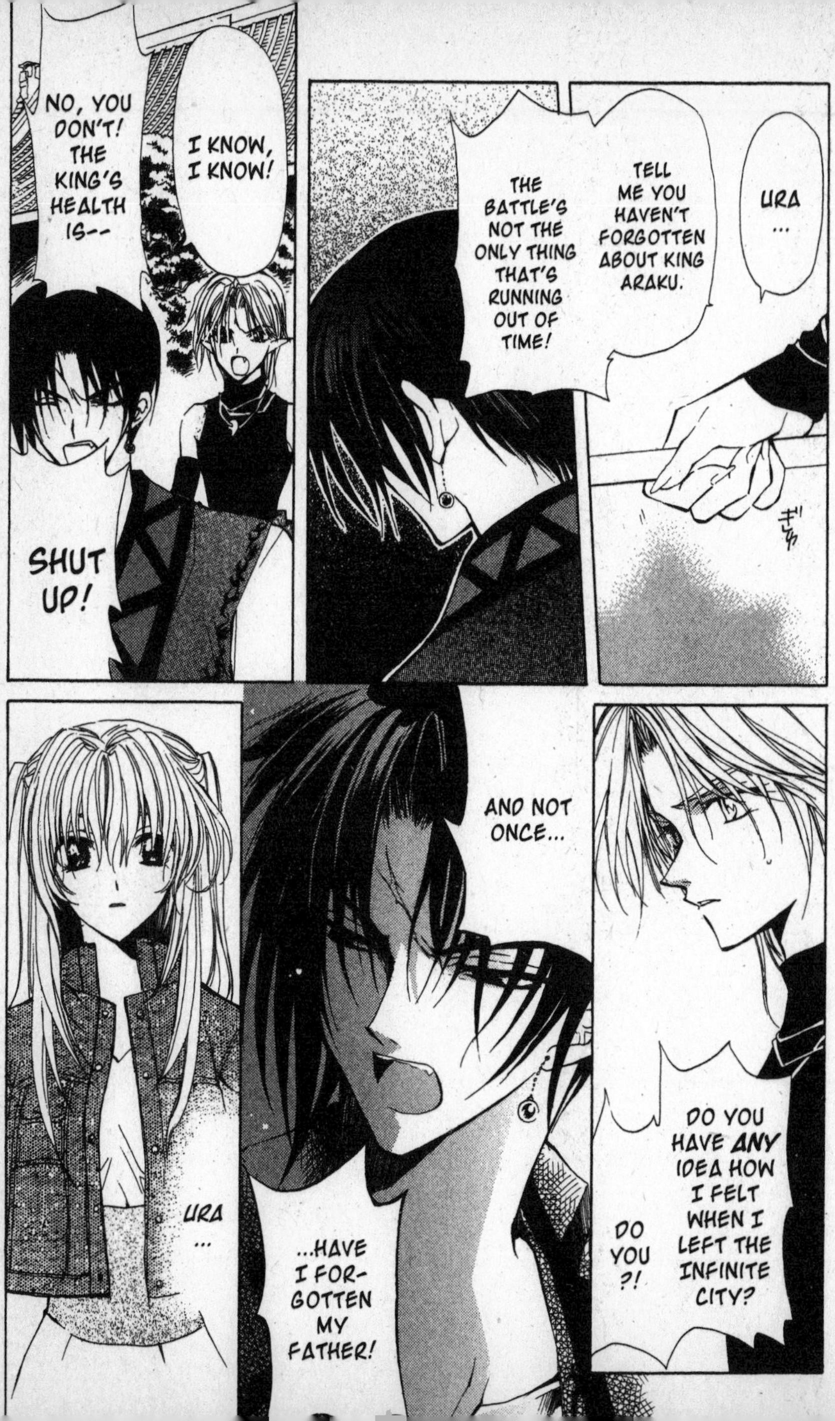
URA ...
TELL ME YOU HAVEN'T FORGOTTEN ABOUT KING ARAKU.
THE BATTLE'S NOT THE ONLY THING THAT'S RUNNING OUT OF TIME!
I KNOW, I KNOW!
NO, YOU DON'T! THE KING'S HEALTH IS--
SHUT UP!
DO YOU HAVE ANY IDEA HOW I FELT WHEN I LEFT THE INFINITE CITY?
DO YOU ?!
AND NOT ONCE...
...HAVE I FOR-GOTTEN MY FATHER!
URA ...

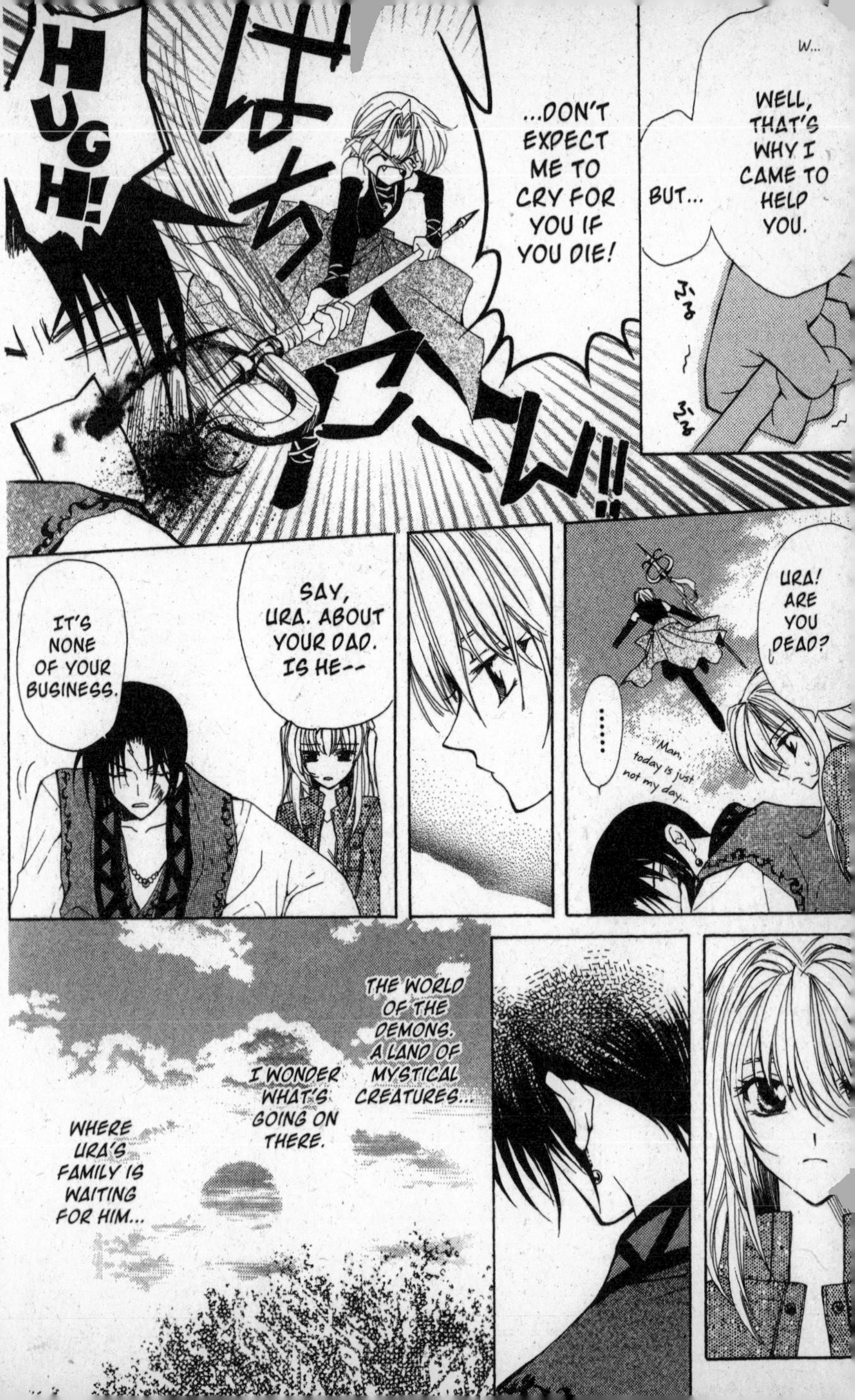
W...
WELL, THAT'S WHY I CAME TO HELP YOU.
BUT...
ぷる~ぷる
...DON'T EXPECT ME TO CRY FOR YOU IF YOU DIE!
ばちこーん!!
HUGH!
URA! ARE YOU DEAD?
......
Man, today is just not my day...
SAY, URA. ABOUT YOUR DAD. IS HE--
IT'S NONE OF YOUR BUSINESS.
!
THE WORLD OF THE DEMONS. A LAND OF MYSTICAL CREATURES...
I WONDER WHAT'S GOING ON THERE.
WHERE URA'S FAMILY IS WAITING FOR HIM...

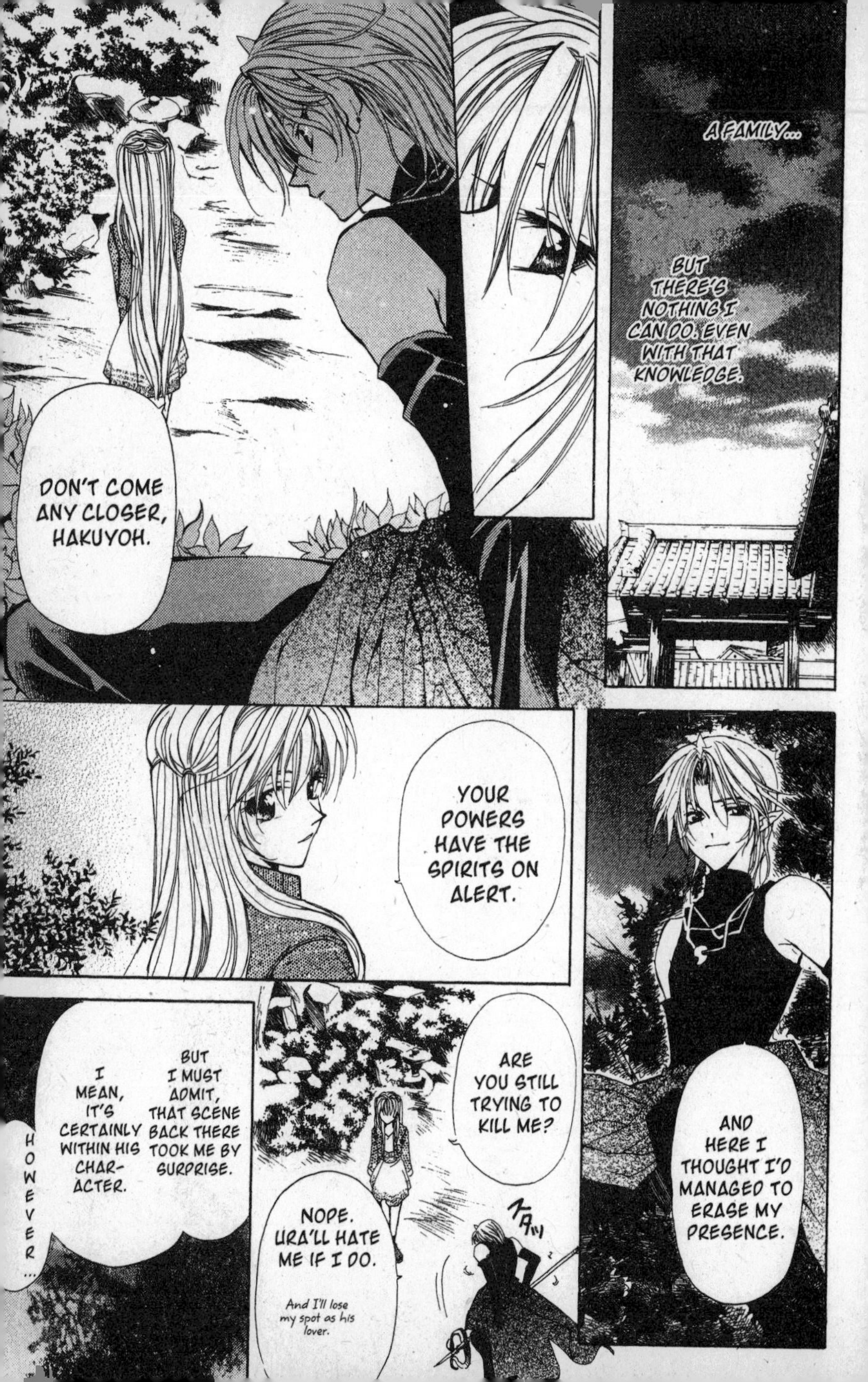
A FAMILY...
BUT THERE'S NOTHING I CAN DO. EVEN WITH THAT KNOWLEDGE.
DON'T COME ANY CLOSER, HAKUYOH.
AND HERE I THOUGHT I'D MANAGED TO ERASE MY PRESENCE.
YOUR POWERS HAVE THE SPIRITS ON ALERT.
ARE YOU STILL TRYING TO KILL ME?
NOPE. URA'LL HATE ME IF I DO.
And I'll lose my spot as his lover.
BUT I MUST ADMIT, THAT SCENE BACK THERE TOOK ME BY SURPRISE.
I MEAN, IT'S CERTAINLY WITHIN HIS CHARACTER.
HOWEVER...

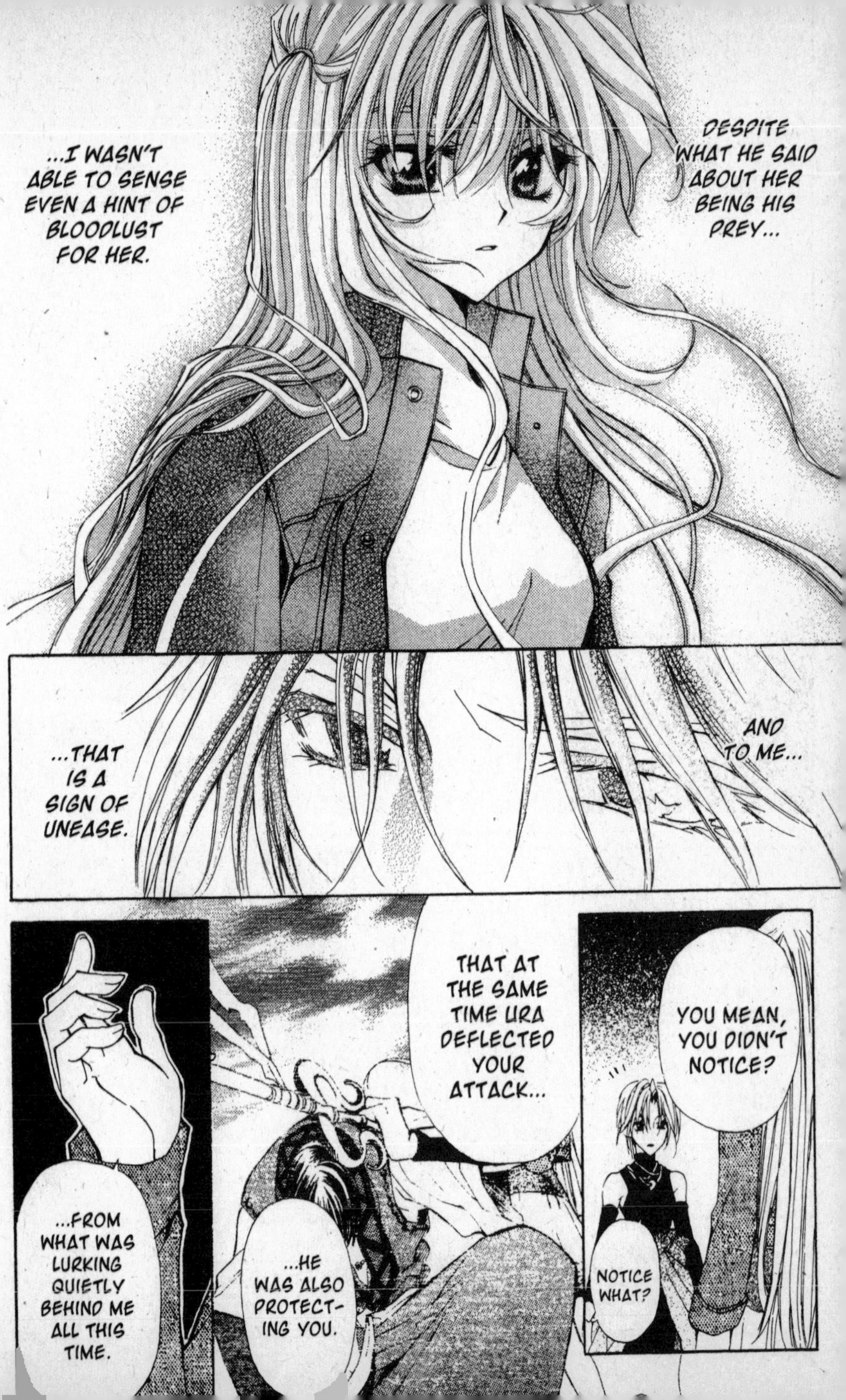
DESPITE WHAT HE SAID ABOUT HER BEING HIS PREY...
...I WASN'T ABLE TO SENSE EVEN A HINT OF BLOODLUST FOR HER.
AND TO ME...
...THAT IS A SIGN OF UNEASE.
YOU MEAN, YOU DIDN'T NOTICE?
NOTICE WHAT?
THAT AT THE SAME TIME URA DEFLECTED YOUR ATTACK...
...HE WAS ALSO PROTECT-ING YOU.
...FROM WHAT WAS LURKING QUIETLY BEHIND ME ALL THIS TIME.

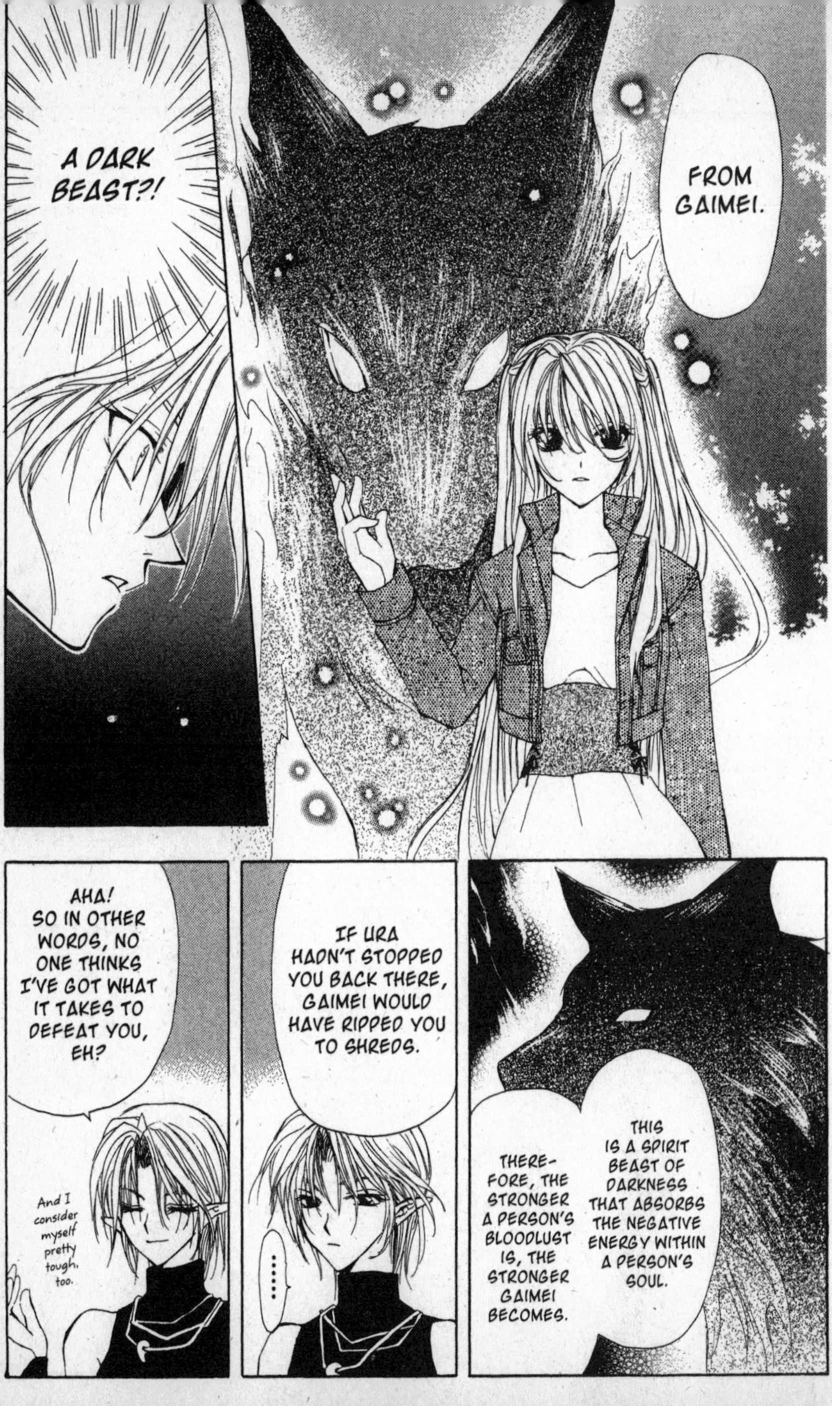
FROM GAIMEI.
A DARK BEAST?!
THIS IS A SPIRIT BEAST OF DARKNESS THAT ABSORBS THE NEGATIVE ENERGY WITHIN A PERSON'S SOUL.
THEREFORE, THE STRONGER A PERSON'S BLOODLUST IS, THE STRONGER GAIMEI BECOMES.
IF URA HADN'T STOPPED YOU BACK THERE, GAIMEI WOULD HAVE RIPPED YOU TO SHREDS.
......
AHA! SO IN OTHER WORDS, NO ONE THINKS I'VE GOT WHAT IT TAKES TO DEFEAT YOU, EH?
And I consider myself pretty tough, too.

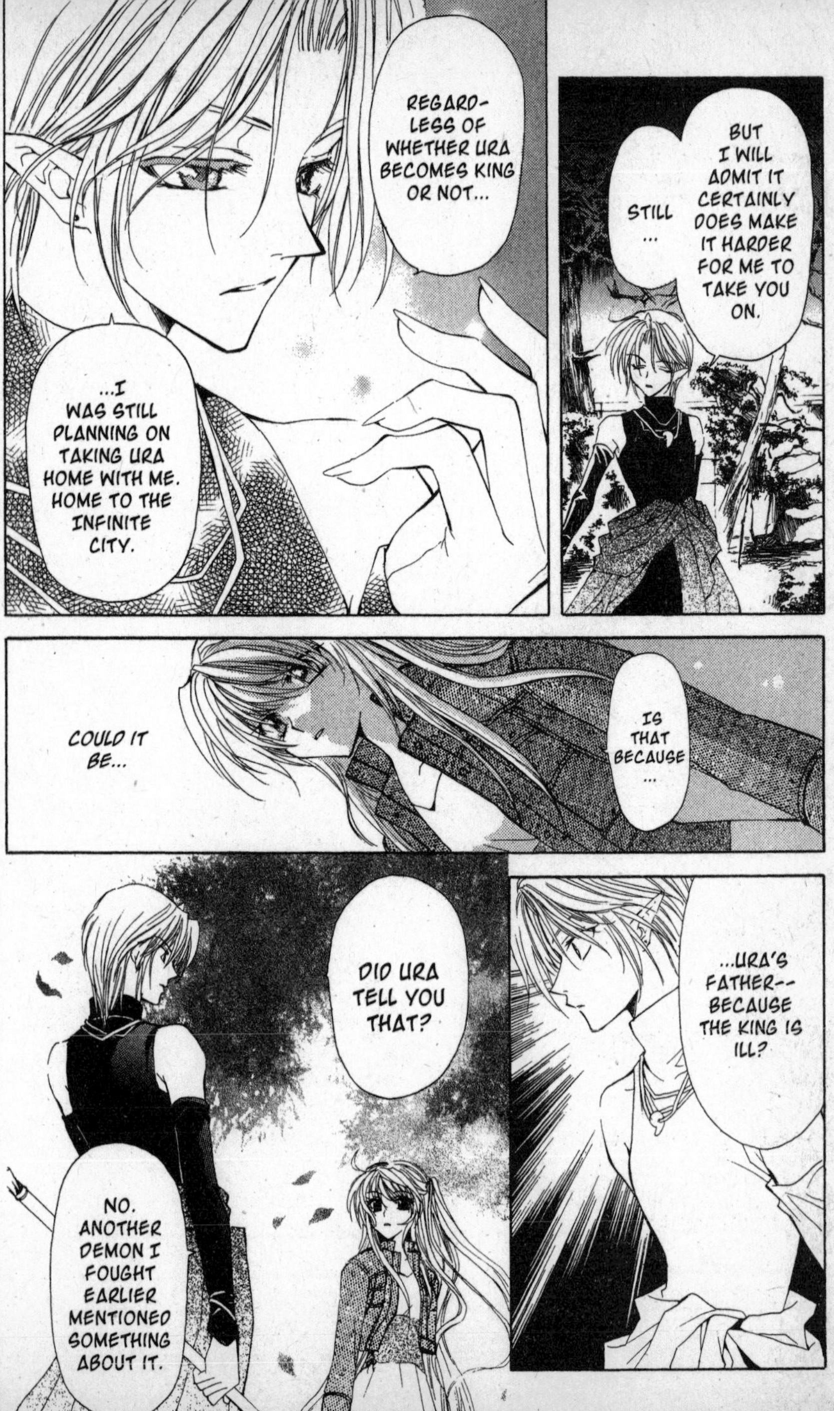
STILL ...
BUT I WILL ADMIT IT CERTAINLY DOES MAKE IT HARDER FOR ME TO TAKE YOU ON.
REGARDLESS OF WHETHER URA BECOMES KING OR NOT...
...I WAS STILL PLANNING ON TAKING URA HOME WITH ME. HOME TO THE INFINITE CITY.
IS THAT BECAUSE ...
COULD IT BE...
...URA'S FATHER--BECAUSE THE KING IS ILL?
DID URA TELL YOU THAT?
NO. ANOTHER DEMON I FOUGHT EARLIER MENTIONED SOMETHING ABOUT IT.

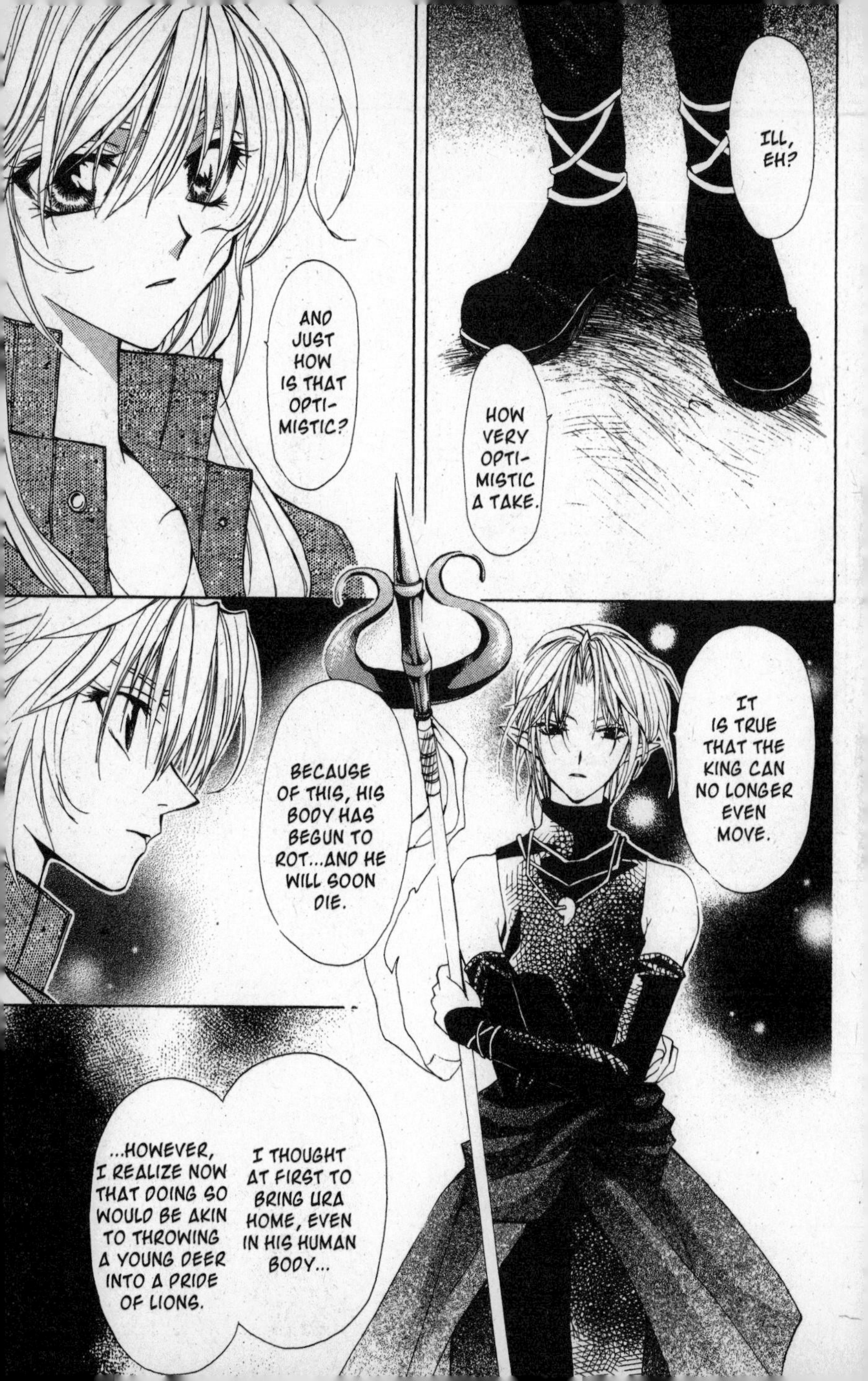
ILL, EH?
HOW VERY OPTIMISTIC A TAKE.
AND JUST HOW IS THAT OPTIMISTIC?
IT IS TRUE THAT THE KING CAN NO LONGER EVEN MOVE.
BECAUSE OF THIS, HIS BODY HAS BEGUN TO ROT...AND HE WILL SOON DIE.
I THOUGHT AT FIRST TO BRING URA HOME, EVEN IN HIS HUMAN BODY...
...HOWEVER, I REALIZE NOW THAT DOING SO WOULD BE AKIN TO THROWING A YOUNG DEER INTO A PRIDE OF LIONS.

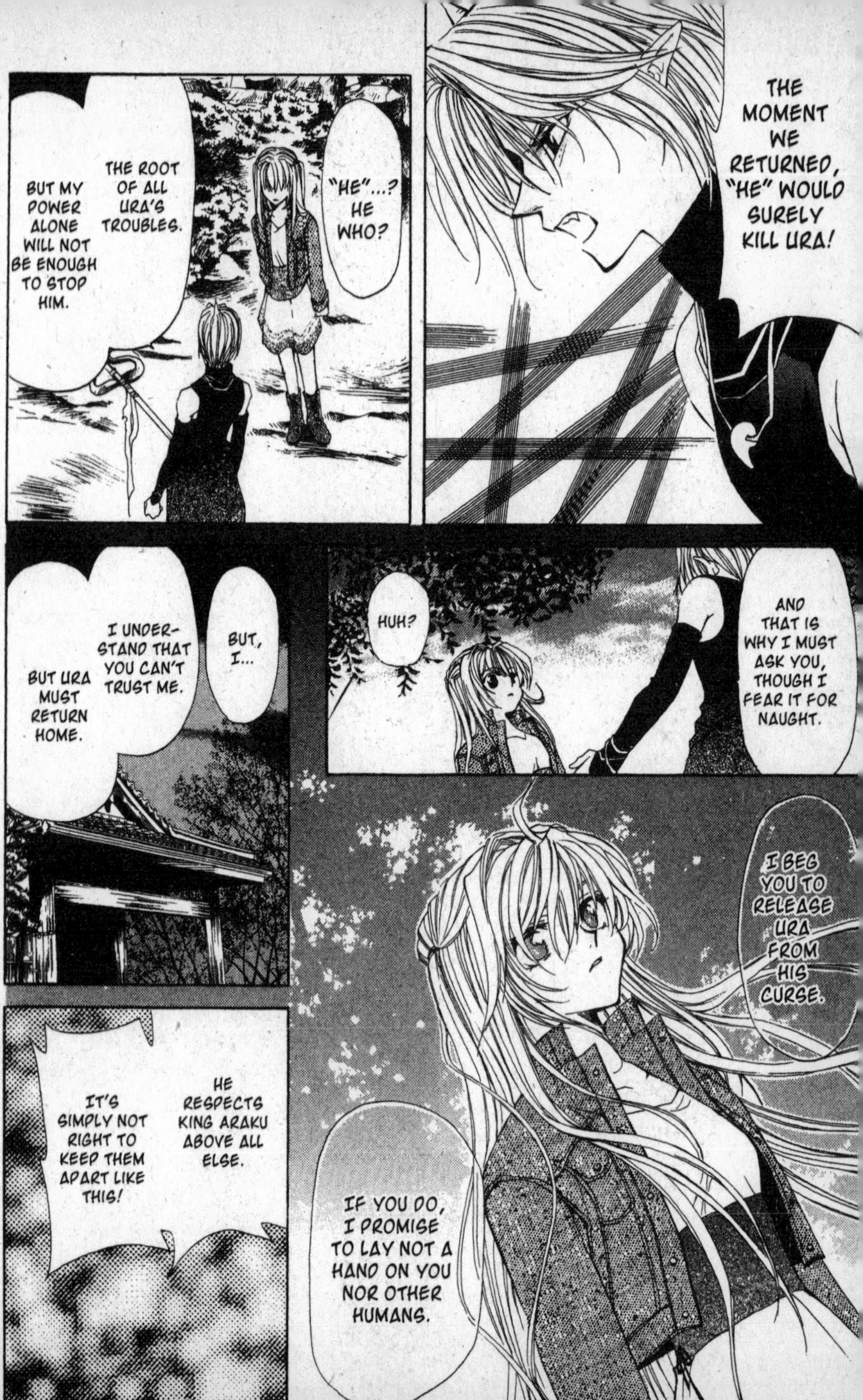
THE MOMENT WE RETURNED, "HE" WOULD SURELY KILL URA!
"HE"...? HE WHO?
THE ROOT OF ALL URA'S TROUBLES.
BUT MY POWER ALONE WILL NOT BE ENOUGH TO STOP HIM.
AND THAT IS WHY I MUST ASK YOU, THOUGH I FEAR IT FOR NAUGHT.
HUH?
I BEG YOU TO RELEASE URA FROM HIS CURSE.
IF YOU DO, I PROMISE TO LAY NOT A HAND ON YOU NOR OTHER HUMANS.
BUT, I...
I UNDER-STAND THAT YOU CAN'T TRUST ME.
BUT URA MUST RETURN HOME.
HE RESPECTS KING ARAKU ABOVE ALL ELSE.
IT'S SIMPLY NOT RIGHT TO KEEP THEM APART LIKE THIS!

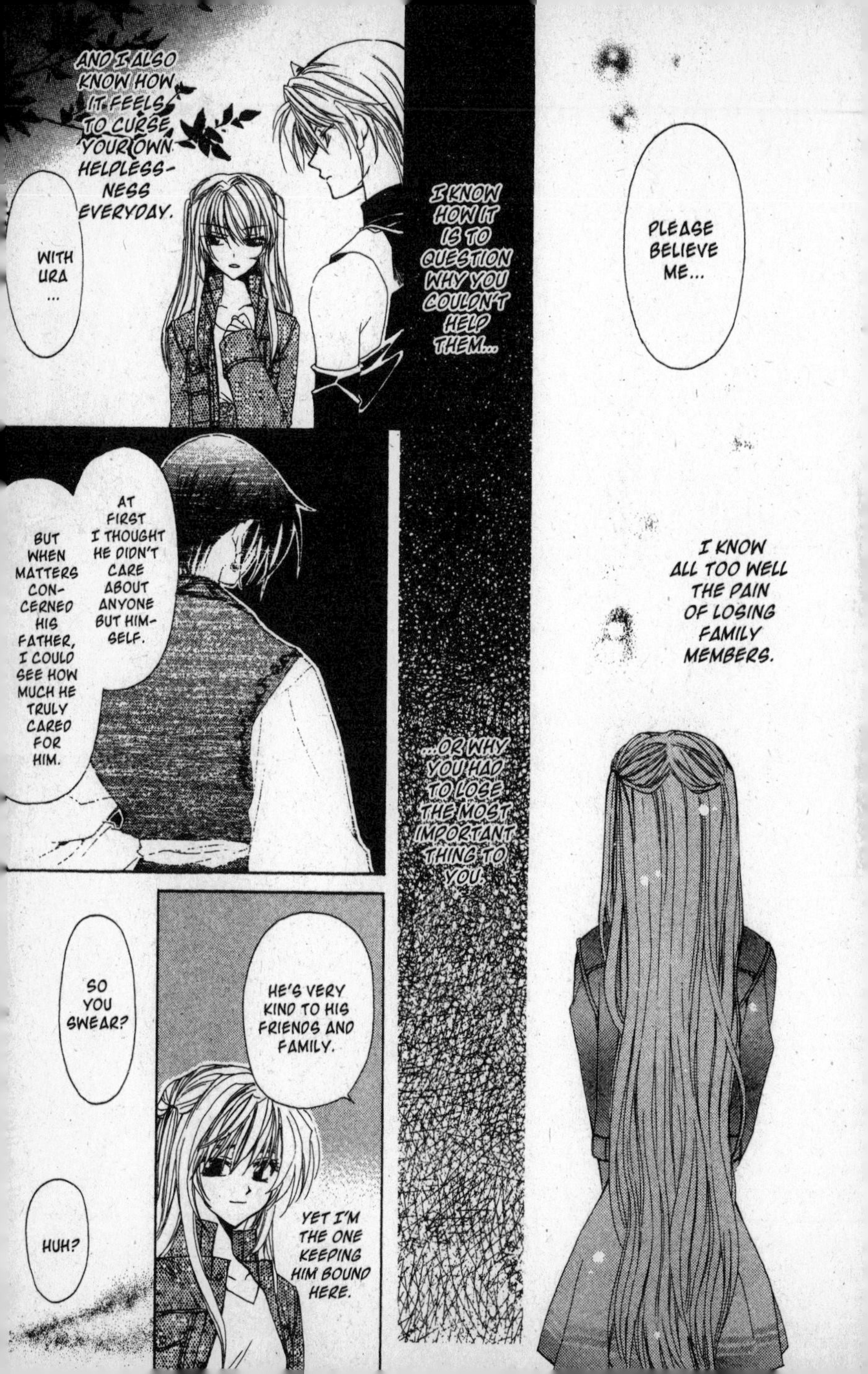
PLEASE BELIEVE ME...
I KNOW ALL TOO WELL THE PAIN OF LOSING FAMILY MEMBERS.
I KNOW HOW IT IS TO QUESTION WHY YOU COULDN'T HELP THEM...
...OR WHY YOU HAD TO LOSE THE MOST IMPORTANT THING TO YOU.
AND I ALSO KNOW HOW IT FEELS TO CURSE YOUR OWN HELPLESS-NESS EVERYDAY.
WITH URA ...
AT FIRST I THOUGHT HE DIDN'T CARE ABOUT ANYONE BUT HIM-SELF.
BUT WHEN MATTERS CON-CERNED HIS FATHER, I COULD SEE HOW MUCH HE TRULY CARED FOR HIM.
HE'S VERY KIND TO HIS FRIENDS AND FAMILY.
SO YOU SWEAR?
YET I'M THE ONE KEEPING HIM BOUND HERE.
HUH?

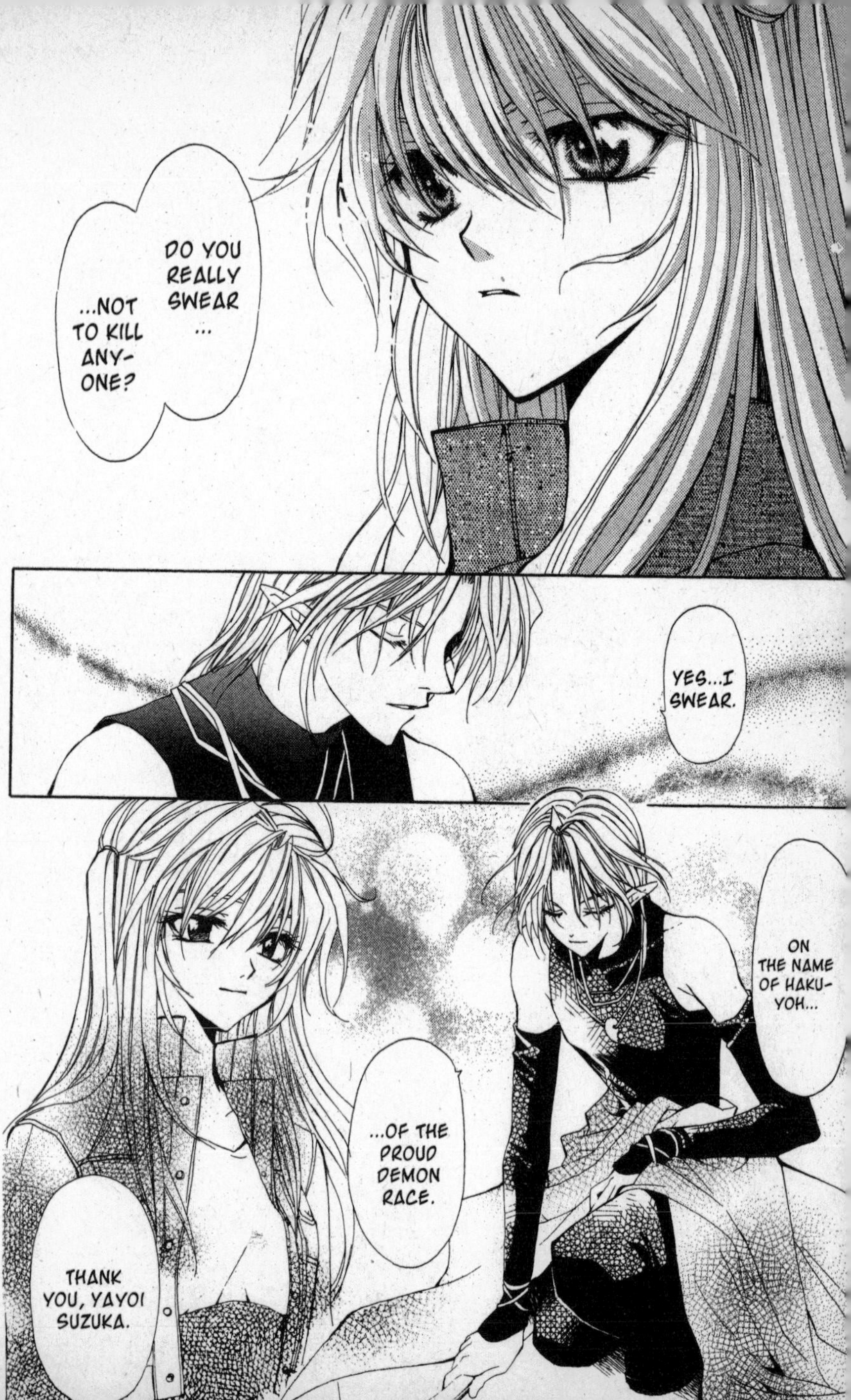
DO YOU REALLY SWEAR ...
...NOT TO KILL ANY-ONE?
YES...I SWEAR.
ON THE NAME OF HAKU-YOH...
...OF THE PROUD DEMON RACE.
THANK YOU, YAYOI SUZUKA.

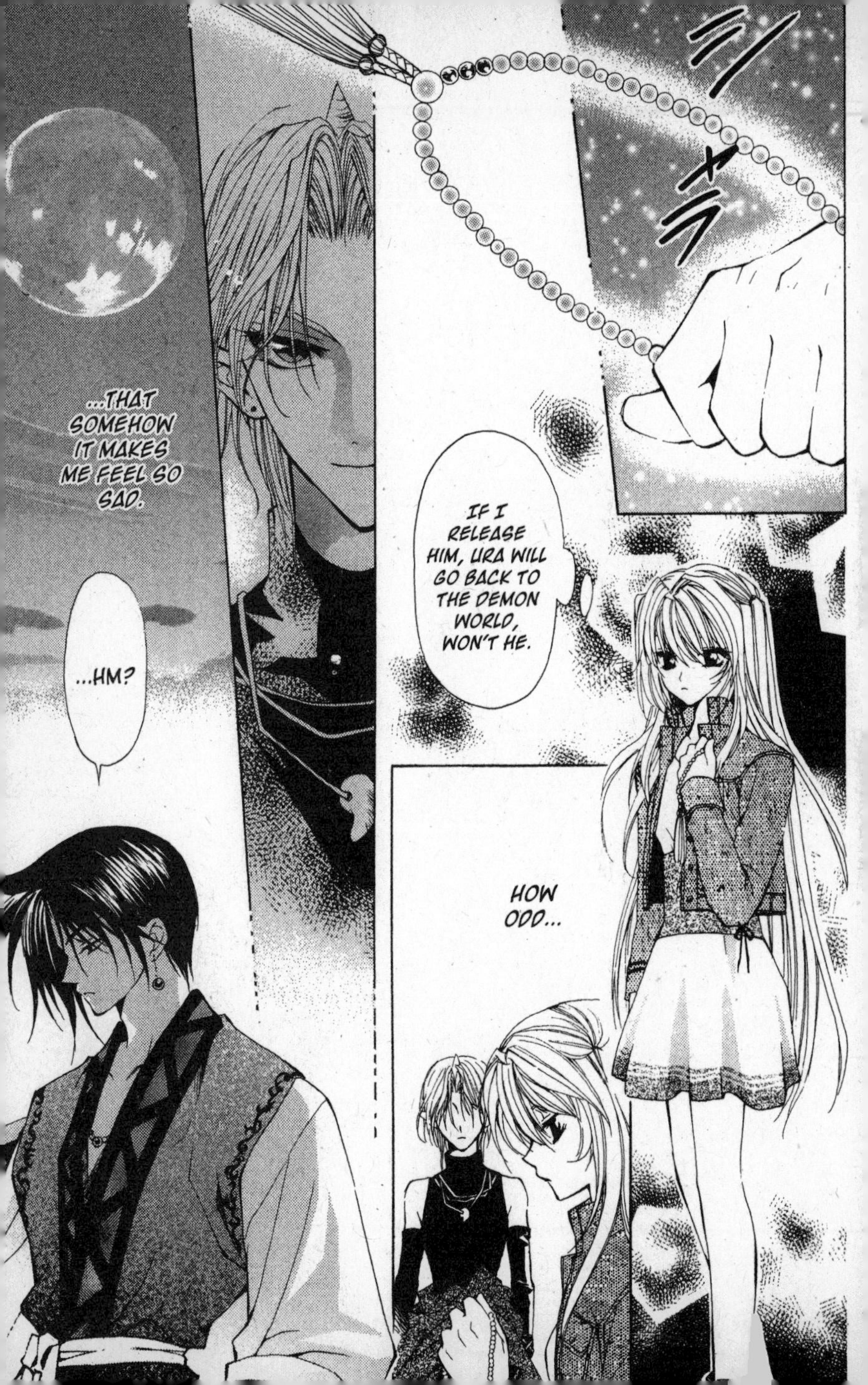
シャラ
IF I RELEASE HIM, URA WILL GO BACK TO THE DEMON WORLD, WON'T HE.
HOW ODD...
...THAT SOMEHOW IT MAKES ME FEEL SO SAD.
...HM?

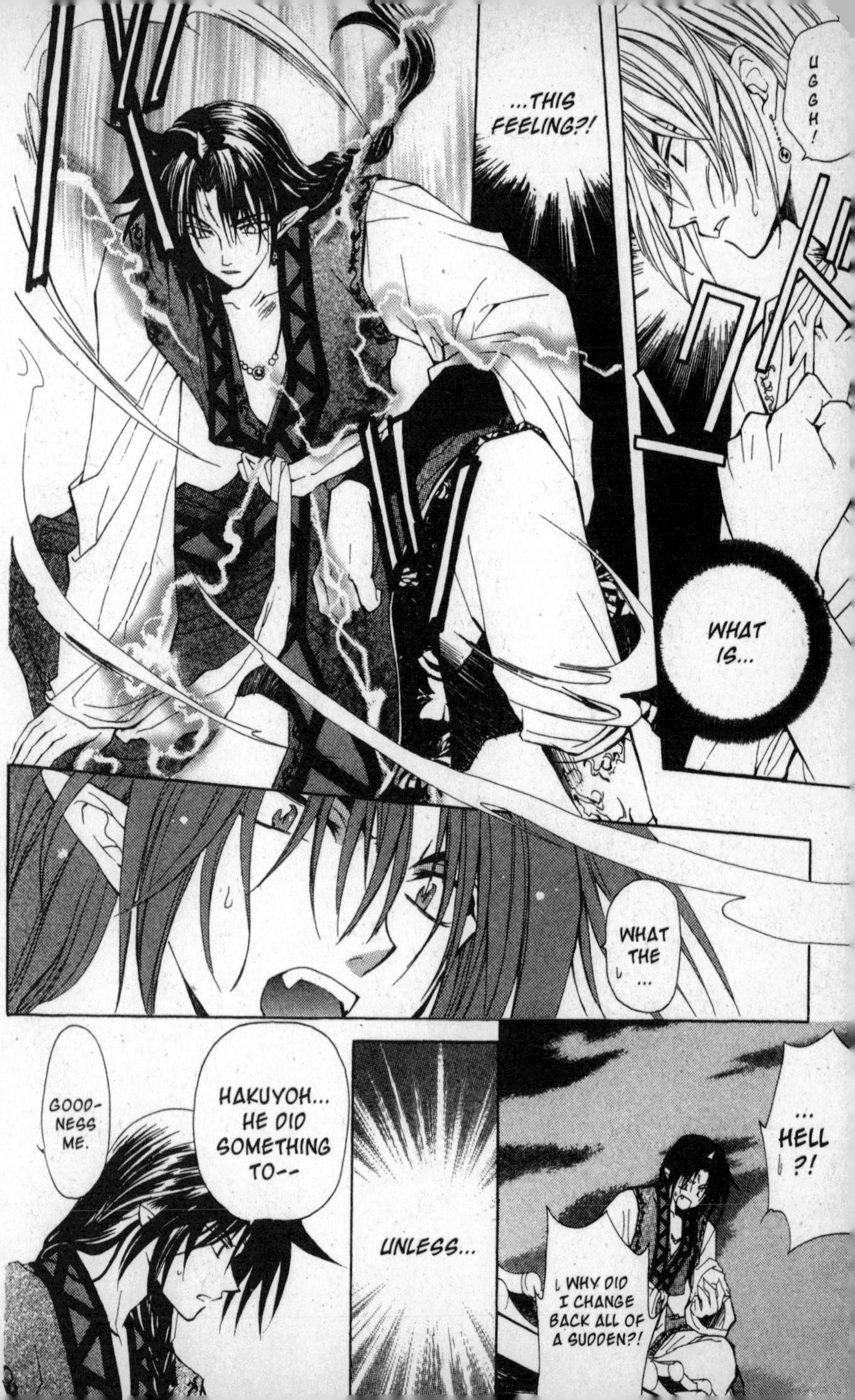
UGGH!
WHAT IS...
...THIS FEELING?!
WHAT THE ...
...HELL?!
WHY DID I CHANGE BACK ALL OF A SUDDEN?!
UNLESS...
HAKUYOH... HE DID SOMETHING TO--
GOODNESS ME.

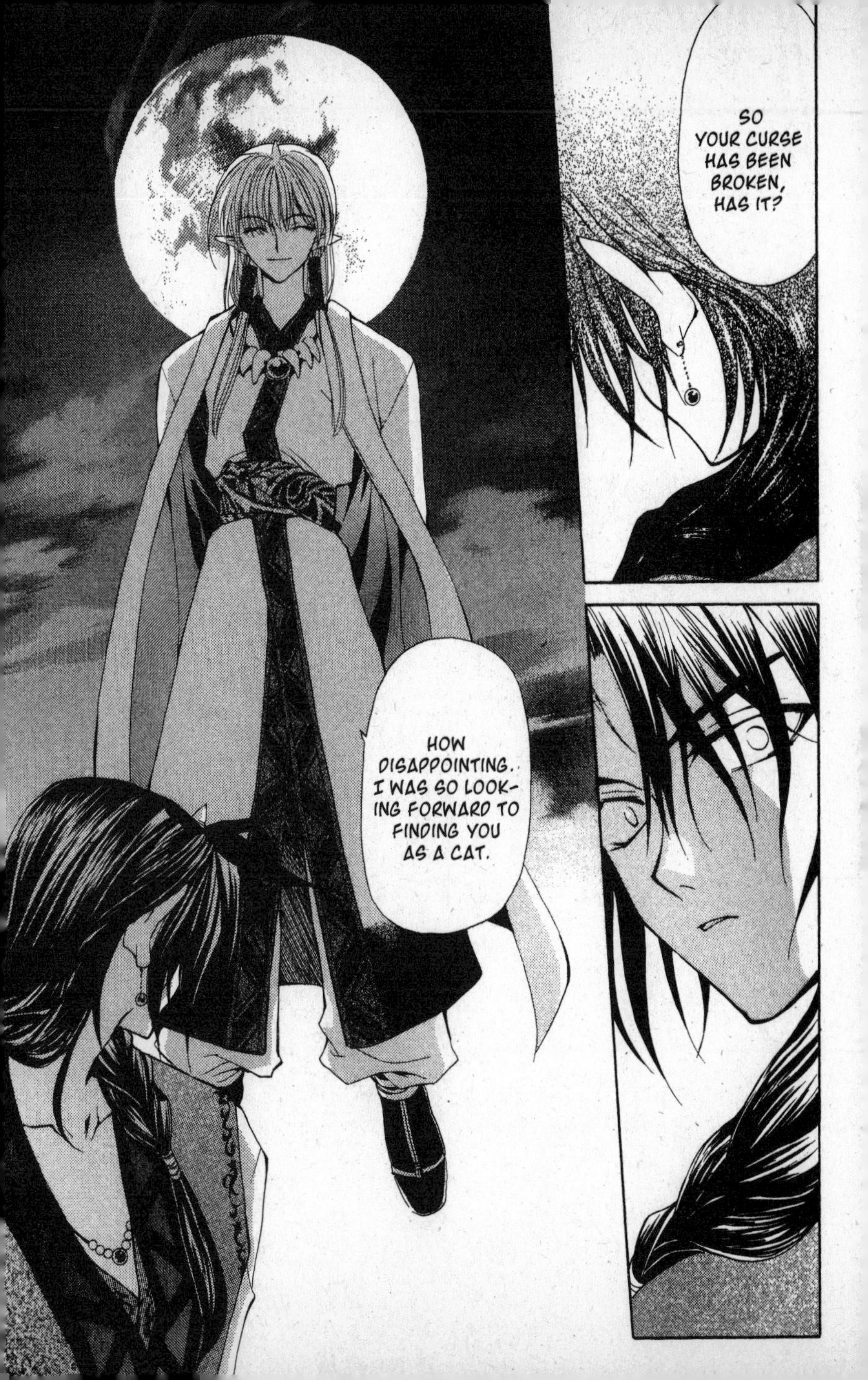
SO YOUR CURSE HAS BEEN BROKEN, HAS IT?
HOW DISAPPOINTING. I WAS SO LOOKING FORWARD TO FINDING YOU AS A CAT.

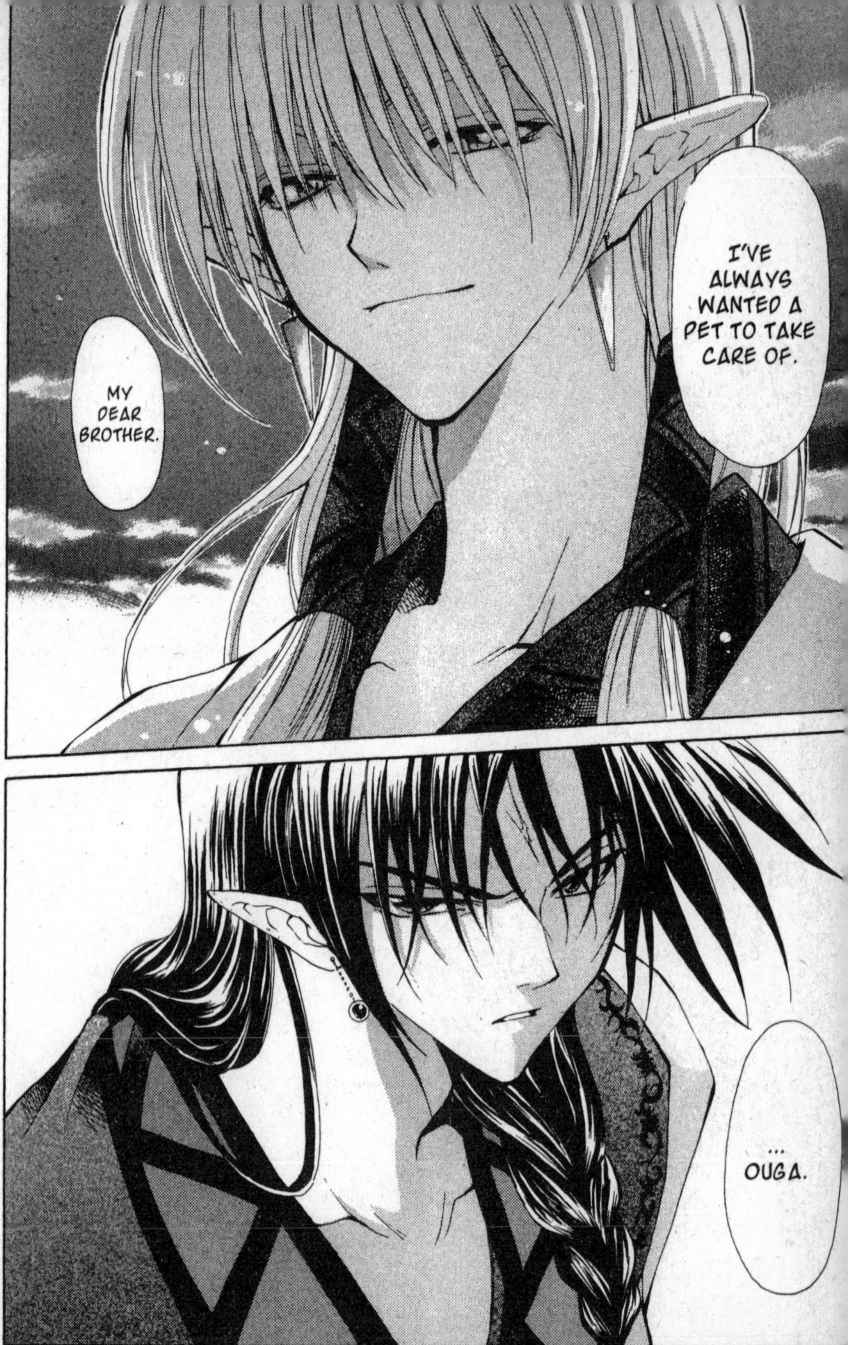
I'VE ALWAYS WANTED A PET TO TAKE CARE OF.
MY DEAR BROTHER.
... OUGA.

Act 4/The End

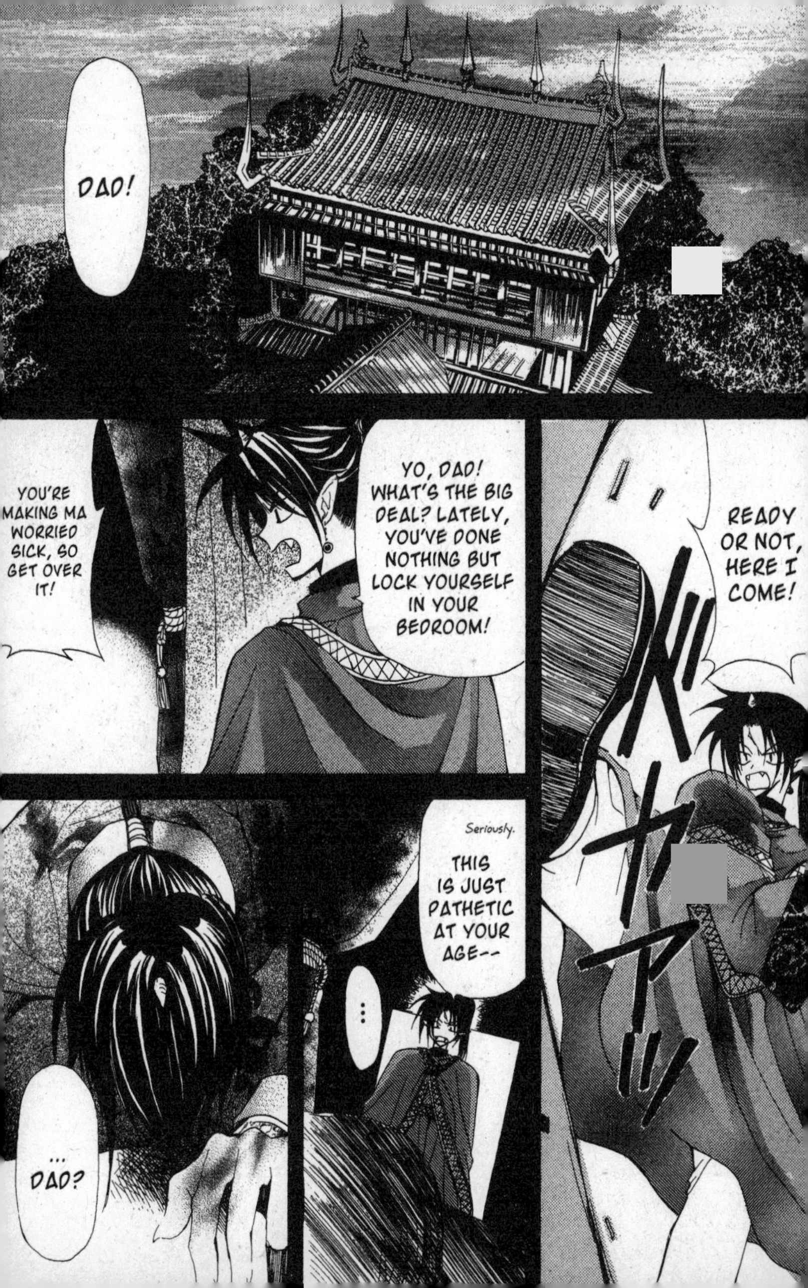
DAD!
READY OR NOT, HERE I COME!
YO, DAD! WHAT'S THE BIG DEAL? LATELY, YOU'VE DONE NOTHING BUT LOCK YOURSELF IN YOUR BEDROOM!
YOU'RE MAKING MA WORRIED SICK, SO GET OVER IT!
Seriously.
THIS IS JUST PATHETIC AT YOUR AGE--
...
... DAD?

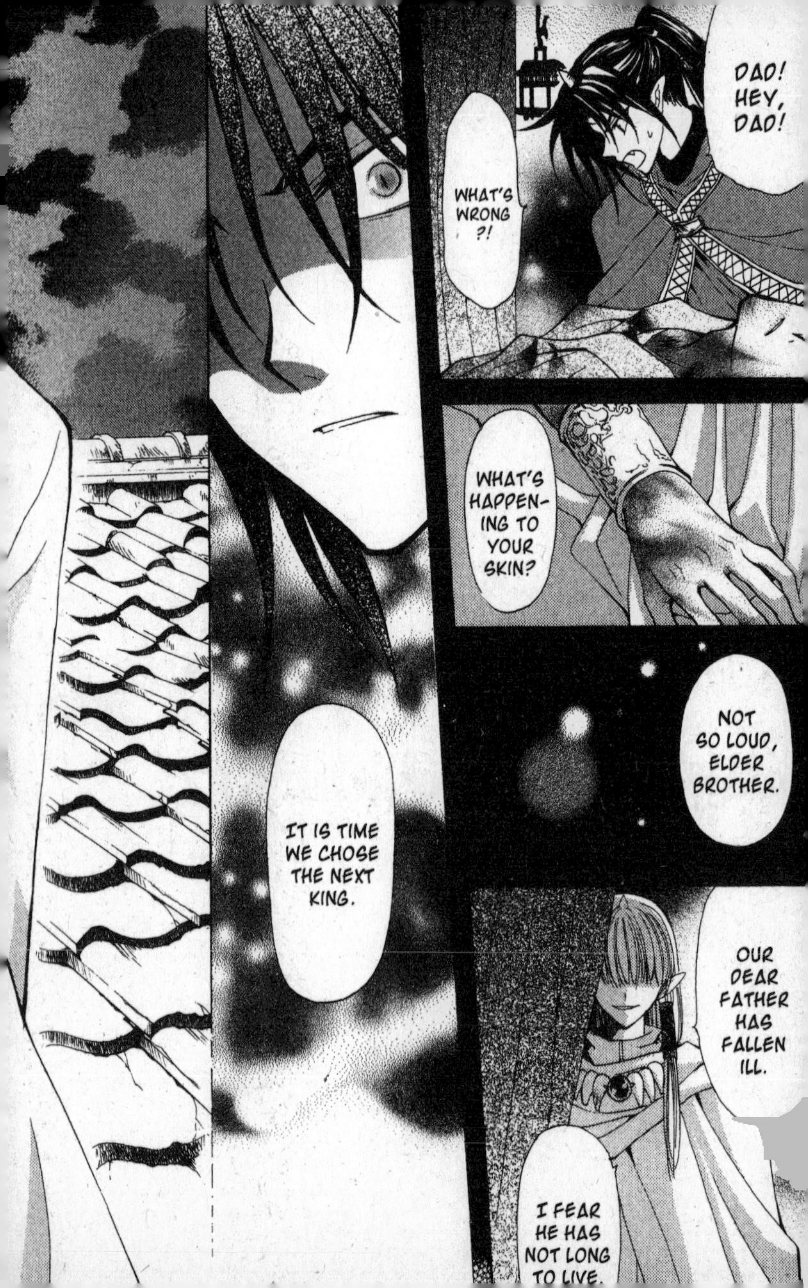
DAO! HEY, DAO!
WHAT'S WRONG ?!
WHAT'S HAPPEN-ING TO YOUR SKIN?
NOT SO LOUD, ELDER BROTHER.
OUR DEAR FATHER HAS FALLEN ILL.
I FEAR HE HAS NOT LONG TO LIVE.
IT IS TIME WE CHOSE THE NEXT KING.

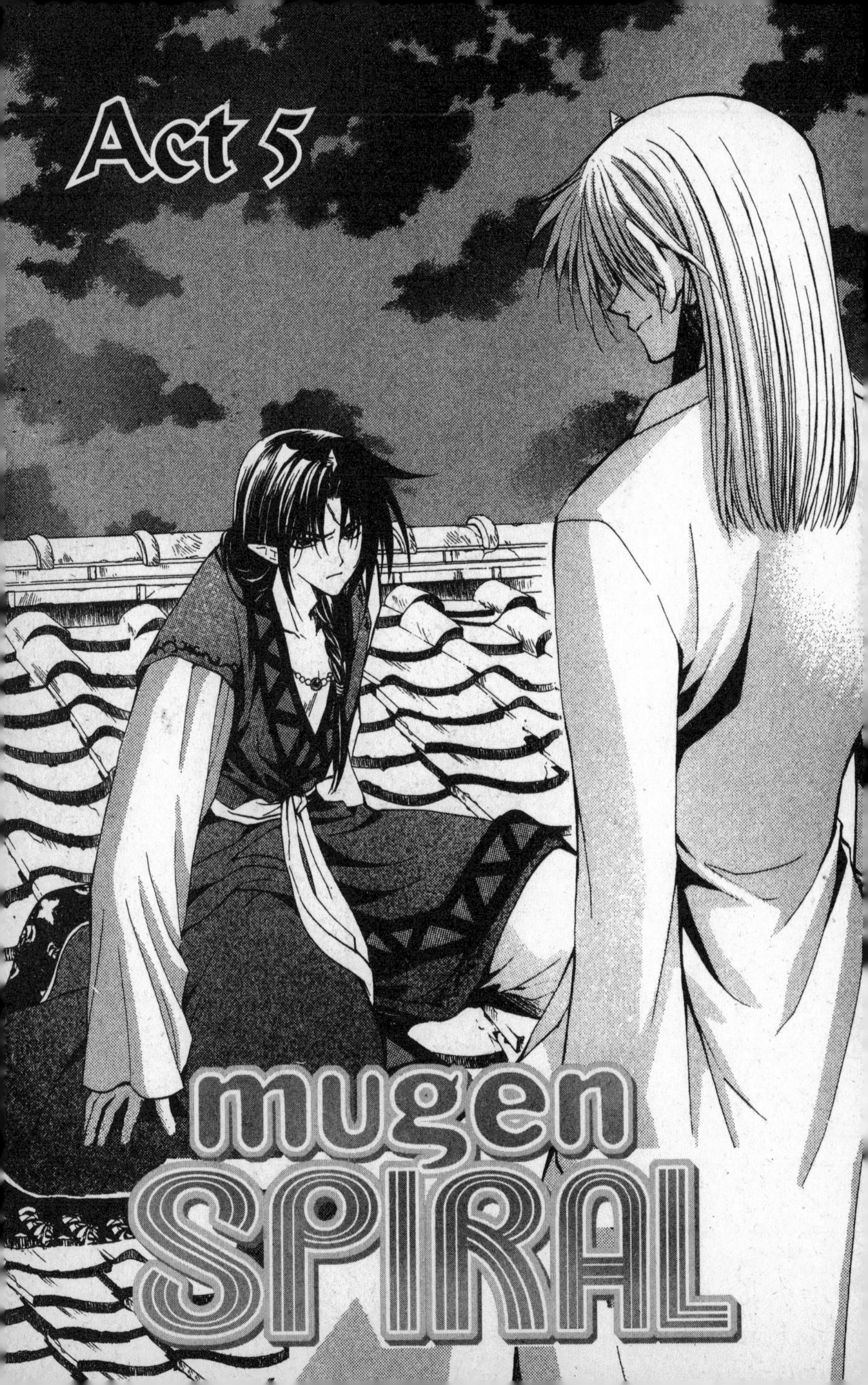
Act 5
mugen
SPIRAL

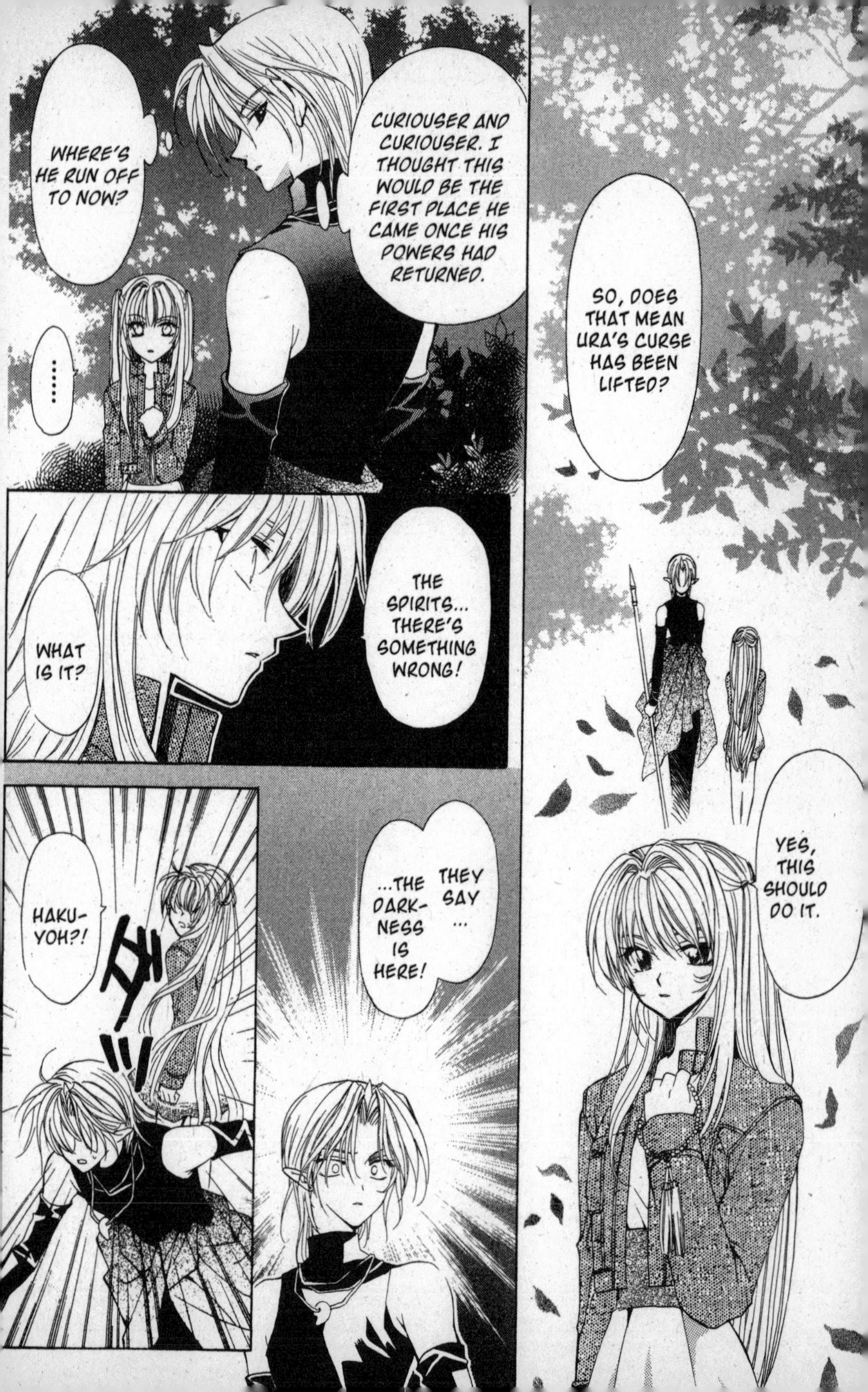
SO, DOES THAT MEAN URA'S CURSE HAS BEEN LIFTED?
YES, THIS SHOULD DO IT.
CURIOUSER AND CURIOUSER. I THOUGHT THIS WOULD BE THE FIRST PLACE HE CAME ONCE HIS POWERS HAD RETURNED.
WHERE'S HE RUN OFF TO NOW?
......
THE SPIRITS... THERE'S SOMETHING WRONG!
WHAT IS IT?
THEY SAY ...
...THE DARK-NESS IS HERE!
HAKU-YOH?!

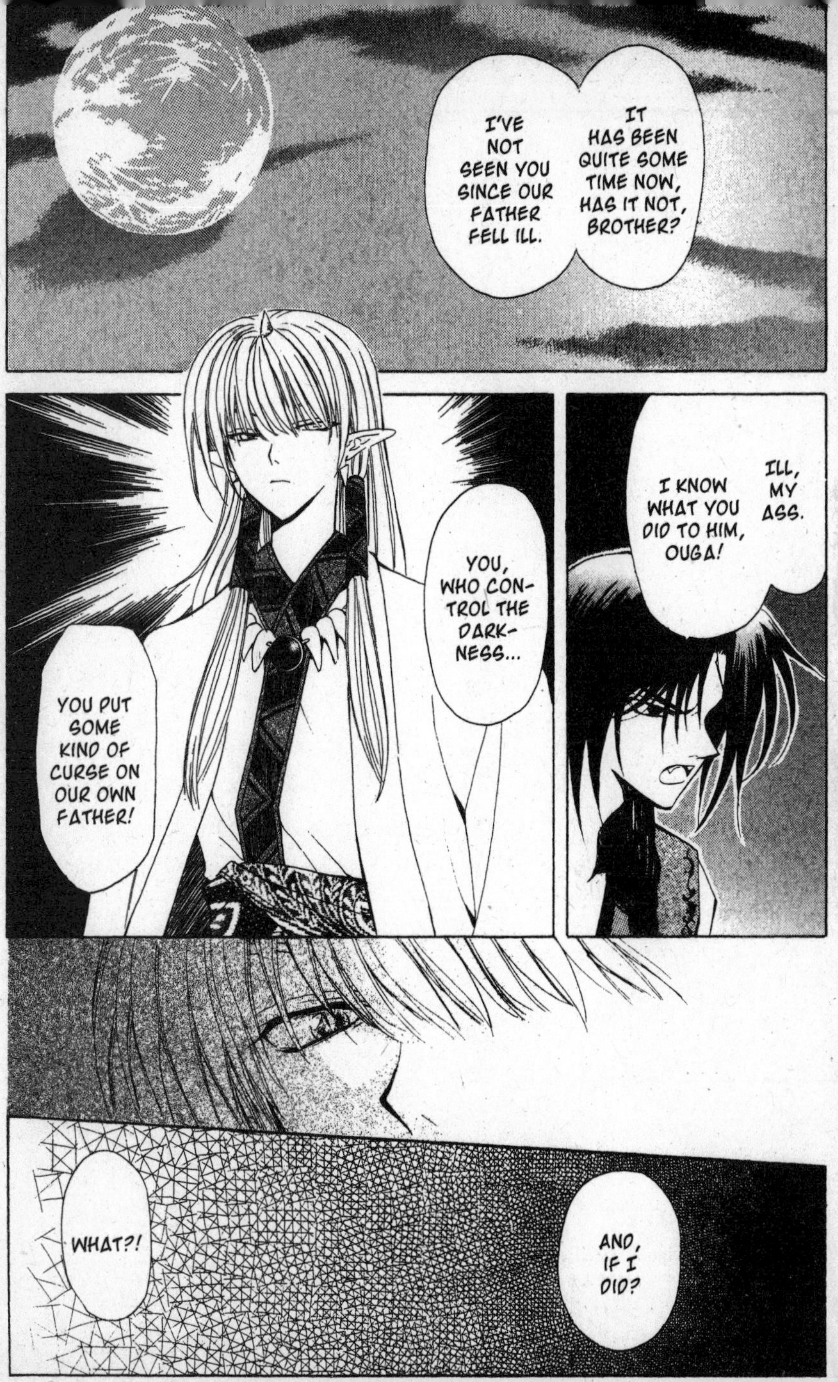
IT HAS BEEN QUITE SOME TIME NOW, HAS IT NOT, BROTHER?
I'VE NOT SEEN YOU SINCE OUR FATHER FELL ILL.
ILL, MY ASS.
I KNOW WHAT YOU DID TO HIM, OUGA!
YOU, WHO CON-TROL THE DARK-NESS...
YOU PUT SOME KIND OF CURSE ON OUR OWN FATHER!
AND, IF I DID?
WHAT?!

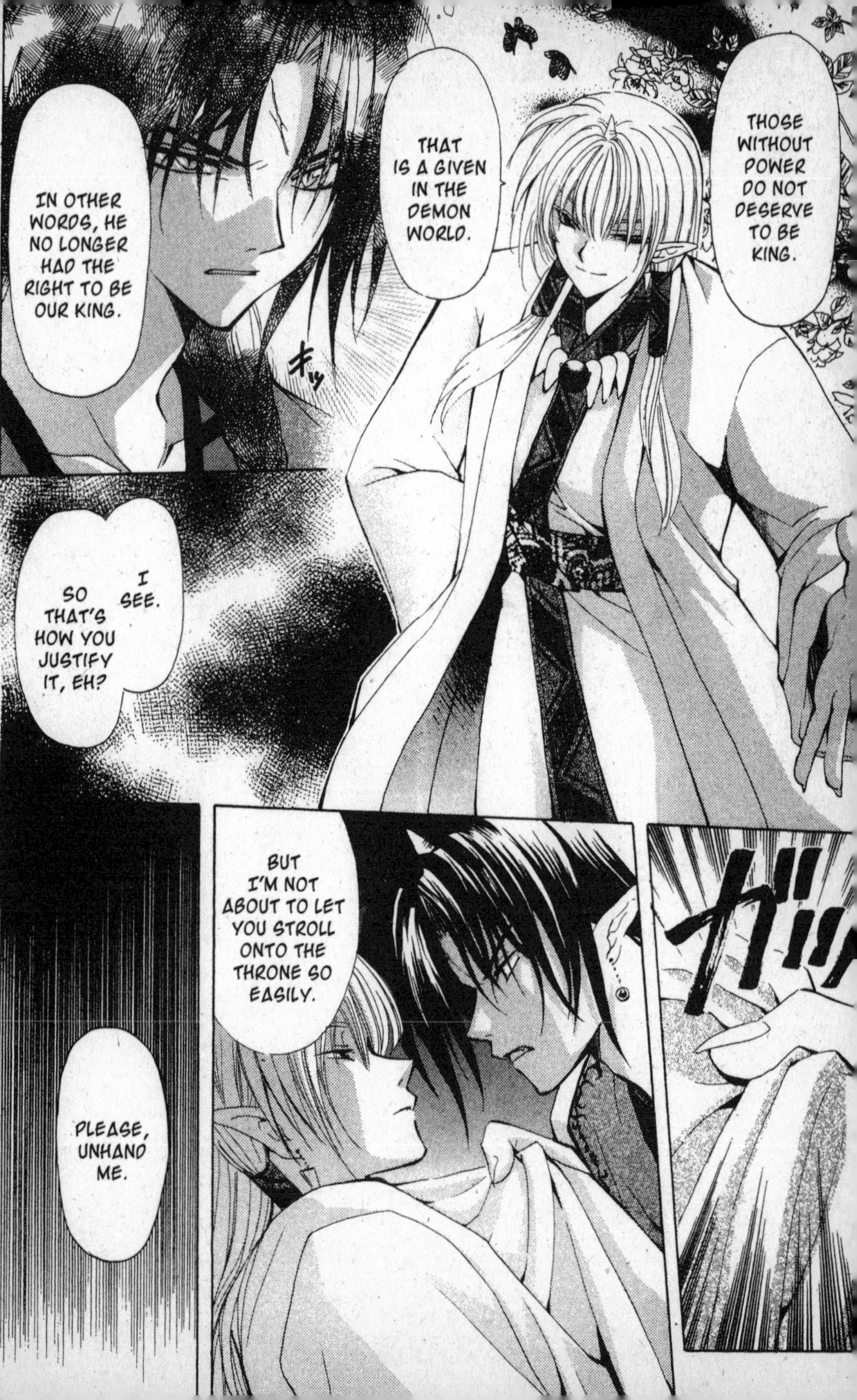
THOSE WITHOUT POWER DO NOT DESERVE TO BE KING.
THAT IS A GIVEN IN THE DEMON WORLD.
IN OTHER WORDS, HE NO LONGER HAD THE RIGHT TO BE OUR KING.
ギッ
I SEE.
SO THAT'S HOW YOU JUSTIFY IT, EH?
ガッ
BUT I'M NOT ABOUT TO LET YOU STROLL ONTO THE THRONE SO EASILY.
PLEASE, UNHAND ME.

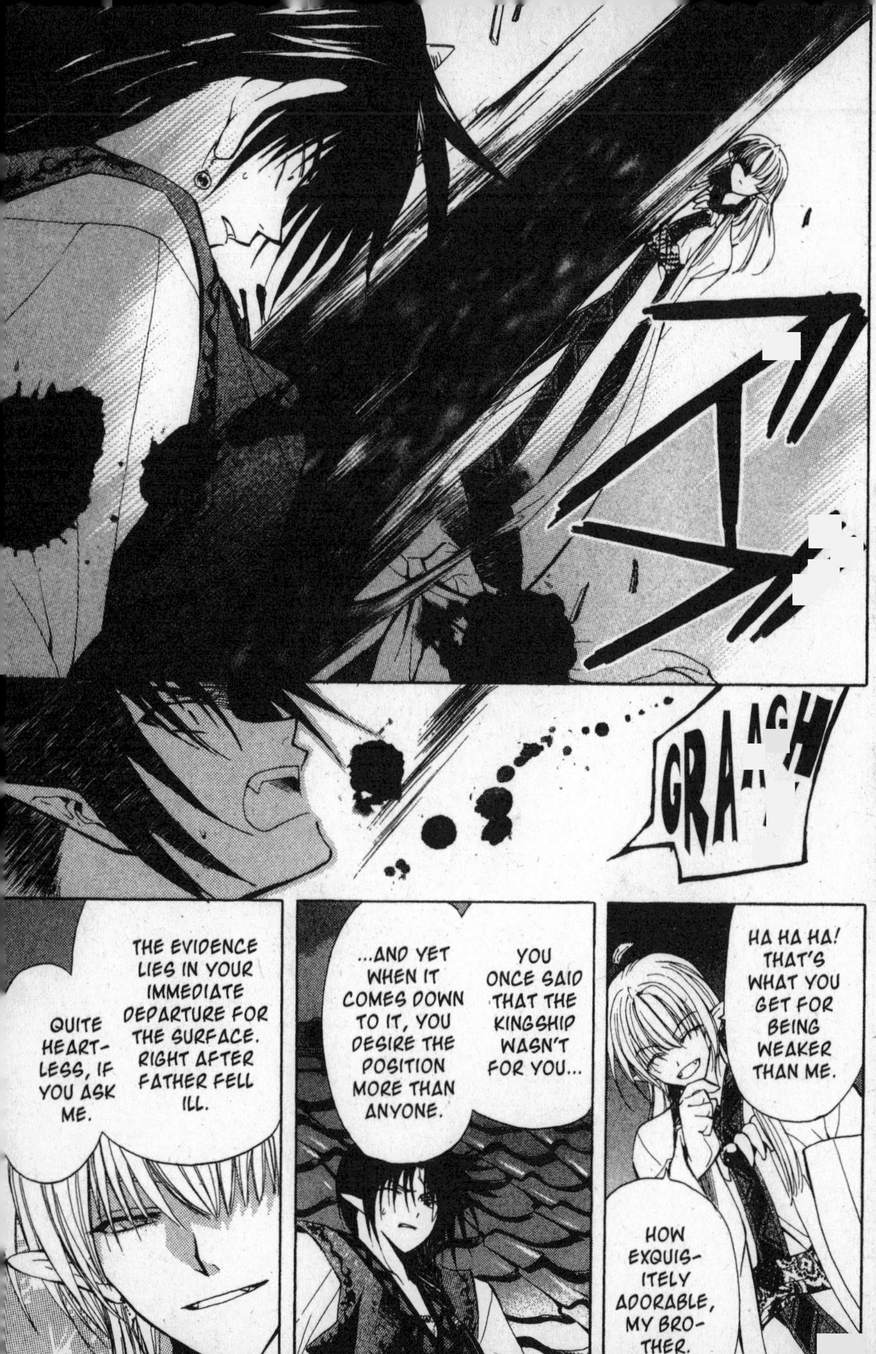
GRA
HA HA HA! THAT'S WHAT YOU GET FOR BEING WEAKER THAN ME.
HOW EXQUISITELY ADORABLE, MY BROTHER.
YOU ONCE SAID THAT THE KINGSHIP WASN'T FOR YOU...
...AND YET WHEN IT COMES DOWN TO IT, YOU DESIRE THE POSITION MORE THAN ANYONE.
THE EVIDENCE LIES IN YOUR IMMEDIATE DEPARTURE FOR THE SURFACE. RIGHT AFTER FATHER FELL ILL.
QUITE HEARTLESS, IF YOU ASK ME.

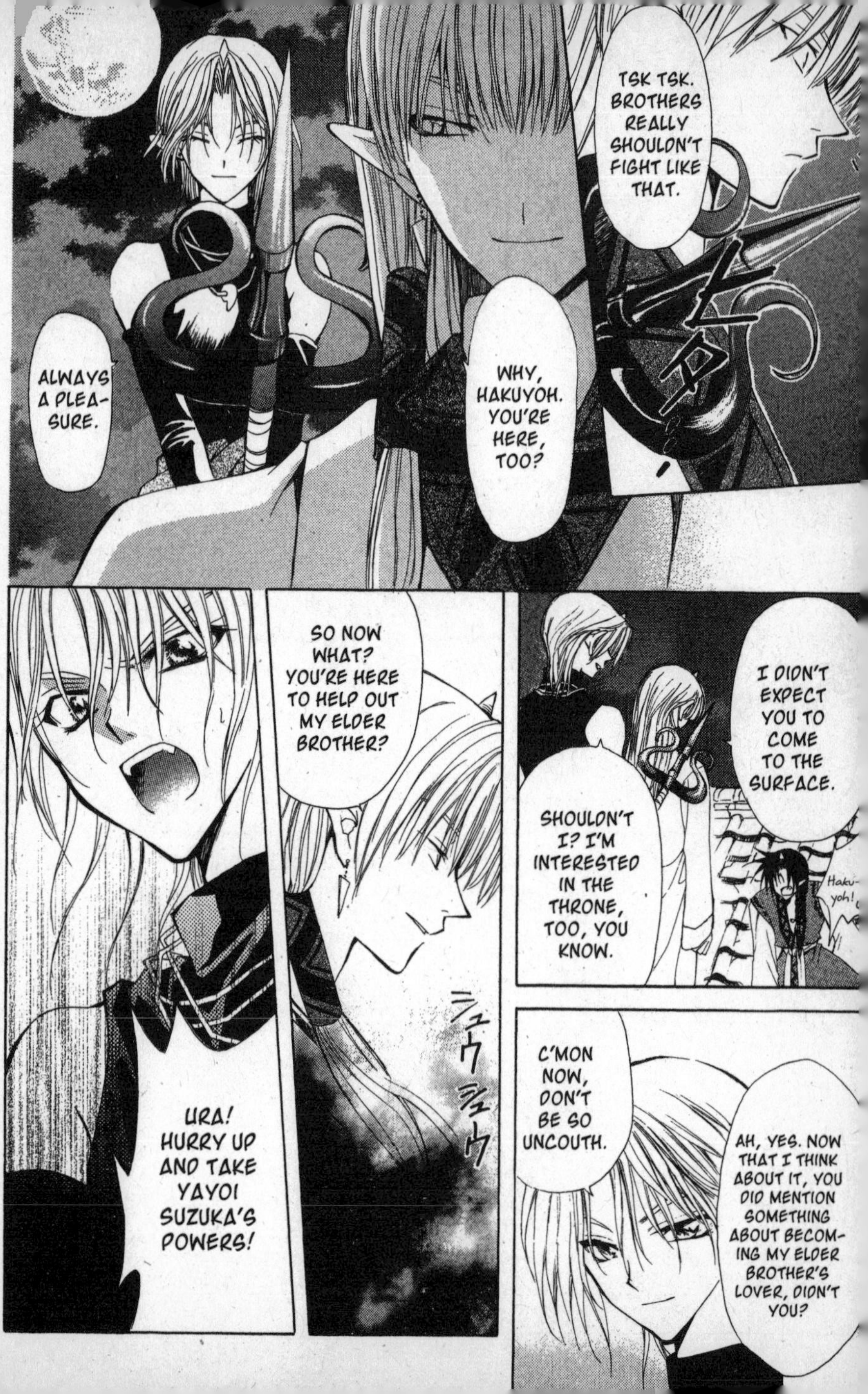
TSK TSK. BROTHERS REALLY SHOULDN'T FIGHT LIKE THAT.
WHY, HAKUYOH. YOU'RE HERE, TOO?
ALWAYS A PLEA-SURE.
I DIDN'T EXPECT YOU TO COME TO THE SURFACE.
Haku-yoh!
SHOULDN'T I? I'M INTERESTED IN THE THRONE, TOO, YOU KNOW.
SO NOW WHAT? YOU'RE HERE TO HELP OUT MY ELDER BROTHER?
AH, YES. NOW THAT I THINK ABOUT IT, YOU DID MENTION SOMETHING ABOUT BECOMING MY ELDER BROTHER'S LOVER, DIDN'T YOU?
C'MON NOW, DON'T BE SO UNCOUTH.
URA! HURRY UP AND TAKE YAYOI SUZUKA'S POWERS!

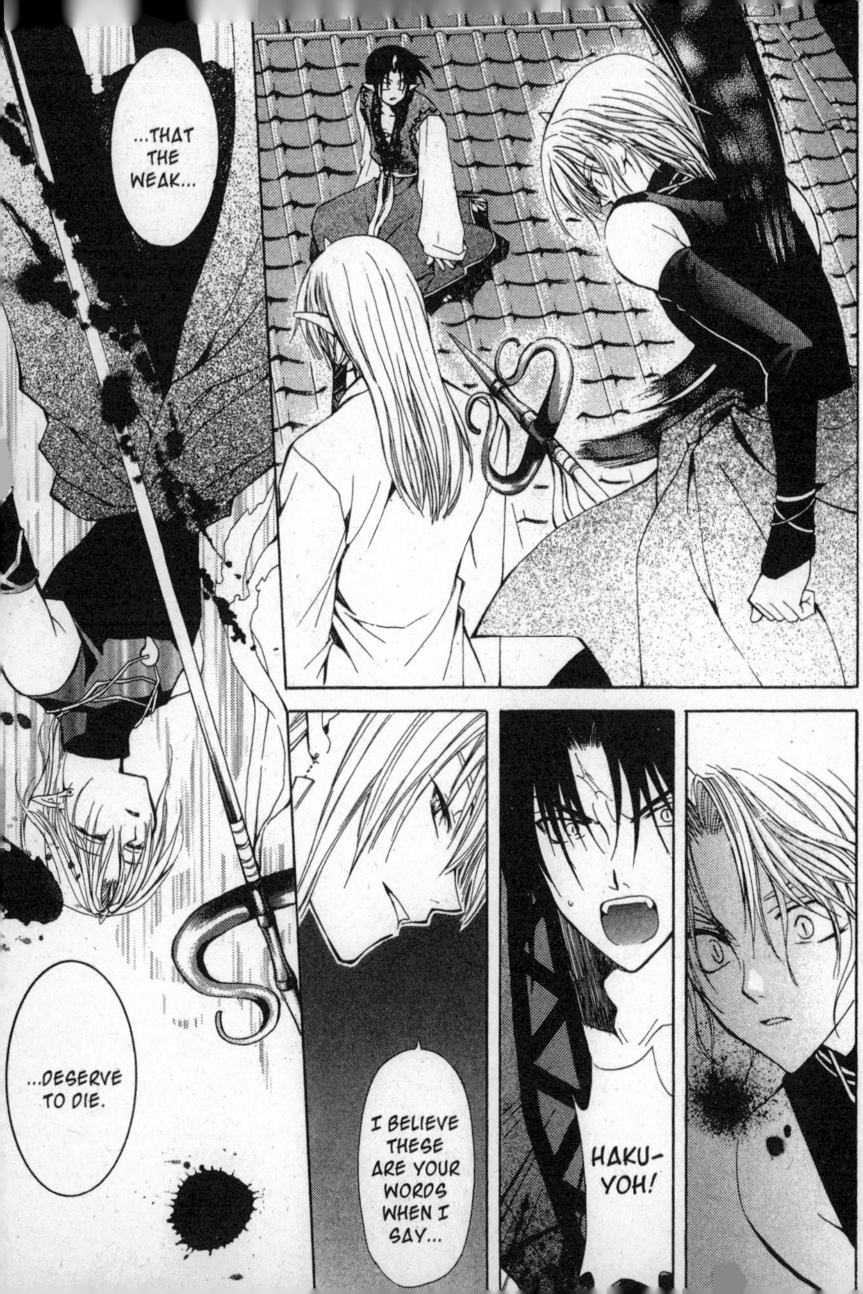
HAKU-YOH!
I BELIEVE THESE ARE YOUR WORDS WHEN I SAY...
...THAT THE WEAK...
...DESERVE TO DIE.

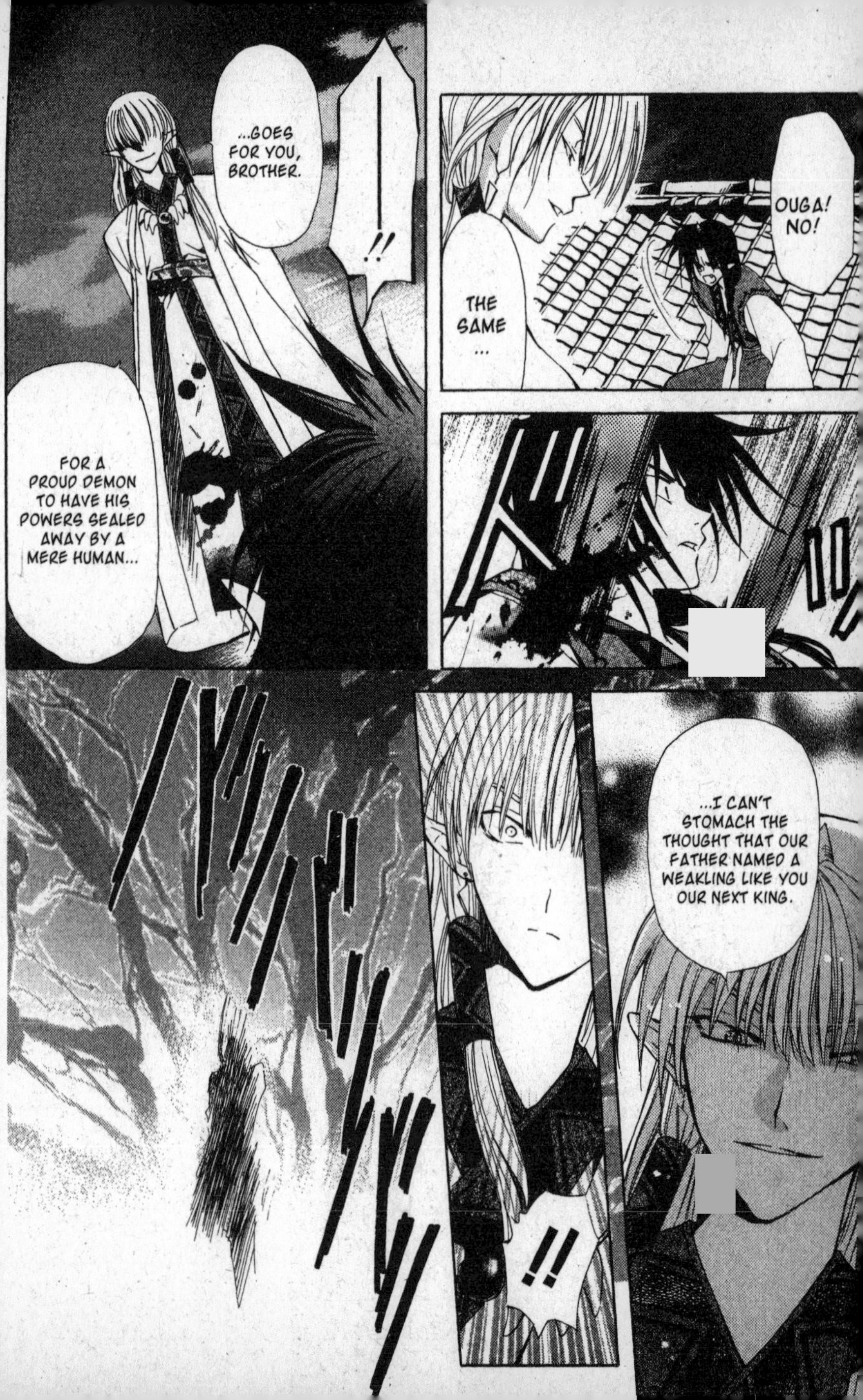
OUGA! NO!
THE SAME ...
...GOES FOR YOU, BROTHER.
!!
FOR A PROUD DEMON TO HAVE HIS POWERS SEALED AWAY BY A MERE HUMAN...
...I CAN'T STOMACH THE THOUGHT THAT OUR FATHER NAMED A WEAKLING LIKE YOU OUR NEXT KING.
!!

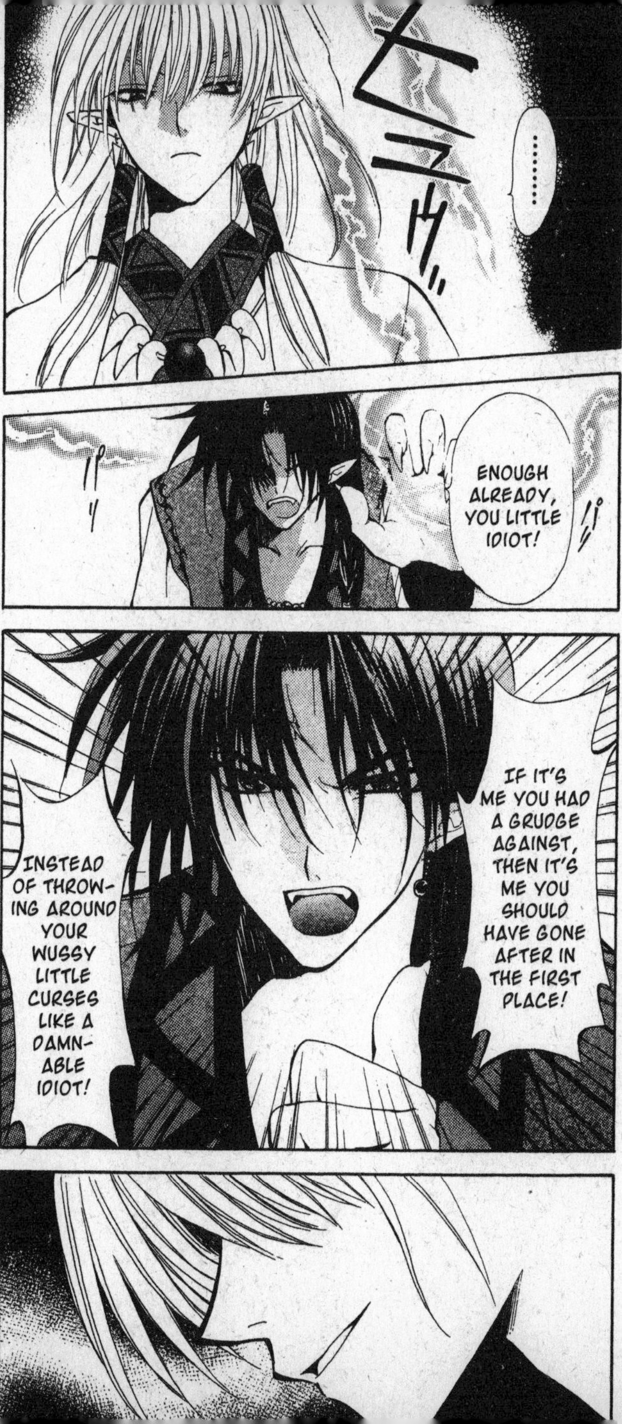
......
ENOUGH ALREADY, YOU LITTLE IDIOT!
IF IT'S ME YOU HAD A GRUDGE AGAINST, THEN IT'S ME YOU SHOULD HAVE GONE AFTER IN THE FIRST PLACE!
INSTEAD OF THROWING AROUND YOUR WUSSY LITTLE CURSES LIKE A DAMNABLE IDIOT!

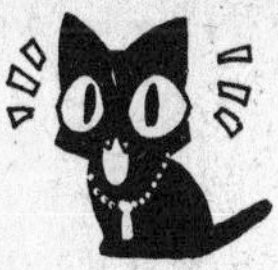

Before it got its present name, Mugen Spiral was named "Mugen Kaiki (Mysterious Demon.)" But the title sounded a little too ominous and thus, it was changed. We must have gone through at least 30 other titles after that. It was almost as hard to come up with a title as the story line itself! I figured if I provided a lot of choices, one was bound to be a good fit... but in the end, nothing came out of that batch. No matter what I proposed, it just didn't quite fit! In my haze, I even suggested "Urara." My manager asked why, "Urara," and the only response I had was, "Because it's about Ura?" (Yes, I was completely lost at the time.) Now that I think about it, once I began to draw this comic, I began to notice a lot more black cats in the neighborhood. They'd come into people's yards or just sleep around all day. I decided to chase them away one day and they got up and left slowly, glaring back at you like, "Fine, human. I'm going, I'm going." Damn you, Ura... So, if you see a black cat, please be sure to call it Ura.

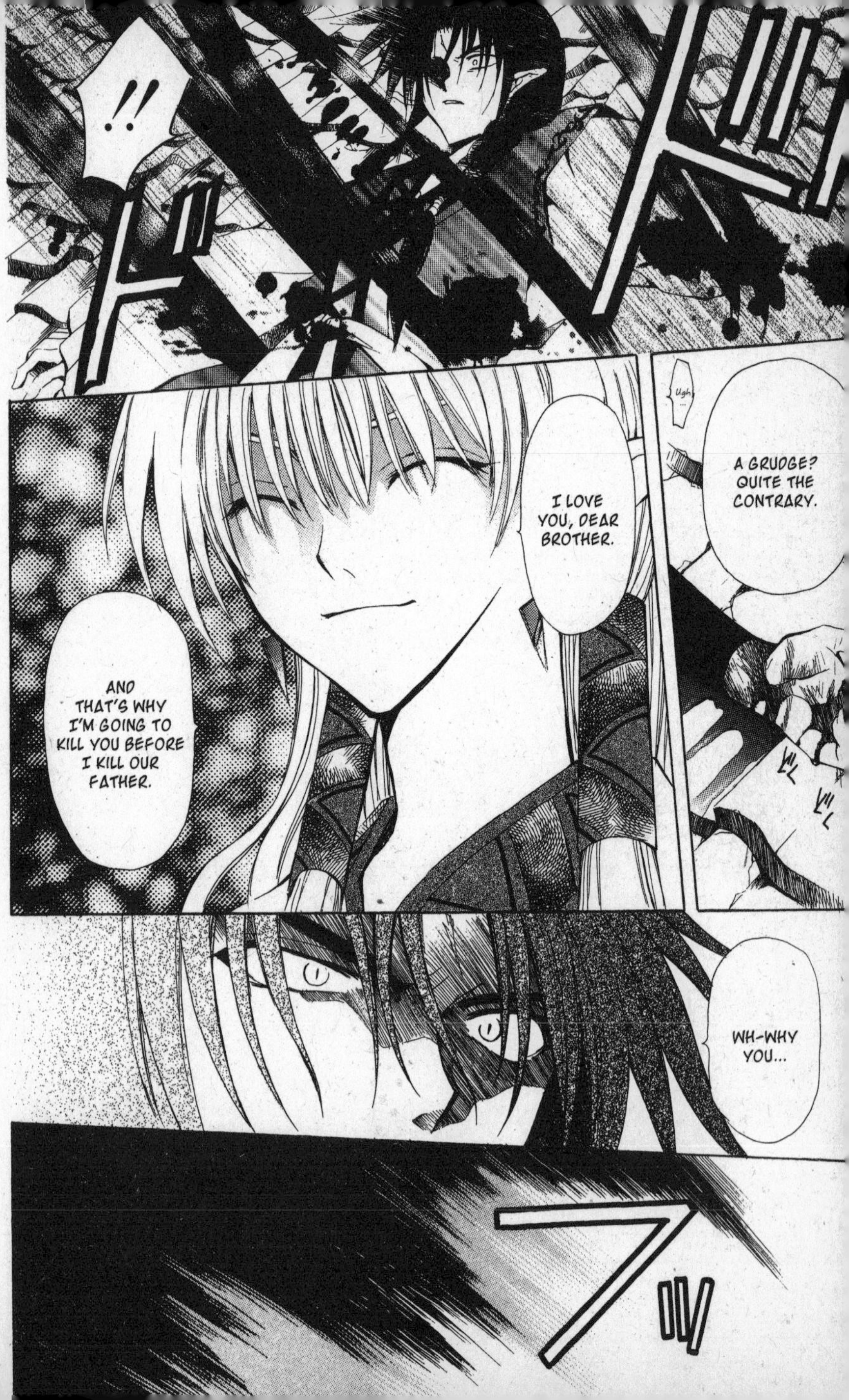
!!
Ugh...
A GRUDGE? QUITE THE CONTRARY.
I LOVE YOU, DEAR BROTHER.
AND THAT'S WHY I'M GOING TO KILL YOU BEFORE I KILL OUR FATHER.
WH-WHY YOU...

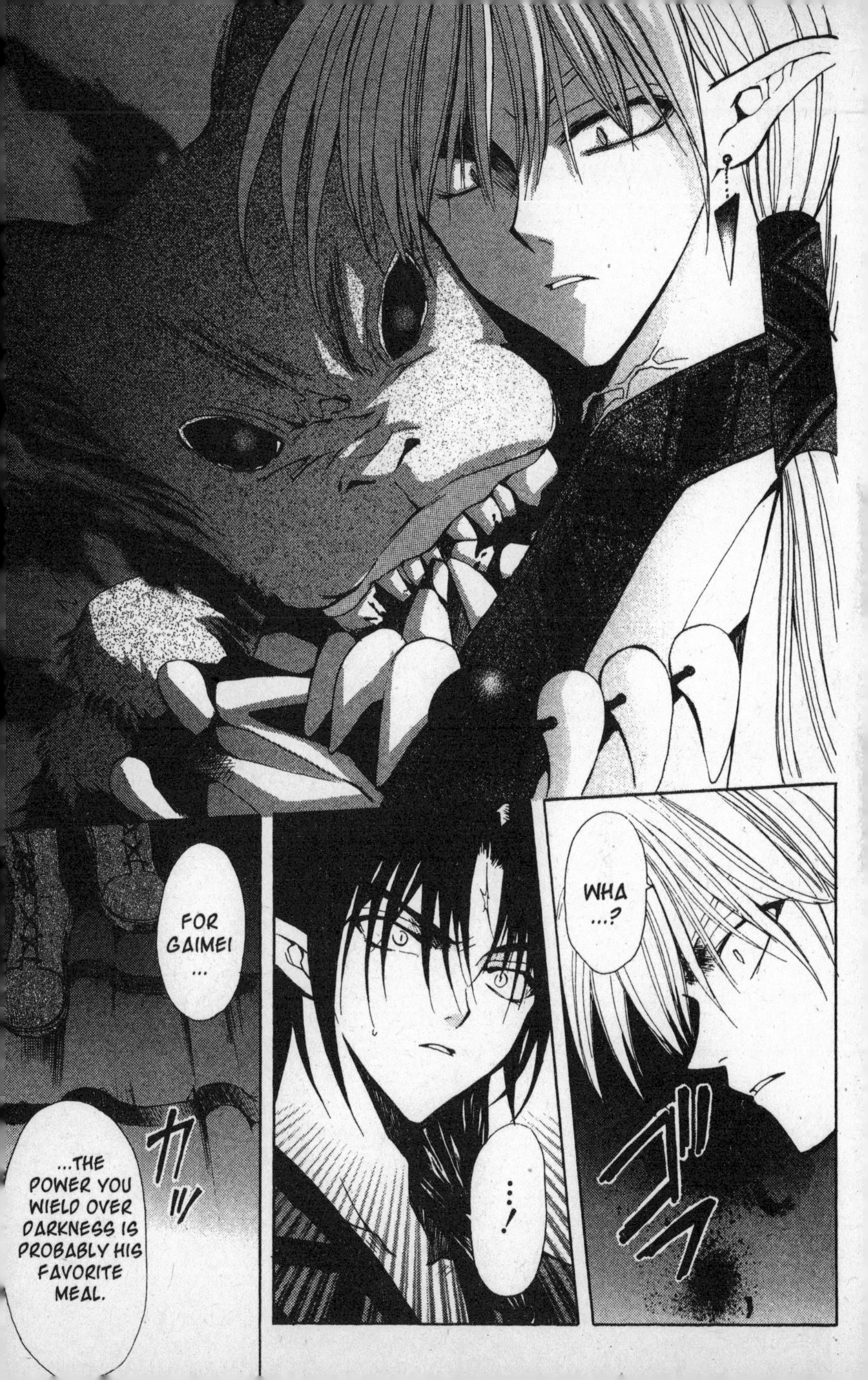
FOR GAIMEI ...
...THE POWER YOU WIELD OVER DARKNESS IS PROBABLY HIS FAVORITE MEAL.
...!
WHA ...?

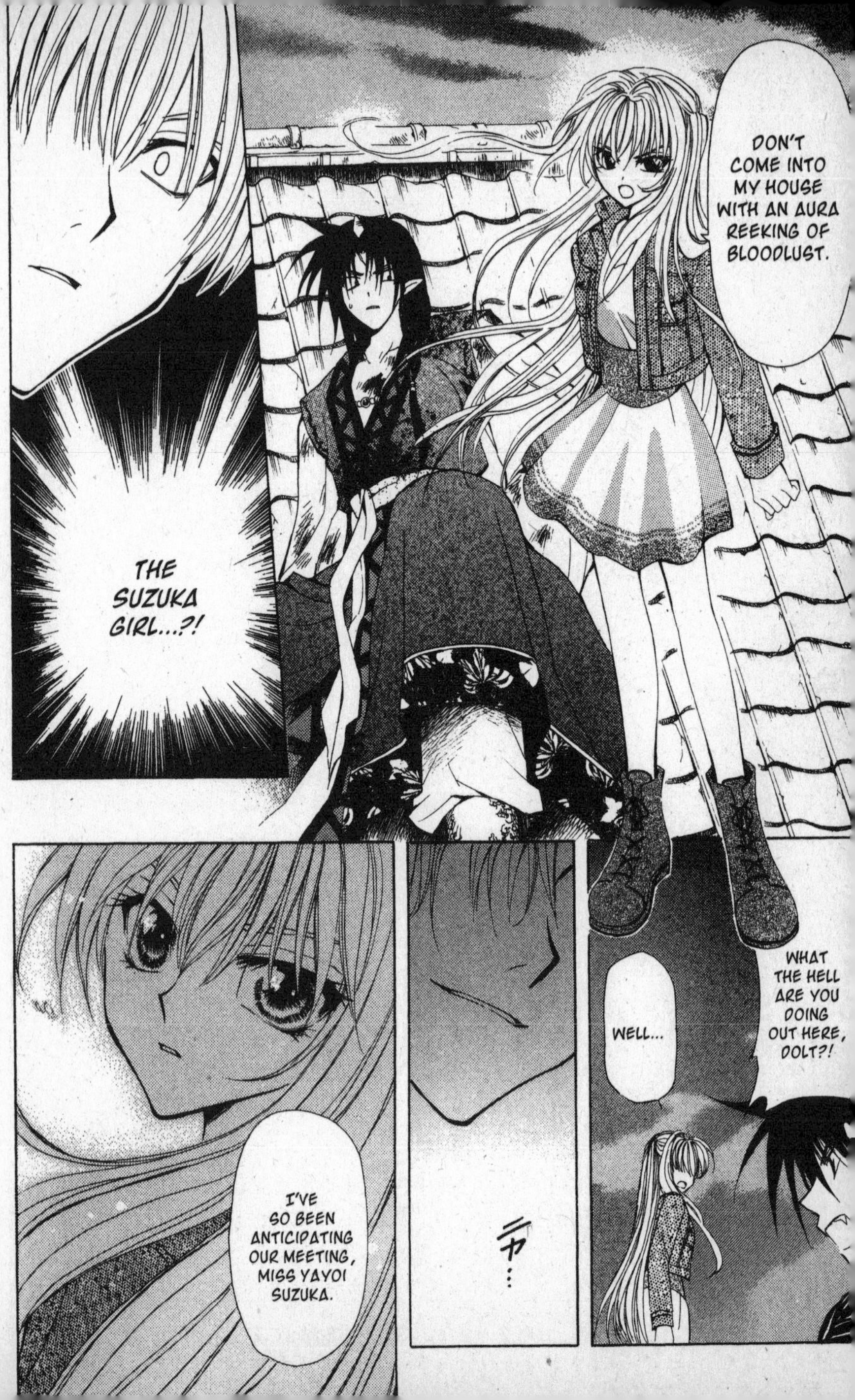

DON'T COME INTO MY HOUSE WITH AN AURA REEKING OF BLOODLUST.
THE SUZUKA GIRL...?!
WHAT THE HELL ARE YOU DOING OUT HERE, DOLT?!
WELL...
ニヤ…
I'VE SO BEEN ANTICIPATING OUR MEETING, MISS YAYOI SUZUKA.

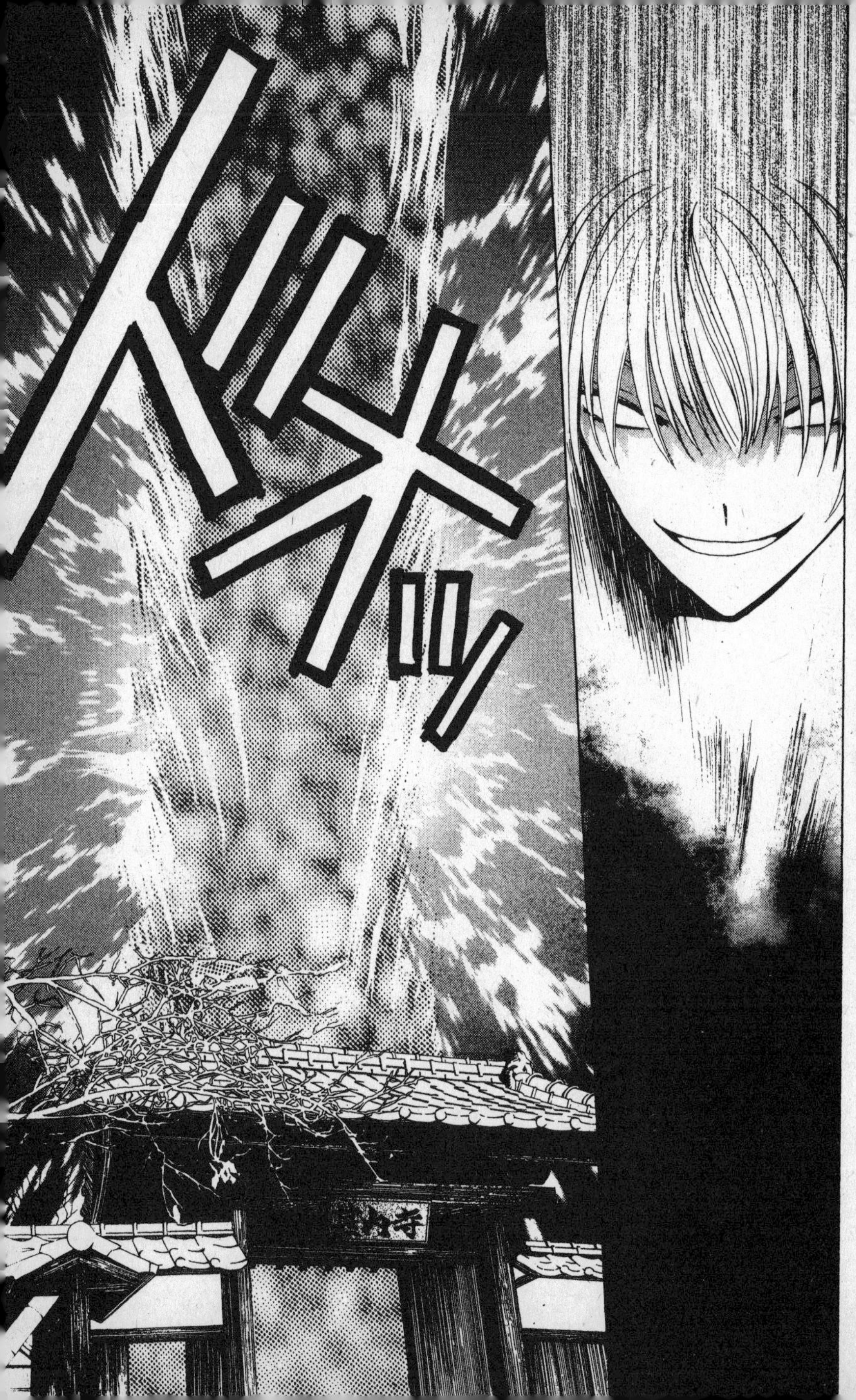
ドオッ

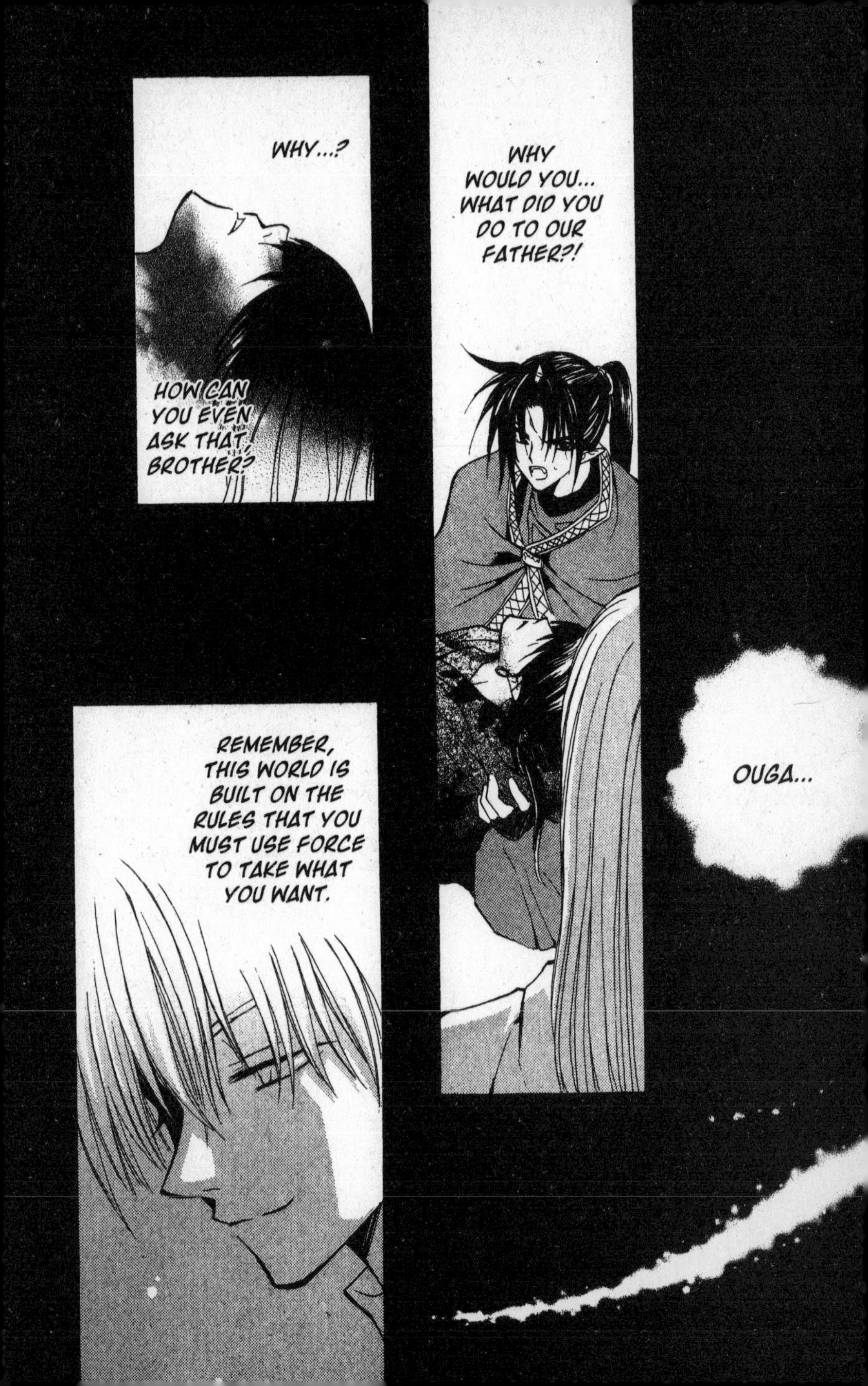
WHY WOULD YOU... WHAT DID YOU DO TO OUR FATHER?!
WHY...?
HOW CAN YOU EVEN ASK THAT, BROTHER?
REMEMBER, THIS WORLD IS BUILT ON THE RULES THAT YOU MUST USE FORCE TO TAKE WHAT YOU WANT.
OUGA...

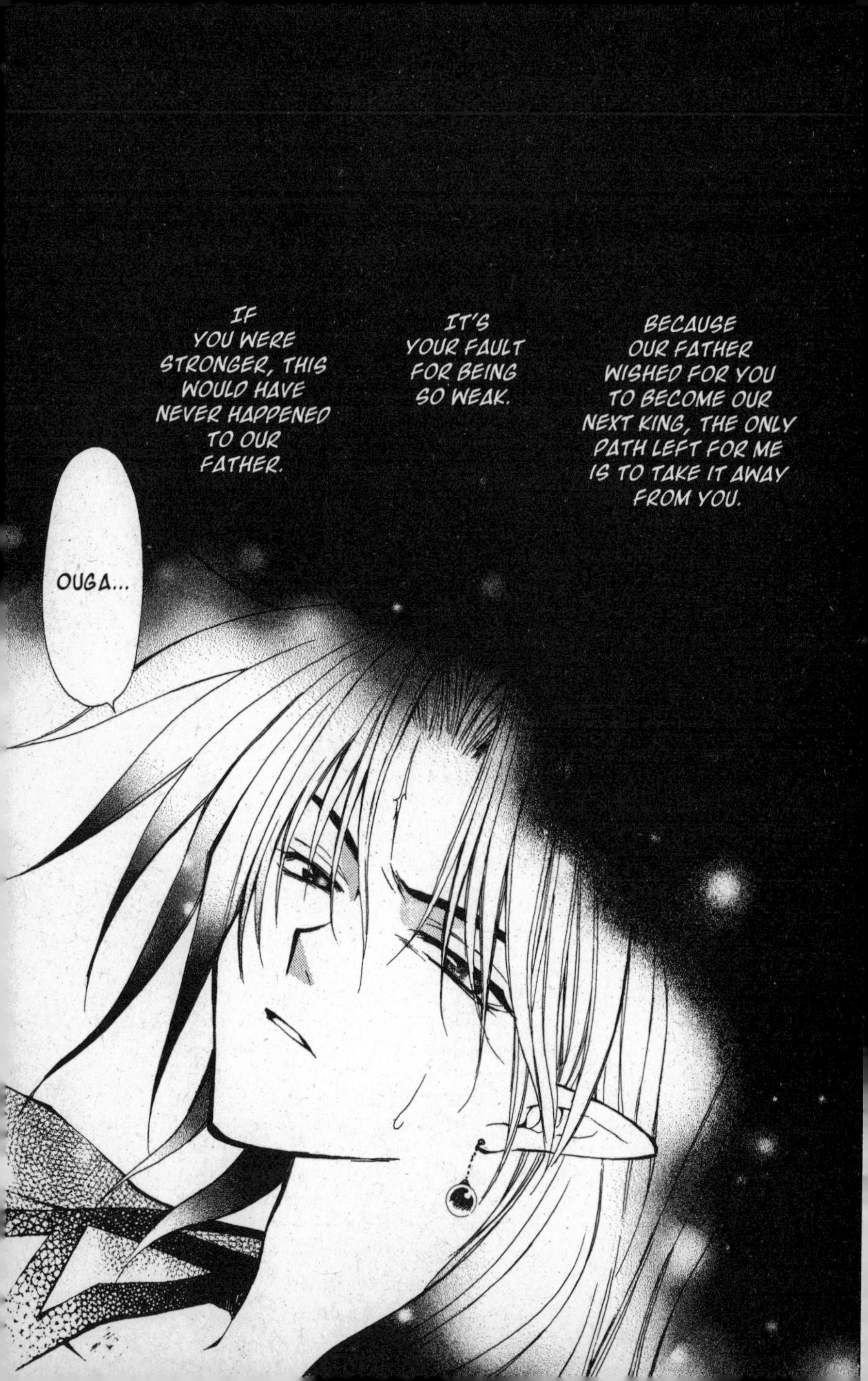
BECAUSE OUR FATHER WISHED FOR YOU TO BECOME OUR NEXT KING, THE ONLY PATH LEFT FOR ME IS TO TAKE IT AWAY FROM YOU.
IT'S YOUR FAULT FOR BEING SO WEAK.
IF YOU WERE STRONGER, THIS WOULD HAVE NEVER HAPPENED TO OUR FATHER.
OUGA...

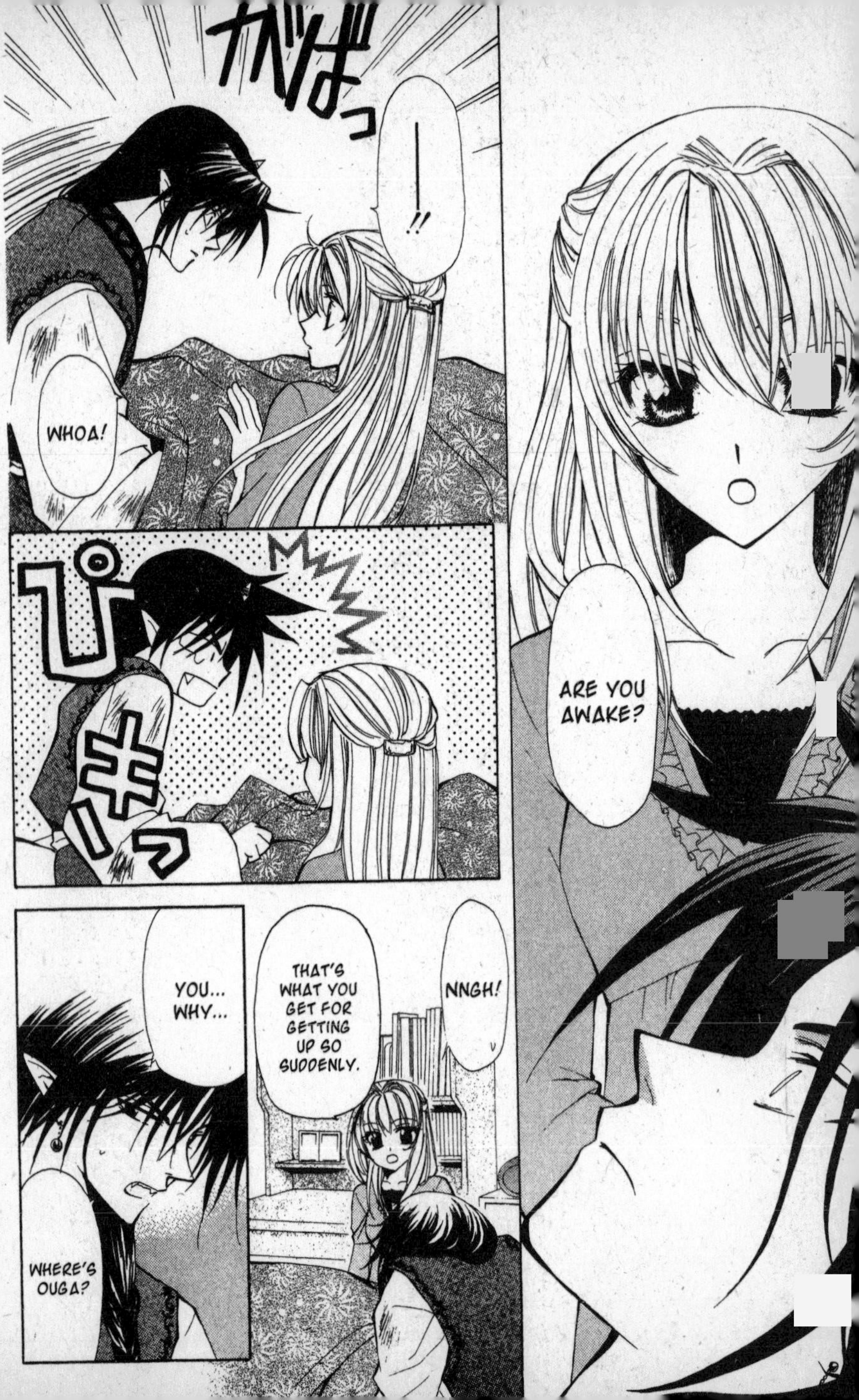
ARE YOU AWAKE?
がばっ
—!!
WHOA!
ぴキーっ
NNGH!
THAT'S WHAT YOU GET FOR GETTING UP SO SUDDENLY.
YOU... WHY...
WHERE'S OUGA?

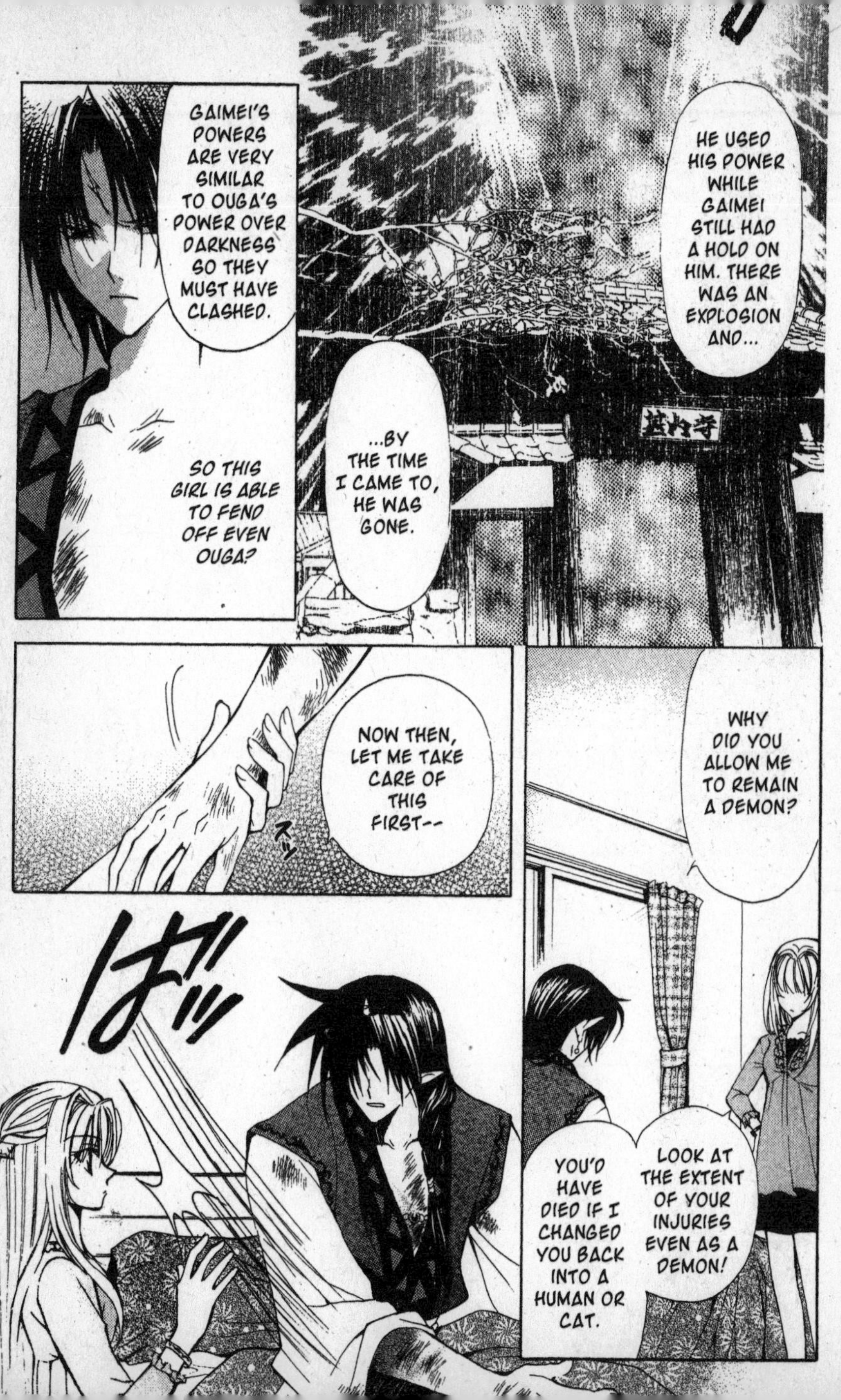
HE USED HIS POWER WHILE GAIMEI STILL HAD A HOLD ON HIM. THERE WAS AN EXPLOSION AND...
...BY THE TIME I CAME TO, HE WAS GONE.
GAIMEI'S POWERS ARE VERY SIMILAR TO OUGA'S POWER OVER DARKNESS SO THEY MUST HAVE CLASHED.
SO THIS GIRL IS ABLE TO FEND OFF EVEN OUGA?
WHY DID YOU ALLOW ME TO REMAIN A DEMON?
LOOK AT THE EXTENT OF YOUR INJURIES EVEN AS A DEMON!
YOU'D HAVE DIED IF I CHANGED YOU BACK INTO A HUMAN OR CAT.
NOW THEN, LET ME TAKE CARE OF THIS FIRST--
ズッ
ばッ

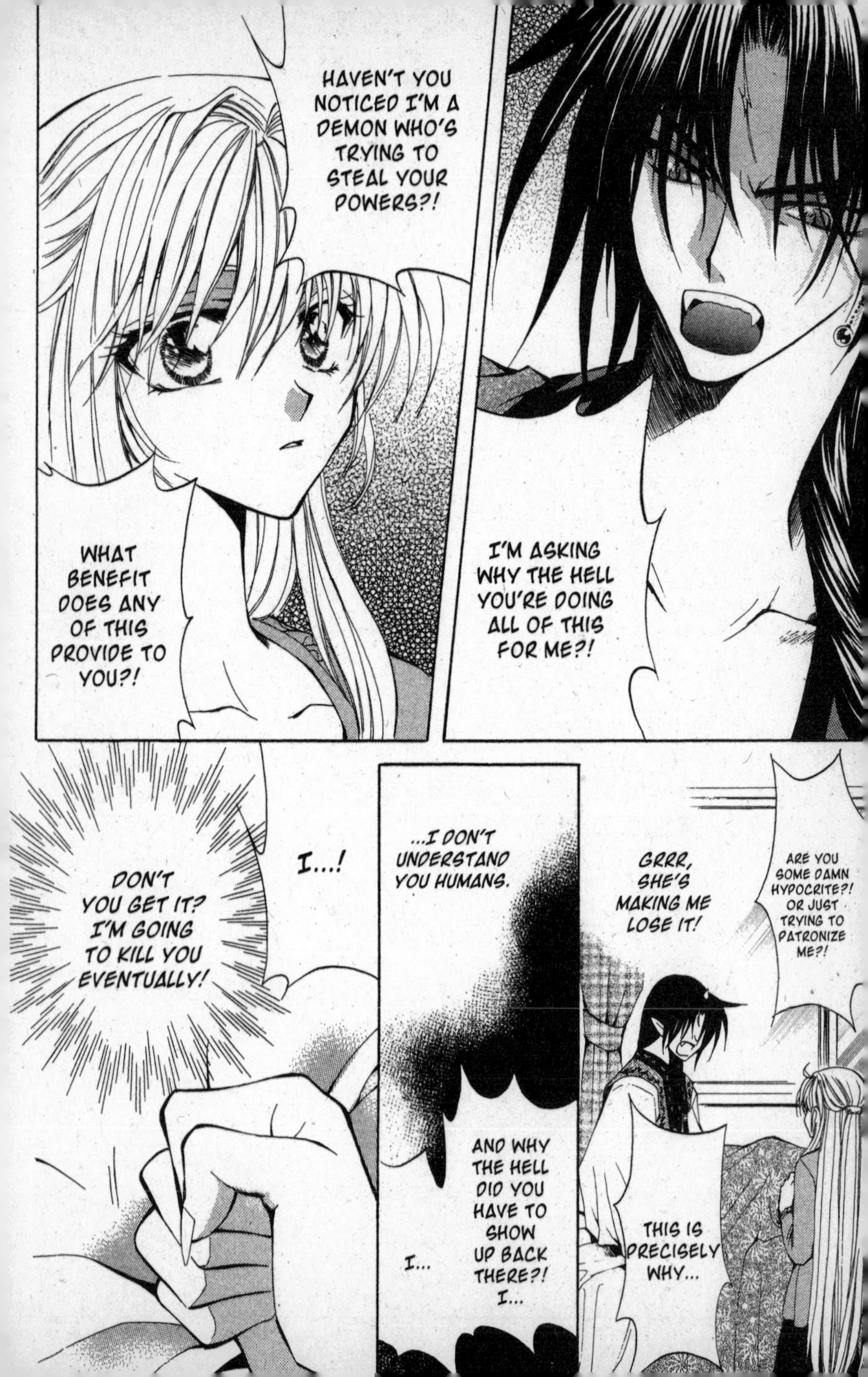
I'M ASKING WHY THE HELL YOU'RE DOING ALL OF THIS FOR ME?!
HAVEN'T YOU NOTICED I'M A DEMON WHO'S TRYING TO STEAL YOUR POWERS?!
WHAT BENEFIT DOES ANY OF THIS PROVIDE TO YOU?!
ARE YOU SOME DAMN HYPOCRITE?! OR JUST TRYING TO PATRONIZE ME?!
GRRR, SHE'S MAKING ME LOSE IT!
THIS IS PRECISELY WHY...
...I DON'T UNDERSTAND YOU HUMANS.
AND WHY THE HELL DID YOU HAVE TO SHOW UP BACK THERE?! I...
I...
I...!
DON'T YOU GET IT? I'M GOING TO KILL YOU EVENTUALLY!

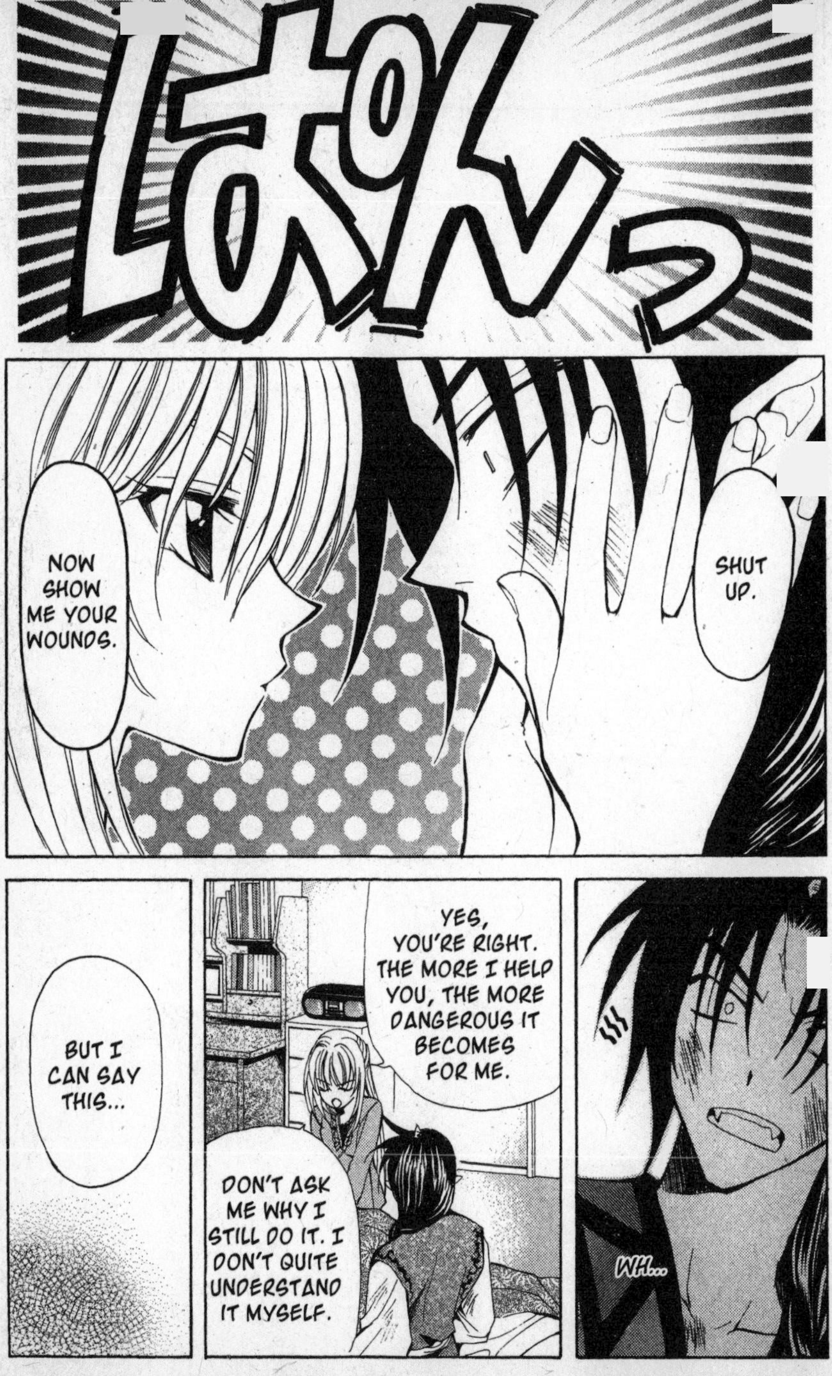
SHUT UP.
NOW SHOW ME YOUR WOUNDS.
WH...
YES, YOU'RE RIGHT. THE MORE I HELP YOU, THE MORE DANGEROUS IT BECOMES FOR ME.
DON'T ASK ME WHY I STILL DO IT. I DON'T QUITE UNDERSTAND IT MYSELF.
BUT I CAN SAY THIS...

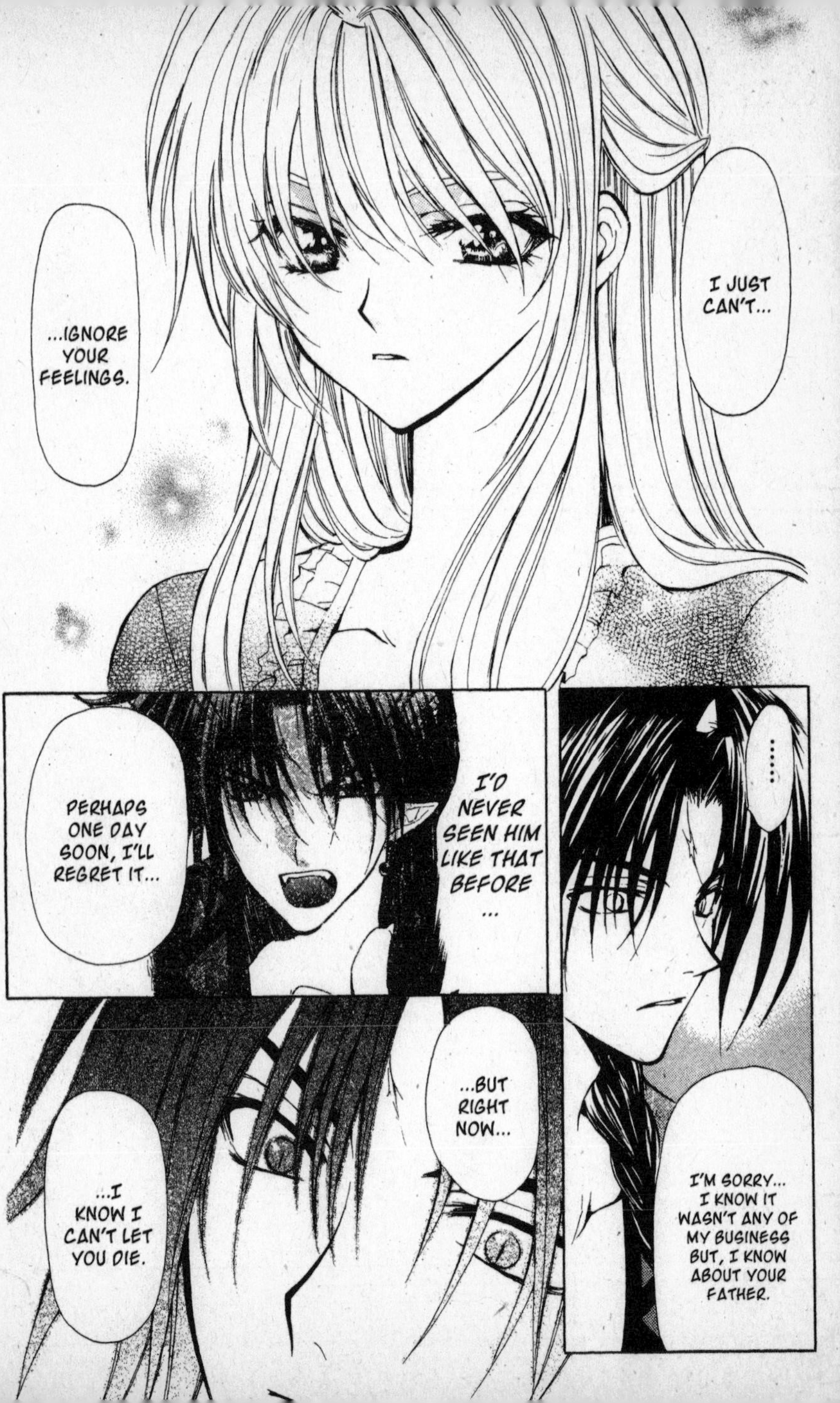
I JUST CAN'T...
...IGNORE YOUR FEELINGS.
......
I'M SORRY... I KNOW IT WASN'T ANY OF MY BUSINESS BUT, I KNOW ABOUT YOUR FATHER.
I'D NEVER SEEN HIM LIKE THAT BEFORE ...
PERHAPS ONE DAY SOON, I'LL REGRET IT...
...BUT RIGHT NOW...
...I KNOW I CAN'T LET YOU DIE.

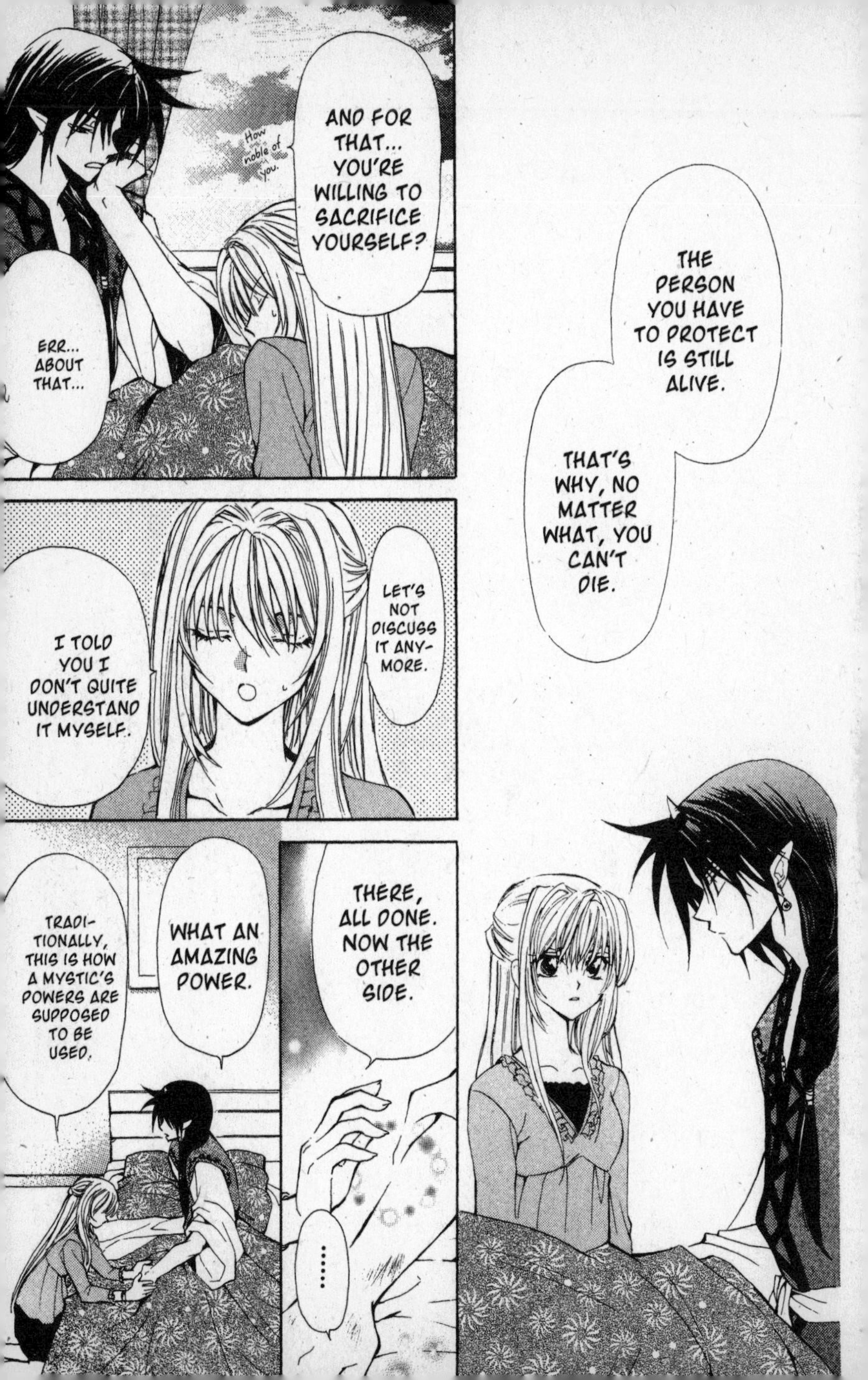
AND FOR THAT... YOU'RE WILLING TO SACRIFICE YOURSELF?
How noble of you.
ERR... ABOUT THAT...
LET'S NOT DISCUSS IT ANY-MORE.
I TOLD YOU I DON'T QUITE UNDERSTAND IT MYSELF.
THERE, ALL DONE. NOW THE OTHER SIDE.
......
WHAT AN AMAZING POWER.
TRADI-TIONALLY, THIS IS HOW A MYSTIC'S POWERS ARE SUPPOSED TO BE USED.
THE PERSON YOU HAVE TO PROTECT IS STILL ALIVE.
THAT'S WHY, NO MATTER WHAT, YOU CAN'T DIE.

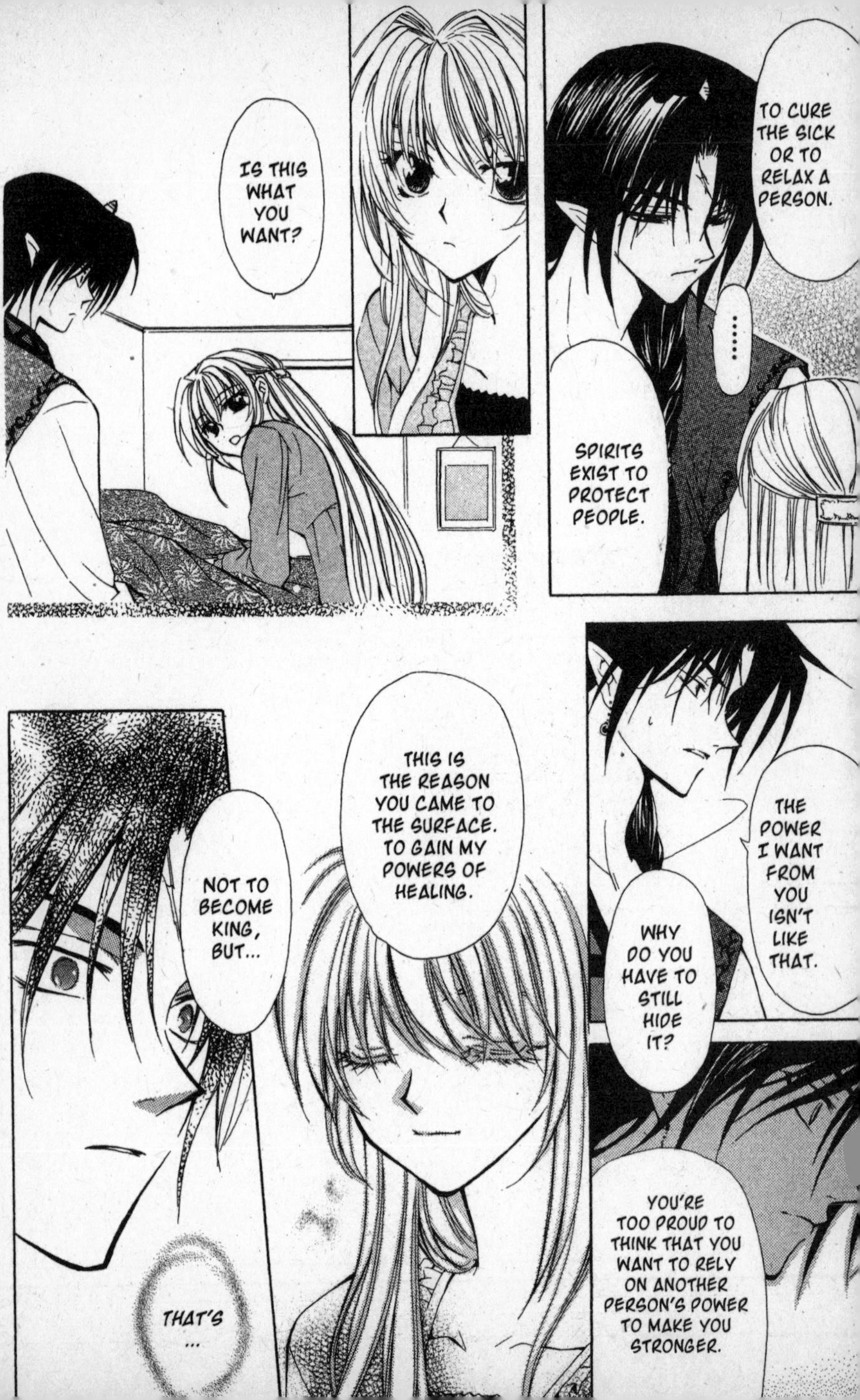
TO CURE THE SICK OR TO RELAX A PERSON.
......
SPIRITS EXIST TO PROTECT PEOPLE.
IS THIS WHAT YOU WANT?
THE POWER I WANT FROM YOU ISN'T LIKE THAT.
WHY DO YOU HAVE TO STILL HIDE IT?
YOU'RE TOO PROUD TO THINK THAT YOU WANT TO RELY ON ANOTHER PERSON'S POWER TO MAKE YOU STRONGER.
THIS IS THE REASON YOU CAME TO THE SURFACE. TO GAIN MY POWERS OF HEALING.
NOT TO BECOME KING, BUT...
THAT'S ...

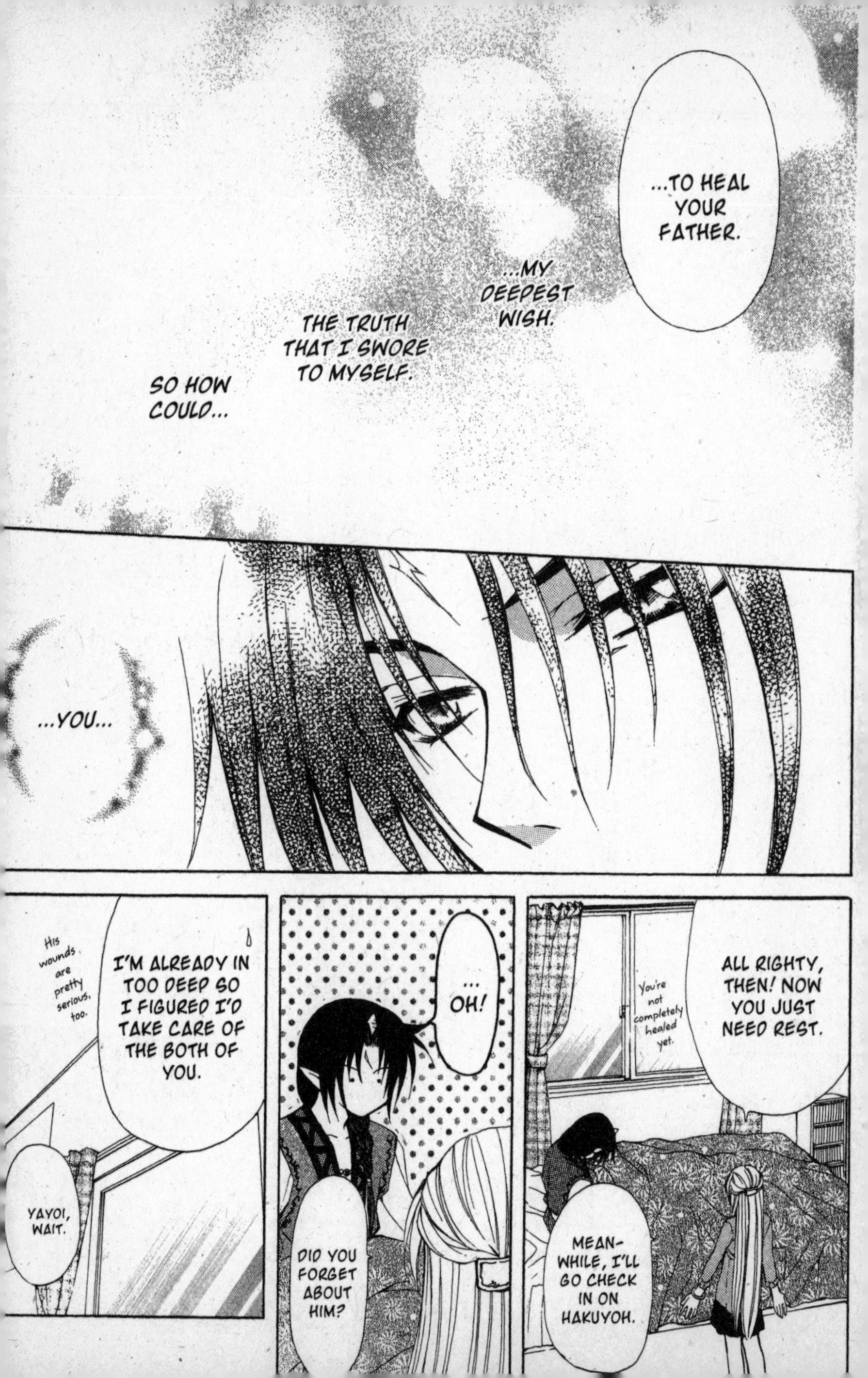
...TO HEAL YOUR FATHER.
...MY DEEPEST WISH.
THE TRUTH THAT I SWORE TO MYSELF.
SO HOW COULD...
...YOU...
ALL RIGHTY, THEN! NOW YOU JUST NEED REST.
You're not completely healed yet.
MEAN-WHILE, I'LL GO CHECK IN ON HAKUYOH.
... OH!
DID YOU FORGET ABOUT HIM?
I'M ALREADY IN TOO DEEP SO I FIGURED I'D TAKE CARE OF THE BOTH OF YOU.
His wounds are pretty serious, too.
YAYOI, WAIT.

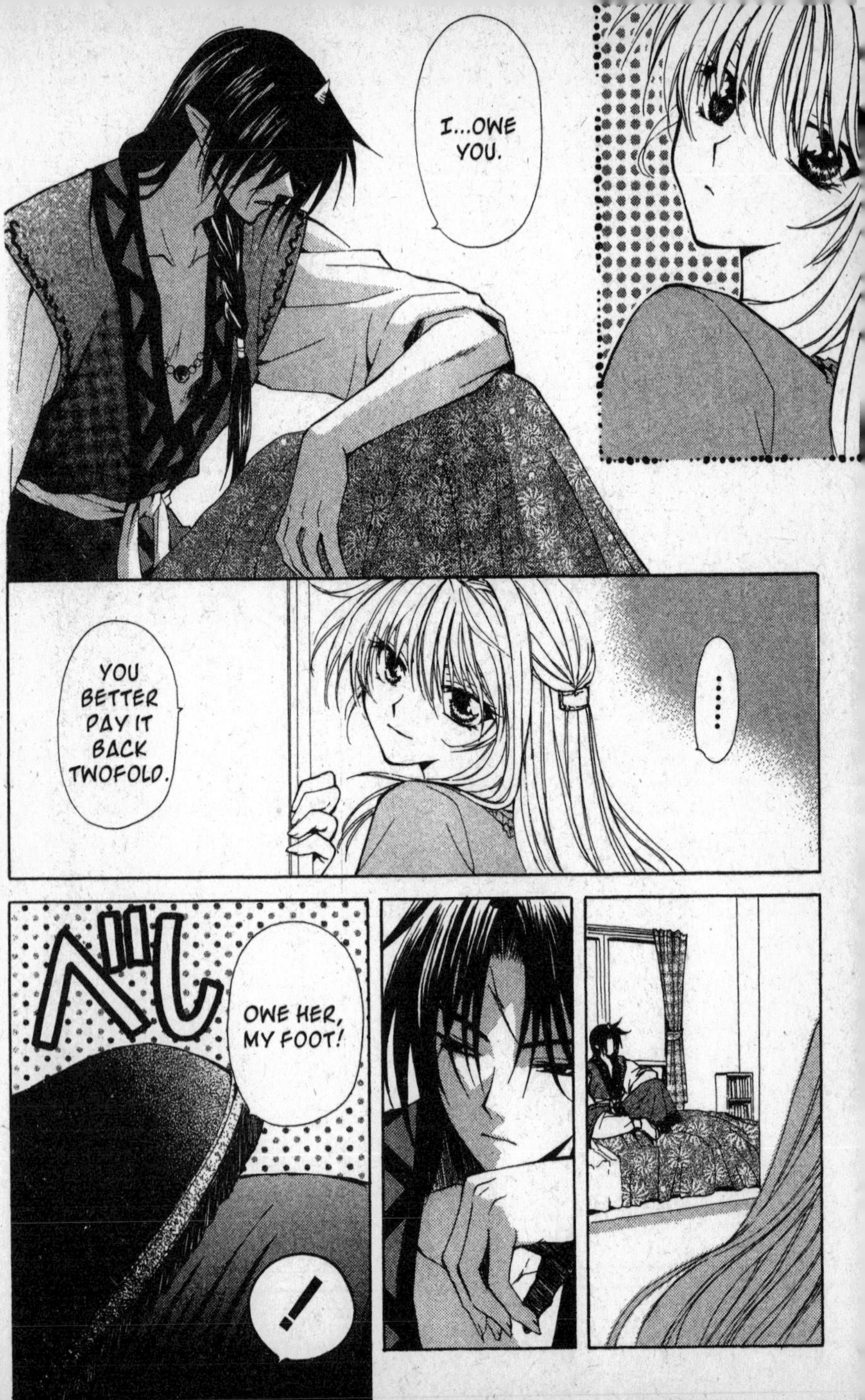

I...OWE YOU.
......
YOU BETTER PAY IT BACK TWOFOLD.
OWE HER, MY FOOT!
べし
!

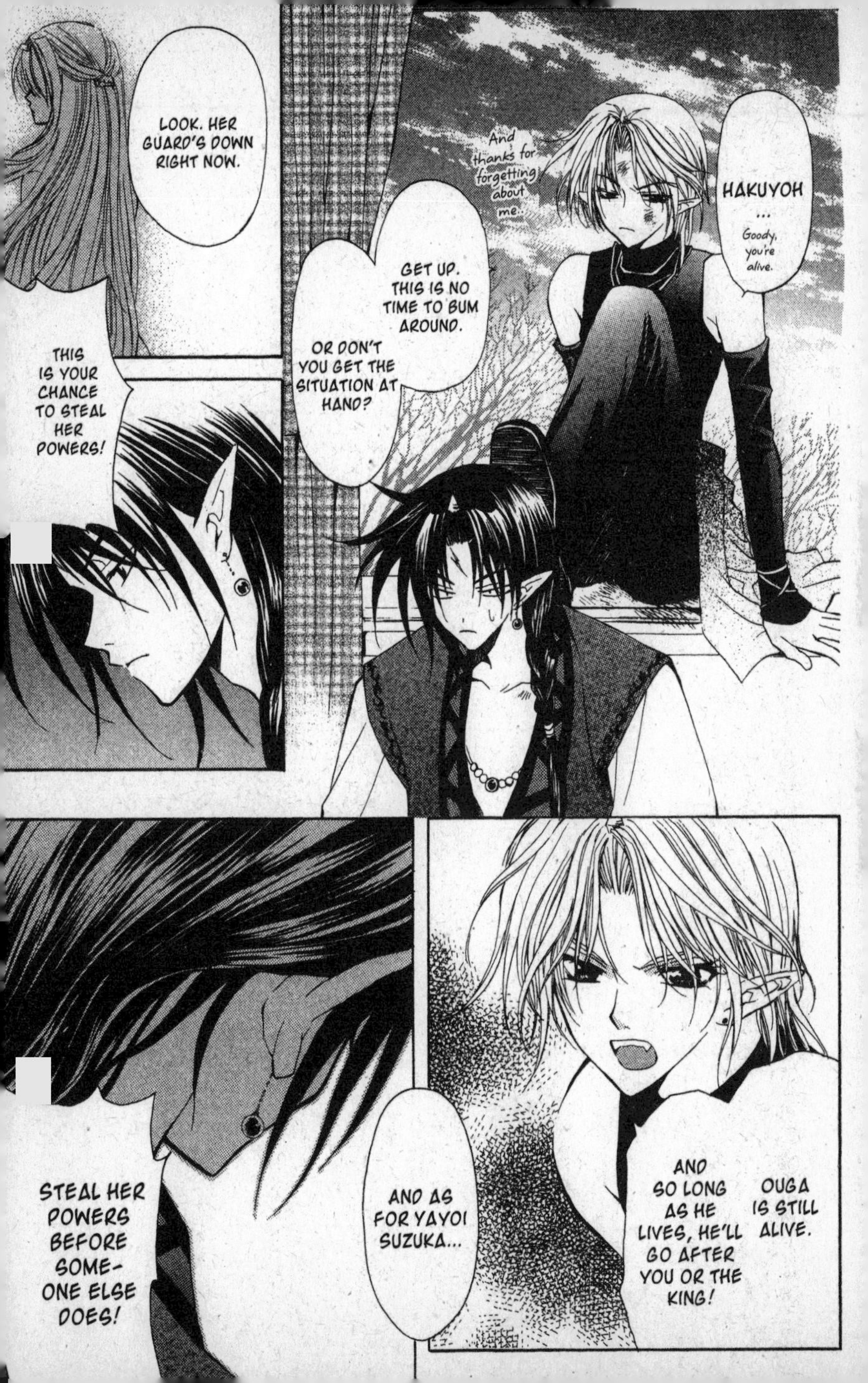
HAKUYOH ...
Goody, you're alive.
And thanks for forgetting about me..
GET UP. THIS IS NO TIME TO BUM AROUND.
OR DON'T YOU GET THE SITUATION AT HAND?
LOOK. HER GUARD'S DOWN RIGHT NOW.
THIS IS YOUR CHANCE TO STEAL HER POWERS!
OUGA IS STILL ALIVE.
AND SO LONG AS HE LIVES, HE'LL GO AFTER YOU OR THE KING!
AND AS FOR YAYOI SUZUKA...
STEAL HER POWERS BEFORE SOME-ONE ELSE DOES!

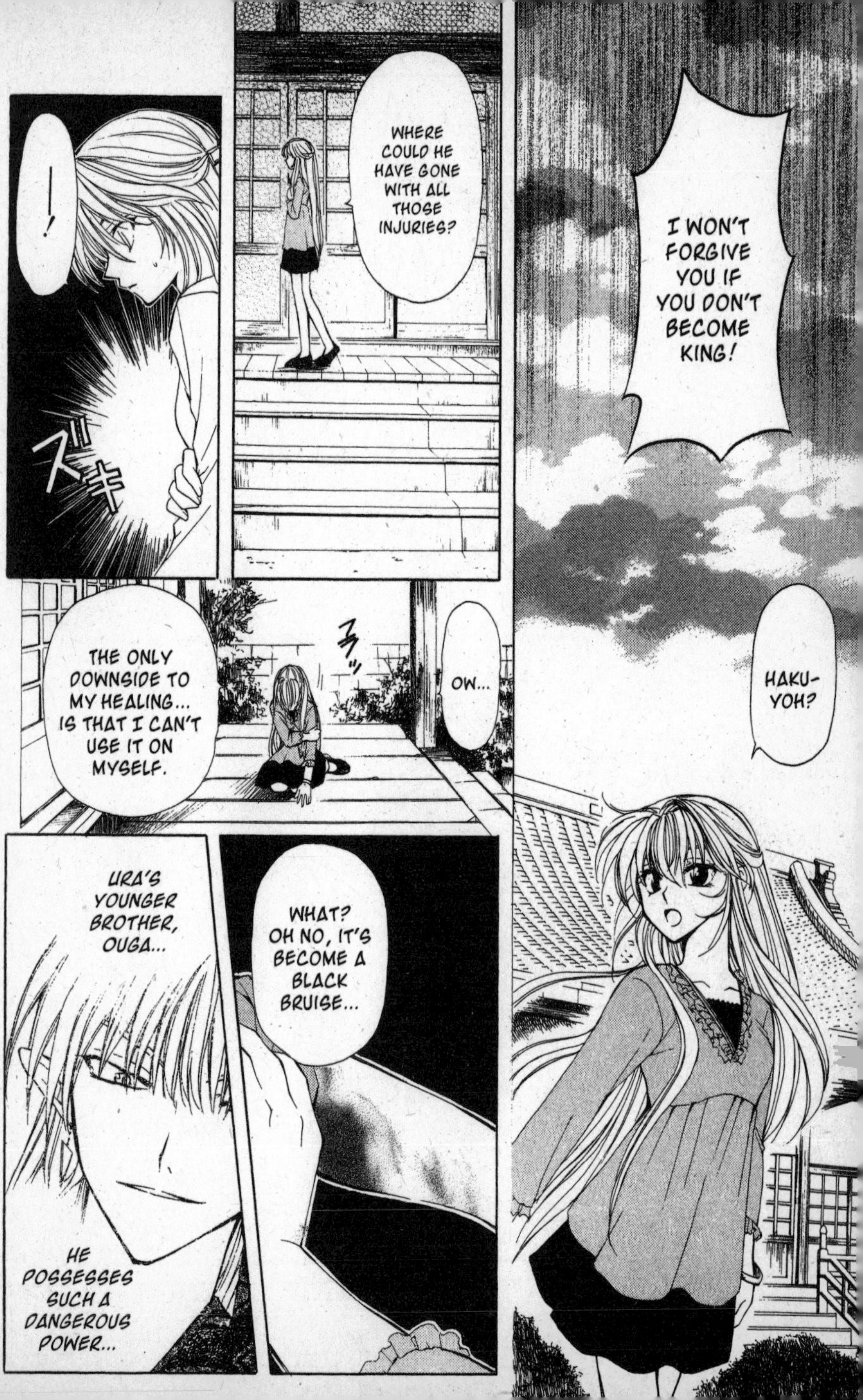
I WON'T FORGIVE YOU IF YOU DON'T BECOME KING!
HAKU-YOH?
WHERE COULD HE HAVE GONE WITH ALL THOSE INJURIES?
!
ズキ
ズッ
OW...
THE ONLY DOWNSIDE TO MY HEALING... IS THAT I CAN'T USE IT ON MYSELF.
WHAT? OH NO, IT'S BECOME A BLACK BRUISE...
URA'S YOUNGER BROTHER, OUGA...
HE POSSESSES SUCH A DANGEROUS POWER...

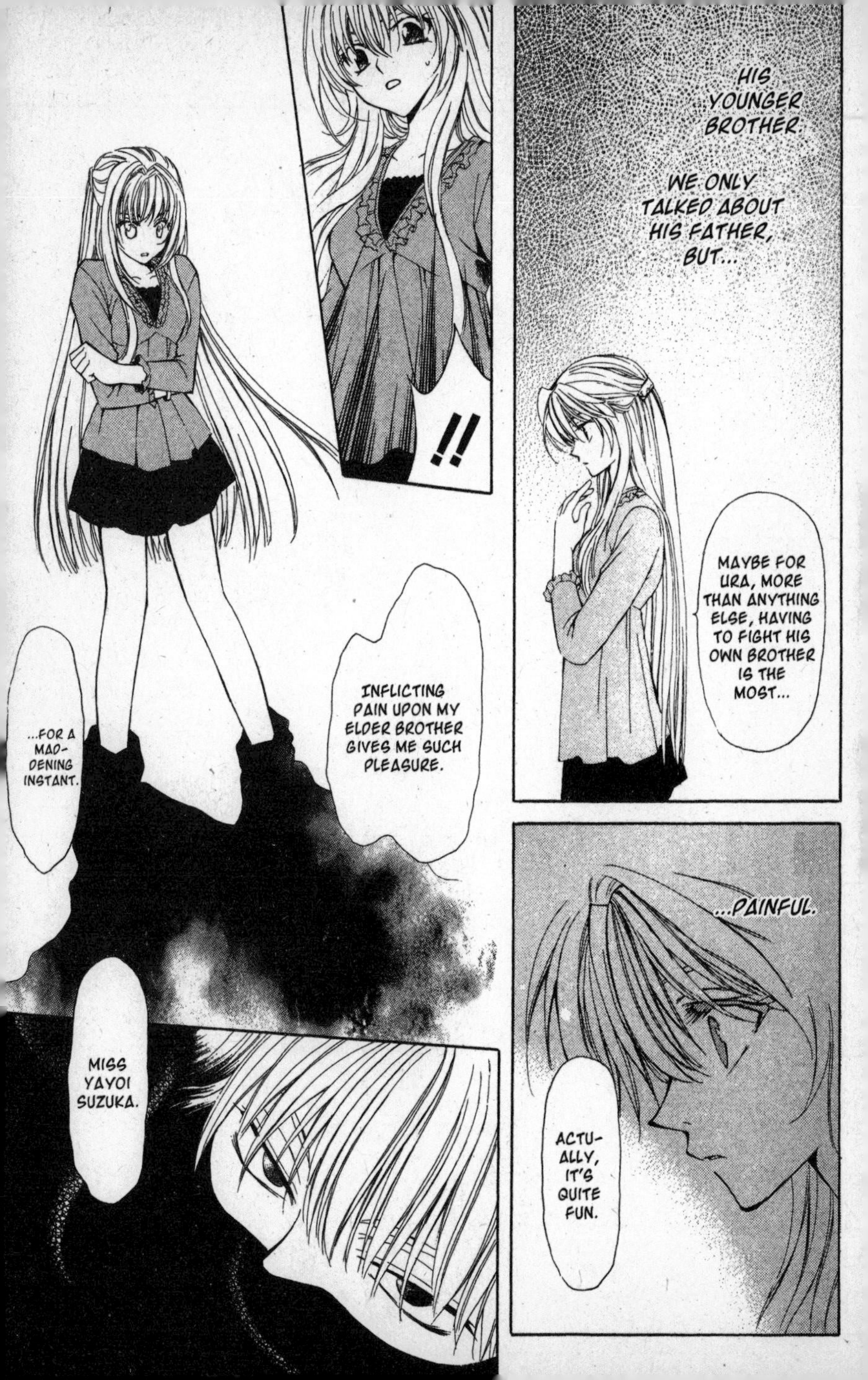
HIS YOUNGER BROTHER.
WE ONLY TALKED ABOUT HIS FATHER, BUT...
MAYBE FOR URA, MORE THAN ANYTHING ELSE, HAVING TO FIGHT HIS OWN BROTHER IS THE MOST...
...PAINFUL.
ACTU-ALLY, IT'S QUITE FUN.
!!
INFLICTING PAIN UPON MY ELDER BROTHER GIVES ME SUCH PLEASURE.
...FOR A MAD-DENING INSTANT.
MISS YAYOI SUZUKA.

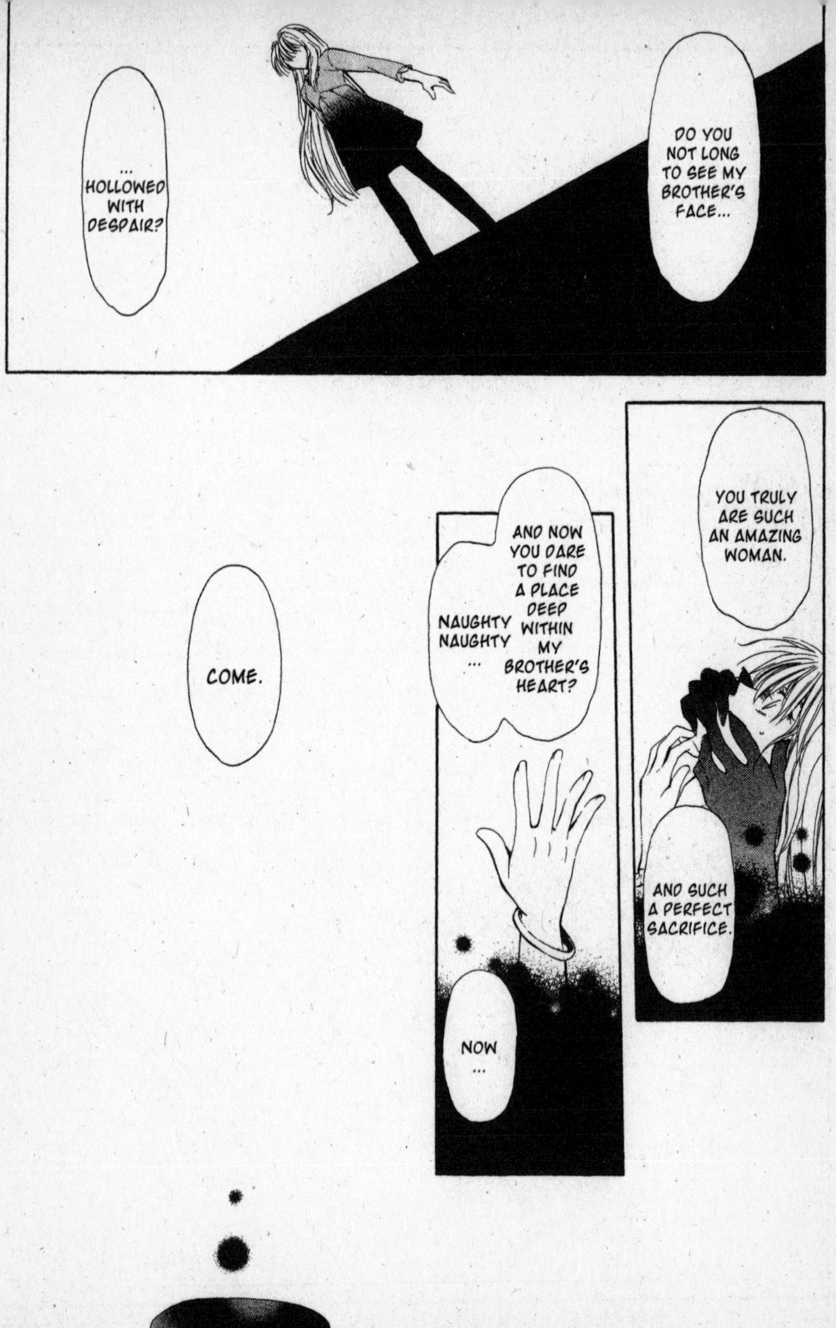
DO YOU NOT LONG TO SEE MY BROTHER'S FACE...
...HOLLOWED WITH DESPAIR?
YOU TRULY ARE SUCH AN AMAZING WOMAN.
AND SUCH A PERFECT SACRIFICE.
AND NOW YOU DARE TO FIND A PLACE DEEP WITHIN MY BROTHER'S HEART?
NAUGHTY NAUGHTY ...
NOW ...
COME.

Act 5 / The End

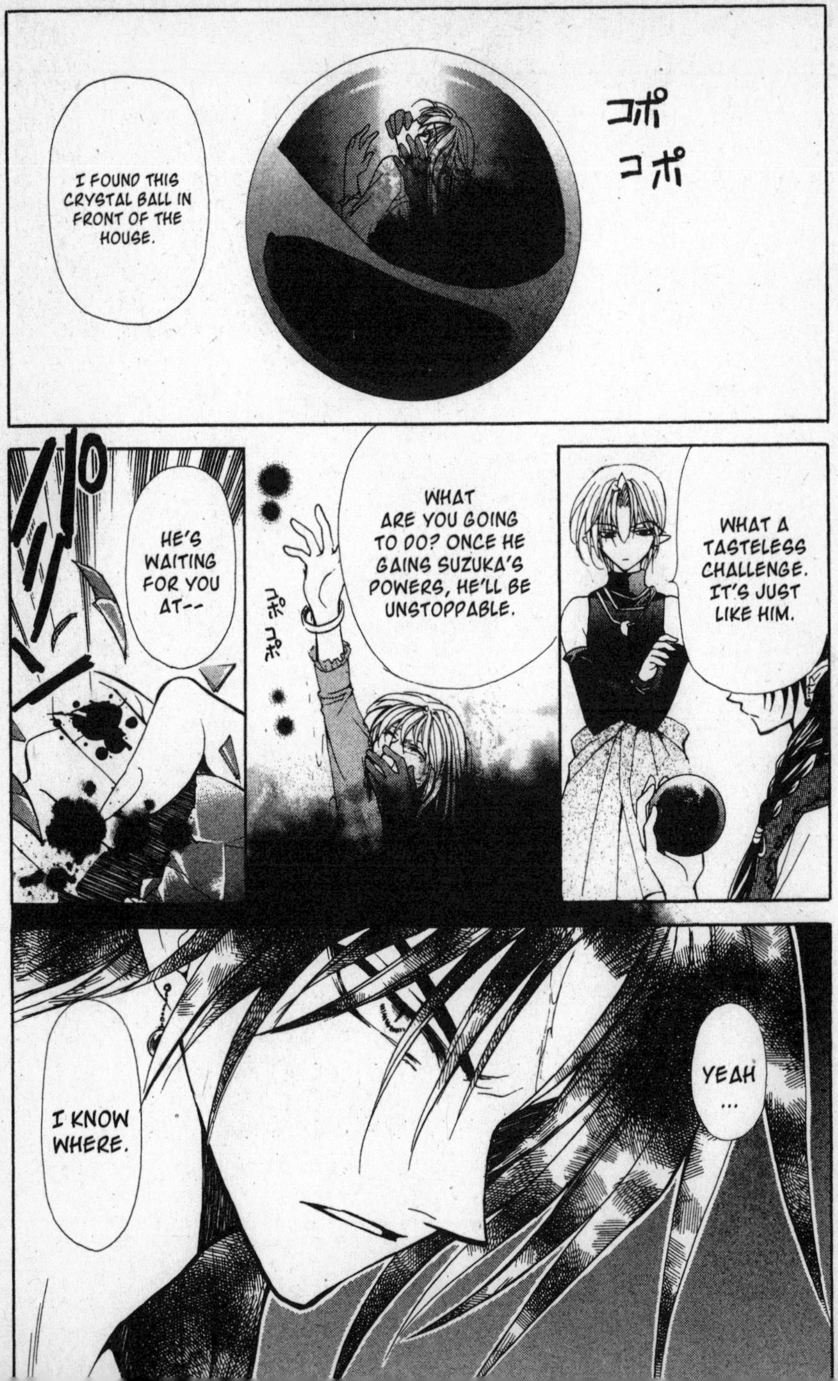
コポ
コポ
I FOUND THIS CRYSTAL BALL IN FRONT OF THE HOUSE.
WHAT A TASTELESS CHALLENGE. IT'S JUST LIKE HIM.
WHAT ARE YOU GOING TO DO? ONCE HE GAINS SUZUKA'S POWERS, HE'LL BE UNSTOPPABLE.
コポ コポ
HE'S WAITING FOR YOU AT--
YEAH ...
I KNOW WHERE.

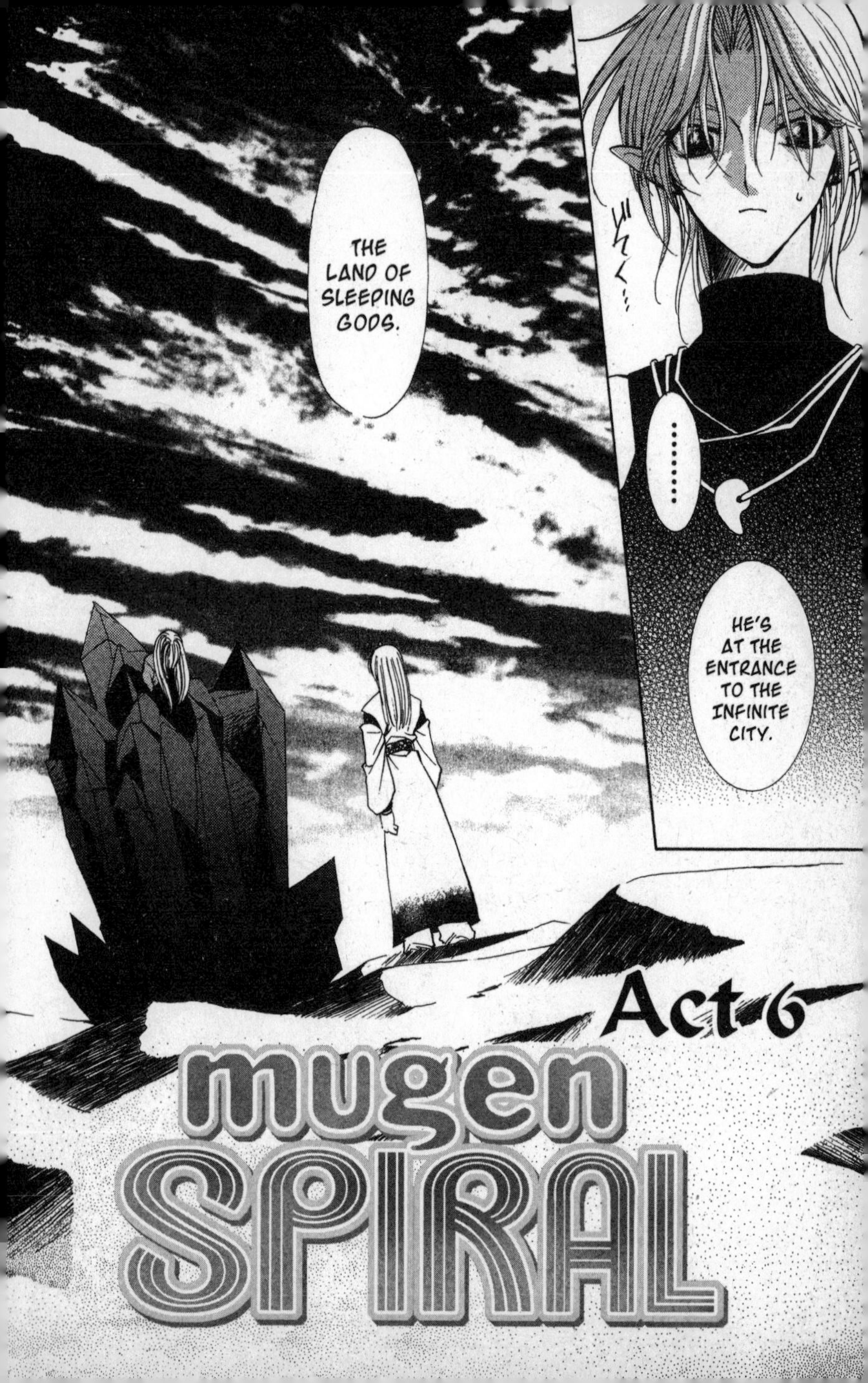
......
HE'S AT THE ENTRANCE TO THE INFINITE CITY.
THE LAND OF SLEEPING GODS.
Act 6
mugen SPIRAL

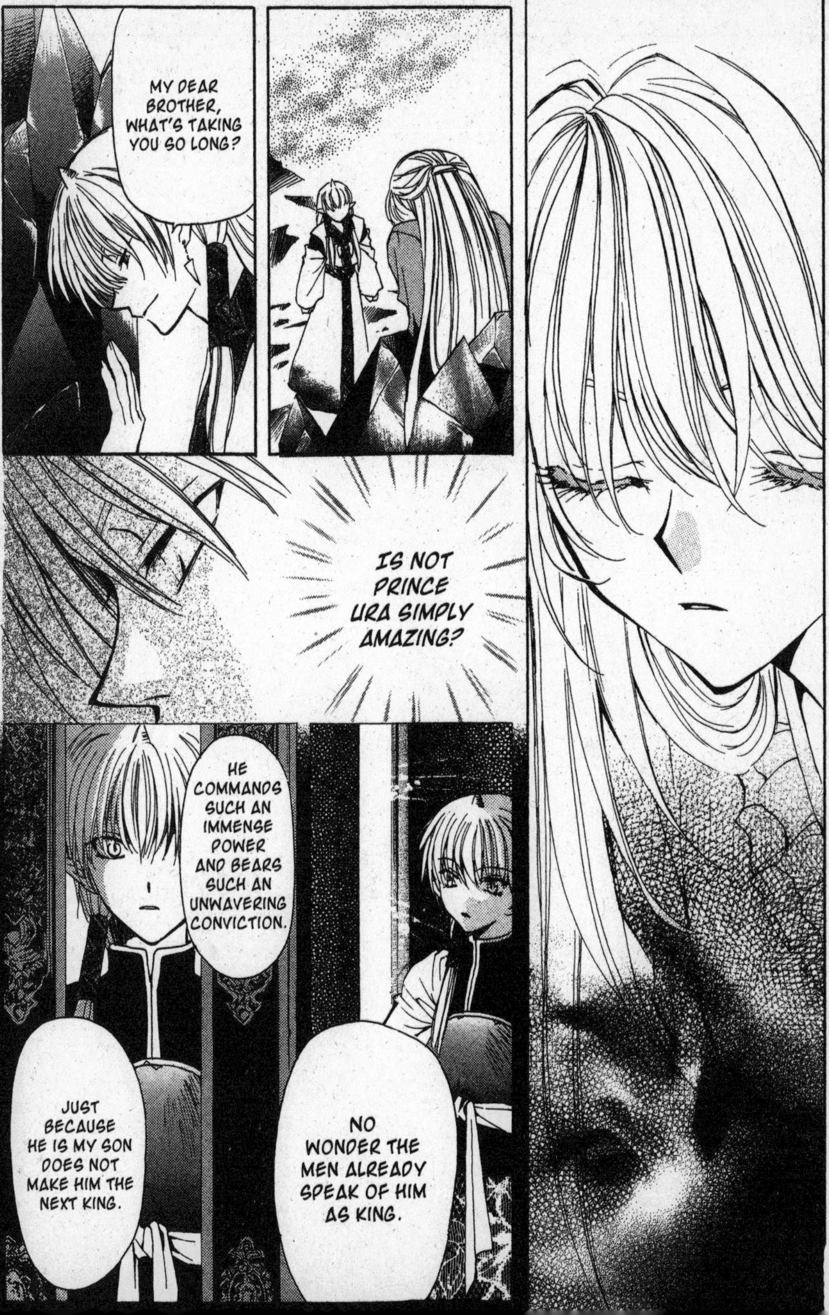
MY DEAR BROTHER, WHAT'S TAKING YOU SO LONG?
IS NOT PRINCE URA SIMPLY AMAZING?
HE COMMANDS SUCH AN IMMENSE POWER AND BEARS SUCH AN UNWAVERING CONVICTION.
NO WONDER THE MEN ALREADY SPEAK OF HIM AS KING.
JUST BECAUSE HE IS MY SON DOES NOT MAKE HIM THE NEXT KING.

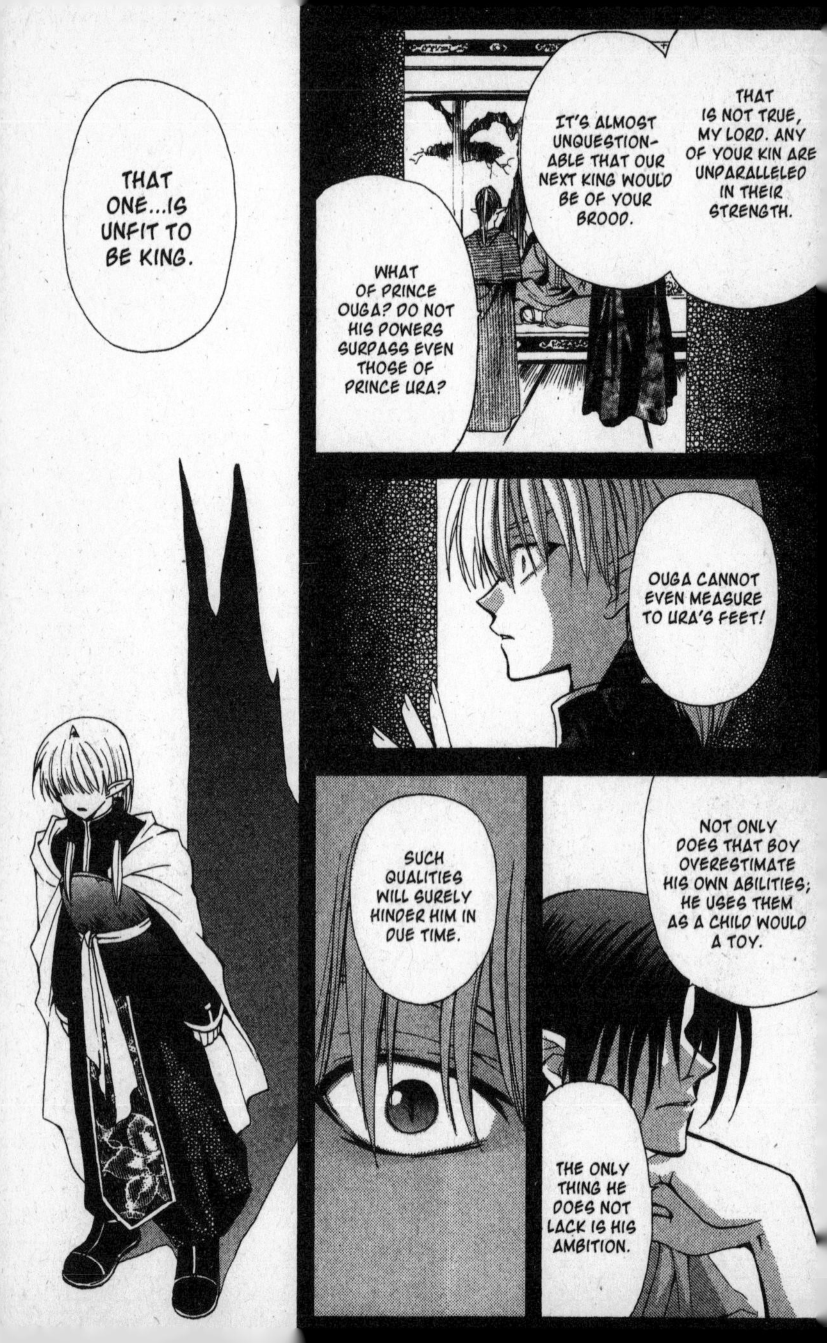
THAT IS NOT TRUE, MY LORD. ANY OF YOUR KIN ARE UNPARALLELED IN THEIR STRENGTH.
IT'S ALMOST UNQUESTIONABLE THAT OUR NEXT KING WOULD BE OF YOUR BROOD.
WHAT OF PRINCE OUGA? DO NOT HIS POWERS SURPASS EVEN THOSE OF PRINCE URA?
OUGA CANNOT EVEN MEASURE TO URA'S FEET!
NOT ONLY DOES THAT BOY OVERESTIMATE HIS OWN ABILITIES; HE USES THEM AS A CHILD WOULD A TOY.
THE ONLY THING HE DOES NOT LACK IS HIS AMBITION.
SUCH QUALITIES WILL SURELY HINDER HIM IN DUE TIME.
THAT ONE...IS UNFIT TO BE KING.

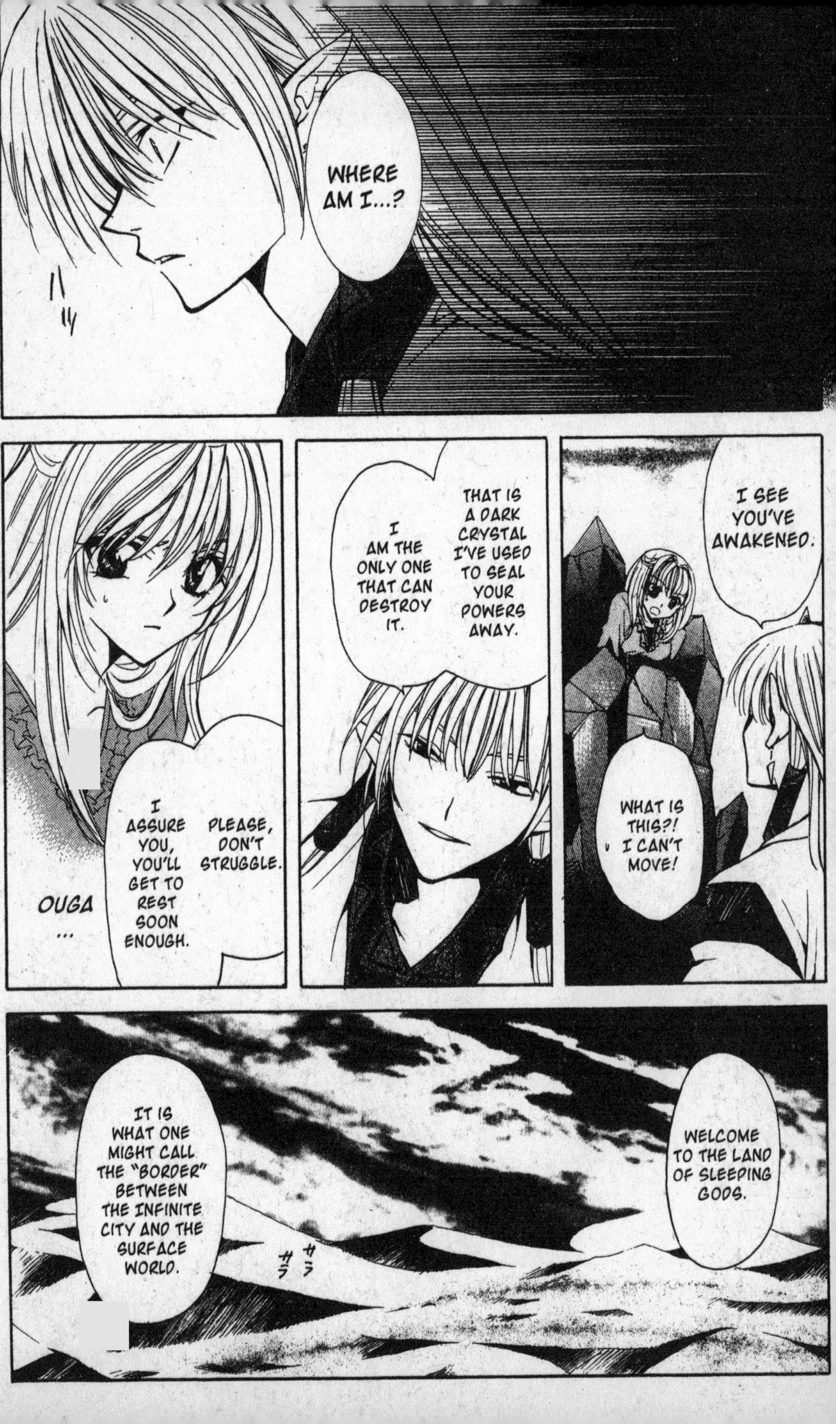
WHERE AM I...?
I SEE YOU'VE AWAKENED.
WHAT IS THIS?! I CAN'T MOVE!
THAT IS A DARK CRYSTAL I'VE USED TO SEAL YOUR POWERS AWAY.
I AM THE ONLY ONE THAT CAN DESTROY IT.
PLEASE, DON'T STRUGGLE.
I ASSURE YOU, YOU'LL GET TO REST SOON ENOUGH.
OUGA ...
WELCOME TO THE LAND OF SLEEPING GODS.
サラサラ
IT IS WHAT ONE MIGHT CALL THE "BORDER" BETWEEN THE INFINITE CITY AND THE SURFACE WORLD.

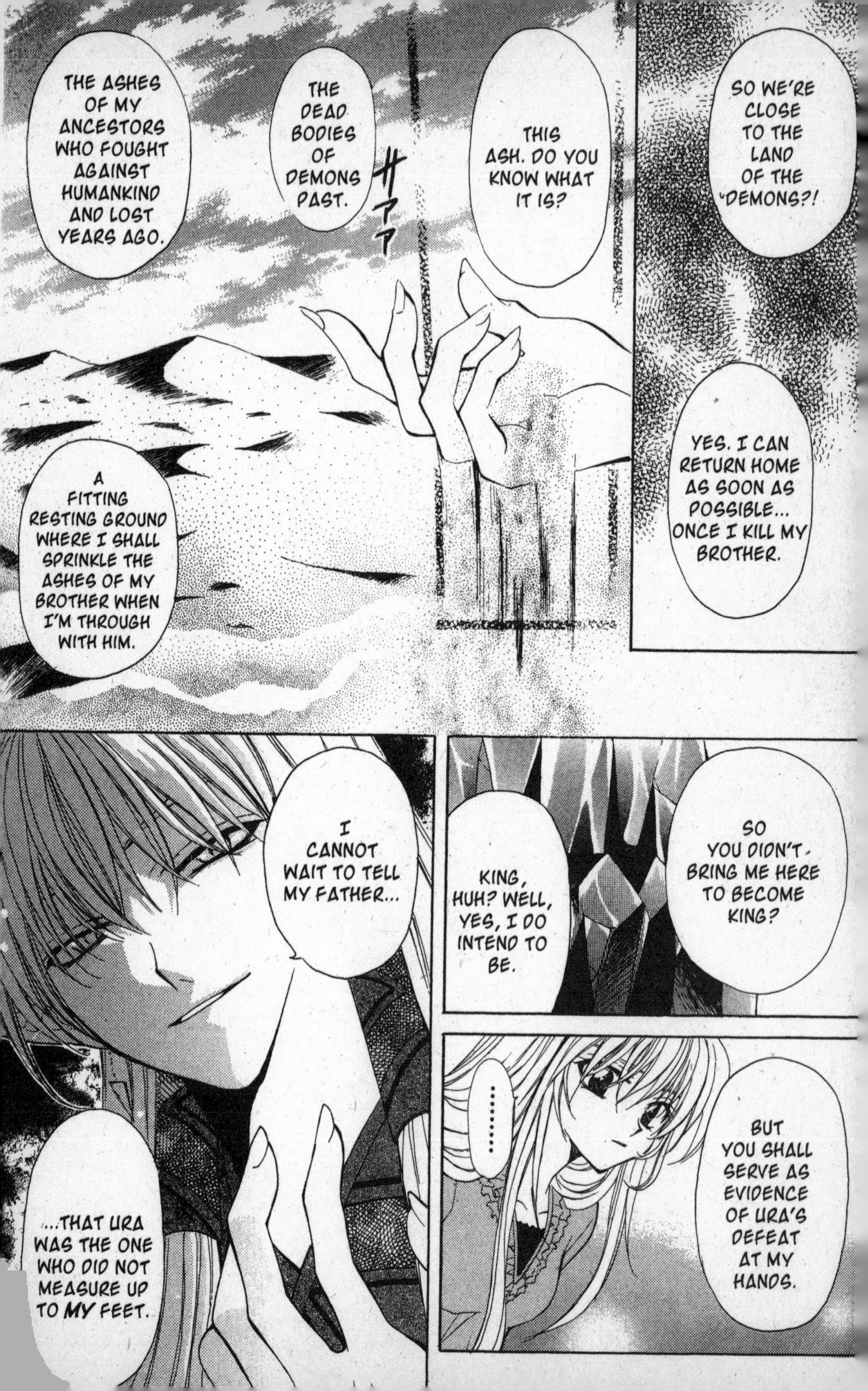
SO WE'RE CLOSE TO THE LAND OF THE 'DEMONS?!
YES. I CAN RETURN HOME AS SOON AS POSSIBLE... ONCE I KILL MY BROTHER.
THIS ASH. DO YOU KNOW WHAT IT IS?
THE DEAD BODIES OF DEMONS PAST.
サァァ
THE ASHES OF MY ANCESTORS WHO FOUGHT AGAINST HUMANKIND AND LOST YEARS AGO.
A FITTING RESTING GROUND WHERE I SHALL SPRINKLE THE ASHES OF MY BROTHER WHEN I'M THROUGH WITH HIM.
SO YOU DIDN'T BRING ME HERE TO BECOME KING?
KING, HUH? WELL, YES, I DO INTEND TO BE.
BUT YOU SHALL SERVE AS EVIDENCE OF URA'S DEFEAT AT MY HANDS.
........
I CANNOT WAIT TO TELL MY FATHER...
...THAT URA WAS THE ONE WHO DID NOT MEASURE UP TO MY FEET.

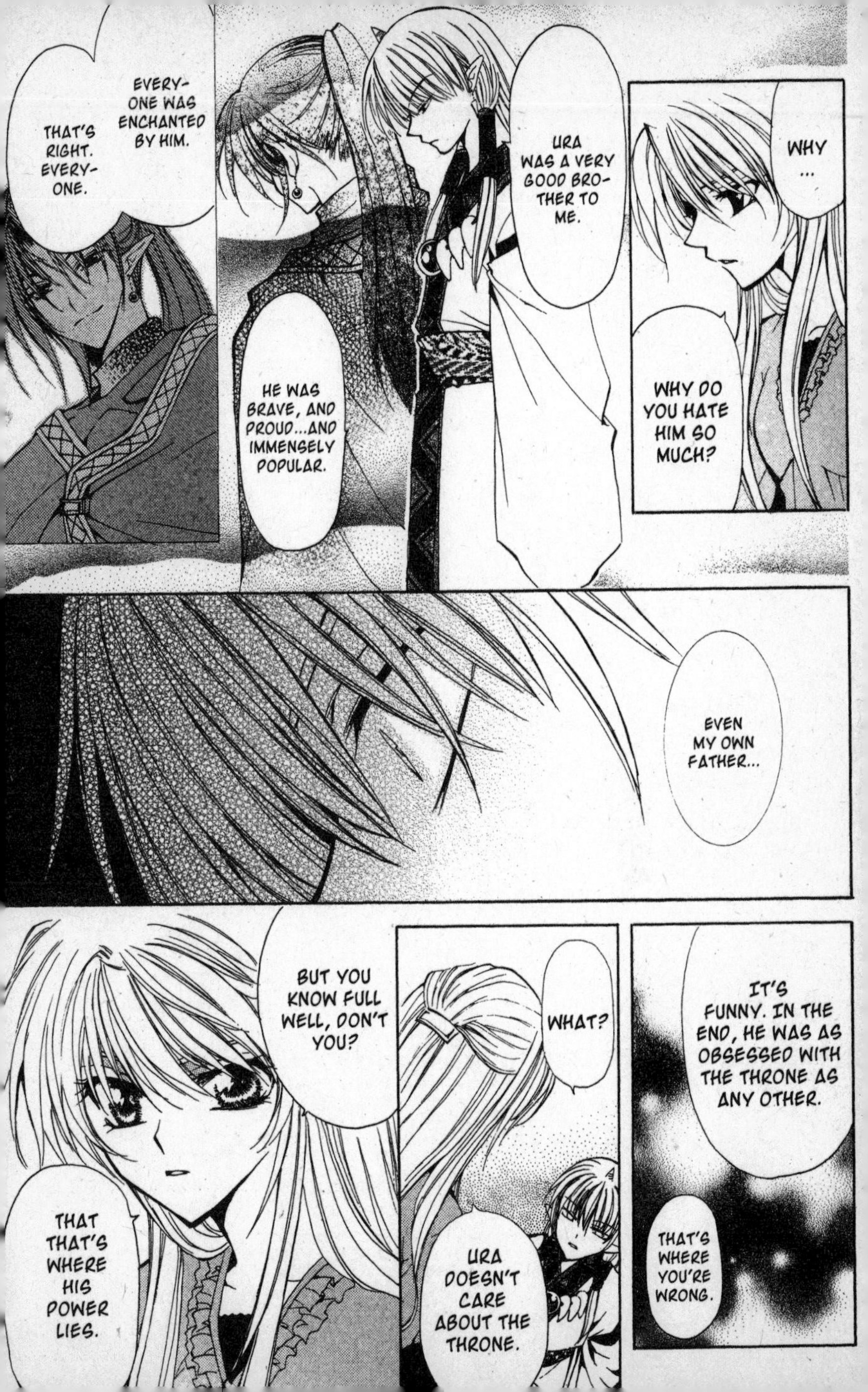
WHY ...
WHY DO YOU HATE HIM SO MUCH?
URA WAS A VERY GOOD BROTHER TO ME.
HE WAS BRAVE, AND PROUD...AND IMMENSELY POPULAR.
EVERYONE WAS ENCHANTED BY HIM.
THAT'S RIGHT. EVERYONE.
EVEN MY OWN FATHER...
IT'S FUNNY. IN THE END, HE WAS AS OBSESSED WITH THE THRONE AS ANY OTHER.
THAT'S WHERE YOU'RE WRONG.
WHAT?
URA DOESN'T CARE ABOUT THE THRONE.
BUT YOU KNOW FULL WELL, DON'T YOU?
THAT THAT'S WHERE HIS POWER LIES.

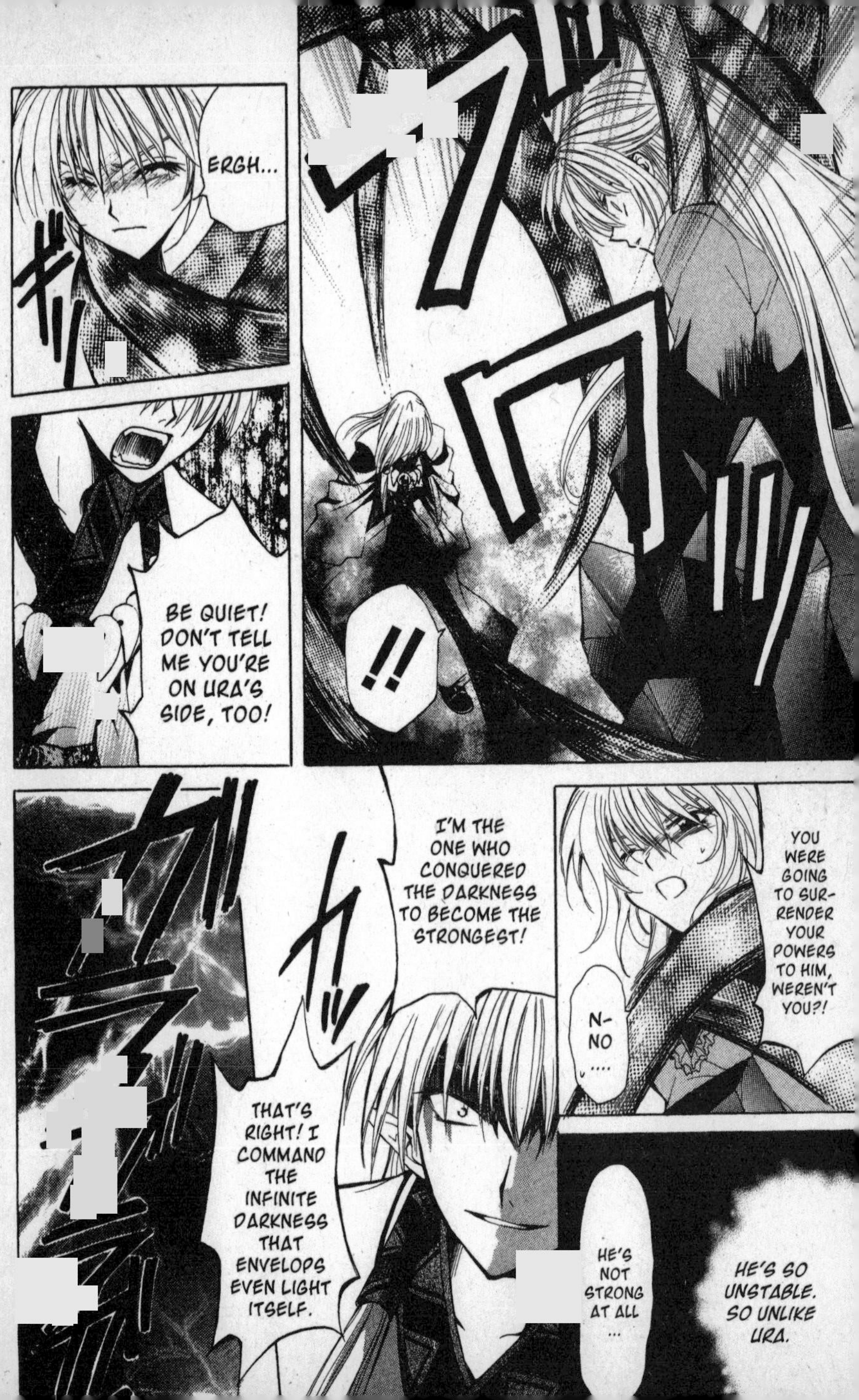
!!
ERGH...
BE QUIET! DON'T TELL ME YOU'RE ON URA'S SIDE, TOO!
YOU WERE GOING TO SUR-RENDER YOUR POWERS TO HIM, WEREN'T YOU?!
N-NO ....
I'M THE ONE WHO CONQUERED THE DARKNESS TO BECOME THE STRONGEST!
THAT'S RIGHT! I COMMAND THE INFINITE DARKNESS THAT ENVELOPS EVEN LIGHT ITSELF.
HE'S SO UNSTABLE. SO UNLIKE URA.
HE'S NOT STRONG AT ALL ...

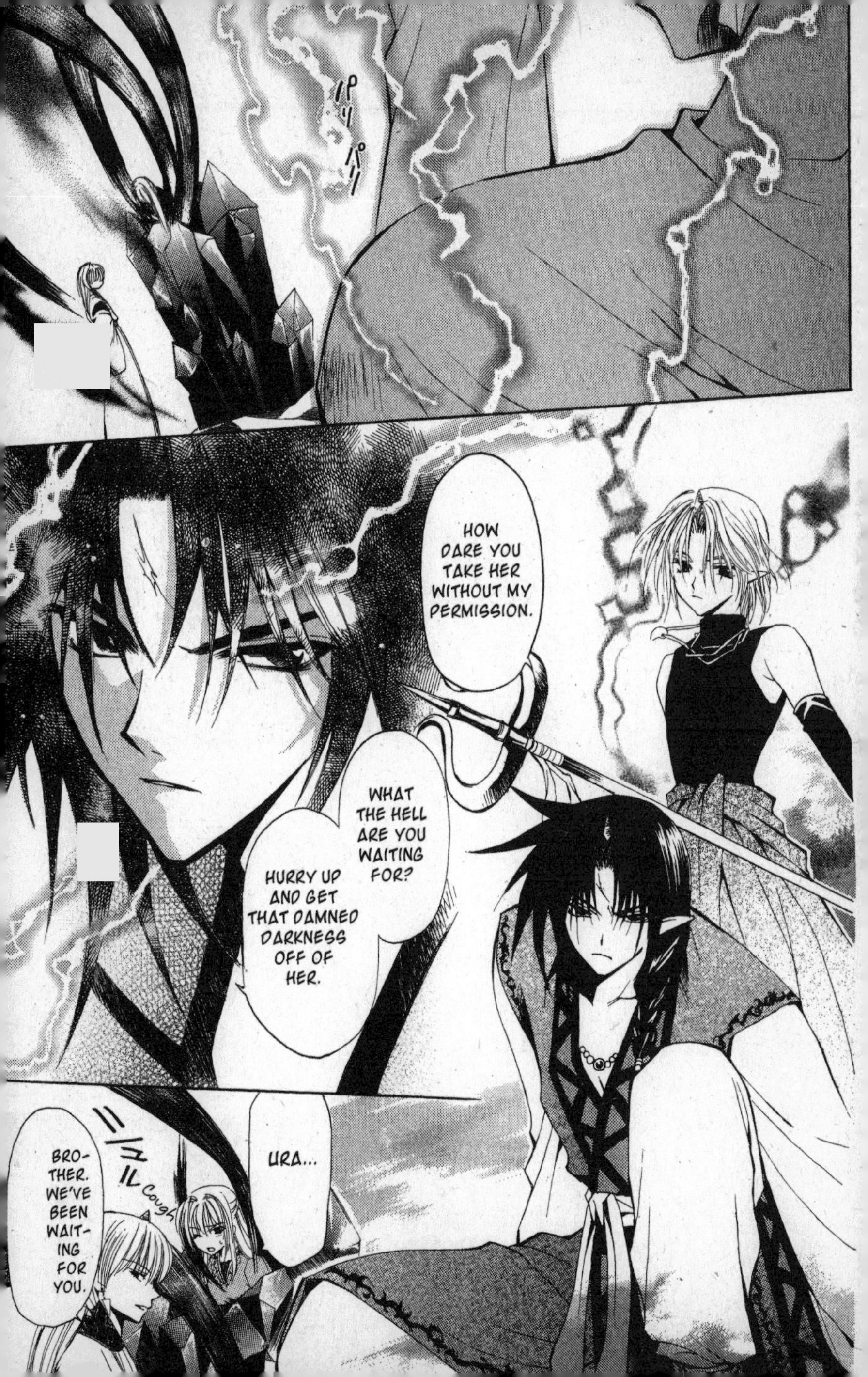
パリパリ
HOW DARE YOU TAKE HER WITHOUT MY PERMISSION.
WHAT THE HELL ARE YOU WAITING FOR?
HURRY UP AND GET THAT DAMNED DARKNESS OFF OF HER.
URA...
ニヤル
Cough
BRO-THER. WE'VE BEEN WAIT-ING FOR YOU.

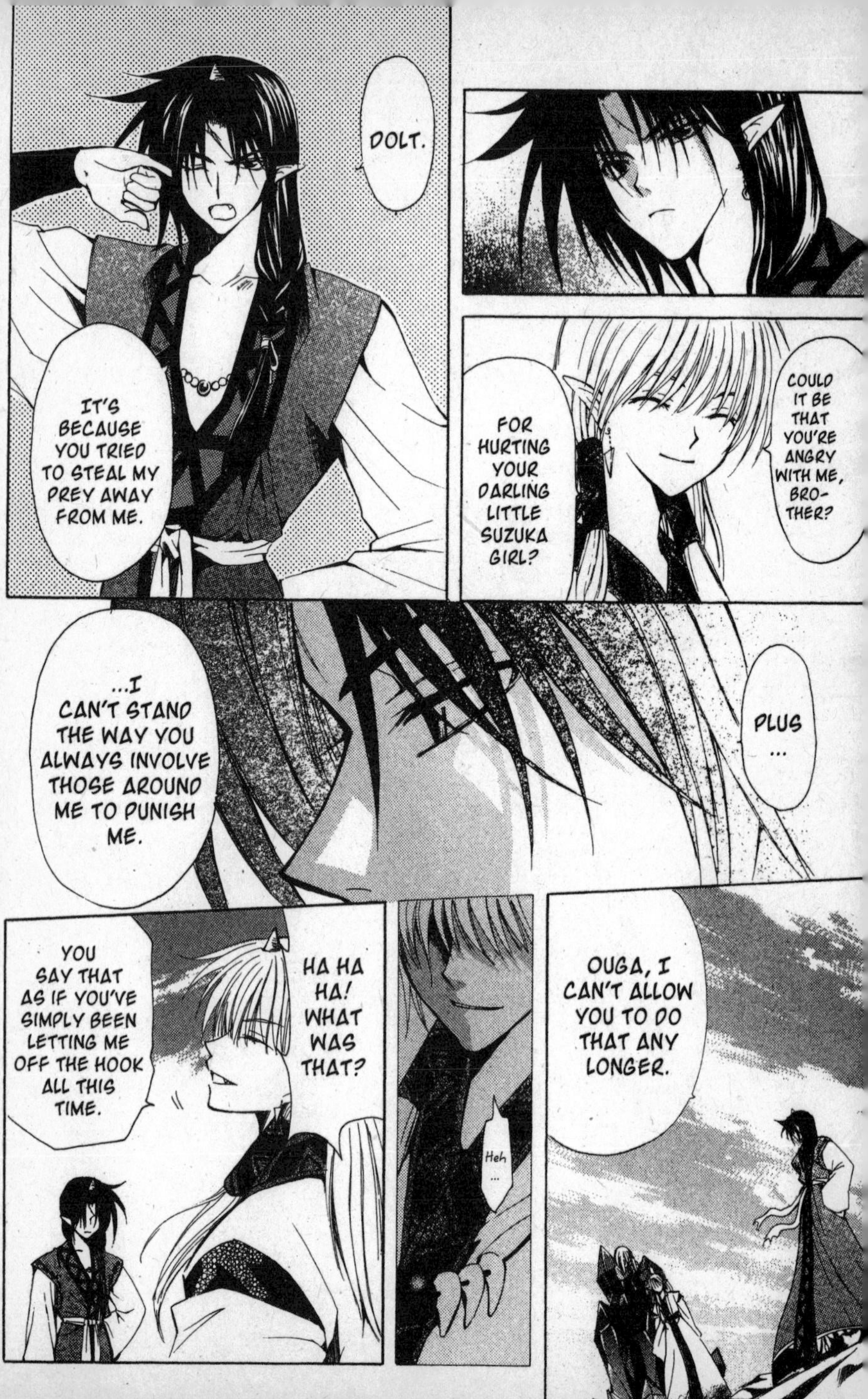
COULD IT BE THAT YOU'RE ANGRY WITH ME, BRO-THER?
FOR HURTING YOUR DARLING LITTLE SUZUKA GIRL?
DOLT.
IT'S BECAUSE YOU TRIED TO STEAL MY PREY AWAY FROM ME.
PLUS ...
...I CAN'T STAND THE WAY YOU ALWAYS INVOLVE THOSE AROUND ME TO PUNISH ME.
OUGA, I CAN'T ALLOW YOU TO DO THAT ANY LONGER.
Heh ...
HA HA HA! WHAT WAS THAT?
YOU SAY THAT AS IF YOU'VE SIMPLY BEEN LETTING ME OFF THE HOOK ALL THIS TIME.

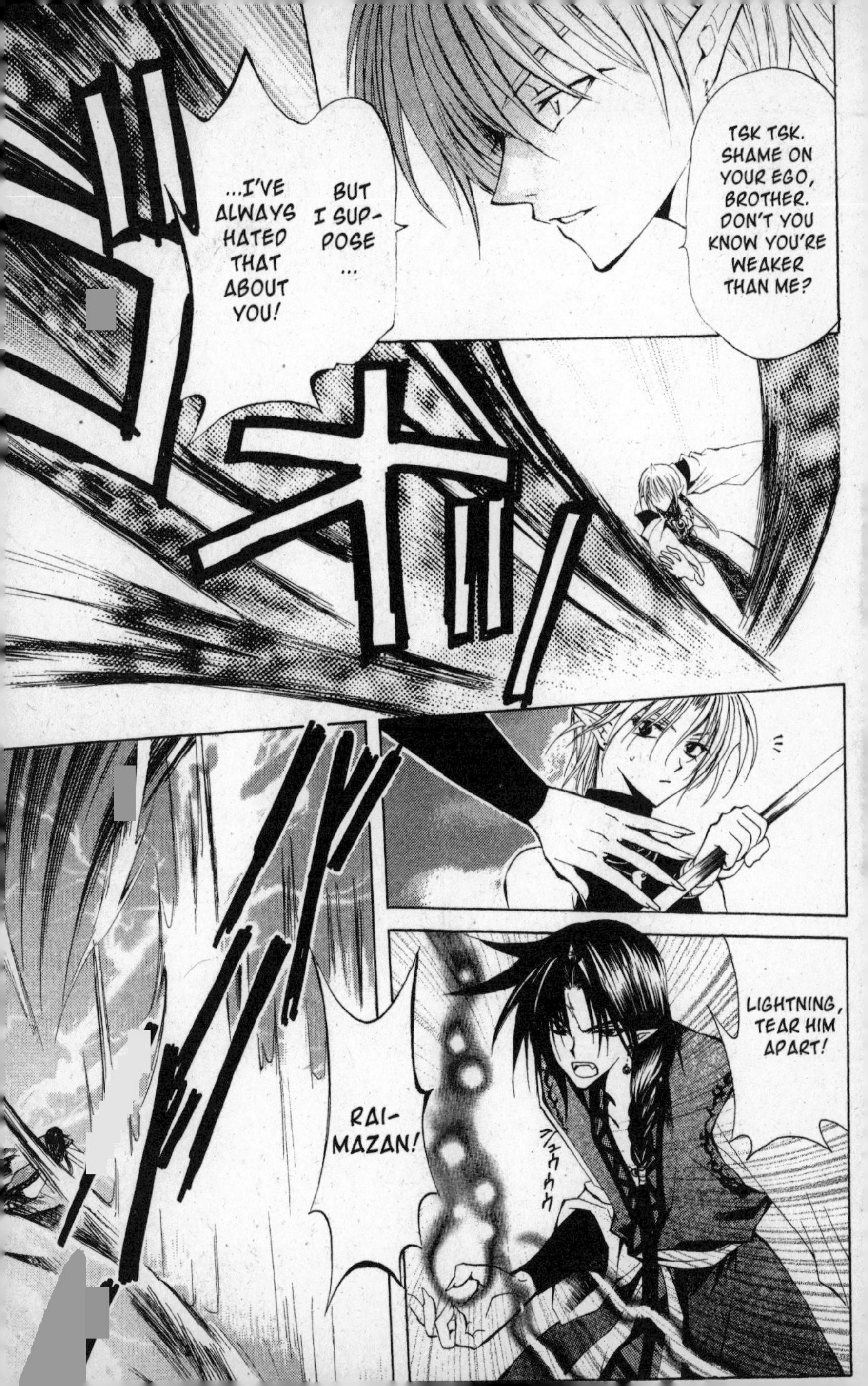
TSK TSK. SHAME ON YOUR EGO, BROTHER. DON'T YOU KNOW YOU'RE WEAKER THAN ME?
BUT I SUPPOSE ...
...I'VE ALWAYS HATED THAT ABOUT YOU!
LIGHTNING, TEAR HIM APART!
RAI-MAZAN!

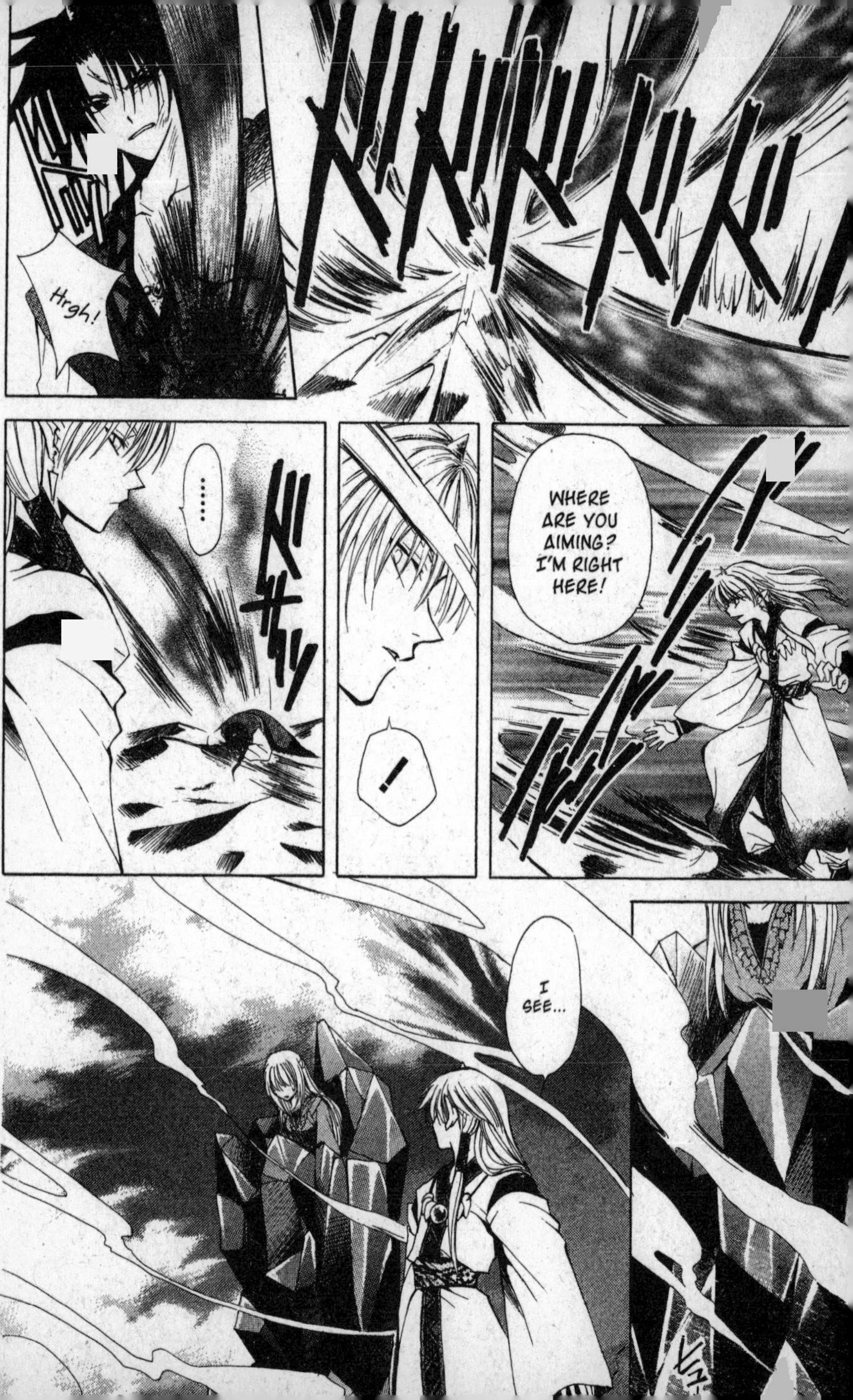
Hrgh!
WHERE ARE YOU AIMING? I'M RIGHT HERE!
!
......
I SEE...

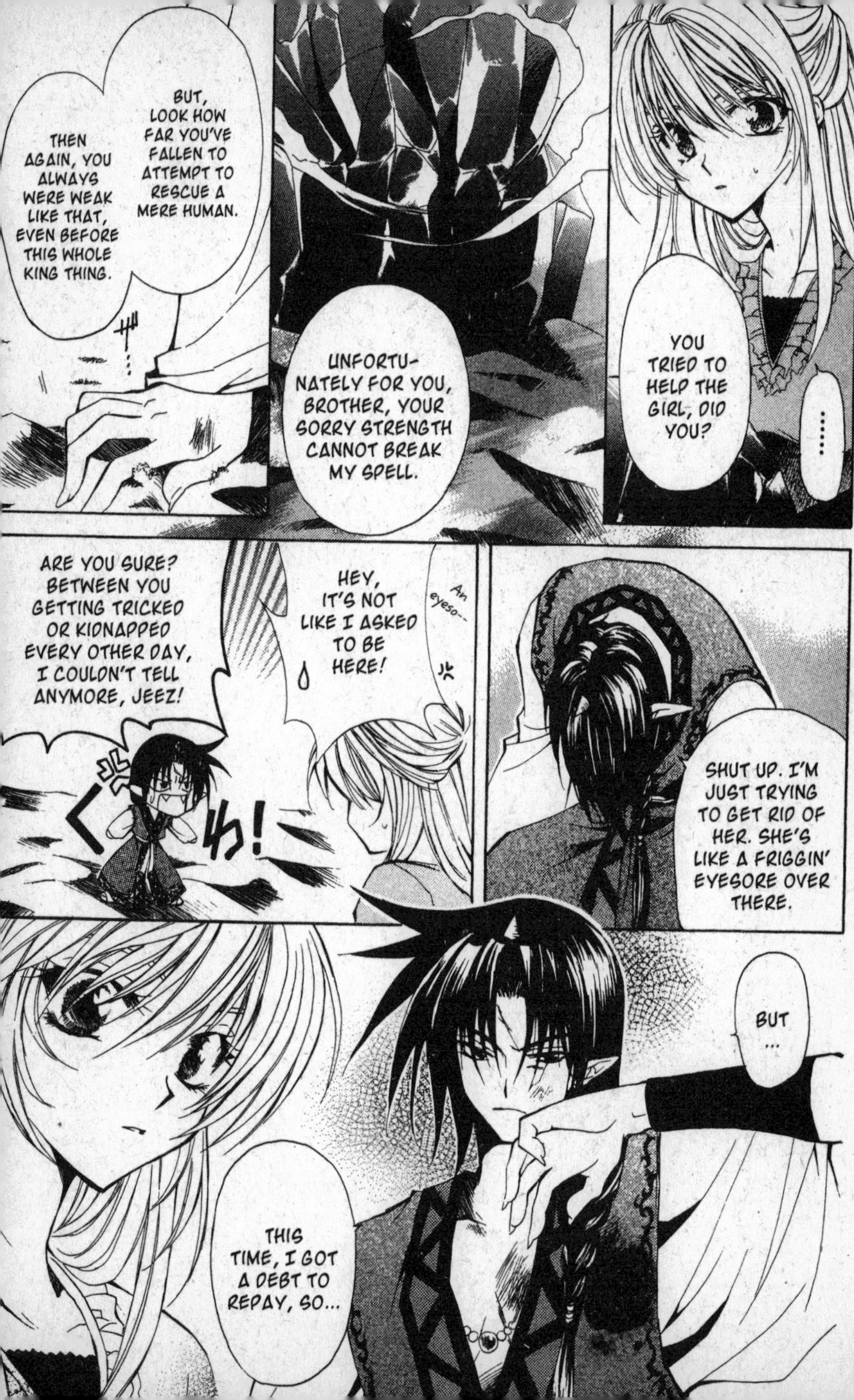
YOU TRIED TO HELP THE GIRL, DID YOU?
......
UNFORTUNATELY FOR YOU, BROTHER, YOUR SORRY STRENGTH CANNOT BREAK MY SPELL.
BUT, LOOK HOW FAR YOU'VE FALLEN TO ATTEMPT TO RESCUE A MERE HUMAN.
THEN AGAIN, YOU ALWAYS WERE WEAK LIKE THAT, EVEN BEFORE THIS WHOLE KING THING.
SHUT UP. I'M JUST TRYING TO GET RID OF HER. SHE'S LIKE A FRIGGIN' EYESORE OVER THERE.
An eyeso--
HEY, IT'S NOT LIKE I ASKED TO BE HERE!
ARE YOU SURE? BETWEEN YOU GETTING TRICKED OR KIDNAPPED EVERY OTHER DAY, I COULDN'T TELL ANYMORE, JEEZ!
くわ!
BUT ...
THIS TIME, I GOT A DEBT TO REPAY, SO...

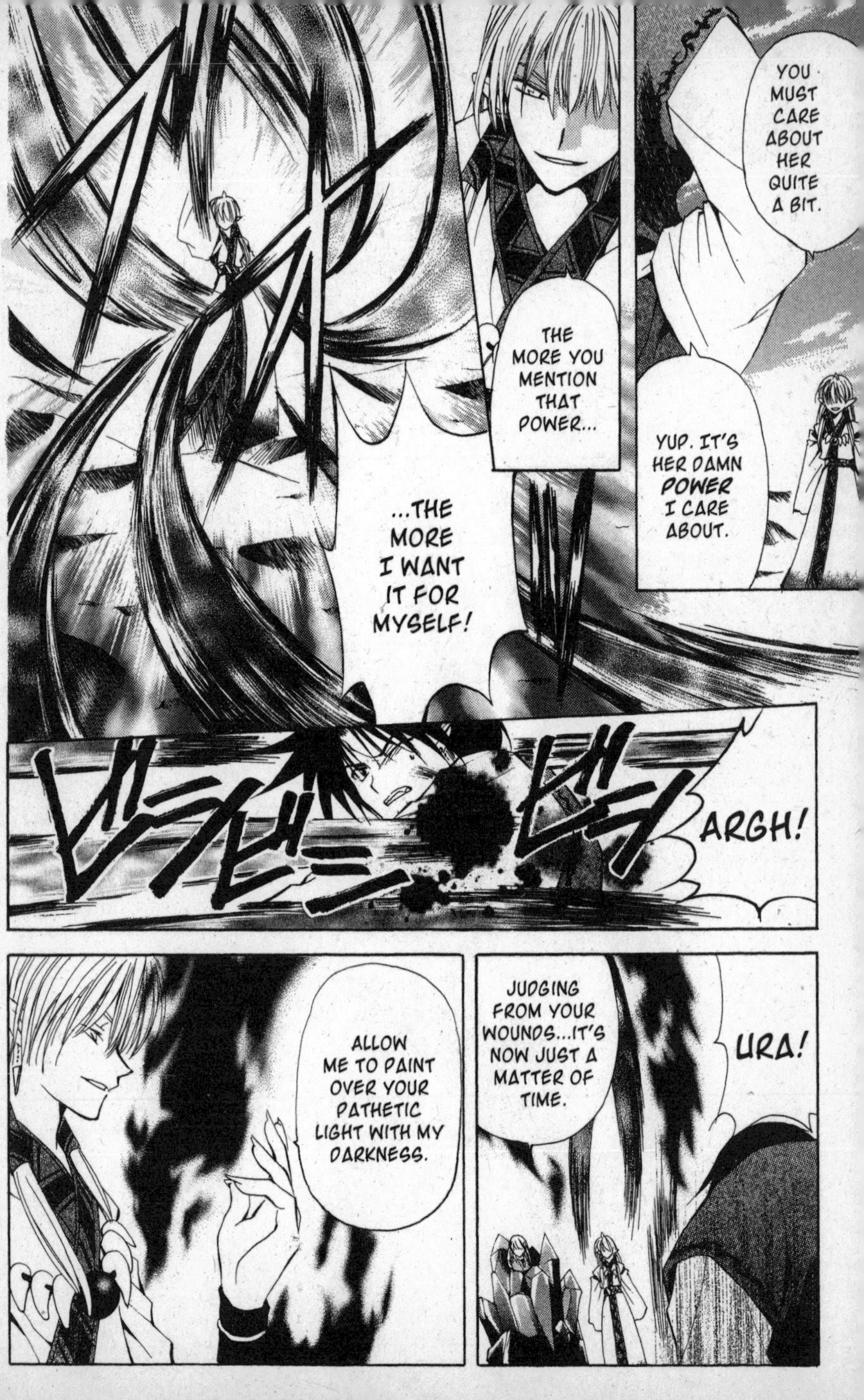
YOU MUST CARE ABOUT HER QUITE A BIT.
YUP. IT'S HER DAMN POWER I CARE ABOUT.
THE MORE YOU MENTION THAT POWER...
...THE MORE I WANT IT FOR MYSELF!
ARGH!
URA!
JUDGING FROM YOUR WOUNDS...IT'S NOW JUST A MATTER OF TIME.
ALLOW ME TO PAINT OVER YOUR PATHETIC LIGHT WITH MY DARKNESS.

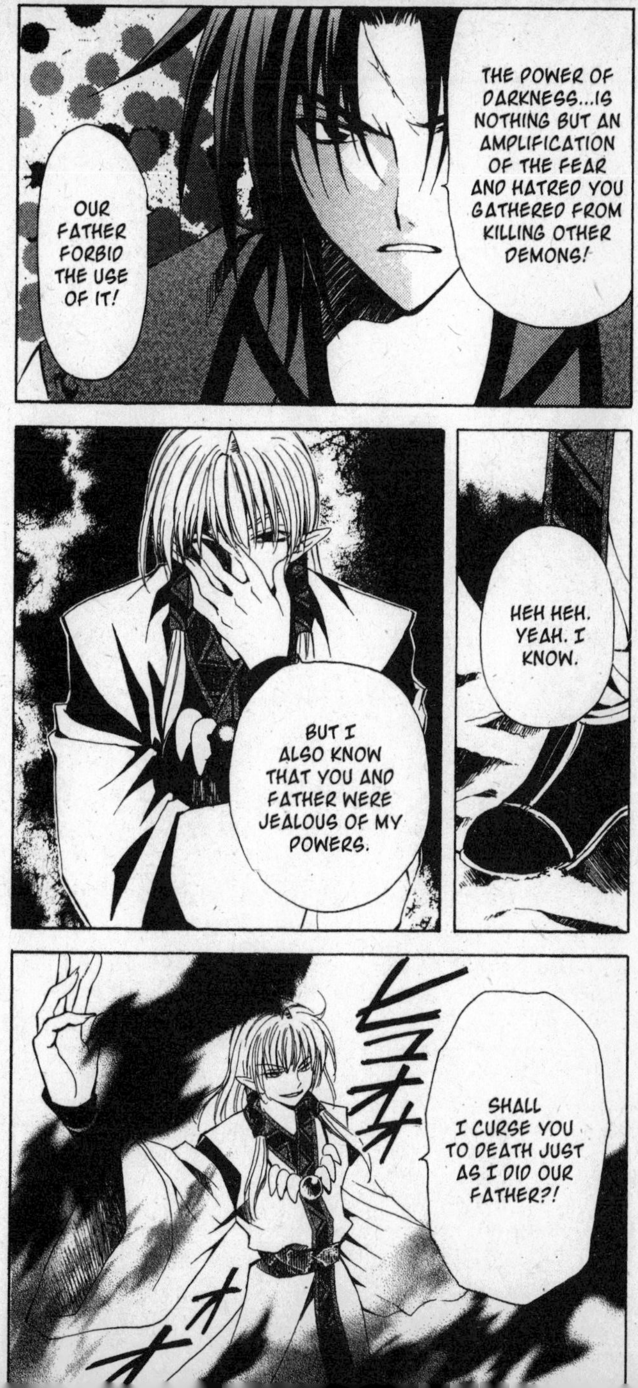
THE POWER OF DARKNESS...IS NOTHING BUT AN AMPLIFICATION OF THE FEAR AND HATRED YOU GATHERED FROM KILLING OTHER DEMONS!
OUR FATHER FORBID THE USE OF IT!
HEH HEH. YEAH. I KNOW.
BUT I ALSO KNOW THAT YOU AND FATHER WERE JEALOUS OF MY POWERS.
SHALL I CURSE YOU TO DEATH JUST AS I DID OUR FATHER?!

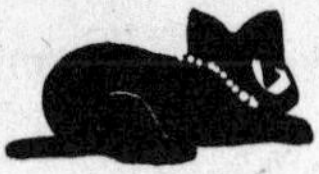

I often receive letters from readers asking that I provide some sort of profile for them, so here it is, short and simple.

**Mizuho Kusanagi:**
(I sort of just came up with a pen name.)

| | |
|---|---|
| Date of Birth: | February 3rd, 1979 |
| Place of Birth | Kumamoto Prefecture |
| Blood Type: | O |
| Hobbies: | I guess, drawing! |

And I also have a super fetish for voices. I love voice actors. I also really like actors with good voices. I'm like a little follower.

**Fave Food:**

I love ramen. I wish I could go around just trying different foods. (But my stomach is small so there goes that idea.) I basically eat a lot a vegetables. I'm not so good with meat.

**Fave Movies:**

Anything Miyazaki. (I'm worried about his health. I just love him!) Sound of Music. Lord of the Rings. If there's anything else you want to know, just send me a letter!

And last but not least, thank you guys so much for all your support!

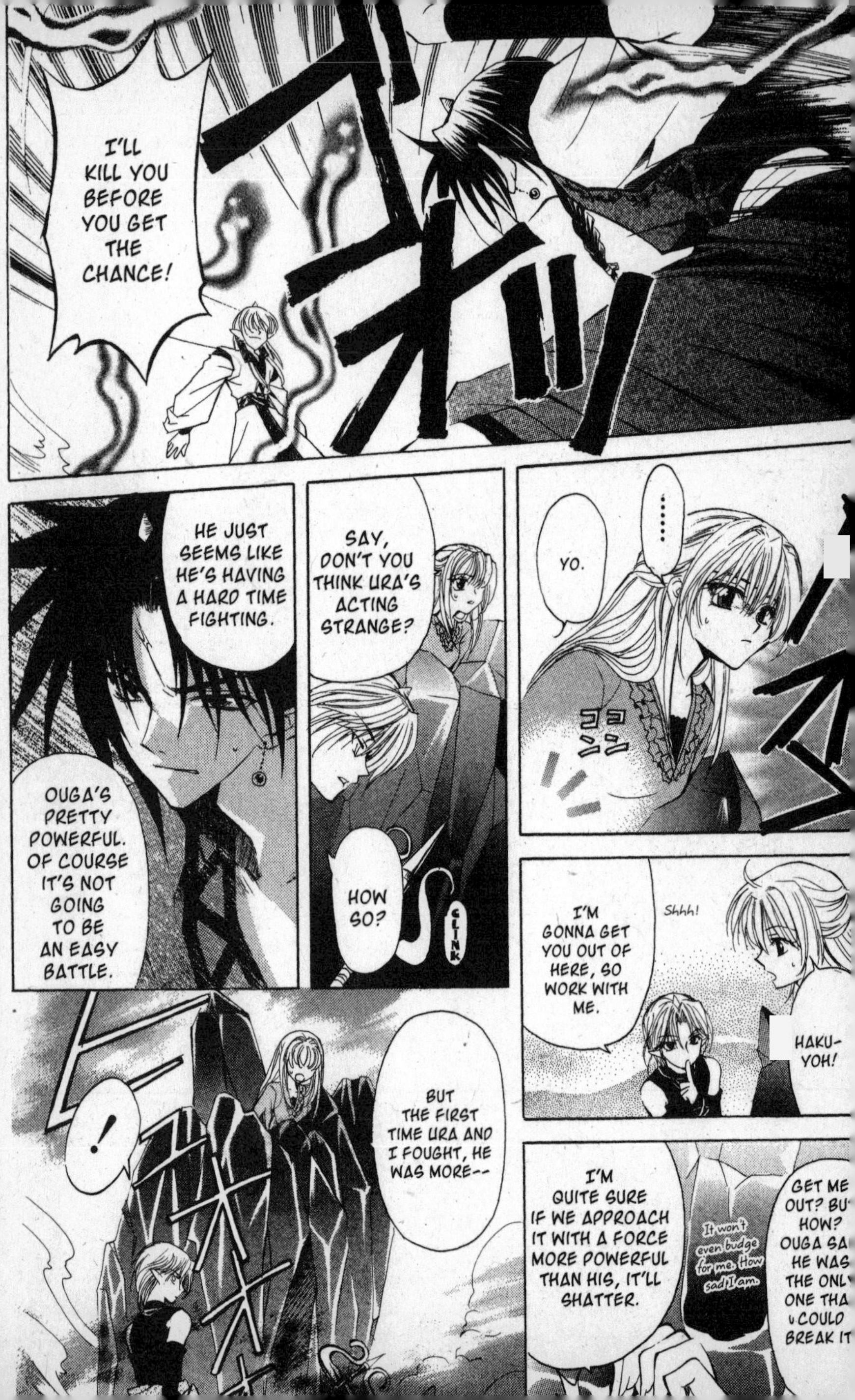
I'LL KILL YOU BEFORE YOU GET THE CHANCE!
YO.
......
SAY, DON'T YOU THINK URA'S ACTING STRANGE?
HOW SO?
CLINK
HE JUST SEEMS LIKE HE'S HAVING A HARD TIME FIGHTING.
OUGA'S PRETTY POWERFUL. OF COURSE IT'S NOT GOING TO BE AN EASY BATTLE.
HAKU-YOH!
Shhh!
I'M GONNA GET YOU OUT OF HERE, SO WORK WITH ME.
GET ME OUT? BU HOW? OUGA SA HE WAS THE ONL ONE THA COULD BREAK IT
It won't even budge for me. How sad I am.
I'M QUITE SURE IF WE APPROACH IT WITH A FORCE MORE POWERFUL THAN HIS, IT'LL SHATTER.
BUT THE FIRST TIME URA AND I FOUGHT, HE WAS MORE--
!

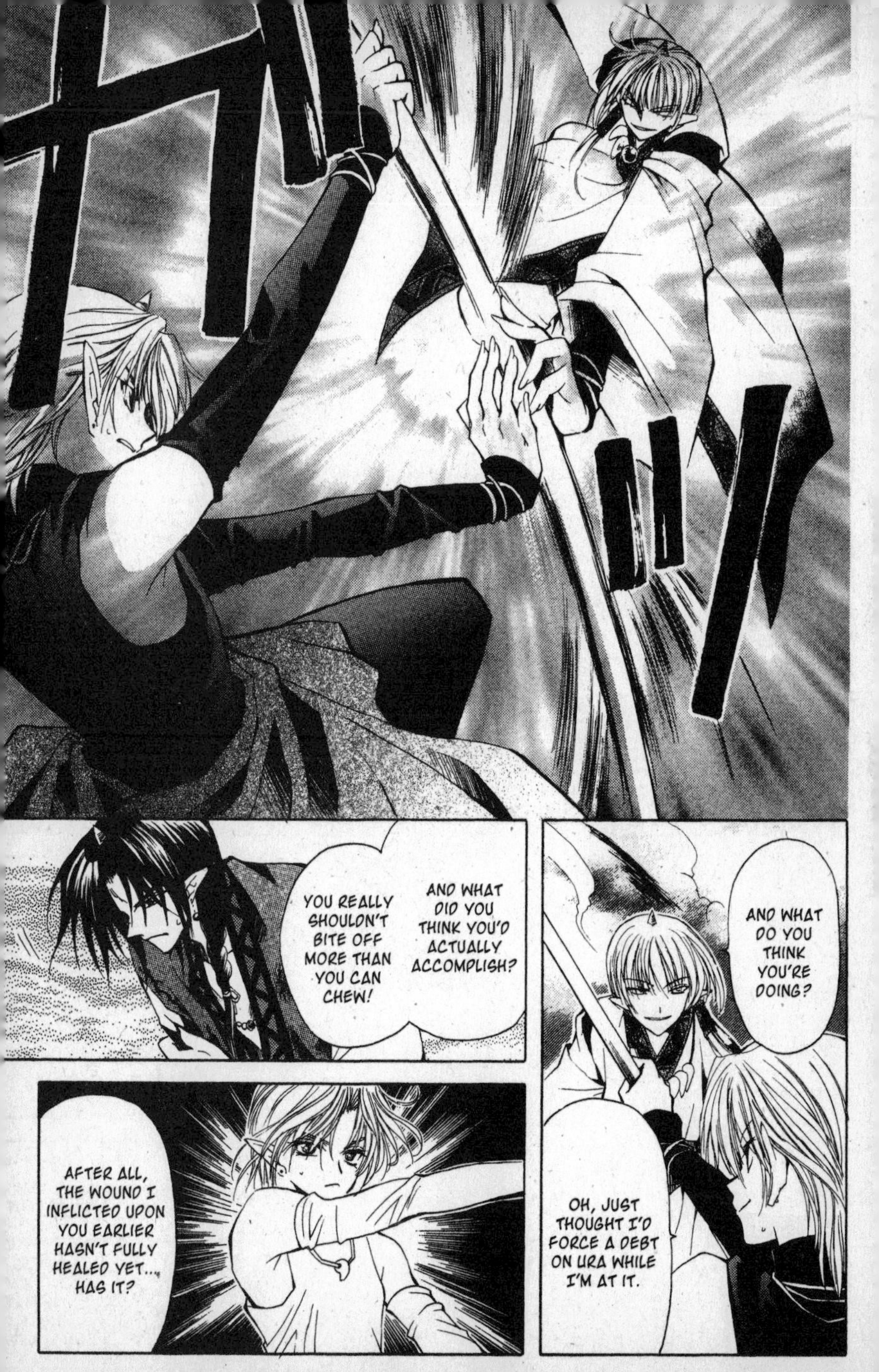
AND WHAT DO YOU THINK YOU'RE DOING?
OH, JUST THOUGHT I'D FORCE A DEBT ON URA WHILE I'M AT IT.
AND WHAT DID YOU THINK YOU'D ACTUALLY ACCOMPLISH?
YOU REALLY SHOULDN'T BITE OFF MORE THAN YOU CAN CHEW!
AFTER ALL, THE WOUND I INFLICTED UPON YOU EARLIER HASN'T FULLY HEALED YET... HAS IT?

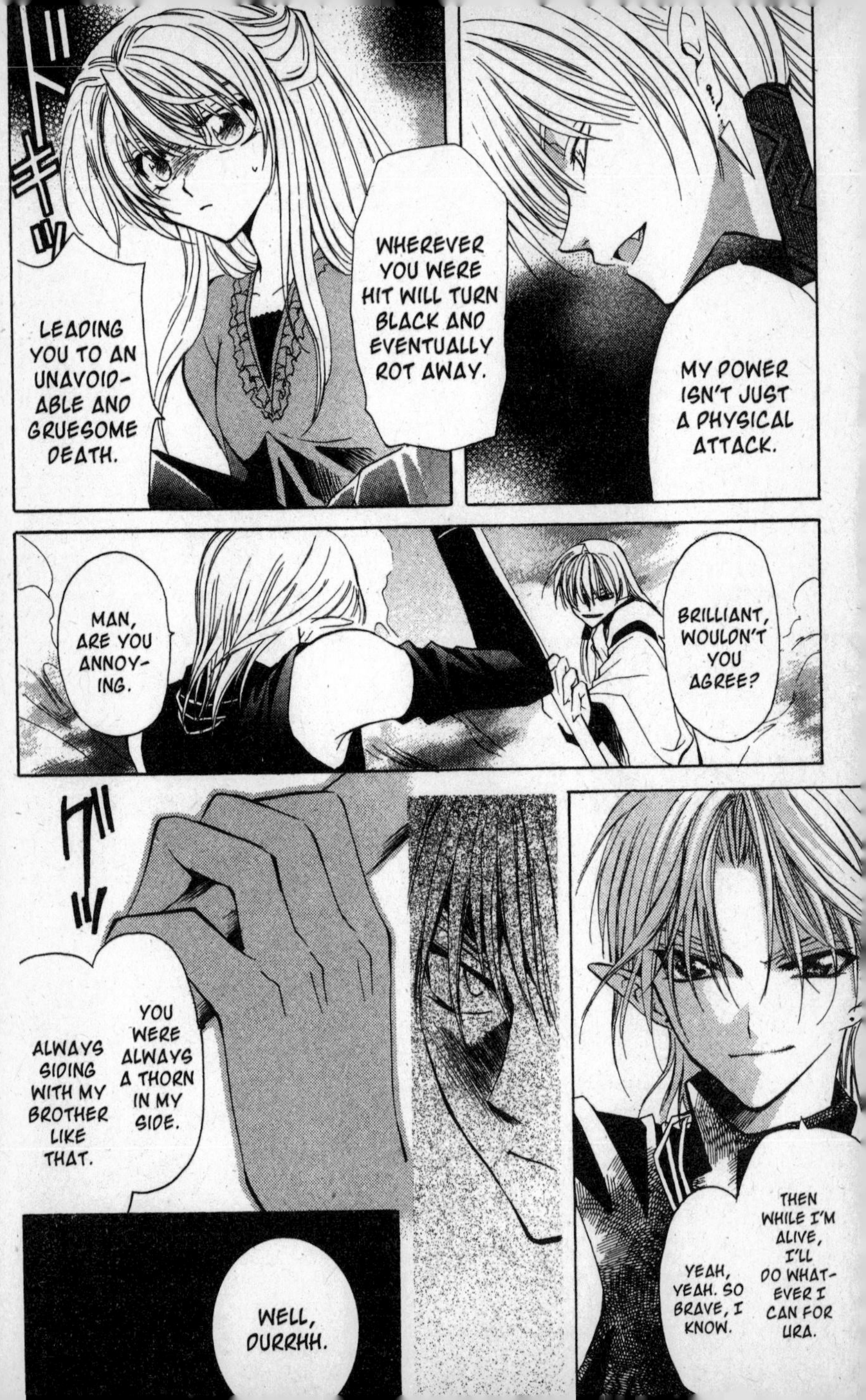
MY POWER ISN'T JUST A PHYSICAL ATTACK.
WHEREVER YOU WERE HIT WILL TURN BLACK AND EVENTUALLY ROT AWAY.
LEADING YOU TO AN UNAVOID-ABLE AND GRUESOME DEATH.
BRILLIANT, WOULDN'T YOU AGREE?
MAN, ARE YOU ANNOY-ING.
THEN WHILE I'M ALIVE, I'LL DO WHAT-EVER I CAN FOR URA.
YEAH, YEAH. SO BRAVE, I KNOW.
YOU WERE ALWAYS A THORN IN MY SIDE.
ALWAYS SIDING WITH MY BROTHER LIKE THAT.
WELL, DURRHH.

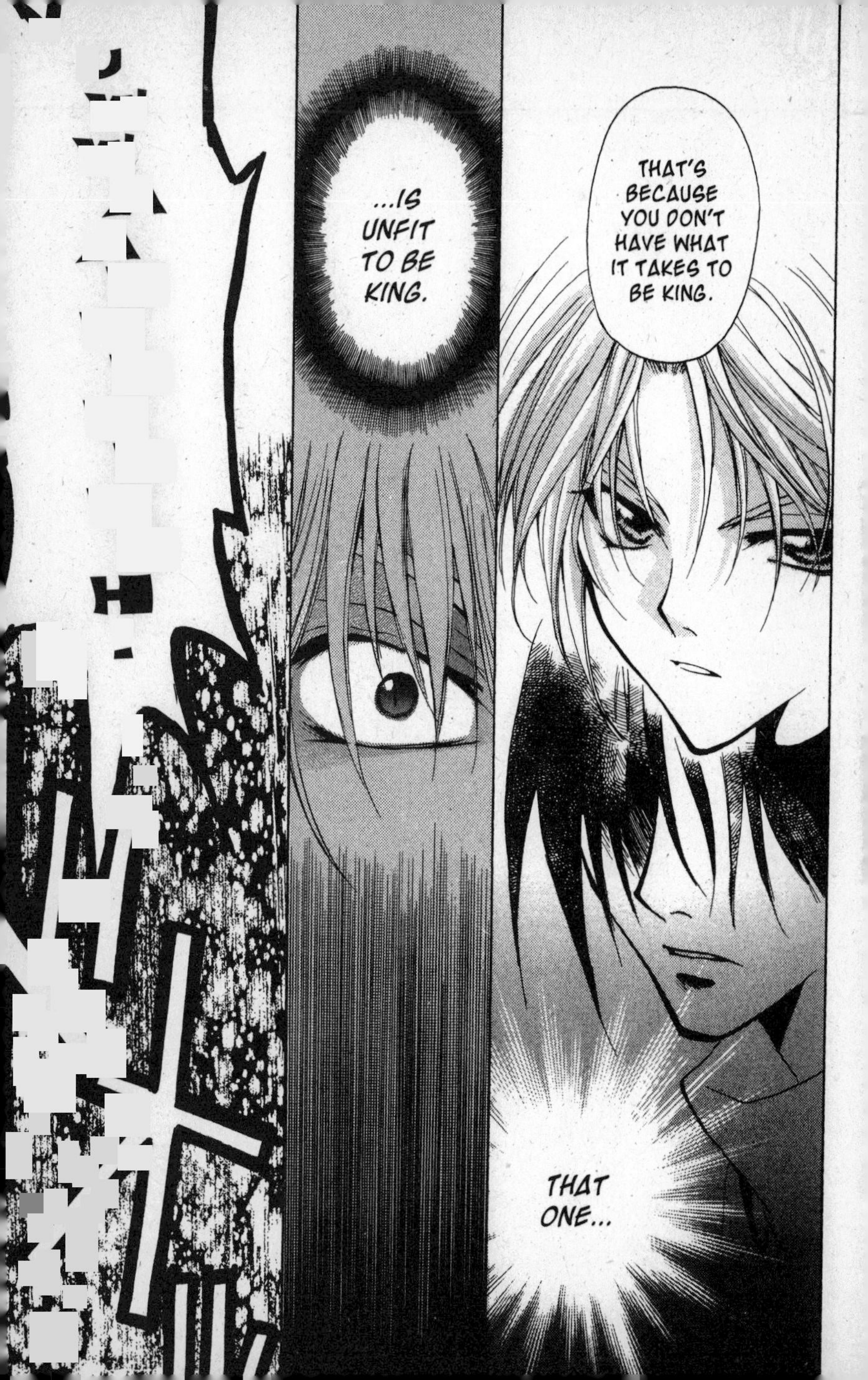
THAT'S BECAUSE YOU DON'T HAVE WHAT IT TAKES TO BE KING.
THAT ONE...
...IS UNFIT TO BE KING.

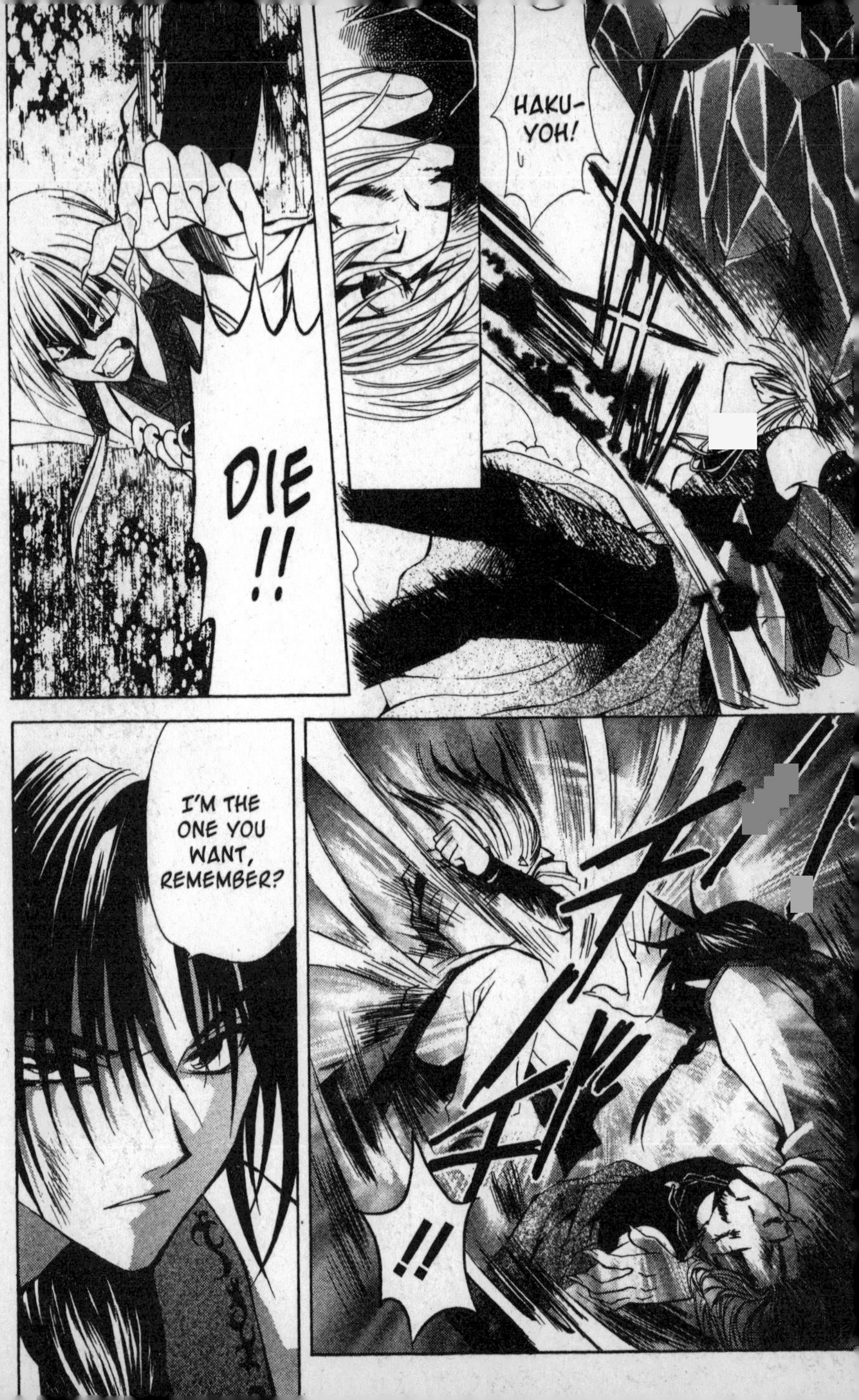
HAKU-YOH!
DIE !!
!!
I'M THE ONE YOU WANT, REMEMBER?

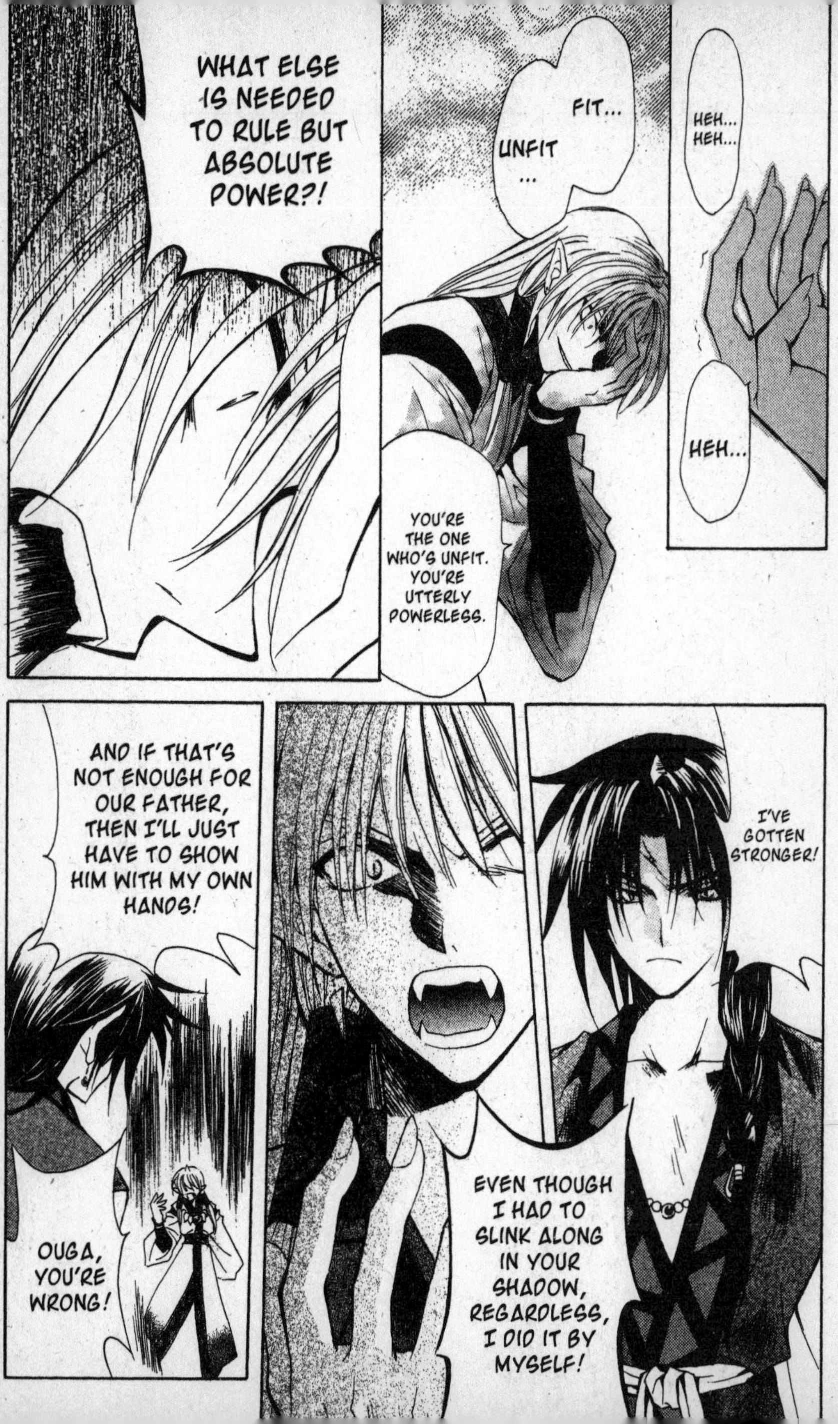
HEH... HEH...
HEH...
FIT... UNFIT ...
YOU'RE THE ONE WHO'S UNFIT. YOU'RE UTTERLY POWERLESS.
WHAT ELSE IS NEEDED TO RULE BUT ABSOLUTE POWER?!
I'VE GOTTEN STRONGER!
EVEN THOUGH I HAD TO SLINK ALONG IN YOUR SHADOW, REGARDLESS, I DID IT BY MYSELF!
AND IF THAT'S NOT ENOUGH FOR OUR FATHER, THEN I'LL JUST HAVE TO SHOW HIM WITH MY OWN HANDS!
OUGA, YOU'RE WRONG!

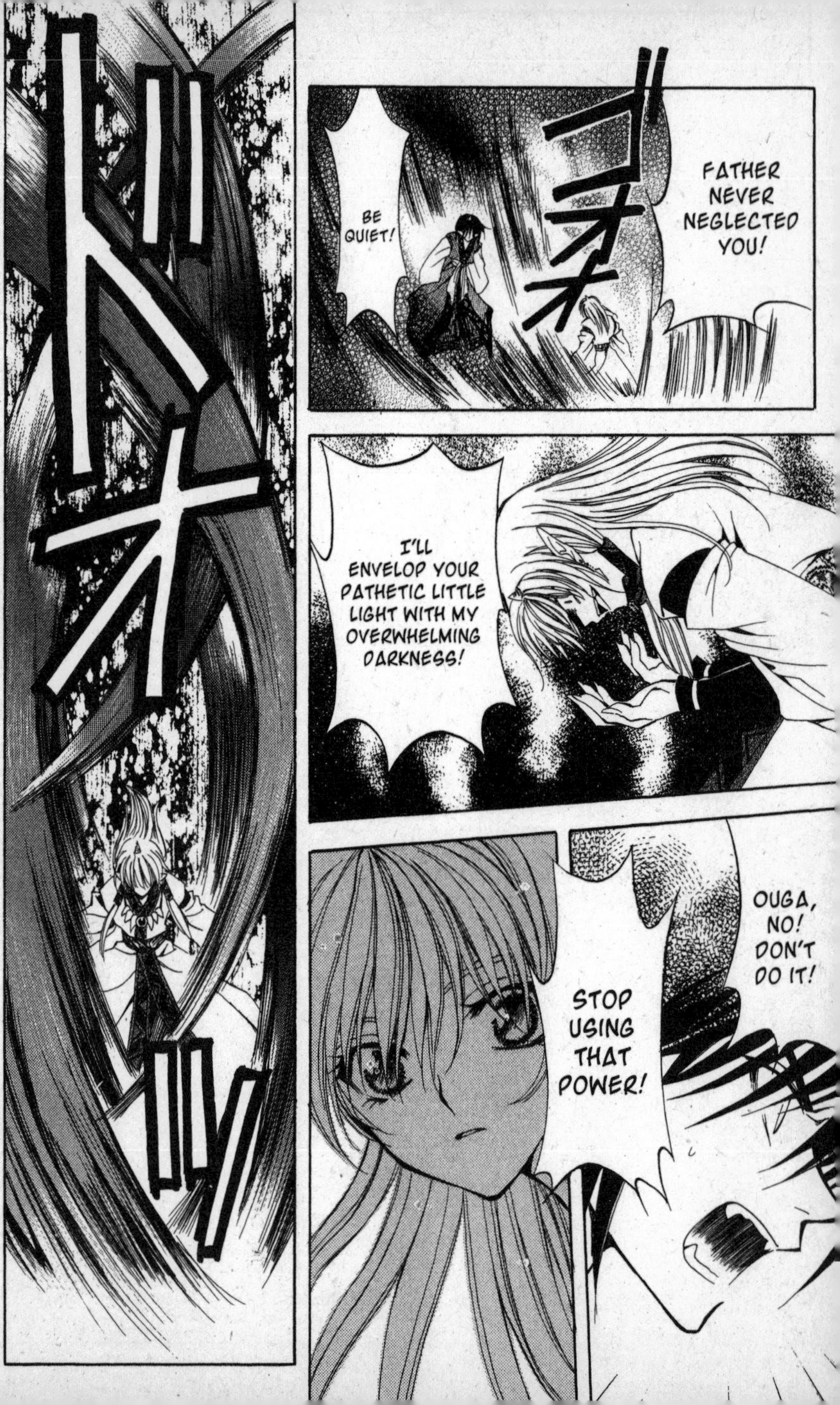
FATHER NEVER NEGLECTED YOU!
BE QUIET!
I'LL ENVELOP YOUR PATHETIC LITTLE LIGHT WITH MY OVERWHELMING DARKNESS!
OUGA, NO! DON'T DO IT!
STOP USING THAT POWER!

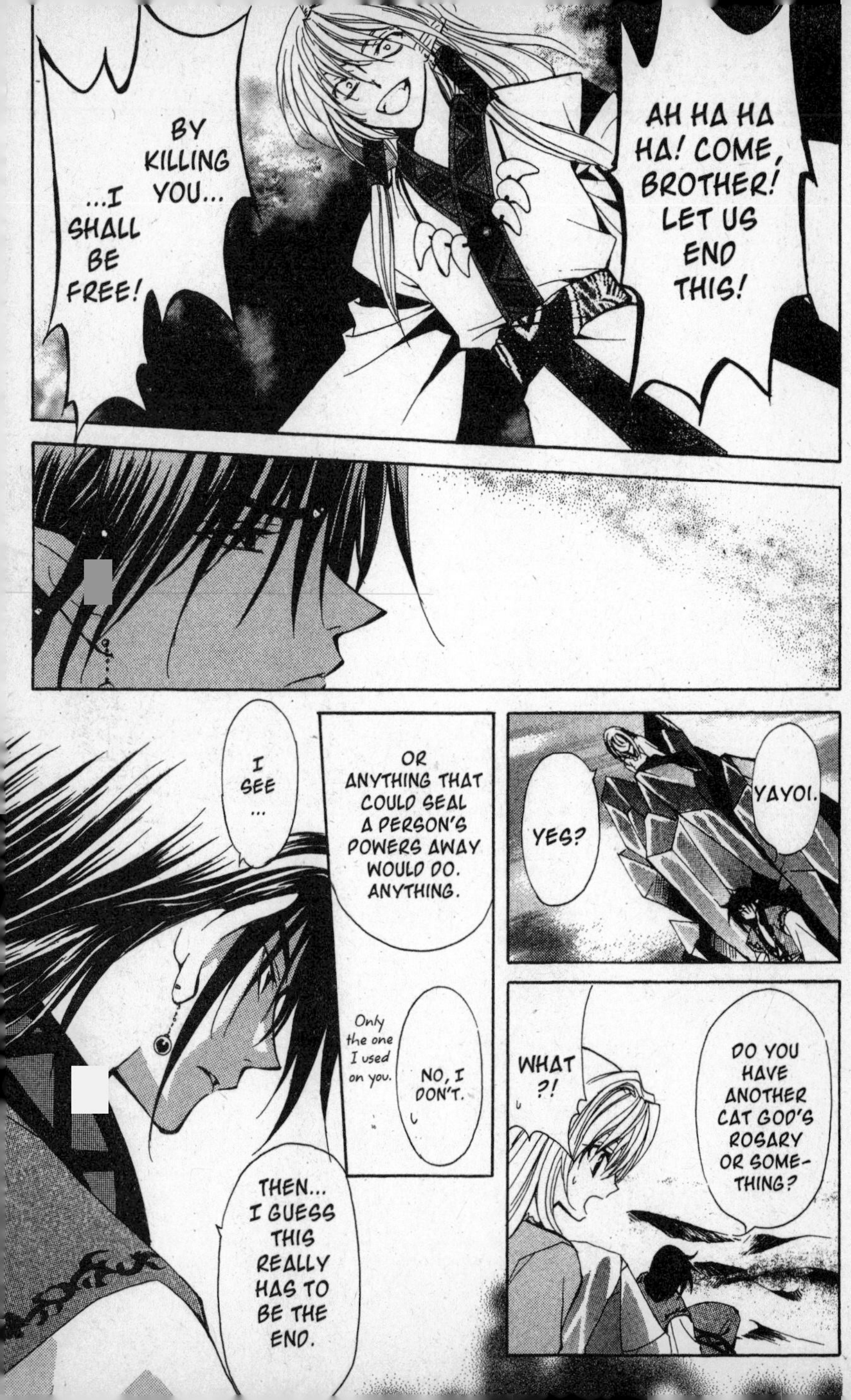
AH HA HA HA! COME, BROTHER! LET US END THIS!
BY KILLING YOU...
...I SHALL BE FREE!
YAYOI.
YES?
DO YOU HAVE ANOTHER CAT GOD'S ROSARY OR SOME-THING?
WHAT ?!
OR ANYTHING THAT COULD SEAL A PERSON'S POWERS AWAY WOULD DO. ANYTHING.
NO, I DON'T.
Only the one I used on you.
I SEE ...
THEN... I GUESS THIS REALLY HAS TO BE THE END.

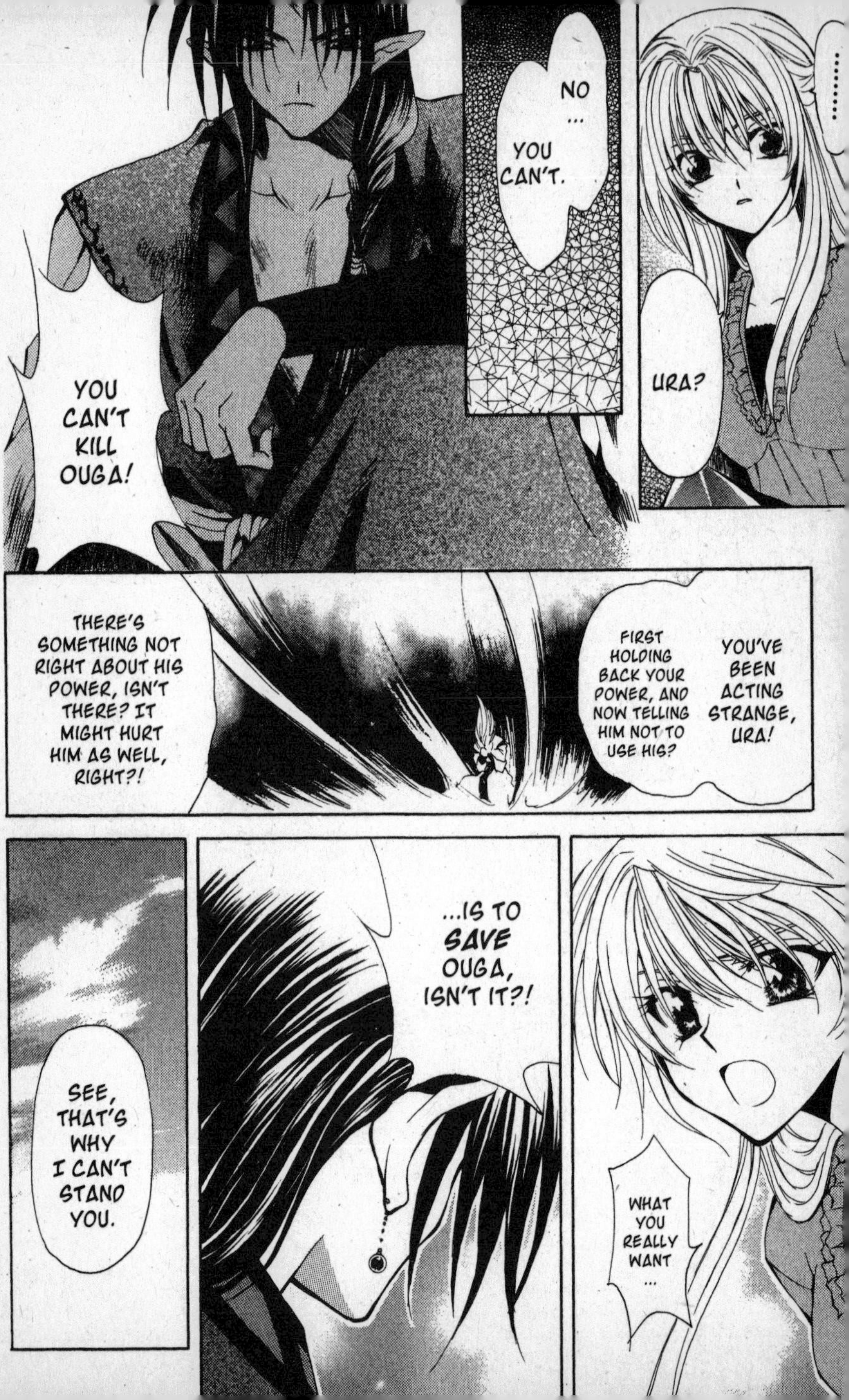
...
URA?
NO ... YOU CAN'T.
YOU CAN'T KILL OUGA!
YOU'VE BEEN ACTING STRANGE, URA!
FIRST HOLDING BACK YOUR POWER, AND NOW TELLING HIM NOT TO USE HIS?
THERE'S SOMETHING NOT RIGHT ABOUT HIS POWER, ISN'T THERE? IT MIGHT HURT HIM AS WELL, RIGHT?!
WHAT YOU REALLY WANT ...
...IS TO SAVE OUGA, ISN'T IT?!
SEE, THAT'S WHY I CAN'T STAND YOU.

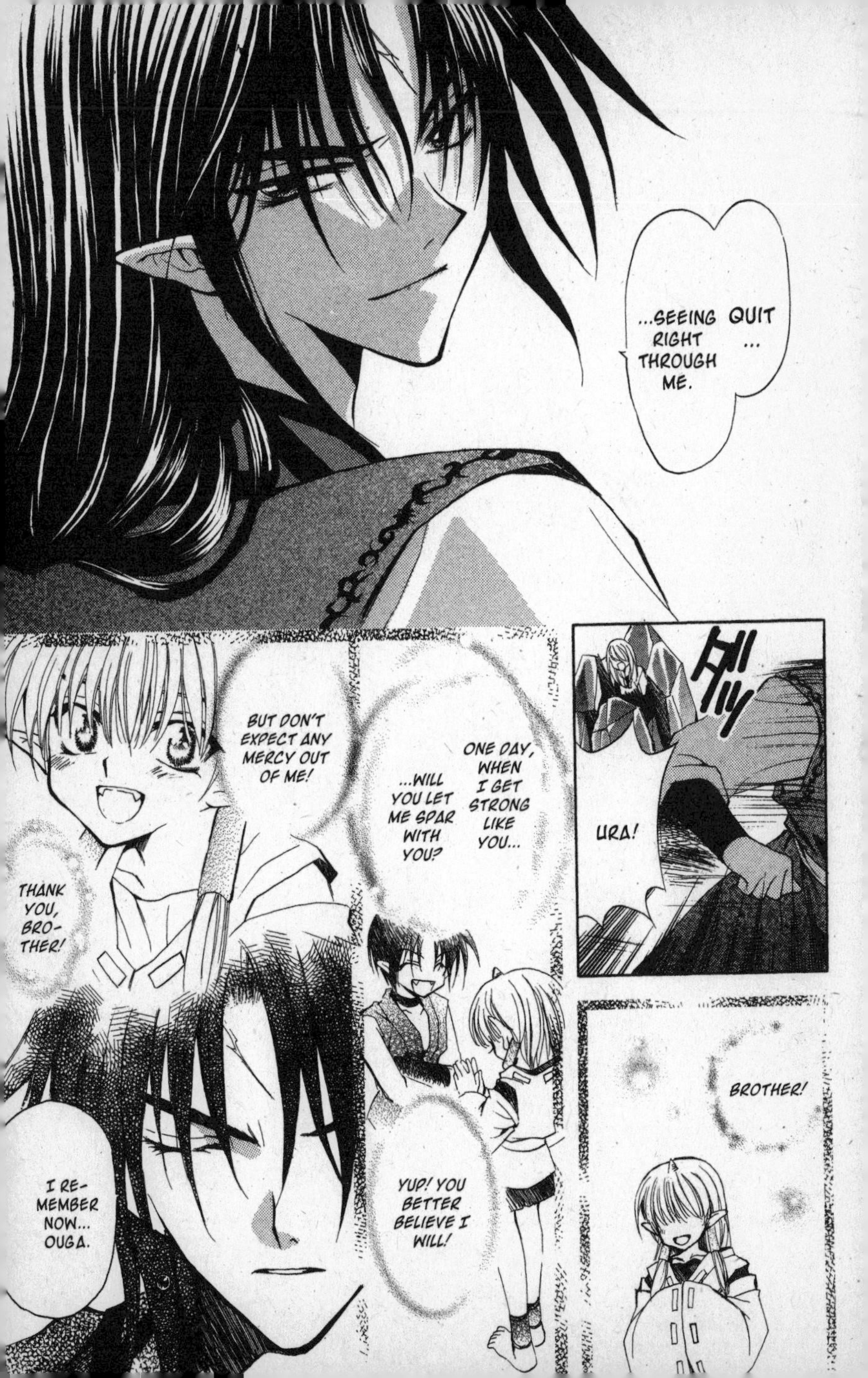
QUIT ...
...SEEING RIGHT THROUGH ME.
ダッ
URA!
BROTHER!
ONE DAY, WHEN I GET STRONG LIKE YOU...
...WILL YOU LET ME SPAR WITH YOU?
YUP! YOU BETTER BELIEVE I WILL!
BUT DON'T EXPECT ANY MERCY OUT OF ME!
THANK YOU, BRO-THER!
I RE-MEMBER NOW... OUGA.

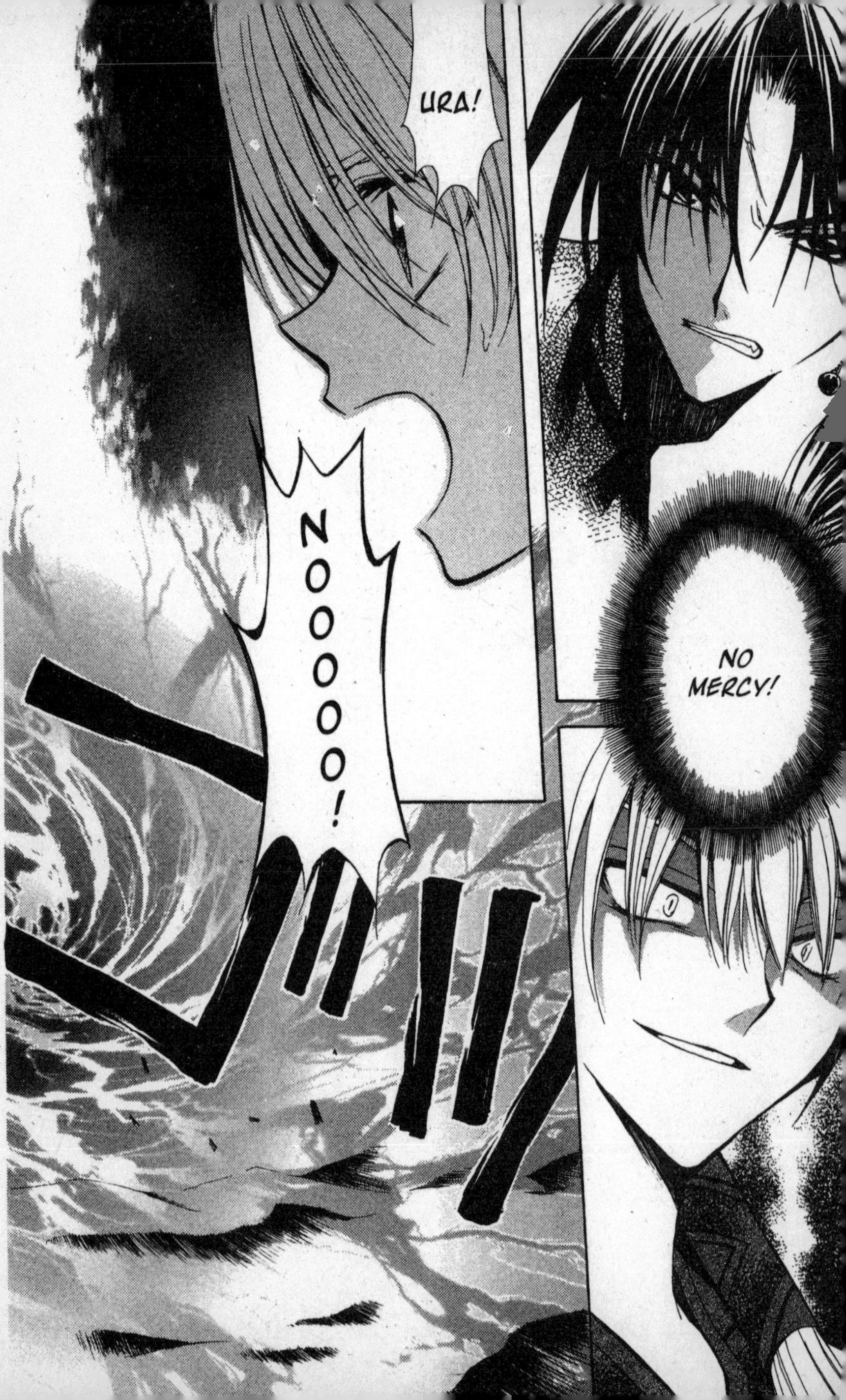
URA!
NO MERCY!
NOOOOOO!

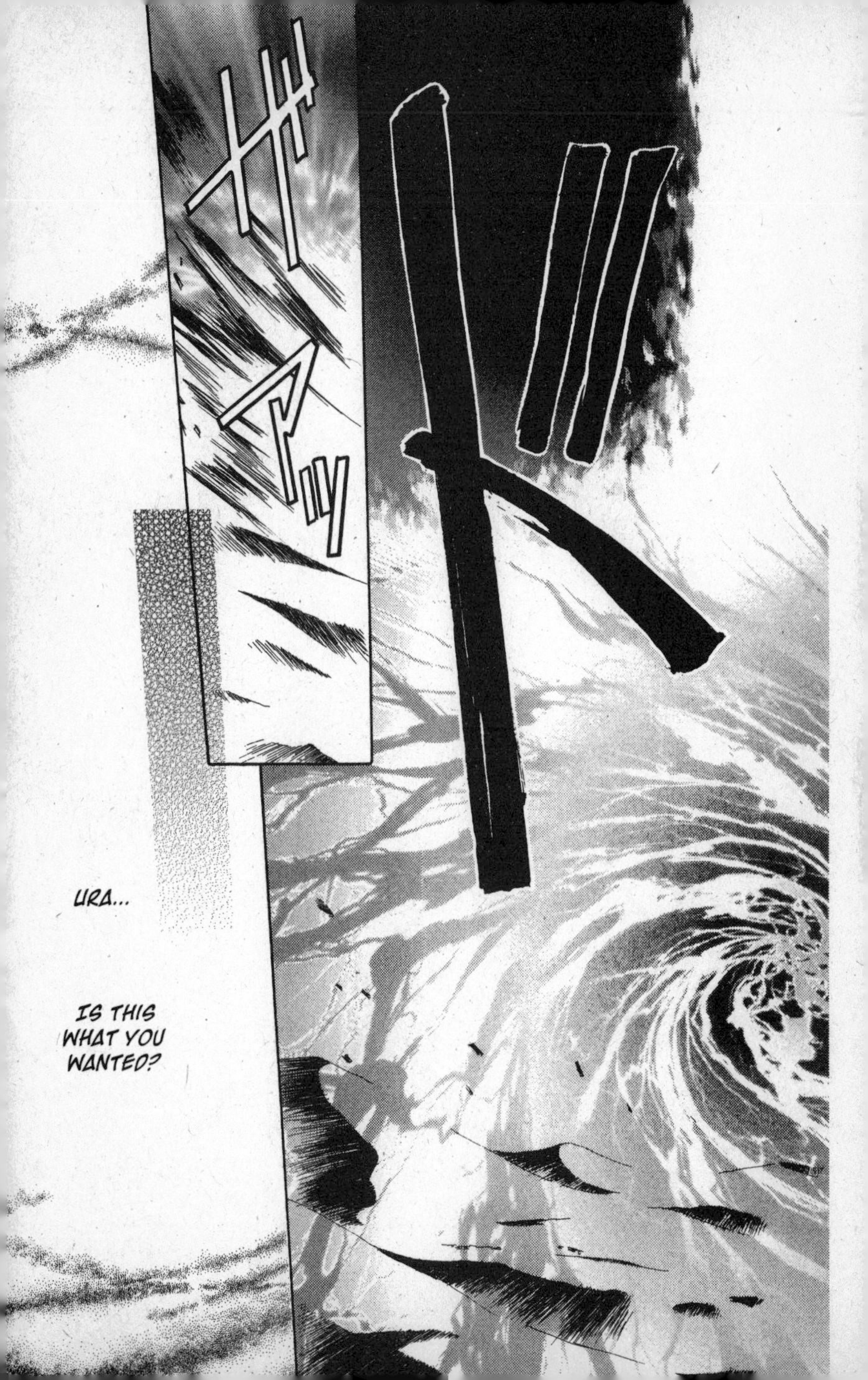
URA...
IS THIS WHAT YOU WANTED?

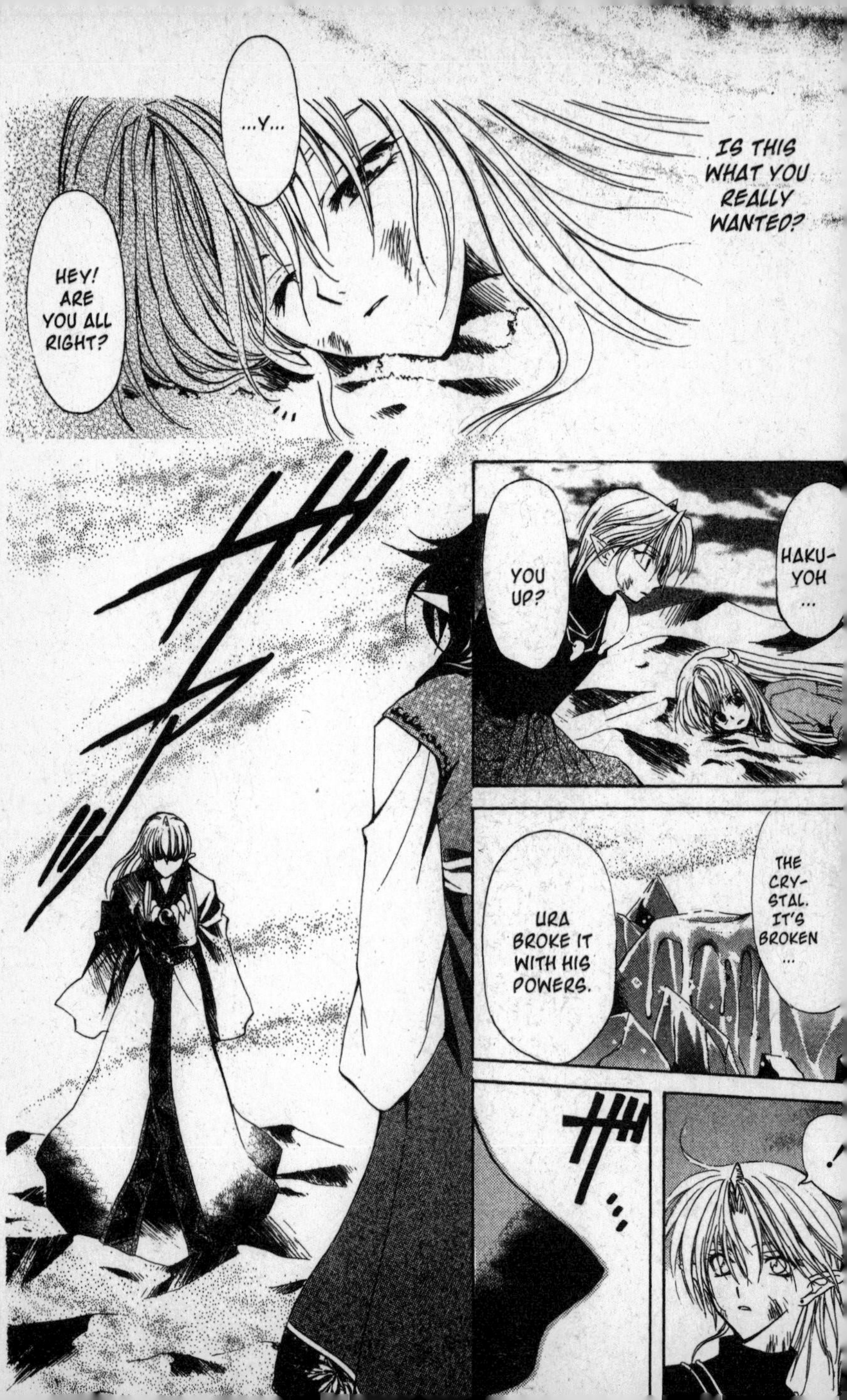
IS THIS WHAT YOU REALLY WANTED?
...Y...
HEY! ARE YOU ALL RIGHT?
HAKU-YOH ...
YOU UP?
THE CRY-STAL. IT'S BROKEN ...
URA BROKE IT WITH HIS POWERS.
!

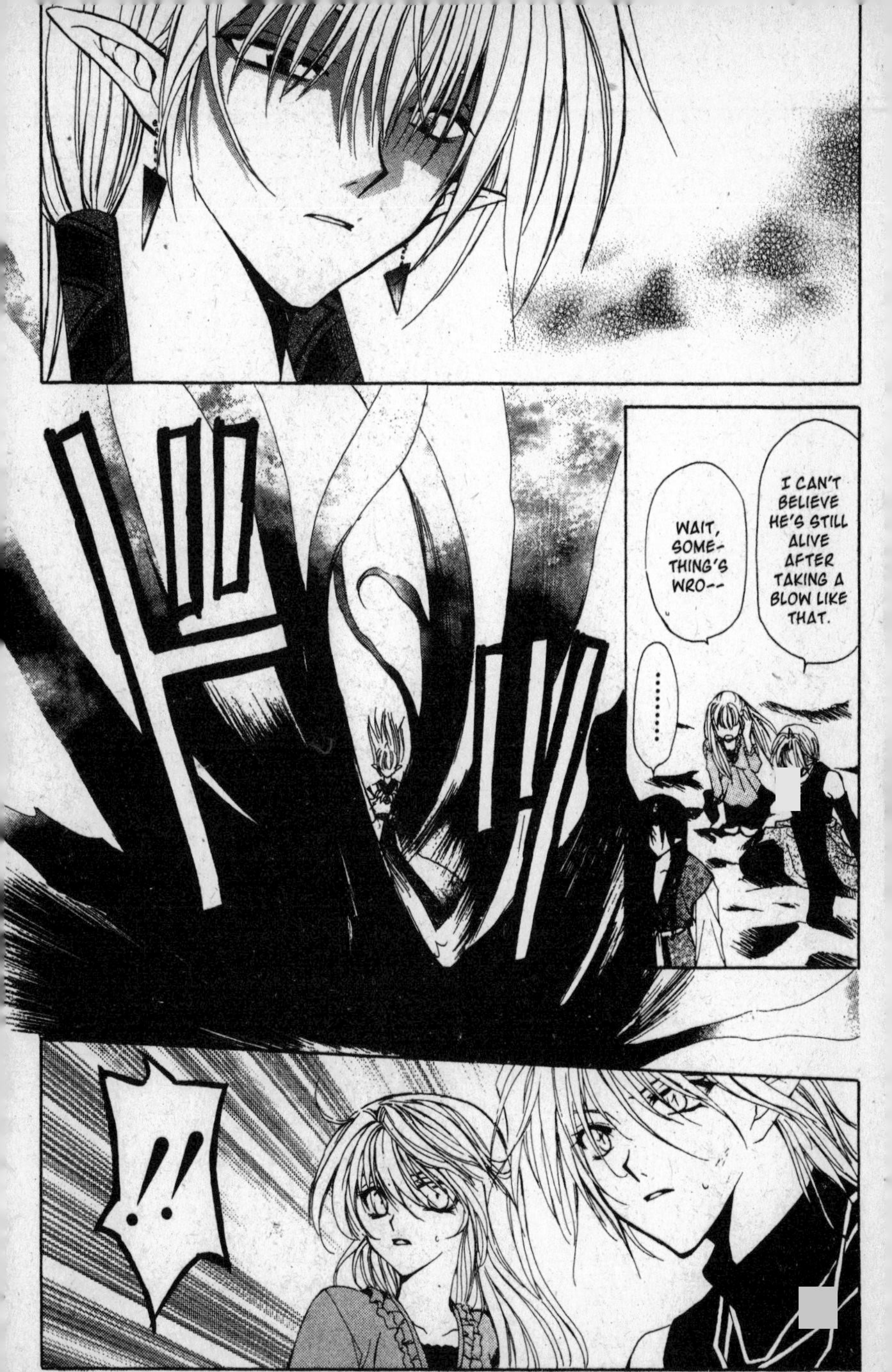
I CAN'T BELIEVE HE'S STILL ALIVE AFTER TAKING A BLOW LIKE THAT.
WAIT, SOMETHING'S WRO--
......
!!

Act 6 / The End

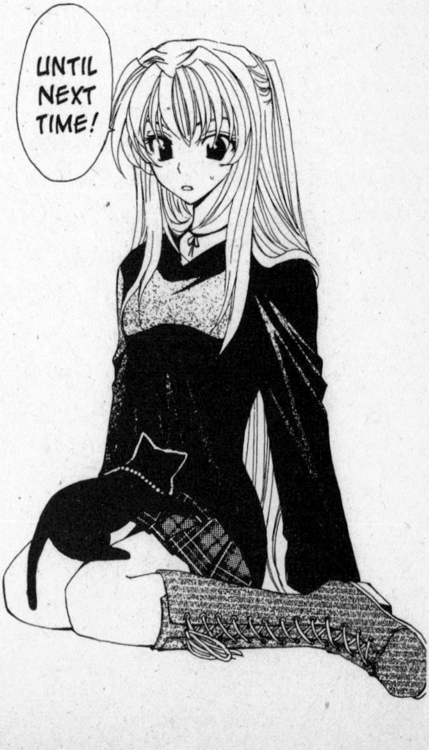
UNTIL NEXT TIME!

# In the next and final volume of

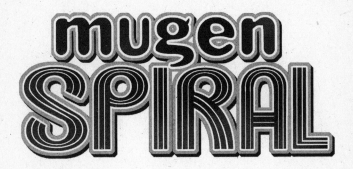

More toil and trouble is on its way as Yayoi and Ura have to face off against an assortment of demons -- first there's Hakuyoh who's determined to make Ura his man, then a rough 'n' tough demon on the high seas, and lastly a trip back in time! But disgruntled spirits aren't the only things ruining their lives. When lives are on the line, there's an attraction growing between Yaoi and Ura that can't be denied much longer...

Reach the conclusion to this tale of sorcery and romance, where a demon may give it all up to gain his humanity.

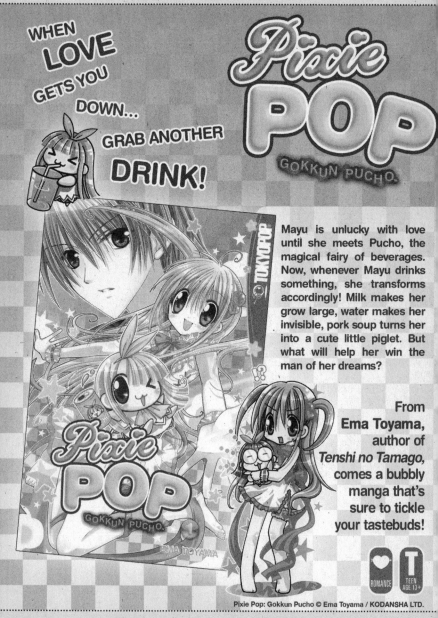

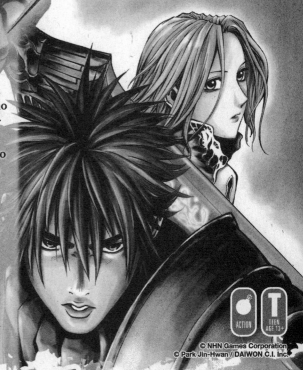

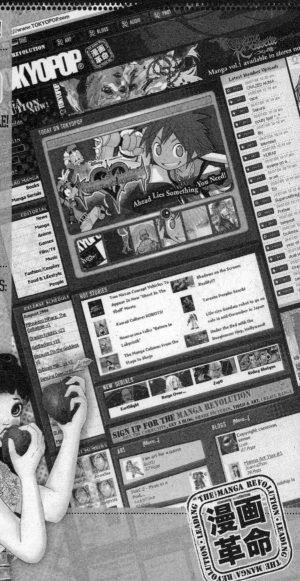

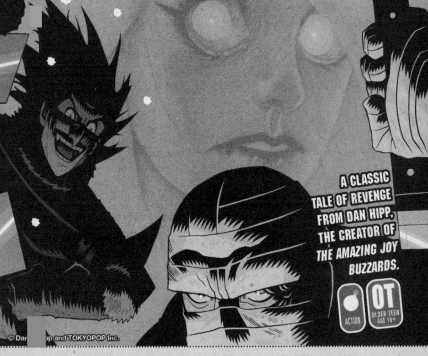

# STOP!

## This is the back of the book.
## You wouldn't want to spoil a great ending

This book is printed "manga-style," in the authentic Japanese right-to-le format. Since none of the artwork has been flipped or altered, readers get to experience the story just as the creator intended. You've been asking for it, so TOKYOPOP® delivered: authentic, hot-off-the-press, and far more fun!

# DIRECTIONS

If this is your first time reading manga-style, here's a quick guide to help you understand how it works.

It's easy... just start in the top right panel and follow the numbers. Have fun, and look fo more 100% authentic manga from TOKYOPOP®!

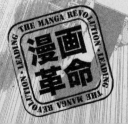

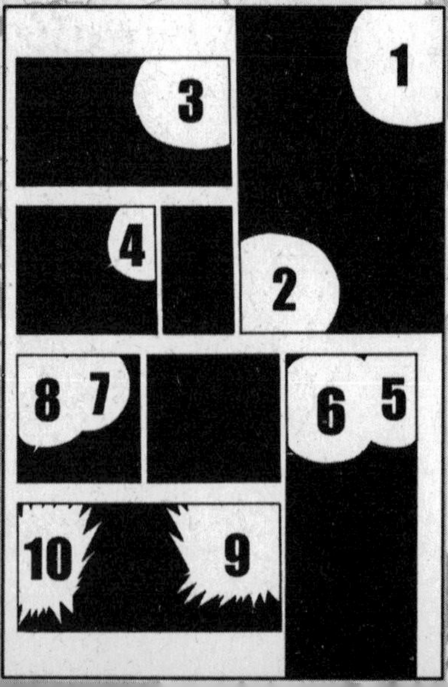

# ANGEL STAR

# JENNIFER MURGIA

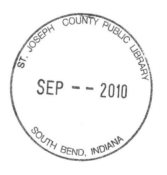

Lands Atlantic
Publishing

Angel Star
Published by Lands Atlantic Publishing
www.landsatlantic.com



This is a work of fiction. Names, characters, places, and incidents are the product of the author's imagination or are used fictitiously. Any resemblance to actual persons, living or dead, events, or locales is entirely coincidental.

ISBN 978-0982500538

*For Christian & Megan ~ my own two angels.*

*And for my husband Chris ~ you have my heart.*

# ANGEL STAR

*For it is written,*

*He shall give His*

*angels charge over thee,*

*to keep thee*

*Luke 4:10*

# Prologue

I knew the moment of death was upon me. Strange how in a matter of a few days it had come to this. I realized I was shaking and had to work quickly before...I didn't want to think it.

I grabbed the tiny dagger. Though deadly, the weapon I held was beautiful. Tiny etchings glinted in the gold handle, retelling the story of the Archangels' fall from heaven, their story delicately carved into the deadly blade.

I swallowed hard. Would God accept *me* now?

Splinters of uncertainty swelled within me, but my mind was already made up.

Without another thought, I plunged the dagger deep into my heart, hoping my plan would work. Gasping, I lurched forward, scrambling for anything my fingers could touch. I found the curtains and brought them crashing to the ground, the rod ripping out of my wall, leaving huge gaping holes. As if mimicking those holes, the velvet night ripped itself open, rain falling to the ground in wet torrents. My eyes closed to the haze that was now enveloping me, and I lay there as the rain quickly stained the weary sky and the heavens wept for me.

# Chapter One

I t was there again.

The fluttering. The wings.

My eyes squeezed shut and I once again convinced myself there was no way this could be real. I was dreaming—again.

But, sure as day, I felt a breeze on my skin, felt my hair shift around my face. The air around me was in motion, my heart beating faster. I gulped down my panic deep into my stomach and did what I knew had to be done.

I opened my eyes.

As awareness slowly wormed its way through my brain, I studied the long, strange shadows that stretched across my ceiling as I recalled the dream.

It was a dream, wasn't it? A dream that was so very real as soon as my eyes closed. A dream that I desperately wanted to wake up from yet struggled so hard to retain once my eyes opened. I could still feel his eyes on me, the color of a storm, pitch black and fearless, studying me as I searched my sleep for dreams more peaceful, more *normal*—but it was over now. I was awake.

My room was hot for March; my tiny fan was waiting in my closet for warmer days. So confusion, of course, surfaced as

I ran a clammy hand through my long, damp hair that moments before had been blowing gently around my pillow. I couldn't remember getting under the covers and falling asleep, but here I was in bed, trembling like so many other nights.

Unable to go back to sleep, I pulled myself out of bed and shuffled over to my computer, which I'd accidentally left on the entire night.

An ad for overstocked Chia Pets stared back at me.

*Ch…ch…ch…bye-bye.*

Two messages were waiting in my inbox and I clicked on them, yawning. The first was a printable coupon for Barnes & Noble.

"Twenty percent off's not bad," I whispered sleepily to myself. Sheepishly, I scanned my bookcase and the overflowing collection it now held. "What's one more?"

My mother, who is a librarian, is forever trying to convince me to borrow books instead of spending my precious allowance on them, but I can't. I can't give up the thrill.

I skipped to the next e-mail and instantly felt my skin prickle with fear. It was from Brynn Hanson—the beautiful, pom-pom shaking, self-appointed queen of Carver High School. I, unfortunately, was her favorite poor soul to pick on. Reluctantly, I opened it.

Only one word had been typed but that single word was enough to send irritation all the way to my toes.

**Freak.**

I read it again. In fact, I read it a few times, disbelieving that her hatred could find its way into my computer—that it

3

was, in fact, meant for *me*. I quickly clicked the icon that would delete the message, as if I was disposing of a slimy bug.

"Wait until I tell Claire about this one," I mumbled to myself, thinking of how my best friend would handle the situation. She would most likely forward it back to Brynn, giving her a taste of her own medicine.

But me? I was still hoping the delete button would erase it forever.

6:12 a.m. glowed from the lime-green iPod dock on my nightstand and I stood up to stretch, crossing my arms over my face, blocking the view of my otherwise seriously outdated bedroom. Evanescence posters and angel sketches covered my pale-purple walls, but there was little hope for the rest. I pulled up my covers, put away my dog-eared copy of *A Great and Terrible Beauty*, and got ready for school, knowing Claire would be honking the horn of her little white Cabrio sooner than I realized. Taking the school bus was most certainly not an option.

Flashbacks of second grade circulated through my head. It was the year Brynn began torturing me, when she poked fun at the crocheted hat my Aunt Karen had made for me. That, combined with the fried-egg sandwich I'd had for breakfast, resulted in my throwing up all over Eddie Carmichael's new hoodie.

That was a bad day.

These days, I still ride the bus from time to time. And Brynn? Well, Brynn got a BMW Z-3 convertible for her sixteenth birthday last year.

4

I wasn't sure why I was at the top of her hate list. In fact, I wasn't sure about a lot of things.

I let my fingers trace over the tiny silver frame on my dresser, the one photo of my father I was lucky enough to call my own. My parents had never married and my mother never spoke of him. Maybe she was dreading the day I would ask about him, dreading the one moment when I would question the strangeness of it all. He had simply vanished. There was nothing else to tell. Other kids had two parents. I had her. It worked. We had a bond between us that stretched and contracted like a rubber band. Best friends one minute, mother and daughter the next. Inevitably, she would cross her arms and huff and I'd roll my eyes, and the elastic between us would snap again.

As I grew older, though, it crossed my mind from time to time that perhaps she was lonely. My father's absence was an unspoken void that lived within our walls, and although I longed for the day I, too, would fall in love, I was fearful. What if the person who would someday hold my heart disappeared too?

"Left you some hot water, honey!" my mother called.

Mom was turning off the shower and if I didn't get my butt in gear I'd miss my ride and have to take the dreaded bus after all.

By the time I arrived at school, my head was pounding from stress. I stood staring at the inside of my locker for what seemed like an eternity, silently cursing Brynn's "happy day" e-mail and the dark eyes of my dream.

"Hellooo? What's with you? You're practically catatonic," Claire said in between bites of a cherry Twizzler.

"My head hurts," I answered quietly and continued selecting the books I needed for the morning.

The noise level in the first floor hallway was beginning to cause a slight tunnel vision effect on me. I wondered if the nurse turned kids away before first period.

"Up late on the computer again? Trust me, Google has been known to cause serious neurological problems with kids our age. Unless…" In an instant Claire had that all-knowing gleam in her bright eyes. "Did you meet a guy on a chat? Do we know him?"

I slowly turned my head to face her. Claire Meyers and I have been inseparable since the third grade but the mechanics of her brain were still a mystery to me.

"I got hate mail from Brynn," I admitted, my less-than-cheerful attitude dropping to an even lower notch.

Claire leaned on the next locker and sighed sympathetically. "Not again?"

"Yep. At least I keep someone up late at night."

"It's for the good of mankind."

"S'cuse *moi*?"

"At least she doesn't pick on *me!*" Claire smiled as she flicked my arm with her finger. She stared me up and down for a few seconds then said in a serious voice, "You need a boyfriend."

I stuck out my jaw and sighed. Like that was going to happen anytime soon.

"You know, someone to save you from the evil witch who walks these halls." Claire's gaze drifted out into the traffic of students.

Just as I opened my mouth to respond, the familiar pit-pat of leather flats came to an abrupt stop behind us.

"Get my message?" Brynn clucked her tongue against her front teeth. Her arms were folded against her crisp white shirt that was neatly tucked into her tartan skirt. Her deep-brown eyes gazed at us maliciously.

"We go to public school, you know," my forever smart-lipped friend quipped. "Perhaps you got lost and forgot to go to Saint Andrew's across town."

Brynn, ever so politely, gave us the finger, then spun on her heels and marched away.

"What?" Claire shoved a stick of gum into her mouth, then threw the wrapper into my locker without a care. "You know you were thinking it. She dresses like she goes to some sort of prep school and we're the dregs. Just ignore her, Teagan."

I heard Claire's voice; in fact, I completely agreed with what she was saying, but I couldn't stop staring after Brynn. I couldn't stop looking at that end of the hallway, where kids were wrestling with their backpacks, where others were opening and closing lockers...laughing, gossiping, talking. It wasn't humanly possible for me to tear my eyes away because at that precise moment the hallway was a dark, suffocating tunnel where I stood at one end and *he* stood at the other.

*Is this possible?*

I felt his black eyes on me just as I had felt them in my dream. I felt my skin reacting in an all-too-familiar chill. My muscles had turned to steel and I was rooted, helplessly, to this

7

one particular spot, yet all I wanted was to make a mad dash in the other direction.

Two large shadows extended from behind the figure. Appendages so enormous that even from this distance I could make out the deep-charcoal wings, leatherlike in texture, beneath the fluorescent lighting.

I drew in a deep breath. Obviously, Claire wasn't paying any attention to this dreamlike intruder down the hall. No one was.

Instinctively, I took a step back and then he was gone.

"She thinks she's perfect," Claire continued, her tone building gradually in my ears as if the volume had been muted and was now slowly rejoining reality.

Shivering, I grabbed my books and took a deep breath, feeling my head automatically nod in agreement.

"It's a sign of insecurity. She has her claws in deep now. She knows what pushes your buttons. Besides, you know it only makes her feel more superior when she can make someone else feel like crap."

I eyed my best friend as if she had just transferred from the moon.

"Claire, didn't you see?" I turned to face where the dark figure had appeared only moments ago.

"Oh, yeah, I see. And he's looking fine."

Forget it. I had lost her.

Ryan Jameson yanked his leather Columbia bag a little higher onto his broad shoulders and stopped in front of us just as the first bell sounded in the hallway.

"Teagan." He nodded, regarding me.

8

I smiled back, trying not to notice how quickly and comfortably Claire's hand slipped into his.

"Maybe you should go to the nurse. You look kind of pale." Claire's eyebrows scrunched up in concern. "See you at lunch, Tea."

I watched her wave as she walked away with her new boyfriend and I slammed my locker shut, feeling the echo reverberate through my pounding head. Gearing myself up for class, I began the boring walk toward the gymnasium, passing lockers and a few obnoxious football players, but my eyes were pulled toward the far end of the hallway, still trying to make sense out of the unreal. Could it just be that I was still suffering from a horrible morning and my mind was playing tricks on me? My nightmare seemed to be lingering, crossing the median into reality and following me into school. Maybe Claire was right. Maybe I needed a boyfriend—or the nurse for that matter—someone to help me keep my mind off my insane life.

Making a split-second decision to skip both the nurse and gym, I purposely wandered out to the courtyard for some fresh air. I dropped my backpack to the ground and slumped down onto a concrete bench. The morning was beautiful, despite the fact that I could still see my breath, but the crisp air was clearing my head, allowing me to see and think more rationally. I stared at the landscaping, the trees, the sidewalk leading to the south stairwell. It was all trimmed and clean and didn't hide any creepy little niches from which a dark-winged creature could suddenly lunge.

I marveled at the pink buds emerging from the recently skeletal branches above me. Even the sky was a perfect, cloudless blue, the kind you see on postcards or commercials; and, yes, it was supposed to make me feel all peppy and cheerful but it just wasn't happening. Cradling my face in my hands, I closed my eyes because somehow the pounding in my head just wasn't going away.

Although muted, a voice managed to penetrate the throbbing. "Are you okay?"

I hadn't heard anyone enter the courtyard, not a single footstep, making his voice seem as if it came from out of nowhere. I must have jumped or shrieked because the look on his face mirrored the uncertain pounding I was now feeling in my chest.

"I didn't mean to startle you."

I cleared my throat. "No, not at all. I mean, I'm okay." Looking up, I found myself staring into an unfamiliar face. The most beautiful face I had ever seen.

The tall boy stood in front of me, his features soft, yet chiseled, and I couldn't help but notice the way the sunlight played with his sandy hair. The way it curled loosely around his face, capturing the specks of light that fell onto us from between the branches. But…his eyes. They were the warmest, most endless aqua—and inhumanly hypnotic. Suddenly, I couldn't recall any sort of discomfort in my head, just a soothing warmth flowing within me, and the panic of the morning—the taunting, the winged mirage in the hall—simply melted away at the sight of him.

10

"I'm Garreth."

I sat like an idiot, staring at his hand, which was extended toward me. To my embarrassment, I couldn't speak. I tried desperately to find my voice but I was entranced. I had to speak soon or he would assume I was socially dysfunctional and at this particular moment that was a fate worse than death.

"Teagan," I replied, at last finding my voice. I took his hand.

It was so warm I didn't want to give it back. He smiled at me and I felt my cheeks redden. I guess I held it a little too long. He was staring at me and I quickly looked away, feeling panic rise in my chest. But it was a good panic. The nice kind.

Garreth unfolded a thin piece of paper that I recognized as a student schedule. His brow furrowed before he looked at me again.

"Would you happen to know how to get to room 303?" he asked with a smile.

"Mythology's actually my next class too. I'll show you if you want."

My hands were clammy as I reached down for my bag, which he politely picked up and handed to me. I stood up slowly to avoid any unwanted dizziness and was surprised to find I felt perfectly stable, despite the odd stammering sensation in my heart.

"Thanks."

I took my bag, feeling a trifle inferior now that I was standing. He easily stood six feet tall. I would have pegged him for a

senior, not a junior, like me; and, feeling like a child next to him, I silently cursed my petite frame.

"Did you just move here?" I asked.

Surely I would have seen him around town if he had just transferred from another local school. Hopewell has three: Carver High, Hopewell Vo-Tech, and Saint Andrew's. Hopewell isn't very big. Just a quiet little town with quaint Victorian and Colonial houses, located in western New Jersey. It was peaceful most of the time, and when the school kids got bored, they would either head down to New Hope or up toward Princeton to escape.

"I came over from Saint Andrew's."

Garreth eased into the conversation, his golden voice gently melting into the air around us as if it were cotton candy, and I found myself stealing glances at him as we made our trek to the third level stairwell.

"Hmmm." I nodded, attentive to every word he uttered while wondering how I had never noticed him before, not even when Carver's football team played against St. Andrew's in the playoffs.

*Everyone* was at that game.

We talked casually during the time it took to reach mythology, catching the curious stares of onlookers as we passed by. Amazingly, Garreth appeared oblivious to everything around us. I briefed him on the mundane benefits of going to Carver High and was absolutely clueless as to why he wanted to come here in the first place. It may have been my imagination but he seemed to hang on every word I said, and I had the oddest sensation of floating on air.

"Well, here we are." I spoke quietly, trying not to appear overly disappointed that the walk to class hadn't taken longer. "Mr. Barry's pretty cool, you'll like him. As long as you're good at distinguishing Greek from Roman, and don't snore during *Jason and the Argonauts*, you'll be fine."

"Thanks, Teagan." He smiled as if he meant it, then turned to hand a note to Mr. Barry.

I smiled back meekly and unwillingly turned to find my seat in the second row. I couldn't help but notice the other girls gawk and whisper as Garreth took his seat at the back of the room. I felt the skin on my arms tingle protectively, as if the last few minutes had allowed me to lay some sort of claim on him. A few of the girls, the snobby elite that were part of Brynn's group, shot cool glances in my direction, but for once I ignored them. My thoughts lingered on the conversation I had just shared, and when I turned to look at Garreth once more, I was filled with delight to find his eyes staring intently and deeply into my own.

# Chapter Two

The rest of my day passed by in a blurry, dreamlike state. Wherever I was required to be on campus, sure enough, Garreth was somewhere nearby. I sought him out easily enough, as though a radar-detection system had been installed in me, and though his presence was most likely coincidental, more often than not I spent the remainder of the day feeling pleasantly flustered. I, like any other seventeen-year-old girl, had already mastered the art of wishful thinking, but I could have sworn he was staring at me, and whenever I was brave enough to meet that stare, he smiled a delicious smile and I felt giddy and stupid. Even Claire noticed at lunch.

"Did the nurse give you some expired Ibuprofen or something illegal?" She inspected me suspiciously.

"Yeah," was all I could muster.

Claire emptied the contents of her orange lunch bag. As usual, it was filled with junk. "There's a buzz going around school." She spoke in a hushed tone, as though it were a giant secret about to get away.

"Hmm?" I was daydreaming, scanning the cafeteria in hopes of spying sandy curls at one of the tables, but Garreth was nowhere to be found. Which I found disappointing. Then

I reminded myself, what if I did see him and he was sitting with a beautiful, bubbly cheerleader?

"Well, aren't you even interested?"

I sighed and stopped looking.

"Two words. Garreth Adams."

"We've already met." I squeezed the words out from under my breath.

Claire's head shot up.

"We have mythology together."

"Uh-huh?" Claire stared at me, prompting me to continue with a wave of her hands.

"What?"

I stared back. I knew what was coming. I was withholding valuable information and she knew it, but I liked playing her game. It was fun making her wait it out. She was practically bouncing out of her seat. It didn't surprise me that the entire school was probably spreading the word about my side job as tour guide today. God only knows what Claire heard.

"From what I hear, he couldn't take his eyes off you. You are so lucky!" Claire was practically bubbling over. "See, I said you needed a boyfriend. Who knew I would become an intellectual *and* a clairvoyant all in the same day?"

I shoved the last bite of my peanut butter sandwich into my mouth and stared across the table at the monster I had created.

Claire was looking quite pleased with herself and it was almost cruel of me to open my mouth and spoil all her fun with this, but I just had to. I used the best diplomatic tone I could drum up.

"Okay, he's nice, but don't read into this like you always do. And don't get any ideas about crystal balls and wearing funky, beaded scarves on your head or anything. He was just appreciative that I helped him out. No big deal. Besides, he's the spitting image of a god, or at least a model, and I'm just…well…I'm me." I finished the last of my Cheetos and chugged the rest of my bottled water. There, enough said.

"Mm-hmm." Claire eyed me over the Devil Dog she was devouring. She reached across and grabbed my hand, opening my palm before her. "Like I thought. It says, 'I have a crush on Garreth Adams.' It says so in your sweaty little palm."

"Does not!" I stood up to drop my bag into the garbage can, turning my back on her.

"Does too! Perspiration doesn't lie!" she yelled after me.

Thank God lunch period was over. Like a magnet in constant motion, I found myself shifting closer, inching my way toward Garreth, no matter where he was. He could be down the hall and my feet would automatically begin to pull me in that direction, whether I needed to be at that end of the school or not. Regardless, I needed to be near him. I *had* to be near him, which sounded romantic, I suppose. Or crazy. Because, in reality, it was just plain insane of me to feel this way. Before today I had never set eyes on Garreth Adams and I already knew…already believed…he was going to be an important part of my life.

At least I hoped.

Not only did Garreth happen to be in mythology, but three of my other classes as well.

In chemistry I tried to pretend he wasn't in the same room. Yeah, right. Like that was easy. It was clear to everyone that Garreth Adams' brain retained information no one else seemed capable of understanding. The poor guy quickly became Mr. Quinn's prize student, reluctantly answering for everyone the entire period. I copied my notes diligently into my notebook, forcing him out of my head with each scratch of my pencil, but I couldn't take it anymore. Twisting ever so slightly in my seat, I pretended to look at the bulletin board at the back of the class, and sure enough, those blue eyes were waiting for me. I turned back around, ignoring his smile but feeling my bones go soft as his presence took effect and weakened my insides to a liquid state. At the same moment, Mr. Quinn breezed past my lab table, passing out lab glasses, and the pair he was handing me smacked me in the face.

"Oops."

"A little extra credit going on back here? Keep your eyes to the front, Miss McNeel."

Brynn snickered at the table diagonal from mine and I knew I had given her solid ammunition against me. Right now, I could only reluctantly pray that Garreth would transfer to an AP chem class, because it was highly unlikely that I would be lucky enough to spontaneously combust, putting an end to my misery.

The bell rang and we all shuffled for the door—and sure enough…

"Setting your sights kind of high, aren't you? New boy's got the pick of the crop here, so don't get all starry-eyed,

17

*Freak*," Brynn hissed as she jabbed me with the corner of her textbook.

As usual, I didn't give her an answer. She didn't deserve one.

Study hall, American history, and English literature came and went and at last the day was over. Claire had accepted a ride home with Ryan. She didn't seem too concerned about leaving her car unattended in the school parking lot. More importantly, she didn't seem too concerned about leaving *me* unattended in the parking lot either. So now my perfect day came to a screeching halt as I prepared to ride the big yellow bus of doom. I made my way across the macadam toward the noxious fumes of the yellow convoy, feeling deflated.

I pulled up the sleeve of my purple T-shirt, and sure enough, a nice black-and-blue mark was developing, thanks to Brynn's dire need to inflict pain whenever necessary. My lips set in a tight line as I yanked down my sleeve.

My eyes followed the flow of students to their buses, to their cars. The afternoon had proven to be beautiful after all and the sun was shining down gloriously. That is, until I spotted Brynn and her friends a few yards away. As usual, Miss Wonderful was smiling. What didn't she have to be happy about? She had the power to ruin everyone else's life. But hers? Hers was just dandy. She appeared to be flirting and I rolled my eyes. Of course *all* the boys thought she was incredible. She was leaning over, practically falling into the open window of a gray Jeep where she was most likely spilling an obscene amount of cleavage. And then, as Sage Fisher and Emily Lawrence

shifted places, I realized whose window she was spilling her cleavage into. It was Garreth's.

"*Teagan.*"

I couldn't tear my eyes away from the two of them. I couldn't stop staring.

"*Teagan.*"

"God, what?!"

A dark shadow flew at me the second I turned around, resembling exhaust but more substantial somehow, and in an instant I couldn't breathe. An invisible hand clutched my throat and my eyes began to water. The world around me blurred. A thunderous flapping of wings rang in my ears, as if a large bird had taken flight directly overhead, but it was coming from all around, bouncing off the pavement, bouncing off my skin. And then I lost my footing, my ankle twisting off the curb as if an unseen hand literally reached down and yanked on it.

Something warm and secure caught me by the arms, lifting me, steadying me. Seriously winded, I managed to focus on who seemed so concerned, on who had just saved me from toppling into the bus lane. Blue eyes looked back at me, inches from my own face.

*Garreth.*

He steadied me and I realized I was now standing on the sidewalk, a good six feet from the curb. The buses were slowly pulling up for the students, creating their usual formation,12A, 4B, and so on. The bustle around me appeared unchanged, as though no one had seen my little mishap. No one showed any

concern except Garreth, whose hand still lingered on my elbow, reluctant to let go.

"Um, thank you," I managed with a quiver to my voice.

*Did that really just happen?*

I could still feel the grip of fingers wrapping around my ankle but, leaning over, of course nothing was there. I felt baffled, disoriented really, and I tried to turn my thoughts away from the very real fact that I could have just been killed.

"Did you see...?" I started to ask, but the rest of my words stuck in my throat.

He looked at me closely. From the concerned look plastered across his face I couldn't be sure. "Did I see what?"

Suddenly, I couldn't remember and then I realized Garreth was asking me something.

"Um, nothing," I answered.

"I was hoping to see you at lunch but I had to fill out a ton of forms in the office."

I stared back at him, not saying anything in response, realizing I probably looked dumbfounded. Again.

"How's tomorrow?" he asked.

"Tomorrow?"

"For lunch?"

"Weren't you just talking to Brynn?" I looked across the parking lot where the two of them had been just minutes ago but she was nowhere to be seen.

Garreth paused. "For a moment." The disappointment I projected must have been easy to read because he leaned closer. "I think she's extremely ostentatious, how about you?"

20

I was beginning to realize that when I looked into his eyes I had trouble concentrating.

"Do you like ostentatious girls?" I asked hesitantly.

He smiled. "Not one bit. May I give you a ride home?"

My eyes detected Claire at Ryan's car across the parking lot. "Um, thanks, but I sort of need to take the bus today." After almost falling into their path, it would be a struggle to take one home. I found myself nearly taking him up on his offer, but I couldn't, no matter how inviting it was. "My mom's expecting me at the bus stop."

The truth was my mom would flip her lid if I accepted a ride with a boy I had just met. Sure, he was nice. *And* hot. But rules were rules, and honestly, I didn't know him yet. Not to mention, I was still trying to figure out what had just happened.

"I'll see you tomorrow?" I offered, heading toward my line.

"Sure. See you tomorrow, Teagan." He winked as he started to back away. "Stay clear of those curbs."

I was stunned for a moment. So he *did* pull me out of the way. I was beginning to think I had imagined it all. I watched him cross the lot until he reached his car and then I unwillingly made my way up the steps and toward the back of the bus, snagging an empty window seat where I had a decent view of him tinkering with his stereo. I realized that for the first time in my entire life I was on the brink of being absolutely and undeniably smitten.

Sinking down into the seat, I plugged in my earbuds as I fumbled with my iPod. It was easy to remember why I hated the bus so much. Buses had a plastic, sour smell to them that

turned my stomach and bounced my insides so violently that it was all I could do to keep everything down. Motion sickness was normal, wasn't it? I was positive bus drivers drove erratically on purpose, just for laughs, knowing full well that the precious cargo they carried had weak stomachs.

Brynn's shiny black Beemer was positioning to cut in front of the bus and through my window I saw her sneer. For my sake, she pointed a manicured finger at the opening of her mouth and pretended to vomit, then erupted into waves of laughter with the other girls.

My body slid lower into the seat as giggles sprang up around me. I closed my eyes, pretending I didn't see, that I was somewhere else...*someone else.* My pulse pounded in my ears and soon I was reliving dual moments, right before Garreth had come to my rescue today, and last night, the sound of dark wings thrumming. The two twisted and blurred in my head, becoming one and the same as the violent whipping to and fro echoed in my skull. I was going to be sick. I needed air.

I felt the bus moving, heard the honk that allowed Brynn to weasel her way in front. I knew I was seated back far enough that she wouldn't see me through the window now. It seemed safe. I pulled myself up and pushed the levers sideways with my thumbs to unlatch the window, then pushed down, welcoming the rush of air that greeted my clammy forehead. I tried to focus my attention elsewhere, so I began to think of Garreth and felt the queasiness slip away.

Why hadn't anyone else noticed my fall? What was that horrible black smoke that, in the pit of my stomach, I knew

22

didn't come from the buses? And how was it that Garreth had gotten there just in the nick of time? Regardless, I owed Garreth a lot. Maybe even my life.

I couldn't help this connection, this attraction that was hitting me like a sledgehammer on the top of my skull. Maybe I had an overactive imagination and I was gullible enough to believe Claire and her recommendation that I needed a boyfriend. I shivered at the thought of my bizarre day. So far, the only worthwhile part was Garreth. Deep down, I knew this crazy dream wasn't just a dream anymore. It was haunting me—and letting someone in on it would be absolutely boy repellant. Maybe a boyfriend wasn't the answer. I needed protection.

The truth was, I needed a life.

I was inwardly laughing at myself when I realized the bus had been stopped for several seconds and a half-dozen sets of eyes were boring holes into my head. The bus had reached my corner and the driver was now directing an impatient stare at me from the gigantic rear view mirror.

I grabbed my iPod and my backpack and hauled myself quickly down the aisle toward the front of the bus, carefully avoiding the stares of the other kids who were now beginning to whisper in low, hushed voices. I mumbled, "Sorry," to the sadistic driver and made my way down the steps to the curb without killing myself in my haste. I would have to speak with Claire about arranging permanent transportation from now on because there was absolutely no way I would ever ride the bus again.

# *Chapter Three*

I woke up bright and early the next morning. My dreams of Garreth had been blissfully uninterrupted—no dark wings—and I found myself energetic and eager to make myself look decent for school.

*Garreth Adams.*

He was unlike any of the other boys I knew from school. For one thing, he carried himself with a level of maturity that ninety-nine percent of the boys in my school seemed to be lacking. He was polite, thoughtful, chose his words carefully, and no matter how sure of himself he appeared to be, he was cautious and I admired that. I thought of his deep-blue eyes and his strong jaw, the way his hands pushed his hair out of his eyes. Instantly, I felt my cheeks warm.

With Garreth in mind, I sneaked into my mom's bathroom, raiding the medicine cabinet for mousse, gel, and shine spray, not having a clue how to use any of them. I was intent on transforming myself into something slightly more than ordinary, a task I was taking on blindly. A rather ordinary face, however, reflected back to me in the bathroom mirror, along with strawberry-blonde hair, light highlights from a box, a somewhat-clear complexion, save for the freckles that

multiplied yearly, and green eyes so light they were almost the color of water and framed by thin, very light-colored eyebrows and lashes. I was often told I was pretty, but somehow the mirror always seemed to lie to me.

I sighed, not convinced the wild array of cosmetics would do any good but I was determined to try. My next victims, the drawers, silently waited and I pounced on them, excitedly uncapping lipstick tubes and popping open eye shadow cases. I felt like a kid in a candy shop.

I bounced downstairs with unusual enthusiasm, catching my mother's shocked look. This was quite a switch from my absentmindedness of last evening when I simply couldn't help my thoughts being elsewhere.

"You look beautiful, sweetie." She eyed me suspiciously, though her compliment was honest. "Big day today?"

"Hey, Mom. Just in a good mood. I hope you don't mind that I borrowed some of your makeup. Did I tell you we have early dismissal today?"

"I have to work until five, Tea. It's Friday." I knew I had blown her away with my chattiness.

Breakfast time usually consisted of a) silence, b) the occasional sleepy caveman grunt, or c) silence. I tried not to look her in the eye over my bowl of cereal since I could feel her staring at me and I could sense her jaw must have dropped a mile at my attempt to look like a normal seventeen-year-old girl. I only hoped she wasn't perceptive enough to guess it had something to do with the opposite sex, though I had my doubts. A familiar honk faintly sounded outside. Claire to the rescue!

"See you later, Mom!"

I rinsed my bowl and dropped it into the sink, then grabbed my backpack and was out the door in a split second. The mental picture of my mother speechlessly staring at the door stuck with me and I wondered briefly if she needed medical attention.

I opened the door to Claire's white Cabrio and hopped inside. Pink was in the CD player and the car was saturated in the scent of the new vanilla-roma tree hanging from the mirror. Claire was rechecking her porcelain complexion then turned in my direction. The look in her eyes mimicked my mother's.

"Do I know you?" She feigned seriousness. "I only give rides to people I know. Please step out of the vehicle and back away slowly."

I let out a small chuckle.

"On second thought," she continued, "who are you and what have you done with my friend?" Claire took my hand in hers and examined my palm with exaggerated interest.

"Aha! Madame Woo says makeup is good idea for landing hunky new boy at school. It also serves as a good disguise for riding the bus again. No one will recognize you." Her eyebrows wiggled up and down.

"You're a nut!"

"You look great!" She was definitely thrilled to acknowledge my attempts to look beautiful. "I never understood why you never wore makeup. Hmm. I guess all it takes is a boy."

I faked a look of innocence, but as the seconds passed the look on Claire's face showed me I had no chance of pulling the wool over her eyes.

"Is it that obvious?" My voice suddenly a timid whisper.

"Only to me." Claire smiled knowingly as she shifted the car into gear and headed down Church Street. "Today, you'll look like the new girl in school and Garreth Adams won't know what hit him."

I smiled to myself as I looked out the window at the passing houses. I could always count on Claire to boost my confidence.

"By the way." The devilish smirk lingered on her face. "Do you think your mom will let me borrow that lipstick?"

The sunlight streaming through the moonroof was warm and comfortable and so I allowed last night's dream of Garreth to sneak into my thoughts once more before school. It was the first pleasant dream I could clearly remember in a long time and I closed my eyes, savoring the moment. His eyes, the deepest ocean blue, peered out from beneath his hair. He smiled radiantly as my heart pulled toward him and then he faded, as if my dream was revealing to me what it truly was. Just a dream.

Then the mist cleared slightly, revealing him once more as he held his hand out, beckoning me to join him. I stepped forward, momentarily blinded by the beautiful colors swirling around me. As I reached out to place my hand in his, the air quickened...electrically charged...static. I stared in wonder as the lines on his upturned palm swirled into a single, continuous thread and transformed into a beautiful eight-pointed star before my eyes, formed from beginning to end in one graceful, sweeping motion. Endless. Gateless. Eternal. Garreth spoke my name softly and the moment I stepped into the mist I knew I was in heaven. Though reluctant to let the dream

fade, I forced it to the back of my mind and tried to focus on the day ahead of me.

Claire was singing along to the next track. "Sorry about yesterday. Did you get home okay?"

"That's a topic you and I have to discuss. I made it home okay, but public transportation is truly humiliating. I'm employing you as my chauffeur."

"Worse than putting up with Brynn and her posse?"

"Hmmm. A close second."

About a block before school, I pulled down the built-in mirror underneath the sun visor above my head. I noted the transparent purple circles surfacing beneath my eyes from lack of sleep and made a mental note to experiment with concealer.

I decided to change the subject and tell Claire about the other night, about the dreams and the wings. Claire was my best friend, the obvious choice to hear all my concerns, but as much as I loved her, she was such a jokester and I didn't know how she would react. I dove in before I could change my mind.

"Um, the night before last I heard some really strange noises."

"What kind of noises?"

"Well, sort of like an animal or a bird flying around my room. I've been having these weird dreams about wings and...Well, I felt a draft."

My tone was serious but I instantly regretted sharing my unnerving evening. How could I expect the ever-joking Claire to sympathize with this one?

"You read too many vampire books."

28

She was right. My fictional track record left me wide open for that one. I felt like the boy who cried wolf.

"Or..." she continued. "Maybe Batman was coming to save you!"

Claire was cracking herself up, flapping her arms above her head while we were stopped at the traffic light. I shook my head and stared out the window. The looming shadow of Carver High School suddenly couldn't be close enough. And then it happened. My stomach lurched into a series of somersaults when I recognized Garreth's Jeep as we pulled into the school's parking lot.

By the time Claire parked, my insides had tied themselves into a gigantic knot. An incredible rush of excitement, eagerness, and panic swept through me all at once, like the first day of high school all over again. I could scarcely will my feet to swing out of Claire's car.

I scanned the campus for any sign of Garreth, my eyes raking over the fellow students I was forced to be herded with day in and day out, but he was nowhere in sight.

Trembling, I walked to homeroom alone.

The morning dragged on endlessly, though it was only just past second period. Anticipation bled into a twisted combination with all-too-familiar disappointment as I fumbled with my locker, and I decided to take on a more reasonable way of looking at the obvious.

*Maybe I was a crutch to get him through his first day?*
*No, no. He seemed so sincere.*
*Could someone that gorgeous really be that nice?*
*Why am I such a moron?*

29

My thoughts turned to panic as I mentally jumped from one scenario to the next. I made it down the hall to third period. I was feeling claustrophobic with all the possibilities and nonpossibilities jumbling themselves in my head, and still he was nowhere in sight.

The bell rang. Fourth period.

I felt jittery. English class passed by in a blur thanks to my elaborate doodling of wings in the margins of my notebook. It was sheer luck I was never called on.

Bell.

I forced myself not to look for him. Claire and Ryan appeared to be lost in some tender adolescent huddle at her locker. I rolled my eyes and walked away.

At lunch, I sat brooding, picking at my sandwich and a measly bag of chips, which Claire happily ate for me when she noticed my nonexistent appetite.

I felt bruised. Dejected.

The end of the day had finally come and I gathered my books from my desk. As I walked slowly to my locker, I reached the inevitable and unwanted conclusion that my mind had played some serious tricks on me yesterday and today I was obviously and understandably being avoided.

My hopes were crashing when…

"Hi, Teagan."

Instantly, my heart tripped at the sound of his voice. *So much for being rational.* I slowly turned to find myself face to face with a set of blue eyes, and all my worries melted down through my sneakers into the tile floor beneath me.

"Hey."

"I'm sorry about lunch. I never realized a meeting with a guidance counselor could last an eternity."

"Let me guess. Transcripts with Mr. Dean?"

Garreth nodded, sincerity gleaming in his eyes as he rolled them. Mr. Dean was notorious for dragging on and on in his especially annoying, especially nasal monotone voice.

"That's okay. I knew you were here. I saw your car."

It had taken only seconds for me to open my mouth and sound like a total idiot. Bravo. I quickly tried to blink away the love-sick gleam I felt clouding my eyes. Yet here he was, speaking to me as if I were the only girl in the school, and my world felt surprisingly complete.

He leaned casually against the row of lockers, appearing as if he had just come from a modeling shoot. The sleeves of his tan button-down shirt were rolled up just past his elbows and I tried not to stare at the fabric straining against his well-defined arms. Beneath the shirt was a black T-shirt, untucked, over slightly worn jeans, frayed at the hems, that wisped over smooth brown Timberlands. He had the look all girls dreamed their boyfriends could achieve, one that brought on immediate breathlessness. He swept his sandy hair out of his eyes as he leaned in closer to speak to me and I swore he could hear my pulse bouncing into the metal interior of my open locker, echoing out into the crowded hallway for all to hear.

"Let me make it up to you," he offered. "Spend the afternoon with me?"

He smiled so sweetly, but I didn't know what to say. Today was early dismissal and I knew I would either end up being bored or doing homework. Still, in all truth, Garreth was a stranger to me. I could almost hear Claire whispering in my ear, "If you get to know him better, he won't be a stranger, now will he?"

I chewed my bottom lip and looked around. Through the window opposite my locker I could see the buses at the curb, the lines of poor defenseless kids lining up to be driven home. Across the parking lot were the *other* kids, the smiling ones, the laughing ones, the thank-God-it's-Friday ones. Brynn was rolling down her windows as her friends piled in, all laughing and free for the weekend.

I looked at Garreth and something close to trustworthiness gleamed back at me. Something felt right.

"Sure," I answered. "But I can't stay out too long."

I glanced at the battery level on my cell phone and then grabbed my books for the weekend and shoved them into my bag before closing my locker. I tried to ignore the surprised looks aimed in our direction as he took my hand. His long, warm fingers entwined with my own and I felt my knees buckle slightly as we walked out into the brilliant sunlight that warmed the parking lot.

As he led me to his car, it dawned on me that I had forgotten about Claire, who I assumed was growing very impatient by now. My thoughts briefly switched to my mother and her rules but they faded quickly into oblivion as Garreth Adams opened the passenger door for me and I slid inside.

# Chapter Four

Butterflies in the pit of my stomach were swarming at an impossible rate, so I took a deep breath. My sense of better judgment told me I should be feeling slightly wary of the situation I had allowed myself to fall into, but I wasn't nervous to be seated where I was, in the unfamiliar car of a boy I had met only yesterday. Quite the contrary, I was overtaken by an astonishing feeling of relief to finally have him to myself.

Because of this, I found myself suddenly scrutinized for my actions by the student body, like a bug under a microscope. I could feel their stares penetrating the glass window that separated us, and I knew if I turned my head to peer out I would surely meet dozens of curious eyes. I knew what they were all thinking because in my own paranoid, self-conscious state I was asking myself the same question.

The only question.

*Why me?*

They were all wondering how quiet, mind-her-own-business Teagan McNeel could suddenly snag the attention of the beyond-humanly-handsome new boy in record time. Claire would have flamboyantly shouted something snotty and sarcastic to them all, but it was more my style to take the quiet

route. My butterflies, however, were jumping for joy in a thousand directions and I dare not let it show.

I allowed myself one quick peek at the audience we were attracting, while Garreth removed the Jeep's top, stashing it in the back. Yep. Eyes. Even some of the teachers had noticed. I turned back to face the mind-blowing fact that I was now sitting in the very car that had caught my eye and everyone else's interest for the last two days. Shaky jubilation filled me.

Garreth opened the driver's side door and flung his backpack onto the backseat. The breeze rustled his clothing through the open framework of the Jeep, bringing the warmth of an incense I recognized. Champa Blue Pearl. How strange. I had burned a stick of that very same fragrance in my room last night.

His car was startlingly clean inside, which really didn't surprise me. It was that mature, clean-cut thing I had noticed earlier. I was pulling my hair into a rubber band when my eye caught the glint of something delicate hanging from the rearview mirror. It was a rosary. It appeared quite old and remarkably fragile with its delicate blue topaz Hail Mary stones wrapped with simple silver wire, dropping to three more stones, slightly larger in size, that fashioned into a cross in what appeared to be genuine marcasite.

"May I?" I instinctively reached up to touch its delicate beauty.

It struck me as unusual that such a thing would be on display in the car of a teenage boy. Garreth smiled and nodded permission.

"Is it antique?"

"It's been…in my family for a long time." He seemed hesitant but obviously pleased by my interest.

"It's beautiful." I found it reassuring that it was in his car on display, like he came from a good background or something, good stock.

"So where to?" I was suddenly aware I had no idea where we were headed, but I didn't quite care. I was thrilled beyond sanity just to be with him. My butterflies had settled down and pure excitement now pulsed through my veins cleansing me of the uncertainties I had felt earlier in the morning. His attention turned to the dashboard and he turned the key in the ignition. The Wrangler rumbled to life.

"I know just the place," he said warmly.

I felt completely at ease sitting beside him, as if I belonged there, though I tried not to get too ahead of myself. So far, this could hardly count as a first date and there was so much I was eager to know yet. I decided to enjoy the moment and revel in the unknown laid out before me.

We were nearing the street now. The long line ahead had trickled down to us and a few remaining cars. The buses had filtered out in the opposite direction, leaving large plumes of exhaust to linger after them, and the parking lot was emptying quickly.

"Oh, no! Claire!" My hand shot up to cover my mouth as I saw her still waiting for me beside her car.

Then I realized the impatient anger on her face was not directed at me for my absence but was aimed instead at the person furiously arguing a few feet in front of her. Ryan's

usually happy-go-lucky demeanor had been strikingly replaced by stone and his dark eyes glared at my best friend as they continued their very public discussion.

"Did you want to stop?"

A wave of guilt suddenly washed over me. I didn't know which was worse, leaving Claire alone to fight her own battles or the sinking feeling that I had witnessed something she wouldn't want to talk about later.

"No. Ryan's with her. I'll...I'll call her later." My voice unavoidably sounded detached with concern. I would call Claire as soon as I got home, not to gloat about my impromptu date, but as a friend.

Garreth put his hand over mine and gave it a gentle squeeze then pushed a CD into the stereo. Soon the car was filled with the soothing chords of Rush's "The Pass," an outdated classic I secretly held close to my heart. I stared at Garreth in wonder and my soul slowly began to fill with something I had never felt before.

We drove down Church Street and pulled into a little shopping center already bustling with the early-afternoon business of high school students free for the weekend. Although I was elated to be with him, this was the last place I wanted to be. All those eyes watching us, wondering, forming rumors, unnerved me. As much as I, too, wanted those whispers to be true, I couldn't help but wish they would mind their own business.

We parked in front of Starbucks and Garreth turned to me, his beautiful smile blinding me; and, just like that, the "eyes" seemed a million miles away.

"Do you like coffee?"

"Love it. It's my one weakness."

*Until now.*

I lowered my eyes, convinced if he stared into them long enough they would surely give me away.

The door to the coffee shop opened and the sharpness of the Arabica beans hit me as I inhaled the penetrating caffeine rush. We stepped inside to take our place in line. It was the only decent place in town to give in to an all-consuming caffeine addiction and was becoming increasingly more crowded by the second; several kids I recognized turned to look at us.

Brynn, unfortunately, was holding court at the back table, conferring with her wicked groupies. As if catching our scent over the bold Colombian cloud, they turned in unison, their dark eyes unreadable. I looked away in hopes of forcing them out of my head as I scanned the menu board on the wall, but I was already distracted and overwhelmed. Making sense of the newly listed coffees for the season was mind-boggling, so when I overheard Garreth ordering a latte I figured that was good enough for me too.

"I'll have the same. Just a tall." I reached for my wallet to pay my share but he was quicker and handed a twenty to the frazzled girl behind the counter, who happened to spare enough time to drink in the tall, blond wonder standing beside me.

We stepped aside to wait for our drinks at the crowded counter and I realized I was self-consciously aware of nearly

everything around me; aware of how close we were standing to each other; aware of the dark scowls Brynn and the other girls were shooting across the room at us; and, very aware of the problem they seemed to have with me getting coffee with Garreth Adams.

"I believe your friends are trying to get your attention." Garreth motioned with a nod of his head.

I followed his gaze but quickly looked away when I realized whom he meant. "Um, they're not my friends."

Sensing my unease, Garreth rescanned the room, resting his gaze on the back table. He defensively stepped between me and Brynn's glare, and to my delight, I felt his hand protectively settle on the small of my back. At last our little white cups materialized on the tiny countertop and we were free to leave. It was entirely too crowded and too hostile in there.

I was hardly aware of the Jeep moving swiftly over the blacktop beneath us. Between sips, I stole glances at him, wondering if he felt the strange comfort I felt when we were together. I wanted to see inside, into his heart, to see if it raced in my presence like mine did when I was in his. Was I the only one affected?

Of course I was. That was logical.

If I looked like Brynn Hanson, perhaps he would show signs of being as physically altered as I was, but then why was I there and she wasn't, never mind the fact that she needed a major attitude adjustment.

Before I could gather my mental and physical bearings we came to a stop in front of a small playground.

"So how do you like Carver?" I asked as we walked toward a pair of swings.

"It's better now that I've met you." He cast me a crooked little smile, watching for my reaction.

I felt the predictable redness spread across my face as I chewed the inside of my cheek and I looked down at the grass.

"I'm sure you've made other friends."

"No," he said matter-of-factly.

"Not a single person besides me? That's impossible."

"Maybe I don't want to make other friends. Maybe I'm happy with the one I already have."

"Is that what I am? Your friend?"

My heart was pounding as his eyes sought mine and held them. Were the questions stewing inside me being answered? Then why was I so confused? Why was he so darned interested in me? And why was it easier to ask that instead of "Why wouldn't he be interested in me?" I wished right then and there that I hadn't been born so insecure.

Garreth pushed off the ground with his long legs, propelling his swing into the air. He held his arms taut as he leaned back, closing his eyes.

"Do you remember doing this when you were little?" he asked, his eyes still closed.

"Yeah, I guess so."

"Did you ever pretend you were flying?"

"Okay, you win. I used to do it all the time."

"Admit it. You still do," he said with a smirk as his swing passed me once again.

I giggled. "Fine."

Was it really so bad if he knew that every so often, when no one was around, I would still swing, that I still leaned back, feeling the air kiss my face like I was flying through the clouds high above the park. I couldn't help myself. It was so much fun.

"Come on," Garreth urged me.

He looked so content with the breeze mussing his hair, splaying his blond curls in all different directions. He looked like an extremely handsome little kid without a care in the world.

My feet pushed hard off the mulch and before long my swing was catching up with his. We looked over at each other and laughed. Then he grabbed the chains of my swing and we were going crooked together, bumping our knees into each other, trying to avoid the steel posts holding us up, which made us laugh harder.

"So tell me, how did your parents come to name you Teagan?" Garreth asked when we were done laughing.

"I don't really know. I think my father was Irish or part Irish, anyway."

"He's not around?" he asked quietly.

"No. He sort of disappeared when I was little so I never got the chance to know him."

"Disappeared?"

"Yes. Everyone tried to convince my mom that he had left us, but she was insistent that it was foul play. I guess lies are easier to swallow than the truth."

"That's a shame."

"Yeah, my mom misses him a lot."

"I meant it's a shame *he* never got to know *you*."

I looked at Garreth swaying on his swing. He had such a way of spreading a warm feeling over me, a way of saying just the right thing, and I realized that played a huge part in why I liked him so much. It wasn't because he was out-of-this-world handsome. It had nothing to do with his looks at all.

Here was a boy, starting over in a new school, who appeared to have everything going for him, so he could have chosen anyone he wanted to bring here today. More so, he could easily choose to be the most popular kid at Carver High School, but he didn't seem to want that. In fact, for today, he made me believe he wanted *me*.

"I think your name is beautiful." Garreth smiled.

Once again, I blushed. "So who picked your name, your mother or your father?" I asked.

"Neither. I don't have parents, biological anyway."

A tiny gasp escaped me and I instantly felt horrible.

"Don't worry. No harm done. I happen to live with a wonderful family."

His beautiful smile told me to let it all go but I couldn't let it evaporate that quickly. My thoughts flickered to asking him if he had a foster family, or was adopted, but I couldn't bring myself to and I muttered a tiny but sincere, "Sorry."

"But it has a pretty cool meaning, though. It means "light."

How does he do that? No matter how stupid I act or feel, all he has to do is smile that perfect smile and it erases everything.

41

"It fits you," I said with a smile.

"Do you have any siblings?"

"No. Just me and my mom."

"So you two are very close to each other."

"Very. We're sort of all each other has."

I thought of my mother and how she probably thought I was doing my homework right now. Guilt was sinking in.

"You don't have to be nervous around me," his soft voice whispered, sensing my unease and interrupting my reverie.

"I'm not, I…"

Garreth looked down at the ground. "You want to ask me about yesterday, don't you?"

"I…" I stammered, making him look up at me.

"I can see it in your eyes." His face was so close to mine.

"I really don't know what happened yesterday," I whispered back.

"Are you afraid to know?"

"Should I be?"

"Tell me something. Do you ever remember your past? I don't mean yesterday or last week, but do you ever wonder if you've lived before?" His voice was soft and reflective, sneakily changing the subject, and I slowly lifted my head to look at him again.

"Do you mean like feeling *déjà vu*?"

"In a sense, yes. But more."

"Sure I do."

I thought deeply for a moment. How else could I explain certain feelings and memories that pop up on me from out of

nowhere, as if they had just happened yesterday? It was very similar to how I felt around Garreth, that strange sensation of being familiar with him even though he was very much a stranger to me. Though I hoped to change that.

"What does this have to do with yesterday?"

"More than you know," he said under his breath as he looked away. "Do you believe things happen for a reason? That it's possible for certain people to come into our lives, to cross paths with us for a certain purpose? A part played in one master plan?"

He took the chains of my swing and pulled me closer to him. Our knees touched and nothing could prepare me for the shock waves that rolled through me. He smelled utterly delicious, as though he were surrounded by an ancient aura, something old and familiar...comforting. I was able to pick up a definite blend of vanilla and something more earthy, like teakwood, spicy and masculine.

"Do you believe that?" His eyes were deep with emotion as they intently searched mine, bringing me back to the conversation.

"What are you trying to tell me?" I whispered, mostly to myself.

It was hard to stay clearheaded around him. I caught that familiar scent again as his face bent toward mine. My incense. My insides twisted with a feeling I couldn't put my finger on, like a strange memory recessed too deeply for me to recall. He hesitated, drawing in a deep breath.

"Do you believe there is a heaven?" Garreth whispered, his face close enough that I could feel his breath on my hair.

"Yes," I whispered back. How could I possibly tell him that if heaven were real it would be here. Now.

"And angels?"

My mind flashed back to yesterday...my foot slipping off the curb...Garreth coming to help me...the strange fact that no one else seemed to notice, as if time had stood still or had been reversed somehow. A couple of seven year olds invaded the quiet, racing for the jungle gym, but they were like silent ghosts to me as Garreth smoothed his thumb across my forehead, as though feeling where my thoughts came from. I felt my pulse quicken, my heart racing behind my ribs...wings came to mind.

I slowly looked up at him and asked what I knew was slightly irrational. "Are you for real?"

"Do you think I'm real?" He flashed a sly smile. Deep down I doubted he was joking.

"I'm not sure I can answer that," I whispered as we hopped off the swings and headed back to his car. I was beginning to feel that everything he had asked me was from a previous conversation, but a conversation I had held recently in my own thoughts.

Then a horrible, sinking feeling hit me. I wasn't ready to have him drive me home and say good-bye just yet. Our afternoon together was entirely too short. I felt teased by it, selfishly wanting more time with him, feeling like I needed to figure him out. To figure me out. I wasn't ready to end the dream.

Still, I tried to make the best of the short ride home to my house, trying not to appear childishly disappointed. Garreth squeezed my hand gently. He had held it practically all

afternoon. I was sure my fingers would go into some sort of shock in his absence.

We turned onto Claymont Street shortly after I gave him directions to my house. My mother would be heading home soon and it was my turn to start dinner. I was trying desperately to push aside the thought of how long it would take for the weekend to pass. Monday felt like an eternity away.

The Jeep came to a quiet stop and slowly idled at the curb.

"Well, thanks for the coffee," I said quietly. I didn't want to say good-bye.

"I'm sorry if I bewildered you with my questions."

"Was that your intention?"

"No. Just curious." He lowered his head and looked up through the fringe that delicately concealed his eyes. "I suppose I'm not too good at this, at getting to know someone. I just don't want to scare you off."

"It's all right. Angels and heaven don't scare me."

I leaned the slightest bit in his direction that I could possibly manage without appearing too eager. His eyes were unreadable to me right now. They appeared almost distant with longing, and wise, as though they belonged to a soul much older than the teenage boy sitting next to me, yet ageless somehow. His hand smoothed a lock of my hair that had loosened during the ride home, triggering something in my subconscious that lingered there.

"I suppose you need to call your friend. Claire, is it?" I was surprised by his attentiveness but completely distracted by how close he was to my lips.

"Yes," was all I could manage. I stared at his mouth wondering, hoping, it would touch mine. My first kiss.

"You never answered my question." His fingers reached out, cupping my face gently.

"Would you mind repeating that question one more time?" I was drowning again, completely lost, submerged in an aqua pool. I didn't want to resurface.

"It was really *your* question, actually. You were wondering if I was a figment of your imagination."

"I still...don't...know."

I was spiraling deeper and deeper into a warm pool of intense and ageless blue. I didn't care if he was my imagination or not, I wasn't going to let this slip away from me. Claire was absolutely right. It was time I had a boyfriend.

"Let's say, hypothetically of course, that you are *not* real, could you visit me in my dreams so I don't have to wait until Monday to see you again?" Was I being bold? I felt our time together coming to a close and was reluctant to get out of his car, reluctant to release myself from the grip I so willingly allowed him have on me.

"Of course. If I'm not real I can do anything," he smiled, playing along.

"Then it's a date."

Garreth stepped out of the Jeep and walked around to my side, opening the door for me like a perfect gentleman. He leaned very close this time, brushing his lips along mine, and then hesitated. I found myself unsteady, and leaning in closer to him, wanting to press my lips against his more

fully but he pulled away slowly. I knew it was time to say good-bye.

It took genuine effort to climb up the five steps to the porch and I was grateful for the railing's support. I twisted my key in the lock then stepped inside. I had roughly thirty minutes to call Claire before I needed to start dinner. But, as much as I wanted to be a good friend for her right now, I couldn't tear myself away from my place in the doorway. I stood watching the gray Jeep getting smaller and smaller as it drove farther away from me.

# Chapter Five

I shut the door and walked in a dazed state down the hall into the kitchen. I honestly couldn't function properly, still feeling his finger trace my lower lip and his warm hand on my face. I still smelled the incense that had saturated his shirt, his hair, his skin, and I felt the pulsing blood beneath my lips from the airlike brushing his lips had given mine, full of newness and hesitation, a kiss that wasn't quite a kiss.

It took all I could to force myself to think of anything else. Then it dawned on me why I was so comfortable with him. He made me feel safe. I felt an undeniably protective bubble around me whenever I was with him.

I looked at the phone and knew I had to call Claire. I wondered if she had noticed I left school with Garreth, but when I checked the answering machine the little red message light wasn't blinking. It glowed steadily, which surprised me.

Then I remembered the argument I had witnessed through the window of Garreth's Jeep. I felt bad for Claire. True, she could stand on her own two feet during uncomfortable situations much better than I ever could. Look at how she had handled Brynn yesterday. But this was different. Her relationship with Ryan was still fresh, still new, and

arguments weren't supposed to happen yet. At least, I didn't think so.

I picked up the phone and dialed Claire's number. It rang several times before I heard her voice on the other end.

"Hey!" I said excitedly. "You'll never guess what I did today. Go ahead and take a guess, Madame Woo."

"Do you have any idea how long I waited for you?" Her voice was a monotone.

"Um, yes. Sorry. I got a ride home with Garreth."

"I know that already, Teagan. Everybody knows that."

"Well, aren't you happy for me? Don't you want to know all the juicy details?"

"Yeah, I'm happy, Tea. But, if I know you, the details aren't that juicy yet."

Okay, that was a stab but for one reason or another it wasn't affecting me. I was still flying high, even though the "Well, what happened" was seriously missing from this conversation. Then I reluctantly shifted to the parking lot confrontation.

"Claire, is everything all right with you and Ryan?"

I heard her sigh into the receiver.

"You can tell me"

"No. I can't."

I twisted the phone cord around my arm. It had become stretched out from years of talking to Claire.

"It's Friday. Why don't you spend the night? You'll feel better. We'll eat chocolate and plan horrible, ingenious ways to get back at Brynn for years of misery. Then Madame Woo can read my future and give me a seaweed wrap."

A giggle surfaced and at last the ice was breaking. "I can't."

At least it was half-hearted. I would definitely take that, although I was hoping for a different answer.

"I'm going out with Ryan tonight."

"Oh. So things are okay between you two?"

"Yeah, they will be."

I said good-bye, still wondering what was going on with Claire. Still feeling a little slighted that she didn't ask about my afternoon with Garreth, the one I'd just had and the one I would continue in my dreams.

With task one completed, I set about taking care of task number two. I set a large pot of water to boil on the stove while I raced around the kitchen, pulling a box of pasta and some basil from the pantry. I emptied tomato sauce and paste into another pot, then added water and a bay leaf. As the sauce began to simmer, I busied myself slicing the bread, hesitating for a moment to glance at the wall clock and scolding myself for staying at the park with Garreth for so long.

As I finished setting the napkins on the table, I heard my mother letting herself in the front door, her footsteps heavy on the hardwood floor of the hall. Without seeing her, I could tell she was tired and I couldn't help feeling relieved that my invitation to Claire hadn't worked out.

"Hi, honey. Mmm. Smells good in here." My mother kicked off her shoes and settled herself into her chair at the small kitchen table. She looked weary. My fun-loving mom, my pillar of strength, appeared as though she had aged significantly since I left for school that morning.

"Do you feel okay, Mom?" I kept my eyes on the steaming colander I was now balancing over the sink. "You sound pooped."

"Just a long day, sweetie. How was your afternoon?"

I shuddered involuntarily. I wasn't very good at keeping secrets from her and I worried that this one could be classified as an outright lie. I knew the time would come around soon enough for her to ask how I had actually spent the remainder of my day, the day I started off so excited about. Surely she would want to know about that. I decided to be somewhat truthful. To a degree.

"I got a coffee after school then spent some time at a park. It was too beautiful to be cooped up here at home."

"Hmmm. That sounds nice. Dinner looks great, by the way."

I was hoping she wouldn't expect me to elaborate anymore on my seemingly ordinary afternoon. I felt guilty about leaving out the more important details, but being completely truthful right now would only open Pandora's box and I wasn't ready to share my can of worms yet.

We ate in silence, which was more the norm for us than the conversation we had shared at breakfast. The time flew by, each of us absorbed in our own thoughts.

"I'll clean up, Mom." I scooped my plate off the table and walked over to the sauce-splattered counter. I wasn't exactly the most organized person when it came to cooking. I felt a twinge of embarrassment as I began restacking the little seasoning jars that had fallen into the dusting of Italian bread crumbs around the cutting board.

"Thanks, hon. Dinner was great." My mother stood up stiffly and laughed a bit as she took in the mess I had created. She shook her head with a smile. "You have your work cut out for you. Are you sure you don't want my help?"

"Nah, I'm sure. I don't have anything better to do."

The truth was, I still felt guilty. The only way I thought I could redeem myself was to make dinner *and* clean up.

I straightened up the kitchen in record time. After one last inspection, and feeling my efforts were worthy of Mom's blue ribbon of approval, I dashed quietly up the steps to my room, wanting nothing more than to relive the hours I had spent with Garreth.

It was Friday night. A girl my age should be getting ready to go out, but the only thing I wanted to do was put on my comfiest jammies, set my iPod to shuffle, and zone out, thinking about the blue-eyed boy I had spent the afternoon with.

# Chapter Six

My intentions of reliving my afternoon with Garreth were but a memory now. I woke to find my room blanketed in darkness, my body slumped over my desk and drenched with sweat. I wrapped my arms around myself, a futile attempt to hold myself together. Hours must have passed since I came upstairs.

Shuffling to my bed, I threw myself on top of my still-tucked covers to think, forcing myself to remember. Since meeting Garreth, my strange, recurring dreams had slipped away from me. I had hoped they were gone for good, but tonight proved me wrong. I couldn't remember the dream but I could still feel the terror beneath my skin. I could still feel eyes watching me, eyes that I had always looked for, knowing they existed...but, still, they eluded me.

This dream was nearly the same as the others, something lurking, keeping a close watch...but this time, I wasn't the only one being watched. Garreth was in my dream, protecting me from an unseen force of... Oh... If I could only remember!

I sat up, pushing my hair out of my face and felt overwhelmingly tired. The dream seemed more of a memory to me

than anything else, though that was impossible. The edges of it were still hazy in my groggy head.

Though my covers were ice cold, I had the sense of feeling warm, as though someone had held me all night, cradling me. The warmth was familiar. Like the soothing comfort of being safe and reassured as a child when I woke up from a bad dream. I used to check my mother's hands over and over after dreams like this, feeling for the warmth I had felt in the night. I had been so sure that she was the one to come into my room to soothe me. Who else could it have been? My mother was amused by my insistence but her hands were habitually cold, and she claimed another theory. That it was a guardian angel who came in to be with me when she could not.

Her theory worked for a while, helping me sleep at night when I was little and afraid. But the day came when I grew too old for such stories, even though the dreams never left me.

It wasn't until lately that I had begun to feel afraid all over again. And I felt silly and inadequate, which is why I read so many books on paranormal creatures and myths. I was stretching my boundaries. I had run out of theories.

So now, sweating and in a panic, I resorted to my old method of comfort. I imagined a beautiful angel with outstretched wings sweeping into my room, chasing away the darkness from the corners, from the shadows. As hard as I tried, I could never picture a face on the angel from long ago. That is, until tonight. I gave it the identity that I knew would comfort me all through the night.

I gave it Garreth's face.

I pictured warm hands, warmer than my own or even my mother's for that matter. Hands warmer than anyone's...save one.

As I tried to concentrate on the hands in my dream-memory, a sudden flood of other near-horrific incidents swelled up from my subconscious, revealing themselves in swift order like an unstoppable slideshow. Glimpses. Accidents I had suppressed deeply into my brain's storage box. Choking. Warm hands. Slipping on ice and whacking my head until black splotches swirled. A voice like velvet, soothing, reassuring, keeping me in the here and now. A voice...not just any voice. One voice I would recognize over anyone else's.

And eyes...the most perfect heavenly blue...aqua...pure and mesmerizing. Something inside me clicked just then. A switch of recognition flipped to the "on" position. Then something fluttered in the corner behind me and I turned around. There was nothing there. The sound was familiar to me—and this time I realized I wasn't scared, not like earlier.

My eyes strained through the darkness of my room, waiting, and then I saw him. I rubbed my eyes, sure I was still dreaming. He walked toward me as though he had every right to be in my room. He stopped at my chair and I looked up at him as he stood in all his glory. He was illuminated by a soft, pale light that surrounded him. It seemed to emanate from within him, centering around his chest and flowing down his arms and out his long, beautiful fingers that had held mine. I felt my hand ache to return there.

"I believe we had a date." He smiled, waiting for me to grasp what was really happening here.

"I *am* dreaming, aren't I?" I blinked my sleep-filled eyes.

How did he get in here? And the light...no matter how hard I thought, I simply couldn't come up with a logical explanation for the fact that Garreth Adams was standing in my bedroom, smiling at me, *glowing*. So I took the only explanation possible. I was still dreaming. This was too wonderfully surreal and he stood before me as if he were truly there. The incense was much stronger now, as though I were burning a stick right now in my room. But it came from his skin and I reached out hesitantly to touch the arm that glowed before me.

"Did you figure it out yet?" he asked softly. His voice melted into my walls.

"You were there, in my dream, but not just my dream. You were *really there*." I couldn't bring myself to elaborate. I was still having a bit of trouble digesting this, even if it was a dream.

"All the other times...you've kept me busy." He held my face in his hands just as he had done in the car and I felt a soft, delicious dizziness overtake me.

"But it's not over yet." Garreth slowly walked over to my window. "He is like a hungry animal, playing with the prey he is about to consume, toying with us—waiting in silence."

"Who?" I edged my way closer to the window. Just beyond the glass I could barely make out a dark haze in the distance, moving away at a thunderous speed. But, as quickly as I took note of the shadow on the opposite side of the glass, it retreated.

"It's morning." He quietly changed the subject.

I followed his gaze, and sure enough, the sun was just coming up over the trees. Dawn. Where had the night slipped away to?

Garreth lifted me gently, placing me on my bed.

"I'll see you in a few hours. I'll explain everything then, I promise." He bent down to kiss my eyelids and they closed at his warmth. His scent lulled me back to sleep for a little while longer.

And then he was gone and I slipped into another dream, inconceivably sweeter than the last.

# Chapter Seven

I slowly opened my eyes to the sun streaming through my curtains in brilliant patches of different lengths. Its light blinded me as it stretched its splendid glare across my eyelids and cheeks. For a moment, I was still lost in the most perfect dream, lost in the warm light radiating from Garreth's chest.

My limbs felt heavy, largely due to the position I had fallen asleep in earlier at my computer. It was only as the sun was beginning to rise that I had found a more comfortable spot, in Garreth's arms, as he carried me to my soft, warm bed where he tucked me in before retreating with the pale intrusion of morning.

He left, promising that he would explain. I certainly hoped so. I found myself still struggling with all that had happened in the predawn hours. I pulled myself from my warm covers and stood up. Methodically, I pulled a pair of worn jeans up over my legs and found a clean, not-too-wrinkled T-shirt from my closet. The night played over in my head as I combed through my hair with my fingers in an effort to smooth it before twisting it into a ponytail.

It was my mother's rotation to work a Saturday at the library. After going downstairs to the kitchen, I found her note

waiting for me on the kitchen table next to a small stack of coupons. Her rushed penmanship apologetically informed me she was once again working late and asked if pizza suited me for dinner. Apparently, she approved of my sparkling house-keeping and was reluctant to have me mess it up again.

I sat down at the table, playing with the coupons. I couldn't stop myself from looking at the ticking clock that loomed over the kitchen sink. I wondered how long it would be before I'd see Garreth again, hoping for some reality in last night's nocturnal visit.

I decided not to put myself through any more torture and went upstairs to shower and get dressed. I tried my hand once more at a makeover; my mother's stash of cosmetics was just too enticing to stay away from now that I knew the effect it had on others. I felt clean and awake, capable of facing the day.

My thoughts drifted back again to the one I had delibe-rately pushed to the back burner of my subconscious. As if on cue, the doorbell chimed in the hallway. Garreth stood on the porch, smiling, and my heart thudded hello.

"I see you're ready." His chuckle touched his eyes.

"Why wouldn't I be? You're supposed to keep your prom-ise today," I said quietly, remembering last night so vividly in my head.

A smile instantly came to his lips and he took my hand, leading me out to his car. My heart quivered behind the safety of my ribcage. I had no idea where he was about to take me, no idea what explanations he would fill my heart with—my soul with. I only knew that I trusted him.

We drove along a winding road in comfortable silence, occasionally asking each other the small questions we had begun to store up in each other's absence: favorite color (his white, mine brown), favorite books, movies, songs, etc. I noticed that his CD collection was as extensive as mine and our tastes were strikingly similar. We kept the conversation simple, never straying toward anything that would allow last night to make further sense to me. It crossed my mind that perhaps it *was* only a dream. A very vivid dream. But then I looked at him and I knew it had been real. The very fact that he had come for me confirmed that.

The center of town was at least a mile behind us now; the houses were thinning out as we sped along. Finally, we slowed and turned left onto a narrow road that, surprisingly, I had never noticed before. My hands began to perspire. I stole a quick glance out of the corner of my eye at the beautiful boy next to me, wondering how I could have lived here my entire life and not know where the heck we were headed right now. I frantically noted the absence of a GPS on the dashboard as the lane narrowed even more. We followed it slowly, burrowing our way deeper and deeper into the thick, overgrown greenery that stretched before us.

One moment we were in the glare of brilliant sunlight, and the next in the dimming, mocked grayness of night. When the veil of the forest began to smother us, I looked up through the open roof of the Jeep in time to see the flanking limbs choke out the rest of the sun. Within what seemed like seconds we were in another world.

Garreth stopped the car in a clearing and stepped out, appearing cautiously excited as he turned to me, his outstretched hand at the ready for mine. The soft ground crunched slightly under the weight of my sneakers and my door shut with a stifled echo. I realized my mouth was hanging open. It was as though we had stepped into some fairy-tale forest one only reads about, a magical place untouched by time.

"This is amazing." I stared at the lushness surrounding us.

"One of my favorite places in the whole world," Garreth said with a smile.

The thick trees absorbed the sounds of our intrusion, covering our presence in the blanket of pine and damp earth. The sun forced its way through the canopy of conjoined oak and hemlocks, teasing its lazy light between the heavy branches.

Garreth led me forward, taking my elbow as we carefully picked our way through the crazy maze of underbrush and twigs, leading us up and over gnarled roots and hollows that twisted out of the earth and pushed the soft mulch carpet to its limit.

I looked all around us. It was breathtaking but unrecognizable as my eyes adjusted to the green cavern we were trailing through.

"Where exactly are we going?" I asked a bit hesitantly.

"You'll see. We're almost there."

Every now and then a twig snapped somewhere in the density surrounding us. I would stiffen but Garreth never let go of my hand.

As if the woods weren't awe-inspiring enough, a perfect little stone chapel soon stood before us. When I walked around

the square building, I was reminded of a miniature one-room castle. A single Gothic stained glass window was set into each of the three walls and a heavy wooden door, arched and aged, took up its fourth. Although the gray stone slab above the door frame was engraved crudely, it was still legible and proudly bore the name Saint Ann's.

"Coming?" Garreth's voice startled me. He was waiting at the top of the stone landing, his hand on the well-worn, tarnished doorknob.

"Are you sure it's safe?" I asked hesitantly. My own voice sounded alien in the undisturbed quiet of the woods. "I mean, is it condemned or anything?"

"Buildings aren't made like this anymore. She might not look it, but she's as solid as granite."

He extended his hand, eager to help me up the steps. His blue eyes shone as if he were the very mason who had laid the stones of the little chapel, eager to show me the precious wonder waiting behind the door. I couldn't help but trust what I saw in his eyes. Carefully, I climbed. The thick door opened, its ancient hinges barely keeping contact with the worn wood. It scraped across the landing and we pushed our way inside.

I walked around the tiny room, taking it all in: wild fern that grew rampant in the corners, stubs of melted candles, massive iron candelabras eaten away by patchy blankets of rust. Beautiful bits of colored glass crunched beneath my feet from stained glass windows of long ago. Although it was in obvious shambles, it was still breathtaking.

"What do you think?" Garreth spoke softly from behind me.

I turned to face him, noting how light it had become compared to the dim green of the forest outside. Looking up, I realized the roof was missing, allowing a glistening stream of gold to flood the tiny chapel.

"I think it's amazing."

"There used to be a tower long ago, but it was destroyed…" Garreth's voice trailed off.

When I lowered my gaze, expecting him to continue, my heart tightened within my chest. It wasn't because the most beautiful boy in the world stood before me, but instead as if for a secret purpose that ray of sunlight spoke to my heart, my senses…making me fully aware that I was seeing what my eyes up until now *couldn't* see.

# Chapter Eight

I t could have been a trick of the light, or perhaps my subconscious finally revealing something suppressed and unknown. I could have tried to explain it to myself a thousand different ways when, in reality, it was right in front of me.

There Garreth stood, embraced by the most splendid set of pure white wings. From the top of his shoulders they arched upward, perfect plumes, soft and white. I had no doubt that if I were to touch them at that very moment my fingers would find a velvet so supple words could not express their softness. They curved and began their gentle descent past the length of his strong arms, to the glass-littered floor below. He was inconceivably beautiful, yet he emanated an indestructibility, an eternal force that left me in awe.

"You're an…" but I was too speechless to continue.

"Yes."

I brought my hand to my mouth. This was so unbelievable, yet it *was* believable. I looked up at him, knowing now that certain things made sense. How many times and how easily had my existence nearly been extinguished if it weren't for the constant protection of my angel kissing life back into me?

*My angel.*

Every molecule inside my body, every ounce of my blood that ran through my veins became acutely aware of only one thing at that one moment. Time stood still for us in the tiny chapel where we were surrounded by the trees, the stones, the silence, and finally, the most important element of all. The truth.

"Are you convinced now that I'm real? That I am just as real to you as every living thing you see in this forest?"

I nodded and, slowly, the shimmering wings folded back into secrecy once again.

Remembering my one vivid dream about him, I reached down and took his right hand in mine. He gave it to me willingly and I knew we had crossed some sort of barrier.

I turned his hand over, palm up, knowing what I would see. My dream foretold his celestial mark. The life line, health line, heart line, chained thumb, all that one would find on a hand, a human hand, did not exist on his. His lines formed a complete circle with eight points. An octagram.

"And this," I glanced down at his palm again. "What does this mean?"

"It's the symbol of rebirth. The octagram allows me to follow you through eternity. From the moment you were created, I was assigned to guard you, to protect you, and guide you. I never realized I would..." He looked at me so deeply, so lovingly, as if he finally found something he'd lost or been without for a very long time. I realized it was the look I had seen on his face the morning I met him in the courtyard at school and every day thereafter.

He looked away for a second, as if searching for the answer to be etched on one of the stones in the wall, so intent was he on choosing the right words.

My instincts prompted me to step closer to him.

"Teagan, this is all so new to me," he said cautiously. "Angels are portrayed and referred to as messengers of God. We're made of light. We represent hope. We're an example of the purest form of love, though for us to love another, as a human loves a human...it's unheard of. But yet, I feel that for you."

His revelation fell on me with the crushing weight of a million mountains so that I could scarcely believe my ears. Yet, while I processed his words, nothing could prevent me from believing them. An angel, *my angel*, Garreth...loved me. His words flowed repeatedly through my brain, shifting and reshifting themselves. I found myself scraping the inside of my hand with what little fingernails I owned just to prove I could feel something because, logically, this really didn't seem possible.

As if sensing the turmoil inside me, Garreth took a step back. "I'm not asking you to feel the same. I'm not asking you to love me."

I shook my head. "I feel something, I...just don't know what yet. This is all so sudden. Please don't be disappointed."

With that, Garreth closed the space between us and took me in his arms. Kissing the top of my head, he said, "You could never disappoint me, Teagan."

This confession was beyond my wildest wishes, and so much more now that it was not just an ordinary human boy proclaiming his feelings for me. Garreth was so much more

than that. I savored the realization of his words as he held me, feeling the wonder of who he was. Then the sweetness sank in. I was his, and in return, he was mine. There was absolutely nothing that could compare to this—an unbroken bond formed long ago in heaven, created and bound for all eternity.

"In my eyes, guarding you is like protecting another angel. Your heart is so pure." He softly swept my hair out of my eyes.

I smiled up at him as his eyes caught and held the gentle golden light of the sun. He seemed a little nervous now that so much had been placed out in the open, wondering if I could reciprocate an emotion so foreign to him. An angel, nervous. It was almost funny to me. Here was a soul, one so perfect, made of love and light, wondering if I could love him back. Silently, I knew he was already everything I ever wanted. He was perfect, but I was trembling inside, wondering if this was all a dream, wondering if my instinct to jump into this blindly was wrong. A mistake.

"Why did you choose to come into my life now? It's so hard to believe that three days ago I had no idea…" I shook my head in wonder as I took his hand in mine and traced the star that was in his skin.

"I couldn't help but be drawn into your world. It was too hard to be outside it any longer," he whispered against my cheek.

Garreth led me to a small bench next to the altar.

"But explain *your* world. You know mine, you're here…you watch me every day." I leaned forward, my elbows resting on my knees. I was eager to learn about this unseen realm, how easily it

fit into the world I lived in. I found it fascinating. "Like this, for example. I want to know everything." I took his hand again, turning it over, tracing the lines of his star with my finger.

"Generally, each point in the star represents a lifetime. You are now upon the Judgment Point of your existence, the eighth point that allows your purpose to come full circle, therefore completing the Order of the Octagram."

"Judgment Point?" I asked.

"The Judgment Point is just as it sounds. It's when your destiny is revealed to you. The circle closes and your star is complete."

I looked at my own hand that was both plain and absurdly human, the bitten nails, the ragged cuticles, and tried to hide what I felt surfacing on my face.

"What happens after that?"

"It depends," Garreth answered.

"Does this mean I'm going to die soon?" I whispered.

Garreth lifted my chin with one finger and tilted his head to one side. "No, you're not going to die. Trust me, the universe has big plans for you."

"But if this is my last life, then...will you still be with me? When it's over?"

"Most likely, but I've never been through this with anyone before. I'm *your* Guardian."

This was all so hard to digest but, somehow, I felt reassured by Garreth's presence.

"Well, either way, you're my angel and you're here with me now."

But instead of the radiant smile I expected, his face suddenly crumpled with concern. Beneath the quiet blue reflecting back at me I saw something deeper.

"What's the matter?" I asked hesitantly.

"I've known you for so long that your life has become mine. I've tried so hard to ignore and to accept that you are my charge, nothing more...but I couldn't."

His brilliant blue eyes were suddenly full of something I couldn't name and there was an edge to his voice that I couldn't put my finger on.

"I asked for something nearly impossible." His voice was distant, reflective, and when my silence prompted him, he continued. "If I could have one moment to know you and for you to know me, in eight days' time, then I would feel my duty as your Guardian is truly complete."

"Eight days?" That was all? I calculated quickly. Five days left. How was my heart supposed to live with that? Now I understood the protectiveness I felt whenever I was with him, the familiarity with him. My soul recognized my protector, my Guardian. And now I would lose him. The moment I first laid eyes on him that day in school, I knew my life was about to change significantly and now there was more to it: the truth, what he is, who he is...what we are to each other. I couldn't give that up.

Not yet.

"Why only eight days?" I asked. It wasn't enough.

Garreth looked at me with intensity, folding my hands within his own. "As each point of the octagram represents an

incarnation, each day that I am allowed here with you is as significant as a lifetime. Life in general revolves around the number eight, the universal symbol for infinity. It's all I have been granted," he whispered softly, almost sadly.

I shifted closer to him, my body suddenly feeling an intense need to close the slightest distance between us. I watched his eyes turn softly toward me, watched the way the muscle beneath his jaw twitched as he focused on the words he was about to speak.

"I came to you to help you understand that light cannot exist without dark. The world cannot have one without the other. It cannot survive on monotony. And no matter how peaceful we make our world, no matter how safe, light is not always prone to strength...it isn't foolproof."

I forced my breathing to return to normal, although I couldn't let go of the fact that we didn't have much time left. And now he was cryptically explaining darkness and light? I was so confused.

Garreth kissed my forehead gently and led me outside. "Darkness takes many forms. The time has come for me to tell you about Hadrian."

# Chapter Nine

There was no obvious reason why I should shudder at the name, yet I was very aware of the prickling sensation on my arms and I looked down to see the light hairs standing on end.

*Hadrian.*

Why should I respond so vehemently to a name my ears had never heard before? The look in Garreth's eyes was clearly unsettling and I, in return, was filled with unfamiliar agitation.

I placed my hand back into the safety of his warm one and asked the question my heart was dreading. "Who is Hadrian?"

Garreth set his jaw tightly. I watched him cautiously.

"He's a dark angel." His sweet voice deepened as he bowed his head.

I realized at that very moment how scared I was beginning to feel. But what frightened me more was the strange feeling coming over me. The same feeling I had from the dreams I couldn't remember. The same feeling that washed over me when I stood at the bus lane.

There had been only one dark angel I had ever learned about and my skin crawled at the thought.

"Is he...?"

"No. But trust me, he's just as lethal, perhaps even a bit more cunning. Hadrian was a Guardian originally, like the other angels. As he became more familiar with his human, much like I am with you, he became curious about how fear, anger, and even hatred could affect your world. It intrigued him. He became… How do I describe this? I suppose "enchanted" is the correct word…with the human psyche."

I sat down on the smooth curve of an uprooted tree, curiously spellbound by his words.

"When the novelty wore off, he craved more. Something darker had settled in. Hadrian was created with all good intent, but the lust for power overwhelmed him. Like the humans he studied, he discovered that it is so much easier to give in to the havoc than it is to disregard it. He eventually set his sights on toying with another society. A hidden society that seemed untouchable, one he knew only too well."

"Other angels?" I guessed as I tried to follow how someone so pure and good could become so corrupted.

"Yes. If he could conquer and control the Guardians then Hadrian would truly be victorious and he would control the most powerful army, an army of vulnerable, unprotected humans, molded into whatever he wants."

"But can't God stop him?" I couldn't understand how this could be happening. If God was the creator of all then certainly this wouldn't be allowed.

"It's been foretold that there will be a second war in heaven, the first being the war of the Archangels, when Lucifer was

banished. Lucifer can influence humans here on earth, bend the will of many to his own liking.

"You see, an angel is sort of a direct link to one's subconscious. We've perfected a way to tap into it. Heaven is here." Garreth placed his fingertip on the center of my forehead. In an instant, I felt the cool breeze of the park we were in yesterday. "Listen carefully the next time you hear the little voice inside your head that steers you. It may not be your own."

With that he gave me the most incredible smile, and although it was somewhat pained, it outshone any sun.

"Hadrian's ultimate goal is to control the angels. Corrupting them will ultimately change how humans here on earth behave. It's a domino effect, to take over what Lucifer has started. Hadrian has the highest advantage. He has the knowledge of a Guardian."

"So heaven isn't a place? I thought it was pearly and white." My head tilted up toward the treetops, which were thickly obscuring any sign of blue sky.

"Heaven starts within. It's your soul's sanctuary. But Hadrian has the power to corrupt psychologically. He's blatantly abusing his power as a Guardian."

"But wouldn't Lucifer prevent Hadrian from challenging him?"

"You would think so. But, you see, that's what gives Hadrian the thrill, the constant hunger for more. Oh, sure, Lucifer will come after Hadrian, that's inevitable. But until that moment comes, Hadrian will stop at nothing to get what he wants."

"Which is gaining control of the Guardians?" I asked as the truth finally hit me.

Garreth looked off into the distance, reflecting. "So he can manipulate all humans on earth."

My heart sank for Garreth. He could protect me but who would protect him? I sat stunned by his words while an icy chill crept through my veins. My heart was racing as my mind played back my nightmares and the strange fluttering in my room as I prayed for sleep. I had hoped it was Garreth popping in to check on me while I slept. Who else could it have been? My mind had forced me to forget, and it all came rushing back in a sickening spiral as my subconscious formed the pieces of the puzzle.

Without trying, I recognized the dark wings in the shadowy corners of my room. My thoughts had fought against it. Garreth didn't reveal his secret from behind a shroud of shadows, he had delivered himself to me in a heavenly glow of light.

I forced the words to escape my lips. "You said darkness takes many forms."

Garreth grew quiet for a moment.

"You're different from other humans, Teagan. You can sense when I'm near and it's made you a bit of a magnet. Do you remember what happened right before you slipped off the curb? Can you recall what you saw?"

"It was black and cloudy. Like thick exhaust coming from the bus, but I think I knew it *wasn't* the bus." I was struggling to remember. "It wasn't anything like I'd ever seen before." I shook my head, trying desperately to recall and escape the memory at the same time. "Was that...?"

"Yes. Hadrian."

I shivered. "He wants me to lead him to you, doesn't he?"

This was too much for me. I shook my head, refusing to believe, but there it was. What a perfect package we made. Tears began to well up in my eyes and I wiped at them furiously with the back of my hand. Angels are used to emotions, but to me Garreth was still a boy, and there was no way he was going to see me cry.

Garreth leaned forward, his face resting in his pale hands, and released a weary sigh. "Hadrian wants you. You're different from the other humans he's collecting for his army. I'm just an obstacle."

"How am I different?"

"Do you wonder why Hadrian is willing to stand up to someone as foreboding as Lucifer?"

I remained silent; it seemed he was avoiding my question.

"Hadrian is Lucifer's twin."

"That explains the dark tendencies," I tried to add lightly.

"Not entirely true. You see, Lucifer was cast out of heaven before he could become a Guardian. He refused. Hadrian on the other hand was the good brother, at first. The light brother, whereas Lucifer was his dark half. Dark by choice."

I concentrated hard on the words he spoke, as though the English language no longer made sense to me, and I instantly regretted not paying attention all those years I had taken CCD.

Garreth continued. "You do know Lucifer was an Archangel, prior to the Great Fall, as was his brother Hadrian?"

I nodded, even though I wasn't sure.

"The essence of the Archangel falls upon the human charge, like a bloodline. *You* are our one hope to stop Hadrian."

I wasn't expecting that revelation. It didn't make sense. "But you're not an Archangel, are you?"

"I wish I were, then I would have power against the darkness, but you, believe it or not, are stronger than I am."

"Me? How?" I fumbled over my words.

Our eyes met in silence and I knew what he was going to say. I felt it in my core.

"Hadrian was your father's Guardian, so it is up to you to destroy him."

# Chapter Ten

My ears still couldn't believe what they had heard. *"My father?"*

For my entire life his existence had been a secret, save for a few pictures lingering around our house. I purposely kept him locked up in the back of my mind to keep from requesting explanations from my mother, explanations I knew would rip her heart open, revealing a wound I was sure had never healed. She loved him long ago. I, on the other hand, held no emotional ties to him. He was a stranger in my universe. Even now, I felt nothing.

"Are you all right?" Concern shone in Garreth's eyes. He was forever watching out for me.

"Why is this up to me?" I was having trouble breathing. This was not what I had expected when I envisioned my Saturday with Garreth.

He looked at me as we slowly began our trek back to the car. "Only a human with an Archangel bloodline can undo the havoc wreaked here. Only the pure of heart can stop this."

"I'm not that pure of heart. I hate Brynn Hanson, remember?"

"Nice try, Teagan." Garreth shook his head and laughed. "Seriously, what's expected of you is important. Don't you feel the slightest bit special?"

I looked at him sideways. "Is that a trick question? Because I'm not finding anything special about this."

The sun no longer peeked through the trees overhead but instead cast shadows at an angle that could only mean late afternoon. Between glances at my shoes, I looked up at Garreth in hopes of deciphering something, anything. I continued walking, picking up my pace. I was anxious to get away from all this green and clear my head. All this responsibility was unnerving me.

"I'm still trying to understand the "bloodline" thing. I'm sorry," I said, shaking my head.

Garreth paused for a moment to find words that would help me grasp this. "It's the essence, the spirit, that is transferred to the human being guarded. It's not blood, nor does it mean you're related in any way. Think of it simply as a succession, like an inheritance being passed down through generations."

I let it sink in. "He had something to do with my father's disappearance, didn't he?" Garreth opened the passenger door for me when we reached the car and I climbed numbly up onto the seat. "Maybe he knew too much?"

"Your father certainly understood that angels, light and dark, existed. Perhaps that was reason enough for your father to be a threat. Either way, something happened to allow Hadrian to turn like he did. Perhaps it was simply a show of power to Lucifer."

Garreth had said the essence of an Archangel flowed through my veins like blood. That I was the only hope for the Guardians. I shook my head in despair. I was barely passing French class. What hope could I be?

There was just enough clearing to turn the Jeep around, allowing us to head out to the main road. We were both quiet as Garreth seemed to respect my need to let my thoughts churn. He took my hand and I sighed. I didn't want to leave him just yet, especially now that I knew we only had a few days left. What made it worse was that I sensed these last days together were not going to be pleasant; they would, in fact, be the darkest days of my entire life.

"Is my mother in on this?" I couldn't help but wonder if this was perhaps a family legacy.

"No. Fortunately, she has no clue what exists outside the human world. Teagan, your father was very heroic but *you* are stronger. The power of the bloodline increases with each generation. You have to believe in yourself. At the end, your father was left to fight alone against his own Guardian, one who used everything he knew about your father as leverage to destroy him."

To my surprise, I felt sad and angry. How strange that I would share a bond so significant with someone I never knew and that my mother could never be a part of it.

Garreth slowed the car to the side of the darkening street and turned to me. Even after spending the entire day with him, the sight of him made me weak yet powerful at the same time. I knew at that moment that whatever I faced, whatever was

expected of me, I could handle, as long as he was by my side. I couldn't bear it if anything happened to Garreth.

Today, a door had somehow opened, allowing what was meant to stay myth or phenomenon to be more real than the world I knew, and now I was facing the impossible. If it were true, could I do the impossible? Could I, me, an ordinary girl, defeat a dark angel? My hands were hot with sweat as I thought about how my father, an adult, failed at this. And now it was up to me.

"Can I ask a dumb question?"

"Sure, but I doubt it's dumb." He was rolling the windows up now against the evening chill that was descending, and once again I caught a whiff of that beautiful incense.

"Is it normal for an angel to have a last name?"

Garreth's brow rose in stunned curiosity. "You go from talking about your father vs. darkness, to angels with last names?"

"I'm just trying to understand all this. It's too much and this is how I deal with it, okay?"

"Let me explain. This hasn't exactly been done before. No Guardian, other than me, has been granted this type of request. For a Guardian to appear like a human is no easy task. We may look the part but we are not like you at all, and in order to create a human identity for myself, I had to adopt a name, for enrollment purposes. Carver High School frowns upon single names. It confuses their filing system. Unless you've reached celebrity status, which most of us haven't yet."

"Don't tell Brynn Hanson that, she'll freak," I interrupted.

His laughter echoed within the space inside the car, erasing the tension.

"I simply chose a last name suitable for what I had been granted. Adam was the first man created by God."

"And you're the first angel to become human on earth?"

"Not human in the true sense. Lineage within our race is nothing like a human's. Guardians simply aren't created the same."

I noticed we were racing back to my house at a speed I never would have attempted. Trees and houses zipped past in a blur.

"Hey, I thought angels were all about safety and preventing accidents. Do you realize how fast we're going?"

Garreth looked at me, the gleam returning to his eyes after all the seriousness of the last few hours. "I'm taking on the daunting task of appearing like a normal teenager. Might as well enjoy it." He reached his arm over and pulled me into his side where I rested my head against his chest. I closed my eyes for a second, wishing later would never come.

We pulled up to my house and I was grateful my mother's car wasn't there. I climbed down out of the seat to the sidewalk, and Garreth was already there, waiting for me. He led me by the hand up the steps to my porch, away from prying eyes. It was dark, private, the moment utterly ours. He cradled my cheek in his hand and I felt a tingling sensation against my skin. Puzzled, I pulled my face away, noticing the octagram in his skin glowing faintly. With a flash, it burst into a brilliant white light, much brighter than the night Garreth appeared to

me in my room. He held it high over my head, the magical blue of his eyes sparkling silver in the glow as the light showered over me, protective and pure. It sank into me, its warmth running through me like white blood as it spread down my legs and into my feet. I watched it seep through me, watched it under my skin as it crept within me, encasing me brilliantly before it faded and dissipated under my flesh.

"Your name means light, and it's almost as if you're giving yourself to me." I held my arms out in front of me, staring at them in wonder.

"I'm giving you all that I am, but it may not be enough. Over the next few days the light that shines from me will grow faint. You need it more than I do right now." He pulled me to him and kissed the top of my head, letting his lips linger in my hair while I let my arms weave around his waist and pressed myself into his chest.

"What do you mean your light will grow faint? I don't understand."

That look returned to his eyes. The look of deep longing, of finding and recognizing something that had been lost, but it was changed now. Different.

"Eight days was my given limit. It's uncertain if that's enough time for me to return."

*Why would that be bad?*

"But then you could stay with me. That's a good thing, right?"

He shook his head. "I would no longer be your Guardian. I'd be earthbound."

"But we'd be together." My voice was getting that excited twinge to it.

"Teagan, I wouldn't have the power to protect you, not like I've done in the past. After all this time, I'm just supposed to stop? And now, facing Hadrian is an absolute certainty."

Why was he arguing with me on this?

"Then we face him together, like you said."

"And what if I fail?"

I swallowed hard at his words. That just couldn't be possible. "You said I might be stronger than you against Hadrian. You need me."

"You're my responsibility. Not the other way around."

Archangel's blood or not, Garreth wasn't going to relinquish his day job anytime soon.

"Teagan, Hadrian is after you more than he is after me. I'm the obstacle in this game."

"Then why give me your light?"

"Because I'm your Guardian. Every time I can prolong your life on this earth is worth it to me. It's worth giving up mine for yours."

What could I possibly say to that?

Garreth looked past my shoulder into the darkness that surrounded the porch. I took a tiny step closer to him. My heart was having trouble finding the good-bye I knew I had to acknowledge.

"But what will you..."

"Shhh. I'll come back tonight. I promise."

I was still afraid, but the newfound courage surging within me was so much stronger than giving in to my fear. Our fingers

touched then slipped away, and I watched him walk around his car, open the door, and get in.

I watched the clouds stretch across the fading light of the day like elegant fingers, curling and crushing the glow from existence. Above the trees the sky was already darkening, as though an ink spill was spreading across the heavens, darker than any night I had ever seen. I took one last look at the blackness that was quickly threading itself into a deep cloud, a blackness that was alive, hovering, waiting. I ran inside and slammed the door.

# Chapter Eleven

I shot a quick glance at the clock as I passed the kitchen, ran up the stairs two at a time to the bathroom, and stared at the face looking back at me. Nothing unusual, just a bit flushed, perhaps. My eyes looked a little wild, but beneath the frantic glimmer in them was something I could only detect as calm. My skin still felt warm from the pure protective light it had just absorbed.

I went to my room and sat down at my computer. It took a few seconds for it to start up and load. I impatiently bit my cuticles as I stared at the screen, waiting for the tiny icons to appear. The arrow of my mouse finally replaced the poky hourglass and I hurriedly Googled the word "angels." Thousands of references came up for me to sift through. I didn't have time for that. I typed in "Hadrian." Nothing. Finally I typed the word "octagram" and at last it seemed I was getting somewhere.

The first listing had mathematical configurations involving the shape but it was the second that proved more promising. The website glowing on my computer screen was one containing information about magical symbols and their meanings. I scrolled down, perusing the contents until at last I found the

word "octagram" and clicked on it. It took only seconds for the beautiful star to appear and take my breath away. There it was, a perfect likeness to what was engraved into the skin of Garreth's right palm and I found myself missing him tremendously. I tore my eyes from the picture and scrolled down to read about it.

*The eight-pointed star, or octagram, represents the cycle of time and the power of regeneration and return. It corresponds with the Wheel of the Year, therefore, representing the circle of seasons...*

I read further, skimming over the parts pertaining to Wiccan and Pagan traditions. *...the unbroken cycle of life-death-rebirth...Gnostic meaning creation...Nordic meaning protection...two forms of the octagram. UNICURSAL is one continuous line forming the star, meaning harmony, knowledge, the future. BICURSAL is made up of two overlapping squares, representing conflict and separation.*

I compared the two and without a doubt it was the unicursal star that was on Garreth's hand. Still intrigued by the beauty of the eight-pointed star, I scrolled down, almost reaching the bottom of the web page.

*The number eight is the number of the harvest, metaphorically allowing one to reap the seeds sown in the past. It is the number of fate, destiny, and justice and is long believed to symbolize completion.*

Garreth had said my star was almost complete. What happens after that? I took a deep breath and pushed the thought to the back of my mind where I knew it wouldn't

stay for long. What good was anything if our time was almost up? Not just a few more days, but eternal time? I couldn't help but feel his time to be my angel was swiftly coming to an end. I was scared of the unknown. Something, lingering in the not-so-distant future, would separate us for eternity, I was sure of it.

I scrolled back up to the top of the page to let myself study the two stars. Where had I seen the other one before? I touched the screen, tracing my finger over the squares that poked in and out of each other and a sudden chill traveled up my spine. I placed the website into my Favorites file for safekeeping just as I heard the door open downstairs, bringing with it the sound of my mother's voice and a mouthwatering aroma wafting through the entire house.

From the moment I strolled into the kitchen, it was clear I was at the mercy of the white cardboard box with red lettering lying on the table. My stomach growled and my mother turned to look at me with a crooked grin.

"Did you skip lunch again?" She turned to the sink, focusing on the suds and the running water. "And I see you forgot about the dishes too."

"Sorry, Mom."

I was still in a state of disbelief from this afternoon with Garreth and I was struggling to cover it up with what I thought was supposed to be normal. I wondered if I looked different, because I certainly felt different. I tried to shake the trancelike stupor I was in and grabbed a dishtowel, but my mother beat me to it, wiping dry the last of the dishes she intended for our pizza.

She still looked tired but she was looking at me with concern now.

"Are you feeling all right, honey? You look a bit flushed." She held my chin in her hand, turning my face to one side, examining it.

"Fine, Mom. Just hungry. Actually, I do have a headache now that you ask." I sat down and opened the lid of the box, studying each delectable triangle.

"You need to remember to eat properly. This crazy work schedule of mine is going to require you to be a bit more independent and responsible for yourself." She took a huge bite then proceeded to douse her slice with a hefty shake of Parmesan cheese.

I found her comment amusing. My mother had no idea. She wasn't aware of any invisible enemy sporting large, dark wings. I chewed my pizza slowly, utterly lost in my own thoughts. I counted again. Five more days. Five more days to spend with Garreth. Five more days to defeat Hadrian.

*Impossible.*

I began to feel the weight of what was expected of me. The shrill ring of the phone momentarily shook me from my thoughts, but it wasn't enough to distract me for long. I slipped back into the black hole of my dilemma, chewing my pizza as I pondered.

"It's Claire." My mother held the phone out to me.

"Hello?" I swallowed the last bit of crust.

"Teagan? What are you eating?"

"Pizza."

"Are we going out? It's Saturday."

"Yeah, I guess so. How was last night? Did you patch everything up? And are you going to tell me what's going on with you two?"

"Only if you promise to tell me about you-know-who."

I wasn't sure if I could trust myself *not* to tell her what was going on. Even if I tried not to, she had a way of pulling it out of me, which would be fine under normal circumstances. Except this wasn't my secret to protect.

"Who wants to know? Madame Woo?" I asked.

"Nah. That was kind of stupid anyway. I just want to know."

Stupid? She certainly seemed to find it funny yesterday. I could hear a shuffling and another voice in the background.

"Is Ryan there right now?"

"No, we're meeting him later."

"Then who…?"

"Gotta go! Pick you up at eight."

I weighed my options. Garreth said he would be back tonight, however I had no idea what that meant in angelspeak. If I said no to Claire, my mother would pry. Saturday night out with Claire was practically a tradition. How could I break it?

I hung up and absentmindedly scratched the palm of my hand. Maybe things were turning around. I didn't feel very lucky but maybe, just maybe, things would work out with Garreth, with Hadrian, with my suddenly frantic and insane life.

I took the crust left on my plate and tossed it into the trash.

"Plans with Claire?" Mom's nose was in the paper.

"Yep. Plans with Claire."

I was thinking about heaven as I went upstairs to get ready. *Heaven.* Immediately, Garreth came to mind and I thought about canceling with Claire and waiting for the one person who would make me truly happy. But that wouldn't work, coming up with an excuse to both Claire *and* my mother. So, heaven would have to wait. Most people waited a lifetime for it. In my case, I was the lucky one. It would wait for *me*, at least until I came home.

# Chapter Twelve

I ran down the steps to the white car waiting below. The dull pounding of bass poured loudly from the stereo and out the door that had been opened for me, the one I quickly shut once I slid inside.

"*What* are you listening to?" I felt myself grimace at the blaring noise that clearly had no right to be labeled music.

"It's Ryan's. Cool, huh?" Claire had to yell over the screeching guitar solo that filled every possible inch of space inside the small car. Strangely, she didn't seem to mind. She peeled away from the curb, the tires of the Cabrio screaming for traction on the pavement. There was no need to answer whether I liked the music or not. My voice couldn't compete with the heavy metal or the peeling rubber. Besides, something told me that she didn't really care anyway.

I felt my face redden at the thought of my neighbors, peering out from behind their curtains at the racket we were causing or, worse yet, the look on my mother's face as we drove away.

"Do you mind turning it down?"

"What?"

"Turn it down!"

I knew that was probably a bad idea. It would open the door to the conversation I wasn't prepared for, my date with Garreth. But, at least, it wouldn't cause me to lose my hearing at an early age.

I was shocked when Claire obliged, turning the knob the slightest bit possible to the left. At least I no longer had to shout.

"Don't you LOVE this?"

"It's not my favorite, but hey, to each his own."

I stared at the stack of newly acquired CDs. I recognized two out of the whole pile. As I thumbed through the case for something milder, I realized her old music had been replaced entirely. What confused me most was the stereo facing me. It was huge and expensive-looking, housing so many buttons and switches that it wouldn't surprise me if a nuclear warhead could be detonated from it.

"What happened to your old stereo? You know, the one your brother installed for your birthday? Four months ago?!"

"Oh, isn't this great? Ryan said the acoustics on my old stereo were junk."

"Old stereo? Junk? Hello? It was brand new! Top of the line!" I couldn't believe my ears. "Simon mowed a lot of lawns last summer to get that for you."

I could only imagine the amount of hurt Claire's older brother would feel when he learned all his efforts had been tossed away. At that precise point, the volume turned up, just enough to conveniently drown me out.

I stared out the window, speechless and desperately wishing I had never agreed to go out with my best friend who was

suddenly a stranger. Claire was not Claire tonight and it was more than her sudden change in musical preference. With each streetlamp we passed under, the inside of the car became illuminated for a few seconds, allowing me glimpses of Claire's transformation: the outfit, the makeup, the very different Claire she had chosen to become tonight.

I ran a compatibility check between the two of us in my head during the six seconds of silence between tracks, which was, amazingly, more deafening than the music had been. I noticed Starbucks pass by my window in a blur.

"Uh, Claire. You missed the turn!" I reached for the knob and twisted it violently to the left as far as it would go. "Claire! You passed it!"

"I know." She looked over at me, a smirk turning up the corners of her mouth. She was deviously calm. "We're not getting coffee. We're getting out."

"Going out or getting out?"

"Take your pick, but I'm not spending another boring Saturday night in this town!"

The big green sign flying past us on the right gave me a red-flag warning and before I could say another word we were leaving Hopewell's city limits and crossing into the next town. I knew with sickening clarity what was happening. It had been going around school but no one had been brave enough to follow through.

"A rave? We're going to a rave?!"

My voice shrilled an octave or two higher than normal and Claire looked at me, disappointed; still, it did nothing to

persuade her to turn the car around. My hand shot out to the dashboard and put an end to the music once and for all, but not without earning a nasty glare.

"Did it ever occur to you that we might have a little problem getting in?"

Reigning in the sarcasm was serious work. I was so ready to explode at her right now, but I knew that would only make things worse. Besides, this wasn't normal for us. We *never* got into arguments, unless it was over which flavor of ice cream to have or which late night rerun to watch. But this? This never happened. This was insanity.

I let my head fall back against the headrest but the pounding in my skull was beyond repair. Sitting up, I yanked my purse from under my seat where it had slid thanks to Claire's erratic driving. Obviously, she had been driving to the beat of the music, which explained a lot.

"That's just great," I huffed, throwing my purse back down.

"What? No license?"

I looked across at her like she had two heads. "No. I don't have any aspirin. But it's not like you care."

"Ryan has IDs for us. Well, for me, definitely. He's working on yours, but don't worry he's really good."

I rolled my eyes. "Like I said."

I let my head fall back against the headrest again, coaxing the throbbing to cease as I concentrated on the hum of the tires on the asphalt beneath us. I contemplated calling my mom to come pick me up when we arrived at the rave, so I stared out the window in hopes of pinpointing a landmark of some sort,

but it was futile. It was too dark and whatever flashed past the window was blurry anyhow. My breath made circular clouds on the glass, and as I lifted my finger to draw a line through the condensation, I realized how cold the car had become. I rubbed my hands up and down my arms.

"It's freezing in here. Wha'd ya do, rip out the heater to make more room for Soundzilla?" I reached for the dial but stopped short when I saw that the heat was already on. It certainly didn't feel like it. I could see my breath forming in front of me. I turned to look at Claire and the leather seat crinkled and crunched beneath me as if it were frozen.

Claire stared straight ahead like a good little driver, on-ly...her breath wasn't escaping her the way mine was. I watched silently in the dim light of the dashboard, waiting for that little puff of carbon dioxide to announce itself, afraid that if I blinked I would miss it.

*Okay, that's weird. I shuddered, wondering if I was just seeing things.*

If I knew I was going to be exposed to subzero tempera-tures, I would have brought my hoodie, but I expected us to be sitting in the cozy back corner of Starbucks with my hands around a warm Grande Caramel Macchiato. I didn't expect to be freezing my ass off in a *car*.

*Maybe I can call my mom now, tell her to drop off my swea-ter. That will make Claire turn around.* I began fishing around in my bag again and yanked out my cell phone.

"Won't get service where we're headed," Claire said, break-ing the silence.

Sure enough, even as I held the phone against the ceiling of the Cabrio there were no service bars. Hiding my discomfort was agonizing.

"I assume we're meeting Ryan there with our new identities?" I certainly hoped she could hear my facetious tone over the new CD she had just popped in.

"Nope. We're making a pit stop first."

She pulled off onto a deep shoulder of the highway that, by the looks of it, was serving as a makeshift tailgating area. There were scores of people. I recognized no one. I rolled down the window as we sat idling but the cacophony of music outside was no better than the one inside. Strangely, it was warmer outside too.

"I understand you want to spend as much time as possible with Ryan. He's your boyfriend. I get it. But don't you want to go back and we'll get some coffee? Maybe go back to my house? I know you've been dying to watch *Napoleon Dynamite*."

She thought about it for all of two seconds. "No."

"Saturdays used to be our thing," I mumbled and turned to the window.

"Teagan, this is fun and you don't look like you're having fun yet."

"What's fun about this? We're sitting in a car with..." I jabbed my thumb at the window, "With them."

That was when I saw the car. At first I thought it was Ryan, but as my eyes adjusted, I realized my error and Claire was gleefully jumping out of her seat. By the time I was able to

get a better look at the figure stepping from the black car, Claire was halfway out the door, waving her arms and giggling.

It couldn't possibly get much worse than this, could it?

Claire skipped her way across the shoulder to the small group of girls who greeted her with unmistakable acceptance. Suddenly my head felt worse as I thought of Garreth's warning of a living hell, and…

*NO, NO, NO! Don't even tell me. I'm right smack in the middle of it already.*

I set my jaw and glared back into the angry brown eyes of Brynn Hanson.

Standing in front of Claire's car, staring at me through the windshield, was the epitome of the evil I knew all too well. I shook my head, truly disbelieving how my night was turning out. I felt the murky coldness pierce the glass, just waiting to suffocate me. Without words, her malevolent, steely stare was a distinct warning. A chill crept across my skin.

I threw the door open and stepped out onto the gravel, the irritating music screaming after me into the unprotected darkness as I stood face to face with a very real, very much alive menace.

"What are you doing here?" I blurted. Finally, I was completely unafraid of her.

She looked me up and down. "I was going to ask you the same thing." Her cocky presence was mere inches away from me and she continued to stare me down.

But I didn't falter.

I didn't waver one bit.

I gave it right back to her this time and it felt good.

I knew the only way to conquer fears was to stand up to them. Claire would be very proud of me, except at this particular moment instead of cheering me on and joining me in my platform on school bullying, Claire was cavorting with the enemy. She was jubilant, enjoying the attention the other girls were lavishing on her. I felt anger and hurt spinning inside me and then I felt my hard-boiled exterior begin to slowly chip away. It wouldn't be long before Brynn would joyfully see me crumble.

*NO! Not now!*

I felt my resistance building up again. I felt it strengthen little by little and Brynn saw it too. I could see it in her eyes.

But then, without even the teensiest snide remark, Brynn sauntered lazily over to where the other girls were congregating and slung her long, toned arm over Claire's shoulders, her skin reflecting an unnatural pallor in the sharp glare of the head-lights. She whispered something in Claire's ear, who was still and attentive, then broke off into a wide grin.

"Come on, Claire. If we're going then let's go." I yelled over to her as my fists instinctively balled at my sides. Claire looked at me with a glazed expression, her eyes appearing almost milky in the light, which caused me to do a double take.

"What the hell is...?"

But Brynn stepped between us and pulled Claire closer. She slowly trailed a finger down Claire's pale cheek then kissed it.

"What sort of game are you playing?" I directed at Brynn. "Claire get back in the car, please. We're leaving."

But Claire refused to answer me, let alone acknowledge that I was even there. I couldn't even begin to piece together what was happening. It was so bizarre.

"I believe your boyfriend's here." The words slithered past Brynn's lips.

I quickly looked at Claire, then back at Brynn as a light approached from behind me. In an instant my heart fluttered as I envisioned Garreth coming to steal me away from all this. But I wasn't the one she was speaking to. I turned to see Ryan approaching with a large high-powered spotlight swinging wildly at his hip, illuminating his distorted shadow on the ground in an almost demonic fashion.

Emily and Sage slinked to Claire's side, beginning a string of flourished comments about her outfit. They certainly played their parts well in all this and Claire soaked up each and every word like an obedient little sponge. Out of the corner of my eye, I saw Lauren produce a small flashlight from her tiny beaded purse and walk over to Brynn. They seemed to be examining a small stack of cards Ryan was holding, most likely the fake IDs. In a flash, Ryan was at Claire's side. His hovering seemed almost protective at first glance, but I instantly understood. There was an undeniable look of control and manipulation in his eyes. Why hadn't I ever noticed that before? Poor Claire was blind to his superficial adoration, and to my horror, Brynn smiled at them approvingly.

Something felt horribly wrong here tonight.

They filed into the thick woods on silent footsteps toward an obnoxious wall of music, hidden well within the trees, that

only a select few, a privileged few, knew about. Claire handed me a small square with a crooked smile. I looked down at the picture and fought against crumpling it in my fist. I suppose in the dark it wasn't half bad and I reluctantly followed the others into the concealing night.

# Chapter Thirteen

I lost my footing several times as I did my best to sidestep the roots and crevices of the black forest's floor. The last time I had been in a setting like this was quite different and I found myself desperately longing for the magical place Garreth had shown me.

Looking back in the direction of the highway, I found the noisy whoosh of tires on asphalt was growing more distant by the second. The music I had heard from the shoulder had definitely been misleading. I assumed we were close to the rave but I was sadly mistaken. This was taking longer than it should have. I became very edgy as I realized we were walking farther and farther away from civilization.

I would have made a run for it if it hadn't been for the tail end of our party keeping a tight watch on me. Brynn guarded my every step, as though predicting I would disappear from our group in a heartbeat. I imagined plans to escape, dreaming that the night would get ridiculously darker and I'd slip away into it; or, maybe I'd get lucky and a branch would snap back and whack Brynn in the face, allowing me to run for it.

My hand itched like crazy to find that branch, but no such luck. I felt Brynn's icy stare carve a permanent hole in

my back. How could Claire possibly think she could bring me here and have me actually enjoy myself? Just when I'd had enough of tripping through the dark and scraping myself silly on thorn bushes, an old warehouse came into view.

The concrete fortress took on a chilling presence as flashing lights and pulsating music bled from its openings. A good crowd had already gathered, forming a line, and to my relief I didn't recognize anyone from school. Leave it to Brynn and her crew to be the only ones from Carver High to make an appearance at something like this.

Brynn stopped babysitting me long enough to push her way to the head of the line with uncanny ease. She was now busy flirting with the bouncer at the top of the steps while the strange glow from a strobe light flickered through the open doorway and bounced off her skin.

With seconds to spare, I tried to take advantage of her absence. "Claire! Come on, let's get out of here!"

Claire turned to look at me with a blank expression that made me want to shake her and drag her back to her car. I wrapped my arms tightly around myself trying to conserve some body heat. I wondered if I was coming down with something.

"Claire, please. I want to go home."

But as she opened her mouth to finally answer me it was Brynn's velvet voice that I heard, not Claire's. "She's not ready to leave yet. Are you Claire?" She stepped closer, linking her arm possessively through Claire's.

I reached out and touched Claire's arm only to recoil at the touch of her skin. It was like ice. Maybe I wasn't coming down with something. Maybe Claire was sick.

"Claire, let's just go back to your car and get coffee like we planned. My head just isn't up to this." I pointed toward the pulsating building.

"Aww. Do you have a headache, Teagan?" Brynn interrupted. "Or are you just concerned about protecting your stellar reputation?"

I hated her mocking tone so I chose not to answer her. This intrigued Sage, Emily, and Lauren, all of whom suddenly stopped ogling the others in line and became interested in what was now taking place on the grass.

Then Ryan came closer and I realized he was the leader of our little group, not Brynn. That misconception alone caught me totally off guard and made me apprehensive about what might transpire here deep in the woods. As seconds became endless, agonizing minutes, it crossed my mind that we were here for something other than a ridiculous rave.

Ryan set the lantern down at his feet where the light seemed to exaggerate his proportions. I felt myself take a step back. In the eerie glow of the lantern his eyes appeared even darker than Brynn's, with no distinction between pupil and iris. My breath caught in my throat. His eyes looked lost…vacant…soulless, yet eerily intelligent. As the others stood around anticipating Ryan's call, I was being silently sized up. Claire had said something the other day about Ryan rubbing off on her intellectually. I wouldn't have believed it

until now. There was something about the way he stared, dissecting me to my core. He was reading my soul as if it were a book, I was sure of it, while the others grew bored waiting. Clearly, they didn't have the ability to read a person as he did. I practically jumped out of my skin when Ryan finally spoke.

"Teagan, why don't you go home."

"If she can find her way back." Sage snorted under her breath.

"Claire obviously wants to spend some *quality* time with her friends," Emily added.

Ryan's words stung me more than those of the other two. I was being dismissed. Without Claire. But I couldn't look him in the eye any longer. I was shaking.

I slowly looked each one in the face, searching for a way out of this—searching for anything. My eyes finally met Lauren's. She was the newest to their group, therefore wouldn't she be the weakest? Her honey-blonde curls framed her face and her blue eyes shone back at me. Yes! It was there, a connection. I pleaded with her in silence, afraid Brynn or Ryan would catch on but they didn't.

"Don't you think that's for Claire to decide?" I asked softly, more for Lauren.

As soon as my words left my lips, the acknowledging light in Lauren's eyes paled. Our connection severed. I was dizzy with fear, wondering if the blasting music had finally taken its toll; that if, indeed, I was seeing straight.

Slowly and deliberately, I studied each face before me. Each one stood stock still, glaring at me, while I shivered in

front of them. My breath streamed out of my lungs, hung in the air in front of me, then dissipated.

Just. My. Breath.

My eyes frantically scanned each one again. Were they even breathing?

Sage…

Emily…

Sharply, I turned to Brynn and Ryan.

When my eyes rested on Claire's face, I could feel threatening tears sting the back of my throat. This time I didn't have the dim light of the car to make me question myself. I could see just fine.

"Claire? Please, let's just go back," I whispered. My voice was raspy and desperate.

Claire's beautiful pale face looked only at Ryan and I watched Brynn's fingers tighten around Claire's arm, forcing her to decide. Without another word, they turned and proceeded to walk to the line with Claire in tow. I hardly noticed Lauren trailing behind them. She lingered long enough to catch my eye, then she blew me a kiss, her breath dancing faintly in the night before turning to catch up with the others.

As I attempted to control the flood of emotions within me, I heard a twig snap behind me. With a little shriek, I jumped. There was Garreth, his face full of relief. I threw my arms around his neck and buried my face into his devastatingly warm skin, breathing the scent of him deep into my lungs. I pressed myself closer to his chest, thawing myself against him with a need for warmth I'd never felt before.

"Claire. She went with them. I think she's in some sort of trouble," I explained urgently.

Fear and anger raged through me like a vicious cocktail as I weighed my chances of following Claire, unseen, to keep an eye on her. But, in my head, I saw only Ryan's dark eyes. I felt Garreth's warm grasp pull me away from the clearing.

"Let her go, Teagan. She's made her choice," Garreth said softly.

But I couldn't. I wanted to race up the steps, grab my friend, and take her home. Yet, in the same moment, I wanted to turn and run away from the eeriness of it all. As soon as one thought formed, my anger answered and interrupted it until they created their own tiny circle that rotated tightly inside my head. My decision was made for me when I saw them fading into the mass of music and bodies.

Garreth took my hand and pulled me with him into the dark tent of trees. I couldn't help turning around once more for a glimpse of the friend I was leaving behind, but she was long gone. They all seemed to know that in some choreographed way Claire would betray our friendship tonight when, in truth, I was the one being left behind.

Then why was I the one to feel guilty?

"I'll take you home, you're tired."

"I'm not tired" My voice sounded weary, even to me.

"Liar. Come here."

With one amazing sweep, he picked me up, cradling me close to him like never before. His arms felt so warm, so comfortable, they made me sleepy. I couldn't resist closing my

eyes just for a second. I heard a soft rustling around us and felt his shirt billow as I leaned in closer to him.

"I think the wind's picking up a bit," I whispered and then all went black.

In a matter of minutes we were at his car; the same clearing on the highway where Claire had parked hers. It felt as though we had descended somehow, his feet landing on the gravel with a slight crunch. He managed to open the door for me without setting me down and had me inside and buckled up by the time I opened my eyes. He gestured to a large cup of coffee in the cup holder, still steaming through the little opening in the black dome lid.

"I thought you could use this."

"How did you know I was…?"

"Just drink."

*Mmm. Caramel Macchiato.*

The bitter liquid burned the raw lining of my throat on its way down but that didn't stop me from taking huge gulps. I couldn't resist its warmth. I was chilled to the bone and my nerves were ripped to shreds.

The inside of the Jeep was toasty, as though it had sat idling with the heater blowing while Garreth combed the woods in search of me. My muscles began to unclench as my body slowly reheated itself. Garreth smiled at me as I sipped my coffee with trembling hands, and listened to the precious silence.

Then it dawned on me how quickly we had made it to his car. My trek with the others had taken much, much longer. I was sure of it.

"How did we get here so fast?"

"You fell asleep."

"You carried me the whole way back?"

I was horrified at the thought of my dead weight in his arms. There wasn't much Garreth couldn't do. His angelic abilities never ceased to amaze me, despite how he claimed he would soon be losing them. I didn't want to think about that right now so I thought of how it had taken a lot for me to navigate my way to the rave, fully alert. I felt guilty about using up the precious warm light he had given me, though a lot of good it had done me tonight. The mental picture of me tripping like an idiot mortified me so I shoved the thought out of my head.

"How on earth did you manage, walking through pitch black woods carrying me? I'm not exactly light."

"Who said we walked?"

Disbelief must have sparkled across my face and he laughed in response to my ability to once again be dumbfounded.

Hesitantly, I found my voice. "Would you...would you show me sometime?"

Garreth cocked his head to the side, as if reading me.

"I meant, would you show me how we got here so quickly?"

"I would show you anything."

My heart pounded in my chest at the sound of his voice. We passed Claire's little white car parked on the side of the turnoff. It made my chest squeeze tighter and I felt the dry lump forming in my throat.

"She'll be all right, won't she?"

"That depends." Garreth's voice was soft but I could tell he was holding back.

"I don't understand."

"Remember when I said things were already set in motion? When a person starts behaving in an unexplainable or uncharacteristic manner than their normal personality, it usually signifies that their Guardian has been...corrupted."

I thought back to how staggeringly different Claire had been this evening—the hair, the clothes, the music. Even the extreme alterations to the stereo and the disregard for her brother were most definitely not typical of the Claire I knew.

"She wasn't herself at all. It was like *Invasion of the Body Snatchers* but...real." I sighed heavily.

The way Claire was adopting Ryan's interests wasn't right; in fact, it was border-line unhealthy. I thought of the icy temperature change I had just experienced. That, paired with the whole no-breathing thing, was way over the top. I just didn't want to go there.

"It's as if she's lost her identity." I stared out the window, letting the motion of the car numb me. "All along, I thought Ryan was a nice guy. I never even knew he hung around Brynn."

"Exactly. Like I said before, uncharacteristic behavior." Garreth sighed, as we drove into more civilized territory. I could see the lights of an Exxon station a few miles down the road and I instantly felt more at ease, although the headache I had been brewing at the rave was in full swing now. And something occurred to me.

"Garreth, what is Hadrian like?"

He slowed the car to a stop and looked at me intently. "Well, he's very...dignified, if you can believe that. There's a certain aura about Hadrian when someone is in his presence. That person is awed by him...almost mesmerized."

I had a disturbing feeling that I just couldn't make clear. My thoughts kept switching from the vexing evening I was now trying to forget, to the dark wings that fluttered in my room on occasion. Something was there...here. Something to be pieced together, only all the pieces weren't available...or perhaps they were, but they just weren't cooperating yet.

I struggled with asking the bizarre. There was something about Ryan, some link to Hadrian I wasn't getting. All I could think of was how I felt when Ryan was sizing me up. It was definitely some psychological game he had played with me but I felt more demoralized, more threatened than humbled by him. No. The puzzle I was toying with in my head wasn't fitting together. Ryan and Hadrian couldn't possibly be one and the same. But, if...

Take the key. Fit into lock. Turn. Bingo.

"Garreth, do you think Hadrian is manipulating Ryan?"

My heart was pounding and I couldn't take my eyes off his face. I was afraid to miss even the slightest reaction to my suggestion.

"Yes, I do. I believe Hadrian is actively targeting the Guardians of those closest to you, to get to you."

I suddenly felt very sick.

"How? How would he do that?"

Garreth turned to face me in the tiny quarters of the Jeep, giving me his full attention.

"This is a game for Hadrian, one he will do anything to win. The Guardians are not human. We have deep emotions, but our basic structure is *thin*. How do I explain this? Like a living soul that bounces between forms. Hadrian can take Guardians when they are in their weakest state, when they are occupied with their human charge. Whether it's protecting or swaying a decision...changing fate."

"I would assume that's when a Guardian would be at its strongest," I interjected.

"Quite the opposite. It's the most vulnerable state."

I chewed on this for a moment. Garreth was vulnerable right now just by being with me. It was *I* who was putting *him* in danger.

"Then what happens to the person whose Guardian falls into that sort of predicament?"

Garreth gazed at me reluctantly, and then began.

"There is an immediate change to the human the moment a Guardian is corrupted. A change so significant, both physically and mentally, that the only thing it can really be compared to is like a soul leaving a dying body." He gauged my reaction and kept going. "Their body temperature even drops slightly as the protective warmth of their Guardian leaves them. It is replaced by something cold and malicious."

"Is that why you feel so warm when I touch you? Like when you gave me some of your internal light?"

# Chapter Fourteen

I was too worried to sleep but I couldn't help closing my eyes as Garreth drove me home. Drifting off to a place far from the middle of the dark forest was inviting. But it wasn't enough to shut out the dark faces and angry words plaguing me. Needless to say, to enter the world of sleep and escape would be a gift. Cradling against the hollow of his shoulder, I let the soothing scent of incense from Garreth's presence fill my lungs, sustaining me as if he were the only air I would ever need.

It was very late by the time we arrived home from Garreth's successful search-and-rescue mission. I turned my key as quietly as I could, using the back door this time to let myself in. I tiptoed past my mother who had fallen asleep again on the couch in the living room, her arm dangling limply at her side, and quietly turned off the television with the remote. Her breathing reassured me that it wasn't likely she would wake up anytime soon.

I had a few moments to myself. It had been unlike me to invite Garreth to sneak into my room, but the very idea of letting my mind twist and play back the evening was too much for me to face alone. I felt too vulnerable. So I asked him to do for me what he's always done...protect me, even if it meant protecting me from my own thoughts. He promised he would

come to me once he parked the Jeep safe from view around the corner. Sleep was now weighing heavily on me once again and I didn't pay much attention to how he was going to get in. Assuming he would find a way, I trudged upstairs.

I peeled off my jeans followed by the brown sweater I had been wearing and stashed them in the hamper in my closet, slamming the lid with disgust as I thought about pulling the burrs off of the sleeves before my mom did the laundry. I replaced my dirty clothes with warm flannel pajama pants and a T-shirt and quickly began texting to Claire, not that she would be checking it anytime soon, let alone answering it. I had to know she was okay, and more importantly, I wanted to let her know that I was concerned. Ryan's dark eyes kept creeping their way into my thoughts and I found my thumbs flying across the keyboard. Anything to get away from those dark, haunting eyes.

**UOK? TXTME**

I waited. Nothing. I slid the pad open again.

**?4U. WTH? B&R??????? H8M!**

Silence.

**WRU@?**

I looked at the clock. It was well after one a.m. I would rather hear her voice than text her, but I had my suspicions she was still out with Brynn and Ryan. There was no way she would be able to hold a conversation.

My anxiety was building, and as if knowing that I needed him, Garreth was sitting at the end of my bed by the time I turned around.

115

"Tying up some loose ends?"

"I guess. She's probably not even home yet."

Something remotely similar to jealousy attached itself to my tone. I couldn't help it. Claire was *my* best friend.

"I just don't get it. I don't mind that she might choose to have a friend other than me, but...there are plenty out there that would be better than *them*. They're not even likable, not to mention I can count a thousand times when she's complained about Brynn Hanson."

Garreth patted the covers next to him, and I shuffled my way over. He pulled me to him without saying a word. His eyes were soft in the pale light of the streetlamp that found its way through my open window. Miraculously, I felt calm, as if he had erased the anxiety that had been simmering inside me.

"How do you do that? How do you calm me?"

"I can't explain it too well. I picture myself being completely in tune with you. I breathe when you breathe. My heart beats when yours beats. I can time them perfectly to each other and then I just...slow it all down. It's really very easy."

I grew reflective as I listened to Garreth, a memory surfacing in my mind.

"What is it?" he asked me.

I sat picking at the loose threads on my quilt, giving my hands some sort of purpose.

"I was just remembering last year when Claire went on vacation with her family. It was the longest week of my life. I had to take the bus every day. I had to sit alone at lunch every day. Not one person offered to come sit and eat with me. Not

even to talk to me. I sat there feeling sorry for myself, feeling like I didn't belong like the rest of them. There was the jock table, the goth table, Brynn and her friends looking over every few minutes, laughing. But I sat alone. And you know? As I sat there, I realized that maybe there was nothing wrong with me—that maybe it was my own fault that I never tried to hang out with other people."

I looked at Garreth. The look on his face was so tender; there was no pity for me at all. It was as if he was remembering it right along with me.

"I decided the next day I would try to weave myself into the lives of everyone else. I was even desperate enough to try it out on Brynn's friends, that maybe if they accepted me, she would too. I was ready to sever my loyalty to Claire out of loneliness."

"But you would be severing loyalty to yourself," Garreth said.

"The following day," I continued in a whisper, "that feeling was gone. There was a rhythm deep inside me that just magically appeared." I let my gaze rest on him. "I felt that calmness you give to me. I recognize it now. It was you, wasn't it?"

Garreth tenderly swept a stray hair from my face, tucked it behind my ear, and nodded.

I could accept now that angels existed, even remember when I had been touched by one. Garreth had always been with me. Always.

His index finger absentmindedly traced my face, beginning at my now perpetually creased forehead, down my nose, to my

cheek, where he let his hand stretch open, warming it. His thumb glided over my lips. Despite the calm he had just generated within me, I couldn't help feel the increased pounding of my blood as it raced to my heart.

His lips hovered just above mine, his breath warming my face, and I closed my eyes to accept his kiss. The instant his lips locked onto mine I felt we were moving, floating upward. I saw a glow behind my eyelids, as if someone had turned on the overhead light. Panicking, I opened my eyes and searched frantically for an excuse as I pictured my mother's astonished face in the doorway, only she wasn't there. My door, thankfully, was still closed. I looked at Garreth, searching for an answer but I was met with an overwhelming feeling of peace.

I realized just then the magnitude of what it means to know your Guardian. What Garreth was sharing with me couldn't be placed into words. What I was experiencing, what he was giving me, was raw emotion. The answers to my endless stream of questions were visible in his eyes...who he was, what he was...the strand that connected us. It was all there.

Weightlessly, I was returned to the comforting mattress beneath me.

"Sleep now. You've been through a lot tonight and I know you're going to need all of your strength soon. If Hadrian has control of Ryan's Guardian then he's even closer than I thought."

I wanted to object and force myself to stay awake but sleep came after me like a warrior and I unwillingly surrendered. The night, the stress, the kiss rained down on me and I found

myself soothed in my angel's arms as he held me, his breath on my ear like a lullaby.

"Stay," I whispered, my fingers curling with his, holding him to me for the duration.

I was beyond drowsy, my eyes refusing to open at that point. As sleep wove its way through my system, I felt reassured that nothing would dare linger in the shadows, not on this night.

But I was wrong.

# Chapter Fifteen

The star kept changing. At first, the points were clear, shimmering in the pale light of the descending sun of my dream, never failing to capture my soul the way it always did. Then the hand on which it was engraved closed, crushing it fiercely, then opened once again. Dust spilled from the open palm and overlapping squares would replace the eight-pointed star that had been embedded before it.

This happened over and over, the constant change of one to the other. The beautiful star insisting it stay and the other overshadowing and pulverizing it. The squares always resurfaced, their outline glowing crimson, dripping, as if lined with blood. It sent me running through a dense wood that was strangely familiar.

I dodged tree after tree, stumbling and regaining my footing, only to fall again. My heart pumped with fear as I raced toward a white light in the clearing, only I couldn't get there fast enough. Even with the trees racing past me, nearly blinding me, I couldn't will my feet to move any faster. I screamed my angel's name until my throat became raw but only my echo had the courage to answer me.

At last I saw white wings, more beautiful than ever, and my heart leaped at the sight of them. "Garreth!"

I pushed myself forward, ready to jump into his arms, ready to float upward again, away from the darkness of the trees, away from the bloodstained star I knew was not far behind me. Tears spilled onto my cheeks. He was so close.

"Garreth!" My voice strained, but I had to call to him. I had to reach him. I had to keep moving.

But I stopped short. The wings before me were no longer soft and white, but thick and leathery. I was mesmerized. My mouth ran dry as I looked up and realized why my beautiful guardian hadn't answered me.

The wingspan that towered over me was enormous, larger than anything I could ever envision. They flapped violently and strangely. I was flung to the ground, overcome with immense fatigue. As I came to, I found myself standing on a rooftop, my arms outstretched at my sides. I heard a voice behind me. Ryan. It was when I looked down at my feet and saw the black boots that I began shaking horribly. *Claire's boots.* I stretched my hands out in front of me and saw the tiny scar on my left thumb. *Claire's scar.* The scar she had gotten eight years ago, the day we met on the third-grade playground, the cut that brought us together and linked us as friends forever.

I felt my blood drain as the wind caught me, my feet no longer steady on the edge. Wings cradled me but only for a matter of seconds before breaking off. Then a swift breeze clawed at my skin, and I screamed in silence as I tasted blood from the back of my throat.

I didn't want to wake up, but a sharp, intrusive light piercing the thin skin of my eyelids finally urged me to open my eyes. I murmured softly into the comfort of my pillow.

"Garreth." My hand reached out to grasp his, knowing he would be there still, lying next to me, but my fingers grabbed a pillow.

I sat up, pushing my hair out of my face and I realized it wasn't morning. Light streamed in from the hallway, bouncing off the glass of my window, mirroring my room back to me instead of allowing me to see the new day on the other side. There was a motion down the hall, followed by the slight padding of my mother's feet, slowing as they reached my door until her form filled the brightly lit space of my open doorframe.

"Teagan? Honey, are you asleep?" Her hesitant voice was laced with worry.

"No, I'm awake." I shook my head, trying to clear it, and quickly scanned my room. Aside from my mother, I was alone. "You were asleep on the couch when I came in. I didn't want to wake you."

My mom stood in the doorway, staring at me.

"What's wrong?"

"Um, the phone. It's about Claire."

It was just like Claire to ignore my text. When she wanted to be heard, that girl sure had a way of making people listen. My brain was preparing me for what I would hear. All the reasons. All the excuses. Why she hooked up with Brynn and the Bitch Squad, why she dragged me into it. Hell, she was probably pissed at *me* for leaving.

"I'm sorry mom. I sent her a text when I got home. She's probably just...being Claire." My annoyance was streaming out of me.

With my covers pushed aside, I hopped out of bed to get the phone so she could go back to sleep but my mother didn't budge. I tried to decipher the look on her face as she stared at me.

"It wasn't Claire who called. It was her mother."

Little bolts of fear pinched me from the inside out. My mom was going to find out eventually that I had crossed the town line and went to a rave, so I guessed now was as good a time as any.

Well, I almost went to a rave.

But what about when I had to explain the part about the IDs or Claire's manipulative, turned-evil boyfriend? That sure as hell wasn't going to go over very well. Not only that, now she would know I didn't get a ride home with Claire.

I let out a big sigh. "I didn't get coffee with Claire. We were supposed to, but she had this crazy idea about trying to get into a club with these new friends of hers."

*Eew. My stomach is churning.*

"I told her it was wrong and I really, really tried to get her to go back home but she was acting strange and I couldn't get through to her. So I found another way home. I'm sorry."

The truth spilled out of me, much like it always did when I was nervous, and then I let my voice fall silent.

"I'm sorry. I guess this means I'm grounded from Saturday nights with Claire for a while, huh?"

I peeked at my clock: 4:23 a.m. My mom studied my face. If she was looking for guilt, I'm sure she found it.

"Teagan, there was a horrible accident." Her face contorted and got that scrunched up look people get when they're holding back tears. She placed a comforting hand on my shoulder.

I stared at my mother as if she had two heads.

"Claire's dead."

In an instant, my dream found its way back to me. I felt the sick swirl of nausea starting in the pit of my stomach. Suddenly my room felt hot and dark and my pulse pounded throughout my body, adding to the strange tone my mother's voice had taken on, like it was trapped in a metal can.

"Oh, sweetie." She threw her arms around me, instinctively protecting me from the words she had delivered. "Thank God you're all right, but I'm so very, very sorry about Claire."

She reached for the tissue box on my nightstand but for some reason I wasn't crying. I was numb.

I looked at her, her mascara smudged beneath her eyes. She was visibly more upset than I was showing. I couldn't believe it. Claire?

Then, suddenly, something inside me snapped.

"We should have stayed together." I was shaking now. "I shouldn't have left her!"

I looked at my mother but it wasn't her face I was seeing. It was Claire's with her vacant stare.

My mother sat down on the edge of my bed slowly, as if not to upset me further. "How did you get home then?"

"Claire wouldn't leave so I sort of found my own way home with someone from school."

I don't think she noticed the quiver in my voice and she didn't press for more. For now, all was safe as far as Garreth was concerned.

Except for Claire.

All was not safe for her.

A tear escaped down my cheek as tiny pieces of my dream began trickling in, the numbness wearing off. My mother wanted to console me but I insisted I wanted to be alone.

It was all starting to become a little more clear.

Hadrian. My father. Claire.

The connections were there, piecing themselves together, and finally tears rolled down my cheeks as I mentally tallied who would be next.

*I can't let this happen.*

I wrapped my arms around my body and for the first time in years, I prayed for someone other than my family.

I prayed for Garreth.

# *Chapter Sixteen*

Feeling a presence, I turned to find my angel standing silently in the corner near my dresser. He had a strange look on his face, as if he was seeing me for the first time.

"What is it?" I asked quietly.

"No one's ever prayed for me before."

I held my arms out to him and he crossed the floor to sit with me.

"I've always heard *your* prayers. You prayed for me to come to you when you had a bad dream. I even heard you pray for a perfect, selfless, superwonderful boy to fall in love with. But I've never heard you pray for *me*."

I couldn't erase the thoughts stirring in my head. "Maybe it's about time someone did."

"Why?" he asked.

"You said Guardians become vulnerable when they are protecting their human. I'm making matters worse."

"Don't even go there, Teagan. Nothing is going to happen to us. Everything will be all right."

He was reassuring, in a defiant sort of way, as if worries like this surfaced all the time. Nonetheless, I was responsible

for placing him in the direct line of danger from Hadrian, and living with this sinking feeling was not at all pleasant.

Without a word, he gently wiped away my tears, soothing me into a calm sleep.

When I awoke, he was gone and I was full of the strangest sensation I could ever imagine. My mind flickered back to Claire. My dream. My mother waking me in the night to tell me the horrible truth that I somehow already knew. Claire was dead. Not missing from my life because she was still angry at me. Not missing because she was still in the woods where I left her.

She was gone.

Dead.

Somehow I accepted it but I couldn't comprehend it.

I reached for my phone. The inbox was empty, as I should have known. Its silence screamed the ugly truth. I wanted to check my e-mail but Claire never e-mailed me. I wanted to look out my window and see her waiting in her car at the curb.

I couldn't stop myself from imagining the normal.

Claire, checking her face in the mirror and singing along to her music in an awkward voice.

Claire, reporting the latest gossip on someone, anyone, *anyone* worth gossiping about except...she wasn't.

She wasn't.

I felt myself sink to the floor but didn't feel myself hit it. I felt wetness on my face. If I hadn't left with Garreth, would I be dead too? Was that what this was all about? Either way I looked at it, it didn't make any sense. So I stopped looking at it. It hurt too much.

I pulled my hair into a ponytail and looked at myself in the mirror with a blank expression. The smell of bacon wafted up the steps as I walked down. I found my mother at the stove, preparing a meal she knew I would never eat, but like the good mother she was, that didn't stop her from going through the motions. I sat down in silence at the table and flicked at the curled edges of the morning's newspaper with my finger.

She shot me a look of motherly concern and turned back to the bacon. "I'm glad you slept. That's the best thing for you right now." She placed a plate of warm, crispy fat in front of me. I just stared at it.

"If Garreth hadn't shown up to bring me home I would...I might be..." She looked at me with a tender expression and I saw her eyes begin to fill up with tears. I couldn't finish. I didn't have to.

"Garreth. That's an unusual name. I'd like to thank him for bringing you home safely. If I didn't know better, I'd say you have a guardian angel." She turned back to the spattering fat in the pan and I felt myself blush.

*If she only knew.*

I guess I always assumed she would be protective but it surprised me how easy this was. A smile appeared without even trying as I thought of her meeting Garreth and approving, but that smile soon faded.

"I heard that Claire's boyfriend is an emotional wreck," she said cautiously. "He told the police he tried to stop her. I just don't understand how a couple of kids could sneak up to the roof unseen."

"Roof?"

Mom sat down across from me and nudged my untouched plate, urging me to eat.

"That building is very dilapidated and should have been shut down years ago, but it never stopped kids from flocking to it." She reached out and took my hand. "Claire slipped from the roof. She fell. At least that's what Mrs. Meyers told me last night. I didn't want to tell you all of it and you didn't ask, so I let it go."

She dug into her share of bacon while I played with mine. A part of me was thankful she didn't gloss it over for my sake. It was better to know. Better to know what I was up against, if Hadrian did, in fact, have something to do with it. I bit off a small piece of my breakfast and crumbled the rest with my fingers. It fell to the greasy plate like ocher confetti.

As she quietly started to clear the table, she leaned down and gently kissed me. This was probably just as hard for her. Someone else close to us lost forever. Gone. Just like that. I looked up at my mother, knowing I should say something, but the words wouldn't come to me. She had turned away and was now facing the sink, busying herself with the daily routine of life. Last night played over and over in my head. Could I have done anything differently?

I sighed heavily and let my head fall into my hands, but not without noticing today's date on the newspaper. Today was Sunday. I only had four days left with Garreth. I realized something horrible was brewing inside of me. Something I was having a hard time controlling. What hurt tremendously

was that I couldn't grieve for Claire like I should. I should be crying hysterically, pining for my best friend of eight years. Eight years of friendship. Gone. And hate was taking its place.

My head shot up with a jerk. The number eight again. Claire and I met in third grade. She was eight years old and I was just turning nine. Eight years later, she's dead and I'm in love with an angel and fighting to save humanity. Eight. The octagram has eight points. Garreth's star. He was granted eight days to be with me. To be human. Claire's life is over. When life ends, an incarnation ends. The Judgment Point. Eight lives. It was spinning through my head and I couldn't stop it. It was meant to happen. Last night. It was all meant to...

The kitchen moved strangely. Tilting. My mother's body spun at an odd angle as she turned and called out my name. The frying pan was suddenly airborne, sending soapy grease everywhere. Then all went black as my head hit the floor.

My mother gently tapped on my door. "Teagan? Are you just about ready?"

I smoothed the front of my skirt with my hands and stared at the girl in the mirror reflecting back at me. Something had changed, her eyes perhaps. I leaned closer to look deeper into the green eyes trapped within the glass. No, she was in there.

*Just checking.*

"Yeah, Mom. I'm ready."

I opened my door and found my mother's warm smile. I couldn't help smiling back.

"You look nice. How's your head? That's quite a fall you took at breakfast, almost hit the table. "

I rubbed the back of my skull and flinched. "Still tender, but it's okay."

"You made me nervous, but I guess it's normal that you slept so long. You had a rough night. Just don't forget to take more Tylenol. We're leaving for the church in a few minutes. Are you sure you're all right?"

I nodded and she gave me another smile, this one a little more apprehensive than the first, then she turned and headed down the steps, her heels clicking softly on the floor. The house still smelled like bacon grease. It lingered, reminding me of this morning. Suddenly, I wanted to get out of the house, far, far away from the smell that was beginning to turn my stomach.

By the time our car pulled away from the curb and headed west toward the church, my head was beginning to clear. The throbbing ceased, allowing me to think, and I was truly thankful that my mother didn't bother filling the empty space of our short car ride with mindless chitchat. I couldn't help thinking about Claire, though in a numb, detached sort of way that both relieved and appalled me. I began wondering all sorts of things, like what should I say to her parents, or was it okay not to say anything at all? Would Ryan be there? Would Brynn and her tagalongs dare show their faces?

Today was a memorial service. The viewing would be to-morrow, followed by the funeral the next day. My head was a gigantic jumble as thoughts wove themselves within it. There

was so much weighing on my shoulders, so much depending on me, that I couldn't help but think I would be of better use somewhere else.

As we drew near the church and rounded the corner, I couldn't help noticing the reflection of a gray Jeep in the side mirror. It was two cars back but had no trouble keeping up with my mother's erratic driving. I smiled to myself.

It was an old church, the type that had hard wooden pews that were smooth and worn and numbed your bottom. An old, comforting smell was always present here, a smell I could never put my finger on but had breathed in every Sunday since I was a child. Sometimes it smelled of incense, especially on holidays, but it could never compare to the tantalizing smell that Garreth possessed. I closed my eyes to conjure that aroma rolling off his perfect skin. With that thought, I opened my eyes and turned around to look for him, hoping I would find him standing somewhere toward the back, but it was becoming crowded.

People were filing in, finding their places among the pews. I tried not to notice their awkward glances, so I stared down at my lap. But I still felt their stares and heard the whispers of Claire's relatives, pointing me out. The sun was beginning to set, creating a warm glow of orange and purple across the open room, across the bridges of people's noses in the fourth row, across the little cabinet that held the Host near the altar.

I heard the first five minutes of the homily before my thoughts began to wander, much like they always did. But part of me purposely tried to drown out the priest's words. He had

no idea what Claire was like and I couldn't pretend to listen anymore. My eyes roamed the room and I smiled back at a lady in a lilac suit.

What would happen if I approached the altar and told them what Claire had been like last night?

*"Hey, everybody, Claire kidnapped me so we could go to this raucous party, and you should have seen her milky eyes. She was downright freaky. She even arranged for fake IDs. But, hey, she spent the last moments of her life with wonderful, loving friends. Me? No, I abandoned her so I could hang out with my boyfriend who, by the way, has wings and is helping me thwart an evil angel's plot against the world. So, if you think we're all going to go to heaven someday, think again, because our futures lie in my hands!"*

Maybe it was better to let the priest have center stage after all.

They would cart me off to the loony bin faster than my mother could tell them I bumped my head this morning, or explain to them why I still smelled like bacon.

The setting sun had faded the faces in the stained glass windows so only their outlines remained. I stared at the blank, fleshy ovals with curiosity. For some reason, the clothing, the robes, were still very much visible but the faces had disappeared and were now eerie and hollow-looking.

As though on cue, it began to rain outside, adding to the thick, somber cloud lingering inside the church. I watched the rain stream down the windows, mesmerized by the way the drops and rivulets altered the colors, graying them, lending a

smeared appearance to the faceless bodies I couldn't seem to tear my eyes away from.

One in particular managed to capture my interest more than the others and was conveniently positioned above our pew, minimizing unwanted eye contact with the rest of the congregation. This glass rendering, this one likeness, failed to disappear like all the others. It was a beautiful angel, its white wings outstretched as though hovering protectively over my seat. At first, it reminded me of *my* angel and I thought for sure it held some significance. But to my amazement, I realized the face was female. It wasn't Garreth. It was *me*.

At that moment, my mother poked my side and pointed. "Look, Teagan, that angel looks just like you. Isn't that the strangest thing?"

She was right. My mother turned her attention back to the priest then bowed her head to pray, but my eyes stayed put. I couldn't look away from the glass angel. The rain was coming down heavier than ever now, dimming the likeness in the glass. A passing car disrupted my thoughts. Its red taillights illuminated the angel from behind in a scarlet glow no one else seemed to notice. I looked around the room. Everyone's head was bowed except mine. My eyes returned to the window above me and I shuddered as I saw the still-red glow penetrate the raindrops and spill down the angel's face like tears of blood.

# Chapter Seventeen

M onday morning came just as all Mondays do, with the alarm screaming in my ear and my hand reaching out to pound the snooze button. If only Monday mornings could somehow stay trapped in the timeless sleep of the night before, forgotten. But, no, not Monday. In fact, if Monday were a student at Carver High School, it would win the stock of perfect attendance awards

I sat up and rubbed my eyes, then flung myself back onto my pillow as the one dreaded thought crept into my head. School. I had forgotten about the chemistry test today, which I hadn't studied for, and the new English paper would be assigned today.

Groaning, I swung my legs over the side of the bed. Why couldn't I have hit my head hard enough to make me absent until graduation? Only the thought of seeing Garreth finally got me moving and out of bed to face the day.

I showered and dressed and applied my own newly acquired makeup. Mom had had a field day when my little experiment proved to be more than a two-day fling.

Back in my room, I stood beside my window, refraining from pulling the curtain aside like I had done out of habit for

so long. My ears told me the street below was vacant, that if I peeked out I wouldn't see the white car waiting below. Eventually, habit won out and I shamefully parted the sheer fabric, and just as I expected, there was no white car.

"Breakfast in five minutes!" my mom shouted from the kitchen below.

So, in the extra time I had before leaving for the bus stop, I pulled up the file I had saved on my computer. A glowing octagram appeared on the screen and I sat completely immobile, studying the double squares. Garreth had already explained that this star was Hadrian's mark, but deep inside I knew I had seen it somewhere else before. The power of *déjà vu* hit hard and I found myself profoundly irritated. Maybe I saw it in a past math class? Frustrated, I closed the file and completely shut down the system. I grabbed my backpack and slung it over my shoulder.

The itching on my palm had resurfaced with a vengeance and I opened my hand to examine it.

*Gross.*

An unpleasant raised line appeared on the surface of my skin and I scratched at it with my stubby nails, careful not to split open the ugly welt now forming. Obviously, I had been exposed to some sort of poison oak or sumac during my trek through the woods the other night. I thought quickly of the contents of our medicine cabinet. Surely it contained some sort of cream that would erase yet another reminder of my last night with Claire. As I turned to head into the bathroom, I stopped dead in my tracks.

A familiar hum had come from my window.

*Claire.*

The ache in my heart spoke her name but I shook my head, knowing there would be no white car waiting at the curb. Yet, the sound of the engine was so familiar. I heard a door open and close.

I turned around and crossed the length of my room to the window. My wishful thinking was never practical and my heart was pounding wildly out of rhythm, but I couldn't stop myself from checking. My eyes widened, expecting to see white. That was what I most desperately wanted. What I didn't expect, however, was to see how beautiful gunmetal gray could appear in the bouncing light of a morning sun. I practically ran out of my room to the top of the stairs, the first aid forgotten.

I tiptoed down the steps and stood in the doorway of the kitchen, watching in silent disbelief. It was one thing to see his car parked outside, but it was something else entirely to see my own personal angel sitting in my kitchen, chatting with my mother as she refilled her coffee mug.

"Hi, honey. It seems you don't need to introduce me to your friend after all. Garreth thought you could use a ride to school since word's gotten out that you loathe the bus so much."

My eyes drifted toward the only light in the kitchen worth looking at, as comfortable as anything in the chair that was usually mine. He smiled that particular smile that I knew was only meant for me.

Calm washed over the room and I knew he was responsible for it. I knew he was timing his heart with mine, using it to

calm me. For that reason alone I had never felt closer to him. Who else's heart would beat in time with mine? Who else would breathe when I did? Or, better yet, breathe for me?

"A ride would be nice, thanks. Is that okay, Mom? That Garreth takes me to school?" My voice sounded pleading. I hoped she wouldn't notice.

"Absolutely. In fact I'm glad you came over, Garreth. I told Teagan I wanted to thank you for the ride you gave her the other night. It means a lot to me that you were there for her. She's very special to me. She's all I have."

"You're very welcome, and you're right, she *is* special."

I was taking a sip of orange juice just as those words slipped from his mouth, and I gulped to keep from choking on it.

"Well, we should be going now. I am so glad you two met." I grabbed my backpack, a piece of toast, and Garreth's arm as I dragged him to the door.

"So nice to meet you, Garreth," Mom called out behind us as I raced ahead of him to the Jeep parked at the curb.

We drove in silence at first but then I couldn't hold back any longer.

"You could have warned me, you know."

"Sorry, I thought I would surprise you. But, if you feel that strongly about it, I think I can catch up to your bus. It's 4E, right?"

I smiled at his joke then I looked at him and lost my train of thought. The sun was shining through the windshield, bringing out the tints in his sandy hair. He was looking straight

138

ahead, concentrating on the road. I let my eyes travel from his perfect profile, down the smooth skin of his neck where the breathtaking incense was strongest, down his arm to the loosely rolled cuff at his wrist, and then out to his strong but delicate hand.

"What are you doing?" he laughed.

"I'm memorizing you." My voice caught in my throat.

He was with me. Here. Now. Yet, as hard as I tried, I couldn't shake the plunging feeling that overwhelmed me at the end of each day, bringing closer the day I dreaded.

"You don't need to memorize me."

"Of course I do. You'll be leaving soon."

"I'm not leaving *you*. You just won't be able to see me as you do right now." A look of remorse spread quickly across his face. "Maybe this wasn't such a good idea, my coming here."

I jumped on his words. "How can you mean that?"

"I've been very selfish coming to you like this. I broke a cardinal rule."

"Which is?" Exasperation seethed within me.

"Putting my own wants first, before your protection. I've endangered you, Teagan. I wanted to know you so much that I placed what should be secret and sacred behind all that. Knowing about Hadrian places you in a danger greater than ever."

"But wouldn't he have found me anyway? The bloodline?"

He continued staring straight ahead, even though we had already arrived at school and were parked in the spot Garreth had claimed for himself these last few days.

"Yes, he would have found you, regardless. I just can't help feeling responsible, like I've brought him closer...sooner than what may have transpired. As you grow stronger, Hadrian is becoming more aggressive."

I could only hope that Hadrian never confronted us. I couldn't imagine Garreth becoming part of a powerless legion of fellow Guardians, forced to watch helplessly as their charges were manipulated. I was picking at my nails, what was left of them, when he took my hand.

"It would have been safer to guide you in my natural form. I can't stop protecting you, Teagan. It's who I am. But my feelings for you have only sped up the inevitable. You are Hadrian's greatest enemy right now. *You* have the power to destroy him."

I leaned into his chest. My eyes closed, for a second, and then the bell echoed over the parking lot.

# Chapter Eighteen

Half of the day managed to go by before I couldn't stand it any longer. I couldn't take walking the halls, staring down at my shoes or straight ahead, avoiding the invisible question marks tattooed across everyone's faces. I had just about thrown a fit when the guidance counselor called me out of class for the third time to "monitor" me. Only one good thing had come of it all: Garreth had appointed himself to be my emotional chaperone.

"This is ridiculous." I hugged my books tighter to my chest, like a shield.

"They're in shock, Teagan. A part of their little world has just drastically changed and they're looking for an answer."

"And they think I have it?"

"They don't know what to think."

"Well, I'm no different from them. I don't know what to think either."

We walked slowly, in silence, past the orange lockers to the bench under a large glass window at the far end of the hall. I had a free period coming up next and I wasn't quite sure how I wanted to spend it. I kept myself focused on the window instead of the people we were passing, until I was filled with

sudden rage. It came on so quickly that it nearly stopped my breath. Then I realized why.

"Are you okay?"

Garreth's perfectly sculptured face twisted awkwardly with concern. His serene blue eyes followed my line of vision and then he understood.

He touched my arm gently, as though holding me back. "That might not be such a good idea, Teagan."

"Oh, it's a very good idea."

As if they had a mind of their own, my feet pulled the rest of my body in the direction of an open locker and firmly planted themselves in front of a very irritated Ryan. Apparently, my fear of him from the other night was completely gone.

"Teagan."

He regarded me icily, as Kid Rock seeped from his earbuds. I noticed the circles under his eyes as he tried to shrug me off. A voice I didn't recognize snarled out of my throat, causing me to jump when I realized it was my own. "How could you?"

Ryan stared at me blankly then turned back to face the inside of his locker. Smugness I could handle, but ignoring me was the wrong move.

"I had nothing to do with it," he said cold-heartedly. Deception rolled off of him in waves, pretending to be worn down with grief.

"Liar."

"What is that supposed to mean?"

"You know what it means. I saw how you changed, how you acted. Just tell me what Brynn has to do with this and I'll piece together the rest."

"I have no idea what you're talking about, Teagan. I'm just as hurt as you are. I loved Claire."

"You are so full of it," I spat. A small semicircle of kids had started to gather behind us but that didn't stop me from lashing out at him. "Why weren't you at her memorial service last night?"

Ryan shook his head. "I don't handle funerals very well."

"Her *funeral* is tomorrow," I shot back.

I knew what I was about to do was an act of desperation. I grabbed Ryan's hand, prying his cool fingers open, looking for some sort of proof that he was being manipulated by Hadrian. Of course, there was no octagram, no mark of a dark angel. Ryan was like me. Human. Although how he appeared to me at the rave made that questionable.

"What the hell, Teagan?" Ryan yanked his arm, pulling his hand away from my grasp. "You *are* a freak."

He stared at me, his eyes darkening at what I had just done, with what I was accusing him of, then his face was covered in shadow as Garreth stood behind me. In that very practiced, very controlled voice, the same I had heard that fateful night in the woods, he began his take on what had happened that night at the rave.

"Brynn was trying to dance with me at the rave, and Claire got a little pissed off. It was crazy. You know, we were having a good time. The music was loud. The place was wild. By the time I turned around Claire was outta there."

"Where did she go?" I heard the chatter of the kids behind me, wondering what we were talking about.

"She was headed up the back steps to the roof. Some other kids were following her, thinking it was a cool idea—especially since it was off limits. By the time I reached her, she was standing right on the edge. *Right on the edge.* Freaked me out. I mean, I've seen some crazy shit, but Claire balancing on the edge of a four-story building? I never expected that to make my list."

Ryan got a dark look in his eyes as he stared out across the hallway, lost in the memory of that night. Then he looked me straight in the eye.

"There's a lot I don't remember about that night. But I won't forget what I saw. No one would forget that."

For a second, I began to doubt the boy I had seen in the woods.

"What did you see, Ryan?" I prompted him.

"Claire was just standing there. Her arms were out-stretched at her sides. Her back was facing us. She was so still. I remember taking a step closer to her. I wanted to grab her arm and pull her away from the edge but this kid stopped me. And then, it was like she was levitating—right there in front of everyone. Like someone had lifted her up, holding her out for the world to see. It was…it was like she was flying. And then she went over the side."

I couldn't speak. I stared silently at Ryan, hearing his words echo in my head, even though he wasn't saying them anymore. In my mind I could picture her. I could see Claire as

144

if I was witnessing the entire thing...no, as if I *were* Claire. The Claire from my dream.

Then I felt the warmth of Garreth's hand on my arm.

"Is everything okay?" he asked.

I snapped out of it and instantly felt a confrontation brewing. Reality was crushing the dream I wanted to see again in my head.

"Hey, back off!" Ryan slammed his locker shut and the hall fell silent again. "Anyway, what does it matter? No one will ever know why she jumped."

I felt my skin freeze inch by inch with tiny stabs of ice that worked their way down my neck and arms. I jumped as Ryan's arm shoved sharply into Garreth's shoulder as he pushed his way past us. Without another word he disappeared down the hall to his next class. My feet had rooted themselves to the floor in front of his locker and I felt as though I was sinking right through the tiles into the bowels of the school.

"Teagan?"

The voice of my angel brought me back. Someone was whispering.

"Come on, I'm taking you home."

I felt myself moving, being led forward by a magical pull I had no control over. Garreth led me down the hall, through the strange, silent cloud that still hovered overhead, past the confused faces of those who had witnessed the showdown between Ryan and me. Past everything. And, if I had eyes in the back of my head I would have seen Brynn Hanson cast a hateful stare in my direction.

We were just outside the main office when I felt my knees go weak and Garreth had to catch me. He opened the door but I pushed it back, closing it against the smell of ink and paper. I could tell he was worried.

"Garreth, my mom spoke to Claire's mom. Claire slipped and fell. No one said anything about her jumping. Claire wouldn't do that." My voice was urgent and fearful.

"You shouldn't be here today. I'm going to ask if you can be excused."

"No. If he's here, then I'm here. I'm not going anywhere."

"We need to get out of here."

He smiled down at me and in a flash of intuition, I knew he meant the one special place where no harm would come to us. Our place. The chapel in the woods.

"There's only one problem, we're stuck here."

Just then my hand went numb. It was the strangest thing. I lifted it to inspect the poison I had forgotten to treat earlier and began to wonder if I should spend my free period with the nurse.

As if reading my mind, Garreth took my hand and gently rubbed his thumb over my palm. "This will have to wait."

"What?"

"There's nothing the nurse can do about this."

"You know something about my hand?"

I turned it over again. It was just raised and red, like a big, gross welt, but Garreth knowing about it freaked me out a little.

"Just trust me. I'll explain the best I can later."

146

Just like that, the feeling in my hand came back, filling my palm with a electric tingling sensation. I opened and closed my fist and wiggled my fingers to rush the feeling back into them. I closed my fist again, knowing that one surefire cure would be to punch Ryan Jameson point-blank in the mouth.

# Chapter Nineteen

No matter how hard I willed them to, the hands on the clock wouldn't move any faster, and so I was stuck in history class, dying of boredom. Ms. Carlson was discussing the progression of war, which led into the topic of when World War Three may or may not occur, which led into the predictions of Nostradamus. Could he have predicted the fate of humanity? Did he have any inkling back in the seventeenth century that something dark was lurking on the horizon, something no one would believe was coming? I stared at the clock and gave up wishing.

It was at that precise moment that I felt the draft.

I turned my head to my left, my hot breath billowing out in front of me, as if the room had suddenly dropped twenty degrees. The boy at the neighboring desk, Seth Robards, stared at me with a blank look on his face, his brown eyes glassy and vacant. His mouth was hanging open slightly, but there was no breath. Each puff of air I released only exaggerated the absence of his. I forced myself to look away.

The classroom filled with a sudden, numbing silence. The shuffling of papers, book pages turning, all came to screeching halt. Although everyone was still moving, their

breath streaming out of their mouths, no one else noticed the chill. Ms. Carlson kept on talking but I couldn't hear the words coming out of her mouth. All I could do was focus on her breath filling the air in front of her face. It was as if the room had become a vacuum. My intuition sparked to life and zeroed in on the only audible sound. It echoed in each corner and swiftly the room became hauntingly claustrophobic.

Everyone was oblivious to the horror only I seemed to know was coming. I felt the blood drain from my face as the noise grew louder. I looked from face to face. Nothing. No one seemed to hear it but me.

There was a rustling of feathers, growing to a deafening roar for my ears alone. The room grew dark, as though a large slow-moving cloud was passing overhead, but no one noticed that either. I couldn't explain what I was feeling. Fear definitely stirred inside me, and strangely, a small feeling of relief. Relief that if it was going to happen, then let it come.

*Bring it on, Hadrian. Let's get this over with!*

I clenched my jaw tightly as I began to absorb the tension building in the room. The cloud moved downward, positioning itself directly in front of my desk, looming larger, touching the ceiling.

It began to take shape. I could see its outline, rough leathery tips that were tattered and frayed, darker than any shade of black I was ever taught in art class. My mouth went dry. I couldn't swallow. My head tilted upward, straining to see the formidable shape before me. The shadow made a graceful

sweeping motion and landed squarely on my desk. I couldn't suppress the bloodcurdling scream that ripped loose from my throat.

"Teagan?" Ms. Carlson's voice broke the silence.

Her voice was different, softer, perhaps even a little scared, and something told me she was no longer lecturing on the aspects of war. It was safe to assume Nostradamus had exited the building quite some time ago.

I sat up, startled, focusing on each confused face staring at me.

*Great, I am a freak.*

The room felt overwhelmingly warm just then and I looked down at my desk and quickly wiped away a glistening smear of saliva with my sleeve.

"May I go to the nurse?"

"Of course you can. Let me get you a pass." She was trying to remain calm and in charge of things but the edginess to her voice was giving her away.

As far as I knew, I had fallen asleep in class, but by the looks on the faces around me, a little more must have happened. I stole a glance at Seth who still appeared dazed.

I gathered my things, avoiding the snickers growing around me that were abruptly halted by the exaggerated clearing of Ms. Carlson's throat. Garreth was right, I had to get out of here. My legs trudged heavily up the aisle, as if sliding through pudding, but thankfully, they led me to the large wooden desk at the front of the room. I took the piece of paper, flashed an apologetic smile, then stepped out into the hallway.

Garreth was already there, waiting for me, his blue eyes distraught and clouded with unspeakable fear. "We have to go NOW."

He handed me a yellow office slip marked "excused." I had never seen him panic-stricken and immediately I was terrified. Had I done something to bring this on? I clearly remembered stating some sort of challenge in my dream, now that I knew it was a dream. Wasn't it?

"How did you know I would be coming out of class?"

"There's no time, we have to go."

"But I had this dream, and..."

Garreth took a second to slow us down, placing his steady hands on my trembling shoulders.

"I'll tell you when we get to the car. Trust me, it'll be okay." He protectively wrapped his arm around me, hurrying us to the main office. "Let me do the talking." He opened the heavy door, and I reluctantly followed.

I stood by his side, as quiet as I could will myself to be, while he impatiently tapped his finger on the long wooden counter until an irritated secretary came over. She took the two passes Garreth handed her and looked at us both, long and suspiciously, then signed them and handed them back. I didn't make eye contact with her, hoping she would take it as intense sorrow and take pity on me, therefore giving our early dismissal a sense of legitimacy.

We walked to the student parking lot as quickly as school rules would allow. Once inside the Jeep, I sat silently, praying the next words Garreth spoke would resemble something that made sense, but he was more silent than I. His hands gripped

the wheel hard as he steered the car out of the school lot and onto the main road.

"Will you please tell me what that was all about?" I asked finally.

His eyes focused on the road, as though on a serious mission to get us far, far away from something. It was only when we were close to a line of trees I recognized that he took a deep breath and seemed more like the Garreth I knew.

"I knew Hadrian would be getting close, very soon too, but I wasn't expecting this."

"What are you talking about?"

"The closer he gets, the more he drains me and I have no way of sensing him anymore. But *you* can. Your dream wasn't a dream. He was in that classroom with you."

Okay, that didn't just frighten me a little, it frightened me *a lot*.

"But, if you can't tell where Hadrian is, then how come you were waiting outside my class, like you knew?"

"Aside from the fact that your scream wasn't exactly silent, I can still feel when you need me near. I have no doubt you rattled the entire school back there."

Great, another reason to transfer to another school.

We made the sharp turn that led us onto the narrow lane within the trees. I found myself eager to see the tiny stone chapel again, to escape all that was rapidly plummeting down on us, even if only for a little while.

Just like the first time I laid eyes on it, it sucked the breath right out of me with its simple beauty: the old stone, the

wooden door, and the broken stained glass windows shrouded in roots and underbrush, as though forgotten by time. Something was different and I didn't immediately know what, but I felt it, like something was waiting. I shook the feeling. After what had just happened in history class, no wonder I was on edge.

He took my hand and together we slowly approached the little stone chapel, looking around us every so often, as if trying to spy something among the trees. It looked the same, nothing appeared damaged, but why did it feel so…*wrong*? Then intuition took over and told me we shouldn't go inside. I didn't know if Garreth felt the warning. I wasn't sure what angelic sense he had left and I was more than confused that I seemed to be the one feeling this extrasensory-perception thing instead of him. Like he said, he was my protector, not the other way around.

Instead, we sat on the fallen tree like last time. He took my hand, the burning one, and looked at it carefully, as though he were a doctor inspecting a freak of nature—which would be me.

"It's forming correctly."

I stared at him as he looked at my hand.

"What?"

"As your Guardian, I was given orders not only to protect you but to also be your witness."

"Um, in English, please?"

"The Judgment Point of your existence has begun, the revealing of your purpose."

153

"But...didn't you already do that? I'm supposed to defeat Hadrian."

He cupped his hands around my face and held them there, warming my skin with what little white light he had left. It was still in him. I felt it pulsing through his veins, felt it tapping against my skin. He closed his eyes and I watched him calm me, forcing his pulse to beat with mine. I had the urge to lean forward and press my lips to his and seal them there forever. But there was so much at stake. I wasn't sure how much more of this I could take. Hadrian...angels... Couldn't he and I just run away and be together?

Garreth opened his eyes and touched his lips gently to my hand, as if obliging the one wish he could give my heart. As soon as his lips met my skin, I felt so much more inside me that connected to him. It wasn't just the life-light, or the calming of my emotions, it was beyond that. I could clearly *feel* that he and I would get through this unscathed.

We pulled apart and then, without explanation, he pressed his palm to mine. I felt searing heat from the octagram slice into my hand, burning it, and I wondered if he was healing the poison welting up my flesh. When the heat subsided and I was given back my hand, I gasped, staring at it in wonder and surprise.

"My hand. It's…"

"It's called the *circle of unity*. It represents the unbroken cycle of life, death, and rebirth."

I held my right hand open in front of my face, so I could look at it more closely. It was absolutely beautiful and it was

mine. I wanted to trace the simple scrolling with my finger but I was scared to. Would it hurt? Would it disappear? The fragile curve began its scrolling descent down across my palm in an elongated "S," then repeated the shape behind itself. It was incredibly feminine and I was amazed how it suited me. It filled me with a strange sense of power and tingled against my skin as if resonating with magic.

So now I was no longer the damsel in distress but an equal to both Garreth and Hadrian. I belonged, inducted into a divine society...and this was too much. I suddenly felt overwhelmed, as if I had been given an expensive gift. Do I give it back and tell them I can't accept? What if I can't do what's expected of me? But it made the task ahead of me all the more meaningful. Somehow, I would have to find the strength to believe I could do this.

I began to shake, the power inside suddenly retreating, leaving in its wake the timid seventeen-year-old Teagan I've always known.

# Chapter Twenty

"Teagan," he whispered, trying to capture my attention.

I had been staring at the beautiful mark on my hand for about ten minutes. A bizarre feeling swept over me but it wasn't just because of my hand; it was all of me, my whole body, my insides.

"I don't know if I can do this. I…"

"You're scared."

I nodded. His gentle words soothed the pain from my hand and the tremors of confusion from my body. And when I looked up into his pure eyes, I had no doubt that I could trust the unknown. He was guiding me. Protecting me.

We had three more days. Three more days to spend together and stop Hadrian and his plan.

Impossible. But was it?

Silently, I accepted my gift.

The sky had grayed quickly, covering the treetops with heavy, threatening clouds that forced me to shudder involuntarily. There was something more than the sudden change in weather that caused my arms to tingle and prickle, but I couldn't figure it out. I looked at Garreth leaning against the imperfect bark and gnarls of the old tree.

"Come on, let's go," Garreth said, sensing my discomfort and looking upward. "I have a feeling the school might call to check on you."

I rolled my eyes. School was the least of my worries these days.

The first plump drops of rain were just beginning to fall as we reached the Jeep. Garreth quickly started the car and turned the dial for the heater.

"You're shivering." He pulled me close and enveloped me with his warmth.

"Didn't you feel strange back there?"

In the dim light, Garreth shook his head slowly from side to side. "What did you feel?"

His handsome face suddenly took on a boyish expression of uncertainty. He looked so innocent. No, he looked...*human.*

"I don't know exactly, but something wasn't right."

With the heater cranked, I felt myself begin to thaw just a little but I couldn't stop trembling.

"What?" Garreth asked of me. He had been studying me intently while I was off somewhere in my brain trying to figure all this out.

I let out a sigh. "I really don't know. Obviously, Hadrian is playing hardball here. I mean, this army of his. There are so many already." I shook my head as if disbelieving my very own words. "I see them everywhere now, the people who are losing their Guardians. There was a boy in my history class, and just like that, his Guardian was corrupted. It's happening so quickly, Garreth."

I let my head fall back against the headrest and I pressed my hands to my eyes. Everything inside me hurt. I realized I hadn't let myself properly grieve for Claire, and that all this happening in my life was like a fast-forwarded episode of *The Twilight Zone*, starring yours truly.

Hadrian's war was psychological, his victims affected mentally. Deep inside, I felt like I was going crazy. Maybe I had Hadrian to thank for that? Maybe I wasn't too far off if I believed that he would soon drive everyone absolutely mad in order to reign. I had been chosen for a reason but, right now, that reason made absolutely no sense to me. I looked at my hand for reassurance. *Everything* happens for a reason. *Nothing* is coincidental.

Gently, Garreth took my hand and placed in it another gift. Only this one was hard and cold and very, very deadly.

The sheer weight of it held me and I couldn't move, let alone take my eyes off the incredibly scary looking knife Garreth had just placed in my hand. I looked at him and he read the confusion in my eyes.

"It's a dagger, by the way, not a knife." He smiled in an attempt to pull me out of my deer-in-the-headlights trance.

"Oh, no. Don't tell me this is how I'm supposed to destroy him?"

"It might resort to this, yes. I need to know that you'll be prepared when the time comes. And it is coming. Soon."

His eyes still held that gentle quality but his words and tone were absolutely serious. I looked down at the knife—excuse me, dagger—and turned it over carefully to admire the beauty of its design.

The gold handle was etched with endless scrolling, very similar in design to the symbol now embedded in my right hand. In fact, I curiously compared them and they matched. Perfectly. When I held the dagger in my right hand, warmth tingled against my skin as though it were teeming with life. The beautiful handle told the well-known tale of the Archangels and the struggle they endured in heaven, the story continuing down onto the shining steel blade. It was obviously very old, priceless in its craftsmanship.

"It just shocks me a little that an angel would be in possession of such a...weapon."

"Under normal circumstances, we don't take part in violence. Of any sort. You're well aware this is not a normal situation. Besides, I'm not holding the weapon."

I looked at my second gift of the day and sighed. "It looks old."

"That it is."

"Is it...yours?"

"It wasn't made for *me*."

Garreth's voice was clear and strong, but it wasn't his words that spoke so clearly to me; it was the fact that the time had come. The deadly instrument that would destroy a dark angel had just been delivered to me, and at that very moment I realized how very precious the circle of time and life is.

# Twenty-one

My mother never questioned why I had come home early. She simply looked at me now and then with a soft worry in her eyes as we cleared the kitchen table of our silent dinner. Garreth had been right, of course. The assistant principal had called exactly ten minutes after I walked in the door, to make sure I had gotten home safely. Surprisingly, she informed me I was excused from all classes tomorrow to attend Claire's funeral, which I had decided not to attend precisely five minutes before she called. But I kept that to myself.

I knew it was wrong. I knew full well that my mother, along with every grown-up in my school, would stress to me that it would give me the closure I needed. They were probably right, and deep in my heart I agreed with them. My mother would leave for work right after the funeral, so at least one of us was going to represent our little unit, leaving me several hours to get my bearings and search for a dark angel. If that was even possible. I didn't know where to begin.

Tracking down Hadrian and following the path I had been led to had become personal—for Claire and for the preservation of my own sanity. There was no telling how much time

was left. No telling who would fall next as Hadrian's victim. No telling how long I had before he came for *me*.

Coming home to an empty house had been a blessing, allowing me to safely hide the ornate dagger under my bed. I wrapped it in a thick towel and covered it with magazines. It terrified me to think that thing was under my bed. I felt as if I had stolen a priceless piece of art from a museum. Every time I thought of its gleaming gold handle and silver blade nestled safely in the towel, I felt lightheaded and sweaty, which added another crease to my mother's forehead by evening.

"Honey, are you feeling all right?"

"I'm fine, Mom," I answered hastily, my mind occupied with thoughts I couldn't share.

"Maybe we should have gone to the doctor after you fainted yesterday. I'm worried you might have a concussion."

"Really, Mom, I'm okay."

I said it with more feeling this time, hoping she would be satisfied, but she didn't take the bait, not that I truly expected her to. My mother is a notorious worrywart. Actually, the more I thought about it, I saw the possibilities that this could work to my advantage.

"You know, Mom, I am feeling tired. I think I'll go on up to bed."

"Sure, sweetie."

Bull's-eye. She shot another look of concern in my direction. Her maternal instincts would go into overdrive soon. Thankfully, I was genuinely tired, so her checking on me once or twice during the night most likely wouldn't bother me.

She went back to paying close attention to the television, watching the news and shaking her head. "It's sad, Teagan. Everywhere you look there's destruction and misery. It's so scary to think our number could be up at any given moment."

I thought of Claire and how destruction and misery had hit so close to home, and then I swallowed the lump that had formed in my throat. Who had any idea Claire's number would be up when she and I joked about Madame Woo, or when I let her finish my bag of chips? Unexpected or not, she certainly didn't deserve to have her sweet young life taken by a malicious dark beast with huge wings and an emblem carved into his hand.

My poor mother. It was her job to protect me from the world. She had no clue as to what was about to transpire over the next day or two. If she only knew what was lying hidden beneath my bed…

I stared at the television. Floods, fires, murder, hatred…the list went on and on. Lucifer's Hell. As I climbed the steps to my room, I was eager to say good-bye to this day. I was exhausted but wasn't sure if I could sleep, knowing a sharp weapon had been stowed under my bed, and even more frightening, what I was going to do with that weapon. But, as my head hit the pillow, I fell asleep almost instantly…dreaming of the funeral I would not be going to in the morning.

I opened my eyes to darkness, lying still and staring at my ceiling. A faint rustling sound had woken me, I was sure of it. My mind drifted, going back to the funeral in my dream, and I saw myself standing above an open grave. I was the only one

left in the cemetery, all the others had gone. I was left alone to think of the gloomy hole Claire would soon be lowered into after I left. I regretted not following her into the rave. I missed her terribly.

A rippling noise filled the air and I felt the hair on my neck rise in a split second of white-hot fear.

*Hadrian.* It was as if even my bones screamed his name.

Behind me, a crow balanced on a branch, keeping a close watch on me. I reached into my pocket, letting my fingers clutch the coolness of the stones and wire. The rosary that had hung in Garreth's car was now at the bottom of my coat pocket. It was *my* rosary and my last gift to my friend, an everlasting symbol that she would always be in my prayers. I turned around to drop the chain onto the casket but was nearly knocked over by the force of a startled scream lodged in my throat.

"I knew you would come." Claire smiled at me.

Her breath smelled rank, of old decaying wood. I hastily grasped for composure. It was difficult to keep from screaming into the gray-blue face of my friend, a face that was just inches from my own.

She hovered there, an eerie specter guarding her own grave. I looked down into the pit before me, which appeared endless and much, much deeper than the required six feet needed for a proper burial. My feet inched back from the edge ever so slightly as I blinked back hot tears. This wasn't the way I wanted to remember her.

Her voice changed suddenly. "Why, Teagan? Why did you leave me with him?" She hissed at me from her moldy mouth.

I could only stare and wonder why she looked so decomposed so quickly after her death. In reality, she wasn't even buried yet.

"You walked off with Ryan and Brynn and the others." I tried to explain, but I knew who she meant.

A stench rose up from the hole, bringing with it a blast of icy air. The Claire floating before me writhed with agony, resembling a hideous combination of Brynn and all of the other breathless faces I had seen. *His* victims. *His* army.

"Claire! Please!" I sobbed but it was too late.

I lost my balance and went tumbling into the musty darkness. As I fell, a familiar hand reached out to me, the hand of my father from the picture on my dresser, trying to pull me up from the empty grave. As he reached for me, I saw a scar on the inside of his right palm, a swirly little scar that would have otherwise been unnoticed since it blended with the natural lines of his palm. Barely visible in the photo, it wasn't significant enough for me to ever question...before now.

I bolted up and knew. My memory flickered back to my computer, to the strange octagram. Still rattled by the disturbing dream, I tiptoed quietly out of my bedroom, down the hallway to the linen closet at the opposite end. The thought of Claire like that...but no, it wasn't Claire, not the Claire I knew. It was only a dream. She was changed, just like me. I realized that I was no longer the quiet, mousy girl I used to be; that over the course of a few days I had been dramatically transformed. I stepped inside closing myself in as I had done as a child, and pulled the small, thin chain dangling above my head.

I remembered hiding in here but I couldn't remember why. Hiding from someone, something. I remembered the dreams from my childhood, the ones that caused my mother to come into my room to help me back to sleep, and now I clearly remembered Garreth, my angel, guarding me even then when my mother had long since left to go back to her own room. He was the one who stayed the entire night with me, protecting me from my dreams, keeping me safe from the monsters in the corners of my room.

It had been Hadrian watching all along, sending me running to the closet to hide.

I reached up and took down the dusty cardboard box of family photos and pulled the chain. Darkness hushed in around me. I opened the door, padding softly back to my room where I set the box on my bed and opened it. I rummaged carefully to the bottom where my fingers found the envelopes containing my long-forgotten baby pictures.

There were only two pictures in existence of me with the man my mother told me was my father. One was safely framed in silver on my dresser. The other I looked upon now with new eyes, scouring each and every square inch of the faded picture that had been folded in half, as if saved long ago from being ripped in two. It was of the two of us, our poses nearly identical to the one I had framed, only this particular shot was different. *He* was different.

It looked like him. He had the same handsome features, the same build, but his eyes reflected back strangely. I turned it at various angles but I was positive the color of his eyes

appeared changed, they were darker...black...and there, one of his hands half hidden by my tiny knee. The angle of the camera had caught part of his open hand facing just the right way; a strange tattoo made up of intersecting lines that could easily be mistaken for the crease where the picture had been folded. This wasn't the mark from the dream. It was hard to tell but I was pretty sure I could make it out. Points. Like half of a square.

*His* mark.

Hadrian.

# Chapter Twenty-two

I sat back on my heels, cradling the photo in my hands. How could my father have the same mark as Hadrian? I brought the picture closer. My father's hand looked red and a little swollen. I wasn't sure, but if I stared long and hard enough I thought I could make out the scrolling detail just beneath the edges of the fresher line. Did he do that to himself? Did he carve an exact replica of Hadrian's mark into his own hand? Was it to pay homage to his Guardian, or perhaps Hadrian did it—some sort of torture.

Somewhere along the way, they both must have realized that I would someday learn what this was all about, even if it would be a very long time before I was capable of understanding it. And, although today brought me closer to the truth, it was still far away from making any sense.

I quickly laid the pictures in the box and stashed them under my bed before climbing under the covers. I knew I had to get some sleep if I was to face tomorrow but I couldn't stop my mind from racing. Then fear seized me like an icy hand. A sensation of heaviness pulled me down at my knees while my upper body went strangely limp. I willed my eyelids to close, to

somehow protect me from what I would see in the shadows, but they wouldn't obey me.

The rustling sound had returned. It began in the corner, growing louder, as if a large bird had taken flight; but, this was too large, too loud; it brought with it the hideous dream of Claire and that awful glaring crow. My body wanted to scream, but a strangled squeak was all I could deliver. I desperately fished around for Garreth's words about strength and purpose but, sadly, this was what I had been reduced to. Then it happened. It rose from the shadows like a cobra, the wings outstretched, the deep ashen veil cutting the dim of my room…

"I'm awake, I'm awake, I'm awake," I whispered to myself in the dark. I had become so used to the dreams that I was in shock that this was finally real.

*"Garreth,"* I willed my thoughts to him, *"please hear me."*

The form first loomed and positioned itself above me, then shifted into shape as my room became hushed in a cold, ethereal silence.

He was remarkable.

I could be honest with myself. Garreth was still my most perfect dream in human form but, as Hadrian stepped out from the shadows, as if taking his place center stage, my inability to tear my eyes away from him hit me like a ton of bricks.

Dressed in dark clothing that accentuated every line of his perfect form, he stood inhumanly still as his black eyes pierced their way into mine; eyes so dark that even from a distance I could tell the pupil and iris blended into one insanely dark orb.

168

But they were deep and cold, and although I shivered under his determined stare, I couldn't look away. The magnetic pull I felt toward his enigmatic darkness couldn't be described with words, and I was so taken by him that I would have done anything he asked, had he spoken, but he only stared at me.

He moved with a gentle fluidity that resembled music come to life. But I knew better. His dark strength was well hidden behind his austere and graceful facade. I had no doubt that he could snap me in two with one swift motion. To my surprise, I realized I had been holding my breath. As I sucked a large gulp of air into my lungs, I felt warmth wash through me, faint, as if a cloud had passed between me and the dark angel before me.

"Leave her alone," Garreth warned.

I clung to his back as though it was shield the second he materialized in front of me. The thunderous noise that billowed out from Hadrian scared me until I recognized it as mocking laughter.

"Ah, Garreth, the white knight come to save his love. All of heaven has its eyes on you, I'm sure. You are, after all, the one who's risked everything for the human girl he loves. How touching."

The symbol in my hand stung with warning, and a surge of intense heat came over me as I realized Garreth was giving me more of his light. I felt Garreth's spine tense and the dark beauty I had been enamored with just moments ago melted away to reveal the grotesque truth. With one sweep of his arm Hadrian struck Garreth, sending him hurtling across my room and into the wall.

169

"No!" I screamed.

I didn't care if my mom came running in, wide-eyed and scared. I wanted her to! How could I have ever thought I could handle this on my own? Was I insane?

Garreth staggered to his feet. I swallowed the bitter taste of bile rising into my mouth as I saw dark red appear at his hairline and trickle in a steady stream down the side of his pale face. Even weakened, he tried to make his way over to me. Strangely, I knew I was witnessing the remarkable; Garreth still shielding me, still protecting me under these horrible circumstances. He was a fascinating mixture of teenage boy and ancient Guardian, fighting to the end for what he was sworn to protect. But his strength was gone. He had given the last of it to me.

An ebony shadow positioned itself above me, spreading its dark fingerlike wings across my ceiling and down the walls on either side of me.

*"It's a trick…"* I told myself.

Surely, Hadrian was using the shadows to make himself look larger to scare me out of my wits. I thought I had outsmarted him until his cunning face was a breath away from my own. His lips curled back bitterly, and duress blasted through to my bones. I would have sworn I was staring into the face of darkness itself, into the indescribable grin of his twin, Lucifer.

Hadrian's wings flung back as if he was defiantly stowing them away. But, instead of following through, they rushed forward in one violent motion that sent a shock wave rolling across my room toward Garreth, sending my bed somersaulting

into the air and splintering my bookcases. I turned to scream for Garreth but was too stunned and stood frozen.

In the wake of it all, Garreth looked at me, his blue eyes calm and gentle, and in an instant the chaos around us paused, melting into the night. With his eyes, he spoke to me without words. I heard him clearly in my head and I learned what I had meant to him all these years, all these incarnations. It would have been indescribable with words.

Although I watched, I still couldn't believe what I was seeing: Garreth, so poised, so incredibly still, while all around us our world, or at least my tiny room within the world, came crashing down. And then, as if someone pressed a button, the whirlwind started up again. The part of my room where Garreth stood suddenly became dark. I could only watch as Hadrian's wrath blasted full force into Garreth and a large chunk of my soul was ripped to shreds.

I dropped to my knees, sweating and trembling. The emptiness inside me was excruciating. It was amazing how much of Garreth had been a part of me, so much I had taken for granted. Thinking it was how *I* felt. What *I* believed.

My room looked like a war zone and I stared silently at Hadrian, who was suddenly beautiful again. I looked at him, seeking an answer, hoping it would somehow become visible to me, hidden within his jet eyes, his pale skin, but I couldn't remember how to speak.

As if surmising my sudden handicap, he turned his attention to me, and for the first time Hadrian addressed me. "He belongs to me now."

"Belongs?" I was suddenly filled with rage. The heat in my hand burned intensely, sending a throbbing fire up my arm and into my chest.

Ignoring me, he turned to leave but I refused to let him. I found the strength to rise to my feet and lunge for his legs.

"What happened to my father? Tell me!" Choking on my words, I was desperately trying not to lose it. I still had a job ahead of me. A seemingly impossible job.

He glared down at me, offering nothing. I thought the glimmer that shot across his face like a meteor was one of intense compassion but he regained his composure quickly.

"I wonder, are you predictable like the others?"

"What do you mean 'others'?"

"Let me ask you, Teagan. What do *you* choose? I can offer you what your father failed to take. I can give you power."

He stepped a bit closer to me, hesitantly reaching his hand out to me. I felt so weak. He was so fascinating, so powerful... I knew taking his hand would be wrong, yet something in his eyes pulled at me.

"I know you better than you know yourself, Teagan. I've known you your whole life, your entire existence. You have so much potential. Heaven would be nothing more than a dream compared to world you and I could create."

Hadrian's cold hand brushed my cheek, triggering a memory deep within me. I had felt another hand on that cheek but it seemed like so long ago.

"I can help you, you know."

"Help...me?"

"You don't know all that you possess?" He took my hand and opened my palm, seductively tracing his finger along the scrolling I had been trying to hide. "Together we can unharness a power beyond description. You should consider yourself exceptional."

I was beginning to feel sick to my stomach, but Hadrian continued, pleased with my reaction.

"I have been ready for a new challenge. I've grown so tired of your kind, so selfish and demanding. It's beyond me why Guardians have so much compassion for such a disgusting race." His voice was saturated with a nauseating hunger and he tapped a heavy boot against Garreth's thigh. "But I have to admit, you've pleased me. I never expected to witness a human transform during an existing life-phase."

I looked at the amount of blood pooling around Garreth's limp body on my floor. It was too much blood.

"There can be others, you know. With your power you can have your pick, although you may just find me to your liking." He caressed my flushed cheek with his cold fingers. Then he turned his back to me.

"You're no angel, you're a monster!"

He spun back around to face me, a look of reproach on his face, as if he was actually considering what I said to be true.

"I think of myself as an angel of mercy. After all, aren't humans always searching for meaning to their meager little lives? Wouldn't you agree that I'm giving them a purpose? Placing them on a new path?"

The playful tone in his voice was gone. It was clear to me he was no longer willing to nicely talk me into assisting him in his plan of havoc. Instead, he would put me there by force if he had to. As he stretched his blackened wings, I fell to my knees, waiting to take my place where I really belonged, by Garreth's side.

The memory of Hadrian's fury slamming Garreth against the far wall of my bedroom was all I could see as I slumped to the floor. It played over and over again, vivid and hovering inside my brain like a serpent striking over and over. I pressed my palms against my temples but the pressure of my sweaty hands couldn't stop the pain. It had been so hard to stop looking at Garreth; but, more so, it was almost impossible *not* to look into the eyes of the one responsible. I was so blinded by the force of Hadrian's eloquence that it briefly shadowed the black heart he hid so well.

Hadrian crouched down in front of me. "You find me intriguing, don't you?"

I refused to answer, turning my head away, but he reached out and delicately ran his fingers through the disheveled strands of my hair.

"Yes, I am complex. You're trying to understand me but you lack the capacity to do so just yet. Very frustrating, isn't it?"

I still couldn't meet his eye and I pulled away from his touch.

Hadrian stood then. "Don't underestimate yourself, Teagan. Remember, I enjoy a good challenge. Won't you reconsid-

er my offer? You can leave all this behind and finally feel like you belong." He held out his smooth, pale hand to me. "I may not offer again, so I suggest you choose wisely."

I can't say why, but I rose to my feet and faced Hadrian, now with strange new eyes. My beautiful angel lay crumpled at my feet but I allowed a vacant mist to spread through my body, numbing me happily. I stepped around the debris that was once my bedroom, picked my way around Garreth's lifeless body and reached for Hadrian's hand even as Garreth lay bleeding. I never knew an angel could bleed, never thought about it before, but he was much more human now than he had ever planned to be.

The dark eyes that sought mine promised so much that nothing else seemed relevant. It was no wonder the others had fallen. Whether human or Guardian, the spell Hadrian wove was fiercely mesmerizing.

It was at that moment I saw the glimmer of something small and yellow barely concealed by the night. As I tried to make out what it was, everything suddenly came into perspective. Could it really be that simple? My hand reached, not for the hand of the dark-winged angel before me but for the instrument that could possibly save us all.

The air shifted as Hadrian tensed, his eyes no longer bright and imploring me with invitation, but instead darkly sinister and hollow. A storm announced itself with thunder clapping like an enormous rip across the sky. Suddenly, the dark wings above me trembled and spread open before me as my arm slid beneath the disheveled mess of my overturned bed. I withdrew

the dagger Garreth had entrusted to my care, awed by its simple beauty, but careful not to keep my back turned to Hadrian for too long. Hadrian quivered with rage, his wingspan full and splendid, nearly knocking out the walls as they filled my room. They overshadowed me like an ashen cloak, lifting him in ferocious beauty off my floor.

I was crouched as low as I possibly could be, fully prepared to feel his wrath, when his face contorted into a sly smile. Then, like a nearly forgotten trophy, Garreth was effortlessly scooped from the floor and Hadrian's dark laughter echoed throughout my skull and then whispered itself away with the wind.

And I was left alone with the dagger.

# Chapter Twenty-three

I expected morning to wake me from the nightmare but there was no light. There was no sun to warm my skin, only the dark of night that was exaggerated by the ever-building storm outside my window. Wading through the shock that quickly invaded my body, I began throwing clothing and blankets over the pieces of furniture that were destroyed. In doing so, I wondered if *I* too could ever be repaired.

I wrapped my quilt tightly around me, as if securing what I had left of myself, and curled up on the floor where Garreth had fallen, closing my eyes, picturing his warm white light, but all that was left was my cold, hard floor.

Silence tried to comfort me, closing in like a soothing whisper. I let it hold me and with it I was able to think about what had happened, but it all came rushing back too fast. The deeper I let myself sink, the more I became aware of a growing rage deep inside me.

Then it occurred to me, the rage I felt wasn't malicious anger. It was strength. The tables had turned now. I had to go after Hadrian if Garreth was to survive. Thunder cracked loudly, making me jump and I pulled the quilt tighter as lightning illuminated the sky, splitting the dark with jagged

streaks. Even though it was early morning, it was as dark as night and I needed to stop the darkness.

I needed to save my light.

I needed to save Garreth.

The mark on my hand burned gently with hope and I knew at last what had to be done. I held the small dagger in my hands, its weight confirming my decision. When Garreth had given it to me, he had meant for me to use it on Hadrian but that wasn't possible just now. Hadrian was more powerful than either of us could ever have imagined, but I knew how to defeat him. I would give him his wish and become his challenge.

As I formed the plan in my head, I knew I had to act quickly. I knew what it would do to my mother when she walked in to say good-bye to me in the morning but I couldn't take the chance of waiting any longer. And, if I took my time, I might chicken out and Garreth was much too important for me to risk that.

My thumb rubbed over the tiny raised octagram that stood out from all the other etchings on the golden handle. About the size of my thumbnail, the tiny sphere reminded me of a miniature sunburst and it glistened, as if revealing the magic it held deep inside. It was my angel calling to me, my sun, my light, and as it sparkled, I knew he was still alive, though he wouldn't be for long. Hadrian had one reason for taking Garreth.

And that was me.

My shaking was nearly uncontrollable, but the picture I held of Garreth in my head was enough to keep me from losing all control. I prayed the thunder wouldn't wake my mother. I

prayed that God would forgive me; this was going against all I had learned while growing up, but this was the only way. I knew very little about the octagram, just what Garreth had told me that day in the chapel, the day I found out he was my Guardian. I stared at the beautiful little star, wondering how such an uncomplicated symbol could be such a powerful gateway between two very distinct worlds.

If an angel could cross into my human world, then couldn't a human cross into the angels' world? Through the same portal? As I thought of Garreth, Hadrian's words interrupted and echoed inside me.

*Heaven would be nothing more than a dream compared to the world you and I could create…*

Wasn't this a new world already? That angels and humans could know of each other and coexist? Garreth told me that heaven started in our minds, that as long as I believed and was happy, it existed.

Well, I do. It exists. Garreth still exists and no one, especially Hadrian, was going to take that away from me.

I took the dagger, its shining blade reflecting the lightning through the glass of my window, shining my reflection back to me as I held it in front of me. My eyes were wild with fear but behind the uncertainty was hope and that hope was more powerful than anything.

The little voice inside my head was telling me to trust that hope, though it wouldn't stop my heart from wrenching the way it did when I thought of Garreth trying to touch my subconscious from another plane.

My room felt cold, and in my head I heard the mimicking laughter of black wings.

Time was running out.

I pulled the blade toward my chest in one quick thrust and felt it slice into my skin with ease, giving me the oddest sensations of warmth and cold. I was no doubt delirious by this point, and for the moment the sharp steel awakened me. At the same instant the smooth slice hit me, the sky opened and I heard rain falling, each drop soaring its way down to its death below, their pelting kisses to the earth amplified in my ears.

My senses began to sift through the numb fog that was filling me. Scared, I reached out in front of me. I heard a strange voice that seemed to be my own whisper, "Please, help me," as the curtains slid limply through my fingers then pooled around me. I felt tingly and tired and before me a mirage of two faces appeared, though I knew they weren't really there.

One had eyes so black they made me shiver, and the other was the incredible aqua blue of a boy I met once in a courtyard at school. The rest faded away as I plunged into darkness.

# *Chapter Twenty-four*

Waking up in death was not what I expected.

I waited for the pain, but strangely it didn't come. I peeked, first with my left eye and then my right, sure it would hit me at any moment. Slowly, both eyes opened and I stared down at myself, grimacing in expectancy for what was still absent.

My shirt held no stripes of crimson evidence. Nothing.

No blood.

No wound.

The only tangible proof the portal had worked was that I was still breathing and the bittersweet taste of urgency hung heavily in the air, reminding me of unspeakable sadness.

All around me I sensed a longing for the untouchable, a yearning for what had been left behind, and also for what might lie ahead, an unknown that was just within my reach.

Garreth.

I suppose I expected to open my eyes to some surreal world, if it was safe to expect anything at all. Perhaps some foreign, otherworldly terrain, a mystical realm, but this was surprisingly earthlike, even though Garreth explained that heaven is more than just a place. It starts with a peaceful state

of mind, but my subconscious clearly expected something else.

Wasn't Garreth supposed to be waiting for me the moment I opened my eyes here? What about Hadrian? Was he somewhere nearby, watching me as he always does?

But I was alone in this sort of purgatory that looked both so familiar and foreign to me. It was my street but there were no people, no houses.

I squeezed my eyes shut.

If Garreth was my heaven and if I was so close to finding him...

*Please, let this be true.*

If Garreth could link his heart to mine and manage to control my fears to calm me, then...

*Oh, God, will this work?*

I had to try. He needed *me* now and if I've been given any sort of—I didn't know what to call it...angelic prepowers?—then I might be able to mesh my heart with his. I could keep him alive. It *had* to work.

Each day Garreth spent on earth put him at risk. His light was dimming and mine was...changing...like an electrical current transferred from one outlet to another. Garreth knew the consequences. He knew he could become earthbound but it didn't stop him from making himself known to me. It didn't stop him from warning me about Hadrian. He was willing to take that risk because...because he loved me.

I had to keep moving.

I had to find him.

He had risked all for me and now I owed it to him to do the same.

It was faint at first, but I was sure I hadn't imagined it, a second heartbeat slightly out of rhythm with my own. As I concentrated only on that one sound it became a little stronger each second. Tears stung my eyes as it pounded away in my ears and then I felt it in my chest, like a confused palpitation.

I couldn't believe I was doing it. I sucked in a large breath of excitement but then forced myself to slow down.

*Take little breaths. Small breaths.*

He was here! I closed my eyes and took a deeper breath this time. I thought of what he meant when he said he would find me but this was different, this was remarkable. I was doing this on my own.

A beautiful scent floated across my face, bringing stinging tears once again. I wanted to catch it and hold in my chest forever. It was *his* scent. That warm, safe, spicy scent that rolled off his skin like magic whenever I was close to him; that heady incense that was his alone, that permeated from the warm light he held within him.

Then, without warning, another scent flashed across my face like a cold wind, bringing with it pine and damp. Instantly, I knew where he was. My nostrils filled with the smell of molten wax while I felt the heat of a thousand candles on my skin and cold stone beneath my feet. Then I felt dizzy, as if something spiraled high above me, spinning, flying, sending the air in waves down upon my face. His breath broke out of sequence with mine. Something was happening, something was

coming from above. I knew my way to the woods but I wasn't sure I could get there fast enough.

I looked down at my feet to find the dagger lying there and I slowly picked it up and examined it. The blade was clean. Panic washed over me. Would they find me at home? What if they buried me? I let out a deep sigh.

*What's done is done.*

Very carefully, I wrapped the blade in the fabric at the bottom of my shirt and tucked the dagger into the front pocket of my jeans. I forced my legs into a run. Back home, in *my* time, the world was covered in the darkness of the night's storm; yet here, in a place of such uncertainty, it was quite the opposite. The blue reminded me of the safe haven I so desperately needed to find again, pushing me forward to find him.

The importance of my task hovered in the air. The more I breathed it, the more I wanted him; and the more he felt farther and farther away

# Chapter Twenty-five

Desperation settled into the very marrow of my bones and steered me on a course over which I no longer had control. My feet knew the way to the woods but getting there seemed to take forever. The entire time, my thoughts were tormented by images of what Garreth might be enduring, and my trying to hold fast to the thin traces of him within me.

I had heard that your life passes before your eyes when you die. And although I wasn't truly dead, I still saw all I held close and dear, like a movie unfolding before my eyes. I saw my mother applying the last bit of hairspray and then walking slowly to my closed door, her hand hesitantly resting midair before knocking.

*"Let me sleep."* I willed with all my might, picturing my words floating to her on an unseen wind. To my relief, her hand dropped to her side and she walked away.

I brought the photo of me and my father to the very edges of my mind, hearing twinkling baby laughter from long ago as he bounced me on his knee. I saw the crease in the second picture flatten and run smooth, as though newly printed from the long-discarded Polaroid it had come

from—and I knew I was being given full reign to clean the slate.

Suddenly, I was thrown to the ground by some unseen force and my hand sprung to my forehead. I felt a warm stickiness but my fingers showed nothing. I wanted to scream out as waves of pain squelched my visions of home. A warmth trickled within me, as if coming to life, and I knew I was feeling Garreth. I knew he was being hurt.

I forced myself to my feet but my legs ached horribly from running. I urged myself on, and before long I arrived at the mouth of the forest. The narrow trail beckoned me and I followed it. Jutting brambles and thorns that were now overgrown in wild anticipation of my arrival caught at my jeans, as if they purposely arched themselves outward to keep me back, making my plight all the more sweet in the end.

My chest heaved. I was openly crying now, on the border of hysterics, fearing I couldn't reach him fast enough. I felt so incredibly alone.

From out of nowhere, the stone chapel took shape in the haze I had been trudging through, rising high like an old castle. This wasn't the simple chapel I had visited before and I realized that what stood in the woods back home was only a scrap of the splendor it used to be. The rubble was revived in this green spotlight, still very much alive within this otherworld.

The smell of hot wax was strong, filling the air with perfumed heat as I quietly made my way across a courtyard to an open hall lined with high, arched passages. I spied a wooden door that spilled a golden glow through its cracks and seams,

warm and inviting. I felt the dancing light from behind it breathe and pulse, begging me to enter.

It reminded me of the concrete fortress a few nights ago where nameless, faceless teenagers entered in droves, music pounding, lights splitting the dark, splattering their beams on the walls and out the door onto the waiting line, like an enticing siren. But my mind quickly cleared, and only a caressing wind could be heard, running its fingers through the overgrown thick of green around me.

I opened the door.

A scream that was half sob wrenched itself loose from my lips. "Garreth!"

Through the arched doorway, in the middle of a large stone vestibule, stood my beloved Guardian, still and beautiful. His skin was paler than ever, his wings hanging crumpled behind his back. As I quickly crossed the uneven stone floor, I noted that his arms were gathered limply at his wrists, bound by a thick leather strap.

"Garreth," I whispered. "Oh, what has he done to you?"

My hand trembled as I reached up to touch the side of his face that a few hours ago had been covered in blood. His skin was ice cold but it didn't deter me from clinging to him. I was so incredibly relieved that I had found him and he was still alive. I wrapped my arms around his chest and pressed my face into him.

"I need to tell you something I didn't fully understand until now. All this time, I've wanted something I wasn't ready for. The dream every girl wants, but I failed to realize what it

really means to have that dream and to hold on to it." I looked up at his beautiful, pale face and with absolute certainty released the words that had been hiding inside me. "Garreth, I love you."

But he looked right through me, his blue eyes reflecting eerie milky white in the candles' glow.

"Can you hear me, Garreth?" I dropped my arms to my sides, completely baffled. I had listened to my heart and finally said the words. But there was no response from him at all.

He stood as still as a statue, seeing nothing, feeling nothing.

I looked around to discover we were not alone. Scores of other angels stood in rows the entire length of the chamber.

The corrupted.

Some were male, some female, others exquisitely androgynous. I hadn't noticed them until now, I had been so intent on finding Garreth. Had I seen the silent group of Guardians upon entering, I still would have had no trouble singling out my Guardian, for he was more beautiful to me than all the others combined.

They were all dressed in hues of white; transparent eggshell, bone, and snow, wings silenced behind their backs with chains. Velvety feathers, all varying shades, littered the stone floor, bringing immediately to mind struggle and defeat. I had seen what happens to a person once their Guardian has been taken from them. I knew of the change in personality, in character, how without a Guardian to breathe choice and decision into their souls they instead became lost.

But seeing a Guardian after a separation was more than I could bear.

Each angel stood still and unseeing. They seemed excruciatingly empty—ripped from their responsibilities. They were mere shells now.

Panic stirred inside as I wondered where Hadrian could be. Where was the one who silenced these remarkable beings into submission?

As though hearing my thoughts aloud, the shadows in the corners stirred to life, sending the all-too-familiar scent of fear across the room to me.

"Garreth!" I pleaded in an urgent whisper.

I pulled at his cold hands but they wouldn't yield. I threw my arms around his neck but my efforts fell short. All I could think of was his warm scent, that thin thread of a lifeline that had reeled me in to this place, connecting us again; but, it was nowhere to be found and I was confounded that the trail should suddenly run cold when it should be at its strongest.

I stood on my tiptoes, looking into his eyes that were lifeless now. He was here, I was here. How could this possibly be so wrong? I kissed his face over and over. Was I too late, then? Was there any chance of breaking this awful trance he was in? Then, to my horror, I realized he appeared just as vacant as the others.

"What has he done to you?" I stepped back, confused. "Garreth, please. You have to come with me." Why couldn't he snap out of it and realize this was our chance? It was here! This was all he had warned me about! It had come!

I tried whispering into his neck, but his warmth was gone. The scent that was always with him was replaced by something cold and empty.

"You risked everything to come to me in my world and now I've done the same to find *you*." I didn't hear the silent retreat of the other angels, never noticed their sudden absence. We were alone now.

Something in the corners moved again, and just as quickly something in Garreth sprang to life. His hands broke free and tightly grabbed my shoulders, as if he were suddenly in pain. There was acknowledgment in his eyes that I had come for him.

"You love me?" Garreth's voice rattled.

"Yes," I nodded my head, tears blurring his beautiful face before me. "I love you." I looked around. The urge to flee this stone chamber was unbearable. "Where is Hadrian?"

A new fear grew inside me. My gaze darted around the empty room. In taking Garreth, Hadrian had to know I wouldn't be far behind. He had to be here, waiting to spring from the shadows, but there was no sign of him and Garreth wouldn't budge. Instead, he stared at me with eyes now deep and black and that's when the familiar chill traveled down my spine, weakening my legs.

Garreth's entire body quivered and I jumped back, not knowing what was happening. I stood frozen as his stunning wings snapped and cracked like breaking bones, caving in on themselves to fit behind his shoulders. He moaned and slumped to the stone floor, as if being tortured by an unseen assailant.

Angel Star

"What's happening?" I went to my knees and reached for him, torn between the urge to run or spend moments we couldn't afford cradling him in my arms. "Garreth, please! I don't know what to do!"

Within seconds, the room became a frosty tomb, despite the welcoming glow of the candles. The chill around me whispered his name. *Hadrian.*

My heart screamed inside me to run but I couldn't as the world and everything in it slowed down to a pace only felt in dreams, and the stones around me began to pitch.

Garreth was motionless, lying on the floor at my knees. I felt a presence behind me and I closed my eyes, knowing once I turned around what I would see. I tightened my grip around the golden handle of the dagger I now held in my sleeve, afraid it might slip from my sweaty hand. Now that I was here, now that I was about to place myself in front of the one I feared, to save the one I loved, I couldn't think properly. I wrapped my fingers tighter around the beautiful knife, feeling its chill through the cloth, like the cold hard truth of what was behind me now.

Very slowly and deliberately, I stood. Each inch that my body distanced me from the inert form of my beloved Garreth felt painful and wrong.

Hadrian's breath whispered on the back of my neck. I knew he was waiting; he knew he was winning. The question was, would I allow him to? Was this all for nothing?

The cold steel in my grasp pulled my senses back to the surface. I had brought myself here by placing it through my heart. Was that what I had to do to Hadrian? How on earth

191

would someone defeat a dark angel? My mind raced, sorting through possibilities and coming up empty. This wasn't like any place I was used to. In the stolen seconds, I allowed myself to think of the safety of home. I realized how alien home had been to me and that I had merely waded through life until now, never really living it. It was Garreth who had brought me to life. He had shown me what I was missing by revealing himself to me.

My blood coursed through my veins at lightning speed; and, with it a fire, something brewing inside me along with the last of what Garreth had given to me, sacrificed for me.

Light.

It was white and hot, like new blood brought to life, and running through me like the night Garreth first gave it to me, only stronger now that it was mixed with my own. My inheritance. The blood essence of an Archangel. That essence was derived from Hadrian's own existence and now I was going to use it against him.

I spun around to face him. "What have you done to him?" I demanded.

Hadrian was silent. Towering over me, his dark wings quivered tensely as he stared down at me in an obvious attempt to intimidate me, but I stepped forward, welcoming the threat. His dark eyes reflected amusement at my resolution. To my surprise, he backed off a little, eyeing me curiously as he paced back and forth across the stone floor, carefully choosing his words.

"Your Guardian, Garreth, was found in violation of—"

"I asked what you've done to him." I felt shaky, as if I might collapse at any second, but thankfully, my voice didn't betray me. To my surprise, I found myself ready to use the dagger that was so carefully hidden in my sleeve, ready to start and end this war.

"My, my, aren't we agitated today? If I may continue?" Hadrian seemed to take pleasure in my endeavor to appear fearless. "As a Guardian he was not permitted to enter the human world and cavort as if he were like the very one he was responsible for. It is unheard of and places the entire society in danger. Your Garreth broke many rules because of his selfishness."

Hadrian's black eyes settled on me, keeping me locked to him.

"Garreth said he had permission. It was never done before, that he was the first. He was allowed to." I looked away, hiding the fresh tears forming that would give away my crumbling resolve.

"And no other will dare make his mistake in the future. I'll see to that myself."

"You don't care about violations! That's not why you're doing this! Haven't you done enough?" I trembled, knowing Garreth lay as still as death behind me. "You'll never have your army. You're no match for your brother," I spat, clutching at straws with which to wound him.

"Ahhh, Lucifer. Garreth was very informative. I may still have my chance; you see, I have a sizeable army already. But I can't risk the naïve emotions of another Guardian such as Garreth. May he be a lesson to us all, for he is no more."

My heart plummeted to my feet at his words. *No more?*

The ripping pain inside my heart mimicked what I saw in Hadrian's eyes.

*He can't be...*

But I felt the pain endured by Garreth as if it were my own. I was too late. My heart was being ripped out of my chest.

Hadrian stepped closer, placing his wickedly perfect face close to mine. "Remember this, Teagan. I am stronger than my brother. I am smarter than the great Dark Prince and I always get what I want."

I was momentarily dizzy, blinded by a light that unexpectedly appeared in the room. Hadrian's breath was still on my face, warm and soothing, and I leaned into it away from the chill of the stone chamber.

"There is something else I desire, something more than the power Lucifer holds in his hands. For, without a taste of it, I fear I am nothing. It is the only way to ensure my existence."

His voice dripped like sweet honey, touching my soul with a deep torch. I wanted to look away but couldn't. It wasn't just his beauty—it was a longing he carried in his dark smile. He touched my forehead with the tip of his finger, leaving an icy heat across my skin, thrusting me into a dream that was so real and inviting I couldn't bring myself to fight it. Slowly, the pain I had felt over Garreth slipped away from me.

I felt like a ghost watching over myself, and before long I was in the dark night of my bedroom, listening to the fluttering that I knew was Hadrian, comforted by the darkness he

shrouded himself in. It was familiar, night after night, never failing—always expected, always anticipated. In my vision, I realized the fear that always accompanied his presence was not what I thought. It was the fear of him *not* returning to me, of him *not* torturing me with the dark eyes that forever watched me, leaving me alone and breathless with fear.

I felt the air shift around us. Hadrian's hands were on my face, closing my eyes with lips I had never felt before. I didn't want him...I... Who did I want? I couldn't remember anymore. I was floating. He was holding me and we were spiraling higher, above the stone floor. His lips were on me, cool and mesmerizing. The downdrafts of his wings pushed us higher off the ground, and I pictured what we must look like from below, the beautiful image of us entwined. It reminded me of looking up at another image, spiraling high above me, but I couldn't see what it was. It was a dream, forgotten now.

Higher and higher we rose, my insides reeling as he pressed his lips to my neck. His black wings carried us, keeping us from falling, and I felt the gentle breeze from them on my skin. Their tips pricked me as they waved to and fro in midflight, bringing to the surface tiny dots of red on my pale, bare hands that smeared with the brush of his lips.

His melodious voice whispered promises in my ear. I tilted my head back, desperate to hear more—the words, the promise Garreth could not repeat minutes before.

I dared to look down to see how high we really were. I turned my eyes toward the stones, the patterns of light that splashed across them on the floor, and I felt the breath leave

me. From here I could see the one thing that would bring me to my senses. The one thing strong enough to break any spell.

Fragmented light from the stained glass windows stretched its way across the floor, appearing haphazard at first, but from this height I saw clearly now that the light broke off into eight points, each pointing to an arched opening in the walls. I traced the lines back to the center where the beams of light touched each other. To my wonder, it formed a perfect circle at its center.

The heart of an octagram.

I saw the beautiful star from where Hadrian held me and my heart crushed in agony. It was his star, Garreth's star, and the moment I saw it I remembered everything. I saw Garreth's light illuminating deep within his chest. I felt the warmth it radiated and instantly felt the searing heat of my hand, the power of my own mark tingling with a simple reconnection to him. I heard his heart beating in my chest stronger than ever before and I smelled him.

He was alive.

# Chapter Twenty-six

Hadrian's hand reached out to caress my face, to bring me back to him. Suddenly, I remembered his mark and my eyes focused on the star that was his. Hadrian's octagram was made up of two squares that stacked diagonally on top of one another. The four points of each square then each became a star point. Entranced, I visually traced the lines on his palm, staring at the octagram until the two squares separated themselves from each other and became two simple squares.

Finally, I understood.

The bottom square represented the light, the Guardian he used to be, and the top square, the darkness he had become.

One on top of the other.

Dark claiming light, yet the light still visible, still trying to break free.

I thought back to the glowing screen of my computer and the peculiar meaning of Hadrian's mark, which suddenly wasn't so peculiar anymore.

*Conflict...separation.*

As we descended. I remembered that hand striking Garreth, sending him across my room in pain. Hadrian's hand inflicted

destruction while my hand held the instrument that would separate light from dark. More importantly, I held in my other hand my own mark. One that could not be claimed or swayed, that had the power to inflict justice. I was the one who could witness what hung in the balance between the two worlds. I was the source of light that would split the darkness and unify the separation between the human and angel worlds.

Hadrian's dark eyes squinted with malice. "You wouldn't."

"Try me. You told me never to underestimate myself."

"Look inside yourself, Teagan, and recognize the real reason you came here. It wasn't to seek out your Guardian. You came because of me." Hadrian's voice was tender now as he approached me.

In his eyes, I saw glimpses of what had just happened between us, like a movie reel rewinding in slow motion. Fleetingly, I had succumbed. The gentle wind from his wings, the sting of the feathers, our arms intertwined. His hand reached for me and I could hear his thoughts.

*"Take it...accept me."*

And just as quickly, I came to my senses.

"No. I love Garreth. And I won't let you destroy him or anyone else's Guardian."

My fingers tightened around the dagger. It was light's turn to reclaim what was now dark and I raised my arm, aiming for the source of Hadrian's power. He saw it coming, his wings spreading wider, flapping like thunder, rolling like the dark clouds that covered the night. His hand was raised, in protest, and his octagram glowed with red fury.

"Remember, my blood runs with yours. You cannot destroy me. We are the same." The dark angel's voice echoed and bounced off the stones surrounding us.

The dagger, aimed true, then plunged downward, straight into his open palm, slicing the overlapping squares neatly in two with one thrust. In the shrillness of his suffering, the stones began to loosen with his anger and began falling around my head. I tried to cover myself from being crushed, but all that fell around me was the soft silence of gray as thousands of feathers floated to the ground.

A brilliant white light shone down on me from above. I lifted my face to it, feeling a soft shower of white that floated down to me, kissing my cheeks and eyelids. It fell as softly as white feathers but melted as soon as it touched my warm skin. I realized it was snowing. Fluffs of white drifted down through the massive opening in the roof where the tower once stood, washing away the darkness. I was sleepy and wanted nothing more than to lie down and dream but the gentle flakes tingled my skin, keeping me awake. I heard footsteps behind me, and as I turned I realized Hadrian was nowhere to be seen. I looked around frantically, wondering what had become of him, what had become of Garreth, but I only found a dusting of white snow on the floor. I was alone.

As the footsteps grew closer, I saw an arched tunnel that was lit by a warm glow that grew in size and moved with the imminent visitor. My heart pounded in hope, for I wanted it so much to be Garreth; but, as the figure entered what was left of

the stone chamber, my heart sank and I began to wonder if Hadrian's words were true.

A Guardian stood before me, aged and regal, white wings tinged with gold folded at his sides. He gestured for me to look to my right. Before me, the shattered walls of stone magically disintegrated and I looked out upon a vast sea of angels, their multicolored feathers blending into a cloud of color as they stood shoulder to shoulder.

In a wise, gravelly voice the angel spoke. "There are thousands of Guardians; one for each person, sometimes two or more. You have done the remarkable. By ensuring that our society still exists, you have begun to save the race to which you belong. The Guardians have been released, but the damage Hadrian has begun cannot be reversed until humans *want* them back, thus restoring order to the balance of all things."

His pale-blue eyes were almost white. Not the eerie, chalky white that I had seen on Brynn and Claire, but the white of the endless sky that hovers beyond the blue. They were eyes that had seen many things. I felt humbled that they looked upon my confused face now.

"But how can a human want their Guardian back if they don't even know they're missing?"

"You are the example of all that is possible. The voice of reason is not only the voice of a Guardian. It is also your own. You should be very proud of yourself. I speak for all the Guardians when I say you have done a great thing."

"May I ask you something?" I said timidly.

"Please, my name is Mathur, and you may ask whatever you wish."

"I came here looking for someone. Is he…? I need to know if he…" My composure was failing me. If I said his name, I knew I would lose it completely.

"Yes, he is well. Do not worry, my child. You will see him soon," the angel reassured me.

I was relieved at his words but I wanted to ask so much more. Where was he? Was he hurt? How long do I have to wait to see him? There was so much I needed to know and still I wouldn't be satisfied until I could feel his arms around me and breathe him into my lungs.

"Your life, even a few days ago was quite different, yes?" Mathur folded his hands together.

I looked at Mathur and smiled, feeling a little more comfortable. He reminded me of a grandfather, warm and wise.

What did I feel? I was still me. I was still the girl I had always been, but there was something remarkably changed about me. I took stock of all that had happened to me in a surprisingly short amount of time. I lost my best friend, stood up to Brynn, fell in love, and was tempted by a dark angel with plans to destroy all the good I have ever known. I learned about my father and felt pity when I thought of how Hadrian had taken advantage of him. Without my father, I wouldn't exist, and without me, Hadrian's plan might have worked. And I never would have known what kind of person I truly am if Garreth hadn't taken the risk to become human and find me.

I looked into Mathur's face, his wrinkles and lines like a timeline of the ages. I silently wondered how old he was and he began to chuckle.

"I am older than time, my child. Yet, somehow, in less than eight days, you learned more than one could in a lifetime. Tell me, do you like what you find inside yourself?"

"Yes."

"Then your Judgment is complete."

"It's complete? I don't understand. Don't I have to stand in front of anyone, like a panel? Don't I have to stand up in front of God?"

"Child, you already have. Your Judgment is your own, and when you can look inward and see that you are changed and like what you see, then it is by your own hand that you are judged. You are His creation, and when you can take the extra step to become more than a simple wish of His, then the purpose is fulfilled."

I didn't know what to say. I kept thinking the hard part was still coming but I had already survived the biggest part of my challenge.

"You look sad, child. What is it that you wish?" Mathur's smile was soft. He knew what I wished for but it didn't count if I didn't ask for it myself.

"I want to see Garreth, please."

Within a breath of my asking, I felt the air around me change and the warm static that swirled from behind me announced his arrival. I closed my eyes, savoring the spicy scent that tingled my nose, and a smile spread wide across my

face. When I opened them he was standing in front of me, looking more beautiful than ever: his sandy hair still hanging in front of his blazing blue eyes, his smile, his jaw, his presence perfectly sculpted for me alone. I threw my arms around him and his arms tightened on me, lifting me off the ground. His embrace was strong yet unbelievably tender. We said nothing, knowing that words could not fully explain what we both felt at that moment.

His warm hands touched my face, tracing it, as though trying to never forget it. "Are you all right?" he finally asked.

I nodded as he smiled down at me. Suddenly, birds were chirping and I turned to see a pair of swings hanging quietly beneath a familiar tree.

"How did we...?"

"Heaven is here, remember?" Garreth kissed my forehead.

I took his hands in mine, feeling their warmth return, and I held them tightly, never wanting to let go again.

"You were bleeding." He held me away from him for a moment, looking at my hands where Hadrian's feathers had pricked me.

"You saw...us?"

Something dark and unwanted passed through me as I remembered the bits and pieces I would rather forget. I felt sick to my stomach, not because Hadrian had placed me under his spell but because a small part of me had enjoyed it; a very small part that, if I could, I would crumble to bits and set fire to it. Garreth lifted my face to his, still holding me, unable to let me go.

"He's very..." I began.

"Persuasive?"

"Is he gone now? Please tell me he's gone."

"Yes, he's gone." His voice was steady with reassurance but I was sure his eyes hid something else. I quickly dismissed it. I was still so shaken by all that had happened it was no wonder I was reading too much into things.

Hadrian had fooled me once already but he was gone now and my perfect angel was the one standing in front of me. I thought of the dagger slicing Hadrian's palm. I had almost aimed for his heart. Who would have known that he held his heart in the palm of his hand: his octagram, the one source of all his power, like any true Guardian.

Hadrian's star was different from Garreth's, linking his light and dark sides, both competing for precedence. It was obvious that neither would win. I let out a deep sigh. Hadrian was gone. So why couldn't I shake this feeling?

I turned my attention back to Garreth. I couldn't take my eyes off him. I was so afraid I would lose him again.

"It's time to take you home," he said.

I nodded. "But you're coming too, right?" There was no hiding the strain in my voice. I just couldn't bear being separated from him again, not even for an instant.

"You know I can't stay long, Teagan." There was pain in his eyes. "Remember that I'm not really part of your world."

"You have two days left, at least give me that much."

Garreth smiled down on me. Even with the wounds Hadrian had given him he still looked like a perfect angel. Yet they made him look human, and even though I knew they

would heal at a rate faster than a human's would, I still couldn't shake the image of him lying in blood. Had he been an ordinary human, he would be dead.

"You'll be home soon. Sleep now."

"I don't want to sleep. I want to stay awake with you."

"Teagan." He was smiling that magnificent smile I loved so much. "There's no reasoning with you, is there?"

"Nope." I stifled an enormous yawn.

"You're impossible. Number one, you're exhausted. You should be in a state of shock after all you've endured. And, number two, you can't stay awake for this. It's kind of against the rules."

"I'm not that tired." I tried to sound convincing but, really, I was pleading. "Besides, don't you think I've already witnessed enough that's against the rules?"

"Have I told you you're adorable when you're flat-out exhausted?" He let out another laugh. "And you babble when you're tired."

I looked at him closely. Tonight was definitely not the best night to risk talking in my sleep, especially when I might let something about Hadrian slip out. But who was I kidding? Garreth was my angel and my life was an open book to him.

"I do *not* babble."

He raised his eyebrows without uttering a peep and a little smile grew at the corners of his mouth.

"I'm afraid you'll disappear if I close my eyes." It was a whisper that trickled out of me, and he took me in his arms, saying nothing in response to my fear.

I pressed my face into his chest. As I listened to the drumbeat of his heart, my eyelids had a preset plan and there was no point in fighting them any longer. I fell into a deep, dreamless sleep.

# Chapter Twenty-seven

I sat up, sweating. My heart was pounding at a dangerous rate. It was dark and it took a bit longer for me to realize where I was. A hand reached out from the dark and swept my hair from my eyes.

"Garreth?" My eyes adjusted slowly. "How long have I been asleep?"

I tried to look at my clock but couldn't find it, and then remembered that a lot of things were out of place in my room. I had a lot of cleaning up to do.

"You've been sleeping for three hours."

"Three hours? You should have woken me as soon as we got back." Didn't he realize how long three hours is? It's a huge chunk of time lost when it should be carefully spent now.

He was grinning, enjoying my distress. "But you were babbling. I didn't have the heart to wake you and deprive you of your...what do girls call it? Beauty rest?"

*Oh, no. Babbling.*

I put my face in my hands. "What was I saying?" I couldn't look at him.

"Well, for starters, you said you loved me and then there were a few things I couldn't quite understand. Like I said, you're prone to babbling."

*Okay, I can look up now.*

"Is it true that you love me?" he whispered, leaning closer.

"Yes. It's true."

Then, leaning even closer, he placed the sweetest, softest kiss his lips could possibly allow on my lips. "You did mention Hadrian's name a few times. Not many, but a few."

"And?"

*Do I really want to know?*

He looked away for a moment, taking his light with him. I felt left in the dark in more ways than one.

*Oops, what have I done?*

"Garreth?"

He turned to me, the dim glow of his skin illuminating my face.

"It was the *way* you said his name. As you slept, there were moments when you sounded downright terrified. I almost woke you up. I feel so guilty for leaving you to face him. And then, when your panic subsided, you...I don't know. You sounded almost as if it was Hadrian you wanted."

He took my hand, carefully cradling it in his own, and looked at my mark, putting an end to that conversation. "Does it still bother you?"

"No, it's all right."

His finger traced the scrolling embedded in the skin of my right hand, then let it follow the tender flesh of my wrist,

trailing it ever so softly up the inside of my arm. I shivered at the warm, prickling sensation it left behind. I watched, amazed his touch didn't leave behind a visible trail.

When Garreth raised his face to mine, I was weakened by how blue his eyes were even in the dim light of my bedroom.

"Thank you for saving me," he whispered.

"You're welcome."

"I didn't realize until now that we've sort of come full circle with each other."

"What do you mean?"

He tilted his head to the side and gazed at me. "I'm so used to being the one to help you that when I was the one in need of help, I... I'm just very grateful."

I smiled back at him. He was right. It was amazing how things had changed over the last few days. How both he and I had changed.

"It makes me feel sort of...human."

"Is that a bad thing?"

"No. Not at all. Now that you seem to be well in charge of things, perhaps becoming earthbound isn't such a foreboding idea."

"But you wouldn't be able to save me from anything anymore."

"Ahh, that's where you're mistaken, my dear." He planted a warm kiss on my lips. "I can save you from the persuasive dark angel in your dreams."

"Are you jealous...of a dream?"

"Very," he answered.

Without warning, his hands were cupped at my jaw and his lips were on mine, only this time his kisses were hard, urgent, wildly human. His hands dropped to my shoulders where he let his thumbs slide the fabric of my shirt away from my skin. I tore at the buttons of his shirt but he stopped me, capturing my hands in his. He let go only to smooth away a lock of hair that had fallen against my neck. When I felt the soft warmth of his breath there, kissing the exposed flesh of my collarbone, it brought goosebumps and odd tremors to my skin.

Soon my hands were in his hair and with the moonlight streaming through my window I saw he was perfectly disheveled when he pulled himself away. His shirt was practically ripped from his chest, revealing the smoothness of his skin. His eyes were so blue and wild that it almost hurt to look at him. He was flawless. Something I would never be, especially after what I allowed with Hadrian. Yet, I had just reduced Garreth to this breathless state. Perhaps there was a bit of power in me after all.

"What *was* that?" Garreth asked me.

As my own breathing became more controlled, I was pleasantly surprised to see he was still struggling.

"Wow. Do I have the same effect on you?" I couldn't hide the smile forming.

"What do you mean?"

Was he really blind?

"You make me feel like this all the time," I admitted softly. I was finding it easier to tell him how I felt.

"Do you mean to tell me I make you feel as if your breath has just rushed out of your chest *all the time*?" he was smiling, inching closer to me.

"Mm-hmm."

"And do you mean to tell me that your heart races just a *teensy* bit faster when my lips are...say, right about here?" His lips were at my neck again. He was enjoying this game immensely. And me? I felt all weak and fluttery, as if I were the one with the wings and they were holding me up as the rest of me just melted away.

His mouth brushed my shoulder. "Mmm, you're so tempting."

"Then stay."

"I did. The sun's coming up."

I looked reluctantly at the pale streak of light creeping its way across my floor.

"Explaining to your mother why I'm here would be awkward, but I have a surprise for you now and one for later."

He could see the disappointment on my face as he pulled me to my feet. I flung my arms around his neck, as if they could stop him from leaving. It was then I noticed my clock, perfectly placed upon my once-upturned nightstand. I spun around, looking in disbelief at my room. It was as if nothing had ever happened.

"When did...?"

I turned to Garreth, searching for an answer, but he was already gone.

# Chapter Twenty-eight

After checking and rechecking my appearance in the full-length mirror for any sign that would send up my mom's red flag, I decided to just get it over with and headed downstairs. I found her busy at the kitchen sink.

"Oh, Teagan. I didn't hear you come down." She stuck half of her upper body into the cabinet below to get a clean garbage bag. "Did you sleep well?"

"Yeah, I guess so."

*Sleep? When did I sleep? Oh, yeah, when Garreth magically knocked me out on our way home from...where had I been again?*

"Are you all right?" She was looking at me kind of funny.

*Oh, geez, here we go.*

"I'm fine, Mom. Why? Don't I look fine?"

"I guess...well..." She let it drop. "You look a little different, that's all. Are you hungry?" My mother turned and went about stuffing the new bag into the almond-colored garbage bin and stashed it back under the sink.

*That's a relief.*

I leaned over and peered into the side of the shiny stainless steel toaster as soon as her back was turned. I looked distorted, but as far as I could tell, there was nothing too

abnormal about my reflection. If she only knew what I had really been through.

"I'll just grab some cereal," I said, making for the stack of clean bowls in the dish drainer.

"Oh, come on. Let me make you some breakfast. Eggs sound good? How about bacon?"

My nose turned up at the word. "Uh, let's nix the bacon."

"Right." I knew she was seeing the same mental picture of the last time this kitchen produced bacon for breakfast. It wasn't a pretty sight, seeing me faint and then splashed with soapy dishwater to bring me out of unconsciousness.

An overwhelming sense of obligation surfaced in me. "How was the funeral?"

"It was nice, honey. Don't feel bad that you weren't there. I'm sure everyone knows you wanted to be and they understand."

I felt a little better, knowing I had avenged Claire's death, and now that Hadrian was gone, it was nice to think of finally getting some sleep around here. But, somehow, I knew he would always haunt me, even if he wouldn't be lurking in the shadows anymore. He would haunt me with the memory of the way he had made me feel at the end, just when I was about to take his life. I closed my eyes, wishing away the thought from my mind, and strangely, a part of me didn't want it to leave entirely. How could I have just spent time making out with my angel boyfriend and then come down here and remind myself of the fleeting moments when Hadrian had almost seduced me? What kind of person was I? *I* felt like the monster.

"Are you seeing Garreth today?" Mom's face beamed with the silly "you-have-a-boyfriend" look.

"He said he has a surprise for me." I shoved my spoon into my mouth so I wouldn't have to answer the questions I saw in her eyes.

"Oh, that reminds me. There's a surprise here for you too."

She made her way to the back door. For a minute I thought she was going to ask me to take out the garbage, but instead she reached up to the hook on the wall and took down an unfamiliar key. It bounced from hand to hand as she playfully flipped it over, but I couldn't read the look on her face. It was happy and concern all jumbled together and I was beginning to think she'd lost her mind. Then, finally, she slid the key across the table to me.

It was a car key. The black rubber end was engraved with the initials VW. My heart stopped when I recognized it. I got up from my chair and slowly walked to the window, and sure enough, parked alongside our little brick garage was Claire's white Volkswagen Cabrio.

Before I had a chance to ask, my mom was by my side, her arm around my shoulders, and we stared at it together in silence.

"Simon's going to graduate school in Indiana and so the Meyers have decided to put their house up for sale and go with him. I think it's a good idea that they all start over, fresh. Looks like you've finally got yourself a set of wheels."

I didn't know what to say except, "I can't take Claire's car."

"Claire's mom says that car is as much yours as it was Claire's. She insisted that you have it. It's a great little car and the best part is that it's paid off. You'll just have to take over the insurance payments." She plopped the key into my hand.

"Which brings me to my next surprise. There's a part-time opening available at the library. It's only ten hours a week but it would be enough to pay for your insurance and gas, along with some extra spending money to go out with friends."

"What friends?" I whispered to the window.

My mother paused at my sadness. "Well, for now it'll be savings money then. And it means you and I can spend more time together instead of you coming home to an empty house. What do you say?"

I couldn't bring myself to destroy the hopeful look on her face.

"Maybe, Mom. Can I think about it? I mean, I guess I need a job now. I'm just not sure if I want to work at the library."

"Sure, sweetie. Maybe you should go out and find your own thing. You could use a fresh start too."

I instantly felt as if I had deflated her but I couldn't promise anything right now.

She left me staring numbly through the glass. I didn't know what to do next. Do I go get ready for school? Do I call Claire's parents and thank them? My thoughts were answered for me.

"Go get ready now. You'll have enough time to call the Meyers to thank them before school."

215

My mom was as cool as a cucumber. I couldn't understand how she could be so calm about me suddenly owning a car, knowing full well that I would want to drive it right away. It occurred to me that perhaps all along I was the worrywart of our family. No, she definitely had her fair share of it too. But, regardless, something in the air had made us both change, both able to let go and accept the changes we normally wouldn't think of allowing ourselves.

A glance at the clock sent me flying upstairs. I still needed a shower, and I remembered that my driver's license was still in my old denim purse in my closet, where it's been since the day I passed my driver's test.

"Are you *sure* you don't want bacon?" my mom's voice trailed up after me.

"Ha-ha," I yelled back down to her and ran into the bathroom, shutting the door on her giggles.

# Chapter Twenty-nine

I pulled into Claire's old parking space.

Everyone looked as if they had just seen a ghost, but when they recognized me through the window, they went on with their lives as before. I sat there for a few minutes, not getting out, not playing with the gigantic megastereo that was still in her car, though the buttons looked pretty tempting. I was feeling the difference between now and all the other times I had sat in that car. And it wasn't just because I was no longer a passenger; Claire had let me practice driving plenty of times.

Now it was just plain lonely.

I flicked the vanilla-roma freshener with my finger, watching it sway, and thought of all the times Claire and I drove around for something to do. It was always the three of us: me, Claire, and this car. There were nights in winter when we rolled the windows down, with the heat going full blast, and anyone who witnessed us singing our lungs out as we drove up and down the streets must have thought we were crazy. I guess a part of me was hoping a piece of that would still be here, embedded in the leather seats, that the memories of Claire would hit me so hard as soon as I sat in the driver's seat that it would be like the old times were still here, strong enough to go

on and last forever. I'd never have to miss her. But it wasn't the same. She was gone.

I closed my eyes and soon the vanilla scent floating around me was sickening. It was letting another crushing reality hit me and it hit me hard. I pictured sitting in a different car, the same boxy shape, but with an entirely different aroma filling me. His car. His scent. A second loss. It was more than I could bear. I got out and locked the door behind me, not turning back to look at the car that was now mine as I walked into school.

Thousands of words floated through the halls, thousands of voices, and yet it was only a splintering silence that I heard. My feet walked, preprogrammed, from class to class where I feigned interest and did what was expected of me. It was the end of the last period and Garreth was still a no-show.

*Some surprise.*

I was instantly reminded of that day when I couldn't find him anywhere. I had felt all jittery and panic-stricken. My heart had pounded uncontrollably at the very thought of running into him, and when I didn't, the pounding in my chest grew unbearable.

All I could think about now was hearing the last bell ring and making a bolt to the car that I still couldn't bring myself to take ownership of yet.

*My car.*

That just sounded too weird.

As the bell rang, I rose from my seat and in a cheerless daze headed out into the hall, the wanting-to-bolt feeling seeping

out of me with each step. Rounding the corner, I headed to the end of the hall to a row of metal lockers, absentmindedly turning the round combination wheel until I heard the lock open with a click.

My week-old gym clothes were in a bag stuffed into the bottom, and as I reached down to grab them, it occurred to me that I was no longer alone. I pulled my head out of my locker the instant I noticed a body behind me, wearing a great pair of faded blue jeans. My heart pounded. It was just like Garreth to make me sweat it out for the day and then show up, knowing I'd cave and forgive him.

"Is this my surprise...?"

I ended up getting a real surprise as I looked up into Ryan's brown eyes. I cringed and wanted to back into my locker. Whatever he had to say to me couldn't be good. Not after the last time I saw him.

"Hi, Teagan."

I was stunned for a few seconds. He was being civil?

"You're not mute all of a sudden, are you?" A wide grin spread across his face, bringing out very deep dimples. He was actually pretty cute.

*Eew! What am I thinking?*

"I'm sorry. Are we having a conversation here?" I turned back to my locker and pulled my backpack out.

"Well, I'd like to if you'd give me the chance." He leaned against the next locker, waiting patiently for me to come around.

I slammed my locker shut. "Fine. What do you want?"

219

He let his gaze wander out into the constant momentum of the hall then reeled it back in, studying the shuffling of one of his sneakers against the other. I was growing impatient.

"I'm sorry, Teagan. I'm sorry I was such a jerk. I still can't remember what got into me."

I thought back to when I had truly feared him, to when I knew him as scary and intimidating, to when the predictable wall between us had crumbled and a lot of terrible questions were left in its place. But now I was looking into the face of a boy, not the same boy he used to be. He was different now. Like me.

It occurred to me that he might not be at fault. He probably didn't even know what happened.

"I'm sorry I accused you…" I responded.

"S'okay. Like I said, I was a jerk."

People were staring now as they walked past us. First, I show up at school in Claire's car, and now I'm in a quiet conversation with her old boyfriend. I knew what it looked like but I didn't quite care.

Ryan let out a deep sigh. "Teagan, I don't even know who I'm supposed to be anymore." He gave me a weary smile. "I really miss her. I can't begin to tell you what it feels like, I can only say that it seems like hell."

I leaned my head against the locker and smiled back. "Trust me, I understand."

Ryan was staring off again, dealing with the ghosts in his head. I knew all too well what he was feeling, and not just

about Claire. I would soon be hit with this feeling all over again when Garreth leaves me. It had been building itself up in me for days now, preparing me, but it still hurt.

"Look," Ryan began, breaking the awkward silence, "I don't expect us to be friends, but do you think it would be so horrible for you to let me talk to you every now and then? It would mean a lot to me. Get me back on track."

He seemed afraid to meet my gaze head-on, but when he did I saw the glimmer of something. Something I'd seen in myself recently.

I smiled at him, catching him by surprise. "Sure, I don't think there's a problem with that."

He smiled back without another word. As I watched him walk away from me and disappear into the crowd, so forlorn and broken, I swore to myself I would never lose sight of who I was.

Not only that, I would never take anything for granted ever again.

Just then, my hand felt tingly, a feeling I wasn't expecting, and I looked down the hallway to see Sage, Lauren, and Emily stomping their way smugly through the crowd. In the center of their little bunch was Brynn, still the reigning queen of Carver High School. She passed my locker, glaring at me, but she didn't utter a word. She just kept on walking.

I watched them long enough to see Emily raise her eyebrows at Sage, apparently wondering why Brynn chose to keep on going, not taking part in her usual "pick on Teagan" ritual. What surprised me the most was that Lauren, lagging behind the others, looked right at me and smiled.

I shut my locker and proceeded to walk the other way.

School was over for the day. I took my time walking across the parking lot to the little white car that had waited for me all day long like an obedient pet. I kept my gaze straight ahead, on the windshield, afraid to look away. I couldn't figure out where that strange sparkle was coming from. As I got closer, my heart tripped a couple of beats.

*Unbelievable.*

I had spent the whole day in flux. Waiting. Searching. He hadn't shown up for school today, and on several occasions throughout the day I couldn't decide if I wanted to cry or scream because of it. I unlocked the car, slid inside, and reached up to the rearview mirror. I couldn't hold back my smile.

The blue topaz rosary hung from my mirror, and inside one of the chains was a tiny scroll of paper. It would have taken me hours to get it rolled as tightly as it was. Very carefully, I unrolled the stationery that was as thin as rice paper and Garreth's absence was instantly forgiven. His amazing scent also unfurled from the delicate paper, filling my car like an embrace, and tears welled up in my eyes. Only a few hours on my own and it hit me how desperately I missed him.

*How am I going to cope when he leaves me forever?*

I wiped my eyes, worrying I would stain the paper with my tears and his message would be ruined.

*I missed you too.*

*Your surprise awaits you...*

*I figured it was about time your*

*boyfriend took you on a date.*

*Ready by 6 o'clock.*

*G.*

My hand trembled. Before I realized it, I had read the note at least ten times. I turned the key in the ignition and the little car sprang to life, its engine humming joyously along with my heart. Together we drove home to get ready for my date.

# Chapter Thirty

"Stop pacing. You're wearing a path in the wood and it's not in the budget to refurbish the floors," my mom called out from the living room.

"Sorry!" I yelled as I peeked out the window for the thousandth time. "He's here! See ya!"

"Just hold on a second. If he's a gentleman, he'll come to the door." My mother walked into the hallway, curious to see if Garreth would pass her test of chivalry.

I rolled my eyes, my impatience to be alone with him getting the best of me. And now my mom expected me to play along with her.

"Mom, we're not going to the prom, you know. It's just a date. No big deal."

"If it isn't a big deal, then how come you've been wearing a hole in the floor for the last half hour?" Her smile rubbed it in that she had won this match, and I was left waiting to hear his footsteps on the porch.

My hand flicked out for the doorknob like a streak of lightning as I gritted my teeth and begged with my eyes for my mother to disappear into the other room.

"Fine, fine, I'll stop hovering. Have a good time." She planted a kiss on my head and walked back into the living room.

Finally, I swung open the door and there stood an absolutely incredible-looking being in a black leather jacket and dark jeans. My eyes drank him in, traveling from his feet upward. I quickly shouted good-bye to my mom and pulled the door closed behind me.

I stopped short.

I was staring into the beautiful face of my date.

I was staring into the face of Hadrian.

I couldn't speak.

"You look nice." Hadrian smiled crookedly, making light of the shock he had just given me.

I didn't answer, wanting to run back into the house, into the safety net of my living room where my mother was glued to the evening news between commercial flips to the QVC channel. Of course, that posed a problem. How would I explain to my mother who Hadrian was. *What* he was?

The hairs on my arms rose and tingled in the evening breeze. I couldn't believe my eyes.

*Hadrian?*

"How? Why…?" I tripped over my words.

When nothing else came out, I simply clamped my mouth shut and stared at him. The familiar trickle of fear pooled deep within me, but even more disturbing was the fact that I felt this need to stay. And it was much stronger than the need to hear why he had come back, *how* he had come back. This was *desire.*

"I understand. You're a bit surprised to see me." He inched his way forward and I felt my own feet move closer in response. I was powerless to stop them.

He looked different tonight. Handsome beyond explanation. Dangerous. But different. And I had no idea why. He held out his hand to me, and as if under a spell, I placed mine in his. The touch of our skin sent my blood screaming through my veins. My house, my street, my neighborhood seemed to melt away and the air felt perilous and enticing.

Hadrian led me off the porch and down the steps to the street below.

"Are we walking somewhere?" I asked.

From his pocket he produced a small black key chain and I heard the familiar click of a car unlocking. I stared at the shiny black Jaguar parked across from us and then turned to look at his face.

"Rides like hot glass," he answered, his laugh melting into the night, along with everything else.

I truly believed my sanity, at that point, was among the missing.

His eyes were shining like the glossy wax job on the intimidating vehicle we were approaching. He opened my door, like a gentleman, then shut it and walked around to his side while I quietly looked across the street, staring blankly at the house that was mine.

Wordlessly, we took off into the night. I had no idea where we were going or what to expect. This was one "surprise" I had never anticipated.

Finally, I couldn't stand it any longer. I shifted in my seat to face him. "Where are we going?" I asked with as much authority as I could muster.

I watched his profile light up with the passing of each streetlight. This all felt oddly familiar to me.

"You got my note, right?" He smiled at me, finally tearing his eyes away from the road ahead of us.

"*Your* note?"

"Well, don't you like surprises?" His eyes grew wide with animation. "My dear, it was only fitting that you would assume the note was from your *Guardian*. I found it pertinent to exclude the actual source."

My insides twisted anxiously. The note hadn't been from Garreth.

It sank in then that I was in a moving car with an angel intent on destruction, and my Guardian never showed up at school today, *or* after school for that matter.

I was a freaking idiot.

I sat numbly, staring straight ahead, trying to figure out where we were going so I could find a way out of this mess I had foolishly gotten myself into.

No, scratch that. How *stupidly* I had gotten myself into this.

With each tree and each sign that passed my window a familiar, uncomfortable feeling tortured me. Something was seriously wrong here. My heart began pounding, I was sure he could hear it. It echoed in my chest and my ears. I looked out the window but it had become so dark suddenly that all I could

see was my own worried reflection. I looked down at my lap where my hands rested quietly, aching terribly for Garreth's.

Perhaps if I…

I slid my left hand over and placed it on top of his, forcing him to abandon the wheel. His dark eyes gleamed with surprise and he took my hand firmly, sending a dark tremor through me.

His hand was like ice.

"Your hand's freezing." It was the first thing out of my mouth. My heart's heavy thumping was nearly uncontrollable now.

I reached out to crank up the heat, seeking normalcy in the situation but got confusion instead as I stared at all the buttons and dials. As foreign as this car and its controls were to me, the complexity of the dashboard wasn't. Now that I was staring more intently at it, it reminded me of the stereo in Claire's… I mean, *my* car.

My emotions were a gnarled mess. I was afraid of where I was, that I was with Hadrian, of what had become of Garreth, what was to become of me… Yet, through it all, an unfamiliar part of me wanted to stay. I *had* to stay.

There was no hiding the hesitancy in my voice. "Wow, what a system. So this is why these cars are so expensive." Perhaps if I tried to act in a normal way, I could get myself out of this.

"Actually, it came with a different one, but I switched it out," he answered.

"You *switched* it? Why?"

"Does that matter? It wasn't what I wanted."

I looked at him long and hard for a moment.

"What? Don't you like the stereo?" Hadrian asked, playing along with my little game.

"It's um…" What was the word I was looking for? "It's a bit…ostentatious."

"That's how I like things. Ostentatious." His smooth, cold hand gestured to the electronic monstrosity.

The car slowed to a stop and I saw we were parked on a barren stretch of road alongside thick woods. Hadrian turned to me and light from the dashboard splashed across his face so that only the deep intensity of his eyes was visible to me.

"Haven't you ever wanted something *else*? Something that perhaps isn't quite up to your standards, something you can bend and shape into what you want?" He leaned closer now. Close enough that I could smell him.

He smelled of something dangerous, something strong that mixed with earth and pine, as if the line of trees next to us were growing right alongside us in the car.

"We're not talking about the stereo anymore, are we?" I whispered, shivering beneath his stare.

I felt my insides turn to jelly; my limbs had forged with the black leather seat beneath me and refused to move. The car, the road, the trees no longer existed, only his unfathomable eyes fixed on mine. I felt him breathing me in, and without any regard I leaned in closer to him, unable to stop myself.

"*You're* what *I* want, Teagan." I felt the strength of his whisper beneath my skin. "You tip the scales when I'm with

you. All I thought I wanted means nothing now that I know you exist." His breath was on my neck, his lips devouring my skin.

I heard something tapping against the roof of the car. It was raining. A streak of white flashed across my eyelids, which were uncontrollably fluttering. Lightning. A second streak invaded the dark, making me open my eyes as he grabbed my wrist. The light flashed across his eyes, blacker than the night and shining with conviction. He was just as mesmerizing as the moment I first laid eyes on him, but I was quickly recovering.

"No!" I pulled away but he held tight. With fear, I realized part of me wanted to stay and my wanting him repulsed me. "You're dead!"

"I'm very real, thanks to you."

"But I killed you."

"Transformed would be more appropriate. You cannot kill a Guardian, merely alter one."

I shook my head. This couldn't be. It just couldn't be. Reality was hitting hard. I needed to get out of there, but Hadrian's firm hand anchored me.

"Before you judge me, please listen to me."

I trembled, inches away from my greatest enemy, as the darkness from beyond the window softly crept into my head. I was dizzy, woozy, and I had no choice but to stay.

# Chapter Thirty-one

I woke up as if from a vivid nightmare. I was lying on the floor, watching streaks of light play and mingle with the colored triangles of stained glass. I rolled over. Hadrian was lighting a red candle, his back turned to me. I could hear rain falling steadily outside the chapel but it did not fall through the open roof above me. I looked up into the dark, waiting to be splashed in the face. I remembered the tower that once stood there, stretching high into the sky, the tower Hadrian and I had floated up into...floating...spiraling... I closed my eyes for a second, seeing two faces: Hadrian's and Garreth's. The spinning sensation came back to me, dizzying me. I sighed in agreement. My life was spiraling out of control.

"You're supposed to dead." My chest rattled with the breath I drew in too quickly.

Hadrian turned immediately at the sound of my voice and walked over to me, slowly, stopping just before I would feel he was too close.

"Haven't you learned that death is a beginning? Besides, I already told you, you can't kill what isn't human." He crouched down and gently took my hand, opening it to reveal

my palm. "You have this power, and still you are unclear as to what it means."

He was so different now, not as menacing as in the car. But, of course, my own fear played a large role in how he appeared to me. He spoke with tenderness and his eyes were full of warmth, though something lingered there...misunderstanding and hurt and I felt too tired to fight or even fear him. My hand was open in front of me, my mark displayed. The etching had become deeper and more pronounced. Daily, it was becoming a permanent part of me.

"I have known you your entire life, Teagan." He gently traced the outline of my mark with his finger. "Close your eyes and you can make it disappear."

"I can't do that! You just want me to get rid of it so I'm powerless against..."

"Just try it. *You* control your mark."

He was smiling at me and I had no choice but to try it. I squeezed my hand shut and then opened it. It was gone! I opened and closed my hand over and over but it was truly gone.

I looked up at Hadrian, anger surfacing. "I want it back."

"Then wish it so."

I expected him to fight me on this, saying it was too late and gone for good. It confused me that perhaps he was simply giving me a lesson. With all my heart I wished for it, and as soon as I opened my hand, it was there again. Relief swept through me. I wanted to cry.

My heart was pounding. "I don't understand."

"You have the power to make things happen." He took my chin in his hand and tilted it up toward the light of the candles. "My feet have worn a path I no longer wish to follow, but that path cannot be erased and I will forever pay for my actions. You sliced the octagram in half, dividing me. For the longest time, I couldn't see who I was because something else was always covering it, and I, too, feared what I couldn't see. You broke that in me. Don't you see, Teagan? That is your power. You are the key to truth. The truth of what is in each and every one of us."

His expression was so serious and genuine. Did he truly want to reform? Was that why I felt drawn to him, because I could see what good was left in him? Could I help repair him somehow?

"Yes, you can. You can help me."

"But how did you know what I was thinking?" I asked, although I wasn't shocked.

"Like I said, I know you so well, Teagan." He leaned closer to me, placing his hand in mine, a hand that felt warmer now. "I fear I have done too much harm here in this world where you belong. If heaven offers me a second chance…" Hadrian looked away and didn't finish.

He tilted his face toward mine again and the light caught his eyes. For the first time, I saw a hint of green behind the ebony.

The darkness was lifting, letting the light he used to be shine through, allowing it to break through what had controlled him for so long. He was beautiful and light, and soon

he would be whole again. He could be what was planned for him so long ago. An angel. I could help him, I knew that now. That was my power. To heal. To bring the truth.

His lips were inches from mine. I breathed him in. I wanted him to stay... I wanted...

I heard a scraping sound come from beneath me. From the corner of my eye, I saw colors of light moving on the floor, sliding across it. The triangles of colored glass met, forming a design.

As if the floor had a mind of its own, it formed a circle around us, the sharp points of the red stained glass forming an octagram. Suddenly, the candles toppled over, the spilt wax merging with the outline. Their tiny flames grew larger and taller by the second. We were trapped inside the circle, inside the heart of the octagram, surrounded by an awesome power.

"Teagan!" Someone was calling me.

I was being pulled out of my dream and I didn't want to leave. It was so warm here, I wanted to stay. But I was yanked away from it and thrown. It was only when I hit the cold floor outside the circle that I could see clearly what was happening.

In the center of the octagram, Garreth and Hadrian stood facing each other as flames licked at their legs, threatening to take one of them down. Two angels. One of light, the other of darkness. Both beautiful. Both powerful. One of love and the other of destruction. And there I was, outside the circle, and I wanted them both.

If Garreth hadn't shown up, I would have been convinced I could change Hadrian. Did I really have the power to make him as God wanted him—and keep him for myself? I unders-

tood then that nothing comes without a price. How far would I have gone before I realized that? I would give anything to have Garreth's invisible and unconditional love around me, then let Hadrian take his place in the human world.

Garreth stood strong as the flames threatened to reach within the circle. He stared into Hadrian's fierce glare, ready for anything and forever my protector. "She seems to see something in you that I don't believe exists."

"Oh, don't let her innocence fool you. She has a dark side."

"Don't you think I know her well enough to know that?" Garreth offered.

Hadrian's laugh sent shivers down my spine. I couldn't deny it any longer; there was something about Hadrian that I needed. That I wanted. But Garreth meant more and I only hoped I could make him believe that.

I frantically searched my thoughts for the purpose I could offer. What price would anyone be willing to pay for the one they loved? I knew, without a doubt, because it surrounds me each and every day. Sacrifice.

I pulled myself to my feet and stepped inside the circle. The flames threatened to take me but the only part of my body that felt intense heat was my right hand. As I moved between the two angels, with my hand held high in front of Hadrian, I let the flames' heat seep into the lines of my palm, activating the power of my Guardian stored within me.

Hadrian's face crumpled as he looked at me innocently, and I trembled inside, questioning just for a second what might have been. Then a pair of strong hands were on my shoulders,

convincing me I was right. Garreth's gentle scent strengthened me, shattering Hadrian's perfect illusion.

The truth to see beyond; to uncover what truly lay beneath the façade. That was all Hadrian really was. A façade.

The world tipped then and the black sky above the ruined tower was now beneath our feet, swirling and spinning below us, an angry hole sucking in anything it could grab from our world. The room appeared illuminated by a thousand fires as shards of colored glass flew past us into the dark, swirling cavity. My hand burned ferociously and I anchored it with my left hand as the full and final power of the light Garreth had given me surged out of it and smashed squarely into Hadrian's chest. I felt sick, wanting to turn away, but Garreth's hold on me was strong and sure.

Hadrian's feet lost hold, and he desperately grabbed onto my hand, clinging to the power it held. I met his eyes, the green of his, flashing in the flames' glow as he tried to convince me to help him. I closed my eyes and willed my beautiful scrolled mark to disappear from my palm.

At last I knew the power *I* could wield.

My eyes opened and the lifeline Hadrian clung to was gone, sending him plummeting down into the darkness. But the floor no longer wished to hold us and Garreth pushed me to the stones outside the circle just as the glass octagram splintered and fell in pieces into the abyss beneath. We stood staring as the colors disappeared after Hadrian.

We were then immersed in a great orange light. The flames were out of control. Soon the tiny chapel was filled with thick,

gray smoke that seemed to tear the skin from the inside of my throat. Within seconds, Garreth and I were lost to each other.

"Garreth!" I screamed. My voice stretched itself over the expanse of the room, seeking him. "Garreth!"

I dropped to my knees, desperate to avoid breathing in the ashes that danced around me like phantoms. I willed myself to crawl, though where I was crawling to I had no idea. My hands reached out in front of me, feeling for anything substantial and I felt the wall give way and crumble to the ground. I clawed my way through the stones, my skin tearing away from my fingertips. At last, I made it to the ground on the other side. I sucked the cool air into my lungs but the woods hung heavy with smoke and shadows as ashes flew and clung to the trees and branches. Tiny sparks projected themselves above the inferno and hovered, airborne and still, as if calculating where they wanted to land before falling gracefully to the ground, setting the dry brush into miniature fires.

Garreth was nowhere to be seen and panic bled itself into my bones.

The fire was spreading. I saw the flames race past the clearing and out toward the road. The air rang with sirens and it felt like the whole town was on fire. I was spent, my legs refusing to move anymore. With my head pressed against the smooth, worn bark of our old tree, I began to sob uncontrollably. My chest was heavy with fatigue. All I could think of was Garreth, and suddenly the hole in my heart ripped all the way open with fear. Hadrian, it seemed, was gone for good, but in the end, I feared Garreth was gone as well.

I felt smoke weave itself around me, clouding my senses. I closed my eyes to the sweet song of the sirens and cried for my Guardian.

# Chapter Thirty-two

I let my head roll to the side as the room spun then slowed around me. At last I could make out white cabinets, a single gray chair, a commercial linoleum floor. I looked for the source of a sound that had been repeating itself in my ears, the constant hum of a machine in the room with me. It sounded like water flowing and briefly I envisioned it to be the contents of my heart pouring out of me. That would explain why I could no longer feel it.

A big metal box on legs was the culprit so I closed my eyes again, preferring sleep to wondering how I managed to be in the hospital. A shuffling sound joined the hum, and I forced my eyes to open.

"Hi, sweetie," My mom leaned over me. She looked as if she hadn't slept for a week. "The doctor will be in soon."

I opened my mouth to speak but my lips felt all dry and cracked. I wanted to ask if anyone had found Garreth. At the thought of his name, I couldn't help but cry again.

"Oh, shhh. Don't, honey, you're going to be okay." My mother glanced over her shoulder and stepped aside.

"Well, now, how's our patient?"

I couldn't see his face from where I lay but I saw a redness flush its way into my mom's cheeks. He stepped into view, pausing to smile at my mother, then he lifted my right hand, which for some reason I failed to notice until now was bandaged heavily with white gauze. I looked at the doctor, then my mom, then back to the doctor again.

"I don't need to tell you how lucky you are, young lady. The whole town practically went up in flames last night and only your hand was injured. You're a hero, you know," he said, nodding his head.

*Hero? Why am I a hero?*

I wanted to interrupt and ask a zillion questions but I couldn't get my tongue to reach the roof of my mouth to form the words. And, whenever I breathed too deeply, it felt like my chest was about to explode.

My mom's gaze dropped to my wrapped hand. "Will there be much scarring?"

"Unfortunately, yes, but the burn looks sort of like a design. It will be a great battle wound to show to your friends." The doctor went to the foot of the bed and began writing something down on my chart.

*Battle wound. Good one.*

The doctor looked up from his notes. "You'll have the use of your hand back in no time. Just a few more weeks of school, huh? Almost time for graduation?"

"One more year," my mom answered for me. She was keeping the conversation going with the doctor, happy to use me as an excuse.

"Junior, huh? I have a daughter your age."

I strained my eyes to see his name tag but the last name didn't ring a bell.

He continued. "I just don't understand how you... All I have to say is, you're both very lucky. If you need anything, don't hesitate to call me. Get better, Teagan. Okay?"

The doctor tapped the foot of my bed with his hand and stepped out of the room, but not without one final smile, which was obviously for my mother.

"What was that all about?" I finally managed to croak.

"I'm not really sure," she admitted, but the look on her face told it all.

Change couldn't be avoided any longer, and whether she was ready for it or not, life had a plan for my mom. In sharing this weird little moment with her, my face inevitably fell and gloom filled me like helium.

"Not what you planned for a first date, was it?" She sat at the edge of the bed, fingering the scratchy hospital blanket.

I turned my head, my eyes were filling with tears again. "Did the whole town really go up in flames?" I asked.

"Just some of it. Mostly fields, though. Bartlett's skating rink is gone. The police are still investigating."

My cheeks burned at the thought of having to admit I was the one responsible for the fire. Mentioning Hadrian and pleading insanity might work, but I couldn't bring myself to do it.

"The fire marshal thinks the cause was electrical."

"Electrical?"

241

"You know, from that old warehouse where the kids have been hanging out? They should have torn down that dump long ago. I'm sure everyone will be happy when it's finally gone." She touched my cheek. "Are you thirsty? I'll run down to the cafeteria for some tea, or maybe I can find a nurse around here."

My mother was up and sticking her head out into the hallway before I could object, then she pulled it back in. "I'll be right back. Just close your eyes and rest." And she was gone.

I did as I was told because there was nothing better to do. Instantly, I regretted it. My mind began to wander in the silence of the sterile room, searching for signs of Garreth. I had never felt so alone. I tried to will fluttering sounds to come from the corners of the little room, or perhaps from behind the curtain, but they wouldn't come.

I was resigned to give up when I heard it. Faint but true. I felt him near me. I smelled him, though it wasn't his scent alone. It was mixed with the fire that had burned around us in the chapel, spicy, pungent, smoky—but still his. I wanted to open my eyes to see if he was really there beside me. But I knew he wouldn't be. Not here. I didn't want to spoil this moment so I kept my eyes tightly shut.

"You can open them, silly." His voice was beautiful, husky.

"I don't want to. You're not really here and if I can't see you I'll be a mess."

"Just open them," he said softly. He lifted my bandaged hand then placed it back gently at my side.

242

I let my eyes open and settle on the brilliant light in front of me. I couldn't see him. Oh, why did I listen? This was how it was going to be from now on, until it was my turn to follow. I might as well get used to it. But then the sun moved behind a cloud, shifting its light and I shook my head in disbelief.

"You're here? You're really here? How?"

I must have looked like an idiot, beaming uncontrollably in my blue-and-white hospital gown. Then it dawned on me and I was even more dumbstruck. Garreth was sitting on the edge of my bed wearing an identical hospital gown and looking incredible in it, in a way I never could. We both broke into laughter and he leaned over to kiss me.

"You're real?" I think it was more of a question I was asking myself but it escaped me and I said it out loud.

"That's some power you have. Even I had no idea of its strength."

I just shook my head. I didn't know what to say or ask.

Garreth continued, "It boiled down to one thing. Truth." He picked up my bandaged hand again. "To create unity within your spirit is a hard thing, but you managed. You held what you believe in your heart, and never let it go. You never lost yourself. Even though you admit that a bit of darkness lures you, you never caved. Seeing through Hadrian was almost impossible and Mathur and the other Guardians are very proud of you."

"But how can you be here with me? I thought you were gone forever. The fire…"

243

His kiss stopped my rambling. "Looks like I'm here to stay."

"You mean...?" I stumbled over my words. "Are you...?"

"No, not completely, like you. What you did, when you came after me, showed me that as long as you believe in something then any risk is worth taking, even if you risk failing. You see, I *have* to stay."

I couldn't believe my eyes and ears. He looked so human, disheveled and worn out, but that would be our secret. And to me he couldn't have looked more wonderful.

"Don't get me wrong, I'll still find a way to protect you." He snickered. "Of course, I might call on *you* for protection now and then. You're going to put me out of a job."

I shook my head back and forth, clueless.

"*You* saved *me* from the fire." His blue eyes were melting a hole right through me.

"I saved *you*? But how?"

*Is this what the doctor meant?*

"You found me lying in the woods. I don't know how you did it but you managed to drag me out. When we got to the road, a car happened to be driving by and you flagged it down. Now we're here."

Then he smiled and leaned over to kiss me. I closed my eyes, imagining it all and it seemed surreal to me.

Except him. He was real. He was here and I was never going to lose him again.

Then something cold came over me. The truth. I had set the truth free.

*Hadrian.*

I pulled Garreth closer, wishing like anything to avoid the questions circling around in my head. But, if he was here to stay, then I owed it to him to be completely and utterly honest.

I took his hand in mine, careful of my bandage. "You told Hadrian that I saw something in him, something you don't think exists. If a part of me *still* sees it, *still* believes that it might be there inside him…" I was confusing myself.

Garreth stopped me by putting a finger to my lips.

"Truth is your power, Teagan. If you believe it to be so about Hadrian, then I can't convince you otherwise. It's a knowledge I lay no claim to and I cannot judge it. You saw through the illusion he worked so hard to create. Perhaps there is no more illusion."

"But what if I'm only seeing what I want to see. What if I'm helping to create that illusion?"

His eyes went soft. "No. I believe you see the truth. Darkness has a way of being very convincing. On the other hand, maybe I was too quick to help bring him down because of what you mean to me. I couldn't lose you to him." He shook his head.

"You said a part of you still sees good in Hadrian. If you sense that, then he still exists. And, if you're the only one who sees it, then he exists only for you. Like I do."

I knew then, that I could never tell Garreth about the confusion I felt twisting around inside me. He was giving up so much to stay. Even though I couldn't be happier that I would no longer be without him, that I could love him here, forever,

the thought, the very idea, that Hadrian might still be out there, waiting for me, lingered. That, like Garreth, he existed because of me. It disturbed me that I was thrilled by his darkness, that somewhere deep inside my soul I yearned for the excitement I found in that. But I loved Garreth. He was mine and I would do anything to suppress my feelings for Hadrian, anything to be true to my angel. But was I worthy of such a gift? Heaven sent Garreth to me for a purpose, but was it really to fulfill destiny or was it a test of some kind?

I remembered Mathur's words, that a person could have more than one Guardian. Was I such a person? Did I have a Guardian for each side of me? Light and dark?

I kissed Garreth, showing him what he meant to me and leaving him breathless under the spell I wanted to weave for him. Yet I shuddered when I closed my eyes and saw Hadrian. Perhaps I was trying too hard to convince myself, to reassure myself. But, sure enough, Hadrian had gotten under my skin.

# Chapter Thirty-three

"Wake up, sleepy."

It is like a breeze gently sweeping over me, his voice. I brush away the feather tickling my nose, then grab it. I have his fingertip.

*Gotcha!*

"Come on, Teagan, you have to get up."

"And what am I getting up for?"

I've been sleeping a lot these days. In the middle of the night, when I feel the warmth of him lying next to me after he's sneaked in, I fall asleep too soundly. Too deeply. No longer on pins and needles.

"You know." He lies back, lengthwise, across my bed, stretching his arms up over his tousled head so that his arms now dangle over my floor in midair.

Garreth has grown entirely too comfortable in his new skin. I've had to remind myself often that he's not what he appears to be. That he's still an angel.

"Do you feel older?"

I groan and bury my head into his side. I breathe him in.

*Spice…mmm…*

It lulls me back to sleep.

"You were babbling again," he teases.

"I've told you. I do not babble." But my argument is muffled. I'm still smothering myself against his skin. "Okay, I'll bite."

I'm sitting up now and suddenly he is serious and for a second I feel a little afraid. It's been months since the fire at the chapel. Months since I've let *his* name force its way to the front of my brain. I've stifled him, tried to break the grand illusion with denial.

And it's worked.

These weeks have been heaven on earth and I'm convinced that my feelings, or whatever I should call them, for Hadrian were a farce, part of his plan to lure me away from the safety net of my Guardian. I've rid myself of the guilt I feel, to a degree, because guilt is a poison.

But I'm quiet. I don't bring my thoughts to the surface. I squelch them and leave them to drown and disappear.

Garreth is studying my face intently. "Where were you just now?"

I look at him, not sure what to say. "Still babbling, I guess. You just couldn't hear."

I smile. I look at the calendar on my desk. It's a silly little propped-up book with a furless cat on it; a little something from my mom. Like I said. Silly. It's my birthday. August eighth. Only this year it seems...not odd, not special, just different. It would mean nothing to me if the number eight held no significance. But it can't be ignored. It stares back at me, repeating itself. Two eights, 8/8. One for Garreth, the

other for Hadrian. It could mean the beginning or the end, but I can't bring myself to think about which one just yet.

"Happy Birthday." Garreth dangles the blue rosary in front of my eyes and kisses me sweetly, letting it curl into my palm. The chain mimics my mark, all scrolled and curly. A perfect fit.

"It's not much of a surprise, but it happens to be the only valuable thing I can give you." His eyes tell me he's not sure I'll appreciate its worth, but it means more to me than I can explain.

"I love it. It's so beautiful." I look at the delicate chain, the shining stones that are the same color as his eyes. It's the perfect gift.

He cups his hand around mine, the one that holds his secret—his angel star—closing the chain between us.

"Like you. Beautiful. Rare. Valuable. Fragile yet very strong."

"Thank you."

He stands up in front of me and pulls me to my feet. I'm finally awake.

Garreth has promised me a real date. It's sort of my birthday present. Dinner, candles...the whole deal.

And it goes off without a hitch. In fact, the evening couldn't have been more perfect.

"Will you do something for me?" I ask Garreth on our way home. I can't say why, but I need to see it one more time.

I stand at the foot of the chapel's steps, peering up at the cracked wall that is now covered in multitudes of green growth. It's amazing how when you leave something alone, even for a

short time, it never fails to change on you. With all the damage the fire did, it amazes me that anything will grow now. But when life demands to break through and bust the seams of chaos, you can't stop it. It goes on.

I picture the beautiful triangles of colored glass, the red candles, inside. I picture the way it was when I first came here with Garreth. An ordinary person stumbling upon this place now would assume time has done its damage. They would never know what transpired here, nor should they. There is no need. No need to know that all could have been changed in the blink of an eye. It is best to let it become covered up and let time erase it all.

It is, after all, just another ruin.

But it was here that I came to know of my angel. It was here that he warned me of Hadrian, and where I learned the truth about my father...about myself. I look at my hand and trace the scar with my finger. I let it fade and become invisible...for now.

I'm accustomed to letting it surface and fade and I watch now as the lines melt safely into the creases of my palm. My back tingles ever so slightly between my shoulder blades. Something else is coming and I smile softly to myself. But for now, happiness is beckoning and I walk toward my angel. No matter how human he pretends to be, for now he is still my angel. I am thinking about all he is giving up for me, the risk he is taking by staying. It scared him once, but not enough to keep us apart. It would be scarier not to take that risk and chance losing what means the most.

To be human, and aspire to become more, is pretty amazing. But to be an angel whose wish is to become human...is a miracle.

There is nothing else I can ever imagine wanting.

My thoughts are interrupted by a sudden shiver that shakes me from head to toe. One name passes through my mind and I know I will have to face him again. Who knows when that someday will be?

He is waiting.

*Hadrian.*

The trees whisper his name.

Always waiting. And in stoic silence, always watching.

# Acknowledgments

My gratitude is monumental to each and every one who has supported the journey of this book.

First and foremost, I must thank my amazing publisher, Lisa Paul. I cannot thank you enough for seeing the story within the story. Your enthusiasm, insight, and determination to make this book possible went beyond my expectations.

Thanks to Sharon K. Garner for the outstanding copyedits and for your ability to decipher my ramblings, and to Kimberly Martin for your talented design skills.

Thank you so much to my parents, Richard and Linda Voigt, for encouraging me to go after the depths of my heart, and to my grandmother, Alice Danner, for being my cheer-leader and friend! The biggest thanks to my "seester," Sharon Murgia, and to Nicole Murgia and Rhonda Powell for being my first readers, and for putting up with the tears, the sighs, and the giggles. You guys are the best! Thanks to my friend and fellow author Shelena Shorts for being a mere e-mail away when I needed someone who would understand.

A humongous hug goes to my husband Chris and to my amazing kids, Christian and Megan. Dedicating this book to you just doesn't seem like enough. I love you so much!

Finally, to the person holding this book, you hold my dream in your hands. Thank you doesn't suffice.

Visit

www.jennifermurgia.com

for information regarding *Angel Star's* sequel:

# LEMNISCATE

# WITHDRAWN

Breinigsville, PA USA
09 September 2010
245168BV00001B/13/P

9 780982 500538